RAF Bomber Command Profiles

50 Squadron

RAF Bomber Command Profiles

50 Squadron

Chris Ward

This edition first published 2020 by Mention the War Ltd., 25 Cromwell Street, Merthyr Tydfil, CF47 8RY.

This squadron profile has been researched, compiled and written by its author, who has made every effort to ensure the accuracy of the information contained in it. The author will not be liable for any damages caused, or alleged to be caused, by any information contained in this book. E. & O.E.

Cover design: Topics - The Creative Partnership www.topicsdesign.co.uk

A CIP catalogue reference for this book is available from the British Library.

ISBN 9781911255543

Also by Chris Ward:

Dambusters- The Definitive History of 617 Squadron at War 1943-1945
by Chris Ward, Andy Lee and Andreas Wachtel, published 2003 by Red Kite.

Dambuster Crash Sites
by Chris Ward and Andreas Wachtel, published 2007 by Pen and Sword Aviation.

Dambusters. Forging of a Legend
by Chris Ward, Andy Lee and Andreas Wachtel, published 2009 by Pen and Sword
Aviation.

Images of War: 617 Dambuster Squadron at War
by Chris Ward and Andy Lee, published 2009 by Pen and Sword Aviation.

1 Group Bomber Command. An Operational History
by Chris Ward with Greg Harrison and Grzegorz Korcz, published 2014 by Pen and
Sword Aviation.

3 Group Bomber Command. An Operational History
by Chris Ward and Steve Smith, published 2008 by Pen and Sword Aviation.

4 Group Bomber Command. An Operational History (Pen & Sword Aviation 2012)

5 Group Bomber Command. An Operational History (Pen & Sword Aviation 2007)

6 Group Bomber Command. An Operational History (Pen & Sword Aviation 2010)

Other RAF Bomber Command Profiles by Chris Ward published by Mention the War Ltd.
10 Squadron
75(NZ) Squadron
83 Squadron
101 Squadron
103 Squadron
106 Squadron
115 Squadron
138 Squadron
300 Squadron
Dambusters – The Complete WWII History of 617 Squadron

Contents

Introduction

RAF Bomber Command Squadron Profiles first appeared in the late nineties and proved to be very popular with enthusiasts of RAF Bomber Command during the Second World War. They became a useful research tool, particularly for those whose family members had served and were no longer around. The original purpose was to provide a point of reference for all of the gallant men and women who had fought the war, either in the air, or on the ground in a support capacity, and for whom no written history of their unit or station existed. I wanted to provide them with something they could hold up, point to and say, "this was my unit, this is what I did in the war". Many veterans were reticent to talk about their time on bombers, partly because of modesty, but perhaps mostly because the majority of those with whom they came into contact had no notion of what it was to be a "Bomber Boy", to face the prospect of death every time they took to the air, whether during training or on operations. Only those who shared the experience really understood what it was to go to war in bombers, which is why reunions were so important. As they approached the end of their lives, many veterans began to speak openly for the first time about their life in wartime Bomber Command, and most were hurt by the callous treatment they received at the hands of successive governments with regard to the lack of recognition of their contribution to victory. It is sad that this recognition in the form of a national memorial and the granting of a campaign medal came too late for the majority. Now this inspirational, noble generation, the like of which will probably never grace this earth again, has all but departed from us, and the world will be a poorer place as a result.

RAF Bomber Command Squadron Profiles are back. The basic format remains, but, where needed, additional information has been provided. Squadron Profiles do not claim to be comprehensive histories, but rather detailed overviews of the activities of the squadron. There is insufficient space to mention as many names as one would like, but all aircraft losses are accompanied by the name of the pilot. Fundamentally, the narrative section is an account of Bomber Command's war from the perspective of the bomber group under which the individual squadron served, and the deeds of the squadron are interwoven into this story. Information has been drawn from official records, such as group, squadron and station ORBs, and from the many, like me, amateur enthusiasts, who dedicate much of their time to researching individual units, and become unrivalled authorities on them. I am grateful for their generous contributions, and their names will appear in the appropriate Profiles. The statistics quoted in this series are taken from The Bomber Command War Diaries, that indispensable tome written by Martin Middlebrook and Chris Everitt, and I am indebted to Martin for his kind permission to use them.

Finally, let me apologize in advance for the inevitable errors, for no matter how hard I and other authors try to write "nothing but the truth", there is no such thing as a definitive account of history, and there will always be room for disagreement and debate. Official records are notoriously unreliable tools, and yet we have little choice but to put our faith in them. It is not my intention to misrepresent any person or Bomber Command unit, and I ask my readers to understand the enormity of the task I have undertaken. It is relatively easy to become an authority on single units or even a bomber group, but I chose to write about them all, idiot that I am, which means 128 squadrons serving operationally in Bomber Command at some time between the 3rd of September 1939 and the 8th of May 1945. I am dealing with eight bomber groups, in which some 120,000 airmen served, and I am juggling around 28,000 aircraft serial numbers, code letters and details of provenance and fate. I ask not for your sympathy, it was, after all, my choice, but rather your understanding if you should find something with which you disagree. My thanks to you, my readers, for making the original series of RAF Bomber Command Squadron Profiles so popular, and I hope you receive this new incarnation equally enthusiastically.

My thanks are due, as always, to my gang members, Andreas Wachtel, photo editor Clare Bennett, Steve Smith and Greg Korcz for their unstinting support, without which my Profiles would be the poorer. My gratitude also to Frank McGrath in Canada, who kindly provided details of his uncle and namesake, along with photographs, and Mike Connock and Neil Cheeseman of the Friends of Skellingthorpe website for kindly allowing access to the photo archive. A special thank you, also, to David Layne, for allowing me to use content from his blog about Wally Layne, *www.wallyswar.wordpress.com.* Finally, my appreciation to my publisher, Simon Hepworth of Mention the War Publications, for his belief in my work, untiring efforts to promote it, and for the stress I put him through to bring my books to publication.

Chris Ward. Skegness, Lincolnshire. May 2020.

This wartime history of 50 Squadron is dedicated to the memories of F/L Les Rutherford, who flew on 24 bomber operations, and passed away on the 1st of December 2019 at the age of 101

W/O Frank McGrath RCAF, pilot, who, with his crew, was lost in the North Sea on the 11th of April 1943, aged 21, and was one of 9,915 Canadians to lose their lives in Bomber Command service during WWII.

Narrative History

Originally formed on the 15th of May 1916, 50 Squadron's initial role was as a home defence unit, patrolling the southern coastal area of England. On the 13th of June 1919, it was disbanded while under the command of a certain Major A T Harris, whose future career would have great significance for Bomber Command. The squadron remained on the shelf until its reformation at Waddington on the 3rd of May 1937, and, at the end of 1938, the squadron received the twin-engine Handley-Page Hampden, the type with which it would enter the Second World War under the banner of 5 Group and the command of W/C Young. Although 5 Group was in action from the very first day of hostilities, when fellow Waddington residents, 44 Squadron, took part in a fruitless search for elements of the German fleet in the Wilhelmshaven area, 50 Squadron was not involved and experienced a gentler introduction to the war. Its main occupation at the start was training, and all serviceable aircraft were dispersed to Tollerton in Nottinghamshire on the 23rd of September, and would return to Waddington only when on stand-by for operations, none of which would actually take place.

On the 29th of September, 5 Group sent eleven Hampdens from Hemswell in two sections to attack enemy warships in the Heligoland area, from which the 144 Squadron element of five failed to return. There would be a number of further small-scale forays by the group, and some of a larger-scale by other groups, during which, the Command learned some expensive but valuable lessons about daylight unescorted incursions into enemy airspace. In 1919, Italian air-war strategist, General Giulio Douhet, had propounded the theory that future wars would be fought between giant armadas of self-defending bombers, flying directly over the front lines in daylight to target the economic centres of the enemy, and, thereby, destroy its will and capability to continue the fight. This theory would gain support in a number of countries, in Britain with Arthur Harris, in America with Billy Mitchell and in Germany with Walther Wever. Fortunately for the conduct of WWII, Wever would lose his life in a flying accident in 1935, and the development of the Luftwaffe put in the hands of army minded strategists, who saw bombing as a tactical extension of artillery. This would prove to be an inspired decision in a short war, and Blitzkrieg was highly successful in rolling up France and the Low Countries. However, an extended conflict would require a strategic bomber force, and by the time Germany realized that fact, it would be too late to catch up. The main flaw in the Douhet theory concerned the suggested ability of bombers to get through in sufficient numbers in daylight to reach the target. During a shipping sweep in the Schillig Roads on the 14th of December, five of twelve Wellingtons would be lost, and twelve out of twenty-two on the 18th. This would force the air planners to take stock, and, ultimately, would lead to all but 2 Group becoming a largely nocturnal force.

It was at Waddington during training on the 17th of October, that 50 Squadron registered its first wartime aircraft casualty, when L4080 suffered brake failure while taxiing in the hands of P/O Lloyd, and was written off in a collision with a hangar, happily though, without damage to the occupants. While at Tollerton on the 21st of October, L4077 struck a dummy gun in the centre of the airfield, killing a member of Sgt Wild's crew and injuring a gunner on the ground. On the last night of the month, Sgt Cordle and crew took off from Waddington for a night training sortie in L4096, but crashed minutes later at Branston, four miles south-east of Lincoln, killing all on board.

The first of a number of short periods of detachment to Coastal Command began on the 24th of November, when W/C Young and S/L Fleming led nine other crews, and one on attachment from 44 Squadron, the other Waddington resident unit, to Wick in Scotland. Two days later, F/L Good was granted the acting rank of squadron leader to enable him to assume command of A Flight. In the event, the squadron would not be called into action during this spell north of the border, and returned to Waddington on the 2nd of December. The first offensive activity for the squadron occurred with the above-mentioned shipping sweep on the 14th of December, when eleven crews were joined by another from 44 Squadron for an 07.40 take-off with W/C Young and S/L Good the senior pilots on duty. They flew out over Skegness, where the section of three led by F/O Vernieux became separated in poor visibility, and continued on independently. The operation, involving twenty-three Hampdens, ultimately, was uneventful, although S/L Good's section was challenged and fired upon by a friendly flak ship, which ignored the flashing of the letter of the day. All aircraft landed safely between 12.20 and 12.40, and there would be no further operational activity in what remained of the year. S/L Fleming RAAF was posted to HQ Training Command on Boxing Day, and was succeeded as B Flight commander by F/L Weir, who was granted acting squadron leader rank on his arrival that day from 44 Squadron.

1940 First quarter

The winter of 1939/40 produced particularly harsh weather, and this would restrict flying massively until a thaw brought relief towards the end of February. On the 11th of January, the 5 Group Operational Instruction N°3 came into effect, and, that night, Waddington launched F/O Corr of 50 Squadron and S/L Watts of 44 Squadron to dispense 324,000 leaflets (nickels) each over Bremen and Hamburg respectively, and both returned from uneventful sorties having fulfilled their briefs. There was no further activity until the 26th, when the squadron dispatched six Hampdens to Lossiemouth led by S/L Good for a further detachment to Coastal Command. They would stand-by for operations when convoys were at sea, but were not called into action until the 8th of February, when six aircraft from each squadron took off at 12.45 for a three-hour sweep of the North Sea, during which no enemy surface vessels were encountered. It was on this day that W/C Young was posted from the squadron as non-effective sick, to be succeeded as commanding officer on the 13th by S/L Reid, who was granted the acting rank of wing commander. The two squadrons returned to Waddington on the 15th, and remained on stand-by, while the snow continued to fall, and the ground remained frozen.

During the course of the 16th and 17th, the armed German tanker/supply vessel, Altmark, had become cornered by elements of the Royal Navy in Jøssingfjord in south-western Norway, and had been fired upon and boarded in what the Germans correctly claimed were neutral Norwegian waters. Altmark had famously acted as the supply vessel for the Admiral Graf Spee pocket battleship, which sank nine merchant ships during its highly productive campaign in the South Atlantic between September and December 1939, before being trapped in the port of Montivideo following the Battle of the River Plate, and, subsequently being scuttled. The crews of the merchantmen had been picked up by Graf Spee and transferred to Altmark, and the three hundred merchant sailors found on board were liberated. Eight German sailors were killed by small arms fire during the action, and the Germans denounced the episode as a gross violation of international law and Norwegian neutrality. The Waddington, Scampton and Hemswell squadrons were put on stand-by on the 17th to attack Altmark or any naval escorts, but, in the event, the thirty-six Hampdens were not called into action. On the 18th, German naval units were reported to be icebound in the Heligoland Bight, and 5 Group was put on stand-by to take advantage between the 19th and the 22nd, but, again, nothing came of it.

Heavy drizzle on the 22nd began a rapid thaw, which left Waddington wet, boggy and unserviceable, and sunshine on the following day melted the last vestiges of the white stuff. S/L Good and crew took off at 17.50 that evening with the intention of delivering nickels to the residents of Hamburg, but managed only three circuits of the airfield before landing with a faulty wireless. The operation was rescheduled, and S/L Good and crew took off from Waddington at 18.15 on the 26th, ten minutes after the departure of F/L Cosgrove and crew on what was referred to as a security patrol over the North Sea. Both flew out over Skegness and headed eastwards, F/L Cosgrove as far as the Frisian Island of Norderney and S/L Good to a position north of Hamburg, with a view to dropping his leaflets over the Kiel area. At Norderney, F/L Cosgrove headed north to Föhr and Sylt, off the western coast of the Schleswig-Holstein peninsular, before returning to home airspace, all the way attempting and failing to obtain bearings from Heston, Waddington, Scampton and Grantham. Landfall was eventually made over Margate in Kent, whereupon the starboard engine seized and a forced-landing was carried out at Manston at 00.30. S/L Good experienced no such difficulties, and returned at 00.20 to report a largely uneventful sortie, with good visibility over Germany and no opposition other than a few searchlights.

P/O Taylor and crew departed Waddington at 17.45 on the 29th to carry out an armed security patrol of enemy seaplane bases, in an attempt to prevent the enemy from dispatching aircraft to lay mines in British waters. They exited the Lincolnshire coast at Skegness, before flying up to Esbjerg, Sylt, Heligoland, Norderney and Borkum, maintaining 4,000 feet for most of the flight and spending the requisite amount of time over each location. They met no opposition and saw nothing of interest, and landed safely a minute before midnight. F/L Bennett and crew had taken off at 21.15 to conduct a similar sortie over the same route, and landed at 03.05, also with nothing of value to report. Twenty-four hours later it fell to F/Os Ayres and French and their crews to take off at 22.10 and 23.00 respectively to reconnoitre Sylt, Heligoland and the East Frisians. They encountered ten-tenths cloud between 4,000 and 10,000 feet, while operating at 1,000 to 8,000 feet, and also had little of interest to report on landing some five-and-a-half and six-and-a-half hours later. Weather conditions between the 2nd and the 15th of March proved to be unsuitable for operations, but a brief window on the 6th allowed three aircraft to take-off at 18.45 that evening for nickelling duties over north-western Germany. P/O Wawn and crew were bound for Wilhelmshaven, Sgt Stenner for Bremen and F/O Lloyd for Hamburg, and, what the A-O-C 5 Group, AVM Sir Arthur Harris, described as toilet paper for the German population, was dispensed from 7,000, 15,000 and 14,000 feet respectively. All three crews returned safely to report favourable weather conditions, but nothing of interest for the intelligence section.

As weather conditions took a turn for the better on the 15th, the squadron launched six Hampdens in two sections of three to carry out a North Sea sweep in search of enemy mine-layers. Section 1 consisted of S/L Good, F/O Lloyd and P/O Bull, who took off at 16.05, five minutes after section 2, containing the crews of S/L Weir, F/O Ayres and Sgt Wild. The patrol area covered a patch of sea beginning around one hundred miles from the Yorkshire coast and extending further to the mid-point between the English and Schleswig-Holstein coasts, perhaps seventy miles or so north of the Frisians. The sorties were largely uneventful, but both sections spotted two neutral merchantmen and section 2 carried out a dummy attack on them. This trio then ran into poor visibility on turning south, and the individual crews lost sight of each other, but all returned safely, section 1 at 20.15 and section 2 thirty minutes later. On the following day, the station commander ordered a repeat of the sea-sweep to enable other crews to gain experience, and this was led by F/L Cosgrove between 12.10 and 16.45. Other than the sighting of a Swedish vessel, the operation, which was undertaken at an average altitude of 2,000 feet, proved to be uneventful.

At 18.35, P/O Bull and crew departed Waddington for a routine patrol of enemy seaplane bases, and they were followed into the air at 19.15 by F/O Ayres and crew. The former flew out over Skegness and proceeded to the northern coast of Holland at 8,000 feet, before being forced to climb a little to avoid the cloud and icing of a cold front. A position was established over the Elbe Estuary and a course then set for Sylt, where cloud increased and it became necessary to descend to 3,000 feet, from where the sea was visible intermittently. The wireless became temporarily unserviceable during the homeward leg at 5,000 feet, and navigation relied on dead-reckoning aided by moonlight. However, cloud was encountered that forced them to climb to 12,000 feet, at which point the a.s.i became unserviceable. They failed to break into clear air, and decided to return to 5,000 feet, upon which, the wireless deigned to function again, and homing signals brought them to landfall sixty miles from Leuchars, where a safe landing was carried out at 01.00. F/O Ayres and crew had been flying at 13,000 feet, and sought homing assistance from Waddington. At this stage of the war, problems were being experienced with the D/F equipment, and not all fixes could be relied upon to be accurate. The Waddington homing station believed the Hampden to be over Lincolnshire, and advised F/O Ayres to descend to 2,000 feet, when, in fact, it was two hundred miles to the north and heading into the 3,000-foot-high Cheviot Hills in the Borders region. L4063 flew into high ground at 03.00 at Cocklaw Foot, some twelve miles north-east of Jedburgh on the Scottish side of the border, and there were no survivors.

P/O Bull and crew departed Leuchars at 14.35 on the 18th to carry out an anti-submarine patrol on their way home to Waddington. The weather was poor as they flew to a point fifty miles east of Leuchars, before heading south on a parallel course with the coast at between 500 and 1,000 feet some thirty miles out to sea. South of the Humber Estuary they were attacked by three Spitfires, which broke off on receipt of the recognition signal, after which, they flew in over Skegness to land safely at base.

At Dusk on the 16th, fifteen enemy bombers carried out attacks on elements of the Royal Navy at Scapa Flow in the Orkneys, hitting HMS Norfolk and killing four of her officers. Bombs also fell close to Hatstone aerodrome and Bridge of Wraith on the road between Kirkwall and Stromness on the island of Hoy, and two cottages were damaged, leading to the death of one civilian and injury to seven others. In retaliation for this, orders were issued on the 19th to carry out an attack on the seaplane base at Hörnum, located on the southern tip of the island of Sylt, off the western coast of the Schleswig-Holstein peninsular. 4 Group made ready thirty Whitleys, and they were assigned a four-hour slot in which to carry out their attacks, to be followed by twenty 5 Group Hampdens from Waddington and Hemswell, who were given a two-hour window later in the evening. 50 Squadron loaded five Hampdens with four 250 pounders each and a container of incendiaries, and dispatched them from Waddington between 22.55 and 23.40 with F/Ls Bennett and Cosgrove the senior pilots on duty. The former flew out over Skegness before setting course for the northern tip of Sylt at 1,000 to 2,000 feet under seven-tenths cloud, and, having reached his pinpoint, turned south to run in on the target. He selected a slipway, onto which the contents of his bomb bay were unloaded, before returning safely to report a fire and searchlight and flak activity, which was not, in his view, troublesome. P/O Taylor made landfall north of Esbjerg before turning south to carry out his attack from around 2,000 feet at 02.30, describing at debriefing numerous fires and intense ground fire. In contrast, Sgt Stenner was not troubled at all by the flak defences, but was denied sight of his bombs bursting by cloud obscuring the ground immediately after release. F/O French favoured a dive-bombing attack, and let his bombs go from 1,000 feet at 250 m.p.h., while F/L Cosgrove spent forty minutes searching for the aiming-point and evading a night-fighter. He carried out his attack from the west, aiming at a hangar at the northern end of the site at 02.10, all the time under fire from a hostile flak and small-arms defence, which they managed to evade.

5 Group recorded that its aircraft had attacked between 23.45 and 01.50 from heights ranging from 1,000 to 10,000 feet, and had delivered a total of sixteen 500 and forty-four 250 pounders along with 660 x 4lb incendiaries. The report added that the hangars were hit several times and direct hits were observed on the living quarters and slipway. The raid was claimed by the crews to be an outstanding success, and would make headline news, until reconnaissance on the 6th of April failed to detect any evidence of damage to the target. As this was the very first intentional attack on German soil, it demanded some kind of recognition, and F/L Bennett became the first Bomber Command pilot to be awarded an immediate DFC for a night bombing operation.

While the above operation was in progress, S/Ls Weir and Good and P/O Thomas departed Waddington between 19.20 and 19.45 to carry out a reconnaissance of the River Elbe, and to deliver leaflets to Hamburg, Lübeck and Cuxhaven. P/O Thomas and crew were assigned to the Elbe Estuary and Cuxhaven, and set course through a layer of nine-tenths cloud between 2,000 and 5,000 feet to find a full moon shining from an otherwise clear sky. They continued on at 6,000 feet, heading for a pinpoint fifteen miles north-west of Cuxhaven, when, after ninety minutes and still ninety miles short of their objective, their starboard engine began to falter. A course was set immediately for home, where they arrived safely at 21.05. S/L Weir's destination was a stretch of the Elbe between the town of Wedel to the north-west and the district of Altona on the North Bank near the heart of the city. He climbed to 12,000 feet and lost sight of the ground because of ten-tenths cloud, and was north of Oldenburg, north-west of Bremen, by the time a gap appeared to provide him with a pinpoint. The nickels were delivered here, and the decision taken to abandon all thoughts of attempting to reconnoitre the Hamburg area. S/L Good and crew pressed on to encounter ten-tenths cloud with tops at 10,000 feet, and icing conditions. Developing cloud partially obscured the moon, reducing the level of illumination and rendering the visibility insufficiently good for a detailed reconnaissance. Despite the navigator establishing a position over Kiel, it proved impossible to make a positive identification even from as low as 5,000 feet. With the intended target still some forty miles to the south, a single searchlight prompted the release of the nickels, more in hope than expectation, before a course was set for home. Equipment failure demanded a return by dead-reckoning (DR), and the first landfall was made over the Dutch coast, where a built-up area, believed to be Amsterdam, was spotted, and an S.O.S signal sent. There was no response to this, and the Hampden was pointed in the general direction of the Norfolk coast. It eventually became clear that they had actually been over Ostend, and their course took them to Margate on the Kent coast, from where they located Manston for a landing under moonlight.

The squadron remained on stand-by for night operations or daylight sweeps over the ensuing days, but the weather proved to be unfavourable, despite which, Hemswell launched aircraft for reconnaissance duties on the 24th, as did 44 Squadron also on the night of the 25/26th, from which one of its aircraft was lost in the North Sea. On the 27th, P/O Jacklin and F/O Corr took off at 19.13 and 19.35 respectively to carry out reconnaissance of seaplane bases on Sylt and Borkum. A recall signal was sent out almost immediately because of deteriorating weather conditions, which included severe icing and electrical storms. F/O Corr picked up the signal and turned back, but P/O Jacklin and crew continued on towards Sylt at a height of 8,000 feet over low cloud at around 2,000 feet. This persisted to within a hundred miles of Sylt, when it dispersed to leave good visibility for the run-in to the Schleswig-Holstein coast, where a few searchlights were in evidence along with slight flak activity. A new course was set for Borkum, where ten-tenths cloud obscured the ground to render further reconnaissance impossible, and a safe return was accomplished after a flight lasting almost six hours.

On the 28th, S/L Weir was posted across the tarmac to 44 Squadron, where he would assume the role of flight commander, before eventually being handed a command of his own with 61 Squadron eighteen months hence. His successor as flight commander at 50 Squadron was S/L Cooper, who was already on the staff at Waddington. Six aircraft remained on stand-by on the 28th and 29th, when adverse weather conditions kept them on the ground, but the 30th brought an opportunity for P/O Bull and F/O Corr to depart Waddington at 18.30 and 18.45 respectively for a further reconnaissance of the islands of Sylt, Borkum and Norderney. The weather proved to be moderate during the five-hour flights, both of which were uneventful and concluded safely to bring the month's operational activity to an end. During the course of March, the squadron operated on nine occasions, and dispatched twenty-six sorties for the loss of a single Hampden and crew.

April 1940

The squadron was in action late on the 1st, dispatching F/O Wawn and crew at 22.30 to carry out a reconnaissance of the Elbe estuary, F/O Vernieux and crew an hour later to cover the stretch from Wedel to the main docks area, and, finally, F/O Lloyd at 23.35 with a similar brief to F/O Wawn. F/O Wawn found the weather conditions deteriorating over the North Sea, but he and his crew were able to pick out the Frisians from 1,000 feet before heading for the target area, where visibility was poor. They spent thirty minutes patrolling the area from 1,000 feet and delivered leaflets to the residents of Cuxhaven before heading home with nothing of value to report. F/O Vernieux employed the Teschelling light vessel as a pinpoint, picking up its light from forty miles distance, and then setting course for Heligoland, where a searchlight sprang into life to port on e.t.a. A patrol of the Elbe revealed lights, but such was the degree of darkness that the banks of the river remained cloaked even from 1,000 to 2,000 feet, which made it impossible to pinpoint the whereabouts of the lights. The return flight took place in good conditions with easy navigation, and was uneventful. F/O Lloyd flew out under clear skies at 4,000 feet, also using the Terschelling light as a pinpoint en-route to the Elbe Estuary, but found the patrol area under ten-tenths cloud. He climbed to 5,000 feet, but saw nothing through the cloud, and spent little time stooging around before heading home via Skegness.

Orders came through on the 6th to prepare seven Hampdens for further nickelling and reconnaissance sorties that night in a number of areas. F/O Donaldson and P/Os Taylor and Jacklin were assigned to the River Elbe, and departed Waddington at 19.10, 19.50 and 22.00 respectively, while F/L Cosgrove and F/O Corr were airborne by 20.20 bound for the Kieler Förde (Kiel Fjord). S/L Good had the longest round-trip ahead of him, and flew over to Bircham Newton in Norfolk at 18.10 as a forward staging post. His patrol area was off Swinemünde on Germany's Baltic coast, where he was to make a detailed reconnaissance of the coastal region and nearby sea-lanes. He and his crew took off at 22.15 and set course for the Terschelling light vessel, before skirting the German Frisians to the Elbe Estuary and crossing the southern Schleswig-Holstein peninsular to by-pass Kiel and reach the Baltic at 12,000 feet. The night was very dark, but a poor blackout at Swinemünde left it visible from fifty miles out, and the crew was able to plot the lights and ascertain that the charts were still current. Nickels were dropped over the port of Sassnitz on the way home, and a safe return completed after seven-and-a-half hours aloft. Meanwhile, F/O French had been the last to take off, at 22.40, for his reconnaissance of the Elbe Estuary, and, in keeping with the experiences of the other crews, headed for the target area in good weather conditions under clear skies and intense darkness. Conditions deteriorated to some extent as they reached enemy air space, but all sorties were completed as briefed and without incident.

On the 9th, Germany invaded Denmark and Norway, prompting a British and French response in the form of a naval assault on the area around the town of Narvik in the north. Elements of the Royal Navy and the Kriegsmarine would come face-to-face on the 10th and 13th, and be followed by landings involving British, French and Polish troops, linking up with Norwegian forces. Bomber Command was prevented by the extreme range from directly supporting the landings, and would focus instead on attacking enemy supplies of men and materials arriving by air and sea in the south. 5 Group responded on that first day by detailing twenty-four Hampdens to attack enemy warships and troop carriers in Bergen Fjord on Norway's south-western coast. 50 Squadron was called upon to provide half of the force, which was divided into two flights, each consisting of two sections of three, and departing Waddington at half-minute intervals from 16.00, with W/C Reid leading the first, S/L Good the second, S/L Cooper the third and F/L Cosgrove the fourth. During the short leg from base to Skegness, haze caused Flight 2 to become separated from Flight 1, and W/C Reid delayed the North Sea crossing for five minutes in the hope that the two might regain contact. This did not happen, and the two flights would thus proceed independently from that point on. A course was set to a position thirty miles south of Bergen Fjord, during which leg the second section of Flight 1 found itself unable to maintain the speed of the lead section, and these also became separated. This meant that three separate elements of 50 Squadron were now making their way independently to the target area, possibly unaware that the other squadron had been recalled. W/C Reid reached the Norwegian coast alone at dusk, having now lost contact with his N°s 2 and 3, and, after searching for some time and finding features inland difficult to distinguish, spotted what appeared to be a warship, towards which he dropped four 500 pounders. It seems that P/Os Bull and Jacklin did not carry out an attack, and all three aircraft of this section proceeded to a landing in Scotland, as briefed.

The second section, consisting of S/L Good, F/O Corr and Sgt Abbott, arrived in the target area twenty minutes after the first section, but could identify no suitable target for their bombs and returned to Scotland. Flight 2 had managed to remain together, having set course at 16.25 in excellent weather conditions after failing to re-establish contact with Flight 1, and crossed the North Sea at between 5,000 and 7,000 feet to make landfall some fifty miles south of Bergen at 19.35. Only at 20.00 did the two sections lose sight of each other, and, five minutes later, section 4 was attracted by smoke to the west, which, on investigation, was found to be from the guns of a cruiser defending itself from an attack by section 3. The latter had chanced upon two cruisers and two destroyers off an island at the mouth of Kross Fjord, and had climbed to 8,000 feet to deliver an attack in line astern in the face of intense ground fire from shipboard and shore-based batteries. Fortunately, the shells exploded below their flight level as one aircraft suffered a hang-up, while the other two dropped eight 500 pounders, claiming a direct hit on one of the cruisers, which was reported later to have sunk. Section 4 arrived on the scene five minutes later to drop seven 500 pounders from 4,000 feet, this time within range of the anti-aircraft fire, and one Hampden sustained a number of holes in its fuselage and elevators. All made their way in isolation and without incident to airfields in Scotland, and returned to Waddington on the following day.

W/C Taafe was posted to the squadron from Finningley on the 10th, a station currently occupied by 106 Squadron, which was acting as the 5 Group pool training unit, feeding fresh crews to the front-line squadrons. He would succeed W/C Reid as commanding officer on the latter's posting to command 44 Squadron. Taafe had been one of three squadron leaders to be promoted with effect from the 1st of March, another of which, W/C Denny, was currently in command of 5 Group's 61 Squadron. On the night of W/C Taafe's appointment, F/L Bennett was dispatched at 23.35 to conduct a reconnaissance of a section of the Baltic Sea. Landfall was made near Esbjerg at a height of 1,500 feet, which was increased to 3,500, above the cloud, for the flight across southern Jutland. Passing out over the eastern coast, the island of Langeland was reached, and height reduced to 1,500 feet for the patrol, but, on failing to break cloud, F/L Bennett climbed again to 4,000 feet, changing course a number of times in a vain search for a gap. Time ran out, and the ground was not seen again until reaching Esbjerg on the way home. On the following night, P/O Wawn took off at 22.55 to search for the Deutschland class heavy cruiser, Admiral Scheer, which was one of three so-called "pocket" battleships. It had been reported to be off the eastern coast of Jutland in the Kattegat, apparently trying to make port with a heavy list to port. Weather conditions were excellent with clear skies and starlight affording good visibility, but, despite an extensive search, there was no sighting of the vessel, and P/O Wawn and crew landed safely after a sortie lasting ten minutes short of eight hours.

Orders were received across the Command on the 11th to prepare for what would be the largest commitment of bombers since the war began, and eighty-three Wellingtons, Hampdens and Blenheims took off during the morning and early afternoon of the 12th to attack shipping in the port of Stavanger. Waddington dispatched a dozen Hampdens, five representing 50 Squadron with seven from 44 Squadron, briefed to form into four sections of three aircraft each, sections 1 and 2 made up of 44 Squadron aircraft, section 3 consisting of S/L Good, P/O Bull and a 44 Squadron crew, and section 4 containing the crews of F/O Donalsdon, Sgt Wild and P/O Thomas. They took off at 08.15 and flew out over Skegness, before setting course for Lister Fjord, and being compelled by low cloud and bad weather to make the North Sea crossing at 300 feet. With the Norwegian coast on the horizon, the weather improved, and the profile of the land confirmed it to be Lister Fjord. Based on 3 Group records, it is believed that the primary target was the heavy cruiser Scharnhorst, which was at sea and making for Stavanger, while her consort, Gneisenau, was on course for Kristiansand, further to the east near Norway's southern tip.

The appointed leader of the Waddington element, S/L Watts of 44 Squadron, was persuaded by the weather conditions not to attempt to intercept Scharnhorst, but to concentrate instead on Gneisenau, and he set course for Kristiansand accordingly. The formation skirted the coast ten miles out, and climbed to 8,000 feet before heading for the harbour, where two large cruisers, three transports and a smaller vessel were sighted. The target was approached from inland on a south-easterly heading with the sections in line astern at one-mile intervals, and were flying at 180 m.p.h when they released their bombs, beginning at 12.15. As far as can be determined, all twelve delivered four 500 pounders each in the face of intense anti-aircraft fire, after which, the leader dived down to sea level at 210 m.p.h., followed by those of the formation that had survived the defences. Not all of the fourth section made it through the curtain of steel, and L4073 was seen to be hit and dive vertically into the sea, taking with it the crew of Sgt Wild. It is believed that L4081 was finished off by a fighter and also crashed into the sea with no survivors from the crew of P/O Thomas. L4083 was attacked and mortally wounded by a BF109 of II./JG77, and was crash-landed in flames by its Canadian pilot, F/O "Weasel" Donaldson, on an island off the Norwegian coast. The survivors were chased out to sea by the BF109s, and L4064 was seen to be losing fuel from a damaged tank. S/L Good flew escort to shepherd the ailing Hampden until the fuel became exhausted at 14.20, when it was forced to ditch at a position some 120 miles east of Newcastle-Upon-Tyne. S/L Good circled the spot while transmitting the precise location for the benefit of the rescue services, and observed P/O Bull and crew getting into the dinghy. Having done all they could, S/L Good and crew headed for home, where they would be the only one from 50 Squadron to make it. At debriefing, gunner Cpl Wallace was credited with shooting down an enemy fighter, and was awarded an immediate DFM.

The attempt to rescue P/O Bull and crew began with the departure from Waddington of P/O Taylor in Anson N9829 at 06.05 on the 13th, with P/O Luxmoore alongside him as second pilot. They returned four hours later to refuel at Driffield before continuing on to Waddington, where they reported finding no trace of the dinghy. Later, a Lockheed Hudson crew of Coastal Command reported observing a dinghy and crew and circling it, before losing it again, and this prompted P/O Wawn and F/O Lloyd and their crews to take off in Ansons N5193 and N9829 at 17.45 and 17.55 respectively for a further search. The latter returned at 22.20 having seen nothing other than a destroyer heading in the direction of the last-known position, while the former ran short of fuel and was written off in a crash-landing at 23.35 near Grimsby. P/O Wawn and his crew sustained injuries, one of them of a serious but not life-threatening nature. Meanwhile, "Weasel" Donaldson and two members of crew had been rescued by two local fishermen, who rowed out from their small village of Trevge after being alerted by the flames. Sadly, one of the gunners had been killed in the engagement, but the survivors were ferried to the mainland for hospital treatment and were well looked after by the hospitable and courageous local people. The locals had discovered an intact BF109, which had been force-landed in a field after running out of fuel during the attack on Kristiansand. They had arrested the pilot and confined him, and hidden the fighter in a forest. Asked if he could fly it, P/O Donaldson declared himself up for the challenge, and was conveyed to the location, where he checked out the aircraft and found it to be fit for flight. While the town was scoured for petrol, the 109 was divested of its seat to enable it to carry three men, and preparations were put in hand to launch it from a field of barely one hundred yards in length. The petrol was not aviation fuel, and this made the engine sluggish and incapable of generating sufficient power to gain flying speed before running out of field. A number of attempts were made, culminating with the wrecking of the aircraft, and another trip to hospital. With the Germans about to enter the town of Mandal, and Cpl Henry not fit enough to leave hospital, P/O Donaldson and P/O Middleton were hurriedly evacuated to the coast, but had to be given up by their gallant helpers after threats of consequences were issued by the invaders. They were sent to PoW camps, where "Weasel" would continue to be a thorn in the flesh of his captors.

The loss of six Hampdens and three Wellingtons confirmed that daylight operations invited disaster, and, had dwindling fuel not compelled the BF109s to withdraw, the losses would surely have been substantially greater. While 2 Group would continue to operate in daylight with its Blenheims, 3, 4 and 5 Groups would become largely nocturnal, as, eventually, would a newly-constituted 1 Group, which was currently settled in France under the title of the Advanced Air Striking Force. A new campaign of mine-laying began on the 13th, to which the Hampden was to prove itself eminently suited. Code-named "gardening", the laying of mines in enemy sea-lanes from the eastern Baltic to the border between France and Spain would continue to the end of the war as a major part of Bomber Command's effort, and would be highly productive, ultimately sinking more enemy ships than the Royal Navy. The "gardens" were identified by horticultural and marine-life code names, the mines were referred to as "vegetables", and the act of delivering them as "planting", and the target area for fifteen Hampdens for this maiden operation was Asparagus, located in the southern reaches of the Great Belt between Denmark's two largest islands of Fyn and Sjælland. 50 Squadron dispatched F/Ls Cosgrove and Bennett and F/O Corr and their crews at 22.15, 22.40 and 23.00 respectively, just as F/O Lloyd was returning from the above-mentioned fruitless search for the Bull crew. They flew out over the North Sea in very poor weather conditions characterized by low cloud and driving rain, which kept them below 1,000 feet until making landfall after three hours respectively south and north of Esbjerg on the west coast of Jutland. F/L Bennett reached the east coast of Jutland without incident, identified Odense on Fyn and then arrived at Sprogo, the small island at the mid-point between Fyn and Sjælland, at 01.55. The two mines were dropped into the briefed location from 600 feet, and a safe return completed after a six-and-a-half-hour round trip. F/O Corr also reached the target area, where, after searching for twenty minutes at between 1,000 and 3,000 feet, he delivered his stores from 500 feet. F/L Cosgrove and crew failed to return in L4065, and it is not known whether or not they completed their sortie. Reports of a Hampden crashing into the sea off Mablethorpe would seem to refer to the 50 Squadron aircraft, and no trace of it or its crew was ever found. F/L Cosgrove was Australian, and his father was the Premier of Tasmania.

F/O Lloyd and crew set off in the Anson at 05.40 on the 14th to conduct a further search for P/O Bull and crew, and they were followed into the air twenty minutes later by F/O French in a Hampden. Because of the restricted range of the Anson, Thornaby, in what is now Teesside, was used as a staging post for refuelling, in order to allow the maximum patrol time over the search area. F/O French and crew searched first, returning after six-and-a-half-hours to report finding nothing, before F/O Lloyd took off from Thornaby at 11.55 on the very final quest to find their colleagues. Sadly, they, too, returned after five-and-a-half-hours having seen nothing, leaving the Bull crew to be declared missing in action. The body of one crew member would eventually come ashore for burial after somehow being carried to the Kiel area on the eastern side of the Schleswig-Holstein peninsular. W/C Taafe ordered S/L Good to search for the other missing crew of F/L Cosgrove, and he took off at 11.30 to focus on an area some twelve miles out from Mablethorpe. Again, no trace was found, and the squadron was forced to come to terms, for the first time, with the realities of an escalating war, in which four crews had been lost from two operations.

That night, 5 Group dispatched twenty-eight Hampdens for gardening duties off Denmark, for which 50 Squadron detailed four crews briefed to return to the Asparagus garden area. P/Os Taylor and Stenner and S/L Cooper took off between 19.20 and 19.40, leaving F/O Vernieux and crew to depart three hours later. Exiting the English coast at Skegness, they set a course for Fanø island south of Esbjerg, which proved difficult to identify because of poor weather conditions and low cloud. The newly-commissioned P/O Stenner altered course for the garden area on e.t.a., and, on e.t.a there, searched in vain for thirty minutes for a pinpoint, before abandoning the sortie and returning to land at Manston. P/O Taylor and crew were more successful in establishing their position, both at Fanø and in the target area at 22.30, for which they were assisted by lights from Nyborg, Sprogo island and the main islands on either side of the Great Belt. They planted their vegetables as briefed, and returned safely also to Manston. S/L Cooper and crew described the conditions in the target area as fairly good with a cloud base at around 4,000 feet, but this was only after crossing Denmark over ten-tenths cloud with a base at 1,000 feet. They descended to 500 feet at 22.40 to deliver their mines into the briefed location, before setting a return course to a position ten miles north of the Teschelling light, and, thereafter, a landing at Manston. At 22.50, F/O Vernieux and crew took off from Waddington on their sortie to the same area, but an inaccurate wireless calibration was picked up at base, and a recall signal was sent. This proved to be the final operation with the squadron for S/L Cooper, who was posted on the 15th to 185 Squadron, which was being reformed as a Hampden unit at Cottesmore in Rutland. This unit would not become operational, and would be disbanded in mid-May, only to be reformed eleven months hence and equipped with Hurricanes for the defence of Malta.

Orders were received on the 17th to repeat the operation that night, for which 50 Squadron made ready four Hampdens in an overall 5 Group effort of thirty-three. Sgt Abbott and F/Os Lloyd, French and Vernieux departed Waddington between 22.45 and 22.55, before crossing the coast at Skegness and heading for Esbjerg at between 2,000 and 4,000 feet in excellent weather conditions and moonlight, which assisted with navigation. It took around two-and-a-half-hours to reach Denmark's west coast, and a further hour to cross Jutland and locate the target area, where Sgt Abbott and crew planted their vegetables at 02.18. They encountered no opposition, other than a challenge from Korsør on the western tip of Sjælland, and returned safely after a trip of almost six hours. F/O Lloyd and crew fulfilled their brief also during an uneventful sortie of six hours, but the remaining two crews would not even reach the English coast. F/O French and crew were back on the ground within twenty minutes after their maps, charts and navigational equipment were sucked out through the open hatch in the navigator's compartment, and, by the time they had replenished the stocks, it was too late to take off again. F/O Vernieux and crew had reached Horncastle on their way to the coast, when an issue with the starboard engine ended their sortie.

5 Group sent out orders on the 20th for further mining operations that night, and twenty-three Hampdens were made ready, seven of them by 50 Squadron, whose crews were briefed for the Eglantines garden, situated in the familiar territory of the River Elbe estuary. They took off between 00.01 and 00.35 on the 21st with S/L Good the senior pilot on duty, but soon lost the services of P/O Jacklin and crew to a wireless issue, and F/O Corr and crew, who were an hour out when an engine developed a fault. The others pressed on across the North Sea,

encountering poor visibility and rain until reaching the east Frisians, where the skies cleared, allowing moonlight to assist with navigation. The vegetables were planted into the briefed locations from 500 to 800 feet, and all returned safely to report many marine and shore-based lights, but no opposition.

Later in the day, 5 Group issued further orders, this time for thirty-six Hampdens to conduct gardening sorties in northern waters that night. 50 Squadron made ready three aircraft, one for the Eglantines area with P/O Jacklin and crew on board, and two for Daffodils, the stretch of water between Denmark's Sjælland island and Sweden's west coast, known locally as Øresund, and to the British as The Sound. The crews of F/Os Corr and Lloyd were assigned to the latter, and the trio departed Waddington between 18.55 and 19.05, making first for Skegness to begin the North Sea crossing. F/O Corr maintained 7,000 feet, and made landfall on the German coast near Husum aerodrome under moonlight so bright that it was possible to map-read all the way to the target area, where the vegetable was planted from 700 feet. F/O Lloyd had decided to head for Hörnum on the southern tip of Sylt, and pinpointed first on Garding, some twenty-five miles to the south, before traversing the Schleswig-Holstein peninsular and skirting the Kiel Canal en-route to the drop zone. The vegetable was planted in the briefed location, and a return made over List, on the northern end of Sylt, where searchlights and ineffective flak were observed. Meanwhile, P/O Jacklin and crew had set course for the German coast, and flew at 6,000 feet for three hours, estimating that they were then in the vicinity of the target area of the Elbe Estuary. They had clearly overflown their pinpoint, however, and, following a thirty-minute search, were unable to identify their location and turned for home.

5 Group put up thirty Hampdens for mining and seaplane base-patrolling duties on the 23rd, three of the former provided by 50 Squadron. S/L Good and P/O Stenner were briefed for a return to the Daffodils garden, while F/L Willan, who had been posted in to replace F/L Cosgrove, was assigned to Melons, which was the Eckernförde, a dozen miles north-west of Kiel on the eastern side of the Schleswig-Holstein peninsular. The Daffodil-bound duo took off at 19.00 and 19.15 respectively, and crossed the North Sea at 6,000 feet under almost clear skies and bright moonlight, before making landfall in the area north of Sylt. From there they climbed to 8,000 feet to cross Jutland, Fyn and Sjælland and, finally, The Sound, enabled by the conditions to map-read all the way. There was no opposition throughout the sortie, and the vegetables were delivered into the allotted locations from 600 feet, after which, safe returns were made. F/L Willan and crew departed Waddington at 19.30 and followed the same outward course as the others, only at 4,000 feet, also making landfall north of Sylt, before heading south-east across the German frontier with the lights of Flensburg as a guide. Navigation was easy in the prevailing conditions, and, as the target drew near, height was reduced to 800 feet for the delivery of the mine. Two searchlights flicked on at Eckernförde, but did not prove to be troublesome, and this was the only opposition encountered. While these sorties were in progress, F/O Shaughnessy and crew conducted a security patrol over the Frisian islands of Norderney and Borkum. Having taken off at 19.40, they flew out at 4,000 feet, taking advantage of the good visibility and moonlight to establish their position first over Borkum, and dropped down initially to 2,000 feet, before being persuaded by searchlights to climb again. On the way home south of Borkum, they shook off a BF109 after diving down to sea level, and were untroubled thereafter, pinpointing on the Terschelling light vessel for the final leg to a safe landing.

The 25th brought further mining operations, for which 5 Group ordered twenty-eight Hampdens to be made ready. There was a new garden for the four 50 Squadron participants, Forget-me-nots, which was located in the approaches to Kiel harbour. F/L Bennett and F/Os Lloyd, Taylor and Vernieux departed Waddington between 23.35 and 23.45, and headed to Skegness as the exit point for the North Sea crossing. Adverse weather conditions in the form of fog and ten-tenths cloud between sea level and 10,000 feet tested the crews' navigation skills as they made for the Terschelling light vessel at between 4,000 and 8,000 feet. On e.t.a at the Westerhever light, on the west coast of the Schleswig-Holstein peninsular, due west of Kiel on the opposite coast, F/L Bennett descended to 1,000 feet, but did not break cloud and saw only flashes of searchlights and flak. He altered course in the direction of the target area, and, on e.t.a again, descended further to 400 feet, still without being able to observe the ground. After climbing to a safe height, a fix was obtained, which showed him to be over Denmark, north of Flensburg, from where a new course was set towards the south-east. The Danish town of Sønderborg was identified through a break in the cloud, and height was reduced to 400 feet, but the gap closed, and, with bleak prospects of a successful outcome, the sortie was abandoned and a return course to Leuchars in Scotland set via Esbjerg. It was a similar story for F/Os Lloyd and Vernieux, who both failed to break cloud and returned also to Leuchars with their stores. F/O Taylor and crew were experiencing the same difficulties, and crossed Jutland at 7,000 feet, enveloped in cloud the whole way. On e.t.a at what they thought was the target area, they descended to 600 feet, and broke cloud over Ærø Island, some thirty miles north-east of Kiel, for which they set course. On approach they could see a ship being loaded or unloaded, and the lights from it lighting up the town, but these were extinguished as the sound of the Hampden's engines drew near. A vegetable was planted from 500 feet, the only one by a 5 Group aircraft on this night, after which they climbed to 12,000 feet with dawn fast approaching. They were still over enemy territory when daylight arrived, but no enemy aircraft appeared, and they, too, landed at Leuchars after six-and-a-half-hours in the air.

Poor weather over the UK and northern Germany curtailed operational activity over the ensuing days, before the squadron was put on stand-by to move to a base in Scotland. The stand-by was cancelled on the 30th, the day on which S/L Crockart was posted in from 106 Squadron to succeed S/L Cooper as a flight commander. Orders were received that day to prepare three Hampdens for bombing operations that night against an aerodrome at Fornebu, near Oslo, in company with seven others from the group. Two other aerodromes, at Stavanger and Aalborg, were to be targeted simultaneously by Whitleys of 4 Group and Wellingtons of 3 Group, which amounted to a total force over Norway of fifty aircraft. The 50 Squadron trio of F/L Willan, F/O Corr and Sgt Abbott, took off at 20.40, 20.45 and 20.50 respectively, and set course from Skegness to Lindesnes on the southern tip of Norway. F/L Willan flew out at 12,000 feet in good conditions, with five-tenths cloud lying well below at 5,000 feet, and made landfall between Lindesnes and Kristiansand. Moonlight and an inefficient blackout aided map-reading, and, with Oslo fifty miles ahead, anti-aircraft fire could be seen, presumably having been stirred into action by the early arrivals. The target was identified from fifteen miles away by a large blaze, and the bombing run was carried out from south-east to north-west at 12,000 feet at 00.55, in the face of an intense searchlight and flak response. The flak was bursting below the Hampden as the six 250 pounders were dropped to the east of the aerodrome, five of them with delay fuses. After bombing, F/L Willan set a course a little south of due west to reach the coast at Haugersund, descending then to 8,000 feet for the sea crossing to Kinloss in Scotland.

When a hundred miles from the Norwegian coast, Sgt Abbott and crew were latched onto by a Dornier Do 18 seaplane with four landing lights displayed. The rear gunner fired a burst, which seemed to enter the assailant, and persuaded it to extinguish the lights, break away and disappear from sight. They attacked the aerodrome from 10,000 feet at 01.15 on an east to west heading, and observed the bombs to fall on the edge of the airfield. They returned to Kinloss to report a large fire and five searchlights co-operating with numerous light flak batteries. F/O Corr approached the target initially at 4,000 feet, but this was in the killing zone for light flak, and it was decided to turn away and come in again at 10,000 feet. The six bombs were dropped at 01.20, but the one fused to explode on impact failed to do so, which meant that the fall of the others could not be determined precisely. Three Hampdens failed to return, and one of them, believed to be from 49 Squadron, became the first to be shot down at night by an enemy fighter. During the course of the month the squadron participated in fifteen operations, and launched sixty-one sorties for the loss of four Hampdens and crews.

May 1940

The squadron was in action immediately at the start of the new month, supporting an attack by six Hampdens on the aerodrome at Ålborg (Aalborg) in northern Denmark. 50 Squadron loaded two Hampdens with six 250 pounders each, all with instant fuses, and dispatched them at 22.35 and 22.45 with F/L Bennett and P/O Stenner at the controls. The latter returned within twenty-five minutes with a failed wireless, and took off again at 00.05 for a second attempt. F/L Bennett and crew flew out at 6,000 feet over a blanket of cloud, which dispersed some forty miles short of the Danish coast, enabling them to pinpoint their landfall at the Lemvig lighthouse on the north-west coast of Jutland. They climbed to 10,000 feet and headed for the east coast, where they turned 180 degrees to attack the target from east to west, descending to 1,000 feet to deliver the bombs in a single stick in the face of intense searchlight and flak activity. The bombs were seen to explode close to the hangars and across the airfield, and the gunners strafed the area as F/L Bennett weaved away until clear of the flak five minutes later. A course was then set for Kinloss, where they landed safely after seven hours aloft. P/O Stenner flew out at 10,000 feet with patchy cloud below, until nearing the Danish coast near Nissum Fjord, when it cleared to leave favourable visibility for map-reading the rest of the way to the target. The first bombing run was thwarted by the intensity and accuracy of the flak defence, but the bombs were successfully released during a second run from east to west at 03.30, during which, a piece of shrapnel entered the tail. After bombing they continued in a westerly direction, shedding height as they made for the coast, and were intercepted by a Me110 at 03.40, which attacked with cannon and machine-gun fire. It was driven off by return fire, but returned with another Me110 a few minutes later, before both were driven off again. Damage to the Hampden was not serious, the crew was unhurt, and a safe return was made to Kinloss. While this operation was in progress, eleven Hampdens were sent mining in the Eglantines garden in the Elbe Estuary. The 50 Squadron Operations Record Book records that one of its own crews took part, but provides no details concerning this sortie, other than that it was concluded successfully.

On the following night, 5 Group sent twenty-six Hampdens to mine the waters of Oslo Fjord (Onions) and Kiel Bay (Forget-me-nots), and among them were four representing 50 Squadron. F/O Taylor and F/O Shaugnessy and their crews took off for the former at 20.15 and 20.25, to be followed two hours later by Sgt Banker and P/O Jacklin bound for the latter.

The course to Oslo Fjord ran from Skegness to a point five miles east of Kristiansand, and this was undertaken in good conditions over some low cloud. Then it was a direct course to the target, on approach to which and four miles ahead, F/O Taylor could see an intense flak barrage directed at another Hampden. He made a dummy run over the aiming-point at 3,000 feet on a north-easterly heading, before descending to 500 feet and running the gauntlet of flak from east to west to deliver the mine into the briefed location. Remarkably, the flak missed, and F/O Taylor climbed to 7,000 feet to cross the mountains en-route to the coast, where a course was set for Kinloss. F/O Shaughnessy flew out at 8,000 feet to make landfall ten miles east of Stavanger, and, on e.t.a at Oslo, turned south-east, hugging the West Bank of the Fjord, map-reading to the drop site, where the vegetable was planted at 01.05 from 500 feet in the face of a moderate flak response.

P/O Jacklin favoured a fairly low crossing of the North Sea, and maintained a height of 1,500 feet to a point four miles north of Husum, where he turned inland to cross the Schleswig-Holstein peninsular, taking care to avoid the flak coming up from Kiel. The garden was located without difficulty and the vegetable planted from 550 feet at 02.21. A reciprocal course was adopted to reach the North Sea via Husum, and, after flying west for fifteen minutes, three Me110s attacked "von hintern, untern", from behind and below. P/O Jacklin responded by climbing for a cloud bank four thousand feet above, pursued by the enemy trio, two of which broke off once cloud had been reached. The third assailant continued the attack until the coast was crossed, the two combatants exchanging fire but not scoring hits, and the Jacklin crew returned safely to Waddington. Sgt Banker and crew crossed the North Sea at 6,000 feet over cloud, which dispersed somewhat twenty minutes before e.t.a, and this should have revealed Denmark below. In fact, they were over Germany, south of the Frisians, and a new course was set towards the north and followed for twenty minutes before they turned east at 4,000 feet, barely able to make out the Danish mainland. They spent the next two hours stooging back and forth in search of a pinpoint, before concluding eventually that they had been over the western Baltic, and, it was not until Eckernförde was positively identified, that they could set a course for the garden. By this time, however, dawn had arrived, and, deeming it too dangerous to continue the sortie in the burgeoning light, they headed for home, where they landed after seven-and-a-half hours in the air.

On a relatively quiet night operationally, 5 Group detailed five Hampdens for gardening duties in the Onions region of Oslo Fjord on the 4th. F/O French, S/L Good and F/O Lloyd departed Waddington at 20.15, 20.30 and 20.55 respectively, and set course for the Kristiansand area of southern Norway, before making their way north-east to the drop zone. S/L Good flew out at 10,000 feet, and, three minutes after making landfall, passed over Kristiansand aerodrome, where a paraffin flarepath had been lit. The next pinpoint was at Råda, some thirty miles south of Oslo, from where the garden could be identified by anti-aircraft fire twenty miles ahead. Having descended to 7,000 feet, S/L Good throttled back to reduce engine noise, and glided down to 500 feet along Bonne Fjord, noting about fifteen merchant ships of between 2,000 and 8,000 tons at berth. No opposition was encountered until shortly before the garden was reached, when intense and accurate searchlight and anti-aircraft fire was encountered, and the Hampden was hit by a shell in the port side, injuring S/L Good and knocking out the intercom. The vegetable was dropped immediately from 400 feet at 01.03, before S/L Good turned sharply to starboard to attempt to escape the cauldron of fire. The pilot was too severely incapacitated to continue at the controls, and, with great difficulty because of his condition and the tight confines of the Hampden cockpit, he and the navigator, who, in a Hampden, was always a qualified pilot, exchanged places. While he flew the aircraft, another member of the crew performed first aid on S/L Good, which was credited with saving his life. A safe landing was carried out at Kinloss at 04.30, and the navigator/second pilot, P/O Gardner, flew the damaged Hampden back to Waddington later in the day. He and S/L Good were awarded a DFC for their exploits. Meanwhile, F/Os French and Lloyd had delivered their vegetables as briefed, the latter doing so from 400 feet at 01.15 after observing the defensive activity stirred up by S/L Good. Both Hampdens managed to dodge the shells, and made it safely back to Kinloss.

As the gallant but doomed Allied efforts to gain a foothold in Norway petered out, 50 Squadron was stood down from operations for a week, unless anything of major importance were to take place. Despite that, orders were received on the 9th to prepare five aircraft for mining duties in three gardens, Hollyhocks, on the approaches to Lübeck at Travemünde, Jasmine, situated off the port of Warnemünde in the Baltic, and the familiar Eglantines in the Elbe estuary. F/Os Taylor and French were assigned to Hollyhocks, and took off at 21.35 and 23.15 respectively, F/O Corr and F/L Willan to Jasmine, departing Waddington at 21.45 and 21.50, and S/L Crockart to Eglantines, for which he and his crew became airborne at 22.55. Exiting the coast at Skegness, the Jasmine-bound pair crossed the North Sea over cloud at 8,000 to 10,000 feet, F/O Corr and crew turning inland after reaching the Cuxhaven area. F/L Willan discovered that he had overflown his intended turning point by sixty miles, blaming wrongly forecast winds, and, by the time he reached the target area, the visibility was poor, and the dawn fast approaching, and he was persuaded to abandon his sortie. F/O Corr and crew ran into intense searchlight activity over Rendsburg and Kiel, and also found the visibility too challenging. After searching in vain for an hour, they also gave up and came home. F/O Taylor, meanwhile, had navigated via the Terschelling light vessel and the Westerhever lighthouse to a point on the west coast of the Schleswig-Holstein peninsular, before setting course directly to the target area, descending to 4,500 feet with the intention of passing to the north of Kiel. They ran into the same searchlight and flak activity as F/O Corr, demonstrating that they were south of track, but escaped retribution for the navigational error, and continued on to the garden, where they planted their vegetable from 500 feet. They climbed to 12,000 feet to begin the return journey, making a detour over the Baltic to avoid Kiel, and flew the rest of the way without incident at 10,000 feet. F/O French and crew enjoyed an entirely uneventful trip to this garden, where they planted their mine as briefed, before completing an equally quiet return flight. S/L Crockart was undertaking his maiden operation with the squadron, and flew out at 10,000 feet over cloud, which dispersed from 5 degrees east to leave good visibility but extreme darkness. He located the target area with ease, and carried out a gliding approach to deliver the mine from 800 feet, before climbing back to 6,000 feet for the flight home.

The storm broke at dawn on the 10th, when German forces began the invasion of Holland, Belgium and Luxembourg, and 5 Group was put on stand-by to attack communications targets to hinder their advance. It would signal the massacre of the Battle squadrons of the AASF in France, and also the Blenheim units of the England-based 2 Group, and, over the course of the ensuing five days, both types would be hacked out of the sky in alarming numbers in an unequal fight against murderous ground fire and marauding Luftwaffe fighters. It would fall to the so-called heavy bombers on the stations of eastern England to hinder the progress of the enemy forces, by attacking bridges, roads and railways behind their lines. 5 Group was not called into action on that first night, but nineteen crews were summoned to briefing on the

11th to be told of their part in the bombing of road and rail targets at Mönchengladbach on the south-western edge of the industrial Ruhr Valley. This would be the first time that a German town had been intentionally targeted. 50 Squadron made ready three Hampdens, loading each with six 250 pounders, three with instant fuses and three with a six-hour delay, and dispatched them at 00.25, 00.30 and 00.35 with F/O Vernieux, P/O Mulloy and P/O Jacklin respectively at the controls. The weather conditions were perfect as they set out from Skegness on course for The Hague at 4,000 feet, before climbing to evade the intense searchlight welcome at the enemy coast. F/O Vernieux climbed as high as 13,000 feet to pinpoint on Nijmegen, before altering course to the south-east on track for the target. This was found to be on fire, which, together with extreme darkness, prevented identification of the precise aiming-point. With dawn breaking and the sky lightening perceptibly, it was decided to head for home, and F/O Vernieux put the nose of the Hampden down, shedding height from 13,000 down to 2,000 feet for the race across the defences to reach the safety of the North Sea. P/O Mulloy and crew observed a built-up area beneath them on e.t.a at 02.40, and dropped their bombs from 5,000 feet, observing one to hit a large rectangular building. P/O Jacklin also bombed on e.t.a, and, on the way home, was harried by a night-fighter, which failed to score any hits. The coastal defences had their say also, but the Hampden weaved its way through unscathed, passing some ten miles south of Rotterdam and reaching the North Sea via the Scheldt estuary.

Three aircraft were put on stand-by later on the 12th, but were not called into action, and all serviceable aircraft were made ready for action from first light to 19.00 on the 13th, before being stood down for the night. 5 Group did operate on this night, when sending six Hampdens to bomb roads and bridges in the Aachen-Maastricht-Eindhoven area, while F/L Bennett took off from Scampton with five others for gardening sorties in the Lettuce garden of the Kiel Canal. Having taken off at 20.35, he and his crew crossed the German coast at 22.50 at 200 feet in deteriorating weather conditions. Uncertain of their position, they deviated, before returning to the original course to cross the Schleswig-Holstein peninsular, and, eventually, pick up flashing buoys in the western Baltic from a height of 300 feet. Stumbling around in the murk, they were set upon by three enemy night-fighters, which chased them into cloud at 900 feet. They remained in the cloud for some time, in the expectation that the enemy had given up the chase, but were surprised and dismayed to find ten fighters waiting for them as they emerged into clear air. They soon found themselves boxed in by assailants positioned above, behind and on each side. Further evasive action took them towards the north and then the east, where they spotted land below, before flying north again for twenty minutes, only to run into three more fighters. The navigator identified the Asparagus garden beneath them (Great Belt), and course was altered to the south-east for another attempt to locate the briefed Lettuce garden. Two of the night-fighters were shaken off, while the third persisted with the chase, until, finally, being lost in cloud. By this time, F/L Bennett and crew were over Lübeck Bay, but, determined to deliver their vegetable, set course again for the garden, and once more encountered the fighters. They found another layer of cloud to hide in, and headed westwards while they obtained a fix to establish a precise position. This took time, and, on breaking cloud, they found themselves to be over the North Sea with dawn breaking and an enemy fighter still on their tail. They had no choice but to focus on losing their shadow, in which endeavour they succeeded, and made it back to Waddington in one piece at 04.35 after a highly eventful sortie.

Orders were received across the Command on the 14th to prepare aircraft for operations that night against communications targets in Germany and Holland and for gardening duties. 5

Group was to contribute a dozen Hampdens to attacks on Roosendaal and a road near Breda, both in south-western Holland, for which S/L Crockart and W/C Taafe departed Waddington at 00.15 and 00.25 respectively. The squadron's five gardeners, F/Os French, Lloyd, Shaughnessy and Vernieux and P/O Mulloy, had taken off more than four hours earlier, and were now battling the poor visibility over the western Baltic in search of the Quince garden in Kiel Bay. The flight from Skegness to the Danish coast had been flown over ten-tenths cloud, that prevented sight of landfall, which, for F/O Lloyd and crew should have occurred at 22.50. On e.t.a., a course was set eastwards for the target area, and, on arrival over the Baltic coast at 23.55, the cloud dispersed, enabling them to identify the port of Nyborg on the eastern side of Fyn, where a 12,000-ton transport vessel was observed. They headed south to the garden, situated off the southernmost point of Langeland island, and planted their vegetable at 00.05, before returning home to report a completely uneventful sortie. Despite extensive searches, the remaining four 50 Squadron gardeners would fail to locate their target areas in conditions of persistent heavy cloud, and would bring their stores home.

Meanwhile, some 500 miles to the south-west, S/L Crockart had crossed the coast at Skegness at 10,000 feet, and altered course for the Scheldt estuary, arriving at the Hook of Holland at 01.20. Throttling back, he glided down to the target area, where a reconnaissance established his position, and a flare was dropped to confirm it, before an attack was carried out from 1,500 feet at 02.20. The two delay-fused 500 pounders fell away, but the two with instant fuses hung-up, and it was difficult, therefore, to plot the fall. Fires were reported before and after the bombing run, and also in the north-eastern quarter of Rotterdam, and anti-aircraft fire was observed in the Dordrecht region. W/C Taafe had exited England over the Norfolk coast at 8,000 feet at 00.59, and arrived at the Dutch coast at 01.30 to find lights blazing in The Hague, and Rotterdam to be on fire and under a pall of heavy smoke rising through 9,000 feet following an attack by the Luftwaffe. Attempts to locate Roosendaal were thwarted by smoke haze extending to 5,000 feet, and the deployment of a parachute flare failed to reveal any recognizable landmarks. Attention was switched to Breda to the north-east, where, after a search lasting forty-five minutes, a road was spotted to the north of the town in the light of the breaking dawn, and the six 250 pounders were dropped across it in a single stick. They crossed the enemy coast homebound at 02.46, and reached the Norfolk coast thirty-nine minutes later.

The RAF's campaign of strategic bombing began on the night of the 15/16th, for which ninety-nine aircraft were detailed from 3, 4 and 5 Groups and assigned to sixteen separate targets in and around the Ruhr. 5 Group detailed thirty-six Hampdens, of which six were made ready by 50 Squadron and loaded with four 500 pounders each, while their crews were briefed for the attack on an oil refinery at Kamen at the north-eastern end of the Ruhr. P/O Jacklin and F/L Willan departed Waddington at 21.20 and 21.35 respectively, and they were followed into the air at 21.45 and 21.50 by F/Os Corr and Taylor, by Sgt Abbott and crew at 22.00, and, finally, by P/O Stenner and crew at 22.30. P/O Jacklin and F/L Willan crossed the enemy coast at the Scheldt estuary and altered course at Helden in southern Holland, before running into intense searchlight activity and being driven off track. All efforts by P/O Jacklin and crew to locate their primary target failed, and they headed for Dortmund as their alternative, where the illumination rendered it easily recognizable. They attacked from around 10,000 feet, and scored a direct hit, which caused an enormous explosion that rocked the Hampden. A great sheet of flame followed, and then they were in cloud and heading back across Holland for an uneventful return home. F/L Willan had descended to 7,000 feet over

Holland, and managed to obtain a pinpoint some twenty-five miles from the target, before dropping flares from 6,000 and 4,000 feet at 00.01 and 00.06 in search of the aiming-point. This remained elusive, until being spotted by the navigator at 00.15, but, on turning towards it, it disappeared from sight again, by which time they were down to 3,000 feet. At that moment a large convoy of motor transports was spotted heading west, and this was bombed from 2,800 feet. While setting course for home, they climbed to 14,000 feet to avoid icing conditions lower down, but found themselves being thrown about by a violent electrical storm. On emerging from this, still deep in enemy territory, they dodged searchlights for an hour before reaching the sanctuary of the North Sea.

F/O Corr crossed the Dutch coast at Ijmuiden at 12,000 feet, and reached the Kamen area at 00.25. The primary and alternative targets could not be identified, and the bombs were eventually dropped on what appeared to be the coke ovens of a steelworks at Soest, situated some seven miles to the north of the one-day-to-be-famous Möhne Dam. Flying back over the Ruhr at 10,000 feet, they were ensnared by searchlights on a number of occasions, but managed to escape their clutches to return safely. F/O Taylor and crew noted the fires burning fiercely in Rotterdam and Amsterdam, and then experienced a torrid time over the Ruhr while flying at between 3,000 and 12,000 feet in a vain search for their objective. Haze proved to be the main problem, but it did not hide a railway junction in the textiles-producing town of Bocholt, north of the Ruhr, where the four 500 pounders were delivered from 4,500 feet at 01.31. Sgt Abbott and crew selected a route that took them over Essen, from where they followed the railway line to Hamm and then a river to the Kamen area. They identified the aiming-point without difficulty, and dropped a stick of three 500 pounders across it, before setting course for home at 01.00. As the last to take off, P/O Stenner and crew, perhaps, enjoyed the best of the conditions, and crossed the Dutch coast at 10,000 feet south of Amsterdam, observing the fires there and at Utrecht. The Ruhr was awash with searchlights, none of which found them as they flew over under clear skies with a hint of moonlight. They reached the target at 01.15, the time at which the auto-bomb sight decided to fail, forcing them to bomb manually from 5,000 feet. Setting course for home at 01.30, they made the North Sea forty-five minutes later, and reached Waddington without incident.

Preparations were put in hand on the 17th for another busy night of strategic operations involving more than a hundred aircraft. 5 Group detailed forty-eight Hampdens to attack oil-related targets in Hamburg, while twenty-four Whitleys of 4 Group were assigned to similar objectives in Bremen and a handful of 3 Group Wellingtons went for railway installations in Cologne. While these raids were taking place over Germany, a force of forty-six Wellingtons and six Hampdens would conduct tactical operations against a road and railway junction in Belgium, through which enemy troop columns were passing on their way to the front. 50 Squadron made ready eleven Hampdens, eight of them to send to Hamburg and three to Yvoir, situated on the approaches to the Ardennes. The main element took off between 20.40 and 21.50 with W/C Taafe the senior pilot on duty, and flew out over Skegness on a night of unlimited visibility enhanced by an almost full moon, which would enable them to map-read to the enemy coast via the lightship at Terschelling and the lighthouses at Westerhever and Heligoland. F/O Vernieux's sortie was over almost immediately, however, after an exhaust manifold came loose and forced him to turn back before reaching the coast. W/C Taafe climbed to 14,000 feet, and navigated to the wide Elbe estuary, before following the river into the heart of the city at 12,000 feet, where the searchlights and flak were ineffective. Ground features stood out clearly as he carried out four dummy runs on a south to north heading, before releasing four 250 pounders and a cannister of incendiaries from 11,000 feet at 00.20. One bomb and the incendiaries were seen to fall close to the aiming-point, and cause a fire which grew in intensity. The other crews assigned to this target reported similar experiences, and bombed from between 7,000 and 12,000 feet either side of midnight, enjoying largely uneventful sorties. Only F/L Bennett and crew reported being engaged by a night-fighter, which was driven off by fire from the lower rear gunner.

The tactical trio departed Waddington between 21.15 and 21.40 with S/L Crockart the senior pilot, he and his crew exiting the Suffolk coast at Aldeburgh and heading at 9,000 feet towards a landfall over Walcheren in the Scheldt estuary. Low cloud over Belgium forced them down to between 2,000 and 3,000 feet, but the pinpoints at Brussels, Namur and Dinant were identified, before they turned 180 degrees to run back over Yvoir to drop the bombs. It must have been hugely frustrating when they hung-up and had to be brought home. F/O Corr and crew spent sixty-five minutes in the target area trying to rectify a faulty bomb-fusing light, and, when the six 250 pounders were released, there was no perceptible sense that they had fallen away and no bursts on the ground as confirmation that they had. An enquiry would determine later that the bombs had dropped "live", and the bursts had simply not been observed. F/O French was also forced to fly beneath the ten-tenths cloud base hanging over southern Belgium at 4,000 feet, and dropped parachute flares to reveal the target. This prompted intense searchlight activity and anti-aircraft fire, through which the bombs were dropped from 3,000 feet at 23.45, before a safe return was completed.

A similar pattern of operations against industrial targets in Germany and communications in Belgium and France would occupy the following two nights, and 50 Squadron contributed three Hampdens to 5 Group's commitment of a dozen aircraft to the night's activities on the 18th. F/Os Shaughnessy and Taylor and P/O Jacklin took off at 21.50 to attack a road junction at Givet, situated on the French side of the Franco/Belgian frontier. They crossed the enemy coast near Zeebrugge, and made their way in perfect weather conditions to the target area via Ghent and Brussels, reducing height to between 5,500 and 8,000 feet to deliver their six 250 pounders each. P/O Jacklin had one bomb hang-up, while an un-activated cut-off switch in F/O Shaughnessy's aircraft led to a complete hang-up.

Twenty-four hours later, seventy-eight aircraft, including thirty-six Hampdens, were poised to carry out widespread attacks on German troop communications in France and Belgium and on railway and industrial targets in Germany. The 5 Group crews were briefed for a number of oil-related targets, those at Waddington learning that a refinery at Salzbergen, situated on the River Ems in the Münsterland, ten miles from the Dutch border, was to be their target. This was, in fact, the oldest refinery in Germany, having been established in 1860, and being run now by the Wintershall company, which operated refineries at a number of sites across Germany. They began taking off at 21.30, with S/L Crockart the senior pilot on duty, with the intention, it seems, of flying out in formation. However, S/L Crockart climbed out at a speed that left some of the others behind, and F/O Vernieux was the only one to hang on to his coat tails until twenty miles out from Skegness, where they separated. F/L Willan and P/O Gardiner remained in contact with each other at 8,000 feet as far as the Dutch coast, before all made their way individually to the target area. F/O Corr and crew headed directly for the target, but the navigator was unable to pinpoint their position on e.t.a at the Dutch coast. An hour-long search was carried out at heights ranging from 4,000 down to 200 feet, but flooding of the Dutch coastal region created difficulties, and, by the time they had detoured to a familiar location on the coast at Ijmuiden, it was too late to carry on. It would be established at base that the map had omitted some major ground detail.

The others pressed on under bright moonlight that should have assisted navigation, and P/O Gardiner and crew approached the target area at 10,000 feet, only to find themselves on e.t.a to be some fifteen miles north-east of where they should have been. They observed ten reconnaissance flares to fall in the direction of the target, but, on seeing no bomb bursts, assumed that this could not be it. An hour-long search ended when a large fire was seen over to the east, towards which a course was set, but, after fifteen minutes, it appeared to remain beyond reach in the available time, and the sortie was abandoned. The remaining crews had, by then, reached the target, where F/L Willan delivered four 500 pounders from 2,000 feet, observing them to fall into the centre of the target and cause huge flames and black smoke. F/O Vernieux picked up the River Ems and ran along it to the target, observing the town of Rheine to be below, just a short distance to the south-east of the refinery. Intense searchlight and flak activity concealed the bursting of the four 250 pounders and container of incendiaries at 00.30, rendering an assessment impossible. The target was already on fire when S/L Crockart arrived, and he dropped his four 250 pounders and incendiaries from 1,000 to 1,800 feet onto oil storage tanks in a nearby wood. F/O French and crew returned to report attacking and hitting the target as briefed from 9,000 feet at 00.15, and observing a large fire develop.

The need to hinder the enemy advance would continue to draw elements of the Command's resources from strategic to tactical bombing, and the 20th called on ninety-two aircraft to attack troops and armour breaking into northern France. 5 Group detailed six Hampdens each from Waddington, Hemswell and Scampton to attack road bridges over the River Oise at Longchamps and Mont-d'Origny, for which 50 Squadron made ready three and dispatched them at 20.55 with F/Os Lloyd and Shaughnessy and P/O Jacklin at the controls. F/O Shaughnessy and crew made landfall at 6,000 feet over Gravelines to the west of Dunkerque, and were fired at immediately from the ground, despite flashing the French "letter of the day". They descended to 3,000 feet en-route to the target, passing close to Cambrai and Saint-Quentin, and noting many fires on both sides of the Franco-Belgian frontier. The target was easily identified in the favourable conditions, and the six 250 pounders were delivered in a single stick to strike the road leading to the bridge. P/O Jacklin followed a similar route, and experience the same hostile reception, before shedding height to 3,500 feet for the run-in on the railway bridge at Longchamps. The bombs were seen to overshoot and hit the road alongside the bridge, and the crew surmised that they may have exploded close enough to have the desired effect. F/O Lloyd and crew also noted many fires along the route, and ran into particularly heavy searchlight and flak activity at Vervins, where an enemy artillery unit had been set up. They identified the aiming-point at 23.10, and delivered their bombs from 2,000 feet, observing them to fall onto the railway lines a hundred yards or so to the east of the bridge.

The focus shifted to railways in Germany on the 21st, to attempt to stem the flow of troops and armour being fed into the battle area. 5 Group contributed twenty-five Hampdens to an overall force of 124 aircraft assigned to numerous aiming-points on lines to the west of Cologne from Mönchengladbach in the north to Euskirchen in the south. The 5 Group effort was to be directed at a twenty-mile stretch of track between Cologne and Düren, situated to the south-west of the Rhineland Capital, and the order was to attack any trains encountered. S/L Crockart and crew were the first of four 50 Squadron participants to take off, becoming airborne at 20.35 and setting course for the Scheldt estuary. On reaching the target area they carried out a reconnaissance, that revealed no trains on the briefed stretch of line, but prompted an intense and accurate searchlight and flak response. Turning their attention elsewhere, they came across a section of track between Liblar and Türnich, also to the south-west of Cologne, and dropped four 250 pounders there, and two others onto a road further west, four miles north-east of Blatzheim. A safe return was made, and the Hampden handed back to the ground crew to repair a hole in the starboard wing.

F/L Bennett and crew departed Waddington at 21.00, before crossing the coast at Skegness and heading directly for the target. When a dozen or so miles north of Mönchengladbach, they descended from 7,000 to 2,000 feet, and map-read their way with ease via canals, railways and roads until reaching Roermond in Holland, which they circled at 700 feet in order to pick up the railway line to Cologne. Some eight miles along the track, they ran into intense searchlight and flak activity, lost their intercom, and had to communicate in writing, which was difficult as they jinked about to avoid being hit. The bombs were dropped onto a stretch of line between four and twelve miles from Cologne at 00.05, and two direct hits were observed. F/O Vernieux and crew took off at 21.05, and flew out over Cromer to make landfall south of Rotterdam at 10,000 feet. Haze made map-reading a challenge from that altitude, despite which, the briefed stretch of track was located and bombed over a length of three miles at 23.30, although, no results were observed. P/O Stenner and crew were last away at 21.15, and they found the line between Cologne and Düren without difficulty, and empty of trains. Three bombs were delivered from 1,500 feet at 23.35, and were observed to fall one hundred, eighty and ten yards from the track at a point between four and seven miles north-east of Düren. The remaining three bombs were dropped onto the railway goods yard at Düren, and hits were registered.

It had been intended that the target for thirty-five Hampdens on the 22nd would be the oil refinery at distant Leuna, near Merseburg, one of many similar plants situated in an arc from north to south to the west of Leipzig. In the event, unfavourable weather conditions prompted a recall, which all but W/C Watts, the commanding officer of 144 Squadron, picked up, and he went on alone to bomb and damage the target. Meanwhile, 5 Group contributed a dozen Hampdens from Waddington and Scampton to attacks on railway bridges and road targets in France, Belgium and Holland. The target for the three 50 Squadron crews of F/O Lloyd and P/Os Gardiner and Mulloy was road and rail communications at Binche, situated between Mons and Charleroi in Belgium, close to the frontier with France. They departed Waddington at 21.45, and crossed the North Sea in improving weather conditions to reach the Belgian coast at various points between Blankenberge and the Scheldt, before locating the target area without much difficulty. F/O Lloyd and crew dropped their six 250 pounders from 1,500 feet onto a railway siding at 23.53, and observed much debris being flung into the air. They dropped two parachute flares in an attempt to identify the debris, but failed to do so. P/O Gardiner and crew followed the canal from Terneuzen to Ghent, before setting course for the target, which was easily identified on e.t.a. They attacked from the north-west from 1,700 feet at 23.45, and observed the first two bombs to overshoot by twenty yards, and the others to fall alongside the track. P/O Mulloy and crew had been briefed to conduct a general reconnaissance before bombing, and observed up to fifty fires in Belgium, many of them close to the border with Holland. However, they were unable to locate Binche because of low cloud and poor visibility, and no troop or transport movements were observed.

It was similar fare on the following night, when fifty Hampdens were among 122 aircraft sent to attack railway communications and trains in motion on either side of the Dutch/German frontier. 50 Squadron loaded eight Hampdens with four 250 pounders and a container of incendiaries each, and dispatched them between 21.00 and 21.15, with W/C Taafe the senior pilot on duty and the first away. They flew out over Skegness in formation at between 4,000 and 6,000 feet, setting course for the Ijsselmeer above a thick layer of cloud. When thirty miles off the coast of Norfolk, they were shot at by a Whitley and three ships, and this was the only event of interest before the enemy coast was reached. Once darkness closed in, the formation separated, and each crew proceeded independently to their respective targets. W/C Taafe and crew altered course to the south, with the River Waal 4,000 feet below them acting as a guide as far as Nijmegen, before running into more dense cloud. On emerging from that, at 23.45, they deployed two parachute flares to reveal a concrete road on the north-western outskirts of Eindhoven. Two bombs scored direct hits, and a near-miss resulted from a second attack on this location thirty minutes later. Despite the poor visibility, F/L Willan succeeded in locating his target area in southern Holland, but, after searching for an hour at between 1,500 and 2,000 feet, he failed to identify the briefed stretch of railway. Had he been over Germany, he would have let his bombs go "live", but not over Holland, and he brought them home.

F/O French and crew deployed a flare, which revealed a railway line at Geldrop, east of Eindhoven, onto which a 250 pounder was released from 1,500 feet only to undershoot by thirty yards. Three more 250 pounders were aimed at a railway junction at Helmond, two of them missing by a hundred yards while the third hung-up. S/L Crockart climbed to between 10,000 and 12,000 feet, before shedding height from the enemy coast in an attempt to pick up ground features, and, hopefully, suitable targets. He was unlikely, in the prevailing conditions, to stumble across trains moving on the network, but his persistence was rewarded when he came upon a railway bridge over the Waal at Zaltbommel, onto which he unloaded four 250 pounders, without observing the results. As he pulled away to the west, to the south he could see two large fires burning in the centre of Hertogenbosch. F/O Vernieux and crew parted from the formation with the onset of darkness, and climbed to 11,000 feet, where they found themselves enveloped in cloud. On e.t.a at the Dutch coast explosions were heard, which were assumed to be flak, and the pilot took evasive action while trying to obtain a fix. Electrical meteorological disturbances knocked out the wireless equipment temporarily, and, when ice began to form on the wings, it was decided to abandon the sortie.

P/O Stenner and crew were over the target area in very unfavourable weather conditions, and searched for forty minutes without finding a single train on the move. Heading towards the west they chanced upon a railway bridge over a canal four miles east of Weert in Holland, and bombed it with two 250 pounders, which scored direct hits. A flare was deployed, and its light revealed twisted girders and a sagging span. About five minutes later a train was seen approaching the bridge at speed some mile-and-a-half away, but it was lost to view before it could be attacked. The remaining two bombs and the incendiaries were dropped on a railway siding at Geldrop, damaging the track and causing a large fire. F/O Corr and crew had searched the area between Roermond and Maastricht without finding any trains to attack, and were heading back towards the Weert area at 1,000 feet when they spotted a railway junction at Meerssen. It was being defended by intense light-calibre anti-aircraft fire, which was lethal at such a low altitude, and this persuaded F/O Corr to deliver all of his bombs in a single salvo. As he beat it for home with a shell hole in his tail, he and his crew gained an impression of the bombs hitting the target. F/O Shaughnessy and crew bombed a railway junction at Sittard in southern Holland from 1,000 feet at 23.50, before continuing on to Maastricht, where intense anti-aircraft fire drove them off, and the remaining 250 pounders and incendiaries were delivered onto the Meerssen goods yard at 00.01 and 00.08.

Fifty-nine aircraft were made ready on the 24th for a repeat of the previous night's operations against enemy communications between Germany and the advancing battle front. 5 Group contributed eighteen Hampdens, of which three represented 50 Squadron, and these, bearing the crews F/L Bennett, F/O Taylor and P/O Mulloy, departed Waddington at 21.15, assigned to attack a fuel dump at Recogne in south-eastern Belgium. F/L Bennett made landfall between Texel and Den Helder at 10,000 feet, and noted that he was being shadowed by enemy night-fighters, which would remain in contact throughout, withdrawing temporarily only when ground fire became intense. This was most apparent in the target area, where around twenty-four searchlights co-operated with flak batteries to make life most uncomfortable for the crew as shells exploded underneath them. The four 250 pounders and the container of incendiaries were dropped between 00.01 and 00.10, and a near-miss registered that caused a fire to break out. They headed for home, passing north of Antwerp, still shadowed, but not engaged by the enemy fighters. F/O Taylor and crew crossed the North Sea at 2,000 feet, before climbing to 10,000 feet to pass between Texel and the Den Helder peninsular. They, too, were greeted by intense anti-aircraft fire in the target area, running the gauntlet as they dropped two 250 pounders and the incendiaries from 5,000 feet at 00.20. Ten minutes later they divested themselves of the remaining two from around 1,200 feet when aiming for hangars on an airfield just to the south of the primary target near Neuvillers. Bursts were observed on the tarmac very close to the hangars as they pulled away, climbing to 14,000 feet to exit the enemy coast over Ostend. It was to be a frustrating night for P/O Mulloy and crew, who suffered a complete hang-up over the aiming-point, and were unable to release the bombs even with the jettison switch.

With the British Expeditionary Force now trapped with their backs to the Channel in a reducing pocket at Dunkerque, the relentless round of operations continued with further attacks on troop positions and communications on the 25th. 103 aircraft were involved, twenty-nine of them Hampdens, which, together with the Whitley element, would focus on road and railway links to the battle front between Düren and Aachen, while the Wellingtons targeted troop concentrations. The 50 Squadron quintet took off between 21.25 and 21.40 with F/L Willan the senior pilot on duty, and adopted one of two courses to the target area. P/O Jacklin, F/O Lloyd, P/O Stenner and F/L Willan followed corridor "G", which made landfall over the Scheldt estuary, while Sgt Abbott flew out via corridor "B", making landfall at the Hook of Holland a few miles further north, before turning south-east at 6,000 feet for the same target area. P/O Jacklin climbed to 10,000 feet on crossing the enemy coast, and, between 23.40 and 23.55, having descended to 2,000 feet, he dropped a 250 pounder onto a road-railway-river junction a mile from Jülich, another onto a railway junction four miles north-east of Düren, and the remaining two plus the incendiaries onto the railway track between Cologne and Düren. Hits and near-misses were reported, as was intense searchlight and flak activity throughout this crew's time over enemy territory. F/O Lloyd set course for Aachen, and carried out a reconnaissance of the railway line from 3,000 feet, eventually spotting a three-way junction east-north-east of Wiesmes, towards which a train was steaming from the south. F/O Lloyd dropped down to 1,000 feet, and, in the face of an intense anti-aircraft defence from the town, attacked it with all four 250 pounders and the incendiaries at

00.37. Direct hits were observed, and fires were seen to break out at intervals, before the Hampden made its escape with half of its port aileron missing. Sgt Abbott and crew searched in vain for trains in motion, but came upon autobahn-railway junctions to the north-west and south-west of Düren, and bombed them from 1,000 feet at 23.55 and 00.05. P/O Stenner and crew searched for ninety minutes for their briefed aiming-point, which, it is believed, was a tunnel on the Cologne to Düren line, but were thwarted by darkness, searchlight glare and the failure to release of their flares. Heading back over Holland, they located the railway line between Roermond and Sittard, and dropped their four delay-fused 500 pounders onto it without observing their fall. F/L Willan and crew failed to find any trains in motion, but came upon a railway junction and sidings, which they bombed from 3,500 feet in the face of a spirited defence, claiming direct hits.

The evening of the 26th brought the first evacuations from the Dunkerque beaches in a heroic campaign that would last until the 3rd of June and would result in the rescue of 338,000 men. Meanwhile, operations continued against enemy communications and airfields in France, Belgium, Holland and Germany, for which forty-three aircraft were detailed, twenty-one of them Hampdens. 50 Squadron briefed the crews of F/L Bennett and F/Os Vernieux, Corr and Shaughnessy, and dispatched them between 22.00 and 22.10 in poor weather conditions, which, fortunately, began to improve over the North Sea. F/L Bennett headed directly for the area between Brühl and Euskirchen to the south of Cologne, where he chanced upon a column of twenty-four heavy transports, which he attacked with four 250 pounders and the container of incendiaries between 00.25 and 00.40. On hearing the Hampden's approach, the convoy had stopped and extinguished its lights, but this did not prevent the bombs from detonating among the vehicles and setting off a series of further explosions that lit up the countryside. F/L Bennett then proceeded to the Ruhr, simply to cause a nuisance by flying over built-up areas. F/O Corr and crew located their target, the railway line between Namur and Liege, and bombed it from 1,000 feet at 00.10, before attacking a junction at Liege with their two remaining 250 pounders three minutes later. They then flew home, passing unopposed directly over the heavily defended Antwerp at 500 feet. F/O Shaughnessy and crew made their way directly to Liege, where they were met by intense searchlight and flak activity, the former so numerous that it was impossible to dodge them all. On reaching the target area between Aachen and St-Vith, darkness proved to be the main problem, and a lengthy search was necessary before the four 250 pounders were dropped accurately onto the track. F/O Vernieux and crew had been briefed to attack the aerodrome at Flushing on the island of Walcheren, and found it with ease, aided by the obstruction lights being lit. They dropped their four 250 pounders and incendiaries in a tight stick from 10,000 feet, and they were seen to fall a hundred yards from the hangars. As they turned for home, a fierce fire could be seen taking hold.

120 aircraft were detailed for a busy night of operations on the 27th, for which 5 Group assigned forty-nine Hampdens to a number of targets. Twenty-four crews were briefed to attack oil targets in Hamburg and Bremen, leaving twenty-five others to attend to communications behind enemy lines in Belgium and Germany. 50 Squadron made ready six Hampdens for an oil refinery in Hamburg, and four others to attack a railway bridge over the River Meuse at Givet on the French side of the frontier with Belgium. Those bound for north-western Germany departed Waddington first, between 22.33 and 22.40, with S/L Crockart the senior pilot on duty, and they were followed into the air by the remaining quartet shortly after 23.00, led by F/L Willan. Weather conditions over the whole of western Europe were less

than favourable on this night for what amounted to precision attacks on specific targets, and, while this would restrict success, it would also result in an absence of bomber casualties. As often seemed to be the case, reported conditions in target areas could vary wildly from crew to crew, and F/O French and crew experienced no difficulty in identifying and bombing the oil refinery in good visibility from 10,000 feet at 01.10. The four 250 pounders were observed to burst on the target, but no fire broke out. They reported many searchlights but little flak, and this was confirmed by P/O Mulloy and crew, although they described low cloud at 2,500 feet, through which they had to descend to obtain sight of the aiming-point. The high explosives and incendiaries were released from 2,000 feet, where the light flak was accurate, but the glare of the searchlights prevented observation of their fall and detonation. When they handed P4288 back to the ground crew, there was a two-inch-square hole, that hadn't been there on take-off!

F/O Lloyd and crew approached the target area via Terschelling and Borkum, and, on arrival, encountered low cloud and fog that rendered an attack impossible. They headed south-west to the alternative target at Bremen, but found conditions equally challenging and set course for the second alternative target, the aerodrome at Flushing. It soon became clear that this would not be reached before daybreak, so they altered course for Norderney, where the bombs were dropped onto the seaplane base from 8,000 feet at 02.15. S/L Crockart spent almost two hours searching for the primary target, but was defeated by the mist and poor visibility, and headed for home with his bombs. On the way, he came upon an unidentified aerodrome with its Lorenz flarepath enticingly illuminated, and delivered his bombs in a stick from 1,000 feet. They were seen to fall close to buildings, but smoke prevented an accurate assessment of possible damage. P/O Stenner and crew confirmed the presence of ten-tenths low cloud, which thwarted their attempts to locate either the primary or alternative targets, despite searching for some ninety minutes, and they brought their bombs home. The identity of the sixth participating crew in the Hamburg operation was not revealed in the record.

While these events were taking place, F/O Taylor and crew were traversing Belgium on their way to Givet. They followed the road from Phillippeville, situated some ten miles short of the target, and, on releasing a parachute flare to aid their map-reading, came upon a motorized convoy, which they strafed from 1,000 feet. Another parachute flare helped them identify the target, onto which they released four 250 pounders, but extreme darkness prevented them from observing the results. Sgt Abbott and crew ran into searchlights and light flak in the Givet area, but dropped their four 250 pounders and container of incendiaries, and watched them fall onto the road alongside the bridge. F/L Willan and crew reached the target at 2,000 feet, and were immediately ensnared, first by one searchlight, and then by others, which prompted the flak batteries to open fire. Driven off at first by the intensity of the defences, they tried again at 1,000 feet with the same result. Climbing to 8,000 feet, they dropped a parachute flare, which failed to ignite, and this persuaded them to head for the alternative target of Flushing aerodrome. This they located and bombed from 600 feet as they raced for the North Sea, and they were rewarded with the sight of a developing fire and further explosions. P/O Jacklin and crew made landfall five miles north of Ostend, which appeared to be in flames, but progressed no further as the starboard engine was beginning to falter.

On the 30th, 5 Group detailed eighteen Hampdens for further operations against Germany's oil industry at Hamburg and Bremen. 50 Squadron prepared three Hampdens for use by the crews of F/O French, S/L Crockart and F/O Corr, who took off between 22.10 and 22.19 and set a direct course for the target. Cloud over the North Sea extended up to 10,000 feet, but, over the target, the base was as low as 1,500 feet, and was penetrated by searchlights and flak. It was impossible to locate the briefed aiming-point, and F/O French bombed the centre of the defended area from 8,000 feet, observing explosions but no results. S/L Crockart had experienced severe icing in the higher reaches of cloud, a regular occurrence on this route, and then ran the gauntlet of flak and searchlights as he followed the course of the River Elbe into the heart of the city. On e.t.a., an attempt was made to descend through the cloud base to clear air, but this proved to be impossible, and the bombs were dropped randomly and singly between 00.37 and 00.50. F/O Corr and crew were also defeated by the low cloud, and dropped their stores onto a concentration of searchlights and heavy flak batteries. During the course of the month the squadron took part in an impressive twenty-four operations, and dispatched ninety-five sorties without loss.

June 1940

The Squadron was in action on the first night of the new month, when supporting 5 Group operations against oil targets and marshalling yards in Germany. Hemswell provided twelve Hampdens for the latter, while Waddington and Scampton put up twelve each to attack an oil refinery at Ostermoor, a location between the western end of the Kiel Canal, and the North Bank of the River Elbe. The six 50 Squadron participants took off between 21.35 and 21.50 with F/L Bennett the senior pilot on duty. F/O Vernieux turned back at the coast with an engine issue, and S/L Crockart and crew took off at 23.05 as a replacement. The weather conditions deteriorated as they crossed the North Sea, and low cloud and extreme darkness in the target area combined with accurate anti-aircraft fire to prevent any attacks from taking place.

The Dunkerque evacuations ended on the 3rd, and, that night, Bomber Command launched 142 sorties, the largest number in one night to date, targeting German industry, particularly oil, at various locations between Hamburg in the north and Frankfurt in the south. 5 Group committed forty-eight Hampdens to the fray, nine of them made ready by 50 Squadron, of which six were assigned to an oil depot in Frankfurt and three to an oil-related target in Emmerich, situated on the North Bank of the Rhine, north-west of the Ruhr. Those bound for Frankfurt departed Waddington between 21.10 and 21.30 with F/L Bennett the senior pilot on duty, and headed via corridor "G" to cross the enemy coast over the Scheldt estuary. From there, they would pass between Breda and Antwerp and Aachen and Cologne on a course to Coblenz, Wiesbaden and Mainz, where they would pick up the River Main south of Frankfurt. They selected their own heights for the North Sea crossing at between 6,000 and 14,000 feet, and, once over enemy territory, encountered searchlights and flak near the main population centres, although nothing of a troublesome nature. F/L Bennett and crew spent forty minutes searching for the aiming-point, hampered by low, patchy cloud, and, having pinpointed on the river, reduced height to 8,000 feet for the bombing run from south-east to north-west. Two of the four 500 pounders were fitted with instant fuses, and they were seen to burst on the island in the middle of the Main. F/O Vernieux and crew made a glide approach aided by parachute flares from other aircraft, and dropped their bombs from 8,000 feet at 00.30. Sgt Abbott and crew flew all the way at 6,000 feet, dodging the attentions of searchlight and flak, particularly as they let down to 5,000 feet heading south over the city to drop their four 250 pounders and container of incendiaries, which were seen to overshoot and fall into the River Main and the inland docks. F/O French and crew were carrying four 500 pounders, which they delivered from 8,000 feet at 00.08 in good visibility, observing them to hit the target. P/O Stenner and crew spent thirty minutes searching for the target, but were unsuccessful, and they decided to head back to the Rhine to gain a firm pinpoint from which to navigate. This done, it was too late to return to Frankfurt, and they set course instead up the Rhine towards Düsseldorf, where a refinery was under attack from other elements of the Command. It could be seen to be on fire from sixty miles away, and the bombs were added to this in the face of a searchlight and flak defence. P/O Jacklin and crew attacked from 10,000 feet, observing three bombs to undershoot and one to fall on the edge of the target.

Meanwhile, the trio of F/L Willan and F/Os Shaughnessy and Lloyd had reached their target at Emmerich after taking off between 22.00 and 22.05 and following corridor "B" to a point north of Amsterdam. F/L Willan had followed the River Waal across Holland on a direct course to the target, aided by a light night, courtesy of a glow in the sky to the north and bright starlight. The aiming-point was picked up easily from 800 feet and the four 250 pounders and incendiaries were seen to strike the western half of the site. F/O Shaughnessy identified the target with the help of a parachute flare and an exploding salvo of bombs from another aircraft, and dropped his load in a single stick at 00.40, before making a reconnaissance at 1,000 feet and observing that they had hit a building in the left-centre of the site, which was collapsing amid small explosions. F/O Lloyd and crew picked up the Rhine at 00.25 and flew along it to reach the target at 00.45, before delivering their bombs and incendiaries in a single stick from 1,500 feet at 00.55 onto the aiming-point.

Twenty-four Hampdens were among fifty-eight aircraft returning to Germany on the 4th, Scampton sending a dozen back to the Frankfurt oil depot, while Waddington and Hemswell provided six each for an oil production and storage plant at Mannheim. The three 50 Squadron participants took off between 21.37 and 21.50 with F/O Corr the senior pilot on duty, but he was forced to turn back with engine trouble before reaching the Norfolk coast. Sgt Banker and crew crossed the North Sea at between 10,000 and 12,000 feet over low cloud, which cleared shortly after entering enemy territory over the Scheldt estuary. Unusually, there was no anti-aircraft fire during the outward flight, but searchlights awaited them over the target, which they reached at 00.50, and left fifteen minutes later after delivering four 250 pounders from 10,000 feet. They were seen to fall on the south-western corner of the target, and fires were observed to break out as the Hampden set course for home. P/O Gardiner and crew found the extreme darkness a problem when map-reading, but they picked up the river to the south on e.t.a., and used that as a guide to carry out a bombing run at 8,000 feet. They stirred the light flak batteries into action, but the shells were falling two thousand feet short of their altitude, and did not disturb the delivery of the four 250 pounders and container of incendiaries. They were seen to score a direct hit on the storage tanks, which erupted in flames, the glow from which remained visible to them for a hundred miles into the return flight.

5 Group stations were busy on the 5th preparing thirty-six Hampdens for an attack on an oil refinery and storage facility at Schulau/Wedel, situated on the North Bank of the River Elbe a dozen miles downstream from Hamburg city centre. The Group would also be providing six Hampdens to resume the mining campaign, focussing on this night on the western Baltic. 50 Squadron made ready six Hampdens, which departed Waddington between 21.37 and 21.45 with S/L Crockart the senior pilot on duty. He and his crew made landfall at 23.59 on Blauort, an island north of the Elbe Estuary, from where they picked up the Kiel Canal to follow to the

Elbe. The outward flight thus far had been uneventful, but, once over enemy territory, they were subjected to an intense searchlight and flak defence as they made their way south at 5,000 feet to drop their bombs. Searchlight dazzle prevented them from observing the results, although S/L Crockart gained the impression of a fire, and, in all, spent one hour and forty-five minutes over land, the entire time under fire, before making it home safely with not even a scratch. Sgt Abbott and crew were in the target area for twenty minutes from 00.32, and delivered their bombs from 11,000 feet running from south to north in the face of persistent searchlights and heavy flak. The bombs were observed to overshoot by some three hundred yards, but, at least, the flak missed! F/O Vernieux and crew were enjoying the amazing visibility as they made their way towards the Schleswig-Holstein peninsular, and could see the Island of Sylt some seventy miles distant as they made landfall at the Westerhever lighthouse. Flying at 14,000 feet, they ran into the same intense flak, and were forced to make a detour to the north over the Kiel Canal, but, even then, had to take evasive action. The flak followed them all the way to the target, and prevented them from identifying it, and they were eventually persuaded to give up and head for home. P/O Jacklin and crew arrived at the target at 00.45, and left it fifteen minutes later having dropped their stores from 9,500 feet. They were not alone as they headed for home, having been picked up by a loose formation of seven unidentified enemy night-fighters displaying navigation lights and signalling to each other. They remained in contact until sixty miles out over the North Sea, and two engaged the Hampden, before being driven off by return fire. F/O French and crew delivered their six 250 pounders from 9,000 feet at 00.55, but searchlight dazzle prevented them from plotting their fall. F/L Bennett and crew identified the southern end of Sylt, before altering course and flying directly to the target, all the time under fire from heavy and light flak. The target was identified with ease, and two bombs dropped in the first pass, one falling in the river and the other on the edge of the target. A second pass was carried out from the south-west at 01.12 at 6,500 feet, and the remaining four 250 pounders were seen to hit the target and cause three fires to break out.

Hamburg was the destination for eighteen Hampdens from Hemswell, Scampton and Waddington on the 6th, when a previously attacked oil refinery was the target. While this operation was in progress, six other Hampdens were to sneak into the Elbe to plant mines. P/O Mulloy, F/O Taylor and F/L Willan took off for the main target between 21.02 and 21.12, but F/O Taylor returned within the hour because of W/T failure. P/O Mulloy and crew reached the target area to find haze and searchlight glare obscuring their view of the ground. They spent an hour in search of the primary target, and another hour seeking out the alternative, the oil plant at Ostermoor further to the west, which also remained elusive. On the way home they flew over Norderney, and bombed the aerodrome flarepath, stirring up a hostile reaction from the ground, and observing hits on the north-eastern corner of the airfield. F/L Willan released a parachute flare to aid his search for the primary target, but this was shot out, and the run at 9,000 feet had to be carried out in darkness. Four 250 pounders and 60lbs of incendiaries fell away, and were seen to cause a fire within the confines of the target.

The main battle for the next week was the vain attempt to rescue France from impending occupation, as German ground forces consolidated their hold on the country and prepared for the assault on Paris. However, it was oil that continued to be the focus for 5 Group on the 7th, when twenty-four Hampdens were detailed to attack the refinery at Misburg, situated east-north-east of Hannover city centre. 50 Squadron was not involved, and, instead, prepared six Hampdens for gardening duties in the Quince garden in Kiel Bay. They departed Waddington between 21.06 and 21.15 with F/L Bennett the senior pilot on duty, and set course via Skegness to Fanø island, south-west of Esbjerg, before crossing southern Jutland to the target area. The lightness of the northern sky helped them to map-read with ease, and all reached the target area, where the mines were delivered from around 500 feet into the briefed locations between 00.19 and 00.50. As they turned for home, P/O Gardiner and crew came under fire without warning, and sustained damage to a bomb door and the tailplane. Turning back over the source of the light flak, they dropped a parachute flare, in the light of which, the assailant was revealed to be either a large destroyer or small cruiser anchored close to the shore. F/O Lloyd and crew spotted two similar ships near the Danish island of Langeland, one of which they strafed from 500 feet, only to receive a hostile response, which left a hole in the starboard wing and forced them to fly home starboard wing-low. F/O Taylor and crew were at 800 feet when they also came upon two vessels anchored off the east coast of Denmark, and machine-gunned one, which appeared to be a warship. They managed to evade the return fire, and made it back to base to report observing four stationary cruisers in Kiel Bay. On the way home, P/O Jacklin and crew strafed Ribe aerodrome near Esbjerg from 300 feet, and registered no hostile response.

5 Group issued orders for a number of operations on the 8th, one of them to attack enemy communications in the Amiens area of France, while other forces attended to industrial targets in Germany. Three 50 Squadron crews attended briefing, S/L Crockart to learn that he and his crew were to attack a road junction at Recogne in south-eastern Belgium, while P/O Mulloy and Sgt Banker would join ten others for a raid on marshalling yards at Euskirchen, situated some fifteen miles south-west of Cologne. S/L Crockart departed Waddington at 22.15, and set course for the Scheldt, and, once over enemy territory, encountered haze and poor visibility, that created challenging conditions for target location. Once found at 01.30, the four 250 pounders and 60lbs of incendiaries were dropped onto it from 800 feet, and were seen to strike home. Turning to the north-west, and just five minutes later, they came upon a large convoy of about eighty vehicles heading south-east along the Perwez to Wavre road, which was winding and hilly, and passed through woods. S/L Crockart pulled away to work out the most suitable location to catch it in the open, and this occurred between 01.55 and 02.15, when, in attacks from 150 feet with all guns brought to bear, hits were scored at various points in the convoy, causing it to split into sections with considerable congestion in the rear. It was clear that extreme disruption had been achieved, but it was too dark to assess how many and what kind of vehicles had been damaged.

Meanwhile, P/O Mulloy and Sgt Banker, who had taken off at the same time as S/L Crockart, set course via corridor "G" for the Scheldt estuary, P/O Mulloy and crew flying above thick haze at 7,000 feet to pinpoint on Aachen. On e.t.a at the target, a parachute flare revealed the marshalling yards beneath, and, while the flare was still burning, an attack was carried out in a dive from 6,000 down to 2,000 feet at 00.30. The four 250 pounders were dropped in a single salvo and were observed to burst across the track and set fire to six warehouses in the yards. Sgt Banker and crew flew out at 4,000 feet, where the haze was so thick that the searchlights were unable to penetrate it, and, initially, they were unable to locate the yards. They flew east to pinpoint on the Rhine, and then back to the west on course for the target, where this time, on e.t.a, it could be identified in the light of a parachute flare. They were over the target between 00.34 and 01.00, and delivered their four 250 pounders and incendiaries from 4,000 feet in a long stick, observing them to burst across the yards. That evening at 20.40, P4289 crashed at Coleby Grange while on approach to Waddington during a training sortie, and, although the Hampden was a write-off, P/O Smettem and his crew walked away unhurt.

Forty-two Hampdens were detailed for operations on the 9th, thirty-six of them to continue the previous night's assault on marshalling yards in and around the Ruhr. Waddington was a hive of activity as 44 and 50 Squadrons each prepared eight Hampdens, while their crews were being briefed to attack one of three yards at Soest, Rheydt, south of Mönchengladbach, and Duisburg, although the last-mentioned was actually the Wedau yards in Mülheim-an-der-Ruhr to the south-east of Duisburg. They took off between 21.54 and 22.10 with the newly promoted S/L Willan the senior pilot on duty, and set course for their respective targets, where they would encounter unfavourable weather conditions for navigation and target-finding. F/O Taylor and P/Os Gardiner and Jacklin were bound for Soest, and not one would manage to locate it. P/O Jacklin and crew, perhaps, came closest, but had to take evasive action to shake off two enemy night-fighters, which forced them to deviate from track. At 00.45, they came upon a railway junction four miles north of Iserlohn at the eastern end of the Ruhr, and attacked it with four 500 pounders, observing three bursts and debris being flung across the track. P/O Gardiner and crew began their search at 00.30, but were defeated by the poor visibility, and, finally, found a railway line thought to be north of Soest. The bombs were dropped in a single salvo from 4,500 feet at 01.07, and were observed to fall four hundred yards to the east. F/O Taylor and crew had also arrived in the target area at 00.30, and, failing to locate it, sought out a target of opportunity. They headed south-west across the Ruhr for some fifty miles before chancing upon a blast furnace on the eastern edge of Düsseldorf at 01.15. The four 500 pounders were released from 7,000 feet, and were seen to undershoot by 150 yards.

F/L Bennett actually located his target at Wedau shortly after midnight, and dropped a single 500 pounder onto it from 7,000 feet, without observing the result. The remaining three bombs were aimed at the welding shop of an engineering factory in Homberg in the west of Duisburg at around 00.30, and it was believed that they had fallen accurately. S/L Willan was unable to locate the same target at Wedau, but spotted a blast furnace near Hamborn on the north-eastern outskirts of Duisburg, and bombed it from 7,000 feet at 01.30, also claiming direct hits. F/O Lloyd and crew were the third to be briefed for this objective, but failed to locate it, and sought out an alternative recipient for their bombs. They found what appeared to be an aerodrome some twenty miles north-west of Cologne, which they attacked with a single bomb from 6,000 feet at 00.30, missing it by a hundred yards. Thirty-five minutes later they identified another aerodrome ten miles west of Düsseldorf, and deposited the three remaining 500 pounders onto it, also from 6,000 feet, observing them to undershoot. The fact that the obstruction lights remain on throughout, suggested that both had been dummy airfields.

F/O French and crew successfully sought out their target at Rheydt while flying at 1,000 feet at 01.12, but, intense anti-aircraft fire from the western side of Düsseldorf hit the starboard side of the cockpit, severing a hydraulics pipe and disabling the bomb-release gear. F/O French sustained a wound, but was able to remain at the controls to bring the Hampden and bombs home. P/O Cockerell and crew were unable to locate this target, possibly because of flying at 10,000 feet, and dropped three of their bombs onto a collection of lights in the Rheydt area at around 00.15. The bursts were followed by a large flash and a fire, which remained visible for three minutes as they headed home towards Holland. It was here, in the

Eindhoven area that they came upon another collection of lights, onto which the remaining 500 pounder was dropped, this time without a burst to identify its fall.

The priority on the 10th, the day on which Italy declared war on Britain and France, was to try to stem the tide of the German advance into Northern France. 5 Group committed twenty-nine Hampdens, the crews of which were briefed to attack railway yards and junctions, along with bridges over the River Meuse at Sedan. 50 Squadron made ready five Hampdens for this activity, and another for F/O Corr and crew to take mining in the Wallflower garden in Kiel Harbour. They departed Waddington first, at 21.25, and would complete an uneventful sortie, successfully delivering their vegetable into the briefed location from 500 feet at 00.10. The others took off between 21.50 and 22.05, with W/C Taafe the senior pilot on duty and the last away on what would be his final operation with the squadron. They were to encounter the most challenging weather conditions over enemy territory in the form of towering cloud with magnetic storms, and accurate navigation would prove to be almost impossible. They were routed out via corridor "G" to cross the enemy coast over the Scheldt estuary, before turning south over Belgium to the target area just across the frontier in France. Failing to observe the ground during the entire outward flight, P/O Mulloy and crew descended to 1,000 feet on e.t.a., and, in the light of a parachute flare, saw a bridge over a river, which they believed was two miles north-west of Sedan. They attacked it at 00.18 with four 500 pounders, which overshot and fell onto the riverbank to the north. F/O Vernieux and crew maintained 10,000 feet, navigating by DR (dead-reckoning) and e.t.a., until becoming lost and returning to the coast to pick up another pinpoint. Near Brussels, static electricity lit them up like a Christmas tree, and that persuaded them to head for home, exiting the enemy coast near Den Helder to make landfall at Skegness. P/O Stenner and crew spent thirty minutes stooging around at 2,000 to 3,000 feet in search of a pinpoint at the Dutch coast from which to navigate, before obtaining a fix from Heston, that located them over Zeebrugge. A course was set to the target area, but, on e.t.a., no landmark was visible, and they returned to the coast to try again. This also proved to be in vain, and they reluctantly turned for home. Sgt Banker and crew experienced the same problems, and eventually came upon an aerodrome, believed to be at Belval on the edge of the Ardennes, a few miles to the north-west of Sedan. Four 250 pounders and a container of incendiaries were released from 8,000 feet and observed to fall across the airfield, while enemy aircraft were operating, and the incendiaries caused a fire in one of the buildings. W/C Taafe and crew searched in vain for the primary target, and also failed to find an alternative objective for their bombs, which were brought home.

Having failed on the previous night to find and hit the communications targets in France, 5 Group detailed thirty-six Hampdens for operations on the 11th, thirty-one of them to return to Sedan and five for mining duties. At the same time, eighteen Wellingtons of 3 Group were to attack the Black Forest in south-western Germany with incendiary devices in an attempt to cause widespread fires, and thirty-six Whitleys would carry out the first attacks on Italy with a raid on Turin. Only nine would actually bomb at Turin, while the ill-conceived policy of setting fire to forests, which would be played out over the ensuing months, would prove to be a monumental waste of resources at a time when the Command had more important matters to focus on. 50 Squadron made ready seven Hampdens for north-eastern France, and they departed Waddington between 21.50 and 22.00 with S/Ls Crockart and Willan the senior pilots on duty. They flew out via corridor "G", before setting course for their respective targets, which formed a triangle with points at Sedan, La Fére to the west and Charleville to the south-west. The target for F/Os Taylor and Jacklin and P/O Gardiner was the railway station at Charleville, which the two first-mentioned reached at the same time at 23.50, before delivering their four 250 pounders and 60lbs of incendiaries from 4,000 and 6,000 feet respectively. Extreme darkness prevented F/O Taylor and crew from observing the results, while the Jacklin crew saw their effort fall one hundred yards short. F/O Lloyd and S/L Willan arrived at their target, the German-occupied town of La Fére, within minutes of each other either side of midnight, and spent up to thirty minutes establishing their bearings before bombing from 5,000 feet and observing bomb bursts and fires within the town. F/L Bennett was on a direct course for Sedan, when he caught site of an unidentified objective of interest at Montherme in the Ardennes, and aimed two 250 pounders at it from 7,000 feet at 00.01. Continuing on at the same altitude, he delivered the two remaining 250 pounders and the incendiaries onto a road/rail junction to the west of Sedan at 00.11, observing a number of fires as a result. S/L Crockart reached the Sedan area well after F/L Bennett, but found the target, the same road/rail junction attacked by F/L Bennett, without difficulty, and bombed it with a single salvo from 1,500 feet at 00.50.

On the 12th, S/L Crockart was granted the acting rank of wing commander to enable him to assume command of the squadron. W/C Taafe went on leave before his official posting to 5 Group HQ on the 17th for air staff duties. A reduced effort on the night of the 12th saw thirty Hampdens and eight 4 Group Whitleys detailed for a return to northern France, while five other Hampdens were assigned to gardening duties. 50 Squadron briefed six crews, four of them to attack the marshalling yards at Charleville, and two for a similar target at Laon, the latter situated some ten miles south-east of La Fére. They departed Waddington between 22.03 and 22.45 with the recently promoted F/L Shaughnessy the senior pilot on duty, but he was forced to land almost immediately with intercom failure, leaving Sgt Abbott and crew to attend to the Laon marshalling yards on their own. Crossing the North Sea via corridor "G", they all ran into a thick bank of ten-tenths cloud, which persuaded F/O Vernieux and crew to turn back when some sixty miles out from the Norfolk coast. The cloud would extend over the Scheldt estuary all the way to the target areas, and would prevent all but Sgt Abbott and crew from locating their briefed target. The Abbott crew, in fact, enjoyed an uneventful outward flight and located their target without difficulty, before dropping two 500 pounders from 2,000 feet at 00.45, observing a direct hit on the track at the western entrance to the yards. Five minutes later, they carried out a second pass to drop the two delayed-action 500 pounders, the fall of which could not be observed. On e.t.a., P/O Stenner and crew tried unsuccessfully to break cloud, which enveloped them altogether for an hour and forty-five minutes and prevented them from establishing their position. They were eventually attracted by a searchlight near Ghent, which revealed an unidentified aerodrome nearby, onto which they dropped two of their 500 pounders, before bringing the others home. P/O Mulloy and crew stumbled around in the cloud at 4,000 feet for more than two hours, until coming across a railway line at Launois, south of La Fére, upon which they unloaded the contents of their bomb bay. F/O Corr and crew experienced the same difficulties, and also came upon the railway line at Launois, which they bombed from 1,000 feet at 00.40, observing their 250 pounders to fall across the track and set fire to woods on either side. The previously-mentioned W/C Watts, formerly of 44 Squadron and now the commanding officer of 144 Squadron at Hemswell, collided with a barrage balloon over Suffolk on the way home, and died with his crew.

163 aircraft were prepared for operations on the 13th, their crews briefed to attack a wide variety of communications targets in France, Belgium and Holland. 5 Group called for a

maximum effort from its three operational stations at Scampton, Hemswell and Waddington, and sixty-four Hampdens answered the call, ten of them provided by 50 Squadron. The crews of Sgt Abbott, P/O Cockerell, F/O Lloyd and F/O Jacklin were briefed for a road junction at Beauvais, situated thirty miles north of Paris, while W/C Crockart, S/L Willan and two unnamed crews were assigned to a railway junction at Laon, and P/Os Stenner and Mulloy to a bridge over the River Seine at Pont-de-l'Arche some eight miles south of Rouen. They took off between 21.53 and 22.35, and faced moderate weather conditions over the North Sea with six-tenths cloud. This would disperse over northern France to leave haze, which was particularly thick in the Laon region, where the moonlight proved to be a hindrance by reflecting off it. P/O Stenner and crew were "hosed" by light flak as they crossed Vernon at 00.10, but located the target despite mist and extreme darkness. They dropped a stick of 250 pounders and the container of incendiaries from 2,500 feet at 00.50, and one was seen to strike the southern end of the bridge, while another fell into the Seine to the east. The incendiaries ignited on the northern bank, and, in their light, it appeared that the bridge had been damaged and that two spans were missing. P/O Mulloy and crew crossed the North Sea at 5,000 feet, keeping below the cloud, and they described visibility over France as ten miles. The target was located with the aid of parachute flares, and bombed in two salvoes, which were observed to hit the southern end of the bridge.

In contrast, the conditions in the Laon area were challenging, with visibility at around 1,000 yards and six-tenths low cloud at 1,000 feet. S/L Willan and crew were unable to identify the target, and bombed a road junction on the outskirts of the town from 1,600 feet at 00.40. W/C Crockart and crew experienced similar difficulties while searching extensively, and eventually dropped their bombs onto a railway at Longchamps from 1,000 feet at 01.53. We are told that the two unnamed crews assigned to Laon attacked alternative targets. At Beauvais, F/O Lloyd's load went down in a single salvo from 3,000 feet at 00.14, and started a large fire among buildings. Sgt Abbott and crew arrived at Beauvais soon afterwards, and the fires assisted identification of the aiming-point. One 250 pounder and the incendiaries were dropped from 2,000 feet at 00.20, and were seen to fall onto the south-western corner of the town square, and these were followed by the other bombs in a salvo onto a road leading from the northern side of the square. P/O Cockerell and crew confirmed the town to be on fire when they arrived at 01.10, before delivering their hardware from around 1,500 feet in two salvos onto the market square and the road leading from it to the west. F/O Jacklin and crew also reported bombing this target, but provided no details.

While 4 Group prepared its Whitleys to continue the losing battle to save France from occupation on the 14th, Wellingtons and Hampdens from 3 and 5 Groups were detailed to attack targets in Germany. In fact, only five Hampdens were mobilized, three at Hemswell and one each at Scampton and Waddington. The Waddington representative was P4288, in which F/O Vernieux and crew were to attack the marshalling yards at Soest, a town with busy railway links to the nearby Ruhr. They took off at 21.45, and set course via corridor "B" to make landfall at the Dutch coast at the Zuider Zee, and had to climb to between 10,000 and 15,000 feet to avoid two cold fronts over the North Sea and the Dutch mainland. Severe icing was encountered, which caused the a.s.i to cease functioning, but they pressed on until shortly before e.t.a, when the clouds parted, and the target could be identified. Four 250 pounders and a container of incendiaries fell away from 8,000 feet, but no mention of the outcome was recorded. Earlier in the day, flight commander-elect, S/L Oxley, had been posted in from 106 Squadron.

There were no operations for 5 Group on the 15th, the day on which the battered remnants of the Advanced Air Striking Force arrived back from France with what remained of their Fairey Battles. 12 Squadron settled in at Finningley and 142 Squadron at Waddington, both temporarily, until they could become part of the newly reconstituted 1 Group, which, after continuing briefly with Battles, would convert to Wellingtons later in the year. Only Waddington was detailed to operate on the 16th, when three Hampdens each from 44 and 50 Squadrons were to carry out mining duties in the Radish garden in the Fehmarnbelt, between the Danish islands of Fehmarn and Lolland. F/O Corr, S/L Willan and F/O Taylor departed Waddington at 20.45, 20.56 and 21.01 respectively, and set course for the Danish coast, flying at around 10,000 feet and encountering cloud at times, but clear skies over the western Baltic. Each planted a vegetable from between 400 and 800 feet between 00.20 and 00.30, without opposition. Five minutes after releasing their store at 00.20, S/L Willan and crew spotted a merchantman of about one thousand tons proceeding westwards at five knots with lights on. They made three strafing attacks from 800 feet, expending seven hundred rounds, but generated no reaction from the vessel or shore batteries, and were unable to assess what damage they may have inflicted.

Thirty-nine Hampdens were made ready for operations on the 17th, nine of those at Waddington belonging to 50 Squadron. While the bomb bays were being loaded either with four 250 pounders and a container of incendiaries, or four 500 pounders, five of the crews were being briefed to attack an oil plant at Harburg on the South Bank of the Elbe, and four to target marshalling yards at Coblenz. The first element departed Waddington between 20.59 and 21.27, and flew out over the North Sea under a full moon and in good weather conditions with a few areas of cloud. All would be subjected to intense heavy and light anti-aircraft fire as soon as they crossed the enemy coast, but F/O Watts and crew, who were the first to arrive in the target area, found it to be ineffective at 10,000 feet. They proceeded to bomb the target at 00.10, observing a large fire to break out, which would remain visible for sixty miles into the return flight. P/O Cockerell and crew were some distance behind, and it was at 00.48 when they carried out their attack on the oil depot from 7,000 feet, but watched their load overshoot by two hundred yards and start a small fire. P/O Luxmoore and crew identified the target at 01.50, and carried out their attack from 10,500 feet, but observed their bombs to overshoot by two hundred yards to the north-north-west, where a large fire was seen to break out. On reaching the target at 5,000 feet at 00.30, Sgt Banker and crew had been blinded by the searchlights and driven off by the flak. They soon abandoned all thoughts of attacking the primary target, and, finding a warehouse and bridge over the Süderelbe almost a mile to the south-east as they headed towards the centre of Hamburg, they dropped their bombs there, observing a large fire to break out. F/O Jacklin and crew encountered cloud at the coast, and descended through it to obtain a pinpoint. This took longer than expected, and, by the time that they had established themselves over the Schleswig-Holstein peninsular, decided that it was too late to reach the target before dawn broke. They found an aerodrome at Heide, close to the west coast, and dropped two 250 pounders onto it from 9,000 feet at 01.45, before spotting a railway junction to the south-west fifteen minutes later, and releasing the remaining two bombs, without observing the results.

While these events were taking place over north-western Germany, the second element was some sixty miles to the south of the Ruhr attending to the railway yards at Coblenz. Having taken off between 21.46 and 22.15 with F/L Bennett the senior pilot on duty, they had reached the enemy coast near Rotterdam, and set a course to the target that took them between Cologne to the north and Aachen to the south, after which, three of them were able to locate the target with ease. F/O Vernieux and crew had taken off late, and decided at Aachen that they would not reach the primary target in time. The found some railway sidings to bomb at Aachen from 8,000 feet after a glide attack, and a small fire was observed, although no details of damage. P/O Mulloy and crew reached the primary target at 00.30, and dropped their load in a stick from 1,000 feet, observing bursts along the length of the yards. In contrast, F/L Bennett chose to attack from 10,000 feet, and saw three bursts at separate locations within the yards. F/L Shaughnessy and crew delivered their four 500 pounders into the centre of the yards from 6,000 feet at around 00.45, but were unable to assess the outcome.

5 Group's workload on the 18th was relatively light, with just eleven Hampdens detailed for gardening duties or to attack railway targets of opportunity on the approaches to the Ruhr. 50 Squadron briefed three crews to lay mines in the Eglantine garden in the Elbe estuary, while W/C Crockart and crew sought out a target near the Rhine in an area between Bonn and Coblenz. S/L Willan led the horticultural trio away at 21.42, to be followed into the air at 22.03 by the commanding officer, and all would benefit from near perfect weather conditions. S/L Willan and F/O Taylor experienced no difficulty in locating the briefed drop zone, the latter reaching the target area first to deliver his mine from 400 feet at 00.29, while the former arrived at 00.40 and dropped his from 800 feet. Afterwards, F/O Taylor and crew set course for Heligoland, which they reached at 00.43 at an altitude of 4,000 feet, and observed seven ships in the harbour, one an 8,000-tonner and the others of around 2,000 tons each. They were dissuaded by anti-aircraft fire from carrying out a closer inspection, and headed home to make their report. F/O Corr and crew were fired upon from the small islands of Scharhörn and Neuwerk, and also by flak ships, which prevented them from planting their vegetable in the briefed location. Instead, they headed out to a point some ten miles to the east of Heligoland, and dropped it there. Meanwhile, W/C Crockart and crew had stooged around their target area for some time at between 1,000 and 11,000 feet without finding any train movements, and all the time under intense heavy, medium and light flak fire. They eventually found a railway bridge over the Rhine three miles east of Neuwied and within sight of Coblenz to the south, upon which they dropped two 250 pounders from 1,000 feet in the face of a continuing searchlight and flak response. No results were observed, before they headed back towards the north at 11,000 feet, and came upon Bonn's main marshalling yards to the north-west of the city centre. They delivered the two remaining 250 pounders and incendiaries onto its southern edge shortly before 01.30, again without observing the results, and, a few minutes later, flew over Hangelar aerodrome with all of its lights on, but had nothing left to throw at it.

5 Group would be out in force on the 19th, when contributing fifty-three Hampdens out of 112 aircraft operating that night against a variety of targets in Germany between Hamburg in the north and Mannheim in the south. 50 Squadron made ready nine aircraft, three to target the recently attacked Harburg oil depot, while six others were to seek out trains and railway communications generally at points north and south of the Ruhr. S/L Oxley was the senior pilot on duty for the first time, and the first to take off, at 21.27, bound for an oil storage depot at Brunsbüttel, situated on the North Bank of the Elbe close to the estuary. Although the weather conditions over Germany and Holland were excellent, ten-tenths low cloud over the North Sea and the coastal region forced him to search for the target at 8,000 feet, where he and his crew came in range of anti-aircraft fire from Cuxhaven and nearby flak ships. It was decided to find an alternative target on one of the East Frisian islands, and the aerodrome on

Norderney presented itself for attack with four 500 pounders from 10,000 feet at 00.10. P/O Jacklin and crew enjoyed an uneventful outward flight before crossing paths with a Blohm & Voss floatplane at 8,000 feet, while it was still daylight. The Hampden turned to give chase, eventually overtaking the enemy after eight minutes and engaging it with the front gun. The enemy's rear guns were silenced, and the starboard engine was seen to emit large quantities of black smoke, as it dived steeply towards the sea to disappear from sight at 800 feet. Thereafter, P/O Jacklin and crew seemed to roam far and wide over the Schleswig-Holstein peninsular, attracting attention from flak batteries at Flensburg and Kiel on the eastern side and Brunsbüttel in the west. It was at the last-mentioned that an attack was carried out with four 500 pounders on an oil storage depot from 5,500 feet at 01.20, and a fire seemed to be spreading as they withdrew to the sea.

The fine weather conditions enabled P/O Luxmoore and crew to locate the Harburg oil depot without difficulty, and they dropped their four 500 pounders onto its north-western side from 9,500 feet at 01.08. F/O Watts and crew were among the six given a roving commission to search for railway traffic in an area stretching from Wesel in the west to Hamm in the east and Coblenz to the south. They crossed the enemy coast over the Scheldt estuary, before setting course for the first target area around Coblenz. No trains were moving, so an attack was carried out from 5,000 feet on a railway junction at Linz-am-Rhein, situated ten miles south-east of Bonn. Four 250 pounders and incendiaries were aimed at it at 00.50, and three of them were seen to be direct hits, while the fourth undershot. F/O Vernieux and crew made landfall in the Rotterdam area, and map-read easily across Holland aided by the light of a full moon and the Northern Lights. They found a railway junction to bomb at Nijmegen in eastern Holland, and dropped their four 250 pounders onto it from 10,000 feet at 00.10, watching them detonate on the track between the junction and the station. F/L Bennett and crew were also enjoying the unlimited visibility, which revealed a train heading eastward twelve miles west of Mönchengladbach. They dived from 10,000 down to 5,000 feet to release the four 250 pounders and incendiaries at 00.40, and the first two were seen to overshoot by one hundred yards, while the second pair hit the track two hundred yards in front of the train, which could not stop in time. Three carriages were derailed and rolled onto their sides, and dense clouds of steam were issuing from the locomotive.

F/L Shaughnessy and crew spotted a moving train on the Lünen to Hamm railway line, about eight miles from Hamm and a few miles north of the eastern end of the Ruhr. Two 250 pounders were dropped from 2,000 feet at 00.50, and they were seen to explode on the road adjacent to the south side of the track. As a major railway hub for the Ruhr, Hamm was always hotly defended, as the Shaughnessy crew discovered when they flew over the town at 4,000 feet and were thrown around by bursting flak shells. They emerged unscathed, and delivered the two remaining bombs and incendiaries from 1,000 feet onto a railway siding at Wiescherhöfen, south-west of Hamm at 01.10. Sgt Abbott and crew also arrived in the Lünen area, where they hit a railway junction with one 250 pounder and the incendiaries from 1,000 feet at 01.19. Afterwards, they attacked two other sections of track from the same altitude, four and eight miles east of the town, between 01.30 and 01.40.

4 and 5 Groups were notified of operations in the Ruhr and in the Münsterland region to the north on the 20th, the latter responding with orders, among others, to Waddington and Scampton to prepare six Hampdens each to attack an aircraft park at Paderborn, situated some forty miles to the east of Hamm. Five 50 Squadron Hampdens took off between 22.05 and

22.15 with S/L Willan the senior pilot on duty, and set course from Skegness to cross the North Sea over ten-tenths low cloud. This cleared as they made their way eastwards over the Dutch/German frontier, and bright moonlight greeted their arrival in the target area, enabling three crews to locate the aerodrome without difficulty. S/L Willan and Sgt Banker and their crews were first to identify the aerodrome, assisted by the flare-path lights, which were extinguished as the sound of engines was heard. Sgt Banker and crew carried out their attack at 01.00, delivering their four 250 pounders and incendiaries in a stick from 3,500 feet, the first bomb bursting on a road to the west of the aerodrome, the second on the airfield and the remainder on hangars on the north-west side. Several explosions were observed, and a fire broke out in the hangar. They spotted the navigation lights of another aircraft in the close vicinity, and this may well have been S/L Willan and crew, who arrived at the same time but at 900 feet, and delivered an unusually heavy load of five 250 pounders and two 500 pounders between 01.00 and 01.15. Direct hits were scored on hangars and other buildings, and a column of black smoke was rising through 2,000 feet as they turned away. P/O Stenner and crew attacked from 5,000 feet at 01.25, but did not observe the bursts of their bombs and incendiaries. F/O Corr and crew failed to locate either the primary or an alternative railway target, and dropped their bombs from 2,000 feet onto an autobahn to the north of the Möhnesee at 01.30. Two minutes later, F/O Lloyd and crew released their bombs and incendiaries onto Münster aerodrome from 800 feet, but observed no results.

On the following night, forty-two Hampdens would represent 5 Group as it and 3 and 4 Groups roamed far and wide over Germany from its central region to the north. The 5 Group targets were oil refineries at Misburg near Hannover and Sterkrade in the Ruhr, moving trains and railway installations in the Ruhr, and an aircraft factory at Kassel. 50 Squadron briefed six crews for Sterkrade-Holten, and dispatched them between 22.07 and 22.20 with S/L Oxley the senior pilot on duty, to set course from Skegness via corridor "B" to make landfall north of The Hague. Sgt Abbott and crew searched in vain for the target for sixty-five minutes, thwarted by the ever-present blanket of industrial haze and intense searchlight and flak activity, which was accurate between 8,000 and 10,000 feet. On the way home they spotted a blast furnace at Terborg, just inside Holland, and this was bombed from 9,000 feet at 01.25 without success. Ten miles from Amsterdam they came upon an unidentified enemy aircraft with navigation lights on, and chased it from 6,000 down to 800 feet before it was lost from sight. It was an entirely different experience for S/L Oxley and crew, probably because they arrived earlier at the target, before the defences had been stirred up, and located it with ease before bombing from 6,000 feet at 00.35. Their problems occurred when trying to locate Waddington in poor weather conditions on return, and they eventually landed at Acklington in Northumberland. F/O Watts and crew were over the Ruhr at the same time as the Oxley crew, but failed to locate the oil plant and attacked what they identified as the Krupp works at Essen as an alternative. Four 500 pounders were dropped from 5,000 feet at 00.30, but no results were observed. P/O Mulloy and crew were not bothered by the defences as they carried out their attack on the primary target from 3,000 feet at 01.15, after which, they dropped a flare to confirm that their four 500 pounders had hit buildings to the east of the refinery's chimney stacks. F/O Taylor and crew located the target area without difficulty, but could not pinpoint the oil plant, and turned their attention instead upon the large marshalling yards north of the River Ruhr between Bottrop and Essen. A stick of six 250 pounders and incendiaries was released from 10,000 feet at 00.30, and they were seen to burst from north-west to south-east across the yards and also hit an adjacent factory. P/O Gardiner and crew were driven off by the defences, and found a factory to bomb half a mile to the west of Drevenack, close to the

Dutch frontier and north of the Ruhr. A stick of six 250 pounders went down from 900 feet shortly before 01.00, and they were seen to burst west of the intended victim.

Bomber Command stayed at home on the 22nd for the first time since the start of the German offensive on the 10th of May. This was the day on which the French authorities signed the instrument of surrender at Compiegne, to leave Britain standing alone against a seemingly unconquerable enemy. Unfavourable weather conditions were to blame for the brief break in bombing operations, but orders were issued on the 23rd to resume the fight, and 5 Group detailed fifty-three Hampdens for that night, thirty-eight of them from Scampton and Waddington to attack the Horten aircraft factory at Wismar on the Baltic coast, and the Blohm & Voss aircraft works at Wenzendorf, south-west of Hamburg. The Waddington squadrons were assigned to the latter, and the nine 50 Squadron participants took off between 21.15 and 21.45 with S/L Oxley the senior pilot on duty. F/O Corr and crew turned back early on with engine trouble, and they were followed home twenty minutes later by F/O Vernieux, who had been seventy-five miles out from Skegness when he became unwell. The others pressed on either above or below the ten-tenths stratus cloud that hung over the North Sea, and enjoyed uneventful outward flights until the coastal defences were stirred up over the Weser and Elbe estuaries, by which time the cloud had reduced and lifted to six-tenths at 8,000 feet. Five crews located the aerodrome near the supposed site of the target, but found no sign of factory buildings, and bombed the aerodrome instead from 1,000 to 8,000 feet between 00.20 and 00.50. S/L Oxley and crew were at 5,000 feet over Stade on the North Bank of the Elbe at 00.30, when hit by shrapnel, which caused what was later found to be superficial damage, but also slightly wounded the navigator in the thigh. Unsure at the time of the extent of the damage, they opted to bomb Stade aerodrome, and dropped their four 500 pounders from 6,000 feet at 00.35, and observed bursts in close proximity to the hangars. P/O Luxmoore and crew spent an hour searching for the target, but the presence of thunderstorms added to their difficulties, and they turned for home at 01.30, narrowly dodging the accurate flak as they passed over Emden at 9,000 feet.

5 Group sent orders to Hemswell, Scampton and Waddington on the 24th to prepare for that night's attacks on marshalling yards at Hamm and Wanne-Eickel, on moving trains in the Ruhr and barges on the Mittelland and Dortmund-Ems Canals. Four 50 Squadron crews were briefed for the canals, and departed Waddington between 22.00 and 22.32 with S/L Willan the senior pilot on duty. All found favourable weather conditions in the target area, with visibility aided by moonlight, and S/L Willan and his crew carried out a reconnaissance of the area between 00.15 and 01.15. They found many barges spaced about one hundred yards apart, which they attacked at 01.20 with eight 250 pounders, one setting a barge on fire, and four others scoring direct hits on another, while one hit the canal bank and two fell into the water. (The map references provided in the ORB are wildly inaccurate and cover an area in the southern Ruhr rather than north of the Ruhr around Münster.) F/O Corr and crew failed to find barges on the Dortmund-Ems Canal, and attacked lock gates on a stretch south-east of Rheine from 1,000 feet, delivering four 250 pounders and observing direct hits followed by blue sparks. The remaining four bombs were aimed at another set of lock gates further south, also from 1,000 feet, but two fell into the water and two missed by twenty yards to the west. P/O Stenner and crew reconnoitred the area from 00.10 to 01.00, before bombing a collection of stationary barges on the Lingen-Ems Canal, six miles south of Lingen from 1,000 feet, observing all eight of the 250 pounders to miss the mark. P/O Gardiner and crew found themselves over the Mittelland Canal north of Osnabrück between 00.45 and 01.10, and

dropped the first two bombs onto barges there from 1,700 feet, before attacking others at a nearby canal junction, on both occasions without success. Observing no further barges, the four remaining bombs were aimed at a railway sidings south-east of Osnabrück from 2,000 feet, and were seen to fall through a warehouse roof, although without evidence of an explosion.

Orders were received across the Command on the 25th to prepare for operations that night against twenty-one separate targets. 5 Group detailed twenty-four Hampdens, the six belonging to 50 Squadron to be made ready for a variety of objectives, and they were led away at 22.04 by S/L Oxley and his crew. F/L Shaughnessy and crew took off at 22.20, but had barely reached the coast before W/T failure forced them to turn back. The Oxley crew were bound for the Dortmund-Ems Canal at the point where it intersected the River Lippe on the north-eastern edge of the Ruhr, and they enjoyed clear skies from Waddington to sixty miles out over the North Sea, where cloud built up to ten-tenths between 5,000 and 10,000 feet all the way to the Dutch coast. This had dispersed by the time that Germany lay beneath them, and a rising moon compensated to an extent for a layer of haze up to 8,000 feet, which restricted visibility to a maximum of six miles. The target was picked up with ease, and the first 250 pounder dropped away from 600 feet at 00.05, only to undershoot by thirty yards. They continued on in a south-westerly direction a short distance to a railway bridge over the Lünen to Recklinghausen railway line, where they dropped the second bomb onto its centre. Next came a river/railway crossing at Bochum, after which, they turned north to find a bridge over a road and canal at Senden, and a railway/canal crossing at Appelhülsen, all attacks taking place from 1,000 to 1,200 feet between 00.05 and 00.31. F/O Watts and crew made landfall at 2,000 feet over the Ems Estuary, avoiding a group of five searchlights, and then made their way south along the river to a point five miles north of Lingen. There they attacked a railway bridge over the Dortmund-Ems Canal with a salvo of three 250 pounders from 700 feet, observing them to explode underneath the bridge and destroy it. The remaining five bombs were dropped onto a railway line on the eastern bank of the canal half a mile further north at 00.30, and one was claimed as a direct hit, while the others fell onto the embankment.

F/O Jacklin and crew took off at 22.07 having been assigned to railway communications north of the Ruhr, and came upon a goods train on the Dorsten to Wesel line, which they attacked from 1,000 feet with three 250 pounders and the incendiaries. Two bombs fell short, while the third and the incendiaries landed ahead of the locomotive without the results being observed. Forty minutes later, they attacked a lock on the Dortmund-Ems Canal five miles south of Münster with three bombs from 1,200 feet, and two were claimed as direct hits. P/O Mulloy and crew also departed Waddington at 22.07, having been briefed to attack barges on the Mittelland Canal, and, during a thirty-minute search, encountered a large concentration two miles east of Alswede, which they attacked with six 250 pounders from 700 feet at 00.50. Shortly after setting course for home, they came upon a goods train two miles east of Ostercappeln, and carried out three strafing attacks from 50 feet, expending one thousand rounds in the process. The train was seen to stop, but no assessment of the damage could be made. F/O Taylor and crew had taken off at 22.15, and ran into heavy anti-aircraft fire eight miles south-west of Düsseldorf, but managed to evade the shells bursting all around them. At the same time, they spotted an aerodrome, but the lights were extinguished before the position could be established. Eventually, another aerodrome was sighted on the German/Dutch frontier, which they attacked from 3,500 feet with six 250 pounders at 00.51, observing all to burst and four fires to break out.

A force of over a hundred aircraft was made ready to send against various targets on the night of the 26/27th, 5 Group contributing thirty-four Hampdens to target marshalling yards, aerodromes, moving trains and canal barges in north-western Germany. 50 Squadron loaded five Hampdens with four 500 pounders each and two with six 250 pounders and incendiaries, before dispatching them from Waddington between 22.15 and 22.25 with W/C Crockart the senior pilot on duty. They were bound via corridor "B" to make landfall at Texel, before flying direct to Langenhagen aerodrome, situated five miles north of Hannover city centre. They encountered occasional thunderstorms over the North Sea and Holland, but conditions were good in the target area, where Sgt Abbott and crew were the first to arrive, at 00.40, to be met by intense searchlight and anti-aircraft fire. Despite searching from altitudes between 2,000 and 8,000 feet, with flak shells of all calibres bursting all around, the target could not be identified, and a course was set for Osnabrück, where the marshalling yards had been briefed as an alternative. These were identified, and a stick of four 500 pounders was sent down from 12,000 feet during a run from east to west at 01.33. Intense searchlight and flak activity here also persuaded them not to hang around, and the results were not observed. P/O Treasure and crew were operating with the squadron for the first time, and found themselves surrounded by bursting flak shells from the target aerodrome as well as from Hannover, and were held in searchlight beams. They reduced height to 4,000 feet to deliver a salvo of four 500 pounders at 01.25, and retreated to the west without observing the results. F/L Shaughnessy and crew carried out a dive-bombing attack, releasing their load eventually from 1,000 feet, observing the last two 500 pounders to score direct hits on a hangar on the north-eastern boundary of the aerodrome and generate a large cloud of smoke.

Sgt Banker and crew ran into light flak when still fifteen miles short of the target, and described it as intense and effective between 3,000 and 6,000 feet. The target was identified without difficulty, and a stick of four 500 pounders aimed at a light railway line within the aerodrome from 3,000 feet at 01.15. F/O Vernieux and crew were driven off by the intensity of the defences, and made their way to the alternative target, which they bombed with six 250 pounders and incendiaries from 8,000 feet at 01.30 without observing the results. A W/T signal was received from W/C Crockart, which stated that he was returning on one engine, and this was followed at 03.59 by a plain language message, "going down". The latter provided only a second-class fix, that suggested a position somewhere between fifteen miles east of Amsterdam and ten miles north-west of The Hague, already over the North Sea. Coastal Command aircraft and a high-speed launch were sent immediately to the area to search, but no trace of P1329 was found, and it would be some time before the body of W/C Crockart came ashore in northern Holland, and that of gunner, Sgt Ingram, on the Danish coast. Having negotiated many operations without loss, this night was particularly sobering for 50 Squadron, as P/O Luxmoore and crew also failed to return in L4078, having fallen victim to the defences in the Hannover area, and crashing without survivors.

5 Group detailed twenty-three Hampdens for bombing and mining operations on the 27th, for which a 50 Squadron quartet of crews was briefed to attack an oil-tankerage site at Nyborg on the eastern coast of Denmark's Fyn Island. They departed Waddington between 21.20 and 21.34 with S/L Oxley the senior pilot on duty, each carrying four 500 pounders, and made their way in predominantly favourable conditions and visibility to the target area. On arrival

they encountered only desultory defensive activity, and S/L Oxley, F/O Watts and P/O Gardiner carried out their attacks from 8,000 feet, while F/O Corr preferred an altitude of 5,000 feet. Sixteen bombs fell onto the target between 00.23 and 00.42, and most were observed to be accurate, although no large explosions were evident, and the results were inconclusive. Earlier in the day, W/C Golledge had arrived to succeed the missing W/C Crockart as commanding officer.

On the 28th, the Command committed 108 aircraft to the bombing of industrial targets in Germany, aerodromes in Holland and gardening activities in Kiel Bay. 50 Squadron made ready five Hampdens to send against the Bayer chemicals factory at Dormagen, situated in the southern Ruhr between Düsseldorf and Leverkusen, which was producing poison gas, and three others to plant vegetables in the Quince garden in the western Baltic. The gardeners took off first, between 21.43 and 21.55, with F/L Bennett the senior pilot on duty, and they were followed into the air by the bombing brigade between 22.22 and 22.32 led by F/L Shaughnessy. Among the latter was the crew of F/O Jacklin, who had flown some 150 miles, when the pilot became unwell and aborted the sortie, leaving the others to press on via corridor "G" in favourable weather conditions. In the event, only P/O Banker and crew would attack the primary target, after picking up the Rhine and running the gauntlet of intense searchlights and flak of all calibres, which burst at the correct level but mostly behind. Violent changes of speed between 110 and 240 mph succeeded in preventing the searchlights from establishing a hold, and the six 250 pounders were released in a stick from 3,500 feet, and were observed to straddle the aiming-point from north to south. Two large explosions were followed by a fire and a large, low, white blanket of cloud, possibly gas, and a column of black smoke was rising through 2,000 feet as they turned away. F/O Lloyd and crew blamed industrial haze for their inability to identify the primary target, and, after a twenty-minute search, they turned north to seek out the Derendorf marshalling yards, situated to the north of Düsseldorf city centre. They encountered the same hostile reception here, with shells bursting all around them as they picked out the aiming-point from 7,000 feet and bombed it with eight 250 pounders at 01.20, without observing the results. P/O Treasure and crew were defeated by the defences and poor visibility over Dormagen, and also headed northwards to the cauldron of Düsseldorf, where they ran across the marshalling yards at 5,000 feet. Following the line of the tracks from south to north, they dispensed the bomb load in a stick, but, again, without observing the results. F/L Shaughnessy and crew arrived at the primary target at 00.50, but were beaten off by the ferocity of the defences, and decided to try their luck at the alternative target at Derendorf. They found this equally unwelcoming, and, between the searchlight beams and flashes of exploding flak, caught a brief glimpse of the marshalling yards, towards which they aimed eight 250 pounders from 9,000 feet at 01.19.

Meanwhile, F/L Bennett and crew had experienced an uneventful outward flight, observing nothing of interest until spotting seven merchant ships of up to 7,000 tons steaming north at a position to the east of Kiel Bay. The vegetables were planted as briefed from 600 feet at 01.41, and a course set for home, which took them over an armed auxiliary vessel. This fired at them without effect, and F/L Bennett responded by dropping two 250lb wing bombs, which overshot. F/O Vernieux and crew flew from Skegness to Sylt, before traversing the Schleswig-Holstein peninsular and reducing height to 400 feet to plant the vegetable at 01.00. Some twenty minutes later, they, too, came upon a small vessel close to the east coast of Jutland, and attacked it with their wing-mounted bombs from 4,000 feet. P/O Mulloy and crew delivered their mine into the allocated location from 500 feet at 01.00, and were fired upon ineffectively by heavy flak at Eckernförde Bay on the way home.

5 Group notified Hemswell and Waddington on the 29th to prepare ten Hampdens each for an operation that night against a dynamite factory at Geesthacht, situated some ten miles south-east of Hamburg. 50 Squadron was to support the operation with four Hampdens, which took off between 21.55 and 22.08 with S/L Oxley the senior pilot on duty. Thirty miles out over the North Sea they ran into a front, which stretched eastwards for 150 miles, and south from the Kiel Canal to cover the target area with ten-tenths cloud at between 2,000 and 7,000 feet. F/O Taylor and crew arrived in the target area at 00.50, and ran immediately into searchlights and medium flak at 10,000 feet, despite which, the factory was somehow identified and attacked with four 500 pounders in a stick from east to west at 01.00. No results were observed, and a course was set for home, while P/O Gardiner and crew searched for the factory at 10,000 feet from 00.45 until 01.00, before giving up and seeking out the aerodrome at Farge, a small port on the Weser, where the largest concrete structure in the world would be built to house U-Boots late in the war. However, with daylight approaching in these northerly latitudes, it was decided to return home with the bombs. S/L Oxley alternated between 2,000 and 10,000 feet, but was unable to establish a pinpoint from which to navigate, and dumped his bombs into the sea on the way home. F/O Corr and crew were surprised by intense flak as they flew over Rendsburg on the Schleswig-Holstein peninsular at 2,000 feet while outbound, but corkscrewed their way out of danger and climbed to 8,000 feet as they searched in vain, first for the primary target, and then the Blohm & Voss aircraft factory at Wenzendorf. Defeated by the low cloud, they turned for home, also jettisoning their bombs into the North Sea.

The last night of the month brought further operations by eighty-eight assorted aircraft against targets in Hamburg in the north to Darmstadt and Hanau in the south and the Ruhr in between. 5 Group would return to the previously targeted Hamburg oil refinery with a dozen Hampdens from Waddington, while twelve from Scampton went for an aerodrome near Dortmund and four from Hemswell attacked the marshalling yards at Osnabrück. 50 Squadron made ready six Hampdens for Hamburg, and dispatched them between 21.00 and 21.23 with S/L Willan the senior pilot on duty. He and his crew approached the target area over the Elbe Estuary, maintaining an altitude of 14,000 feet, and being harried by flak all the way south-east along the river to the target. The refinery, actually situated in Harburg on the South Bank, was located at 23.59, and attacked with six 250 pounders and incendiaries, the detonation of which was not witnessed. The presence of low cloud, ferocious anti-aircraft fire and searchlight dazzle persuaded Sgt Abbott and crew to seek an alternative objective after searching for the primary between 23.50 and 00.16, and they found what they were looking for on Norderney in the form of its aerodrome, which they bombed from 9,000 feet at 00.48. F/O Jacklin and crew chose to make landfall over Texel, before setting course via Harlingen and Delfzijl to pass four miles south of Emden. They arrived in the target are at 23.59 to be greeted, like the others, with extreme hostility, although, at 15,000 feet, they were above the danger, and the target was located ten minutes later. Six 250 pounders and the incendiaries fell away, and were seen to detonate some five hundred yards north-west of the aiming-point, but a large fire was seen reflected in the tops of the clouds at 10,000 feet, and a column of black smoke was emerging through into clear air. P/O Banker and crew were at 14,000 feet over Bramstedt with fifty miles still to go to the target, when they became aware of two unidentified aircraft shadowing them half a mile behind. They were seen to have wide wing-spans and navigation lights burning, but they were lost from sight after ten minutes. The bombs went down from 13,000 feet at the same time as those of F/O Jacklin, and were seen to burst across the target setting off rapidly-spreading fires. F/O Lloyd and crew were unable to identify the primary target, but found one of the alternatives, another oil plant in the city (A7), and bombed it from 10,000 feet at 00.23, only to see their effort undershoot by three hundred yards. F/O Watts and crew reported a similar story on return, after being thwarted by the low cloud from identifying the primary, and seeking out yet another oil plant (A8). They bombed it from 10,000 feet on a south-westerly heading, and observed three direct hits by the 250 pounders and another by the incendiaries. These caused a fire to break out, but the extent of the damage could not be determined.

During the course of the most hectic month of operations to date, the squadron participated in thirty-one of them, and dispatched 158 sorties for the loss of three Hampdens and two crews.

July 1940

The new month began as the old one had ended, with operations on the 1st against industrial and communications targets in Germany and gardening. 5 Group detailed a dozen Hampdens from each of its operational stations, six of those from Waddington to conduct mining operations in the Endives garden of the Little Belt between the east coast of Jutland and Fyn Island, while six others attended to the marshalling yards at Osnabrück. 50 Squadron contributed three to each endeavour, and dispatched the gardeners, P/O Treasure, F/O Corr and F/L Shaughnessy and their crews, first, between 21.27 and 21.30, to be followed by the bombing brigade consisting of P/O Mulloy, F/O Vernieux and F/O Reed either side of 22.00. When 120 miles east of Skegness, F/O Vernieux noticed low oil pressure on one engine, and turned back, only for the problem to rectify itself when thirty miles from the English coast. It was too late to make for the primary target, and a course was set for the alternative, a concentration of invasion barges in the River Lek to the east of Rotterdam. On arrival, haze and low cloud obscured the ground and prevented the target from being located, persuading the crew to bring their bombs home. P/O Mulloy and crew found the marshalling yards with little difficulty, but had to face a hot reception from searchlights and heavy and medium calibre flak as they delivered their four 500 pounders from 11,000 feet. They observed them to hit the target, but haze and searchlight glare prevented a detailed assessment. F/O Reed and crew braved the defences at 8,000 feet, and delivered their bombs in a stick from east to west, observing only one to burst.

Meanwhile, two of the gardeners had arrived over the western Baltic to encounter clear skies and excellent visibility, which enabled them to identify their target area without difficulty. F/L Shaughnessy and crew delivered their vegetable into the briefed location from 600 feet at 00.27, and F/O Corr and crew followed up from 700 feet eight minutes later. On the way home, the Corr crew dropped two 250 pounder wing-mounted bombs from 5,000 onto a flak ship thirty miles east of Sylt, after it had fired on them. The Shaughnessy crew was also targeted by a flak ship when sixty-seven miles west of Fanø Island, and they responded with their two wing bombs from 3,000 feet at 01.21. Neither crew could confirm hits, but both ships ceased firing immediately, presumably as their crews took cover. P/O Treasure and crew had been unable to establish their position at the German coast on e.t.a., and began a search for a pinpoint at 00.02, which they abandoned at 01.00, before setting course for home after deeming it too late to head for the alternative garden in the Elbe Estuary.

On the 2nd, Hemswell and Waddington received orders to prepare ten Hampdens each to send to Hamburg, the former to attack the dynamite factory at Geesthacht, and the latter to take another swipe at the Harburg oil refinery, while six others from Scampton took care of the gardening. In the event, the Hemswell element was cancelled, leaving the five 50 Squadron representatives from Waddington to take off between 21.29 and 21.50 with S/L Willan the senior pilot on duty, and make their way to north-western Germany with their 44 Squadron colleagues. F/O Taylor and crew located the primary target, and had to run the expected gauntlet of searchlights and flak as they delivered their four 500 pounders from 14,000 feet at 23.52. P/O Banker and crew arrived thirty minutes later, and elected to carry out their bombing run from 7,000 feet, from where they observed the first two bombs to undershoot by a hundred yards, and the third to score a direct hit, which produced a blue explosion and fires. It was only after bombing that the defences opened up on them with heavy and medium calibre flak, and a piece of shrapnel blew open the lower hatch, almost sucking out the observer. He was halfway to oblivion before the wireless operator dragged him back inside the fuselage with great difficulty, and there he collapsed with shock, taking two hours to recover his wits. F/O Watts and crew were the last to reach the primary target, and delivered their attack from 10,000 feet at 00.45, without observing the results. As they flew back over Bremen, they noted six barrage balloons tethered amazingly high at 11,000 feet, which they were, perhaps, lucky to avoid. While outbound over the North Sea, S/L Willan lost an exhaust stub, exposing the exhaust flame and making the aircraft highly visible to enemy aircraft and ground defences. Rather than abandon the sortie altogether, he proceeded to one of the alternative targets, the seaplane base on Norderney, and bombed it from 10,000 feet at 00.08. F/O Lloyd and crew had reached the primary target area, but low cloud and haze prevented them from identifying the refinery. They, too, opted to attack the seaplane base on Norderney, and carried out their attack from 7,000 feet at 01.10, observing one 500 pounder to find the mark and the others to fall into the sea.

5 Group detailed fifteen Hampdens for operations on the 3rd, when the marshalling yards at Osnabrück and the banks of the Dortmund-Ems Canal were the objectives for the bombing brigade, while six Waddington crews attended to gardening duties. The three 50 Squadron crews of W/C Golledge, who was undertaking his first operation with the squadron, and P/Os Stenner and Treasure, departed Waddington between 21.05 and 21.25 bound for the Quince garden in Kiel Bay. It was shortly after crossing the Lincolnshire coast that the exhaust-stub malaise struck again, depriving P/O Treasure of the one on his starboard engine, and forcing him to abort the sortie. W/C Golledge and crew found the target area without difficulty, and descended to 500 feet to release the mine, only for it to remain firmly in the bomb bay as the release gear failed to function. The mine was brought home, where no fault with the release system could be found. This left just P/O Stenner and crew to fulfil their brief, and their outward flight was uneventful and undertaken in good conditions until reaching 5 degrees east, where they encountered eight to ten-tenths cloud with a base at 1,000 feet and visibility at no more than two miles. Despite the difficulties, the garden was identified, and the mine released from 500 feet at 00.23, after which, they were chased out of the target area by medium and light anti-aircraft fire from two flak ships.

It was at this point that the pace of operations slackened to a small degree, the fall of France having reduced the requirement to the extent that crews could expect to operate from now on every third rather than every other night. Hemswell and Scampton took the strain on the night of the 4/5th, when the target for sixteen Hampdens were a graving (dry) and a floating dock in the Krupp-Germania shipyard at Kiel, one of which was believed to be holding the under-repair cruiser Scharnhorst. There were no claims by returning crews, and a second attack was scheduled for the 5th, which would involve fifty-one aircraft, including a dozen Hampdens from Waddington. The six 50 Squadron participants took off between 21.32 and 21.52 with S/L Willan the senior pilot on duty, and made their way across the North Sea in poor visibility with cumulus cloud between 4,000 and 10,000 feet. F/O Vernieux and crew were thirty miles out when they discovered that there was no dinghy on board, and returned to collect one. This put them too far behind schedule to reach the primary target, and they would attempt in vain to locate and bomb the seaplane base on Norderney as their alternative. The others pressed on to encounter good weather conditions in the target area and moderate visibility, but had to endure the attentions of a hundred searchlights and all calibres of anti-aircraft fire. P/O Banker and crew were, perhaps, unwise to venture into such well-defended territory at 2,000 to 3,000 feet, and suffered the consequences as small nuggets of hot shrapnel entered the fuselage, narrowly missing the occupants, and tore away the starboard flap. They flew out over the sea to turn around and approach from east to west at 3,500 feet, from which height their four 500 pounders straddled what they identified as a pocket battleship in N°6 graving dock and Scharnhorst at the floating dock at 00.20. One bomb was seen to explode close to the pocket battleship, and a red glow was observed with a dark centre. As S/L Willan and crew closed on the target from the north-west at exactly the same time, following the course of the Elbe at a more sensible 12,000 feet, they also felt the attention of the defences and noted shells bursting ahead of them at their flight level and up to two thousand feet higher. The bomb bursts were lost in the glare of searchlights and the flashes of tracer and exploding flak shells, which they were happy to leave behind them, having not received even a scratch. P/O Gardiner and crew ran in from north-east to south-west at 10,000 feet, but the need to take avoiding action would deny them the opportunity to plot the fall of their four bombs. F/O Reed and crew arrived after the others, at 00.50, at 12,000 feet, and adopted a glide approach from the north-east before releasing the bombs from 7,000 feet at 00.50 with, now, few searchlights to bother them. However, it seems that this attack stirred the defences into action again, and F/L Shaughnessy and crew felt the full force when they carried out their attack on an east-west heading from 9,500 feet five minutes later.

Waddington was alerted on the 6th to provide a dozen Hampdens for gardening duties that night in the Quince region of Kiel Bay, for which 50 Squadron made ready five aircraft. They took off between 21.25 and 21.46 with F/Os Watts and Lloyd the senior pilots on duty, and set course from Skegness to Esbjerg on the west coast of Jutland. They experienced adverse weather conditions of rain, sleet and occasional icing as they traversed the North Sea, and F/O Watts and crew flew at 1,500 feet to remain below the 4,000-foot cloud base. They reached Denmark's western coast at 23.50 and came under accurate fire from "pom-pom" batteries at Esbjerg as they turned inland for the forty-minute, one hundred-mile crossing of the Schleswig-Holstein peninsular. On arrival over Kiel Bay, they found cloud at between 3,000 and 5,000 feet with visibility at up to six miles, enabling the drop zone to be identified without difficulty, and the vegetable to be planted from 700 feet at 00.32. This was supplemented by the others from 300 to 500 feet, before the crews set course for home, and to seek out suitable targets for their two 250lb wing-mounted bombs. P/O Mulloy and crew attacked Hörnum seaplane base from 4,000 feet with two wing-mounted 250 pounders at 01.07, and observed large orange and red explosions along with fires in a large, square building, which appeared to be destroyed. The others failed to locate a target, and mostly jettisoned their bombs in the North Sea.

All three 5 Group operational stations were to be in action on the 7th, Hemswell taking care of the gardening activities and a small-scale attack on the Dortmund-Ems Canal, while Scampton attended to an oil refinery at Offenbach and Waddington to marshalling yards at Soest. Three 50 Squadron Hampdens were made ready for the last-mentioned, and took off between 21.58 and 22.09 in the hands respectively of F/O Vernieux, Sgt Abbott and F/O Taylor and their crews. They flew from Skegness to Texel in good conditions, before running into a fifty-mile wide bank of cloud beginning twenty miles inland from the Dutch coast and ending before the target was reached. They were fired upon by the defences at Münster, Hamm and at the target, where many searchlights co-operated with all calibres of flak to buffet the Hampdens with exploding shells. F/O Vernieux and crew dropped their six 250 pounders from 10,000 feet, but saw nothing of their impact in the glare of the defences and the need to take evasive action. Sgt Abbott and crew ran in at 00.40 from south-east to north-west at 5,000 feet, from where they were able to confirm two hits on the west corner of the yards and three undershooting misses. F/O Taylor and crew could see fires already burning as they released their load at 00.48, and observed five bursts, followed by fresh fires, but it was difficult for anyone to make a meaningful assessment in the cauldron of searchlights and exploding flak shells.

The squadron was stood down from operations on the 8th while the move took place to a new home at Hatfield Woodhouse, located across the county line in Yorkshire, five miles north-east of Doncaster. This was a brand-new airfield, completed in June, and 50 Squadron would be its first resident unit. To prevent confusion with the Hatfield in Hertfordshire, which was home to the de Havilland aircraft factory, Hatfield Woodhouse would be renamed in August to become Lindholme, after a country house and hamlet on the eastern boundary of the airfield. Training continued at Waddington while the move went ahead, and P4288 crashed at Branston on approach to Waddington on the 9th, while in the hands of P/O Mulloy and his crew, who walked away unhurt. Having been allowed two days to familiarize themselves with their new surroundings, the squadron's crews returned to operations on the 13th on what would be a busy night for the group involving fifty-seven bombing and mining sorties. The squadron made ready a record eleven Hampdens for another crack at the explosives works at Geesthacht near Hamburg, referred to now in the ORB as Krümmel, and they took off between 21.32 and 22.07 with S/L Willan the senior pilot on duty and F/L Corr operating for the first time in his new rank. Crews were becoming accustomed to occasional unfavourable weather conditions between the English coast and the Hamburg area, and, on this night, they were particularly unhelpful for purposes of target location. Only P/O Banker and crew were able, somehow, to identify the primary target through the nine-tenths cloud that lay between 2,000 and 12,000 feet and contained violent electrical storms. They arrived at 01.55 and departed seventeen minutes later after delivering four 500 pounders from 10,000 feet. They were unable to assess the results, but believed that the target had been hit. The others were unable to locate either the primary or the alternative target, the oil refinery coded A7, but S/L Willan found an aerodrome thirty miles east of Hamburg, and bombed it from 4,500 feet at 23.59. P/O Stenner and crew attacked the aerodrome on Texel with a stick of eight 250 pounders delivered on a south to north heading from 7,000 feet. They were seen to burst, but darkness prevented observation of detail, and, these apart, the others returned their bombs to store.

5 Group detailed twenty-one Hampdens on the 14th, a dozen for an operation that night against the Blohm & Voss aircraft factory at Wenzendorf, and the remainder for gardening duties. 50 Squadron made ready five aircraft for the former, which departed Hatfield Woodhouse between 21.27 and 21.38 with S/L Oxley the senior pilot on duty and the first away. They were under fire from accurate flak bursting at up to 12,000 feet all the way from Texel to the target area, where F/O Watts and crew arrived first, in good conditions, to deliver an attack from 8,000 feet onto the adjacent aerodrome at 00.20. One minute later, Sgt Abbott and crew bombed the factory from 10,000 feet, and it was a further twenty-four minutes before the next stick of four 500 pounders went down on the primary target, these from 6,000 feet from S/L Oxley's aircraft. P/O Gardiner and crew were also unable to identify the factory, and aimed their bombs at the flare-path of the aerodrome from 10,000 feet at 00.55, and P/O Mulloy and crew were the last to reach the target area, where they, too, attacked the aerodrome from 10,000 feet at 02.00. It was a disappointing operation generally, as both of the crews that identified the primary target, acknowledged failing to hit it.

5 Group alone was required to operate on the 15th, and thirty-three Hampdens were prepared for an aircraft park at Paderborn, an oil refinery at Misburg near Hannover and gardening duties. 50 Squadron's ten crews were briefed to mine the waters of the Daffodil garden at the southern end of The Sound (Oresund) between Sjælland Island and Sweden, and took off between 20.35 and 20.47 with W/C Golledge the senior pilot on duty and first off the ground. It turned out to be an uneventful operation for all crews, who benefitted from favourable weather conditions, and only isolated and ineffective opposition, which enabled them to deliver their stores into the briefed locations from 500 to 700 feet between 00.13 and 00.45 and return safely. There was no operational activity by the group on the 16th because of adverse weather conditions, and 50 Squadron had no suitably rested pilots available on the 17th.

Orders were received by the squadron on the 18th to make ready ten Hampdens for another operation that night against the aircraft park at Paderborn, situated to the north-east of the Ruhr beyond Hamm. This was one of a number of operations by the group involving thirty-eight Hampdens in all, the remainder assigned to the Krupp works at Essen, marshalling yards at Cologne and an aerodrome at Eschwege. The Hatfield Woodhouse element took off between 21.29 and 22.02 with S/Ls Oxley and Willan the senior pilots on duty, but soon lost the services of P/O Potts and crew, who had to turn back with an engine issue. The others pressed on to reach the target area after largely uneventful flights, but neither of the flight commanders was able to identify the target in the conditions of darkness and haze. S/L Willan attacked an unidentified aerodrome with two 250 pounders from 4,000 feet at 00.30, and observed one to burst in the middle of the airfield and the other near the eastern boundary. S/L Oxley dropped four 250 pounders from 3,500 feet onto a railway siding at Wewer, a couple of miles south-west of the primary target, at 00.35, and, as he pulled away, saw the aircraft park under attack by his colleagues. By this time, P/O Gardiner and crew were already on their way home having also failed to identify their briefed objective. They found a stretch of railway line further north between Gutersloh and Bielefeld, and dropped their four 500 pounders onto it from 3,000 feet at 00.15. The others managed to locate the primary target, and attack it from a variety of altitudes ranging from 1,000 to 8,000 feet between 00.05 and 00.42, and all returned safely, mostly to report hits on, or, very close to hangars and other buildings.

On the following night, the group detailed nineteen Hampdens from Scampton, Waddington and Hatfield Woodhouse to send respectively against the cruiser, Admiral Scheer, at Wilhelmshaven, to mine the waters of the Kattegat, and to return to the aircraft park at Paderborn. The six 50 Squadron crews took off between 21.38 and 22.01 with F/Ls Corr and Shaughnessy the senior pilots on duty, and all reached German airspace without incident. As F/L Corr and crew passed close to Münster at 00.15, they came under fire from accurate light flak, which exploded all around them, rocking the aircraft in a way that gave the impression that it had been damaged. The bombs were jettisoned on this erroneous assumption, and the sortie was abandoned. F/L Shaughnessy and crew were unable to locate the primary target because of cloud and poor visibility, and dropped their bombs onto De Kooy aerodrome near Den Helder from 6,000 feet at 02.44 on the way home. P/O Wawn and crew experienced similar difficulties, and found a road and railway junction to attack from 6,000 feet as a last-resort target, observing direct hits on the track. F/O Lloyd and P/Os Banker and Potts experienced no difficulty in identifying the intended target, but would report inconclusive results after attacking it with their 500 pounders from 3,000 to 5,000 feet at around 00.20.

Ground crews at Hatfield Woodhouse were kept busy on the 21st preparing a dozen Hampdens for operations that night, eight for mining duties in the Nasturtium garden at the northern end of Oresund (The Sound) between Denmark and Sweden, and four to attack the Horten aircraft factory at Wismar on the Baltic coast. The gardeners took off first, between 20.37 and 20.54, with S/Ls Oxley and Willan the senior pilots on duty, and were followed immediately into the air by the bombing brigade of F/O Taylor and P/Os Mulloy, Stenner and West either side of 21.00. F/O Jacklin soon turned back with engine trouble, leaving the others to press on to their respective target areas in favourable weather conditions. F/O Taylor and crew approached the Horten factory at 12,000 feet shortly before midnight, and lined up their attack unopposed, to deliver four 500 pounders at 00.02 and cause large fires to break out. However, no sooner had the bombs struck home, than cloud slid across the aiming-point to obscure the ground, and it was not possible to assess whether or not the attack had been accurate. When P/O Mulloy and crew arrived at 4,000 feet eight minutes later, the aiming-point was visible, and the bombs went down at 00.15 to score two direct hits on two buildings in the south-west corner of the target. A large explosion was followed by a fire, which remained visible for thirty miles into the return journey. It was a further thirty minutes before P/O Stenner and crew arrived on the scene at 10,000 feet, and cloud prevented them from assessing the accuracy of their bombing. It was probably this cloud that prevented P/O West and crew from locating the target, and they dropped their load onto the seaplane base on Fehmarn Island from 8,000 feet on the way home.

The gardeners, meanwhile, had experienced an uneventful outward flight, and delivered their vegetables into the briefed locations from 500 to 800 feet between 23.50 and 00.25. It was on this night, that 1 Group, which had been formed out of the shattered remnants of the AASF, began operations with Fairey Battles flown by 103 and 150 Squadron crews, who attacked invasion barges in Dutch ports. During the course of the autumn and winter, the group would convert to Wellingtons and be ready to join the Command's campaigns in small numbers late in the year.

5 Group detailed twenty-three Hampdens for a variety of targets on the 22nd, three of them representing 50 Squadron, and assigned to the important marshalling yards at Hamm. F/Ls

Corr and Shaughnessy and P/O Banker departed Hatfield Woodhouse between 21.40 and 21.50, and all reached the target area to encounter cloud and haze, which prevented the two senior crews from identifying the target. Seeking out an alternative, F/L Corr and crew found a stretch of railway line south of Ahaus, which they bombed with four 500 pounders from 10,000 feet, but, apart from registering the burst of one of them on a siding, could not identify the fall of the others. F/L Shaughnessy and crew spotted the railway track running across the frontier between Zutphen in Holland and Vreden in Germany, upon which they dropped eight 250 pounders from 500 feet at 01.15, but observed no bursts. This left just P/O Banker and crew to attack the primary target, which they did in the face of ineffective searchlights and flak from 4,000 feet at around 00.15.

Aircraft factories at Wenzendorf and Wismar were assigned respectively to nine Hampdens from Hemswell and four from Hatfield Woodhouse on the 24th, the latter element taking off between 20.51 and 21.03 with W/C Golledge the senior pilot on duty. Weather conditions over the North Sea were found to be challenging, with a bank of cloud between 500 and 10,000 feet, and this persuaded W/C Golledge and P/O Jacklin to turn back at the German coast. P/O Potts and crew spent the outward flight dodging storms, and, having been thwarted by the conditions from locating the Horten factory, found the seaplane base on Borkum, and unloaded their four 500 pounders onto it in a stick from 4,000 feet on a north-westerly heading. In contrast, Sgt Abbott and crew reported locating the target without difficulty, and aimed four 250 pounders and incendiaries at it from 3,000 feet, observing them to fall onto the riverbank opposite the factory and start a fire that remained visible for thirty miles.

A busy night of operations on the 25th involved 166 aircraft, the crews of which were briefed to attack one of seven targets in the Ruhr and aerodromes in Holland. 5 Group detailed forty-one Hampdens to target oil refineries in the Ruhr, and eighteen from Scampton to attack the Dortmund-Ems Canal at Ladbergen. Eleven Hampdens were made ready at Hatfield Woodhouse, where five of the crews, those of S/L Oxley, F/L Corr and P/Os Bell, Mulloy and Treasure, were briefed to attack the oil refinery at Castrop-Rauxel in the eastern Ruhr, while six others were assigned to a similar target a mile or two to the west at Wanne-Eickel, situated between Gelsenkirchen and Herne. They took off between 21.09 and 21.37 with S/L Oxley the senior pilot on duty, and all reached the Ruhr to encounter the expected industrial haze and hostile reception, with a scattering of cloud as an additional impediment to target locating. The conditions and searchlight glare prevented S/L Oxley and crew from identifying their aiming-point, and their bombs went down from 13,000 feet into the aerodrome at Gelsenkirchen as an alternative at 00.45. F/L Corr and crew observed large concentrations of searchlights as they homed in on the target, and suspected that they were co-operating with night-fighters, which were releasing red cartridges over open country short of the industrial region. Other searchlights and anti-aircraft fire protected the target area, despite which, they were able to identify the refinery and aim their four 500 pounders at it from 9,000 feet at 23.40. One bomb was seen to start a fire, but haze prevented a detailed assessment of the results. P/O Treasure and crew found what appeared to be an active blast furnace near the target, and bombed it from 8,500 feet at 23.55, while P/O Bell and crew were defeated by the searchlight dazzle and let their load go onto a railway line near Herne. A message was received from P/O Mulloy DFC and his crew at 02.15, stating that they had lost their port engine over Cuxhaven and were making for Calais. This was an unlikely destination from north-western Germany, and was probably misread. Further fixes on P1321 were obtained at 02.29 and 02.57, but nothing more was heard until a message was received that the crew of a heavy gun battery at Happisburgh on the Norfolk coast, south-east of Cromer, had watched a bomber crash at the low water mark at 03.00, and that they had removed three bodies. They provided the serial number that confirmed it to be the 50 Squadron Hampden, and stated that shrapnel damage was clearly visible. It had, apparently, approached the crash site from the land side, having established its position, and it was assumed that P/O Mulloy was attempting a forced landing on the long and flat stretch of the beach. Sadly, he lost control at the very last moment, and the aircraft disintegrated on impact, killing all on board.

The Wanne-Eickel-bound crews experienced similar conditions, and F/O Vernieux and crew described intense searchlight and flak activity from Wesel all the way to the target, the sky over which was illuminated to such an extent that it was impossible to hide. They carried out their attack from 7,000 feet, and believed that a number of fires resulted, but the glare blinded them to any meaningful assessment of what was happening on the ground. P/O West and crew crossed the Ruhr at between 12,000 and 15,000 feet, hoping to evade the attentions of searchlights, but this proved not to be possible, and they dropped their bombs towards the target from 14,000 feet, losing sight of them as they plummeted into the kaleidoscope of light, exploding flak shells and tracer. P/O Gardiner and crew identified the target at 23.55, and bombed it ten minutes later from 12,000 feet without observing the outcome. F/O Taylor and crew had crossed Texel outbound at 6,000 feet at 23.10, causing all lights to be extinguished, and, on arrival in the target area on e.t.a., were unable to distinguish features on the ground through the haze and six to eight-tenths cloud. Driven off by the defences, they attacked a railway line at Dortmund from 12,500 feet at 00.20, and observed four fires to break out. F/O Reed and crew found themselves at 12,000 feet over Essen with flak shells bursting at heights up to 16,000 feet, and decided to seek a target of opportunity, which they found on the southern bank of a canal to the north-east of Essen. Three bursts were seen, followed by three fires that remained visible for a short time. P/O Wawn and crew abandoned the search for the primary target, and settled for the aerodrome at Lohausen at Düsseldorf, which they bombed from 6,000 feet at 00.40.

Scampton took care of the group's business on the following night, when targeting oil plants in north-western France, while the other stations stood down. On the 27th, orders were received for 50 Squadron to prepare seven Hampdens for operations that night against the oil refinery in Harburg, and S/L Willan was the senior pilot on duty as they took off between 20.58 and 21.11. Sgt Abbott and crew were contending with an engine issue as they approached the Frisians, and knew that they would not reach their assigned target. When the seaplane base on Borkum appeared beneath them, they dropped their six 250 pounders onto it from 12,000 feet at 23.15, but were prevented by cloud from observing the fall. The weather conditions were generally favourable as the others approached the enemy coast, and, while low cloud prevented some from picking up ground detail, a ferocious defence outlined the route from the Elbe Estuary all the way into Hamburg, where intense searchlight and flak activity would deflect all but two of the bombers from their purpose. F/O Watts and crew fought their way to the target, and identified it, but, during the bombing run at 15,000 feet, the defences became so intense, that it was lost from sight, and they ended up bombing a nearby heavy flak battery at 00.35. Some shrapnel did penetrate the cockpit, and F/O Watts had his cigarette case to thank for stopping a piece from hitting him. F/L Shaughnessy and crew also followed the Elbe all the way to Harburg, somehow avoiding the flak while flying at 12,000 feet. At 01.05, they dropped a stick of 500 pounders from east to west across the target area, before beating a hasty retreat with no clue as to the result of their courageous efforts. S/L

Willan was beaten back, and went in search of the seaplane base at Borkum as an alternative target, but failed to locate it, and, with dawn approaching, turned for home at 02.00 with his bomb load intact. F/O Jacklin and crew did find Borkum, after fending off the attentions of a night-fighter, and were subjected to a defence almost as hostile as that at Hamburg, with shells bursting at up to 13,000 feet. They dropped six 250 pounders from 8,000 feet at 00.20, and observed three bursts among searchlights on the aerodrome as they turned for home. P/O Stenner and crew had flown close to Norderney on the way out, and, having found the Hamburg defences too intense to penetrate, returned to attack the seaplane base from 8,000 feet at 00.50, observing the burst of two of their 500 pounders. P/O Potts and crew had lost their heating system over the North Sea, and were suffering extreme discomfort from cold as they reached the Elbe Estuary. The decision was taken to attack the Ostermoor refinery situated between the South Bank of the Kiel Canal and the North Bank of the Elbe, but the fall of the six 250 pounders from 9,500 feet towards the northern corner of the site was masked by searchlight dazzle.

Another busy night of operations for 5 Group on the 28th required the preparation of sixteen Hampdens at Waddington and eight at Hatfield Woodhouse for attacks on oil refineries at Hamburg and Bremen, while a dozen others from Scampton took care of gardening duties. 50 Squadron briefed eight crews to attack the Korff AG refinery in Bremen, with the naval docks at Wilhelmshaven as the alternative, and they took off between 21.27 and 21.54 with F/L Corr the senior pilot on duty. On approach to the enemy coast they ran into a bank of cumulo-nimbus cloud between 3,000 and 12,000 feet, along with extreme darkness, which prevented them from observing ground detail. These already challenging conditions for target locating became compounded by an intense searchlight and flak response. In contrast to the reports of others, P/O Treasure and crew described an uneventful outward flight and no difficulty in finding the target. They delivered their six 250 pounders from 10,000 feet while being subjected to an intense but inaccurate flak barrage, and it was this and the darkness that prevented them from observing any results. P/O Gardiner and crew approached the target from the north, and were still ten miles short at 12,000 feet when they ran into the flak, which accompanied them all the way to the aiming-point. They delivered their four 500 pounders from 11,500 feet at 00.12, and, such was the intensity of the searchlights, that they illuminated the Hampden through four thousand feet of cloud. F/O Taylor and crew carried out their attack from 14,000 feet at 00.20, and observed their bombs to burst, but could not assess the accuracy or possible damage. As for the others, F/L Corr could not locate the primary target, and bombed the aerodrome on Texel from 10,000 feet, while F/O Vernieux was beaten back by the ferocity of the defences, and attacked the docks at Wilhelmshaven at 00.20 instead. P/O Wawn and crew bombed the seaplane base on Borkum from 10,000 feet, and F/O Reed and P/O Bell brought their bombs home.

When orders were received on the last day of the month, 50 Squadron learned that it would be responsible for maintaining the mining campaign, and a dozen Hampdens were made ready to send to the Radish and Forget-me-not gardens, respectively, the Fehmarn Belt and Kiel Harbour in the western Baltic. They took off between 21.00 and 21.33 with S/Ls Oxley and Willan the senior pilots on duty and assigned to the Forget-me-not region, but immediately lost the services of P/O Treasure and crew from their section, after they turned back because of excessive vibration. The outward flight was undertaken in poor weather conditions, but was uneventful, and the target areas were reached without difficulty, although a layer of ten-tenths cloud was encountered over the Fehmarn Belt that lay from 2,000 feet down, in places, to 200 feet. S/Ls Oxley and Willan, F/O Read and P/O Wawn carried out their briefs in the Forget-me-not garden from 500 to 800 feet between 00.25 and 00.54, and all returned safely, although S/L Oxley's P1327 was found to have been overstressed during an incident on the way home. While attempting to swap positions, S/L Oxley and his second pilot had lost control, causing the Hampden to plummet towards the sea. In arresting the fall, the controls were strained, and they landed at Driffield to have them checked out. They flew back to base later, where a further inspection declared the aircraft to be beyond repair, and it was reduced to a ground-instruction airframe. P/O Wawn and crew reported being fired upon on the way home as they approached Toftlund on the Jutland peninsular, and dropped their two wing bombs onto the offenders from 6,000 feet at 01.37. Sgt Abbott and crew had been unable to locate the target area, and brought their mine and bombs home.

Meanwhile, F/O Taylor and P/Os Banker, Gardiner and Stenner had successfully fulfilled their briefs in the Radish garden from 500 to 700 feet between 00.13 and 00.50, while P/O Potts and crew had been unable to locate it, and were heading for home when they came upon an unidentified aerodrome in south-central Jutland. They attacked it with their two wing-mounted 250 pounders from 1,000 feet, and two bursts were observed on the flare-path. This was close to the location of the attack by the Wawn crew, and may well have been the same one. Contact with P/O Bell and crew in P4383 was lost at 04.10, when it was plotted to be some forty to forty-five miles off Flamborough Head. Aircraft were sent out immediately in search, along with two high-speed launches and two naval vessels, and a dinghy with four persons aboard was eventually spotted from the air at 20.20, but, sadly, lost forty-five minutes later.

Although not recorded in the squadron ORB, it seems that F/L Bennett was posted from the squadron during the month, his name not appearing on the Order of Battle after late June. He would go on to command 144 Squadron between February and July 1942, and, after a spell at 1 Group HQ, become the first commanding officer of 550 Squadron in November 1943. During the course of the month the squadron undertook twenty operations, and dispatched 127 sorties for the loss of three Hampdens and two crews.

August 1940

The squadron dispatched nine sorties in search of P/O Bell and crew during the course of the 1st, and efforts began again at dawn on the 2nd, but, despite a further twenty-one sorties by the squadron, and fifteen more on the 3rd right up until darkness arrived, nothing positive was found. One report from an aircraft late on gave a faint hope, and another 50 Squadron crew set off to cover that area on the morning of the 4th, but nothing was found, and the search had to be abandoned. Six weeks later, P/O Bell's body would come ashore on the Dutch coast to be buried at Bergen-op-Zoom War Cemetery. August's operations would follow a similar pattern to those of July as invasion fever increased, and 5 Group divided its effort on the 2nd between the oil refinery at Misburg for the Hemswell crews and mining for those from Scampton. On the following night, the Scampton element was sent in search of the cruiser Gneisenau at Kiel, while Hemswell went for the Dortmund-Ems Canal and Waddington took care of the gardening. There were no operations for the group on the 4th, and so it was the 5th before Hatfield Woodhouse found itself once more on the Order of Battle.

Briefings revealed that nine Hampdens from Scampton and eight belonging to 50 Squadron were to seek out the Bismarck, which was under the final stages of fitting-out in Hamburg. At Hatfield Woodhouse, four 500lb semi-armour-piercing bombs were loaded into each aircraft, which took off between 20.33 and 20.55 with F/L Shaughnessy the senior pilot on duty. Engine problems forced him to turn back after twenty minutes, and twenty minutes after he landed, F/O Vernieux also returned because of faulty instruments, having only reached the coast at Flamborough Head. F/L Shaughnessy and crew jumped into a spare Hampden, and took off again at 21.53, but, when 130 miles out over the North Sea, a faltering engine forced them to abandon the sortie again and jettison the bombs. The remaining six crews pressed on to reach the target to face the expected hostile response, which combined with haze, cloud and extreme darkness to conceal the location of the battleship. F/Os French and Reed bombed the docks in the area where Bismarck was believed to be, doing so from 14,000 and 10,000 feet respectively, the former at 00.22 without observing results, and the latter reporting two bursts. By this time, F/O Taylor had attacked a "self-illuminating military objective" in the Hamburg area from 13,800 feet at 23.30, at the same time as Sgt Abbott and crew dropped their load into the general docks complex from 14,000 feet. P/O West and crew found an electrical power station at Hastedt, situated on the North Bank of the Weser, south-east of Bremen, as an alternative objective to aim at from 14,500 feet at 00.03, and, at 01.45, P/O Wawn and crew emptied the contents of their bomb bay from 7,000 feet onto an aerodrome at Neuenburg, south-west of Wilhelmshaven.

It was the turn of Hatfield Woodhouse to provide the gardening element on the 7th, and seven Hampdens set off between 20.15 and 20.50 to plant their vegetables in the Quince garden, situated in the western Baltic off the southern tip of Denmark's Langeland Island. W/C Golledge was the senior pilot on duty as they climbed away to encounter unfavourable weather conditions in the form of ten-tenths cloud, electrical storms and barely moderate visibility. F/O Jacklin became indisposed shortly after take-off, and, such was the urgency of the situation, that he landed at Finningley en-route to base. F/O Watts and P/Os Banker, Potts and Treasure and their crews each successfully delivered their mines from 500 to 800 feet between 23.22 and 00.07, the Banker crew also dropping their two wing-mounted 250 pounders on what was believed to be a ship in the channel south of Svendborg at the southern end of Fyn Island. P/O Stenner and crew established a pinpoint on the Danish coast, but could not locate the garden through the cloud and darkness, and turned for home. F/O Vernieux and crew cited the weather conditions, particularly thunderstorms, as the reason for their failure to locate the target area, and they, too, abandoned their sortie.

Only Scampton operated on the 8th, to target an oil refinery at Oppau, near Ludwigshafen, and the entire group remained on the ground on the 9th because of adverse weather conditions. On the 10th, nine Hampdens each were made ready at Hemswell and Hatfield Woodhouse to operate that night against the Bergius oil refinery at Homberg, situated on the West Bank of the Rhine opposite Duisburg. The 50 Squadron element took off between 21.39 and 21.58 with W/C Golledge and S/L Willan the senior pilots on duty, and departing among them, at 21.47, was a tenth Hampden, P4382, which was embarking on a night training sortie to the Dutch Frisian island of Vlieland with the freshman crew of P/O Nolan on board. Sadly, they would never be seen again, and it must be assumed that they were swallowed up by the North Sea. The bombing brigade faced challenging weather conditions as they made their way to the enemy coast, and only three crews would manage to locate and attack the primary target. According to the timings recorded in the squadron ORB, F/O French and crew attacked the primary target with four 500 pounders from 12,000 feet at 23.35, one hour and fifty-five minutes after taking off, having covered a distance of 350 miles, and landed back at 02.20, to complete the round-trip in a remarkable four hours and forty minutes. In ideal circumstances this is possible, but one wonders whether GMT has been used rather than BST for the bombing and landing times. P/O Banker and crew found the target immediately on e.t.a., and attacked it from 7,000 feet at 23.50, straddling it, they believed, and stirring the defences into intense activity. This and the presence of cloud, prevented as assessment of the results to pass on at debriefing. F/O Reed and crew encountered eight-tenths cloud between 3,000 and 6,000 feet, and spent thirty minutes positioning themselves and gliding down through it to 2,500 feet. It was from that altitude that they delivered their six 250 pounders and incendiaries at 00.55, and observed several large explosions, followed soon afterwards by an extensive fire that lit up the sky. They enjoyed an uneventful return flight, and landed safely at 03.55 after a round trip of almost six hours. Of the others, W/C Golledge was defeated by the cloud, and bombed an unidentified Dutch aerodrome from 7,000 feet at 00.30, only for his four 500 pounders to undershoot. F/Os Lloyd and Watts both attacked an aerodrome at Krefeld from 10,500 feet at 23.45, the former claiming the destruction of a taxiing enemy aircraft, while P/O West and S/L Willan reported bombing an aerodrome at Duisburg from 11,000 feet at 00.01 and 01.00 respectively. S/L Willan later recorded that his bombs may have fallen elsewhere, into the large Ruhrort inland docks complex to the south of the city centre. P/O Wawn and crew found a searchlight and flak position twenty miles east of Arnhem for two of their 250 pounders, which they aimed from 3,000 feet without observing their fall.

5 Group detailed thirty-one Hampdens on the 12th to send against the Dortmund-Ems Canal at Ladbergen, the Wintershall oil refinery at Salzbergen and mining in the Quince garden off Langeland Island in Kiel Bay. The Dortmund-Ems Canal would become a 5 Group preserve for the remainder of the war, and, on this night, would result in the first Bomber Command VC, awarded to F/L Learoyd of 49 Squadron. At Hatfield Woodhouse, 50 Squadron loaded nine Hampdens with a mine each and dispatched them between 20.52 and 21.08 with S/L Willan the senior pilot on duty. His P4287 developed an engine issue while outbound over the North Sea, and the mine and bombs were returned to store. F/O Vernieux and crew were flying at 3,000 feet and were some eighty miles east of Flamborough Head on course for Sylt, when two lights were spotted at 23.05, about four hundred yards apart flashing S.O.S. They circled the spot attempting to obtain a fix, which took forty-five minutes in the prevailing atmospheric conditions, which they relayed to 5 Group HQ for action, and were then ordered to return to base as they would be too late on target. The others pressed on to reach the target area and locate their drop zones without difficulty, and the mines were delivered as briefed from 400 to 700 feet between 23.59 and 00.50. On the way home at 01.00, P/O Wawn and crew dropped their two 250lb wing bombs from 3,500 feet onto a railway junction at Haderslev in southern Denmark.

Airframe factories came under the spotlight on the 13th, when 5 Group assigned twenty-eight Hampdens to attack the Junkers works at Dessau in eastern Germany and Bernburg in north-east-central Germany, twenty miles south of Magdeburg. F/O French and P/Os Banker and West took off between 21.01 and 21.11, but F/O French was immediately compromised by technical problems and was back on the ground within twenty minutes. P/O Banker and crew set course from Skegness and flew all the way to Texel in cloud at 2,000 feet, before climbing to 9,000 feet to break into clear air. They were fired upon as they passed close to Hannover and then Braunschweig (Brunswick), and, three minutes before e.t.a., began a glide down until breaking cloud at 7,000 feet. The visibility remained poor, and a ten-minute search was required before the aiming-point was located and bombed from 4,000 feet at 00.22. One of the four 500 pounders was seen to hit a large building, causing an explosion that sent debris into the air, while the remaining bombs burst on the adjacent aerodrome. The attack stirred the defenders into life, and the Hampden was caught in a cone of fifteen searchlights as it scurried away, chased by exploding flak shells. P/O West and crew experienced the same difficulties when searching for the target, and found themselves still in cloud at 1,500 feet in the target area. They turned for home, and bombed a gun emplacement on Texel from 8,000 feet at 03.00.

A change of focus on the 14th would pitch the group against oil production and storage facilities at Pauillac, situated on the West Bank of the Gironde on the approach to Bordeaux in south-western France. The target code recorded in the squadron ORB was Z161, but Z was the prefix for an aerodrome, while A was the prefix for oil, so, perhaps we should conclude that the oil storage facilities were located on the site of an aerodrome. Seven of the eight 50 Squadron participants took off between 21.15 and 21.37, leaving F/O Vernieux and crew on the ground for a further thirty-four minutes, while a problem with the intercom was fixed. This left them so far behind schedule, that the long flight down to the Bordeaux region was out of the question. The station commander ordered them to proceed to an alternative target, the aerodrome at Cherbourg, and, on a night of most favourable conditions, they flew out via Abingdon and Lyme Regis to locate it with ease. They attacked from 1,500 feet with six 250 pounders and incendiaries, stirring up a hornet's nest of a dozen searchlights, which held them and blinded them to the fall of the bombs. By this time, the others were approaching the Gironde estuary, led by S/Ls Oxley and Willan, and were being drawn on by the fires already burning at the target. This and the excellent conditions enabled all to carry out their attacks with great accuracy from a very low 1,500 feet (F/O Reed) to a more conservative 11,000 feet (F/O Watts) between 01.20 and 01.56, and the target was left a sea of flames that remained visible for up to 130 miles into the return flight.

Remarkably, S/L Oxley's substantive rank was flying officer at this time, and, on the 15th, he was elevated to flight lieutenant, while retaining his acting squadron leader rank to remain in the role of flight commander. The squadron had no rested crews to contribute to the group's operations on this night, but was able to muster eleven for briefing on the 16th, when the oil refinery at Leuna, near Merseburg, was revealed as the target. This was one of many oil production and storage sites situated in an arc to the west of Leipzig from north of the city to the south, and it would be an area of major interest to the Command from mid-1944 onwards. That was in the distant future, when a thousand sorties might be launched in a single night, while on this night, the commitment of 150 sorties represented a major effort.

The Hatfield Woodhouse Wanderers took off between 20.40 and 21.45 with W/C Golledge and S/L Oxley the senior pilots on duty, and disappeared into a fine night with gentle moonlight to illuminate their path. Once over enemy territory, however, low cloud slid between them and the ground, happily, to disperse as the target area drew near. Despite the clear skies and the brightness of the moonlight, some crews experienced great difficulty in identifying the well-camouflaged complex, and spent a long time searching before finding it or giving up. Curiously, W/C Golledge identified it in the illumination provided by a number of parachute flares in the sky and fires in the general neighbourhood, and, one wonders why the others failed to do so. He bombed from 9,000 feet, but was blinded to the results by flashes and searchlight glare. Sgt Abbott and crew searched for forty minutes, before carrying out their attack from 10,000 feet at 00.45, and observing hits on buildings near the northern chimney, that resulted in an explosion. Approaching Derby, short of fuel and uncertain as to the visibility for landing at base, Sgt Abbott decided to put P1356 down in a field near Repton, striking a high-tension cable in the process, but causing only minor damage to the Hampden. F/O French and crew ran into heavy anti-aircraft fire over the target, where haze proved to be an added impediment, and the starboard engine began to falter. The four 500 pounders were released from 11,000 feet at 00.50, after which, they turned immediately for home without observing the results of their efforts. F/O Watts and crew attacked at precisely the same time from 10,000 feet, and observed six bursts, and were followed ten minutes later by F/O Taylor and crew, who only recognized the target from 1,200 feet by observing the hydrogenation plant to be ablaze. They made their first run at 01.00, only for the bombs to hang up, but a second pass five minutes later was successful, and direct hits were observed on a line of sheds at the base of the northern chimney. After a long search, P/O Banker and crew finally delivered their six 250 pounders and incendiaries from 3,000 feet at 01.28, observing them to burst and set off a fire that remained visible for fifteen miles into the return journey. F/L Shaughnessy and crew were unable to locate the primary target, and jettisoned their bombs in open country at 01.50. P/O Stenner and crew followed suit fifty minutes later after failing to establish their precise position, while feeling terrorized by the defences and fearful of running out of fuel or being intercepted by night-fighters. F/O Reed and crew made it all the way to the target, where a misunderstanding between the pilot and bomb-aimer led to the bombs being retained. S/L Oxley and crew searched in vain for an hour, before jettisoning their load over open country, while P/O Potts and crew stooged around the target area until 01.00, constantly under fire and hampered by the failure of their intercom. They eventually came upon an unidentified "self-illuminating target", and bombed it from 10,000 feet without observing the outcome.

Later, on the 17th, Hatfield Woodhouse underwent the change of name as described earlier, and would now be known as Lindholme. F/O Jacklin had already concluded his first tour of operations, and was officially posted on this day to 16 O.T.U., to pass on his skills to others. There were no further operations for the squadron until the 21st, even though 5 Group operated successfully on the 19th against another oil target near Bordeaux at Bec-d'Ambes in the Dordogne River. The dual targets for forty-four Hampdens on the 21st were a ship lift at the eastern end of the Mittelland Canal at its junction with the Elbe, and a Bergius synthetic oil refinery (hydrogenation plant), both located in the same Rothensee district to the north of Magdeburg city centre. Also, on the target list was a second ship lift at Hohenwarthe, close by to the north-east, which, in reality, had not been built, and, as a result of the war, would not be. 50 Squadron made ready ten Hampdens for the refinery, and dispatched them between 20.26 and 21.07 with S/Ls Oxley and Willan the senior pilots on duty, although the latter's sortie was abandoned a few miles out from Skegness because of an engine issue. The others pressed on to run the usual gauntlet of flak from numerous hotspots, particularly when passing between Hannover and Celle either side of 23.00, although the poor weather conditions, which included thunderstorms and rain, provided a degree of protection.

They encountered varying amounts of cloud in the target area, which F/O Lloyd and crew reached at 4,000 feet at 23.20, only to find the ground concealed and intense searchlight and flak activity making it a very uncomfortable place to hang around in. They didn't, and five minutes later jettisoned the bombs on the route back to Celle, noting with surprise a number of resulting explosions and a silvery fire visible briefly through a break in the cloud. P/O Potts and crew were among the earlier arrivals, reaching the target at 23.50, before gliding down through a break in the cloud, and following the course of the Elbe to drop their high-explosives and incendiaries from 6,000 feet three minutes later. They spent a further ten minutes observing the scene, and noted violent explosions and a large fire that appeared to be spreading. F/O Reed and crew attacked from east to west at 2,000 feet at 00.03, delivering four 500 pounders in a stick as they raced across the target under heavy fire and blinded by the searchlights. They emerged unscathed on the other side, before concealing themselves in the cloud for the uneventful home journey. P/O West and crew came close to disaster when at 8,000 feet over the southern end of Texel on the way out, after being targeted by the flak battery there. They survived by taking violent evasive action, and, at 00.10, they added four 500 pounders from 8,500 feet to the hardware falling in the target area, although, like most of the others, they would not be able to comment on the outcome. F/O French and crew observed widespread cloud at 3,000 feet as they crossed the aiming-point at 10,000 feet to drop six 250 pounders and incendiaries. They saw the flash of the detonations, but had no chance of making a meaningful assessment. F/L Shaughnessy and crew were hampered by patchy cloud at around 6,000 feet, but moonlight helped to illuminate an autobahn and a wood, which then led them to the built-up area. They found the target to be clearly visible from 7,000 feet as they bombed from west to east at 00.40, but flak and searchlight glare ensured that they saw no results. P/O Wawn and crew attacked from 2,500 feet at 00.45, and observed three 500 pounders burst alongside the northern edge of the target and start one fire. S/L Oxley carried out his attack from 10,000 feet, but was another too occupied with evading the defences to notice where his load fell. Sgt Abbott and crew spent forty minutes searching for the refinery, and came under heavy fire from the nearby aerodrome, sustaining slight damage as a result. While making a dummy run over the northern end of the target at 3,000 feet at 00.55, the bombs were accidentally released, and their fall not plotted.

On the 22nd, 5 Group detailed twenty-three Hampdens for an operation that night against an aircraft components factory at Frankfurt, while a dozen others from Scampton took care of the gardening duties. 50 Squadron made ready five Hampdens, which took off between 21.25 and 21.51 with S/L Willan the senior pilot on duty. P/O Stenner and crew were less than an hour out when engine trouble ended their sortie, and they brought their bombs home. The others pushed on to cross Belgium and reach the target area, where cloud concealed the ground from view and presented challenging conditions for target location. P/O Banker and crew, who, during past operations, had demonstrated a determination to find and attack their briefed objective, alone identified this one. Three minutes before e.t.a, they glided down to break cloud at 7,000 feet, only to encounter barrage balloons tethered at 9,000 feet and hiding in the cloud. This removed a low-level attack as an option, and, having climbed again to 9,000 feet, they spotted a bend in the River Main close to the target, and turned onto a reciprocal course to drop their bombs in a long stick at 00.18. They were unable because of the cloud to plot the fall, but they had the satisfaction, at least, of pressing home another attack. S/L Willan and crew searched for an hour without breaking cloud, and headed home via Rotterdam, where they ran into intense anti-aircraft fire that persuaded them to jettison their bombs as they weaved their way clear. F/L Corr and F/O Taylor experienced similar difficulties and aimed their bombs from 10,000 and 12,000 feet respectively at a flak position to the west of Frankfurt on the way home at 00.12 and 00.11.

5 Group was handed responsibility for gardening duties on the 23rd, and four 50 Squadron crews were among a total of forty briefed to ply their trade in the Jellyfish garden on the approaches to the U-Boot base at Brest. The 50 Squadron quartet took off in a five-minute slot either side of midnight with S/L Oxley the senior pilot on duty. They exited the English coast at Lyme Regis, and reached the target area to find excellent conditions with bright moonlight, and the defences already stirred into action by earlier arrivals. S/L Oxley and crew were at 10,000 feet as they closed in on the target area at 02.30, when the defences were at their most hostile, and decided to wait for them to become less aggressive, before throttling back and gliding down to 600 feet to drop the vegetable at the entrance to the harbour at 02.40. On gunning the engines for the "getaway", the defences opened up again and chased them out to sea and into the safety of a bank of cloud. P/O Wawn and crew dropped down to 350 feet to plant their vegetable at 02.44, before aiming their two 250lb wing-mounted bombs at a flak position, which stopped firing immediately. F/L Shaughnessy and crew also adopted a glide approach to deliver their vegetable from 600 feet at 02.48, and they, too, dropped their two 250lb wing-mounted bombs onto a flak position from above cloud at 4,000 feet. P/O West and crew braved the ground defences to get into position, only for a short in the electrical circuit of the bomb release system to prevent the mine from dropping away. This was not instantly apparent as they focussed on escaping the cauldron of fire, but, at least, they still had their wing bombs, and these were dropped from 9,000 feet onto one of the offending batteries.

On the following night the mining shifted south along the Biscay coast to the Cinnamon garden off the port of La Rochelle, another haven for the Kriegsmarine's U-Boot fleet. Twenty-nine Hampdens were detailed, seven of them at Lindholme, and they took off between 21.36 and 21.59 with S/L Willan the senior pilot on duty. They soon lost the services of P/O Smettem and crew, who were unable to extinguish their forward recognition light and had to abandon their sortie. The others were to enjoy an uneventful operation in favourable weather conditions, and planted their vegetables into the briefed location from 450 to 600 feet between 01.05 and 01.50. Opposition in the form of light flak came at them from various locations, but it was inaccurate, and this encouraged some to drop their wing bombs onto suitable targets on the way home. Sgt Abbott and crew released theirs over Rennes aerodrome from 1,000 at 01.18 just as an aircraft was landing, and scored direct hits on a hangar, while S/L Willan found a battery on a wharf to attack from 8,500 feet at 01.55. P/O Banker and crew were alerted to a coastal battery when it opened fire on them, and they returned the favour from 7,000 feet.

In retaliation for the bombing of London on the night of the 24/25th, the War Cabinet sanctioned the first raid of the war on Berlin to take place on the 25th. 5 Group responded with the preparation of forty-six Hampdens, thirty-four from Scampton, Waddington and Lindholme to attack an electrical power station, while twelve from Hemswell targeted Tempelhof aerodrome. The five 50 Squadron participants took off between 21.50 and 22.05 with S/L Oxley the senior pilot on duty, and made their way to the target over ten-tenths cloud, which prevented sight of the ground. F/O Taylor and crew approached the target area at 18,000 feet, and delivered eight 250 pounders through the cloud at 01.23 without observing the results. F/L Shaughnessy attacked two minutes later from 16,000 feet, and both returned safely from uneventful sorties to land after more than seven-and-a-half hours in the air. P/O Potts and crew were unable to locate the primary target, and were subjected to intense anti-aircraft fire as they searched, and suspected that they may have sustained some damage. They eventually bombed a heavy flak position on the city's north-eastern outskirts from 4,500 feet at 02.25, before setting course for home and reaching the Dutch coast, where the starboard engine cut out through fuel starvation. They crossed the North Sea on one engine, making landfall at Scarborough, but, with no aerodrome within reach and now flying on fumes, they force-landed P2124 at 07.50 four hundred yards off the beach. They were picked up by a fishing vessel, which made an attempt to tow the Hampden to shore, and it remained afloat for twenty minutes, before sinking while still some two hundred yards out. S/L Oxley and crew were the last to land at Lindholme, at 07.10, and they reported failing to locate the primary target, and bombing a flak position near Neustadt from 8,000 feet at 02.45. P/O Wawn and crew contacted Heston by W/T at 04.15 requesting a bearing, and acknowledge the receipt of four, but not the fifth. The fix seemed to place the Hampden somewhere in the Brussels area, but it seems that P2070 actually force-landed at Lautersheim, south-west of Frankfurt at 06.35, and the crew fell into enemy hands.

Another busy night of operations on the 26th saw the preparation of twenty-two Hampdens from Hemswell and Waddington to attack the Leuna oil refinery near Liepzig, while six others from Waddington were assigned to a gas production plant in the city itself. Lindholme's six crews were briefed for an assault on the aerodrome attached to the aircraft factories at Leipzig-Mockau, with the factories themselves as alternative targets. They took off between 20.19 and 20.33 with no senior officers to take the lead, but S/L Willan was on the Order of Battle on this night, assigned with a crew from Waddington to attack the old aqueduct of the Dortmund-Ems Canal at Ladbergen. He and his crew departed Lindholme at 22.15, only to be greeted by ten-tenths cloud over the target with a base at 5,000 feet, and, based on recent experiences, this was too low to go in alone at such a well-defended target. The weather conditions were equally unhelpful to the others as they passed between Münster and Osnabrück on their way to the Leipzig area, coming under heavy and accurate fire, and again later on as they bypassed Celle. F/O French and crew located the primary target, and dropped six 250 pounders and incendiaries onto it from 10,000 feet at 23.39, without observing the results through the cloud cover. They were followed a minute later by P/O Stenner and crew, who raced across the aiming-point from east to west to deliver their load from 7,500 feet. Sgt Abbott and crew had to search briefly before identifying the target, and then bombed it from 2,000 feet, from where they could observe hits on buildings to the north-west of the aerodrome. The anti-aircraft fire was intense, and a shell punctured the starboard fuel tank, despite which, an uneventful return flight took them as far as Hemswell, where they decided to land with what reserves of fuel remained. They joined the circuit and were two miles south of the flare-path when the starboard engine cut out, compelling Sgt Abbott to put P1317 down in a field. This he did successfully, and, although the Hampden would never fly again, the crew would, having emerged from the wreckage unscathed.

Scampton took the strain on the 27th, taking care of both the gardening duties and attacks on the oil plants at Bec-d'Ambes and Pauillac near Bordeaux, but all stations were in action on the 28th, preparing thirty Hampdens to send to Berlin to target the Siemens aircraft components factory in the Siemensstadt district of Spandau, north-west of Berlin city centre. The 50 Squadron quartet of F/L Shaughnessy, F/O Lloyd, P/O Potts and S/L Oxley and their crews departed Lindholme between 20.37 and 20.59, the last-mentioned having been delayed by a hitch during the bombing-up process. Within a short time of crossing the coast, they decided that they would not be able to reach the target and return before the advent of daylight, and abandoned the sortie. P/O Potts and crew were the first from the squadron to reach the target area, at 00.03, and observed three concentrations of searchlights and intense anti-aircraft fire already being directed at other aircraft. They reduced height from 10,000 to 8,000 feet, from where the factory was easily identified, and took advantage of the defenders' focus elsewhere to glide down to 5,000 feet to release the six 250 pounders and incendiaries in a stick at around 00.20. One large building was hit, and began to emit clouds of smoke, before beginning to glow and, finally, burst into flames. This alerted the defences to the Hampden's presence, and it seemed as if the whole of Berlin were firing at them as they dived steeply to 3,500 feet, and, then on full power, back up to 7,000 feet to evade the searchlights. F/L Shaughnessy reached the target area two minutes after the Potts crew, and ran straight into the intense searchlight activity and a hail of anti-aircraft fire, which screened the aiming-point from view. They ran across the estimated position of the factory at 14,500 feet, and dropped four 500 pounders at 00.12, before wheeling away to return home with a frequently cutting-out starboard engine and an unserviceable wireless. F/O Lloyd and crew carried out their attack from 15,000 feet eleven minutes after F/L Shaughnessy, also on the estimated position of the target, but failed to observe the outcome.

On the 29th, Hemswell and Waddington dispatched twenty Hampdens between them to an unspecified oil refinery at Gelsenkirchen in the Ruhr, which may well have been the Scholven-Buer plant situated north of the city and some two miles to the north-east of Gladbeck. This was to be the target also for five 50 Squadron crews twenty-four hours later, while fourteen Scampton Hampdens flew further afield to the recently attacked Bergius hydrogenation plant at Magdeburg. The Lindholme quintet took off between 20.49 and 21.00 with S/L Willan the senior pilot on duty, and made their way towards the Ruhr in favourable conditions, which enabled S/L Willan and crew to map-read with ease from the Dutch coast and establish a pinpoint ten miles from the target. They continued on at 10,500 feet, and were soon ensnared in a cone of searchlights, which completely blinded them to ground features. They had little choice but to pull away and seek an alternative target, which they found in the form of an aerodrome, believed to be some twelve miles south-east of the frontier town of Emmerich. As they made an approach, another aircraft carried out an attack, and all lights were extinguished and aircraft, perhaps night-fighters, were seen to take off. They proceeded northwards, and ran into another searchlight concentration that held them for ten minutes until they left the area, to return minutes later higher up at 14,000 feet. As they ran in on what they believed to be Haskamp aerodrome, situated some twenty miles north of Osnabrück, they were rocked by a vibration, and suspected a flak-hit to be responsible. They dropped their six 250 pounders and incendiaries onto the airfield from 12,000 feet at 00.12, and watched them undershoot. On landing, it was discovered that the vibration had been caused by the gills being open. F/O Reed and crew were defeated by the four-tenths cloud and searchlight glare, and found an alternative target east of Gelsenkirchen to bomb from 11,000 feet at 00.01. It was a similar story for F/O Ruth and P/O Mulligan and their crews, who were undertaking their first operation with the squadron. The latter bombed an unidentified alternative objective from 10,000 feet at 23.20, while the former dropped their bombs onto another unspecified target to the north-west of the Gelsenkirchen district of Horst from 14,500 feet at 23.48. L4079 failed to return with the crew of P/O Smettem and crew, who had registered a somewhat chequered and stuttering operational career thus far. It was learned later that they had all lost their lives in a crash at Angerlo, a dozen miles east of Arnhem in Holland.

All four of 5 Group's operational stations were in action on the last day of the month, as preparations were put in hand to attack an aero-engine works and Tempelhof aerodrome in Berlin, and the Rothensee oil refinery at Magdeburg. Scampton and Lindholme were to be responsible for the last-mentioned, and five of the fifteen Hampdens detailed would be provided by 50 Squadron. They took off between 20.11 and 20.20 with S/L Oxley the senior pilot on duty, and headed out in weather conditions that were moderate at best for target location, with up to ten-tenths cloud in the target areas. P/Os Potts and Stenner were the only two to identify the target, P/O Stenner and crew arriving first at 22.55 to bomb from 9,000 feet, while the former's load went down from 6,000 feet five minutes later. Neither was able to observe the results in the face of poor visibility and the ferocity of the defences, and it was these factors that prevented the remaining three crews from carrying out their attacks on the primary target. F/O Lloyd and F/L Shaughnessy and their crews were on their way home with their hardware still in the bomb bay when they came upon Langenhagen aerodrome as they skirted the northern rim of Hannover. The former released six 250 pounders and incendiaries from 12,000 feet at 00.20, but observed no results, while the latter, arriving five minutes later at 10,000 feet, found a fire already blazing, and added four 500 pounders, which resulted in another fire. S/L Oxley spent thirty minutes searching in vain for the primary target, before attacking an unidentified aerodrome to the west of Magdeburg from 4,000 feet at 01.00. During the course of the month the squadron took part in sixteen operations and dispatched 106 sorties for the loss of five Hampdens and three crews. It also waved goodbye to F/O Vernieux, as he moved on to N°4 Ferry Pilot's Pool on the 31st at the end of his operational tour.

September 1940

While the Battle of Britain was reaching a crescendo overhead, and invasion fever was gripping the nation, the overriding priority for the Command in September would be the destruction of the invasion craft being assembled in ports along the Occupied coast. That said, the new month began for 5 Group with small-scale attacks on industrial targets at Stuttgart and Ludwigshafen and marshalling yards at Mannheim on the 1st. Lindholme was not called into action, but was on the 2nd, when two Hampdens each were made ready to target the marshalling yards at Hamm and the aqueduct section of the Dortmund-Ems Canal at Ladbergen. They took off together between 20.15 and 20.17, S/L Willan and F/O Ruth bound for Hamm, and F/O Reed and P/O Banker for Ladbergen, and the former would be beset with visibility problems caused by five-tenths cloud and mist. On e.t.a at Hamm, S/L Willan observed lights, which he concluded came from the marshalling yards, and searchlight and flak activity seemed to confirm this belief. At 22.55 he delivered six 250 pounders and incendiaries from 13,000 feet, and, although their fall was not plotted, bursts were observed and a fire resulting from the incendiaries. F/O Ruth and crew dropped flares to aid their search, but the ground remained hidden, and it was decided to attack an aerodrome noted on the way out. This was either at Hengelo or Rijssen, and was found to be well-illuminated as they attacked it from 11,000 feet at 23.50, observing the 250 pounders to overshoot slightly and the incendiaries to undershoot.

Meanwhile, P/O Banker and crew had reached the enemy coast at Amsterdam, before passing over the lighthouse at Harderwijk with the weather improving towards the east. The target area was located without difficulty, and was circled for ten minutes, while the crew established a method of attack. It was at this time that a thick smoke screen was emitted from six generators to the west of the target, which actually aided identification of the aiming-point. Lining up on the canal, they dived from 7,000 down to 3,000 feet to release a stick of eight 250 pounders, which were seen to burst through the smoke, although it was not possible to confirm hits on the aqueduct. F/O Reed and crew arrived on the scene later when only the eastern branch of the twin aqueduct section was visible, and they dropped a long stick from 6,000 feet on the stroke of midnight, observing bursts but no details.

Lindholme was stood down on the 3rd, while twelve Hampdens were made ready for a raid on a power station on the outskirts of Berlin, while nine others were to target the Rothensee oil refinery at Magdeburg. On the 4th, twenty-three Hampdens were detailed on all four operational stations and made ready for a long-range operation to an oil refinery at Stettin. Bircham Newton was to be used as a forward base, and the five Lindholme crews took off between 18.35 and 19.00 for the short journey to the Norfolk station, where they would top up their tanks. They set off for north-eastern Germany between 20.28 and 20.53 with S/L Willan the senior pilot on duty, but lost F/L Shaughnessy and crew at the coast to a burnt-out wireless lead. The others set course for Heligoland to make landfall on the Danish coast south of Sylt, from where they were able to map-read their way to the target area in favourable conditions that offered ten miles visibility. P/O Stenner and crew identified the target straight-away, and attacked it from 10,500 feet at 23.35, observing their four 500 pounders to burst along the southern edge of the site, although they were unable to determine the effects. F/O French and crew found the searchlight and anti-aircraft fire over Denmark to be both accurate and troublesome, but came through unscathed to deliver their attack from 10,000 feet at 00.27, registering three direct hits that caused explosions and white fires visible for fifteen minutes and from fifty miles away. S/L Willan and crew spent thirty minutes searching for the target, before bombing it from 7,000 feet at 00.30, and observing their four 250 pounders and incendiaries to burst on buildings at the southern extremity of the site, causing fires with white flames that remained visible for twenty miles into the return flight. P/O Banker and crew bombed the target at the same time, having adopted a slightly different outward flight that made landfall first on Terschelling. They had found a thick haze lying over Denmark, which dispersed as they neared the target area, and, having identified the refinery, they carried out a dive attack from 7,000 to 3,000 feet. The four 500 pounders were seen to fall across the centre of the complex and cause three tall chimneys to collapse, and the resultant large fires could be seen for forty miles into the return journey.

Lindholme sat out a busy night for 5 Group on the 5th, when a return was made to the Stettin oil refinery, while other elements attended to a similar target in Hamburg and the Dortmund-Ems Canal. When orders came through on the 6th, 50 Squadron found itself assigned to gardening duties in the Læsø Channel in the Kattegat, better known to the crews as Yew Tree, while an oil refinery at Dortmund and four marshalling yards from Hamm to Mannheim hosted other elements of the group. The 50 Squadron quartet departed Lindholme between 20.29 and 20.37 with F/L Shaughnessy the senior pilot on duty, and made their way to the west coast of Jutland, some finding German beacon stations to be helpful in establishing fixes. Low cloud lay over the Danish mainland at under 1,000 feet, which prevented P/O Mulligan and crew from locating the garden, and they abandoned their sortie before returning, as briefed, to Kinloss. Sgt Brooker and crew were the first to reach the target area, and, having negotiated the ten-tenths cloud over the garden, delivered their vegetable into the briefed location from 700 feet at 23.46. While searching for the target area at 1,200 feet, F/L Shaughnessy and crew were fired upon by light flak from two unidentified vessels at 23.50, but they found the drop zone twenty minutes later, and planted the vegetable from 600 feet. On the way to a landing at Kinloss, unreliable fixes led them astray and north of their intended course, and it was only as they flew north over Wick that the error was noticed, enabling them to turn back and reach Kinloss after nine hours aloft. F/O Ruth enjoyed an uneventful sortie, which culminated in the delivery of the vegetable from 600 feet at 00.25, followed by a safe return to Scotland.

The first concerted effort to eliminate invasion barges in Channel ports was undertaken on the 7th, when 5 Group contributed twenty-nine Hampdens to attacks on concentrations at Ostend. 50 Squadron supported the operation with five aircraft, which departed Lindholme between 19.52 and 20.04 with S/L Oxley the senior pilot on duty and F/O Woodward and P/O Davies and their crews undertaking their first sorties with the squadron. They set course via corridor "G" towards the mouth of the Scheldt, before turning to the west and running in on the target. A mist lay over the area, and light from a quarter moon reflected upon it to decrease visibility, but the main impediment to target identification and assessment of results was the hostility of the flak and searchlight defences. P/O Banker and crew arrived at Ostend ahead of schedule, and circled the area to establish their bearings. The visibility was poor, but the searchlights gave an indication of the whereabouts of the target, and a steep diving attack from 7,000 to 3,000 feet at 21.20 directed the bombs towards the edge of the canal. The glare was too intense to even catch a glimpse of the barges, however, and they turned away with nothing of value to report at debriefing. F/O Woodward and crew found the target area well-illuminated by flares, and carried out a glide approach from 10,000 to 8,000 feet to deliver their load in a stick at 21.24. One minute later, F/O Lloyd and crew delivered their load from 6,000 feet, and believed that they had hit a railway line next to the wharf. On e.t.a., S/L Oxley glided in to release a flare, before returning to the sea to begin a bombing run, culminating in a dive attack from 6,000 down to 1,500 feet to deliver eight 250 pounders in a stick at 21.35. Only three were seen to burst, one on the bank and two in the canal, and it was not possible to determine anything further. P/O Davies and crew came upon the target at 4,000 feet, but too late to bomb on their first pass. They climbed to 8,000 feet on a reciprocal course, and then turned back towards the target, finding it difficult to identify it from so high. A fire provided a clue to its location, and a dive attack was carried out at 21.57, resulting in a number of further fires.

5 Group sent orders to all of its operational stations on the 8th to prepare for a major operation that night against a section of the Blohm & Voss shipyards in the Altona district of Hamburg to the west of the city centre. The actual aiming-point was recorded as lying five hundred yards south-east of the centre of the yards, and was probably a capital ship, perhaps Bismarck. Forty-nine Hampdens were made available, six of them at Lindholme, which took off between 21.17 and 21.39 with W/C Golledge and S/L Willan the senior pilots on duty. At 00.15, the Lindholme operations room received a call from Group to say that Scampton had picked up a message from P4287 at 23.59, to the effect that the Willan crew was "Jumping for it over Germany". The time suggested that they had reached the target area before running into trouble, although, when F/O French and crew arrived over the target a few minutes later, they saw no evidence of other aircraft having attacked, and did not report the defences being active. This probably placed both crews at the tip of the spearhead, minutes before the searchlight and flak defence sprang into life. News that the Willan crew members had all survived and were in enemy hands, would be received at Lindholme remarkably quickly later in the day. Meanwhile, F/O French and crew identified the target and attacked it with six 250 pounders and incendiaries from 10,000 feet at 00.07, and bursts were observed, although haze prevented a meaningful assessment of the results. When P/O West and crew began their search for the aiming-point, a number of fires were already burning and appeared to be

spreading. By this time, searchlight dazzle and gun flashes were compounding the difficulties caused by haze and rendered target identification something of a challenge. At 00.20, they released their four 500 pounders from 13,000 feet, and observed three bursts in the target area but no detail. On the way home they reported large fires at Cuxhaven, but they were probably observing Emden, which was another of the night's targets. The newly promoted F/L Reed and his crew were aided by the defences to identify the target, but soon found themselves held in searchlights at 15,000 feet. They shed five thousand feet to drop their 500 pounders at 00.40, and observed three bursts but nothing else through the haze and glare. P/O Potts and crew found patches of cloud hampering their attempts to draw a bead on the target, and eventually released their load from 10,000 feet on a southerly heading in the face of a spirited defence, sensing that their 500 pounders had undershot the mark. On e.t.a at the target, W/C Golledge and crew began a search that would last an hour in conditions of poor visibility. At some point, they found themselves in the middle of a searchlight and flak barrage, and it dawned on them, ultimately, that they were over Kiel, some fifty miles north of their intended position. It was too late to head for Hamburg, and a course was set for home, the bombs being jettisoned off Flamborough Head because of adverse weather conditions over Lindholme.

S/L Taylor was posted to the squadron on the 9th to succeed S/L Willan as flight commander, but he would not remain for long. That night, twenty-one Hampdens were detailed to return to Hamburg for another shot at the special target in the Blohm & Voss shipyards, and the 50 Squadron element of four took off between 19.34 and 19.47 with F/L Shaughnessy the senior pilot on duty. The weather on this occasion was excellent, with clear skies and a quarter moon to light the way and aid map-reading. F/L Shaughnessy and crew made landfall north of Nordstrand on the Schleswig-Holstein peninsular, before turning south to run in on the target at 12,000 feet and release their six 250 pounders and incendiaries at 22.56. Bursts were observed near the aiming-point, and fires broke out that remained visible for thirty miles into the return journey. P/O Mulligan and crew crossed the North Sea at 11,000 feet and also made landfall in the Pellworm/Nordstrand area, before setting course for the target and coming under fire all the way. They released their bombs and incendiaries in a stick from 14,000 feet at 23.00, and believed that they had fallen into the target area. Sgt Brooker and crew had become adept in tuning into German navigation beacons, and used them on this night to guide them to the target, where they dropped their four 500 pounders from 15,000 feet at 23.15, and watched them burst close to the aiming-point. F/O Ruth and crew found the target area without difficulty, and carried out a wide left-hand circuit to the south of the city to enable them to attack on a northerly heading. Their four 500 pounders went down in a stick from 13,000 feet at the same time as those of Sgt Brooker, but sight of their fall was denied them by searchlight dazzle, gun flashes and the need to take evasive action. They believed them to have impacted well within the target area, and this was their report at debriefing.

More than a hundred aircraft were in action on the 10th, eighteen of them 5 Group Hampdens assigned mostly to invasion barges at Ostend and Calais. 50 Squadron briefed the crews of F/L Reed and F/O French for Ostend, where concentrations of craft were reported to be eight or nine deep on the eastern side of the outer harbour. They took off shortly before 20.00, and crossed the North Sea at 7,000 feet to encounter seven to ten-tenths cloud in the target area, that severely hampered their attempts to establish a position. F/O French and crew descended to 3,000 feet and dropped flares, but still failed to locate the aiming-point, and, couldn't even determine whether they were over sea or land. After thirty minutes of fruitless searching, and rather than waste the effort, they climbed to 10,000 feet and flew towards the Ruhr in search of something worthy of their 250 pounders and incendiaries. They reached Duisburg at 23.30, where they spotted moving lights reminiscent of rolling stock, and bombed them at 23.35, without observing any results. They returned alone to Lindholme, where they waited in vain for F/L Reed and crew to join them. They would learn later that L4097 had been shot down into the sea off Ostend with fatal consequences for all on board, and only the remains of F/L Reed and his second pilot would be recovered for burial.

For the third time in four nights, the Blohm & Voss shipyards were to be attacked on the 11th, and twenty-one Hampdens were made ready, five of them at Lindholme. They took off between 18.35 and 18.55 with no senior pilots taking the lead, and flew out via Flamborough Head to make landfall in the area of Sylt. When F/O Lloyd and crew arrived in the target area at 21.30, they found it to be partially concealed beneath six to ten-tenths cloud between 3,000 and 12,000 feet. This hampered identification of landmarks, and persuaded them to seek an alternative target, which they found in the form of an aerodrome three miles south-east of Stade and west of Hamburg. They aimed six 250 pounders from 13,000 feet at 22.14, but cloud slid between them and the ground to deny them sight of the impact. F/O Woodward and crew were able to identify the target through breaks in the cloud, and attacked from 11,000 feet at 21.52, but could not determine the outcome. P/O West and crew reported a reduced level of searchlight and flak activity compared with recent experiences at this target, and dropped four 500 pounders through cloud from 13,000 feet at 22.00, also without observing their impact. P/O Banker and crew adopted an approach that would become a regular feature of 5 Group operations from 1943 onwards called the "Time and Distance method". This required them to identify a landmark, work out how long it would take to reach the aiming-point, and drop the bombs on that e.t.a. They let their 500 pounders go through the cloud at 22.15, and could only hope that they were accurate. P/O Davies and crew were the last to carry out an attack, but, after failing to locate the briefed aiming-point, they unloaded the contents of their bomb bay from 11,000 feet onto quays in the general vicinity of the target at 22.25. This was one of three crews to drop "Razzles" onto wooded areas on the way home in an attempt to set them alight and burn the Third Reich into submission. These incendiary devices would be persisted with for a period, being used extensively in the Black Forest region of south-western Germany, but they would prove to be ineffective, and would soon be consigned to the "It was worth a try" file.

Following two nights on the side-lines, the squadron was notified on the 14th of a return to Ostend by thirty Hampdens to target the concentration of invasion barges. Lindholme was required to provide ten aircraft, while four others were made ready to send against the marshalling yards at Mannheim. With further to travel, the Mannheim quartet took off first between 19.48 and 19.57, with W/C Golledge the senior pilot on duty, to be followed into the air between 20.35 and 21.30 by the main element led by S/Ls Oxley and Taylor. P/O Banker and crew were climbing out when the lower rear door fell off, and they were forced to turn back, leaving the others to head via corridor "G" towards the Scheldt estuary. S/L Oxley and crew arrived in the target area to find patches of low cloud, and dropped a flare, which ignited just below the cloud base to reveal the entire docks complex, and, according to the rear gunner, upwards of one hundred barges. An attack was carried out from the land side at 3,000 feet at 22.06, after which, the searchlights and light flak opened up to chase them at low-level out to sea. Sgt Crum and crew attacked from 5,000 feet at 22.29, and watched bursts across the Bruges Canal and the harbour works, but could not determine the results. S/L Taylor and F/O Ruth favoured a medium level approach, the former running in from west to east at 8,000 feet at 22.30, and dropping his load onto the outer harbour, only for low cloud to obscure their fall. The latter bombed from 9,000 feet with a similar outcome. P/O Mulligan and crew were intent on a glide approach from 10,000 down to 7,500 feet at 22.37, and F/O Woodward followed suit eight minutes later in a descent from 8,000 down to 4,000 feet. Sgt Brooker and crew glided down to 2,000 feet, unnoticed by the defences, until releasing their load at 23.12 and opening up the engines to climb away, when everything but the kitchen sink was thrown at them. F/O Lloyd and crew made two passes over the target, gliding from 4,000 to 1,000 feet on each occasion, but intense searchlight and flak activity beat them away, and the final run was made at 23.35 from 8,000 feet. The 250 pounders were seen to burst among the docks, but, precise details could not be determined. P/O Hindley and crew were the last to brave the defences, when delivering their attack from 3,000 feet at 23.47, and they, too, had to be content with an impression of hitting the target.

While the above was playing out, three of the four crews assigned to Mannheim were carrying out their briefs. The absentee was W/C Golledge, who had lost his intercom as the Dutch coast drew near, and decided to seek out the first military objective for his bombs before turning back. The aerodrome at Deurne, near Antwerp, presented itself, and the six 250 pounders and incendiaries were dropped in a stick from 11,000 feet at 22.50 in the face of an intense searchlight and flak response. The others continued on to reach the target area, in the case of P/O Potts and crew, ten minutes ahead of schedule, and, following three unsuccessful passes across the aiming-point, carried out a dive attack to release the bombs from 3,500 feet at 23.11. F/O French and crew adopted a north-west to south-east course over the yards, and aimed their four 500 pounders from 11,000 feet at 22.44, believing that they fell across the tracks. The intense searchlight and flak defence blinded them to the detail, and barrage balloons, tethered up to 13,000 feet, provided another distraction. P/O Davies and crew went in at 4,000 feet at 23.05, and believed that at least four of their 250 pounders had found the mark.

P/O Stenner was another of the squadron's stalwarts to conclude his tour during the month, and became attached to 16 O.T.U. on the 15th pending his official posting. He would return to the operational scene with 106 Squadron in 1941. This was the day on which the Battle of Britain reached its climax, and, by dusk, enemy losses had been sufficient to persuade Hitler to call off Operation Sealion, the invasion of Britain. This would not be apparent to the British authorities, however, and anti-invasion operations would continue, as would the Battle of Britain at a reduced intensity for another six weeks. 50 Squadron remained at home that night, while thirty-three Hampdens from Scampton and Waddington attacked invasion craft at Antwerp. The following night was one of those rare occasions when the entire Command stayed on the ground, but the 17th would bring a return to normal activity, with barge concentrations in Channel ports the objectives for most of the record number of 194 aircraft dispatched. In fact, 50 Squadron had been scheduled to launch thirteen Hampdens to mine the waters of the Artichokes garden off the U-Boot port of Lorient on the night of the 16/17th, and the first participant, P/O Banker and crew, took off into the teeth of a gale at 00.45. It was at that point, that the operation was called off, but the Banker crew failed to pick up the message, and, contrary to orders, continued on without receiving the "Go" confirmation. They battled the headwind to within sight of the French coast, where they realized that they had been pushed so far behind schedule that they would not be able to complete the operation in darkness. They turned back and touched down at 06.15 to make their explanations to the squadron commander.

Preparations were put in hand on the 17th for another major night of operations involving 174 aircraft, mostly in support of the campaign against invasion craft, for which 50 Squadron made ready six Hampdens. The Lorient gardening operation for 50 Squadron had also been rescheduled for this night, and the eight participating Hampdens took off between 19.43 and 19.55 with S/L Taylor the senior pilot on duty. They flew out via Oxford, Bridport and Guernsey in perfect weather conditions, and located the garden area without difficulty, attracting, in most cases, only a small amount of shore-based flak. The vegetables were planted from 500 to 800 feet between 23.01 and 00.14, the last-mentioned time that of Sgt Crum and crew, who, fifteen minutes earlier, had dropped their two 250lb wing-mounted bombs from 800 feet onto a flak battery at Paimpol on the northern extremity of the Brest peninsular. They claimed a direct hit, and, on return to Lindholme, reported being subjected to intense anti-aircraft fire from the mainland as they planted their vegetable. Sgt Brooker and crew dropped their pair of 250 pounders from 3,000 feet onto the aerodrome at Lannion, a few miles to the west of Paimpol, on the way home at 00.10, while F/O Ruth and crew found an unidentified aerodrome to bomb from 8,000 feet five miles west of Flouay.

The bombing element had taken off for the docks at Antwerp between 22.47 and 23.10 with S/L Oxley leading, and they all reached the target area to encounter six-tenths patchy cloud at 8,000 feet that impeded their attempts to line up on the aiming-point. F/O French and crew dropped their bombs from 9,000 feet in a long stick heading north at 00.35, and, being the first to arrive, were not subjected to the cauldron of anti-aircraft fire that awaited their colleagues. P/O Davies and crew made their attack from 11,000 feet on an east to west heading at 00.55, and observed their bombs to fall in a stick across the docks. F/O Woodward and crew approached under cover of cloud, and cruised around at 13,000 feet, attracting the attention of searchlights and coming under intense fire from heavy flak. The six 250 pounders and incendiaries were seen to fall directly onto the docks to the north of the town at 01.00, and two fires were seen to break out close by. P/O Potts and crew carried out a glide approach from south-east to north-west, and were almost over the aiming-point at 3,000 feet when they were ensnared in searchlight beams. They released the bombs seconds later at 01.00, while under an intense barrage of light flak, which chased them out of the target area and scored a number of inconsequential hits. S/L Oxley spent ninety minutes circling the area, spotting the docks intermittently, and eventually dropped his four 500 pounders from 12,000 feet at 01.15 without observing the results. P/O Mulligan and crew decided to attack invasion craft at Ostend as an alternative target, and enjoyed excellent visibility as they unloaded their four 500 pounders from 10,000 feet at 00.43. They observed no bursts, and concluded that the bombs had fallen into water.

P/O Bushnell had been one of three officer pilots to join the squadron on the 15th, and was flying the station's communications Miles Master, T9676, on the 19th, when he crashed near Thorne, nine miles north of Doncaster, with fatal consequences. The Command had sent out orders earlier in the day to continue the anti-invasion campaign against Channel ports, and the 5 Group element included a dozen Hampdens from Lindholme. The crews were briefed to attack barge concentrations at Flushing (Vlissingen) on the southern coast of Walcheren Island in the Scheldt estuary, and took off between 01.47 and 02.27 on the 20th with S/Ls Oxley and Taylor the senior pilots on duty. They soon ran into challenging weather conditions over the North Sea, with driving rain in a band of cloud between 1,000 and 10,000 feet, and this would prevent most from fulfilling their brief. Sgt Crum and crew were at the Norfolk coast when an engine issue persuaded them to turn back, and they were approaching the Lindholme circuit when they became caught in violent weather. The port engine appeared to be on fire, and the order was given to abandon the aircraft, which the navigator did, to land safely in the middle of Hemswell aerodrome. The bale-out order was then rescinded, and the Hampden landed safely with its bomb load intact. P/O Hindley and crew also aborted their sortie because of engine problems. S/L Taylor abandoned his sortie as impossible to complete on reaching the Dutch coast, and headed straight back home.

The others made a genuine effort to reach the target in conditions that became worse the further they progressed towards the enemy coast, but P/O Potts and crew were another to head for home with their bombs. Sgt Brooker and crew tried their best at very low level, but came upon the aiming-point suddenly on each occasion, with insufficient time to take aim, and they, too, gave up. P/O Mulligan and crew approached Walcheren in heavy rain, and descended to 3,000 feet, flying for five minutes after e.t.a without breaking cloud, before they decided to turn back. F/O French and crew were defeated by the conditions, and went in search of an alternative target, finding one at Bergen-op-Zoom aerodrome in south-western Holland, which they bombed from 3,000 feet at 03.35. P/O Davies and crew went in low at Flushing, beneath the cloud base at 500 feet, from where they dropped six 250 pounders and incendiaries in a stick from south to north across the Verbreed Canal and inner docks at 03.30. Despite the challenges, F/L Shaughnessy and crew located the target, and dropped eight 250 pounders from 700 feet at 04.00 in the face of intense searchlight and flak activity, observing them to hit barges and collapse a warehouse. S/L Oxley and crew climbed to 13,000 feet over the North Sea in a vain attempt to break into clear air, before shedding height to 1,000 feet on e.t.a., and eventually establishing a pin-point four miles north of the target. They experienced turbulence as they ran across the aiming-point at 800 feet on a north-easterly heading to drop their bombs across the canal and inner harbour at 04.20. When F/O Ruth and crew descended to 2,000 feet to establish their bearings, they found that they were some forty miles north of the target, and it took a number of attempts before they located it and attacked it from south to north at 04.35. One bomb hung up, but the others were seen to fall across a concentration of barges at the southern end of the canal and cause fires to break out. F/O Woodward's search lasted an hour and forty minutes, before he and his crew gave up and went in search of a suitable alternative. They came upon a stretch of the canal between Veerge and Middelburg to the north of Flushing, and dropped seven 250 pounders onto the banks from 1,000 feet at 05.00.

The squadron had no rested crews to offer for operations on the night of the 20/21st, when most of the 172 aircraft prepared for operations were assigned to the anti-invasion campaign. It was similar fare for ninety-two aircraft on the following night, which the fog-bound crews at Lindholme were forced to sit out. F/L Tom Rippingale was posted to the squadron on the 22nd, to fill the vacancy for a flight lieutenant created by the loss of F/L Reed. Thirty Hampden crews were briefed on their various stations late on the 22nd to launch against five Channel ports in the early hours of the 23rd, the seven Lindholme participants learning that they were to return to Flushing. They took off between 02.42 and 03.12 with S/L Taylor the senior pilot on duty, and made their way via corridor "G" to the target area, where conditions were good and visibility excellent. F/O French and crew were the first to arrive, and delivered their load in a stick from north-west to south-east from 8,000 feet at 04.10, observing them to fall across the harbour works. One 250 pounder hung up, and this was dropped onto the nearby aerodrome from 6,000 feet a minute later. P/O Banker and crew glided down from

7,000 down to 3,000 feet to release their load at 04.15 across the outer and inner harbours, but saw no bursts, while P/O Hindley and crew attacked from 10,000 feet at 04.22, and also failed to register the detonation of their eight 250 pounders across the target area from the Walcheren Canal to the outer harbour. Sgt Brooker and crew made two passes across the aiming-point, the first to release four 250 pounders from 8,000 feet on a north to south heading across the harbour works between the inner and outer harbours at 04.20, and the second five minutes later from east to west. P/O Davies and crew located the target with ease, and chose a high-level run at 13,000 feet, from where the eight 250 pounders were seen to burst in the target area at 04.28. Two minutes later, F/L Shaughnessy's load went down from 10,000 feet during a run from south to north, but no bursts were observed to confirm the accuracy. S/L Taylor and crew crossed the North Sea at 16,000 feet, before gliding down to 12,000 feet to release their bombs in a stick at 04.49, and watched two of them burst in the target area.

Ground crews were kept busy on all operational 5 Group stations on the 23rd, as forty-five Hampdens were made ready for that night's attack on an electrical power station in Berlin's western district of Moabit. The five 50 Squadron participants flew over to Bircham Newton as a forward base, and topped up their tanks, before taking off between 20.00 and 20.15 with S/L Oxley the senior pilot on duty. Each carried four 500 pounders and "Razzles" as they flew out at high-level, in order to put themselves above a front that lay between the Dutch coast and a point 150 miles from Germany's Capital. P/O Mulligan and crew were mid-way between Bremen and the target when the heating system broke down, and the prospect of being turned into blocks of ice persuaded them to abandon all thoughts of reaching the primary target. They turned towards Hamburg to seek out an alternative objective, but were diverted by intense anti-aircraft fire as they passed over the town of Salzwedel, and set course instead for Bremerhaven. A glide approach to the port from 12,000 down to 9,000 feet culminated with the release of their bombs, which were seen to explode across the docks and cause a fire that remained visible for forty miles into the journey home. S/L Oxley was barely fifty miles from Berlin when it became clear that the oxygen supply would not last if they continued on. They could not reduce altitude because of the conditions, and turned back with the intention of bombing the docks at Flushing. On the way, they dropped Razzles between Minden and Rheine, before noticing night-flying in progress at Soesterberg aerodrome in central Holland. They decided that this was an opportune alternative target, and bombed it from 10,000 feet at 00.15 without observing any results. P/O Potts and crew were confronted by poor visibility as they approached the western extremities of Berlin, and began a glide from 12,000 down to 4,500 feet to gain a glimpse of the ground through the thick local ground haze. The BMW works at Spandau, located some four miles short of Moabit, lay directly under the flight-path to the primary target, and probably offered itself as an inviting alternative as it emerged from the murk. The bombs fell away at 23.15, with indeterminate results, and Razzles were dropped on the way home. F/O Woodward and crew carried out their Razzling on the way to Berlin, before, then, somehow identifying the power station from 14,000 feet. The four 500 pounders went down, and three of them were seen to burst nearby and start two fires. F/O Ruth and crew reported an entirely uneventful sortie, with no difficulties at any time, other than the inability to identify the target on their arrival at 22.55. A short search confirmed the futility of persisting, and a S.E.M.O., (self-evident military objective) was found in the form of a number of lights partially obscured by haze among heavy flak batteries, towards which the bombs were directed from 13,500 feet. They Razzled their way home, where they were the last to land at 04.15.

A total of twenty-three Hampdens was made ready on the four operational stations on the 24th, four of them at Lindholme, whose crews, all recent additions to the squadron, were briefed to attack barge concentrations in the port of Calais. They took off between 23.37 and 23.47, and all reached the target area, where Sgt Crum and crew were the first from the squadron to arrive. They decided on two runs at 1,500 feet, each to deliver four 250 pounders, the first pass at 01.21 and the second fifteen minutes later. Bursts were observed, and three fires broke out in N°6 dock. F/O Liddell and crew made landfall three miles east of the target, and bombed from 8,500 feet at 01.35 in the face of a moderate defence. No results were seen because of cloud, although, when P/O Powell and crew carried out their attack from 6,000 feet fifteen minutes later, they described the visibility as good. They watched their 250 pounders explode on N°7 dock and start a fire a few minutes later, and picked up a small shell hole in the tailplane for their trouble. Sgt Coad and crew missed their landfall at 4,000 feet because of haze, despite the fact that the port was already alight. They were soon alerted to their position, however, as they came under fire and observed barrage balloons, which persuaded them to climb to 7,000 feet. The eight 250 pounders were released from this altitude at 01.55, and were seen to detonate in the target area, although precise details were rendered unobtainable by cloud.

On the following day, plans were put in hand to send four Hampdens to Bircham Newton as the launch pad for another assault on a Berlin power station. They departed Lindholme either side of 19.00, and landed safely some forty minutes later, only to be delayed by late refuelling, and then grounded because of an air-raid Red Warning. This ended all hopes of taking off for Berlin, and they would spend the night as guests of Bircham Newton, while seventeen other Hampdens continued with the operation, and a handful of others attacked marshalling yards at Osnabrück and Trier. 5 Group would divide its forces on the 26th, sending a dozen Hampdens to attack the cruiser Scharnhorst at Kiel, and six to take another swipe at the Dortmund-Ems Canal at Ladbergen. 50 Squadron's seven crews were briefed to attack barge concentrations at Calais, with Boulogne as the alternative, and they departed Lindholme between 18.52 and 19.25 with S/Ls Oxley and Taylor the senior pilots on duty and F/L Rippingale undertaking his first sortie with the squadron. They climbed out through ten-tenths cloud, which would cover the route all the way to the target, and lie over northern France at 4,000 feet. S/L Oxley climbed initially to 5,000 feet, before ascending further to 11,000 feet twenty-five minutes before e.t.a., and, on reaching the target, circled for forty-five minutes. Presumably, he was descending during this period, because the 250 pounders and incendiaries were released from 1,500 feet, after which, small fires were seen to break out. F/L Rippingale and crew were hampered in their search by cloud, but delivered their attack from 10,000 feet at 21.30, without observing any results. P/O Hindley and crew carried out a glide approach to 1,000 feet, at which point, the entrance to the harbour lay directly beneath them. They dived immediately to drop a stick of eight 250 pounders from 200 feet onto barges in N°2 dock, before being chased inland at 60 feet by intense light flak, which robbed them of their wireless aerial and left holes in various places. P/O Mulligan and crew delivered their bombs through the cloud from 11,000 feet at 21.10, and saw nothing of the outcome. On return to Lindholme in poor landing conditions at 23.50, they crashed into a tree, writing off L4062, and leaving P/O Mulligan and his navigator bruised and suffering from shock. P/O Davies and crew spent thirty minutes searching for the target, and eventually dropped their load onto a searchlight and flak concentration from 10,000 feet. S/L Taylor lingered for an hour over Calais, before being attracted by a searchlight and flak concentration ten miles to the west at Boulogne. They bombed it from 8,000 feet at 21.20, and flew home with no clue as to the outcome. Sgt Thomas and crew also attacked Boulogne through cloud from 11,000 feet, and the bursts were followed immediately by a red glow.

The anti-invasion campaign continued on the 27th, when five 50 Squadron crews were briefed to target barges, motor torpedo boats and U-boots at Lorient, which, early in the coming year, would be the site of a massive civil engineering project to construct three huge concrete U-Boot facilities. They departed Lindholme between 19.21 and 19.38 with no senior pilots to lead the way, and exited the English coast at Chesil Beach, before passing to the west of Guernsey, where some attracted the attentions of searchlights and flak from surface craft. It was at this point, that F/O Liddell and crew noticed an unsettling vibration in one of the engines and decided to turn back. They continued on for some fifteen minutes, however, until crossing the French coast and, unaccountably, unloading their bombs onto the unsuspecting town of Sainte-Brieuc from 7,500 feet at 21.30. Sgt Coad and crew crossed the English coast at 20.55 and the French coast at 22.05, but were unable to establish a pinpoint, and found themselves ultimately to the west of Brest, where they, too, attacked an undeserving French town, in this case, the coastal resort of Douarnenez, from 10,000 feet at 22.35. F/O Woodward and crew arrived at the target to find clear skies and a spirited searchlight and flak defence, through which they bombed from 7,000 feet, but were blinded to the results by glare and flashes. Sgt Crum and crew located the target without difficulty, and released their bombs in a stick from 6,000 feet at 22.44, observing each individual burst, followed by five fires, one of them large enough to remain visible as they headed out to sea. P/O Powell and crew had crossed the French coast at 10,000 feet, and descended, thereafter, to start their bombing run at 6,500 feet, before releasing their bombs from north to south at 22.53 and observing explosions followed by a large fire.

50 Squadron had no rested crews to offer for operations on the 28th, when 5 Group dispatched twenty-five Hampdens to attack barges, marshalling yards and the Dortmund-Ems Canal. F/O "Bill" Russell, a future commanding officer of the squadron, was posted in on the 29th, the day on which marshalling yards in Germany again featured prominently on the target list, along with a Bosch electrical component factory at Stuttgart. Four Lindholme crews were briefed for the last-mentioned, while two others would take on the previously-attacked marshalling yards at Soest. The two elements took off at the same time between 18.50 and 19.30, those bound for southern Germany led by S/L Taylor, while it was the freshman crews of P/O Thwaites and Sgt Thomas who made their way via corridor "B" towards the Dutch Frisians and the northern-eastern Ruhr. The outward journey via corridor "G" was undertaken at 10,000 feet above the cloud, and some crews encountered icing conditions as they climbed through. P/O Hindley and crew had been the first to take off and were the first to reach Stuttgart a little over three hours later, before delivering their bombs from 12,000 feet at 22.07, and then climbing into cloud to escape the attentions of heavy flak. P/O Davies and crew provided no details of their sortie, while F/L Rippingale reported arriving in the target area at 22.50, and carrying out the attack from 12,000 feet. There was no report from S/L Taylor and crew, whose return was awaited in vain, and no clue to the fate of X2902 and its crew has ever surfaced. Meanwhile, P/O Thwaites and Sgt Thomas had emerged from the cloud over England to find it dispersing as they crossed the North Sea to their target at Soest. The skies over enemy territory were clear, and Sgt Thomas and crew found the railway yards well illuminated as they bore down on them. The lights were quickly extinguished, but their illumination was replaced by a flare from the Hampden, once it had been dislodged after

becoming jammed in the flare-chute. The attack took place from 10.000 feet at 22.05, and stirred up the defences, which chased the Hampden out of the target area. P/O Thwaites and crew arrived considerably later, when they described the darkness as extreme, rendering the task of identifying the target a challenge. They located it eventually by adopting a "time and distance" run from Hamm, and delivered their four 500 pounders from 14,000 feet at 23.00, observing a line of white fires to break out as a result.

On the 30th, 5 Group instructed Scampton, Hemswell and Lindholme to prepare for an operation that night, and nineteen Hampdens were made ready, four of them belonging to 50 Squadron. The crews learned at briefing that their target was to be the Air Ministry building in Berlin's Leipziger Strasse, a main thoroughfare, that ran from the Tiergarten (zoo) in the west through the city centre and across the River Spree. The Lindholme quartet began taking off for the forward base at Bircham Newton at 18.40, leaving F/O Liddell and crew to launch their gardening sortie to the Eglantines region of the Elbe estuary from Lindholme at 20.40. Having topped up their tanks, the Berlin-bound crews were scheduled to take off at intervals, beginning with S/L Oxley, but he lost an engine before leaving the ground, and P4395 was severely damage in the ensuing crash. The crew was unhurt, but the incident, and problems with refuelling, delayed the departure of other aircraft, and Sgt Crum and crew, who should have taken-off at 21.51, eventually got away at 23.05, preceded at 22.25 by Sgt Coad and crew and followed into the air by P/O Powell and crew at 23.15. By the time that the Crum crew reached Bremen, it was clear that insufficient time remained for them to continue on to Berlin and get back to the Dutch coast before the advent of daylight. They sought out railway installations in Bremen as an alternative target, and dropped three 500 pounders from 9,000 feet, only to be denied by poor weather conditions from observing their impact. Sgt Coad and crew made landfall at the northern end of Texel, but could not establish a position again because of extreme darkness. They also realized that time was against them, and turned back, dropping their load onto Schiermonnikoog Island as they passed over it at 10,000 feet at 03.45. This left just P/O Powell and crew of the original four assigned to Berlin, and they made landfall at the southern end of Texel at 23.39, before setting course for the target area. They maintained that heading for the next three hours and ten minutes, at which point they found themselves over Wandlitz, some fifteen miles north of Berlin. They ran into intense and accurate ground fire over the centre of Berlin, and, failing to locate the primary target, bombed what looked like a large factory from 8,000 feet without observing the results. They were off Terschelling on the way home when a fuel leak caused the port engine to catch fire, a situation that lasted barely five minutes, but left the engine faltering. They eventually came in over Cromer at dawn, and, while trying to land at Docking, hit a mound of earth on the perimeter, and ended up in a tangled heap, from which P4411 would never recover. The crew, however, emerged from the wreckage, no doubt shaken, and were soon back in the bosom of the squadron.

While the above was ongoing, F/O Liddell and crew were making landfall at Heligoland at 23.25 at 8,500 feet in good weather conditions, and located the Eglantine garden area without difficulty to plant their vegetable from 700 feet at 23.50. During the course of another very busy month, the squadron undertook twenty-four operations, and dispatched 114 sorties for the loss of three Hampdens and crews and one pilot.

October 1940

There would be changes at 50 Squadron at the start of the new month, beginning with the posting of P/O Banker and F/O French to 106 Squadron, which had just become operational after spending the first year of the war as the Group Pool training unit. F/L Shaughnessy, F/O Ruth and P/Os West and Potts were posted to 16 O.T.U on the following day, but a never-ending supply of fresh recruits would maintain the numbers and keep the squadron at the forefront of operations. It was five crews of the old guard that opened the squadron's October account on the 2nd, after sitting out the previous night's forays against industrial targets in Germany and gardening in northern waters. The target was an oil refinery and storage facility in Hamburg (A8), for which they took off between 18.20 and 18.40 with no senior pilots on duty. They soon lost the services of P/O Hindley and crew to engine trouble, however, leaving the others to press on towards the Elbe estuary, on approach to which, Sgt Brooker and crew observed barrage balloons tethered at 6,000 feet over Wilhelmshaven. They ran into the usual corridor of intense searchlight and flak activity as they followed the course of the Elbe south-east towards the heart of Germany's Second City, and delivered six 500 pounders from 6,000 feet at 22.00, observing them to overshoot the aiming-point. P/O Davies and crew arrived thirty minutes later amidst bursting light flak shells at 8,000 feet, with others of heavy calibre exploding above, and carried out a glide attack from 9,000 feet to a perilously low 2,000 feet. The bursts of six bombs and incendiaries were observed in the centre of the target area, followed by explosions and enormous red and yellow fires accompanied by clouds of thick, black smoke, which remained visible for fifty miles. Sgt Thomas and crew encountered cumulus cloud to the west of the target, and spent some time searching an area to the north, before deciding to bomb the docks as an alternative objective. The attack was carried out from 10,000 feet at 22.55, and the burst of one bomb and the incendiaries was observed, followed by four red and orange fires that merged into one as they left the target area. P/O Thwaites and crew provided no detail of their sortie, other than to report the starboard engine faltering and then cutting out while over the target. They flew back to Scotland on one engine, and, with dwindling fuel reserves, decided to risk landing on a dummy flare-path. They overshot the approach, and stalled as they tried to climb away, which resulted in X2896, crashing in a valley at Woodhall Innerwick, south-west of Dunbar on the east coast near Edinburgh. The Hampden was wrecked, leaving the pilot and two others shaken and bruised but intact, while the rear gunner sustained a broken leg.

On the 5th, Sir Charles Portal relinquished his post as Commander-in-Chief of Bomber Command, and took up his appointment as Chief of the Air Staff. He was replaced at the helm of Bomber Command by ACM Sir Richard Peirse, whose tenure would be dogged by the inadequacies of the equipment available to him, and the increasing and often unrealistic demands of his superiors. That night, a dozen 83 Squadron Hampdens were sent to bomb the Nordstern Oil refinery at Gelsenkirchen, while eight others belonging to 50 Squadron targeted mostly marshalling yards at important locations north and south of the Ruhr. The Lindholme crews took off for their respective targets between 18.05 and 18.36, but soon lost the services of P/O Hindley and crew to a failing engine shortly after crossing the English coast, P/O Powell to severe icing while embedded in cloud at 6,000 to 7,000 feet, and F/L Rippingale with compass deviation. This left just one crew each to target the marshalling yards at Hamm, Eiffeltor in Cologne and Soest, and it was for the first-mentioned that F/O Liddell and crew had been the first to become airborne. They had set course from Skegness at 18.30, to reach Harderwijk on the eastern shore of the Ijsselmeer at 19.40, having flown through ten-tenths ice-bearing cloud all the way. A new course was set for Hamm, which was reached fifteen minutes ahead of schedule, standing out in the light of the moon, with a south-bound train conveniently revealing itself by burning all of its lights. A gentle glide approach from 10,500 to 9,000 feet preceded the delivery of the bomb load through a gap in the cloud, and two fires were thought to be the result. Sgt Crum had been assigned to the yards at Soest, where he carried out a high-level attack for which no details were forthcoming. The recently-arrived P/O Grylls and crew had the Fokker aircraft factory at Amsterdam as their target, and attacked it at the end of the gentlest of glides from east to west from 1,200 down to 1,000 feet at 20.00. They thought the bombs had gone, and were horrified later to learn later that the power bolt had not been on, and that the bombs had accompanied them home. F/O Woodward and crew ran into an intense searchlight and flak defence as they closed in on the yards at Osnabrück, and the poor weather conditions added considerably to the challenges of searchlight glare and the need to take evasive action, while trying to locate the aiming-point. They were driven off to seek an alternative, which they found three to four miles to the south-west of the primary, and, whatever it was, they attacked it from 10,000 feet at 20.50. P4417 was lost without trace at some point during its sortie to the Eiffeltor yards in Cologne, and the names of Sgt Brooker and his crew were added to the growing list of 50 Squadron airmen missing in action.

Orders were received on 5 Group stations on the 7th, to prepare for attacks that night on six marshalling yards north and south of the Ruhr, six crews from Lindholme finding themselves divided between those at Mannheim and Osnabrück. They all took off together between 18.32 and 18.52 with F/L Rippingale, P/O Hindley and Sgt Coad heading out via Corridor "G" for the Scheldt, while P/Os Davies and Powell and Sgt Thomas pointed their snouts towards the Lincolnshire coast to follow corridor "B". F/L Rippingale and crew were able to pick up a pinpoint on the River Rhine south of Coblenz and follow its course all the way to Mannheim. There, clear skies prevailed, and six 250 pounders and incendiaries were delivered from 10,000 feet at 21.55 on a south-easterly heading in the face of a spirited searchlight and flak defence. Orange and yellow flames were observed, but the glare of the defences and smoke haze prevented a detailed assessment. P/O Hindley and crew dropped "Razzles" onto wooded areas between Liege and Kaiserslautern, before attacking the railway yards from 12,000 feet and observing bursts, but nothing else. The wing bombs hung up at first, and were released over the city seconds later. Sgt Coad and crew made landfall over the Scheldt at 20.15, and located the target ninety minutes later to attack it from 12,000 feet at 21.50, observing their bombs to straddle the yards. On the way home they ran into anti-aircraft fire over Mainz, but evaded it and landed safely at base after six hours and forty minutes aloft. The second trio was less successful, and P/O Powell and crew arrived home with their bomb load intact after failing to establish their position at any time during the sortie, despite carrying out an extensive search. Sgt Thomas and crew had to dodge searchlights and flak as they passed close to Amsterdam, and then lost their intercom at 21.00, while still some distance from the target. Having identified the aiming-point, they positioned themselves for an east to west bombing run, and let the bombs go from 10,000 feet at 21.34, observing bursts but nothing more. P/O Davies and crew had to contend with a frozen and inoperable a.s.i., without which the navigator could not establish ground speed. They reached the target area, where they watched an aircraft fall to the ground in flames, but, ultimately, attacked Schiphol aerodrome from 12,000 feet at 22.55, observing seven bursts across the flare-path.

The Admiralty was acutely conscious of the threat posed by Germany's mighty battleships Bismarck and Tirpitz, and there was a constant pressure on Bomber Command to deal with them before they began their careers as surface raiders. With no rested crews to offer, Lindholme remained inactive on the 8th, while Scampton and Waddington sent nineteen Hampdens to attempt to hit the Tirpitz at berth at Wilhelmshaven. On the following day nineteen Hampdens were made ready to target the Krupp works at Essen, for which S/L Oxley and F/O Woodward would represent 50 Squadron. Three other crews, those of F/O Liddell, P/O Grylls and Sgt Crum, were briefed for gardening duties in the Artichokes region off the port of Lorient, in company with three crews from Waddington, and these took off first between 18.00 and 18.15. The bombers took off twenty minutes later, and flew, initially, into fine weather conditions, with excellent visibility that enabled them to pinpoint on Vlieland and map-read inland to Elburg, shortly after which, they ran into a bank of ten-tenths cloud some fifty miles west of the target. When the a.s.i froze, S/L Oxley tried to break cloud, but ice began to form on the wings, and he opted to remain in the less cold layer of cloud at around 15,000 feet. On e.t.a., they delivered their bombs across whatever lay beneath them, and had nothing to report to the intelligence section at debriefing. F/O Woodward and crew failed to locate the primary target, and returned to Amsterdam, where the docks area was bombed from 8,000 feet, and then a railway a mile-and-a-half to the south-east. The bursts were followed by six white and two red fires. Meanwhile, the members of the gardening trio were enjoying more favourable conditions in their target area, after inviting the attention of some ineffective coastal flak on the way out. F/O Liddell pinpointed on Lisveur, to the south of Lorient, before gliding for five minutes to the release-point and delivering the vegetable from 850 feet at 22.15. P/O Grylls and crew had already delivered their mine eight minutes earlier, and were heading north with their bombs primed and ready to drop onto a target of opportunity. This they found in the form of a flak battery at Lannion, which they attacked from 8,000 feet. After releasing their mine from 500 feet, Sgt Crum and crew found two merchant ships close by at which to aim their wing bombs from 1,500 feet, but watched them fall short. Undaunted, they carried out a strafing attack, before proceeding to another strafing run across a fully-lit aerodrome.

The promise of bright moonlight on the night of the 9/10th may have been a consideration in scheduling another assault on the battleship Tirpitz at Wilhelmshaven, for which thirteen Hampdens were made ready, nine at Waddington and four at Lindholme. A simultaneous operation would be conducted against Kiel dockyard by an element from Scampton, while Hemswell attended to the mining of the Kiel Canal. The 50 Squadron quartet took off widely separated between 19.10 and 20.15 with F/L Rippingale the senior pilot on duty, but he was back on the ground an hour later with an unserviceable heating system. P/O Hindley and crew reached the target area, but, during the initial bombing run, the power bolt froze up, preventing the bombs from being released. The intensity of the searchlight and flak defence dissuaded the crew from making a second pass, and the alternative target in the dockyards (D12) was attacked from 12,000 feet at 22.40, with flak shells bursting above and below at between 10,000 and 15,000 feet. On their arrival in the target area, Sgt Thomas and crew proceeded northwards until spotting the dockyard glinting in the moonlight. They carried out their attack from east to west, dropping four 500lb SAP bombs from 10,000 feet at 23.00 and observing the last one to explode three hundred yards from the centre of the floating dock. P/O Davies and crew also attacked the primary target, in their case from 12,000 feet, and observed four bursts but no detail in the glare of the searchlights.

The pursuit of the Tirpitz continued on the 11th, with preparations for another attack, for which 50 Squadron made ready five Hampdens, while a sixth flew over to Hemswell to join crews from there to target the Blohm & Voss shipyards at Hamburg. Take-offs from Lindholme for Wilhelmshaven were again spread out between 18.00 and 19.15, with W/C Golledge the senior pilot on duty and the last to depart, while F/L Rippingale left Hemswell at 19.45 bound for Hamburg. He and his crew encountered challenging weather conditions on their way to the target area, and, on arrival in ice-bearing cloud, considered that they had no chance of identifying the aiming-point, and chose to join their colleagues some seventy miles to the west. They found the conditions over Wilhelmshaven little better, and carried out a high-level attack on estimated position, as did Sgt Crum and crew, whose bombing run was guided by the intensity of the flak coming up through the clouds. P/O Grylls and crew had climbed to 16,500 feet as they approached the target area, and, with no prospect of seeing the aiming-point after circling it for thirty minutes, they bombed the alternative at Wesermünde at 21.15. Experiencing similar difficulties, S/L Oxley and crew turned their attention upon the aerodrome on the Frisian island of Langeoog, which they attacked from high-level through cloud. W/C Golledge and crew approached the target initially from the north-west, before running across the top to carry out their bombing run from north-east to south west in a glide from 14,000 feet. They were carrying a 2,000lb armour piercing bomb, the explosion of which was observed in the form of a huge flash beneath the cloud. F/O Liddell and crew had set course from the lighthouse at Flamborough Head at 19.15, and had pinpointed in good visibility on Wangerooge, before encountering medium cloud. They glided in over the target area from the west at 12,000 feet down to 8,000 feet, all the time under fire from heavy flak, and delivered their load at 21.15, the results obscured by cloud and the need to take evasive action.

While other elements of the group were made ready to conduct operations against targets in Germany on the 12th, four 50 Squadron crews found themselves assigned to gardening duties in the Artichokes and Beeches gardens, which were situated respectively off the Biscay ports of Lorient and St-Nazaire. They departed Lindholme between 17.55 and 18.20, and all reached the target areas after uneventful outward flights. Having faced a number of attacks in recent weeks, the coastal defences at Lorient were alert, if inaccurate, and a number of flak-ships were operating in the bay. On their way to St Nazaire, the freshman crew of P/O Tunstall made landfall five miles north-east of Plestin-les-Gréves, south-west of the Channel Islands, and encountered six searchlights and inaccurate flak from the Guingamp area. They ran into intense searchlight activity and all calibres of flak as they passed close to Lorient, and observed flak-ships off the Ile-de-Groix. They located their garden some sixty miles to the south-east, and delivered their vegetable, while a heavy flak battery on the headland fired a number of shells at them. The wing bombs were dropped from 2,000 feet towards two vessels anchored two miles south-west of the garden, but no results were observed. F/O Woodward and crew also located the garden without difficulty, and pinpointed on the Charpentier lighthouse before gliding down from 4,000 to 600 feet for a forty-five-second run to the release point. On the way home they searched for shipping to attack with their wing bombs, but found none, and dropped them instead onto the aerodrome at St Helier on Jersey from 700 feet. Meanwhile, Sgt Thomas and P/O Davies and their crews were being targeted ineffectively by the shore and shipboard defences at Lorient, and planted their vegetables from 600 feet, the former at 21.21, the only one to record a time. This was the last time that operations took place against invasion craft in Channel ports.

P/Os Everitt and Walker were posted in on the 13th, the former to become a mainstay of the squadron, while the latter's time on the squadron would be brief. Neither would feature in that night's operation against the Tirpitz at Wilhelmshaven, for which thirty-five Hampdens were made ready, seven of them at Lindholme. They took off between 17.55 and 18.55 with F/L Rippingale the senior pilot on duty, but F/O Liddell turned back within an hour because of an engine issue, leaving the others to press on. Initially, they flew out over three-tenths cloud, but, ahead, beginning at the mid-point of the North Sea crossing, lay one of those enormous fronts that frequently barred the route into north-western Germany. Characterized by ice-bearing and storm-laden towering cumulus, they were a nightmare to negotiate, and too enormous to circumnavigate. The icing layer on this night extended from 6,000 to 12,000 feet, with rainstorms from 1,000 to 12,000 feet, which had crews climbing and descending in a vain search for clear air, before, in most cases, seeking an alternative target. Sgt Richardson and crew ran into searchlights and heavy flak over what they believed to be the island of Borkum, and carried out an attack from 2,000 feet without observing any results. P/O Hindley and crew abandoned their attempt to reach the primary target, and patrolled the Frisians as far south as the Ijsselmeer in search of an alternative, but severe icing eventually persuaded them to turn for home. Sgt Coad and crew climbed to 14,000 feet without breaking cloud or escaping the icing belt, and bombed the approximate position of Texel aerodrome on the way home. Half an hour from the primary target, while at 10,000 feet in ten-tenths cloud, P/O Grylls and crew decided to descend to ascertain the height of the cloud base. The cloud remained solid as they passed through 3,000 feet, at which point, south of Borkum, both engines cut out, and the order was given to prepare to abandon the aircraft as P/O Grylls turned towards the mainland and jettisoned the bombs at 21.00. The engines began to pick up again, and, ten minutes later, a course was set for the Norfolk coast with the intention of landing at Marham, but, conditions over England allowed them to reach Lindholme for a safe landing. F/L Rippingale was another to be defeated by the conditions, and, after failing to break through the front, headed south in the hope of finding Flushing aerodrome. Having still not emerged from cloud and with oxygen running low, he abandoned the sortie and went home. Sgt Crum and crew did penetrate the front as far as Wilhelmshaven, but the absence of searchlight and flak activity left them without any reference for a bombing run. They attacked from 9,000 feet on estimated position on a south-easterly heading, but had no clue as to the fall of their bombs.

The group detailed twenty Hampdens on the 14th for another shot that night at the Air Ministry building in Berlin, on a night when cities in eastern Germany were targeted by fifty aircraft from other groups. The three 50 Squadron participants landed at Bircham Newton in the late afternoon, before departing with full tanks, F/O Woodward and crew at 20.50, and Sgt Thomas at 23.00. No take-off time was recorded for P/O Davies, and he and his crew failed to return in X2993, after it was shot down by a night-fighter near Kalbe, some eighty miles from Berlin. It is not known whether they were outbound or homebound at the time, but the pilot and second pilot/navigator lost their lives, while the two gunners were taken into captivity. Sgt Thomas and F/O Woodward and their crews reached the target area to encounter haze, and both spent time either circling or making dummy runs from a variety of directions in order to familiarize themselves with the lay of the land and to establish the best method of attack. F/O Woodward faced searchlight and flak activity, and also noticed a number of barrage balloons tethered at up to 15,000 feet. The distractions caused by these defensive measures caused the first two runs to overshoot the aiming-point, but a clear view of the post office and station was secured on the third. A long stick of four 500 pounders was dropped from high-level, along with some Razzles, and the fourth bomb was observed to hit the railway track. Sgt Thomas and crew had approached Berlin at 10,000 feet, and experienced little opposition before the target. They climbed to 15,000 feet on e.t.a., to make their dummy runs, and, after twenty minutes, returned to 10,000 feet to carry out their attack from south-east to north-west, and deliver five of their six 250 pounders and 60lbs of incendiaries. Bursts were observed, and the incendiaries started three white fires of appreciable size.

Oil targets featured prominently on the 15th, when 134 aircraft were detailed for wide-ranging targets in Germany and the Channel ports. 5 Group directed the bulk of its effort of thirty-three Hampdens against oil targets in Magdeburg, principally the Rothensee plant that they had attacked last in early September. 50 Squadron made ready six Hampdens, which departed Lindholme between 18.30 and 19.00 with F/L Rippingale the senior pilot on duty, and set course, it is believed via corridor "G" to the mouth of the Scheldt. F/L Rippingale and crew observed an aircraft above them at the Scheldt displaying a white light, and, shortly afterwards, they ran into the Antwerp defences, where they throttled back to avoid being noticed. Thereafter, the wind took them to the south of their intended track, and they found themselves over Leipzig, where they bombed marshalling yards from 12,000 feet. Sgt Richardson and crew crossed the enemy coast at 20.30, and reached the target area on the stroke of midnight, but were denied sight of the ground by a band of cloud between 3,000 and 6,000 feet. Breaking cloud over a searchlight and flak concentration, they pin-pointed a canal to the north of the city, and began their bombing run from there. The four 500 pounders were dropped from 2,500 feet onto buildings to the south of the target, and were then chased into cloud by the intensity of the defences. Sgt Crum and crew negotiated the route between Skegness and the target without difficulty in what they described as perfect weather conditions. They attacked with 250 pounders and incendiaries from 10,000 feet in the face of a spirited defence, and observed clouds of black smoke following the bursts. P/O Grylls and crew, in contrast, failed to identify the primary target in conditions of poor visibility, and emptied the contents of their bomb bay onto warehouses at Antwerp from 10,000 feet at 00.05. F/O Liddell and crew reported haze, ground-fog and cloud at 7,000 feet over Germany, but they did manage to pick out the horseshoe-shaped lake and the River Elbe to the north-east of the city, before delivering an attack from 11,000 feet at 22.20. P/O Thwaites and crew enjoyed excellent visibility all the way to within fifteen miles of Magdeburg, where they encountered eight-tenths stratus at around 3,000 feet. They descended to the cloud base and dropped flares, which proved to be ineffective, and, while taking evasive action, noticed white smoke emanating from what appeared to be a power station. They selected this as their alternative target, and attacked it with 250 pounders and incendiaries from 6,000 feet, observing yellow and orange fires to follow the explosions.

Lindholme was stood down on the following night because of adverse weather conditions, while thirty-six Hampdens from the other stations targeted an oil refinery at Leuna and U-Boots at Bordeaux. It was a good night to remain on the ground, as ten Hampdens came to grief in foggy conditions on their return. There was little activity generally on the 18th, but 5 Group detailed nineteen Hampdens from Scampton and Lindholme to target the Bismarck at berth in Hamburg. The seven 50 Squadron representatives took off between 23.30 and 00.03 with no senior pilots on duty, and lost the services of P/O Hindley and crew to icing-related engine problems when eighty miles out over the North Sea. The others pushed on to the target area, where, on arrival over the Elbe estuary, they encountered eight to ten-tenths cloud that severely inhibited their attempts to locate the aiming-point. P/O Thwaites and crew managed to find it through the layers of cloud, and began a glide approach, which began at 13,000 feet and ended at 1,000 feet, from where two bombs were seen to burst. Sgt Coad and crew established a pinpoint on the Elbe through a gap in the clouds, and attacked from 14,000 feet without observing the outcome. The remaining crews attacked alternative targets, among them a circle of red lights, a searchlight and flak concentration and Stade aerodrome, before a return was made to Leuchars in Scotland, where conditions for landing were favourable.

Berlin was posted as the target for 5 Group on the 20th, while more than a hundred other aircraft roamed far and wide, as far east at Pilsen in Czechoslovakia. The 50 Squadron element flew over to Bircham Newton as the forward launch pad, but, on a night of enemy intruder activity, a bomb was dropped onto the airfield, and the participation from there was cancelled. Lindholme was fogbound, thereafter, until the 23rd, when nine crews were briefed for a return to the Rothensee synthetic oil refinery at Magdeburg. They took off between 00.01 and 01.15 with F/Os Liddell and Woodward the senior pilots on duty, but P/Os Tunstall and Thwaites returned early respectively with ice-related engine issues and the failure of the heating system. The others carried on over nine to ten-tenths cloud after selecting their own points of exit between Skegness and Great Yarmouth, but, as the last to take off following a delay, P/O Hindley and crew soon realized that they would not reach the primary target in time. Through the seven-tenths cloud with a base at 6,000 feet, they spotted an unspecified S.E.M.O on the western outskirts of Osnabrück, and attacked it with four 500 pounders from 12,000 feet at 03.30. They saw no bursts, but a bluish-yellow flash lit up a very large area. Sgt Richardson and crew had also taken off late, just five minutes before the Hindley crew, and they made the decision to seek out an alternative target, selecting a railway junction on the southern outskirts of Osnabrück, which they attacked from 4,000 feet. Sgt Crum and crew crossed the Norfolk coast at 01.11, and found a five thousand-foot lane of clear air and good weather between the lower cloud tops at 7,000 feet and the base of the upper layer at 12,000 feet. They ran into accurate anti-aircraft fire in the Hannover area, but got through it, and, as the target drew near, they descended to 6,000 feet, from where ground detail could be identified. They picked up the aiming-point and bombed it on a north-east to south-west heading, observing three of their 250 pounders and the incendiaries to burst and cause an extensive fire to break out. F/O Liddell's Hampden became a victim of ice-accretion as it ascended through the ten-tenths cloud, and the crew was blinded temporarily by the Perspex freezing over. The cloud dispersed over the Dutch coast, and the ice with it, but now the crew became concerned about the time left to complete the sortie if they pressed on to the primary target. The decision was taken to bomb the Misburg refinery near Hannover as an alternative, and they found the cloud thickening to eight-tenths as they drew near. The rear gunner threw out nine incendiary bombs (probably Razzles), before an attack was carried out from 11,000 feet in the face of intense searchlight and flak activity. No bursts were observed, but a large brownish fire and a long line of small, white ones were seen. P/O Walker and crew carried out their bombing run at 14,000 feet at 04.57, while Sgt Thomas and crew were unable to locate the refinery, and backtracked to Hannover, where they bombed railway yards on the western outskirts of the city from 10,000 feet at 04.35. F/O Woodward and crew had flown above cloud the whole way, but, having been able to establish a positive pinpoint at Hannover, were able to navigate to Magdeburg without difficulty, where they dropped five 250 pounders and incendiaries from 11,000 feet without observing the results.

Just two 50 Squadron Hampdens were required for operations on the night of the 24/25th, F/O Russell and P/O Everitt departing Lindholme under moonlight at 01.00 and 01.10 respectively, bound for the Jellyfish garden off the port of Brest. They ran into poor weather conditions twenty miles south of Torquay, and would not see the moon again until crossing the English coast on the way home. F/O Russell found the cloud base to be as low as 1,000 feet in places, but, while climbing to find clear air, encountered a band of icing at 5,000 feet that persuaded him to remain beneath. He and his crew spent an hour in search of a pinpoint in the garden area, but failed to establish their position, and headed for home. It proved difficult to obtain a wireless-fix over the Channel, and a thunderstorm compounded the problems, delaying their return until they landed eventually at the aerodrome belonging to the Avro Company at Woodford in Stockport after almost eight hours aloft. P/O Everitt and crew reported an entirely different experience, locating the garden with ease and planting their vegetable as briefed from 600 feet, before returning to base after a six-hour round-trip.

The main focus on the 25th would be Germany's oil industry and shipbuilding, and 5 Group sent out orders to Hemswell, Lindholme and Scampton to prepare eighteen Hampdens to attack the Krupp-Germania shipyard at Kiel, while Waddington took care of the gardening requirements. 50 Squadron contributed six Hampdens, which took off between 17.45 and 18.30 with S/L Oxley the senior pilot on duty, but P/O Tunstall and crew were forced to return early after icing of the air intakes caused a loss of power in both engines. The others pressed on towards the target, on one of those nights when the reports of returning crews would be sufficiently at odds to suggest that they had been at different locations. F/O Woodward and crew made landfall over the Frisians to be greeted by accurate and heavy anti-aircraft fire, but reached the target area intact to encounter a layer of ten-tenths cloud between 3,000 and 6,000 feet. A fifteen-minute search for the target proved unsuccessful, and a course was set for Cuxhaven on the southern bank of the Elbe Estuary, where the skies were clear. An attack was carried out with six 250 pounders and incendiaries from 12,000 feet, and the bomb bursts were followed by two fires and an explosion. In contrast, P/O Walker and crew found no cloud over the target, and located it with ease, guided by the intensity of the searchlight and flak defence. They bombed it from 12,000 feet, but were too busy negotiating the flak to observe the results. On the way home, they dropped a single incendiary onto a flak battery at Friedrichskoog on the northern bank of the Elbe Estuary, and watched it start a large fire that remained visible for fifteen minutes. S/L Oxley and crew exited the English coast at Flamborough Head, before setting course, according to the ORB, for Hannover, situated some 130 miles south of the intended destination of Kiel. They did report being well to the south of the target and turning north, where they came upon it under clear skies and well-illuminated by searchlights. The attack was carried out from 14,000 feet, and the incendiaries left a long line of fires in their wake that remained visible for fifteen miles. On e.t.a., the intensity of the defences left P/O Thwaites and crew in no doubt that they had found the target area, and they delivered their four 500 pounders from 13,000 feet at 21.20, oblivious to the outcome because of the need to take evasive action. P/O Powell and crew blamed seven to ten-tenths cloud for their inability to locate the target, even though heavy flak shells were bursting at between 9,000 and 13,000 feet all around them. They reported delivering an attack from 10,000 feet onto an unidentified alternative objective on the opposite bank to the north-west of the target, and four bursts were observed close to fires already burning.

On the following night, 5 Group dispatched nineteen Hampdens to Berlin, while 50 Squadron sent the crews of P/Os Tunstall and Cooke to plant vegetables in the Deodars garden in the mouth of the Gironde in south-western France. The former was recorded as taking off at 22.38, while the latter departed at 23.50, which may be accurate or may suggest that one of the times is incorrect. The former failed to locate the target area because of mist, and set course for home, temporarily losing the use of their radio equipment at 07.00 while trying to obtain a fix. They eventually landed at Benson in Oxfordshire at 08.15, after more than nine-and-a-half hours in the air, assuming their take-off time had been correctly recorded. P/O Cooke and crew ran into electrical storms and icing conditions while outbound, and the wing bombs were jettisoned into the sea. They located the drop zone and planted the vegetable entirely unopposed at around 04.00, and also experienced difficulty in obtaining a fix on the way home, before landing at Gravesend at 07.45.

Orders were received at Lindholme on the 27th to prepare seven Hampdens to contribute to a 5 Group attack on the Harburg oil refinery south of the Elbe at Hamburg. Shortly before take-off, a Henkel 111 bombed and strafed the aerodrome, leaving just three Hampdens sufficiently serviceable to proceed after a thirty-minute delay. They took off between 18.25 and 18.34 carrying the crews of P/O Powell, F/O Liddell and Sgt Crum, but the first-mentioned turned back with engine trouble after thirty minutes. F/O Liddell and crew noted activity over the Frisians as they made their way towards the Elbe estuary, but little in the Hamburg defence zone until reaching Elmshorn on the North Bank, where searchlights sprang into action. The flak was fairly intense over Hamburg itself, and a layer of cloud contributed to the crew's inability to locate the primary target. They spotted an area of dockyard, which they realized later was the site of the Blohm & Voss shipyard, and attacked it with four 500 pounders from 10,000 feet at 21.55. No bursts were observed, but a series of explosions and a fire with white flames turning to yellow was an indication that something combustible had been hit. Sgt Crum and crew were also defeated by the cloudy conditions over the primary target, and dropped their four 500 pounders from 12,000 feet onto an alternative, which they identified as F12, believed to be an aircraft factory, possibly the Klockner Aero-Engine plant.

Twenty-four hours later, Hamburg would host another visit from 5 Group, ten Hampdens from Hemswell and Lindholme assigned to the Harburg oil refinery, while ten others from Scampton and Waddington targeted dock installations. The 50 Squadron element of four took off between 17.00 and 17.30 with F/L Rippingale the senior pilot on duty, and they soon ran into eight to ten-tenths cloud at 3,000 to 6,000 feet, which persisted all the way to the enemy coast and made it difficult to establish a pinpoint. F/L Rippingale and crew found Hamburg to be completely obscured, and set course for Wilhelmshaven, where, despite repeated efforts to dislodge the bombs, they resolutely remained in the bomb bay and had to be brought home. P/O Everitt and crew found the cloud had dispersed as they reached the Elbe, which they followed towards the city centre, running the gauntlet of searchlights and flak. The bombs were dropped from 12,000 feet at 20.50, but the intensity of the defences prevented as assessment of the results. P/O Mulligan and crew glided from 12,000 to 10,000 feet before releasing their two 500 and two 250 pounders and incendiaries, and watched them straddle the target. F/O Russell failed to locate the primary target, blaming poor visibility and the intensity of the defences, and he and his crew dropped their load from 13,000 feet onto Cuxhaven instead, finding the defences there equally hostile.

Berlin was posted as the destination for twenty 5 Group crews on the 29th, where, among a number of targets in the Capital, was the Danziger Strasse Gas Works situated to the north-east of the city centre. Five 50 Squadron crews found themselves on the Order of Battle, and departed Lindholme between 17.55 and 18.28, only for P/O Tunstall and crew to be forced by intercom failure to turn back. The weather conditions were reasonably good for the outward journey until some sixty miles from the target, where the cloud thickened and extended above 16,000 feet. F/O Woodward and crew descended to 8,000 feet without breaking into clear air, and, when approximately ten minutes from e.t.a., they found themselves in the centre of a flak barrage while still in cloud. All thoughts of seeking out the primary target were abandoned, and they headed towards the west with the intentions of bombing Amsterdam, but were unable to find it either and brought their load home. P/O Thwaites and crew had been delayed at Lindholme by a fault in the oxygen system, and then, as they closed on the enemy coast, the heating system failed. They, too, sought out Amsterdam as an alternative target, but, on the way, came upon a well-illuminated aerodrome with flying in progress and light signals being passed between flying control and aircraft in the circuit. The lights were extinguished as the Hampden was heard approaching, but the flare-path was already in the bombsight graticule and the bombs were released from 10,000 feet. F/O Liddell and crew exited the English coast at Skegness, before climbing through icing conditions for an hour. They made landfall at Egmond on the Den Helder peninsular, and then ran into a thick layer of cloud at 12,000 feet at 21.15. They climbed to 14,000 feet in an attempt to escape the rain and sleet, but failed to break cloud, and increased speed, while descending again to 8,000 feet until within twenty-five minutes of e.t.a., when they turned back. However, they found themselves under fire, and, after dropping the wing bombs, concluded that they must be over Berlin. They dropped their 1,000 pounder from 10,000 feet, and, with intense flak bursting all around them, beat a hasty retreat towards the west. Meanwhile, P/O Walker and crew had encountered snow and icing conditions at around 23.00 when some fifty miles west of Berlin and flying at 16,000 feet. They shed six thousand feet hoping to find clear air, but were still in cloud and decided to turn back. They ran into heavy flak over what they believed to be Brandenburg, and, struggling to maintain power because of icing of the air intakes, dropped their bombs from 12,000 feet, hoping to hit the offending batteries. They limped home, crossing the Yorkshire coast, and attempting to raise the Regional Control Centre at Linton-on-Ouse for assistance as the engines continued to falter. It eventually became necessary to part company with X3000 at 04.30, and all crew members drifted safely to earth, no doubt singing the praises of the parachute packers, while the Hampden crashed near Linton aerodrome. Sadly, this reprieve would be extremely short-lived.

During the course of the month the squadron carried out twenty operations, and dispatched ninety-one sorties for the loss of four Hampdens and two crews.

November 1940

By the onset of November, the Battle of Britain had run its course, and the fear of invasion banished for the time being at least. Industrial Germany would now become the main focus of attention as the winter took hold, with oil related targets at the head of an impressive list drawn up by the Air Ministry in a new directive issued three weeks after the enthronement of C-in-C Sir Richard Peirse. 5 Group hoped soon to have a new weapon in its armoury in the form of the Avro Manchester, a twin-engine replacement for the Hampden, which would soon be delivered to Waddington. The new type was to be introduced to operational service by 207 Squadron, which was reformed on this day, and, while the Manchester would prove to be hugely disappointing, its offspring would become the war's most successful bomber.

The first target of the new month for 5 Group was one of Berlin's many power stations, for which seventeen Hampdens were detailed from Hemswell, Lindholme and Waddington, while Scampton and Finningley took care of gardening duties. Four aircraft were made ready by 50 Squadron, and were taxiing their way to take-off when the one carrying Sgt Richardson and crew ran over the Chance light, and damaged its propellers. This left P/Os Everitt and Thwaites and F/O Woodward and their crews to depart Lindholme between 23.00 and 23.25, and head out over the North Sea. They ran into a bank of ice-bearing cloud before reaching the Dutch coast, and P/O Thwaites turned back after his starboard engine iced up and began losing revolutions. P/O Everitt and crew climbed to 14,000 feet, where the a.s.i froze before failing completely, leaving them without a vital instrument for accurate navigation. They opted to press on, and found themselves in a one-hundred-mile-wide belt of rain, before closing on Berlin at 12,500 feet, over five-tenths cloud that lay six thousand feet beneath them. This, ground mist and the absence of the a.s.i denied them any chance of identifying the primary target, and the four 500lb bombs went down onto a concentration of searchlights and flak. A large fire was observed to break out, which remained visible for thirty miles into the return trip, the glow lingering even longer, and it was, perhaps, this fire that F/O Woodward and crew reported homing in on from 14,000 feet, after also admitting defeat in the quest to find the briefed target. No results were observed through the curtain of searchlights and flak, but the fire seemed to be developing into a raging inferno that remained visible for a hundred miles. Conditions on the way home were challenging for both crews, with snow and electrical storms to contend with, but P/O Everitt's a.s.i returned to life as the English coast drew near, and the engines were running on fumes and spluttering as they landed.

The weather continued to challenge the raid planners, and most of the Command remained on the ground for the ensuing few nights. On the 3rd, 50 Squadron welcomed the arrival of S/L Augustus (Gus) Walker on attachment, prior to being installed as the commanding officer of 83 Squadron at Scampton. Commissioned in 1933, he had occupied a non-flying administrative post in R & D, until attending a course at 16 O.T U in June, and then being put in command of the 16 O.T.U Operational Flight between the 15th of August and 22nd of October. He became attached to Station HQ Finningley while he awaited his posting to Scampton, and came to 50 Squadron to gain some operational experience. On the 5th, he was granted the acting rank of wing commander, and, at some point during the month, on paper, at least, he was recorded as being posted to 83 Squadron, although this does not appear to have taken place physically.

5 Group sent ten Scampton Hampdens to Kiel on the night of the 3/4th, after cancelling the participation of the Lindholme and Hemswell elements. It was the 5th before the other groups stirred into life again, detailing ninety-seven aircraft for operations over Germany, Italy and the Occupied countries. The target for 5 Group's eighteen Hampdens was the Rothensee oil refinery at Magdeburg, for which 50 Squadron made ready seven aircraft, plus one to attack a shipyard at Bremen and another for mining duties in the Willow garden off the Baltic port of Sassnitz on the island of Rügen. It was the last-mentioned, P/O Grylls and crew, who took off first at 23.33, when weather conditions over eastern England were reasonably good. They reached the target area after an outward flight of four hours and twenty minutes, and circled at 1,200 feet for ten minutes above a blanket of ten-tenths cloud, before admitting defeat and turning for home. At 04.38, a gap appeared in the cloud, which revealed them to be two miles north of Fehmarn Island in the Radish garden, and the vegetable was planted there. The main element departed Lindholme between 00.10 and 00.45, and soon ran into ten-tenths cloud, which would deny them a sight of the ground until they returned. They would be dogged by icing conditions and rain throughout their sorties, and not all would have the determination to press on. P/O Tunstall and crew were unable to escape the icing band despite ascending and descending, and they turned back, as did P/O Powell and crew after an electrical storm over

Holland robbed them of their wireless communications. P/O Thwaites and crew lost a number of instruments to icing, before they, too, abandoned their sortie, and X2907 crashed north-east of Almelo, close to the Dutch/German frontier, with fatal consequences for P/O Walker and crew. This left just three crews to battle their way to the target, among them that of P/O Everitt, who approached the target at 14,000 feet and dropped a flare in the vain hope that it might reveal the ground. The bombs were delivered onto a concentration of searchlights and flak seen dimly through the cloud at the estimated position of the target. P/O Whitecross and crew were undertaking their first sortie since joining the squadron three weeks earlier, and they bombed the estimated position of the target from 14,000 feet at 04.40. Sgt Thomas and crew spent forty minutes over the estimated position of the target, before releasing their bombs from 8,000 feet onto a searchlight and flak concentration at 04.35. The reward for their persistence was a wall of snow, frost and static as they fought the conditions to be the last to land at 08.40. P/O Ainsworth and crew were another operating with the squadron for the first time, and had been the last to take-off for their target at Bremen, which they reached over ten-tenths cloud with a base at 2,000 feet. With no chance of identifying the shipyards, they bombed a searchlight and flak concentration as they passed Oldenburg on the way home.

The prospects for decent weather conditions were again bleak twenty-four hours later, when 5 Group dispatched twenty-five Hampdens to the twin cities of Mannheim and Ludwigshafen, which face each other from opposite banks of the Rhine in south-central Germany. 50 Squadron's three representatives, Sgts Crum and Richardson and F/O Woodward and their crews departed Lindholme between 00.10 and 00.30 bound for one of the main marshalling yards in Mannheim, and this left F/L Johnston and crew to take off two hours later for a similar target at Hamm. F/O Woodward climbed to 2,000 feet and had been flying for thirty minutes when the heating system failed, forcing him to turn back. The others pressed on through unpleasant weather, which relented in the target area to leave what Sgt Crum and crew described as perfect conditions. They attacked from 7,000 feet at 03.50 and watched their 1,000 and two 250 pounders burst in the northern section of the yards, before re-entering the foul weather for the homeward journey. A strong wind drove them south of their intended track, and they found themselves making landfall over the Thames Estuary. Sgt Richardson and crew located the target by dropping a parachute flare, but also had intense searchlight and flak activity to guide them to the aiming-point. Four 500 pounders were delivered in a low-level attack from 3,500 feet, and they were observed to burst across a row of buildings on the dockside. Meanwhile, F/L Johnston and crew had found a small gap in the ten-tenths cloud that had concealed the ground most of the way from the Dutch coast, and this enable them to establish their position over Hamm. As an important railway hub serving the Ruhr, it was always hotly defended, and searchlights and flak were much in evidence as they released their four 500 pounders from 11,000 feet. Three bursts were observed but no detail, and then it was a case of struggling through the severe static and icing conditions to reach home, having also been driven by the wind as far as the south coast.

On the 7th, 2, 3 and 5 Groups combined to send sixty-three Blenheims, Wellingtons and Hampdens to attack the Krupp works at Essen in the heart of the Ruhr. 5 Group detailed thirty aircraft, eight of them made ready at Lindholme, and they took off between 20.30 and 21.00 with F/O Liddell the senior pilot on duty, as the absence on operations of the squadron's senior officers continued. All reached the target area after crossing the North Sea and Holland over cloud, and, although Essen also lay under a protective blanket, crews were able to pick up a distinctive bend in the Rhine to the south of the target area, and plot a course from there.

P/O Cooke and crew identified the target by the bursts of bombs and the intensity of the defences as they approached from the south, and their bombs went down from 12,000 feet at around 23.00. P/O Tunstall and his crew encountered accurate searchlights at their flight level at 17,000 feet as they approached the target area, and remained at that altitude to deliver their bombs at 23.05. P/O Ainsworth and crew arrived over the Ruhr at 23.10 and circled for fifteen minutes in search of the aiming-point through occasional gaps, all the time under fire from all calibres of flak. The bombs were dropped from 14,000 feet at 23.25, and three bursts observed, but no detail. P/O Everitt crossed the aiming-point at 13,500 feet heading north, and saw a number of bursts, but, again, no detail. P/O Whitecross and crew were subjected to inaccurate searchlight and flak activity most of the way from the Dutch coast, but it became more troublesome as they circled in search of a pinpoint from which to make their bombing run. They selected the Rhine south of the city, and ran in at 11,500 feet to drop their four 500 pounders at 23.27. F/O Russell and crew might well have been over a different part of Germany, as they located the target without difficulty, and claimed to see smoke emanating from the factory chimneys in the light of a parachute flare. They carried out their attack from 13,300 feet, but were prevented by industrial haze from observing any results. Sgt Ormonroyd and crew were undertaking their first sortie with the squadron, and located the target area, before the challenging conditions persuaded them to return to Texel to bomb the seaplane base. They dropped a stick of four 500 pounders from 9,000 feet, but the eight-tenths cloud obscured the results. F/O Liddell and crew carried out their attack from 10,000 feet at 23.15 in the teeth of an intense searchlight and flak barrage, and, after setting course for home, found that they could not fly straight and level. This led them to the conclusion that they had been hit, particularly as the wireless became unserviceable and prevented them from receiving fixes to establish their position. On e.t.a at the English coast, there was only sea below, and various courses were adopted without success, until searchlights were encountered and it was realized that they were over Holland. The nose was pointed to the west, and, after a tense hour's flight, landfall was made at Southwold with ninety minutes of fuel remaining. They intended to land at Bircham Newton, picked up the beacon, and were given permission to land at the satellite aerodrome, but, after circling for some time, received a red. No response at all was received from West Raynham, and when the starboard engine cut out through fuel starvation, it was time for the crew to hit the silk. They abandoned X2994 at 3,000 feet, leaving F/O Liddell on board, doggedly determined to land the Hampden, and he kept it flying for a further twenty-five minutes before the port engine cut. F/O Liddell baled out at 1,500 feet at 07.00, and landed safely to be reunited with his crew, who then walked to West Raynham to report their survival. Despite the claims of returning crews, it was highly unlikely that any bombs fell in Essen, and the few photographs developed showed only woods.

On the 8th, 5 Group notified its four main stations of an operation that night against a marshalling yard in Munich, for which twenty-three Hampdens were made ready, four of them at Lindholme. They took off between 18.20 and 18.30 with F/L Johnston the senior pilot on duty, and he and his crew enjoyed an uneventful flight to the Dutch coast. Ten minutes later, a layer of ten-tenths cumulus cloud obscured the ground until they were some twenty miles from Frankfurt. It was determined at this time that the groundspeed was insufficient to allow them to reach the target area, still some two hundred miles distance, in good time, and it was decided to seek out an alternative target in Frankfurt or Mannheim. In the event, Rotterdam was selected, towards which the single 1,000 and two 500 pounders went down from 10,000 feet at 20.50, and were seen to detonate between two fires that were already burning. A strong wind, which may have been responsible for the low ground speed, blew the

Hampden south of track on the way home, and a fix was obtained near Hastings. The port engine of P/O Grylls's L4075 cut twice over the North Sea, possibly due to inefficient operation of the petrol cocks, and they, also complained of insufficient ground speed. They opted to bomb Mannheim, where they found almost clear skies, and delivered their attack from 10,000 feet at 22.05 on the second run, after the bombs hung-up on the first. F/O Woodward and crew described their outward flight as very good with regard to weather and opposition, but, on reaching Mannheim, they were blown south and found themselves over a mountainous region, which they concluded to be the Bavarian Alps. They searched for the target for as long as they dared, before retracing their steps, and unloading the contents of their bomb bay from 10,000 feet onto a searchlight and flak battery at Antwerp at 01.35. Sgt Richardson and crew established a pinpoint on Stuttgart, before losing their way and passing over Augsburg, from where a fresh course eventually led them to Munich. After flying from west to east across the city, they turned 180 degrees to approach from the east, and dropped their four 500 pounders from 6,000 feet at 22.05 in the face of an intense searchlight and flak barrage, which, fortunately, proved to be inaccurate.

5 Group sent out orders on the 10th to prepare twenty-eight Hampdens for a number of long-range operations that night, with destinations from Mannheim in the south to Danzig in the north-east and Merseburg, near Liepzig in the east. 50 Squadron briefed eight crews, three to attack the synthetic oil refinery at Leuna, near Merseburg, four to target a power station at Mannheim and one to go for an oil plant located in Mannheim's inland docks area. As Lindholme was severely flooded, the Hampdens flew over to Waddington to be fuelled and bombed up, and then took off together between 23.00 and 23.40. The weather conditions outbound proved to be very poor, with cloud obscuring the ground for most of the way to both regions. P/O Tunstall and crew negotiated one front on the way to the power station at Mannheim, but were unable to climb through a second one of towering cumulo-nimbus, and, while flying at 17,500 feet, the instruments became unreliable through freezing up. They could not locate the primary target, and failed also to find a suitable alternative in Belgium and Holland, where the cloud base was as low as 1,500 feet. Bound for the same target, P/O Whitecross and crew dropped their bombs onto a railway junction near the Moselle river from 11,000 feet at 02.10, and were so concerned about the conditions encountered as they passed through a front over the North Sea on the way home, that they sent out an S.O.S. Sgt Ormonroyd and crew were, likewise, defeated by the weather, and attacked installations on the Walcheren Canal in the port of Flushing. Sgt Thomas and crew did not return in L4149, and news came through quite quickly that the rear gunner was in enemy hands. Information that the Hampden had crashed into the sea and taken with it the other three crew members, was not received for some time. P/O Ainsworth and crew had been assigned to the oil plant at Mannheim, but experienced the same impossible conditions, and, although reaching the target area, searched in vain from 02.20 until 03.00. The squadron ORB records this crew as then attacking the Leuna oil refinery from 10,000 feet at 02.50 as an alternative, but this is an error, and should have cited the Mannheim power station.

F/O Russell and crew were unable to locate either the Leuna refinery or a suitable alternative target through the cloud, and brought their bombs home. Sgt Crum and crew tried unsuccessfully to climb out of the cloud, suffering severe icing in the process, and were nearing the target when the intercom system broke down after someone inadvertently pulled out a plug. Unable, thereafter, to communicate with his crew, Sgt Crum dived onto the target and released the four 500 pounders from 5,000 feet without observing any results. This must have alarmed the crew, who might have believed that the dive was caused by a terminal malfunction and could well have led them to consider abandoning ship. The rear gunner found the errant plug during the return flight, and was able to restore crew communications and enable Sgt Crum to explain his actions. P/O Everitt and crew realized, that to have any chance of identifying the target, they would have to descend through the icing belt, an unappetising prospect, and decided to remain at 13,000 feet and drop their 500 pounders onto a flak position in the target area.

The 5 Group targets for eighteen aircraft on the 12th were much closer to home, and were oil refineries in the Ruhr located at Wanne-Eickel, north-east of Gelsenkirchen, and Dortmund. Three Hampdens were made ready at Lindholme, and were dispatched for the first-mentioned between 02.10 and 02.30 with the crews of P/Os Cooke, Powell and Thwaites on board. They ran into heavy cloud over the North Sea that extended beyond the target area, and, with no prospect of identifying the briefed target, P/O Thwaites attacked a searchlight and flak concentration at Buer, north of Gelsenkirchen, from 14,000 feet at 04.08. P/O Cooke found a similar alternative objective at nearby Recklinghausen to bomb from 11,000 feet two minutes later. P/O Powell descended to 3,000 feet without breaking cloud, and decided to fly north, where he came upon a railway junction at Dorsten. The four 500 pounders went down from 1,600 feet, and the bursts were followed by a huge column of steam, an explosion, and two very vivid green flashes.

Thirty Hampdens were detailed for operations over Hamburg on the 13th, but the Lindholme element was cancelled by the station commander because of poor visibility. Lindholme was found to be waterlogged again on the 14th, when Hamburg was again to be the destination for twenty Hampdens and Berlin for ten. The six 50 Squadron participants flew over to Waddington for bombing-up in preparation for their trip to Germany's Second City, where five were to attack the A8 oil refinery and one the Blohm & Voss shipyards. They took off for their respective targets between 00.45 and 01.20 with S/L "Gus" Walker the senior pilot on duty for the first time. F/L Rippingale and crew were some seventy miles out from Skegness when the a.s.i failed and forced them to return after jettisoning their bombs. S/L Walker exited the English coast between Ingoldmells and Chapel-St-Leonards, and set course for a position south of Cuxhaven, from where he turned directly for the target. For a change, the weather conditions were excellent, and the target was picked up without difficulty, but intense heavy flak followed the Hampden all the way to the release of the four 500 pounders from 13,000 feet at 03.05. Three bursts were observed, but the need to take evasive action took priority over a detailed assessment of the results. Walker's rear gunner on this night was Sgt Richard Algernon Dacre Trevor-Roper, a larger-than-life, rebel-rouser of a character and black sheep of his aristocratic and academic family. In May 1943, he would occupy the rear turret of W/C Guy Gibson's Lancaster on Operation Chastise, the epic attack on the Dams. P/O Weston and crew, who were operating with the squadron for the first time, climbed to 15,000 feet over the North Sea, and made landfall on the Dutch coast before passing close to Wilhelmshaven and coming under fire. They began their attack at 18,000 feet in a glide that culminated with the release of the bombs from 14,000 feet at 03.40, and the bursts on the east side of the target were followed by a very large orange explosion and a fire that remained visible for twenty miles. P/O Everitt and crew attacked from west to east with a 1,000 and two 500 pounders from 12,000 feet, but the wing bombs hung up, and a second and third run were required before they eventually fell away and started a fire. F/L Johnston and crew blamed ground haze for their inability to identify the primary target, and they picked out the docks on the south side of the Elbe to attack on a south-easterly heading from 12,000 feet. The incendiaries were observed to start a fire that remained visible for forty miles. P/O Tunstall and crew had been assigned to the Blohm & Voss shipyard, which they approached over the mouth of the Weser, before coming under fire from Bremen. They were also subjected to intense anti-aircraft fire over Hamburg, but, at their flight level of 17,000 feet, they remained largely untroubled by it and the inaccurate searchlight activity. The four 500lb bombs were released at 03.10, immediately after which, the Hampden fell into a spin, preventing the occupants from observing the bursts. Control was quickly regained, however, and a safe return made at 07.20.

Hamburg was posted as the destination for twenty-five Hampdens again on the 15th, this time to target the power station at Altona on the North Bank of the Elbe to the west of the city centre. 50 Squadron made ready six aircraft, which departed Lindholme between 00.20 and 01.35 with F/O Woodward the senior pilot on duty. Sgt Ormonroyd and crew were back on the ground after fifteen minutes because of a.s.i failure, and they were followed home by P/O Powell and crew with a starboard engine issue. This left the remaining four to push on through difficult weather conditions over the North Sea, which included heavy ice-bearing cloud between 1,500 and 11,000 feet and driving rain. The skies were clear over the target area, however, and this would offer the chance to attack from relatively high level. F/O Woodward and crew approached from the south to come up on the eastern side of the city, before turning to the west to glide in over the densely populated working class districts that would be destroyed in the 1943 firestorm, traversing the centre and Sankt-Pauli to the aiming-point, where the four 500 pounders went down from 13,000 feet. The bursts were followed by a fire that remained visible for thirty minutes, and another stick was seen to start three large fires and many small ones. P/O Thwaites and crew were carrying a 1,000 and two 500 pounders, which were delivered from 14,000 feet at 03.07, and P/O Grylls and crew dropped their three 500 pounders on a north-easterly run across the aiming-point at 10,000 feet. The fourth bomb had been dumped into the North Sea to save weight during a spell of icing. X2908 crashed onto houses in Dunhill Road, Goole in Yorkshire at 07.07 on return, killing Sgt Richardson and two of his crew, while one of the gunners survived with just cuts and bruises.

For the third night running, Hamburg would host a visit from 5 Group, but, on this occasion, only those among thirty-four Hampdens that managed to make it all the way on another night of hostile weather conditions. 50 Squadron made ready four Hampdens, whose crews had been briefed to attack the industrial areas of Veddel and Peute, located on the islands in the Elbe in the heart of the city. W/C Golledge was the senior pilot on duty as they departed Lindholme between 00.45 and 01.17 and headed into a weather front that contained all kinds of unpleasant surprises. Sgt Crum and crew experienced a torrid time as they battled the elements, their aircraft gripped by ice, which froze the starboard engine at 9,500 feet. They dropped through the cloud to a warmer band at 1,000 feet, where the engine thawed, and, as they climbed again, found themselves in a severe snowstorm that ended their resolve. They sought out an alternative target, which they found in the form of an undefended aerodrome on the Frisian island of Spiekeroog, after descending through the cloud base to 1,500 feet. Two bombs struck buildings on the northern side of the airfield, and two overshot, and then to end a thoroughly miserable night, they crashed on landing, fortunately without injury to the crew, and X3022 was deemed to be repairable. W/C Golledge and crew lost their a.s.i soon after take-off, and it remained unavailable to them until shortly before landing. They were prevented by cloud from identifying the target, and turned their attention instead onto dock installations at Wesermünde, which they bombed from 9,500 feet at 04.35. The starboard engine cut out four times over the North Sea on the way home, the wireless became unserviceable and the operator fainted, otherwise, it was an uneventful sortie. P/O Everitt and crew found themselves exactly where they expected to be on e.t.a., and descended from 14,000 to 11,000 feet to carry out their attack through a gap in the cloud, but F/O Russell and crew searched in vain for a gap to appear for them, and they brought their bombs home.

Adverse weather conditions at home and over Germany caused the cancellation of 5 Group operations on the following two nights, and when orders were received on the operational stations on the 19th, they contained details of that night's long-range operations, by eight aircraft to the Skoda armaments works at Pilsen in Czechoslovakia, and by seventeen to an oil refinery at Lutzkendorf near Leipzig. Included in the number for the latter was a 50 Squadron element, which would be withdrawn late on because of very poor visibility around Lindholme. The target posted on the 20th was much closer to home, requiring a trip to the East Bank of the Rhine at Duisburg in the Ruhr, where Germany's largest inland docks, Duisburg-Ruhrort, lay to the south of the city centre. Seven Hampdens were made ready at Lindholme, and they took off between 22.45 and 23.05 with F/L Rippingale the senior pilot on duty. F/O Russell and crew arrived in the target area early, when only a few fires were burning south of the port complex, and these were soon extinguished. They found clear skies, moonlight and excellent visibility to aid their search for the aiming-point, and adopted a north-easterly heading to release their four 500 pounders from 13,500 feet. Three bursts were observed at the western end of the docks in the vicinity of bridges, and these gave rise to six fires that remained visible for forty miles into the return journey. F/L Rippingale and crew flew out over Wainfleet, and made landfall south of Den Helder, before pinpointing on Enkhuizen on the edge of the Ijsselmeer. Having identified the Rhine, they kept it in view all the way into the target area, where they attacked from north-west to south-east at around 01.10. P/O Cooke and crew crossed the Dutch coast at 14,000 feet, and began a gentle glide from a point five miles north-west of the aiming-point to deliver their load from 13,000 feet at 00.50. P/O Everitt and crew bombed from 14,000 feet, while P/O Powell and crew carried out their attack from only 8,000 feet, from which altitude they were blinded to the results by the intense searchlight and flak activity. Sgt Ormonroyd and crew ran into the first searchlight concentration some twenty minutes before reaching the target, and, although flak was slight here, they could see ahead to the curtain of steel over the target, and decided to alter course to cross the Rhine south of the docks and carry out their bombing run on a northerly heading. They followed the river, letting down from 13,000 to 9,000 feet, and dropping their mix of 500 and 250 pounders and incendiaries in a stick to burst close to the bridges. As they turned away, they realized that the wing bombs were still attached, so circled back to let them go, by which time two large fires had broken out, which would remain visible for thirty miles. P/O Whitecross and crew were carrying a 1,000 pounder, which they released from 12,000 feet along with the two 500 pounders, but saw nothing of the impact through the searchlight glare. F/O Russell reached the English coast at Yarmouth at 03.46, and set course for Lindholme, only to be driven back out to sea by a gale. The congestion caused by returning aircraft delayed receipt of a fix, and they were off Whitby before their position was established, leaving them the last to land at 07.07, more than two-and-a-half hours after the others.

On the 22nd, AVM Harris relinquished his command of 5 Group on his appointment as second deputy to the Chief of the Air Staff, Sir Charles Portal, and he was succeeded by AVM

Bottomley. Fifteen months hence, to the day, Harris would return to lead the Command and rescue it from the brink of disbandment. On the night of his departure, 5 Group sent a small force back to Duisburg-Ruhrort and another to attack an aerodrome near Bordeaux, and, twenty-four hours later, returned again to Duisburg-Ruhrort, while also sending five Hampdens to Gelsenkirchen. 50 Squadron had sat out these operations because of adverse weather in its corner of southern Yorkshire, but was back on the Order of Battle on the 24th, for a raid by eleven aircraft on the Blohm & Voss shipyards at Hamburg. The six Lindholme participants took off between 01.20 and 01.50, with F/L Rippingale the senior pilot on duty, and soon ran into six to ten-tenths cloud with tops at between 4,000 and 6,000 feet. P/O Weston and crew turned back after thirty minutes because of an intercom issue, and they were followed home by F/O Liddell and crew, who had lost their oxygen system after an hour. This left the others to battle the conditions, which remained challenging all the way to the target, which F/L Rippingale and crew failed to locate. They were homebound when they chose Wilhelmshaven docks as an alternative objective, and attacked them on a north to south heading from 12,000 feet at 04.05. The bombs were seen to burst, and the ensuing large, vivid, white flash illuminated the aircraft. P/O Thwaites and crew ran into a searchlight concentration as they made landfall at Den Helder, and were subjected to intense anti-aircraft fire on e.t.a at the target, where the bombs were released from 13,000 feet. P/O Grylls and crew struggled against a strong headwind as they crossed the North Sea with the a.s.i showing just 100 mph, while flying at 6,000 feet. They jettisoned a 500 pounder to help their cause, and reached the target over a complete cloud cover to let the remaining three go from 10,000 feet in the face of intense anti-aircraft fire. F/O Woodward and crew were guided to the estimated aiming-point by the intensity of the searchlights and flak, and dropped their four 500 pounders from 12,000 feet in a slow stick from east to west

On the following night Hemswell and Lindholme joined forces to send ten Hampdens to attack the Deutsche-Werke shipyard at Kiel, where the heavy cruiser, Gneisenau, had been built between 1935 and 1938. The four 50 Squadron aircraft took off between 17.00 and 17.20 with S/L Oxley the senior pilot on duty on a night of wasted effort. P/O Powell and crew turned back after twenty minutes, to be followed by P/O Whitecross and crew, both with wireless communications issues. S/L Oxley reported good weather conditions over the sea, but a layer of nine to ten-tenths cloud lay over the target area, preventing them from locating the target. The four 500 pounders were dropped on the north-western side of the port from 13,000 feet at 19.31, and bursts were observed, but no detail. Sgt Crum and crew estimated the cloud base to be at around 1,500 feet as they bombed a searchlight and flak concentration on the western side of the port from 6,000 feet, without observing any results. As they approached the Lincolnshire coast north-east of Louth, fuel was becoming critical, and Sgt Crum force-landed X3125 at Saltfleet, near the Lincolnshire coast, at 03.15. The Hampden was written off, and the crew sustained injuries, which, according to the ORB, were not serious.

Cologne was posted as the destination for sixty-two aircraft on the 27th, which would be allotted to five separate aiming-points within the city. Ten 5 Group Hampden crews were briefed to attack what was described as a "land armament factory", and the four 50 Squadron participants departed Lindholme between 02.30 and 02.45 with S/L Walker the senior pilot on duty. They were routed to make landfall over the Scheldt estuary, where they found their way inland barred by a bank of towering, ice-bearing cumulo-nimbus cloud, extending from 6,000 up to 15,000 feet. F/O Liddell was already dealing with intercom failure, when the severe icing persuaded him to turn back. S/L Walker and crew fought their way through snow and electrical storms to reach the target area, where they bombed on estimated position from 9,000 feet at 04.50. P/O Whitecross and crew struggled with navigation, and, by the time they reached the target area, had insufficient time before dawn to search for the primary target. An attack was carried out from 12,000 feet on what they described as the Eschweiler Works, near a railway junction, and this may refer to a power station in the Eschweiler district of Aachen. P/O Weston and crew claimed to have identified the primary target with the aid of a parachute flare, and bombed it with high explosives and incendiaries from 14,000 feet at 04.50. Bursts were observed in the south-east corner of the target, and a large orange and several white fires were still visible some ten minutes later.

Hemswell and Lindholme were the stations called upon on the 28th to provide aircraft for operations against a naval stores at Mannheim, and the inland port on the other side of the Rhine at Ludwigshafen. Six Hemswell crews were briefed for the former, and five from Lindholme for the latter, and 50 Squadron would also provide one crew to attack the Veddel and Peute industrial area in the heart of Hamburg. They took off between 17.20 and 17.35 with F/L Johnston the senior pilot among the main element and F/L Rippingale heading in the opposite direction, but the latter was soon on the way home with an unserviceable intercom system. It proved extremely difficult to establish a landing protocol after gaining a fix from Heston, and landing permission was sought in vain at Lindholme, Waddington, Mildenhall and Bircham Newton. While flying through four-tenths cloud at 7,000 feet, a beacon was spotted, and they landed eventually at Swanton Morley. F/O Woodward and crew were climbing out over Lindholme when the heating system failed, but, to their credit, they decided to press on as far as the enemy coast to try to do some damage there. The found a road and railway bridge linking the islands of Walcheren and Beveland, and attacked it in a pass from west to east at 5,000 feet, observing the four 500 pounders to overshoot by two hundred yards. They arrived home in the middle of enemy intruder operations, which would create difficulty for some aircraft trying to land in the area. F/L Johnston climbed to 13,000 feet for the North-Sea crossing, and made landfall over the Scheldt on e.t.a., before establishing a fix on the target. For some reason this was not usable, and other attempts to locate the target by radio fix became confused. After circling the target area for twenty minutes, during which time a flare was dropped, they turned for home, and, somehow, found themselves over Düsseldorf, where the bombs and incendiaries were dropped from 10,000 feet, and were seen to start fires. P/O Thwaites and crew encountered icing conditions over the North Sea, which left the a.s.i frozen and showing 190 m.p.h. They found that the enemy coast was blotted out by cloud, and decided to attack Antwerp as a last-resort target, aiming their four 500 pounders at the flashes from a flak concentration from 11,000 feet at 19.25. P/O Powell and Sgt Ormonroyd and their crews were the only ones to fulfil their briefs by bombing the primary target, the former enjoying an uneventful sortie, before attacking through cloud from 10,000 feet. The latter established firm pinpoints on the English and Dutch coasts, before encountering seven-tenths cloud at 6,000 feet over the target with large gaps. The high explosives and incendiaries were released from 8,000 feet in the face of intense searchlight and flak opposition, which masked sight of the results.

This was the final operation of another busy month, in which the squadron operated against twenty-two targets, including mining, on fifteen nights, and dispatched eighty-two sorties for the loss of four Hampdens and two crews.

December 1940

The new month began for 5 Group with the briefing of ten Scampton crews on the 1st, for an operation that night against shipbuilding yards at Wilhelmshaven. Adverse weather conditions reduced the number reaching and bombing the target to three. The weather continued to be unfavourable and kept the group on the ground until the 4th, when orders were received to prepare for a raid on the Derendorf marshalling yards, situated just to the north of Düsseldorf city centre. Scampton and Lindholme detailed five Hampdens each, and the latter took off between 03.26 and 03.35 with F/L Rippingale the senior pilot on duty. They began to run into cloud from the mid-point of the North Sea crossing, and this built into a towering front of ice-bearing cumulo-nimbus starting at 4,000 feet, and extending in places to a height of 18,000 feet over enemy territory. F/L Rippingale managed to find a gap over the target area, and dropped his four 500 pounders through it from 12,000 feet, but, apart from a single burst, saw nothing of value to report at debriefing. P/O Grylls and crew had remained above the cloud at 14,000 feet until fifteen minutes from e.t.a., when they plunged into a bank of it and the temperature plummeted to minus 20ºC. They turned back to seek an alternative target, and spent twenty-five minutes before giving up and setting course for home with their bombs. On the way they had to battle a severe storm with snow, icing and static, and only survived by using the de-icer equipment and descending to 3,000 feet. P/O Cooke and crew claimed to have encountered cloud at 20,000 feet, and also had to rely on their de-icing equipment to keep the propellers turning as they descended. Even so, they began to lose revolutions, with, eventually, both engines cutting out at 6,000 feet, and only restarting one at a time at 2,000 feet. The bombs were jettisoned near Brühl, south of Cologne, and the return journey was undertaken at 2,000 feet with the starboard engine continuing to operate at reduced power for thirty minutes. F/O Russell and crew were twenty minutes from the target when they turned back, and P/O Everitt and crew even closer when all of their instruments froze up and the engines began to splutter, with the revs on the port side dropping off alarmingly. They tried to descend to break into clear air, but were still in cloud at 7,000 feet, and, after turning north in a vain attempt to find better conditions, gave up and took their bombs home.

On the 6th, ten Scampton Hampdens were sent on intruder sorties over Luftwaffe bomber aerodromes in the Occupied Countries, while twenty others from Scampton, Hemswell and Waddington pioneered a new role for the type, conducting offensive patrols over Bristol to seek out and destroy enemy bombers. 50 Squadron remained at home on this night, and received orders on the 7th to prepare to return to Düsseldorf that night for an attack on the Mannesman Rohrenwerke, which, it is believed, was manufacturing heavy gun barrels. Eight Hampdens were loaded with four 500 pounders each, and dispatched from Lindholme at 18.00 with F/O Liddell the senior pilot on duty. They headed into another ice-bearing front over enemy territory, which would force a number of crews to jettison their loads in order to remain airborne, and only three would report bombing the target. P/O Thwaites and crew climbed to 19,000 feet over the North Sea, and remained above the ice-bearing cloud until reaching the target, where the skies were clear and the visibility excellent. They carried out their attack from 11,000 feet, a thousand feet above the barrage balloons, at 20.13, and observed two bursts but no detail. P/O Everitt and crew arrived twenty minutes later after also completing an uneventful outward flight, and, during their first pass over the target at 13,000 feet, found that the bomb doors had frozen. The second run was successful, and one burst was observed before the pilot pulled a tight turn, preventing a view of any further results other than the impression of a small fire. They experienced the severe icing conditions on the way home, but landed safely to make their report. F/O Russell and crew were able to map-read their way to the aiming-point, and were above marshalling yards on the east side of the Rhine when they released their bombs in a long stick to see them impact on a nearby railway junction.

It seems that the above crews, as a result of recent experiences, had decided from the outset to put themselves above the front, rather than attempt to fly through it, while those who crossed the North Sea at lower altitudes paid the price. P/O Whitecross and crew crossed the coast at Orfordness at 6,000 feet, and climbed to 9,000 feet before running into a band of cloud. Hoping to climb above it, they changed course to the north and south seeking a path, but could not coax more than 11,000 feet out of their labouring Hampden. They jettisoned two 500 pounders, and managed another one thousand feet before accepting that they could not reach the target by the cut-off time of 21.00, at which point, they turned for home. On entering the cloud, F/O Liddell and crew succeeded in climbing through it to 15,000 feet, but picked up so much ice on the way that the de-icing equipment could not deal with it, and they, too, abandoned their sortie and returned their bombs to store. Sgt Ormonroyd and crew crossed the English coast at 9,000 feet, still climbing, and, twenty minutes later, entered cloud at 13,000 feet, before re-emerging shortly afterwards into clear air. As they reached 16,000 feet, they were engulfed again in thick cumulus cloud, and, with ice forming rapidly on the wings, the bombs were jettisoned, and the sortie terminated. F/O Woodward and crew climbed to 12,000 feet, and, shortly before reaching the Dutch coast, ran into the towering front, which they attempted to climb through. Even at 17,500 feet they were still enveloped, and the port engine failed because of iced-up intakes. The bombs were jettisoned "safe" some ten miles off the enemy coast, but the Hampden continued to sink, and the ammunition was also thrown out. On reaching 6,000 feet, the intake thawed, the engine picked up and a safe return was completed at 21.55. The return of Kiwi, F/O Mulligan, and his crew in X3004, was awaited in vain, and no trace of the Hampden and its crew was ever found. The likelihood, on a night of little enemy activity, is that they fell victim to the icing conditions over the North Sea.

On the 8th, Hemswell and Lindholme joined forces to send fourteen Hampdens to Düsseldorf to target a steel works, the five 50 Squadron participants taking off between 17.20 and 17.35 with S/L Walker the senior pilot on duty. Each was carrying four 500 pounders and two 250lb wing bombs to the Ruhr, and the early signs for the weather were good in contrast to what had been endured on recent raids, with relatively clear skies as far as the Rhine. Thereafter, nine to ten-tenths cloud lay across Germany's industrial heartland between 8,000 and 15,000 feet to create a challenge for target locating. P/O Ainsworth and crew crossed the Dutch coast north of Rotterdam, and had little difficulty in finding the target area, assisted to an extent by the presence of accurate searchlights and flak on e.t.a. They attacked from 11,000 feet at 20.00, and observed five bursts but no detail. S/L Walker and crew made landfall further south, over Schouwen at the mouth of the Scheldt, before heading north and coming under accurate searchlight and flak activity near The Hague. They were able to map-read to within twenty miles of the target, and noted the aerodrome at Eindhoven to be illuminated and operational. An intense searchlight and flak defence greeted them over the target, and they were stooging around in search of a gap when the bombs from another aircraft created a huge flash, lighting up the riverside built-up area and providing an aiming-point. They immediately went in to attack from 13,500 feet, but the results were masked by the cloud. P/O Grylls and crew arrived in the target area at 10,000 feet at 19.20, and spent forty minutes trying to find a gap in the cloud, until deciding that the intense searchlight and flak activity was providing an adequate indication of where the city lay. They released their bombs at 20.00, before beating a hasty retreat to the west, where they came upon the Luftwaffe activity at Eindhoven. Gliding down to 500 feet, they strafed the aerodrome with all guns, claiming hits on parked aircraft. P/O Weston and crew failed to identify the target, and sought out an alternative, which they found in the form of Kleve (Cleves), close to the Dutch frontier north-west of the Ruhr. They dropped their hardware from 10,500 feet without observing the results, and headed for the Dutch coast, where they were lucky to survive the flak thrown up at them from the Voorn/Rotterdam defences. P/O Cooke and crew reached the target area at 15,000 feet, but failed to carry out an attack and brought the bombs home.

Two nights later, 5 Group sent orders to Scampton and Lindholme to prepare six Hampdens each to target the inland docks on the West Bank of the Rhine at Mannheim. The 50 Squadron element took off between 20.25 and 20.40 with F/Ls Johnston and Rippingale the senior pilots on duty. The Rippingale crew was one of two to return early, in their case after two hours with an unserviceable heating system, and they were followed home twenty minutes later by P/O Thwaites and crew, who had been put off by a towering bank of cumulo-nimbus that extended from 1,500 to 14,000 feet across their path at the Dutch coast. Both crews returned their bombs to store. F/O Woodward and crew exploited the initially good conditions to establish firm pin-points on their way to landfall at the Dutch coast, where they, too, were confronted by the cloud, and decided to attempt to climb over it to avoid icing. They reached 20,000 feet, where they were in and out of the cloud tops, but could not drag another inch out of the Hampden. They pressed on to the target, dogged by static and with the heating system operating at reduced power and threatening to condemn them to frostbite. On arrival, they jettisoned the pairs of 500 and 250 pounders "live" from 19,000 feet at 23.00, and landed three hours and twenty minutes later after a heroic effort to fulfil their brief. F/L Johnston and crew also tried in vain to climb into clear air, and, after about thirty minutes in a temperature of minus 35°C, abandoned all thoughts of reaching the primary target. Forty minutes later they succeeded in breaking out of the cloud, and, thirty minutes after that, found a gap and established their position over the Rhine at Duisburg. They bombed from 12,000 feet and observed two fires to break out, but were in no mood to hang around to glean further detail. The report from P/O Everitt and crew suggested that they remained in clear air until twenty minutes from the target, when they hit a bank of cloud with tops at 14,000 feet. After five minutes, both engines began to falter, despite the use of the carburettor de-icers, and, while the starboard motor picked up, the port one failed completely, as did the a.s.i.. They turned back and jettisoned the bombs along with any removeable equipment, before spending the next forty-five minutes flying on one engine on reduced power and sinking to 2,500 feet with the probability of having to abandon the aircraft. The port engine unfroze at that point, and they were able, eventually, to reach 6,000 feet after the starboard engine returned to full power. F/O Liddell and crew failed to return in X3117, which had fallen victim to flak and had crashed without survivors in the Eifel region of Germany near Aachen.

W/C Golledge reported to Nº2 Personnel Dispatch Centre (PDC) on the 15th pending his posting overseas, and he would be succeeded as commanding officer by W/C "Gus" Walker, whose physical posting to 83 Squadron, it seems, never took place. He presided over his first operation that very night, when 5 Group ordered an attack by thirty Hampdens on various targets in Berlin. The 50 Squadron element of five was assigned to an electrical power station at Wilmersdorf, situated in a south-western suburb, and they departed Lindholme between 00.15 and 00.30 with F/O Russell the senior pilot on duty. P/O Thwaites and crew were back on the ground after two hours because of a faulty artificial horizon, which was an indispensable piece of kit when flying in cloud. P/O Powell and crew became concerned about excessive fuel consumption at 03.00, and decided to make for Hannover, where they delivered an attack from 6,000 feet in the face of intense searchlight and flak activity and in the presence of a night-fighter. No results were observed, and the night-fighter was shaken off by evasive action. On the way home, they came across a factory at Osnabrück and a section of railway near Rheine, both of which they strafed from 500 feet. P/O Ainsworth and crew flew out over Skegness and set course directly for Berlin, encountering nine-tenths cloud over the North Sea, but nothing below them until reaching the target, where they found around eight-tenths at 5,000 feet. This obscured the primary target, but not the previously attacked Air Ministry building in the city centre, upon which they dropped four 500 pounders in the face of a hostile searchlight and flak defence. This prevented a detailed assessment of the outcome, but the impression was that the bombs had overshot and started a number of small fires. P/O Weston and crew reported that they had experienced no flak activity in the outer Berlin defence zone, but this changed over the city itself, where ten-tenths cloud obscured the primary target. They attacked Potsdam railway station from 14,000 feet on a northerly heading while under fire, and observed only three white explosions after one of their 500 pounders hung up. F/O Russell and crew located the primary target without difficulty, and released their bombs from 12,000 feet through a curtain of anti-aircraft fire that blinded them to the outcome. They believed the bombs had overshot the mark, but a fire in an area to the north that remained visible for sixty miles, may have resulted from their efforts.

Orders came through from 5 Group on the 16th to prepare fifty-eight Hampdens to attack various targets in Mannheim in two waves. At briefings, crews learned that this was to be a major operation involving two hundred aircraft under the codename, Operation Abigail Rachel, launched in retaliation for recent devastating raids on English cities, particularly Coventry and Southampton. The plan called for eight of the most experienced 3 Group Wellington crews to open the attack on the centre of the city with all-incendiary loads, and start fires that would act as a beacon to those following behind. As the day drew on, it became clear that the weather conditions over the bomber stations might cause problems, and the force was cut to 134 aircraft. It had been intended that 50 Squadron would provide six aircraft for each wave, taking off at 21.00 and 00.30, but the threat of fog led to the withdrawal of the Lindholme element from the second wave, leaving the first-wave crews to take off between 20.45 and 21.20 with W/C Walker the senior pilot on duty and last away. They were part of a 5 Group contribution to the first wave of twenty-nine Hampdens, and had been given the Motorenwerke Mannheim in the northern outskirts of the city as their aiming-point. This is curious, as the purpose of the raid was to cause as much damage as possible to the central districts of the city in what was the first officially-sanctioned area attack. A number of early returns would severely reduce the squadron's presence over the target, and they began with the return of F/L Rippingale and crew at 22.35 with an engine issue. On approaching the Dutch coast over the Scheldt Estuary, F/L Johnston and crew encountered ten-tenths cloud at around 5,000 feet, and, having reached Flushing, decided that the conditions were too bad to continue. P/O Grylls and crew also blamed the weather conditions for not pressing on, while F/O Woodward and crew lost an engine when about to enter Germany. S/L Walker and crew exited the English coast at 4,000 feet, before climbing through the cloud to 10,000 feet to cross the Dutch coast. The ground remained obscured, but, on e.t.a., they managed to establish a pin-point on the Rhine south of the city, and followed the anti-aircraft and bomb bursts to the release of their load from 10,000 feet. On the way home they climbed to 19,000 feet to remain above the cloud and avoid the icing conditions. P/O Everitt and crew carried out a glide attack, and released their bombs from 12,000 feet into the middle of the target area, where three bursts and one large explosion were observed. Post-raid reconnaissance revealed that the operation had not produced the desired results, after the "pathfinder" element had missed the city centre and the subsequent bombing had been scattered. Even so, local reports provided a figure of 240 buildings either destroyed or seriously damaged, with more than a thousand people bombed out of their homes.

The weather kept 5 Group at home on the ensuing two nights, while very small forces returned to Mannheim. The teleprinters on 5 Group stations burst into life on the 19th to reveal plans to attack the Wesseling oil refinery, situated on the West Bank of the Rhine south of Cologne. Forty Hampdens were made ready across the group, five of them at Lindholme, where take-off was completed safely between 16.25 and 16.42. P/O Powell and crew lost an engine to icing, and returned to base after three hours with their bombs still on board. P/O Ainsworth and crew crossed the North Sea at 16,000 feet above the ten-tenths cloud in order to avoid a similar fate, and managed to establish a pin-point on the Dutch coast through a gap. However, the cloud tops were even higher inland, and the wing bombs were jettisoned to enable the Hampden to claw a few extra feet of altitude. The target area was reached, but the primary target not located, and the bombs were returned to store. Sgt Crum and crew were contending with ice-accretion as they reached the Cologne area at 3,000 feet, and identified the approximate location of the aiming-point by the volume of flak coming at them. They cruised around for a time in a vain search, before following the course of the Rhine south to Bonn, where they attacked a marshalling yard from 1,500 feet and witnessed a mighty explosion, which shook the aircraft. As they headed for home, they saw a large fire beginning to develop out of their incendiaries. P/O Thwaites and crew gained a navigational fix, that enabled them to home in on the target area, and, on e.t.a., as if to order, the cloud cleared sufficiently to reveal a built-up area beneath, which they attacked from 15,000 feet in the face of very accurate light flak. They saw nothing of their bombs' impact, and had to climb to 19,500 feet on the way home to avoid the consequences of icing. P/O Burrough and crew were on their first operation with the squadron, and lost their intercom shortly after crossing the English coast, rendering crew co-operation something of a challenge. To their credit, they opted to carry on, and, ultimately, dropped their bombs onto the approximate position of the target from 14,000 feet.

The 20th would mark the resurgence of 1 Group, which had been reconstituted on return from its role as the major part of the AASF in France for the first nine months of the war. The Fairey Battles had been replaced, and, with four squadrons of fanatical Poles added to its ranks and working towards operational status, this night would see the first six operational sorties in Wellingtons. 5 Group detailed a dozen Hampdens for Berlin and thirty-one for a return to the Wesseling synthetic oil refinery at Cologne, both operations benefitting from the support of 50 Squadron. F/O Woodward and F/L Rippingale and their crews took off first at 00.17 and 00.35 bound for the Schlesinger railway station in the Capital, and, quite why they had been held back until then is unclear, particularly as the 83 Squadron element had departed Scampton either side of 17.00. The Lindholme crews would be under time pressure throughout, conscious that they would struggle to vacate enemy territory before the arrival of daylight, and this would prove to be the case. F/L Rippingale exited the English coast at Skegness, before climbing to 11,000 feet and making landfall twenty miles west of Cuxhaven. This provided an e.t.a at Berlin of 06.16, which meant that they would be returning over Holland in daylight, and the common-sense decision was taken to bomb Hannover instead. However, even this proved to be impossible in conditions of thick cloud and impenetrable darkness, and when they came upon a searchlight and flak concentration at Nienburg, south-east of Hannover, they attacked it with two 500 pounders and incendiaries from 12,000 feet, observing a large white glow to appear and light up the clouds. F/O Woodward and crew reported perfect conditions, and were easily able to obtain a pinpoint some forty miles from Berlin. They lacked the time to seek out the primary target, however, and attacked the alternative, marshalling yards, from 16,000 feet, failing to observe the bursts as an unidentified aircraft dived beneath them at the moment of release.

Meanwhile, the seven crews assigned to Wesseling had departed Lindholme between 03.15 and 04.07 with S/L Oxley the senior pilot on duty. They encountered little opposition as they crossed enemy territory in near perfect conditions, which would persist all the way to the target. P/O Whitecross and crew had been the last to take-off, and this left them barely enough time to complete their sortie before the advent of daylight. They were forty miles from the target when they decided to go for an alternative, and dropped their four 500 and two 250 pounders from 7,000 feet onto river traffic two miles north-west of Jülich, observing bursts on both banks of the Rur (Roer). The others took advantage of the conditions to identify the refinery, part of which was already burning, and carry out their attacks from 1,500 feet (P/O Grylls) and 16,000 feet (S/L Oxley), adding substantially to the fires, which remained visible for some distance into the return journey. P/O Grylls and crew also strafed the site from 1,000 feet, in what appeared to be one of the more successful operations undertaken against an oil target.

5 Group detailed twenty-four Hampdens for operations on the following night, when an electrical power station at Halle, situated to the north-west of Leipzig, was to be the target. (The 5 Group ORB states Halle, while the squadron ORB refers to it as south-eastern outskirts of Dessau). Four 50 Squadron crews departed Lindholme in a five-minute slot from 21.15, with W/C Walker the senior pilot on duty, and set course from Skegness for eastern Germany in excellent weather conditions. Map-reading was a simple task until they ran into a bank of ten-tenths cloud from Osnabrück, at which point, the ground became totally obscured and decisions had to be taken about how to respond. P/O Everitt and crew found that the cloud extended to very low level, but they caught sight of an unidentified railway, and bombed it from 3,000 feet without observing the outcome through misted-up Perspex. Sgt Crum and crew found a gap in the clouds over Magdeburg, and dropped their load from 8,000 feet, while P/O Ainsworth and crew were ten minutes from e.t.a., when they stumbled into intense searchlight activity. They descended to 1,000 feet to strafe the offending battery, before abandoning their search for the primary target at 02.30. On the way home, they spotted a railway junction two miles south of Bielefeld, upon which they unloaded their four 500 pounders from 3,500 feet. Breaking cloud fifteen minutes before e.t.a., W/C Walker and crew found themselves over the River Mulde, which runs south from the Elbe, and passes close to Dessau, and flew up and down the valley in search of the primary target. The cloud was almost at ground level in places, making it an impossible task, when, suddenly, a collection of very large factory sheds came into view, with the central building dwarfing the others. They completed a circuit to line up on the main shed, and dived from 7,000 to 1,500 feet to deliver

two 500 pounders onto it and two onto those nearby. The roof was seen to lift, and red flashes emanated from windows on all sides. (This may well have been the Junkers aircraft factory, where the JU52, known in Germany as Tante Ju or aunty Ju, was being manufactured).

Lindholme and 50 Squadron would now enjoy a week away from the operational scene, while Scampton and Finningley took care of 5 Group business on the 22nd, Hemswell on Boxing Day, and Hemswell and Scampton on the 27th. The last two-mentioned operations had been against Merignac aerodrome in France, and it was to the French coast that 50 Squadron would send ten Hampdens on the 28th to bring its 1940 campaign to an end. The targets were U-Boots in the docks at Lorient, where, as already mentioned, the Germans were about to embark on a massive U-Boot bunker building programme. The Lindholme element was to be joined by five others from Scampton, and took off between 15.59 and 16.45 with F/L Johnston the senior pilot on duty. F/O Russell and crew turned back with wireless failure seventy miles into the outward flight, leaving the others to carry on towards the exit point over the Dorset coast. They met no opposition on the way to the target, which was located with ease by some and with difficulty by others, because of up to ten-tenths cloud. They all found it to be hotly defended by searchlights and all calibres of flak, and this was probably the cause of the loss of X3141, which crashed at Lanester, two miles north-east of Lorient, killing three members of the crew. P/O Ainsworth alone survived, and news would eventually filter through from the Red Cross that he was in enemy hands. The others searched diligently for the aiming-point, but F/O Woodward was defeated by the cloud and set course for Boulogne, which he also failed to locate. He and his crew cruised along the coastline as far north as Flushing, before ultimately abandoning the sortie and taking the bombs home. The seven remaining crews carried out their attacks mostly from between 8,000 and 11,000 feet, although P/O Burrough and crew decided upon a low-level glide attack from 3,000 down to 1,500 feet. Sadly, the intercom failed, preventing the bomb-aimer from receiving the order to release the bombs, which were jettisoned into the Channel on the way home. Returning crews reported observing bursts and flashes, and one very large fire that lit up the sky, but none could provide an accurate assessment of the raid.

During the course of the month the squadron operated against eleven targets, dispatching sixty-three sorties for the loss of two Hampdens and crews. It had been a year of discovery for the Command, and some lessons had been learned, but the means to deliver a telling blow were not yet to hand, and the coming year would see little improvement in tactics and performance. It would be a case of treading water for at least the next twelve months in the face of an, as yet, dominant enemy, and the Command would have to work hard to keep its head above the surface.

Sgt Charles F Stenner was posted to 50 Squadron at Waddington on the 25th of May 1937, and completed his first tour of operations in September 1940. Following a spell as an instructor, he returned for a second tour, this time with 106 Squadron. He survived the war eventually rising to the rank of wing commander DSO, DFC.

1940. RAF Lindholme. 50 Squadron.
Sgt Stenner is seated third from the left in the second row. His first sortie was a "nickelling" (leaflet) trip to Bremen on the 6th of March 1940.

Two 50 Squadron Hampdens with pre-war codes at Waddington.

50 Squadron Hampdens

50 Squadron Hampden air and ground crew.

F/O French DFC and crew, April 1940

A second successive severe winter would restrict operations at the start of the year, when most of the effort would be directed at French and German ports. Bremen was posted as the year's first target on New Year's Day, for which 5 Group detailed thirty Hampdens as its contribution. The briefing to ten crews at Lindholme provided details of the target, the Korff A.G. oil refinery, which the ORB suggested was also a depository for food stocks. Take-off took place in unpromising weather conditions between 16.30 and 16.59 with F/Ls Johnston and Rippingale the senior pilots on duty, but the numbers were soon depleted by the early return of P/O Thwaites with engine trouble, F/O Woodward because of an unserviceable wireless and F/L Rippingale after his a.s.i froze. The last two-mentioned also cited the weather conditions as contributing to their decision to turn back. As always, there were contradictory reports concerning the weather during the outward journey, P/O Powell and crew describing it as good, while F/L Johnston complained of a snowstorm over eastern England that extended as high as 11,000 feet. Sgt Crum and crew reported icing conditions as they climbed over the North Sea, before finding a funnel of clear air, within which they circled while gaining further height to 9,500 feet.

There was agreement, however, that the cloud built to between eight and ten-tenths as the target drew near, despite which, some crews located it without difficulty, aided in part by the intensity of the defences. Sgt Crum and crew delivered their four 500 pounders from 6,000 feet, but saw little of the results through the cloud before turning for home, and losing their heating system for the last two hours. P/O Powell and crew had to search for thirty minutes before identifying the aiming-point, and their first run was unsuccessful, after which they bombed a marshalling yard from 8,500 feet. F/L Johnston and crew found the target in the light of flares, drawn on by the sight of fires already burning and tracer shells whizzing past to a height of 10,000 feet. P/O Weston and Sgt Ormonroyd and their crews carried out their attacks from 12,000 and 10,000 feet respectively, both observing their efforts to undershoot. P/O Whitecross and crew lost the use of their intercom ten minutes short of the target, and, while options were considered, the wireless operator spent twenty minutes vainly attempting to affect a repair. The decision was taken to abandon the sortie, and the bombs were dropped from high-level onto a bridge over an unidentified waterway west of Oldenburg. P/O Burrough and crew were unable to positively identify the primary target, but came upon a collection of large, blazing buildings, which they thought may contain the refinery, and this area was attacked from 10,000 feet. On arrival in the Lindholme circuit, they encountered a snowstorm and a cloud base at 600 feet, which resulted in X3143 being written off in a landing crash at 00.27. Local reports from Bremen confirmed a modest amount of damage, citing the Focke-Wulf aircraft factory as among the industrial buildings hit, while fourteen apartment blocks were destroyed, and three hundred others damaged.

5 Group returned to Bremen with eight Hampdens twenty-four hours later on a night of technical failures and wasted effort, but enjoyed greater success at the same target on the night of the 3/4th, when Scampton provided all fifteen participants. Earlier on the 3rd, the new bomber station at Coningsby had been declared open on a Care & Maintenance basis, and would shortly welcome its first resident unit. Also, on this day, it was decided to draft all Rhodesian aircrew into 44 Squadron as they became available, and to add the name, Rhodesia, to the squadron number. 50 Squadron remained off the Order of Battle until receiving orders on the 4th to prepare nine Hampdens for an operation that night against an

unnamed Hipper class German cruiser in a dry dock at Brest. A process of elimination suggests that it was the Admiral Hipper herself, which had been raiding in the Atlantic following her part in the Norwegian campaign. The Lindholme element was to be part of an overall force of fifty-three aircraft, of which thirty were provided by 5 Group, and they took off between 18.45 and 19.10 with W/C Walker and S/L Oxley the senior pilots on duty. Flying out over the Dorset coast at Chesil Beach in good conditions, they soon encountered a layer of eight-tenths cloud over the Channel at between 3,000 and 6,000 feet, which persisted all the way to the French coast and beyond. The target was easily identified on approach by the reflection of the searchlights in the cloud, and the volume of tracer breaking through it to reach 12,500 feet. Crews spent up to seventy-five minutes orbiting the target area and running across the estimated position of the aiming-point, seeking one of the few gaps in the nine to ten-tenths cloud cover. Eventually, all but F/L Rippingale delivered their mixed loads of 500 and 250 pounders and incendiaries from between 8,000 and 12,000 feet, before returning safely to make their reports.

The naval shipbuilding yards at Wilhelmshaven were scheduled as the target for thirty-two aircraft on the 8th, while sixteen others were assigned to Emden, some forty miles to the west. The aiming-point for the main element was the battleship Tirpitz, for which 50 Squadron briefed six crews and four others for gardening duties in the Eglantine region of the Elbe estuary. They took off together between 17.20 and 18.00, and, for a change, the weather conditions would act in their favour, although this was not immediately apparent. Ten-tenths cloud blanketed the North Sea right up to the Dutch coast, where it began to break up gradually, and, by the time the target area drew near, crews were able to map-read under clear skies and bright moonlight. Two crews would not benefit from the conditions, P/O Powell and crew of the gardening quartet returning within thirty minutes with an engine issue, to be followed seventy minutes later by Sgt Crum and crew from the bombing brigade with W/T failure. The others pressed on to find a heavy flak barrage over the town and its port, which presented a clear and present danger to any aircraft venturing into its path, but petered out some four miles to the south-west. F/O Russel and crew tried three times to reach the aiming-point, but, on each occasion, they became coned in searchlights and bombarded by flak, which forced them to dive from 13,000 to 8,000 feet to break free. They were hit as they passed through 9,000 feet at 20.45, and then deposited the wing bombs onto a searchlight concentration to enable them to regain the lost altitude. They abandoned thoughts of attacking the primary target and turned for home, releasing the rest of the load over Borkum aerodrome from 11,000 feet. The others carried out their attacks from between 12,000 and 16,000 feet without observing the results in the glare of the defences. Meanwhile, the three gardeners, P/Os Weston and Whitecross and Sgt Grainger and their crews, had located the briefed drop zone, and planted their vegetables from between 600 and 1,000 feet. The Whitecross crew dropped their wing bombs onto a torpedo boat or flak ship off the island of Scharhörn from 3,000 feet, while the Grainger crew selected a road bridge over a railway line south of Esens, west along the coast from Jade Bay. They claimed a direct hit on one end, before strafing with all guns a small army convoy on the road.

Sir Richard Peirse had decided on launching one major raid each month on an important industrial city, for which Gelsenkirchen was selected on the 9th, and a force of 135 aircraft assembled. 5 Group detailed the Hemswell squadrons to take part, and the crews were briefed to aim for one of the synthetic oil plants, while four Finningley crews went mining in Kiel Bay. On the following night, the Scampton squadrons went in search of the Tirpitz again at

Wilhelmshaven, and Waddington took care of gardening duties. Lindholme was notified on the 12th that it would be responsible for bombing operations that night, along with an element from Hemswell, when the target for the second time was the Hipper class cruiser at Brest. The five 50 Squadron Hampdens took off between 16.00 and 16.40, four of them loaded with four 500 and two 250 pounders, while P/O Everitt and crew were carrying a single 2,000 pounder. F/L Johnston was the senior pilot on duty as they climbed away into nine to ten-tenths cloud that persisted all the way out over the Dorset coast and the Channel. It was only as the French coast drew near that the cloud began to disperse, and, by the time they reached Brest, the skies were clear and the target area clearly visible under the light of the moon. An intense searchlight and flak defence awaited them as they focussed on the dock layout, which could be identified, but none claimed to pick out the target vessel. The bombing runs were carried out on a variety of headings, and the bombs delivered from between 9,000 and 14,000 feet. After observing the impact of his 2,000 pounder, P/O Everitt reported red sparks followed by a pillar of white smoke rising to a few hundred feet from the water's edge. All were diverted to aerodromes in south-western England on return, because of continuing bad weather at home.

Gardening sorties awaited a dozen 5 Group crews on the 13th, who learned at briefing that the Jellyfish and Beech areas were to be their destinations, respectively off the Brittany ports of Brest and St-Nazaire. 50 Squadron assigned five crew to the former and two to the latter, and they departed Lindholme between 02.30 and 04.25, with F/L Rippingale the senior pilot on duty and last off the ground. It was clear from the start that the lateness of the take-off had put him and his crew under time pressure, and, on reaching Upper Heyford, they decided to turn back. This left four crews bound for the Jellyfish garden, and among them was the crew of P/O Burrough, who had lost oil pressure on the starboard engine shortly after take-off. They returned to Lindholme and circled the aerodrome until the pressure issue sorted itself out, before setting course again, only to adopt a track ten degrees south of the one they should have been on. This led them into barrage balloons at Gloucester, which they managed to avoid, before crossing the coast at 2,000 feet, below the cloud base. Clear skies greeted them at the French coast, and many small ships were seen, until cloud slid between them and the ground as they neared the target area. Pinpointing the drop zone became difficult even at 1,000 feet, and they were forced to take violent evasive action as they became the target for light flak. The vegetable was planted from 700 feet, while the wing bombs were to be dropped onto the previously spotted ships on the way home, but these were no longer visible because of cloud. P/O Thwaites and crew failed to establish a pinpoint from which to make a timed run to the drop, and chose a spot a mile-and-a-half south-south-east of the Saint-Mathieu lighthouse. Sgt Grainger and crew enjoyed a largely uneventful sortie up to planting their vegetable from 600 feet, and dropping their wing bombs on St-Malo from 1,000 feet. On the way home, however, they ran into severe icing conditions that caused the port engine to cut out repeatedly. They decided to put down at the first available airfield, which turned out to be St Eval, where they landed safely despite losing the starboard engine on final approach. F/O Russell and crew failed to identify the drop zone, and brought their vegetable and wing bombs back, having to dodge the Plymouth defences as they came within range between 09.00 and 09.15.

F/Os Weston and Whitecross and their crews had been assigned to the Beech garden, the former pinpointing on the Charpentier lighthouse, before making their timed run to deliver the vegetable from 450 feet. A vessel had been spotted off the lighthouse, and, once the mine had gone, this had been intended to be the target for the wing bombs, but a thirty-minute search failed to re-locate it. The 250 pounders were eventually released over what looked like an airfield near Meucon, north of Vannes. F/O Whitecross and crew delivered their store from 600 feet, before losing their W/T transmitter, which created problems for locating homing-beacons on the south coast on return. They cruised up and down a clear patch of the coast until daylight, when they were able to map-read their way home.

The Air Ministry had decided in a directive issued on the 15th of January, that an all-out assault against oil related targets would eventually take its toll on the German war effort, and operations from now on would reflect this. A list of seventeen sites was drawn up, the top nine of which represented 80% of Germany's synthetic oil production, but it was to be February before Peirse was able to comply. In the meantime, Hemswell sent seventeen Hampdens to Wilhelmshaven on the night of the 15/16th, and Waddington and Scampton a further fifteen on the 16/17th, on the latter occasion in adverse weather conditions and extreme cold. Lindholme remained inactive on these nights, and would continue to do so for the ensuing twelve nights, as a combination of heavy snow, thaw-generated flooding and fog conspired to keep 5 Group on the ground for the longest spell since the balloon went up in May.

When operations finally resumed for 5 Group on the 29th, Wilhelmshaven, or more specifically, the Tirpitz, was posted as the target yet again, for a force this time of nine Hampdens from Lindholme and twenty-five Wellingtons. A dozen 50 Squadron aircraft had been detailed, but technical difficulties grounded three of them late on, leaving the others to take-off between 02.55 and 04.04 on the 30th, with W/C Walker and S/L Good the senior pilots on duty, the latter having returned to duty after being on the sick list. F/O Woodward and crew had not even reached the coast before engine problems curtailed their sortie and forced them to return home. The others pressed on to encounter ten-tenths cloud that lay over the coastal regions and the North Sea at between 600 and 2,000 feet, preventing some from observing either the English of Dutch coasts. The usual flak greeting from the Frisian islands gave a clue to positions, and, by the time the target area drew near, the cloud had dispersed to leave clear skies and ground haze. Even so, not all would identify the aiming-point in the face of a spirited searchlight and flak response, and the late take-off would create a time pressure and discourage some from pressing on with the threat of daylight looming. P/O Grylls and crew bombed Borkum aerodrome from 2,000 feet after throttling back to fool the defences, and then strafed a searchlight and flak battery. P/O Thwaites and crew found no evidence of the target on e.t.a., and, with dawn fast approaching, attacked a flak concentration near Oldenburg on the way home. P/O Weston and crew failed to establish their position, and were somewhere in the target area when the probability of being trapped in daylight over enemy territory persuaded them to turn back at 07.10. W/C Walker and crew located the target area without difficulty in the light of flares from other aircraft, and carried out their attack from 13,000 feet, as did P/O Everitt and crew on their second run, observing three bursts followed by about twenty brilliant flashes and a fire. S/L Good and crew had been the last to take-off, as the reserve crew, and they were alerted to the target at 06.15 by the intensity of the flak. They bombed from 10,000 feet at 06.30, and observed a fire of reasonable size to break out. P/O Burrough and crew attacked from north-east to south-west from 11,000 feet, and several explosions were followed by a white fire estimated to be half-a-mile long. P/O Whitecross and crew were the others to locate and bomb the target, doing so from 14,000 feet and observing fires to break out.

In comparison with the second half of 1940, this had been a low-key month with just seven operations involving fifty sorties for the loss of a single Hampden in a landing crash, from which the crew walked away.

February 1941

A slow start to the new month meant that it was the 4th before twelve 50 Squadron crews were called to briefing, although the group had dispatched a dozen Hampdens to Brest on the night of the 2/3rd, and eleven more to lay mines off the port twenty-four hours later. In a new departure for the Command, 3, 4 and 5 Groups were assigned to their own individual targets, which, for 5 Group, would see thirty Hampdens heading for Düsseldorf in the Ruhr. The Lindholme element took off between 17.00 and 18.00 with F/Ls Johnston and Rippingale the senior pilots on duty. (The ORB lists only eleven crews). They exited the English coast at Orfordness before setting a direct course via the Scheldt estuary to the target, and enjoyed clear weather conditions up to within about ten minutes of the target, when eight to ten-tenths cloud obscured the ground. All reached the target area, where an intense searchlight and flak defence left them in no doubt that they were over the target, whether or not they caught a glimpse of it through small gaps in the cloud. P/O Powell and crew descended to below the cloud base at 3,500 feet, from which point they were able to map-read along the Rhine all the way to the city, where a dummy run was greeted by intense light flak, that left a hole in the starboard wing. A second run was made at 1,200 feet, and the high explosives and incendiaries were seen to burst, starting one very large fire in the centre of the target area. This low-level attack was the exception, and, apart from one by Sgt Crum and crew from 6,000 feet, the others chose bombing heights of between 10,000 and 14,000 feet, aiming mostly at the concentrations of flak and searchlight activity. Sgt Grainger and crew were put off by the low cloud, and turned towards the north-west in search of Wesel, a last resort target, where they attacked a railway junction and buildings to the east of the town from 4,000 feet. P/O Whitecross and crew were also defeated by the low cloud while flying at 8,000 feet, and went in search of a last-resort target, descending further until coming upon an aerodrome, which they bombed from 1,200 feet. The bombs fell among buildings, while the incendiaries overshot, and, almost immediately thereafter, a military vehicle was seen approaching, and was attacked with front guns. This forced it to turn up a side road, where it was fired upon by the rear gunners, and curious onlookers emerging from an adjacent factory were driven back inside by further bursts.

The weather deteriorated again to keep 5 Group on the ground on the next two nights, but the Group Meteorological Section staff managed to find a window of acceptable weather across the Channel on the north-eastern coast of France on the 7th. A dozen Scampton and fifteen Lindholme crews underwent briefing for a raid on shipping and dock installations at Dunkerque, for which the 50 Squadron element took off between 21.17 and 22.22 with W/C Walker the senior pilot on duty. His sortie lasted until the port engine began to overheat over the North Sea, and he jettisoned the bomb load over the Wash on the way home. The others were successful in reaching the target in perfect visibility that included moonlight, and identified the aiming-point, which was defended by searchlights and only heavy calibre flak. Bombing took place from a variety of altitudes between 4,000 and 10,300 feet either side of 23.00, and many detonations were observed across the docks. P/O Moore was temporarily blinded by a light coming on in the cockpit, while he and his crew were at 12,000 feet over the North Sea, but having regained his night vision, he pointed the Hampden's snout towards a concentration of searchlights and flak, that he assumed to be Dunkerque. On reaching the coast he turned onto a parallel course, and cruised up and down until dropping the bombs from 12,000 feet onto what turned out to be Ostend.

Lindholme sat out 5 Group operations by fifteen Hampdens to Mannheim on the night of the 8/9th, and by twenty-three on the following night, when the target was the Tirpitz at Wilhelmshaven. On both occasions, they were the only Bomber Command aircraft in action, and each attack was ineffective in the face of complete cloud cover. C-in-C Peirse had not yet implemented the January directive against Germany's synthetic oil industry, but would, once his monthly "Big" effort against a major industrial city had taken place. The northern city of Hannover was selected on the 10th, and a record number of 222 crews briefed to attack a variety of aiming-points. 5 Group notified all of its operational stations, and forty-six Hampdens were made ready, fourteen of them at Lindholme, where take-off was safely accomplished between 22.47 and 23.22, with S/Ls Good and Oxley the senior pilots on duty. The weather conditions were ideal, with clear skies and bright moonlight to assist navigation and map-reading, and all of the 50 Squadron participants reached the target area, pinpointing, initially, on the Steinhuder Lake to the west and then the Maschsee to the south of the city centre. The defence appeared to be limited to inaccurate light flak, which enabled crews to circle, if necessary, to establish their positions and decide on a method of attack. Some glided down from 10,000 to 8,000 feet, among them P/O Powell and crew, who continued to descend after bombing, and strafed three large barges on a canal from 100 feet. The others mostly favoured a higher-level attack from between 10,000 and 14,000 feet, and all reports by returning crews confirmed many explosions and fires, with buildings standing out black against the background of flames. A fire in the north of the city remained visible for fifty miles into the return flight, but, no reports came out of Hannover to confirm or deny the success of the operation.

On the following night, eleven Hampdens and eighteen Wellingtons returned to Hannover, while a force of seventy-nine aircraft, including five 50 Squadron Hampdens, set off for Bremen. They departed Lindholme between 17.50 and 19.00 with W/C Walker and S/L Good the senior pilots on duty, the latter the last to take off, after having to swap to the reserve aircraft. This put him and his crew well behind schedule, and, on the way across the North Sea over ten-tenths cloud, the decision was taken to attack Osnabrück as an alternative target. However, a faulty navigational instrument sent them off course, and, by the time a fix was obtained, which put them somewhere near Texel, they were already too late to carry out an attack and be back home by 23.59 as ordered. W/C Walker and crew set course over Skegness, and arrived over the cloud-covered Dutch coast reliant upon dead-reckoning to take them to the target. When close to e.t.a at Bremen, flares from other aircraft were observed, while black smoke puffs from exploding heavy flak shells and a few searchlights confirmed their close proximity to the primary target. The 1,900lb bomb was released from 10,000 feet and a photo taken, and a yellowish flash in the target area was followed by a fire. F/O Weston and crew found the flak to be intense and the heavy calibre particularly accurate as they bombed from 12,000 feet, but cloud hid the results. P/O Whitecross and crew found a small gap in the cloud that revealed the River Weser below, and the bombs were dropped from 11,000 feet as the gap closed to conceal the outcome. F/L Rippingale and crew were unable to locate Bremen through the cloud, and continued north to seek more favourable conditions at the coast. The coastline was identified at Wilhelmshaven, and the bombs were released over the port from 9,000 feet in the face of intense anti-aircraft fire. The flashes of bomb bursts were followed by a huge explosion, the glow from which remained visible for fifteen minutes. Fog over the bomber stations at home caused twenty-two aircraft to crash or be abandoned by their crews, but there were no such incidents involving Lindholme crews among the three from 5 Group.

5 Group sat out bombing operations against oil targets at Gelsenkirchen and Homberg on the 14th, but ordered Lindholme to send eleven Hampdens to the Deodars garden in the Gironde estuary region of south-western France. They all flew to St Eval in Cornwall as a forward staging post, and took off from there between 01.20 and 02.28, with S/L Good the senior pilot on duty. The weather conditions were generally fair, apart from rain showers emanating from seven-tenths cloud in the target area with a base at 3,000 feet. Pin-points were established with ease on nearby landmarks and timed runs made to the drop zone, where the vegetables were delivered from between 600 and 800 feet. Wing bombs were dropped on a variety of targets, shipping in the Gironde, a flak position at Pointe-de-Grave, the largest vessel in a convoy, aerodromes at La Rochelle and Les-Sables-d'Olonne, and ships at berth in the harbour at Concarneau. F/Os Russell and Woodward reported observing a large fire at 04.30, with black smoke rising from it, half a mile inland on the South Bank of the estuary. On investigating it from 100 feet, F/O Russell believed it resembled a crashed Hampden, and the failure to return of X2983 with the crew of P/O Tunstall was confirmation that the squadron had lost its first crew in 1941. News would eventually be received that both pilots had lost their lives, and that the gunners were in enemy hands.

On the 20th, Finningley was transferred out of 5 Group to be taken over by 7 Operational Training Group, and the evicted 106 Squadron moved south to take up residence at Coningsby. 5 Group would be out in force on the 21st when sending forty-two Hampdens to plant vegetables in the Jellyfish garden off the port of Brest. 50 Squadron would be responsible for fourteen of them, and they departed Lindholme between 18.20 and 18.45 with S/L Good the senior pilot on duty. They exited England over the Dorset coast, and set course for the target area in predominantly favourable conditions, encountering cloud over the Channel, which had dispersed to five-tenths at 2,000 feet by the time that the target area drew near. Pin-points were established with ease in good visibility, particularly at Pointe-Saint-Mathieu on the headland west of the port, where searchlights ensnared some of the attackers and flak ships took pot-shots at them as they made their timed runs. All successfully planted their vegetables into the briefed locations from between 450 and 900 feet, before returning safely to land either in south-west England or at base.

5 Group would spend the next two nights on the ground, while a small force of Wellingtons targeted enemy warships at Brest on the 22nd and the docks at Boulogne twenty-four hours later. When orders arrived on 5 Group stations on the 24th, they signalled the introduction to operations of a new squadron and aircraft type. 207 Squadron had completed its working-up programme with the Manchester at Waddington, and would contribute six of the type to this night's raid by fifty-seven aircraft on enemy warships at Brest. It had been a difficult gestation period for the squadron, and the coming operational career of the Manchester would be dogged by grounding orders caused largely by the unreliability of its Rolls-Royce Vulture engines. Despite this, and ignorant of the full extent of the problems that would occur, orders would be issued on the following day to reform 97 Squadron as the second Manchester unit.

5 Group detailed eighteen Hampdens to join the Manchesters on this night, and thirteen of them were made ready at Lindholme. They took off between 17.50 and 18.10 with W/C Walker and S/L Good the senior pilots on duty, but the commanding officer was forced to land at Upper Heyford to rectify an ailing accumulator. When running up the engines prior to taking off again, the one on the port side was found to be dropping revolutions and the sortie was abandoned. P/O Cornish and crew also returned early with an engine issue, leaving the others to press on to find the target under clear skies and good visibility, although searchlights and flak had advertised the whereabouts of the port from some distance away. Bombing took place from between 10,000 and 15,000 feet in the face of numerous searchlights and intense flak of all calibres, although few observed the bursts in the glare of the defensive activity. P/O Weston and crew ran up on the target at 8,000 feet, only to realize that it was the wrong dock. They pulled away to make another approach, and climbed to 10,000 feet, whereupon the starboard engine failed, and the second pass had to be carried out on one engine. The defences were at their most intense at the time, and the Hampden was becoming difficult to control, which persuaded P/O Weston to release the bombs short of the aiming-point on the eastern side of the dock. They escaped the flak, and the dead engine came back to life just after crossing the French coast homebound, but it would fail again five miles from base and force a single-engine landing.

Lindholme Hampdens were not included among the twenty-two detailed to join fifty-eight other aircraft from 1, 3 and 4 Groups for a raid on Düsseldorf on the 25th, which probably focused on oil-related targets. Poor weather conditions and ten-tenths cloud attended the operation, and only around seven bomb loads fell within the city. Cologne was posted as the target on the 26th, for which twenty-eight Hampdens and five Manchesters were made ready on 5 Group stations, ten of the former at Lindholme. The crews were briefed to attack one of two specific aiming-points in the city, and took off as part of an overall force of 126 aircraft between 18.40 and 19.10 with F/Ls Johnston and Rippingale the senior pilots on duty. The newly-promoted F/O Weston and crew had barely exited the coast at Orfordness when the oxygen system failed and forced them to turn back, leaving the others to continue on in favourable weather conditions. They reached the target under clear skies, guided by the many fires already burning and huge pillars of smoke rising from the centre of the target area. Numerous searchlights ringed the city, but the flak was remarkably light for such a well-defended target, and one crew spent an hour circling, while seeking out the briefed aiming-point. Most picked up the Rhine to the south of the city, suggesting, perhaps, that the Wesseling oil plant was the specific target, and crossed from east to west to deliver their bombs from between 7,000 and 14,000 feet. Returning crews were confident of a highly successful raid, while local reports mentioned only ten high-explosive bombs and ninety incendiaries falling on the western edge of the city, with more hitting three villages.

Lindholme sat out the final 5 Group operation of the month on the 28th, which was another cloud-ruined wasted effort to hit the Tirpitz at Wilhelmshaven. The irreconcilable dichotomy between Bomber Command claims and local reports would continue throughout the year and beyond, and would culminate in a damning report in the coming August that would threaten the very existence of an independent bomber force. During the course of the month the squadron took part in eight bombing and gardening operations, dispatching ninety-four sorties for the loss of a single Hampden and crew.

The new month began with a return to Cologne on the night of the 1/2nd by an initial force of 131 assorted aircraft, of which forty-four Hampdens were provided by 5 Group. The eleven 50 Squadron aircraft departed Lindholme between 19.20 and 20.15 with W/C Walker and S/L Good the senior pilots on duty, and lost only F/L Rippingale and crew to an overheating engine and unserviceable intercom. The remainder enjoyed favourable weather conditions over the North Sea, and were able to firmly establish their positions as they made landfall over the Scheldt estuary and headed across Holland. They arrived in the target area to find clear skies and easily identifiable ground features, predominantly the distinctive bends in the River Rhine, which provided most with the references they required to run in on the briefed aiming-point. Bombs were delivered from a variety of altitudes up to 16,000 feet in the face of an intense defensive response, those from the lower levels after a glide or dive attack. Sgt Grainger and crew were held in a searchlight cone at 10,500 feet, and released their bombs as they passed through 6,000 feet on their way down to 3,000 feet, where they were chased by a night-fighter with a searchlight in its nose. It was driven off by two bursts from the rear gunner, before two light flak batteries in the north-west of the city were strafed from 2,000 feet and silenced. On return, and after flying around the area for some time in deteriorating weather conditions, X2984 crashed into high ground at Wold Newton, nine miles north-west of Bridlington in Yorkshire, at 03.35. P/O Pexton and two others survived with minor injuries, and returned to the squadron next day to report the sad news that the second pilot/navigator, Sgt Richards, had lost his life. He would be buried with full military honours in the Hatfield Woodhouse cemetery. Other returning crews claimed to have observed many explosions and fires in Cologne, and local reports confirmed substantial damage to warehousing in the docks areas on both banks of the Rhine, the sinking of two Rhine steamers and the destruction of more than eighty houses.

Lindholme would now spend an extended period off the Order of Battle, and would miss operations against the Hipper class cruiser at Brest on the 2nd and 3rd, and a return to Cologne also on the 3rd. Thereafter, the weather took a hand to keep most of the Command on the ground for the next week, and it was during this period, on the 9th, that the Air Ministry responded to the urgent and burgeoning threat posed by U-Boots, which were claiming a massive tonnage of shipping crossing the Atlantic in convoys with vital war supplies. A new Directive was issued, which would unleash a concerted campaign against this menace and its partner in crime, the Focke-Wulf Kondor long-range maritime reconnaissance bomber. These two threats were to be attacked where-ever they could be found, at sea, in their bases in the occupied ports, and at their point of manufacture in the shipyards and in the assembly and component factories. A new target list was drawn up, which was headed by Kiel, Hamburg and Vegesack (Bremen), all of which were home to U-Boot construction yards, and Bremen itself, which also boasted a Focke-Wulf aircraft factory in its south-eastern Hemelingen district. Other related targets included the diesel engine plants at Mannheim and Augsburg, aircraft factories at Dessau, and, of course, the U-Boot bases at Brest, Lorient and St Nazaire. Until otherwise instructed, this was to be the focus of Peirse's efforts, and, only occasionally, would he be able prosecute the oil campaign.

When 5 Group resumed operations on the 10th, only Hemswell and Waddington were involved in sending nineteen Hampdens back to Cologne, where good results were claimed by returning crews. The new directive would be implemented first on the night of the 12/13th, at the end of a day of hectic activity across the Command, as aircraft were made ready for three major raids to be conducted that night. Eighty-eight aircraft were to attack the Blohm & Voss shipyards at Hamburg, while eighty-six other crews were briefed for the Focke-Wulf factory and the city of Bremen, and, finally, seventy-two aircraft were prepared for the long slog to Berlin to target two aiming-points. 5 Group was to support the first-mentioned with forty Hampdens and four Manchesters, and the last-mentioned with thirty Hampdens, and, with the addition of a single freshman crew on gardening duties, this represented the largest effort undertaken by the group thus far in the war. The four Manchesters and three 4 Group Halifaxes at Hamburg would be the first of their type to operate over Germany. 50 Squadron was to be involved in both operations, briefing eight crews for Germany's Capital City and six for its Second City, and it was the latter element that departed Lindholme first between 18.53 and 19.15, with F/L Rippingale the senior pilot on duty. The Berlin element would remain on the ground for a further three hours before getting away between 22.30 and 22.47 led by S/L Good, by which time their colleagues would be in the thick of it over Hamburg.

They had arrived in the target area to find what were described as perfect weather conditions, which allowed easy identification of the aiming-point, once they had run the usual gauntlet of intense searchlights and flak from both banks of the Elbe. P/O Cornish and crew dived from 15,000 down to 12,000 feet to release the bombs, and Sgt Grainger and crew from 13,000 to 9,000 feet, while three others attacked on the straight and level from between 11,000 and 14,000 feet. F/L Rippingale found X2919 reluctant to climb on reaching the North Bank of the Elbe, and dropped two 250 pounders from 6,000 feet onto the Kiel Canal at 22.45 to get rid of some of the weight. Following an unsuccessful run across the aiming-point, the remaining bombs were dropped onto a large railway junction on the north-eastern outskirts of the city, and, although searchlight dazzle prevented observation of the bursts, a large fire was seen to develop as he and his crew beat a retreat. The effectiveness of the operation was confirmed by local reports, which spoke of substantial damage to the Blohm & Voss yards, where offices and slipways had been hit, and four other shipyards had also been afflicted.

Meanwhile, P/O Thwaites and crew had turned back from Berlin because of an engine issue when two hours out. Further to the east, S/L Good had pinpointed himself some thirty miles south of Berlin at 04.15, and concluded that it was too late to push on to the target. It was decided to bomb factory buildings at Elster, a town some fifty-five miles south west of Berlin as a last-resort objective, and this was carried out from 14,000 feet and resulted in six fires. Afterwards, it became a race against time to reach the safety of the North Sea before dawn broke, and the use of full throttle all the way ensured success. P/O Burrough and crew inadvertently stumbled over Brandenburg on the way to Berlin, and found themselves in the centre of a searchlight and flak barrage. There was no escape from the defences as they carried out a dive attack on the aiming-point from 12,000 feet, before a change in wind direction sent them back over Brandenburg for a further dose of pain on the way home. F/O Russell and crew blamed haze and smoke for their failure to locate the aiming-point, and they bombed a railway junction at Nowawes, two miles east of Potsdam from 14,000 feet, claiming a vivid, yellow flash followed by a fire that remained visible for some distance. Three other crews returned to report carrying out their attacks from between 11,500 and 13,000 feet, and this left just F/L Johnston and crew unaccounted for. AD721 had crashed somewhere in the Berlin area, and there had been no survivors from this experienced crew, whose presence at Lindholme would be missed.

Weather conditions remained favourable as preparations were put in hand on the 13th to return to Hamburg that night with a force of 139 aircraft, including a contribution from 5 Group of thirty-four Hampdens and five Manchesters. 50 Squadron made ready six Hampdens and dispatched them from Lindholme between 19.00 and 19.25 with F/L Rippingale the senior pilot on duty. They crossed the Yorkshire coast over Flamborough Head and made their way independently of each other, as was the practice at this stage of the war, towards the enemy coast. P/O Cornish and crew were some ten miles north of the Frisian island of Borkum heading east, when a Me110 passed two thousand feet beneath them on a northerly course. A few minutes later it appeared on the starboard quarter lining up for an attack. P/O Cornish throttled back immediately to 110 m.p.h., and, at point-blank range, one of the gunners fired several bursts. The assailant was seen to dive steeply, chased by a long burst of .303 shells from the rear gunner, and was lost to sight just above the surface of the sea. They continued on to the target, where moonlight helped with identification of the aiming-point, and the bombs were released from 14,000 feet. P/O Hill and crew found themselves in the thick of accurate searchlights with heavy flak shells and light tracer in close proximity, and tried the tactic of throttling back to evade attention. The ploy was unsuccessful, and they beat a hasty retreat after delivering their bombs from 13,500 feet. P/O Thwaites and crew found the heavy flak to be inaccurate, and remained unmolested as they carried out their attack from 12,000 feet on a north-westerly heading. P/O Moore and crew approached from the north to drop their load from 14,000 feet, and observed huge fires already burning on the bank opposite the target, along with large volumes of smoke. F/L Rippingale and crew attacked from 11,000 feet, confirming the presence of fires and the intensity of the defences. X3146 failed to return with the crew of Sgt Grainger, who were duly posted missing. The expectation that news would eventually arrive to shed light on the missing aircraft and crew was disappointed, and no trace of aircraft and crew was ever found. Returning crews were enthusiastic about the outcome of the raid, and this was confirmed by local reports and post-raid reconnaissance, which revealed further damage to the Blohm & Voss shipyards and 119 fires in Hamburg generally, thirty-five of them classed by local authorities as large.

A raid on the Hydriewerk-Scholven synthetic oil refinery at Gelsenkirchen was briefed out to twenty-one Hampden crews on the 14th, four of them representing 50 Squadron. They were part of an overall force of 101 aircraft assigned to a number of similar targets in the city, and departed Lindholme between 19.05 and 19.15 with F/O Russell the senior pilot on duty. They made landfall over the Scheldt estuary, and observed large fires from the oil storage tanks at Rotterdam, which had just been attacked by Whitleys and Blenheims. The glow was still visible from the Ruhr as they closed on the target, where fires were also already burning and smoke beginning to drift across to obscure ground detail. F/O Russell attacked from 10,500 feet on an east-south-easterly heading at 22.20, and the bomb bursts were followed by a dull, orange fire that emitted a column of black smoke rising through 11,000 feet as they turned for home. P/O Whitecross and crew carried out the initial approach at 13,000 feet before gliding down to release the bombs from 6,000 feet onto a large factory, which may have been the refinery, but was, at least, close to it. Sgt Ormonroyd and crew were unable to identify the primary target through the smoke and industrial haze, and bombed the approximate position from 10,000 feet heading south-west. By the time that P/O Grylls and crew arrived over the Ruhr, the haze and smoke from Gelsenkirchen had become impenetrable, and they made their way to the south-west to run across the centre of Düsseldorf and empty their bomb bay from 10,000 feet near some fires that were already burning. Local reports suggested that this was the most destructive raid yet on Gelsenkirchen, where some useful damage had been inflicted on the Scholven-Buer refinery, which lost total production for a brief spell, and adjacent workers housing had also been hit. It was, however, still pinprick stuff, and it would be a further two years before this and other Ruhr production centres felt the full force of a Bomber Command attack.

Hemswell, Lindholme and Waddington were notified of a return to the Ruhr on the 15th, this time to attack a specific target in Düsseldorf. 50 Squadron made ready six Hampdens, and dispatched them between 18.49 and 19.15 with S/L Good the senior pilot on duty. After experiencing haze over base, they enjoyed good visibility with cloud east of the Trent all the way to the Dutch coast, where the skies cleared. With ten miles to go they hit a wall of searchlights, but, surprisingly, no flak, and S/L Good employed the "throttle-back-and-glide" method to avoid attracting attention. The moon had risen as the crews were outbound, and its light glinted off the Rhine to offset the effects of the industrial haze and provide a firm pinpoint. S/L Good and crew noticed that some incendiaries had been dropped on the wrong side of the river as they delivered their load from 12,000 feet, now under fire, and buildings stood out in the flash of the detonations. P/O Burrough and crew underwent an eventful outward flight, first coming upon a flarepath, and falling into the clutches of a concentration of searchlights, which proved difficult to shake off. At the target, they then found themselves under intense anti-aircraft fire that forced them down from 13,000 to 3,000 feet, but climbed again to 12,000 feet to deliver their bombs. On the way home they strafed an aerodrome in Belgium from 50 feet, firing four hundred rounds into an open building, before being diverted along with the others to Tangmere, near the Sussex coast. They landed safely at 01.25, minutes after which, the flarepath was bombed by the Luftwaffe, S/L Good managing to sneak in between salvoes. The remaining crews reported carrying out their attacks from between 8,000 and 14,000 feet, P/O Cornish and crew specifying a marshalling yard as the target for their bombs.

It fell to Scampton and Coningsby to provide eighteen Hampdens on the 17th for a force of fifty-seven aircraft targeting shipyards in Bremen. The raid took place in excellent conditions in the presence of the first Stirling to operate over Germany, and returning crews claimed a successful outcome. Thirty-eight Hampdens and two Manchesters were detailed by 5 Group on the 18th for an operation that night against the Deutsche Werke U-Boot yards at Kiel, which would also involve fifty-seven Wellingtons and Whitleys. 50 Squadron dispatched eight Hampdens between 18.20 and 19.00, with the intention that they would fly out in formation until daylight faded, but P/O Grylls and crew were soon forced to drop out with an unserviceable artificial horizon. F/L Rippingale was the senior pilot on duty as the rest made their way out over Flamborough Head to encounter ten-tenths cloud that persisted all the way to the target. This prevented him and his crew from establishing a pinpoint on the enemy coast, and it was only when approaching e.t.a., that searchlight and flak activity alerted them to the location of the target area. Even so, the bombs were withheld, and a course set for home, and it was soon afterwards when a collection of lights appeared through a gap in the clouds, and the bombs were released. P/O Burrough and crew bombed from 13,000 feet on estimated position on a southerly heading, and F/O Weston and crew followed suit from a thousand feet higher. In contrast, Sgt Ormonroyd and crew established an excellent pinpoint on Nordstrand, and followed the searchlight and flak activity to the southern boundary of the target, before running across it from east to west, observing the gun flashes to reflect in the harbour water. The bombs were released from 14,000 feet, and the bursts witnessed, but no detail could be gleaned in the searchlight glare. F/O Russell and crew seemed to be in the thick of searchlight and flak activity from the moment they made landfall on the enemy coast. They ran across the target area from north to south at 13,000 feet to deliver their bombs, which were seen to burst and be followed by a large explosion. P/O Moore and crew had arrived north of the target, and circled to make their approach to the aiming-point from the north-west at 17,000 feet, whence no results could be observed. P/O Powell and crew circled round to the south at an even higher 19,000 feet, and dropped their load onto the estimated position of the target. Local reports would claim this to be the heaviest raid yet on Kiel, mentioning an increase in the number of incendiaries, and confirming damage to the U-Boot yards.

The main effort on the night of the 20/21st was directed towards the mining of the waters off the Biscay ports of Brest, Lorient and St Nazaire, for which forty-three Hampdens were made ready, while a force of twenty-one Whitleys and three Manchesters turned their attention upon the U-Boot base being built on the Keroman peninsular on the southern extremity of Lorient. The first phase of the massive construction project had begun just weeks earlier, and would continue until January 1942, by which time K1, K2 and K3 would be completed and capable of sheltering thirty vessels and their crews under cover. The complex would boast a revolutionary lift system, which could raise U-Boots from the water and transport them across the facility to repair and servicing bays. The thickness of the concrete would, ultimately, render the structure impervious to the bombs available to Bomber Command at the time, and attacks would be directed predominantly at the town and its approaches to prevent German access by road and rail. However, that lay in the future, and the Waddington-based Manchester crews had been briefed to aim their SAP bombs at U-Boots if they could be found. 50 Squadron loaded a vegetable into each of ten Hampdens, while briefing the crews for the Artichokes garden in the approaches to Lorient, through which U-Boots would have to pass on their way in and out. They departed Lindholme between 18.15 and 18.27 with S/L Good the senior pilot on duty, and crossed the south coast in daylight, most to enjoy a quiet outward flight to the target area, where the port defences were in action against the bombing brigade. The skies were clear, with visibility at around five miles as they planted their vegetables into the briefed locations from 500 to 800 feet from 21.30 onwards. P/O Moore and crew dropped their wing bombs onto an aerodrome from 10,000 feet on their way to the garden at 20.30, while most found no suitable targets for theirs and brought them home. As they were homebound at midnight, Lindholme was asked to provide another crew for mining duties in the Jellyfish garden off Brest, and W/C Walker put himself and his crew forward. It was, perhaps, fortunate that P/O Burrough had found an aerodrome or seaplane base for his wing bombs on one of the small islands to the north-west of Lannion, as he undershot the flarepath on approach to Lindholme at 00.32 and wrecked AD742 to register his second incident of the year. W/C Walker and crew took off at 02.20, after the others had all landed, by which time the Channel was covered by fog and haze that concealed navigational pinpoints from view. Fortunately, visibility improved markedly at the French coast, and the moon rose as the garden was reached. The vegetable was planted unopposed from 600 feet, and it was only after setting course for home that the tracer from light flak batteries came up through the clouds behind.

Twelve Hampdens returned to Lorient on the night of 21/22nd, and encountered poor visibility that led to scattered bombing, while, a handful of others went mining in the Deodars garden off the Gironde Estuary on the approaches to Bordeaux. With the moon out of commission for a period, and weather conditions over northern Germany unfavourable, 5 Group sent thirty

Hampdens to Kiel on the 23rd, three representing 50 Squadron, while Berlin played host to a force of sixty-three Wellingtons and Whitleys. Two of the Lindholme trio, Sgt Ormonroyd and P/O Moore, took off at 19.10, to be followed at 19.35 by P/O Grylls, and P/O Moore and crew were well out over the North Sea when the intercom gremlins struck and forced them to turn back. The other two encountered heavy cloud over the North Sea until reaching the enemy coast, where it thinned sufficiently to allow pinpoints to be identified. Sgt Ormonroyd made landfall near Sylt and attracted the attention of a number of searchlights and accurate flak. They arrived in the target area at 16,000 feet, and glided down to 11,000 feet for the release of the bombs, which were seen to burst and set off a fire. P/O Grylls and crew crossed the Danish coast, and set course for the eastern side of the Schleswig-Holstein peninsular, where the horizontal visibility was good, but mist concealed ground detail. After searching for thirty minutes, they dropped the bombs from 15,000 feet, and observed the incendiaries burning, but no other results. At Berlin, cloud cover had led to scattered bombing, and returning crews had nothing of use to report at debriefing.

Düsseldorf was posted as one of the targets on the 27th, for which a force of thirty-nine aircraft was made ready, consisting of twenty-two Hampdens, thirteen Whitleys and four Manchesters representing 207 Squadron. Industrial haze provided the usual challenges, and no assessment of the results could be offered. On the 29th, the German cruisers Scharnhorst and Gneisenau were reported to be off Brest, and 50 Squadron was ordered to dispatch six Hampdens from Lindholme to carry out a cloud-cover daylight attack. Such operations would come to be known as "moling". The arrival of the vessels must have been expected, because Lindholme had been standing-by at two-hours readiness for seven days when the order was received. W/C Walker led them away between 16.40 and 16.45, and they formed into two vics of three to fly out via Upper Heyford, Start Point and the Lizard, until insufficient cloud cover over the Channel forced them to turn back. That night, twenty-five Hampdens were dispatched to mine the approaches to the port, but, by the following day, the warships had taken up what amounted to a permanent residency. Their presence at Brest as a fleet-in-being would represent a constant distraction for the Command, and necessitate the mounting of frequent operations against the port over the next eleven months. W/C Walker again took the lead as six 50 Squadron Hampdens took off shortly after 14.00 on the 30th to meet up with another six over Hemswell. They then adopted the same course as on the previous day, and, on reaching the Lizard, could see forty miles of clear sky stretching out before them. Despite this, they continued on for thirty miles, at which point, with clear blue sky as far as the eye could see, they abandoned the operation and returned home with their bombs.

During the course of that day, 109 aircraft were made ready to carry out the first concerted effort to bomb the vessels, and among them were fourteen Hampdens and four 207 Squadron Manchesters. 50 Squadron was not involved in the operation, which scored no hits on what would prove to be an elusive pair of targets, but sent four Hampdens to join forces with six from 106 Squadron to mine the waters of the Jellyfish garden off Brest. The 50 Squadron ORB provides no details of the crews involved or take-off times, but the timing of a strafing attack on a flak ship off Pointe-Saint-Mathieu at 22.25 provides an indication, while the Coningsby element remained on the ground until departing either side of 01.00. One 50 Squadron crew failed to locate the target area after slogging through ten-tenths cloud and sleet showers over the Channel, and finding intense darkness to add to the challenges over the garden. The other three crews reported a layer of three to four-tenths cloud between 2,000 and

4,000 feet over the garden, where two of them successfully planted their vegetables, while the third one found an alternative location.

During the course of the month the squadron took part in thirteen operations, and dispatched seventy-nine sorties for the loss of two Hampdens, one complete crew and one other crew member.

April 1941

The first week of the new month was reserved exclusively for operations on and around Brest with the intention of disabling its lodgers. It began with 5 Group launching a dozen Hampdens from St Eval in Cornwall for a daylight attack on the 1st, when all but one turned back in the absence of cloud, and the one that continued on, failed to return. 49 and 83 Squadrons sent six Hampdens each from their Scampton base to St Eval for another attempt on the 3rd, with similar results. Ninety other aircraft were made ready on the 3rd to attack the German cruisers that night, and returning crews reported that it had proved difficult to identify them. While that raid was in progress, 5 Group Hampdens had conducted mining sorties in the waters off Brest and La Rochelle.

On the 4th, Gneisenau entered a dry dock, which was to be drained on the following day for an inspection of the vessel, while, over at Waddington, 207 Squadron was called into action to make ready four Manchesters for yet another attempt on the enemy cruisers that night as part of a force of fifty-four aircraft. Five of the eleven participating Hampdens carried out low-level attacks, and among these was the 106 Squadron commanding officer, whose aircraft was seen to be shot down. A claim was made of a direct hit on one of the ships, while the Continental Hotel in the town was also struck by bombs just as dinner was being served, and a number of naval officers were killed. When Gneisenau's dry dock was drained on the following day, the 5th, a single unexploded bomb was found nestling at the bottom, and the ship's captained decided to move his vessel out into the harbour while it was dealt with. The dock was refilled to allow Gneisenau to vacate it, and she was spotted by a reconnaissance aircraft at some point, which led to an operation being planned by Coastal Command to be carried out at first light on the 6th.

In the meantime, on the 5th, 44 and 50 Squadrons were ordered to prepare six Hampdens each for another daylight operation to be launched from St Eval. The 50 Squadron crews took off between 12.00 and 12.06, and formed two sections of three aircraft, section 1 consisting of S/L Good, P/O Macrossan and P/O Cornish, and section 2 of P/O Burrough, Sgt Willett and P/O Moore. The weather conditions were extremely poor, with ten-tenths low cloud, and, by the time that they had passed south of the Isles of Scilly, they were in rain at 500 feet. In the second section, Sgt Willett and P/O Moore lost contact with P/O Burrough, and, with no prospect of being able to fulfil the brief, decided to turn back. As they did so, the Moore crew observed a burst of flame spreading across the sea, but had no clue as to the cause. Now alone P/O Burrough and crew were in the process of losing contact with the lead section, when they were almost hit by another Hampden, which appeared to be out of control and heading for the sea. P/O Cornish also witnessed the incident involving AD753, which contained the crew of P/O Macrossan, who were operating with the squadron for the first time. They watched it turn violently to port and dive, before being lost to sight and leaving a trail of flames on the sea along with pieces of wreckage. S/L Good had already decided to break formation because of the impossible conditions, and was aware that P/O Macrossan had fallen behind and crashed. He climbed to 5,000 feet where the cloud was broken, and instructed the others to follow him, P/Os Burrough and Cornish complying, and doing their best to hang on as they turned towards the target and climbed to 8,000 feet. The weather became even worse as they navigated by dead-reckoning towards Brest, and, somehow, they managed to remain in contact, until the order to attack was given. As S/L Good dived down, he caught sight of the ground from 3,000 feet, and finally broke cloud at around 400 feet, finding himself to be to the west of Douarnenez Bay. It was at this point that he threw in the towel and headed for home, to be followed by P/Os Borrough and Cornish, the latter having dropped his bombs on e.t.a., after also descending and failing to break cloud.

The Coastal Command operation on the 6th took place in poor weather conditions, which led to the six Beauforts becoming separated while outbound, and F/O Campbell and his crew alone pressed home an attack, which caused damage to Gneisenau that would require six months to repair. In the face of the most concentrated anti-aircraft fire, the Beaufort stood little chance of getting away with it, and was shot down without survivors. F/O Campbell was posthumously awarded a Victoria Cross for his actions.

The naval port of Kiel was posted as the target for a major operation on the 7th, for which a force of 229 aircraft was assembled. 5 Group contributed sixty-one Hampdens, nine of which were made ready at Lindholme. They took off between 20.10 and 20.35 with S/L Good the senior pilot on duty, but lost the services of P/O Powell and crew to a starboard engine issue shortly after crossing the coast at Flamborough Head. The others set course for Rømø Island on Denmark's western coast, where they would turn east to a position north of Flensburg, in order to approach Kiel from the north. They encountered cloud at 6,000 feet for the first fifty miles of the North Sea crossing, but then clear skies for the remainder of the outward flight. The defences had already been stirred into action by the time that the 50 Squadron participants arrived, but, at least, the bright moonlight helped to tone down the glare from dozens of searchlights. Medium calibre flak batteries were hosing shells up to 12,000 feet, with heavy flak reaching as high as 18,000 feet, and the light stuff awaiting any crew foolhardy enough to try to sneak in lower down. The Lindholme crews bombed from between 12,000 and 17,500 feet, noting many fires, which remained visible for up to eighty miles into the homeward leg. Returning crews were confident that the raid, which had taken place over a period of almost five hours, had struck a major blow against this important target, and this was confirmed by local reports of widespread damage to housing in the town, and to port facilities and the eastern docks area. The nightshift workers at the Germania Werft and Deutsche Werke U-Boot construction yards had been sent home, causing a number of days' loss of production.

A force of 160 aircraft was made ready during the following day to return to Kiel that night, and among them were twenty-nine Hampdens and twelve Manchesters, four of the latter belonging to 5 Group's latest addition, 97 Squadron, which would be operating for the first time. 50 Squadron briefed eight crews, who departed Lindholme between 19.45 and 20.20 with W/C Walker the senior pilot on duty. Five of the Hampdens were carrying a single 1,900lb bomb and incendiaries, while the others were loaded with a mixture of 500 and 250 pounders, also with incendiaries. They were to follow the same route as on the previous night, and, once again, they met a band of cloud at Flamborough Head that extended from 3,000 to 6,000 feet. Climbing through it they encountered severe icing conditions, and F/L Rippingale struggled to 10,000 feet, still coated, with chunks of ice smashing against the fuselage as they were flung from the propellers and hubs. Unable to gain further altitude, he descended to 1,500 feet to seek a channel of milder air, and, on failing to do so, turned for home. The cloud dispersed from 5 degrees east, to leave clear skies and bright moonlight that would aid map-reading after landfall, but P/O Cooke and crew were forced to turn back with engine problems when within thirty miles of the Danish coast. The others pressed on to establish firm pinpoints, and each adopted a glide approach to bomb, all but one releasing their load from between 13,000 and 17,000 feet. The exception was P/O Powell and crew, who glided down from 12,000 to 9,000 feet, and watched their bombs burst on the quayside. They continued to shed altitude to 7,000 feet as they swung back towards the north, only to be ensnared by a searchlight co-operating with a night-fighter that latched onto the Hampden's tail. The rear gunner drove the assailant off with a burst, and then the starboard engine cut, sending the aircraft into a flat spin. This was corrected, but it was not possible to maintain height, and the crew was preparing to ditch, when the engine returned to life at 3,000 feet, and gave no further trouble. They couldn't know, but they had just exhausted their ration of good fortune.

Lindholme was not involved in a raid on Berlin on the night of the 9/10th, which 5 Group supported with twenty-four Hampdens, but orders were received on the 10th to prepare for a joint 4 and 5 Group effort against Düsseldorf. The main operation on this night was another assault on Brest and its guest enemy warships, for which fifty-three aircraft were made ready, including five Manchesters of 97 Squadron to represent 5 Group. A rare training accident that afternoon cost 50 Squadron the recently arrived Sgt Campbell and one other, when AD830 crashed at 15.30 into houses in the Evington district of Leicester, where a civilian was also killed. Eight 50 Squadron crews took off between 19.30 and 19.50, with another new recruit, twenty-seven-year-old S/L William Mulford the senior pilot on duty. He had been posted in to succeed S/L Oxley as flight a commander, the latter having completed his tour of operations. He and his crew had actually taken off at 19.40, but had to return immediately to have the aerial repaired, and got away again last at 20.00. They were part of a 5 Group force of twenty-nine Hampdens and twenty-four Whitleys, on what would prove to be a sobering night for the former. They were routed out over Orfordness, Knokke and Aachen, and had to contend with poor visibility as the headed out via Orfordness to encounter haze and cloud over the North Sea. Conditions were not appreciably better over enemy territory, but most were able to map-read their way to the target area, which was found to be covered by the usual industrial haze and medium-level cloud.

By that time, P/O Pexton and crew had turned back, having reached Ostend at 14,000 feet and noticed a drop in oil pressure in the port engine. F/L Rippingale and crew seemed to find the target very easily after picking up the Rhine through the haze, and carried out their attack from 12,000 feet, reporting an unusually modest flak response, but many searchlights working in cones. S/L Mulford and crew maintained a height of 18,000 feet before descending to 13,000 to search for the target, which proved elusive until being identified after more than thirty minutes. P/O Cooke and crew found themselves making landfall over the French coast after a navigational error had led them astray, and experienced difficulty in establishing pinpoints as they set a new course for the target. On e.t.a., they circled, but failed to recognise any ground features, and dropped their bombs from 16,000 feet onto a large factory on the West Bank of the Rhine some nine miles south of Düsseldorf. Another new crew, that of Sgt Maries, spotted a number of fires burning on e.t.a., but were prevented from adding their bombs by the failure of the bomb doors to open, probably as a result of freezing. Sgt Willett and crew searched the target area for thirty minutes before a port engine issue persuaded them to take their bombs home, while P/O Moore and crew dropped their load on the estimated position of the target from 16,000 feet after a search lasting forty minutes. Five Hampdens failed to return, two of them belonging to 50 Squadron, both falling victim to night-fighters over Holland within a minute of each other as they headed for home. AD789 crashed at 22.54 near Roermond after crossing paths with Lt Reese of I./NJG1, and only P/O Cornish survived to fall into enemy hands. AD828 was shot down by Ofw Herzog of III./NJG1, and crashed at 22.55 four miles north of Maastricht, killing P/O Powell, and delivering his crew into captivity. While this operation was in progress, the Brest force had scored four confirmed hits on Gneisenau, and reports coming out of the port told of fifty Germans killed and a further ninety injured.

50 Squadron remained on the ground on the night of the 12/13th as fifteen Hampdens and six Manchesters continued the campaign against the enemy warships at Brest, while fifteen others were involved in the bombing of Merignac aerodrome and mining in the Jellyfish garden off Brest. Persistent technical problems continued to afflict the Manchester, particularly in the engine department, where overheating and component failures were seriously affecting the squadrons' rate of serviceability. As a result, the first of a number of grounding orders was issued on the 13th, while investigations were carried out into the engine-bearing problem, and modifications were put in hand. This meant that no further operations would be undertaken by the type during what remained of the month. Also, on the 13th, Lindholme was ordered to prepare ten Hampdens for mining duties that night in the Cinnamon garden off the port of La Rochelle, where they would be joined by seven others from the group. The crews were also briefed to drop their wing-mounted bombs on a hotel south of Quiberon, which, presumably, was home to U-Boot personnel. They departed Lindholme between 21.45 and 23.05 with S/L Good the senior pilot on duty, but he turned back after half an hour with an engine issue, and was followed home by Sgt Willett and crew, who had got as far as Upper Heyford when they, too, developed engine trouble. The others exited the English coast over Chesil Beach, and ran into ten-tenths cloud with a base at 2,000 feet and lower in places. F/L Rippingale was unable to establish a pinpoint on the French coast, and abandoned the sortie, while those pressing on found clear skies and excellent conditions in the garden area. Sgt Ormonroyd and crew dropped their wing bombs on an aerodrome from 9,000 feet, before gliding down to 6,000 feet to release the mine, coming under fire as they did from the Ile-de-Re and shore-based light flak batteries, that scored hits on the starboard wing. P/O Pexton attacked the hotel from 10,000 feet, and Sgt Maries and P/O Moore from 6,000 feet, while P/O Burrough went in at 1,500 feet and P/O Weston from an even more daring 800 feet, all under accurate fire from light flak batteries. P/O Weston's starboard propeller was hit by a cannon shell, and the intensity of the defensive action prevented an observation of results.

The pattern of operations was now set for the remainder of the month, in which Brest and Kiel would continue to be the principal objectives. Low cloud was again responsible for an ineffective attack at Brest on the night of the 14/15th by an initial force of ninety-four aircraft. This number included twenty-five Hampdens, but none from 50 Squadron, which remained off the Order of Battle. Kiel was posted as the target for ninety-six aircraft on the 15th, for which 50 Squadron contributed ten of the nineteen Hampdens. Nine of them departed Lindholme between 22.25 and 22.50, and climbed away into cloud, that would dissipate over the North Sea, but return to largely conceal ground features inland of the enemy coast. S/L Mulford remained on the ground for an unspecified reason for a further twenty minutes, and, by the time that the Danish coast drew near, it was clear to him that insufficient time remained to attack the primary target. He selected the island of Sylt as an alternative objective, and glided down towards it from 18,000 feet to deliver the bombs from 13,000 feet. He came under fire from heavy but inaccurate flak, and had the satisfaction of observing bomb bursts, followed by a large fire. P/O Pexton and crew had been outbound for ninety minutes, when low oil pressure in the port engine persuaded them to turn back and jettison the bombs into the sea. P/O Maries and crew were flying at 14,000 feet in X2919, the Hampden with the reluctant bomb doors that had let them down over Düsseldorf on the night of the 10/11th. Wisely, they decided to test them before reaching the target, and found them again refusing to open. They tried once more at 10,000 feet with the same result, and had no choice but to head for home and return the bombs to store. The others continued on across the Schleswig-Holstein peninsular, some to find the target fleetingly visible through gaps in the cloud, and others to bomb on estimated positions after a timed run from a coastal pinpoint. The bombing was carried out from between 11,000 and 16,000 feet, immediately after which, F/L Rippingale lost his port engine, sending the Hampden into a dive to port with the loss of three thousand feet before control was regained. As they retreated from the target area, the engine picked up again and gave no further problems. It had been impossible to assess the outcome, and local reports would suggest an ineffective raid that had caused little damage.

Berlin was posted as the target for 118 aircraft on the 17th, thirty-nine of them Hampdens, of which seven belonged to 50 Squadron. The Lindholme crews were briefed to attack an unspecified railway station, and took off between 20.15 and 20.35 with S/Ls Good and Mulford the senior pilots on duty. They were routed out over Skegness, running immediately into ten-tenths cloud at 12,000 feet until reaching Holland, where it began to disperse. There were clear skies over Germany, but haze blotted out ground detail, and, those reaching Berlin would find it difficult to locate the planned aiming-point. This was of no concern to S/L Mulford and crew, who had lost the use of a number of vital instruments during the North Sea crossing, and had been forced to turn back. S/L Good and Sgt Maries and their crews had each noticed flames issuing from their starboard engine exhausts, and sought out alternative targets, S/L Good bombing the southern side of the port of Emden from 16,000 feet in the face of intense anti-aircraft fire but no searchlights. As they withdrew, they were approached from astern by a Me109, at which the rear gunner fired a long burst at 150 yards range, causing the fighter to bank to starboard, and be hit again by a second burst. The fighter was lost from view and was claimed as damaged. As they descended for the homeward leg, the exhaust flame could be seen to extend for eight yards. Meanwhile, Sgt Maries had found an aerodrome, believed to be at Verden, near Bremen, from where an aircraft was taking off, and the flare-path was extinguished as they carried out their attack.

F/O Whitecross and crew spent thirty minutes over Berlin, and established a position over the River Spree, but could not pick out the primary target through the haze. They bombed the estimated position from 16,000 feet, and dispensed a few nickels (leaflets) for the residents to read, before returning safely home. F/O Weston and crew crossed the Dutch coast outbound at 13,500 feet, and found a Me109 on their port quarter just fifty yards away, into which the rear gunner fired a long burst. The enemy was observed to roll onto its back and fall vertically with smoke pouring from it, and would be claimed as destroyed. They pressed on to Berlin, where they released their bombs on the estimated position of the target from 15,000 feet, and saw only the flash of their detonation. P/O Moore and crew made a time-and-distance run from the Tegeler See, situated to the north-west of the city, and bombed the approximate location of the target from 16,000 feet, observing a large flash, but little other evidence of a raid taking place. A fix was established on AD730, which placed it some five miles south-west of Watton in Norfolk, but P/O Hill and crew failed to arrive home. News came through later that the Hampden had crashed on a hillside near Blessington in County Wicklow, Eire, after flying over England and the Irish Sea, and all on board had been killed.

While eleven Hampdens joined fifty others to raid Cologne on the 20th, a further nine were detailed for mining duties in the Jellyfish garden off Brest. Six were provided by 50 Squadron, and they departed Lindholme between 23.30 and 00.25 with S/L Mulford the senior pilot on duty. They set course via Upper Heyford and Chesil Beach, and crossed the Channel just below the cloud base at 3,000 feet to encounter clear skies and extreme darkness in the garden area. This caused difficulties for P/Os Moore and Pexton, who ultimately planted their vegetables about a mile from the allotted positions, while the others managed to locate the briefed drop zones to deliver their stores from between 800 and 1,100 feet, some in the face of intense light flak and searchlights. All returned safely, although the weather produced challenging conditions for landing. Mining would occupy small elements from the group on the succeeding nights while Lindholme remained inactive.

While ten Scampton crews set off for Kiel on the 24th, three 50 Squadron freshmen were briefed to join three others from Waddington for an attack on the docks and shipping at Le Havre. Theirs was to be a very late take-off, and, in the meantime, W/C Walker led six from the squadron to plant vegetables in the Daffodil garden in the southern straits of The Sound off Copenhagen. Five were airborne by 20.30, leaving Sgt Maries and crew to take-off forty-five minutes later, as it turned out, too far behind schedule to complete the operation under darkness. They made landfall at 01.20 in the Lymfjord region of north Jutland, with insufficient time and fuel to complete the sortie as planned, and turned for home. F/O Weston and crew also ran out of time after flying too far north, and eventually identifying Gothenburg, which left them with a further 140 miles to negotiate before reaching the target area. W/C Walker and crew found themselves to be thirty miles north of their intended track, but were assisted by the Northern Lights to map-read in conditions of excellent visibility. They were not impressed by the quality of the blackouts in Danish towns, while Sweden positively sparkled with illumination. As they approached Copenhagen harbour from the south, they were suddenly coned by searchlights from ship and shore-based batteries, and found themselves the target for streams of tracer, to which the Hampden's gunners replied. Violent evasive action succeeded in bringing them through the hail of shells to plant the vegetable in the briefed location, and a quiet return flight ensued. The others managed to locate the garden, pinpointing on the lights on the Swedish coast, and delivered their mines as briefed. It was 01.00 before the first of the bombing trio departed Lindholme, to be followed at ten-minute intervals by the remaining two, and all encountered eight to ten-tenths low cloud that blotted out most of the ground detail. Sgt Baker and P/O Cooke dropped their bombs from 13,000 and 14,000 feet respectively on estimated positions, while Sgt Hughes and crew attacked a flak and searchlight concentration from 10,000 feet, after attempting and failing to get beneath the cloud.

While Lindholme remained off the Order of Battle for the next few nights, 5 Group targeted Kiel again on the 25th and an unidentified specific target in Hamburg on the 26th, on both occasions in unfavourable weather conditions, which severely affected the ability of the crews to identify and bomb as briefed. Lindholme was recalled to action on the 28th to make ready five Hampdens for mining duties in the Cinnamon garden off the Biscay port of La Rochelle, while a predominantly Wellington force attacked Brest further to the north. The 50 Squadron quintet took off between 20.10 and 20.30 with S/L Good the senior pilot on duty, and set course for Chesil Beach for the Channel crossing, and, ultimately, Quiberon Bay, a little to the north of the target area. The thick cloud blanketing southern England dispersed over the Channel, but mist covered north-western France to provide challenging conditions in which to locate the target area. Sgt Willett and P/O Cooke and their crews searched in vain for the garden area before turning back, and only F/O Weston and crew would return having fulfilled their brief. At 23.59, a message was received from F/O Whitecross and crew to the effect that an alternative area had been mined, and that the port engine was failing. They did not return, and it was established eventually that AD834 had crashed at Loudeac on the Brest peninsular, killing both gunners and delivering the second pilot/navigator into enemy hands. F/O Whitecross managed to evade a similar fate, and would return to the squadron in August. Also missing was AD728, which disappeared into the sea, and took with it S/L Good DFC and his crew. Three bodies were eventually recovered for burial at various locations along the French coast, but S/L Good was not among them, and he is commemorated on the Runnymede Memorial.

On the following night 5 Group contributed fourteen Hampdens to a target at Mannheim, while a dozen less-experienced crews joined others to attack oil storage tanks at Rotterdam. 50 Squadron briefed four crews, which departed Lindholme in a ten-minute slot either side of 21.00. They flew immediately into a band of ten-tenths cloud between 2,000 and 4,000 feet, and Skegness passed beneath them unseen as they began the North Sea crossing. The cloud had diminished slightly to seven-tenths in the target area, but any benefit was nullified by ground haze that blotted out identifying features. P/O Pexton and crew were unable to pinpoint on the Dutch coast, and spent fifty-five minutes searching for the target, guided by searchlights and modest amounts of flak, before giving up and returning the bombs to store. Other aircraft dropped flares, and, in their light, Sgt Maries and crew bombed the approximate location of the target from 18,500 feet, before dropping a consignment of tea bags over the Hague. They were stamped with the legend, "The Netherlands will rise again". Sgt Baker and crew attacked a searchlight and flak concentration in the target area, and delivered their precious tea over the suburbs of Rotterdam. Sgt Hughes and crew were the only ones to positively identify the oil depot, and bombed it from 12,500 feet in the light of flares.

The final night of the month brought another raid on Kiel, for which eighty-one aircraft were made ready, thirteen of them Hampdens. Ten-tenths cloud concealed the target area, and the forty-nine crews claiming to have bombed, did so on estimated positions. During the course of the month the squadron carried out eleven operations and dispatched seventy-seven sorties for the loss of seven Hampdens and six-and-a-half crews.

May 1941

As if in atonement for the casualties of April, May would be much kinder to 50 Squadron, despite a busy schedule of operations. The new month began with the posting of an operation to Hamburg on the 1st, but this was subsequently cancelled, only to be reinstated on the following day, for which a force of ninety-five aircraft was made ready. The grounding order on the Manchester had been lifted, and three of the type representing 207 Squadron would join nineteen Hampdens as the 5 Group contribution. 50 Squadron briefed six crews for the main event and three for mining duties in the Nectarine garden off the Frisians, and all departed Lindholme between 20.55 and 22.00 with P/Os Cooke and Pexton the senior pilots among the bombing brigade and S/L Mulford leading the gardeners. The bombers were routed out over Flamborough Head, and set course from there to Neumünster, a town situated some thirty-five miles to the north of Hamburg, from where the bombing run would begin. The weather for the outbound flight was fairly good with just a little low cloud, but this increased over Germany to eight-tenths to create poor visibility. The take-off of the Pexton crew had been delayed for an hour by a recalcitrant TR9 transmitter, and, with insufficient time available to reach the primary target, they attacked Cuxhaven from 16,000 feet instead, commenting on return on the thirty or so searchlights in a box formation all moving as one, clearly under a master controller. Sgt Willett and crew were unable to climb above 13,500 feet, at which height they tried three times to bomb Wilhelmshaven, but, having been driven off by the defences, let their load go onto the outskirts of Emden from 11,000 feet. Hamburg was always well defended by searchlights and flak, which lined the route in on both banks of the Elbe from the mouth of the estuary right into the heart of the city. Despite this, the remaining four crews attacked the primary target through the cloud from between 12,000 and 16,500 feet, and delivered leaflets at the same time. Local reports mentioned thirteen large fires, but no significant damage. Meanwhile, the gardeners encountered much flak along the Frisian island chain, but identified the target area through three-tenths cloud, before gliding down from as high as 15,000 feet to below 1,000 feet to deliver their vegetables into the briefed locations, largely unopposed. During the course of the night, the squadron dropped eighteen 500 and six 250 pounders, along with 1,440lbs of incendiaries, and three mines.

5 Group put up twenty-seven Hampdens and two Manchesters on the 3rd, in an overall force of 101 aircraft bound for Cologne, while a predominantly Wellington force continued the assault on Brest and its lodgers. Lindholme was not involved in either operation, and while there were no confirmed hits on the warships at Brest, nine-tenths cloud and poor visibility ensured that no more than ten bomb loads fell in Cologne. 5 Group contributed twenty-one Hampdens to the next attack on the cruisers at Brest, for which a force of ninety-seven aircraft was prepared on the 4th. The 5 Group ORB offered the thought that the warships must be crippled by now following repeated attacks, but effective camouflage and smoke screens ensured that the British authorities actually had no clear picture of the vessels' state of serviceability, and the raids would continue. Lindholme was not called into action on this occasion, when a number of claims of direct hits were not confirmed.

Mannheim was posted as the primary target for a major operation on the 5th, for which 5 Group would contribute thirty-three Hampdens and four Manchesters. Orders were received at Lindholme to make ready seven aircraft for the main operation and a singleton for mining duties in the Nectarines garden around the Frisians. The main element took off between 20.55 and 21.10 with S/L Mulford the senior pilot on duty, and flew towards the south coast to exit England at Beachy Head. S/L Mulford turned back with an engine issue shortly after taking-off, leaving the others to break cloud at 6,000 feet as they crossed the Channel, and make landfall on the French coast over ten-tenths cloud that would persist all the way to the target area. They set a course to follow the Franco-Belgian frontier until south of Luxembourg, at which point they would cross into Germany, still over ten-tenths cloud, although some gaps began to appear as the target drew near. Even so, it was the concentration of searchlights and flak that guided them to Mannheim, where bombing took place on estimated positions from between 12,000 and 19,500 feet. The lower altitude was that of Sgt Willett and crew, who had climbed to 12,000 feet for the outward journey, but lost their oxygen system after three hours and had to remain at that level for the attack. It was P/O Pexton and crew who bombed from high level, before their heating system broke down, leaving them shivering in a temperature of minus 30 degrees Centigrade. Sgt Broderick and crew had taken off at 22.10, and found nine-tenths cloud at 2,000 feet over the garden, where they delivered the vegetable into a position one mile west of the briefed location.

115 aircraft were detailed for an attack on the Blohm & Voss shipyards in Hamburg on the 6th, an operation supported by 5 Group with twenty-seven Hampdens and four Manchesters. In the event, cloud and poor visibility prevented any crews from identifying the aiming-point, and bombs were dropped on estimated positions or on alternative targets. Lindholme sat this one out, and also the following night's attempt by an initial force of eighty-nine aircraft to hit the cruisers at Brest. Eighteen Hampdens did take part in quite favourable conditions, but the claims of direct hits remained unconfirmed. All 5 Group operational stations received orders on the following day to prepare aircraft for what would be a record-breaking night of activity involving 364 sorties. 188 aircraft were to attack Hamburg, 119 of them assigned to the Blohm & Voss shipyards, and sixty-nine to target the city, while 133 Whitleys and Wellingtons would attend to the A.G. Weser U-Boot construction yards in Bremen. 5 Group contributed a record seventy-eight Hampdens and nine Manchesters to the Hamburg forces, ten of the former representing 50 Squadron, their crews briefed for the shipyards.

They took off between 22.00 and 22.45 with S/L Mulford the senior pilot on duty, and flew out over Flamborough Head to pinpoint on Neumünster and approach the target from the north, with conditions promising to offer a reasonable chance of identifying the aiming-point. Sgt Broderick and crew turned back after failing to climb beyond 15,500 feet, at which altitude the tail vibrated violently, and the intercom broke down. Sgt Willett was unable to coax AD766 above 13,500 feet even after jettisoning the wing bombs, and bombed Cuxhaven instead after gliding down to 8,000 feet. S/L Mulford reached the Danish coast at 15,500 feet, but could not ascend any further, and the decision was taken to turn back to Sylt to attack a target of opportunity. The bombs were dropped from 14,000 feet, and were seen to burst on a railway junction in the centre of the town of Westerland. P/O Cooke and crew were over the Danish coast when the starboard engine began to show signs of distress, forcing them to seek an alternative target. The railway line near Hastrup in southern Jutland presented itself, but the results were not observed as the failing engine demanded the crew's attention. It cut out as they crossed Sylt on the way home, restarted some minutes later, but continued to fluctuate, as did the port engine, to the extent that an S.O.S signal was sent out in the expectation of having to ditch. In the event, they made it home after flying uncomfortably close to the balloon barrage over Sheffield. The others found the target without difficulty in good visibility, and described the defence as intense but inaccurate as they delivered their bombs from between 13,500 and 19,500 feet, the last-mentioned altitude that of the Pexton crew, whose rear gunner suffered miserably in the temperature of minus 32 degrees Centigrade. Bomb bursts were observed in the general area of the briefed aiming-point, and up to a dozen fires were reported by returning crews. Local reports confirmed that an accurate and effective raid had taken place, describing eighty-three fires, thirty-eight of them large, with some destruction of housing, and the highest death toll yet in a German city of 185 people.

The main operation posted on the 9th revealed the twin cities of Mannheim and Ludwigshafen to be the targets, for which 146 aircraft were made ready. 5 Group detailed twenty-four

Hampdens and eleven Manchesters for this endeavour and three Manchesters for a token visit to the "Big City", Berlin, by five aircraft. The aiming-point for the 5 Group element was the Badische Anilin & Soda-Fabrik (BASF) works in Ludwigshafen, which was part of the infamous I.G Farben company, the largest manufacturer of chemicals and synthetic oil products in the world. 50 Squadron dispatched seven Hampdens between 21.15 and 21.30 with no senior pilots on duty, and they followed the same route as for the recent Mannheim operation, enjoying favourable conditions all the way into southern Germany. A faulty intercom led P/O Collins and crew to lose their way while flying over a cloud-covered area of France at 11,000 feet, and it was only on e.t.a., when the Rhine failed to appear beneath them, that the error was discovered. They set a reciprocal course to return to the French coast in the hope of finding an aerodrome for their bombs, but none was found, and the ordnance was returned to store. Sgt Willett and crew had penetrated fifty miles into France, when a troublesome port engine persuaded them to turn back and bomb the docks at Calais from 7,000 feet in the face of a hostile searchlight and flak reception. The others encountered a little low cloud in the target area, which may well have been smoke drifting across the Rhine from Mannheim, but carried out their attacks from between 13,000 and 15,000 feet, observing the bombs to burst and set off a number of fires. Local reports would confirm that some useful industrial damage had been inflicted on both cities, and more than 3,500 people had been left homeless.

Hamburg was posted to face its fourth major operation of the month on the 10th, for which a force of 119 aircraft was assembled and the crews briefed to aim for shipyards, the Altona power station and the general city area. 5 Group put up thirty-five Hampdens and a Manchester for the main operation, and six Manchesters for Berlin as part of a force of twenty-three aircraft. Lindholme remained off the Order of Battle on this night, which was blessed by excellent weather conditions that allowed crews to identify their respective target areas without effort. Crews returning from Hamburg were enthusiastic about the outcome, and local reports confirmed that 128 fires had broken out, forty-seven of them classed as large, with extensive damage resulting in the city centre.

There would be no respite for Germany's Second City as plans were already in hand to send ninety-two aircraft back there twenty-four hours later, while eighty-one others, including thirty-one Hampdens and two Manchesters, sought out one of the Deutsche Schiff und Maschinenbau Aktiengesellschaft shipyards in Bremen. Abbreviated to Deschimag, this was a co-operation of eight shipyards, the largest of which was the A.G. Weser company. 50 Squadron loaded six Hampdens with a mix of either 1,000 and 250 pounders or 500 and 250 pounders plus incendiaries, and dispatched them from Lindholme between 22.15 and 22.35 with no senior pilots on duty. They had been briefed to head out via Flamborough Head to make landfall north of the Frisians, and four crews complied with instructions, experiencing searchlight and flak opposition from the enemy coast to the target, while two others chose a different route, one to the north and the other to the south, and both would report flak-free outward flights. All reached the target to find favourable conditions, and would report on their return that they observed no evidence of other aircraft having attacked. The bomb loads were delivered from between 13,000 and 16,000 feet, four of them falling within the target area and two overshooting, and a number of resulting fires remained visible for twenty minutes. The consensus was of a successful attack, with local reports confirming that many bombs had fallen in the docks area, where a floating dock belonging to the AG Weser Company had been sunk. The main damage, however, was inflicted in the city, where housing was the principal victim.

The squadron would not be called into action again until the 15th, and, in the meantime, a force of 105 aircraft, including a 5 Group contribution of forty-one Hampdens and four Manchesters, raided Mannheim and Ludwigshafen again on the night of the 12/13th. They were divided between the two cities 65/40, but, despite clear skies and bright moonlight, ground haze prevented most from identifying the target, and only around ten bomb loads fell within the target areas. Twenty-six crews seeking an alternative target found more favourable conditions over Cologne, and reported bombing it and hitting a number of industrial buildings. The weather precluded operations on the following two nights, and it was the 15th when the northern city of Hannover was posted as the target for 101 aircraft, for which 5 Group detailed twenty-seven Hampdens, while a simultaneous raid on Berlin would involve eight Manchesters and six Stirlings. The briefed aiming-point was the main post office and telephone exchange, which, in reality, identified this as an area attack. 50 Squadron made ready eleven Hampdens, which took off between 22.00 and 22.30 with S/L Burrough the senior pilot on duty and, flew out over Great Yarmouth on course for the Dutch coast, where thick cloud would obscure the ground and render accurate navigation something of a challenge. Sgt Maries and crew turned back with an engine issue shortly after reaching the North Sea, leaving the remaining ten to reach the target area, harried all the way across enemy territory by intense searchlights but little flak, and it was only when close to Hannover that the batteries opened up with a heavy and accurate barrage. The city area was identified by the River Leine to the north-west and the Maschsee to the south-east, and the bombing was carried out from between 10,000 and 16,000 feet. All returning crews reported that their bomb loads had fallen within the built-up area of the city, but no local report was forthcoming to confirm the level of damage.

The following two nights were devoted to Cologne, while 50 Squadron remained at home, but neither operation, by initial forces of ninety-three and ninety-five aircraft, including twenty-four and twenty-three Hampdens respectively, would be attended by favourable weather conditions. Few bombs found their way into the city on the first occasion, while some damage was inflicted upon housing and public and commercial buildings during the second raid, mostly in districts south of the city centre. Seventy aircraft were made ready to attack Kiel's shipyards on the 18th, and among them were eighteen Hampdens, six of them representing 50 Squadron. A further four Hampdens at Lindholme were loaded with a mine each for delivery into the Forget-me-not garden in Kiel Harbour. The two elements took off together between 21.45 and 22.10, with S/L Burrough leading the bombing brigade, and began the North Sea crossing at Flamborough Head, setting course for the island of Rømø, situated off the west coast of Denmark, before turning east to a point north of the target. S/L Burrough and crew were approaching the enemy coast, when port engine trouble forced them to turn back, while thick haze over the entire Schleswig-Holstein peninsular made it very difficult for the others to establish a pin-point. The gardeners encountered ten-tenths cloud at 2,000 feet over their target area, which added to the challenges facing them. Three gardeners eventually found the drop zone and delivered their vegetables, while the fourth searched in vain for two hours before giving up and returning the mine to store. The bombing element battled the conditions and accurate heavy flak most of the way from the coast to the target, but only Sgt Maries and F/O Fox and their crews made a positive identification of Kiel. They let their loads go from 12,000 and 13,500 feet respectively, and the incendiaries from one were seen to start several small fires that merged into a single large conflagration as they departed the target area. Three crews bombed searchlight and flak concentrations at various locations as alternatives from between 12,000 and 19,000 feet, and all returned safely from what was a frustrating night of activity.

The weather kept the Command on the ground during the ensuing four nights, while Blenheims carried out daylight "Circus" operations and shipping sweeps. Cologne was posted as the target on the 23rd, for which fifty-one aircraft were made ready, twenty-four of them Hampdens. Lindholme was not called into action, and the operation was yet another failure in the face of complete cloud cover. 5 Group operated alone on the 25th, committing forty-eight Hampdens to mine the approaches to Brest and St-Nazaire, the former, in particular, anticipating the arrival of the Bismarck, which, it was correctly believed, was racing for sanctuary with the Royal Navy snapping at its heels, determined to avenge the shocking sinking of HMS Hood on the 24th. Lindholme was again inactive on this night, when the cloud base was found to be down to around 600 feet, and only half of the force located the target area. In fact, the Bismarck's rudder would be crippled by a Fleet Air Arm torpedo during the 26th, rendering the vessel unable to manoeuvre, and restricted to a top speed of ten knots.

Later that night, 5 Group sent thirty-eight Hampdens to continue mining the approaches to Brest, and, among them this time were thirteen representing 50 Squadron. They took off between 22.20 and 22.35 with W/C Walker and S/L Mulford the senior pilots on duty, and flew out via Chesil Beach, before following the Brittany coast to the garden area. Once again, the weather conditions were unhelpful, with a layer of five to eight-tenths cloud at between 1,000 and 8,000 feet dispensing hail and rain. This allowed only eight of the Lindholme crews to locate the garden, some assisted by shore-based searchlights, after spending up to ninety minutes searching. The navigator in the crew of F/L Potts sustained a foot wound courtesy of intensive light flak while searching for the drop zone, and he was unable to carry out his duties. The pilot took responsibility for locating the garden, enabling the vegetable to be planted eventually in the face of a continuing hostile response, followed by a safe return to Boscombe Down and a landing with zero brake pressure. In the event, the pride of the Germany navy would never come within range of Brest. At first light on the 27th, multiple units of the Royal Navy closed in on the helpless ship, and, from 08.47, engaged it with guns and torpedoes until it slipped beneath the waves at 10.39. This left her consort, Prinz Eugen, at large, and the mining at Brest would continue over the succeeding nights in case she put in an appearance.

The above action proved to be the last of the month to involve 5 Group, and 50 Squadron was heading towards a loss-free May, when AD867 stalled during an air-test on the 30th, and crashed at 11.20 two miles north-west of the airfield, killing P/O Cunningham and the other occupant. During the course of the month, the squadron undertook eleven operations, and dispatched seventy-four sorties without loss.

June 1941

June began with an operation against Düsseldorf on the night of the 2/3rd, for which 5 Group put up forty-three Hampdens in a force of 150 aircraft. 50 Squadron made ready ten Hampdens, which departed Lindholme between 22.40 and 22.55, with the recently promoted F/L Fox the senior pilot on duty. After exiting the English coast at Orfordness, most set course for Brussels, while a few headed directly for the southern Ruhr, all having to contend with far from ideal weather conditions. A layer of ten-tenths cloud stretched along the entire route at 2,000 feet, with broken medium cloud at 9,000 feet and another band at 17,000 feet, but this dispersed sufficiently to leave six to eight-tenths in the target area, through which glimpses of the Rhine provided an indication of the location of Düsseldorf. Even so, bombing took place on estimated positions from between 9,000 and 17,000 feet in the face of considerable searchlight and flak activity, and P/O Abbott lost the central panel of his windscreen to shrapnel. Returning crews reported fires in the centre of the target area, but no precise results were observed. Absent from debriefing was the crew of P/O Hodgson, who had all lost their lives when AD797 crashed in Belgium.

Thereafter the group, and, in fact, most of the Command, was kept on the ground by an unprecedented period of adverse weather conditions during the best part of the moon period. This was a source of monotony and massive frustration, until, finally, on the 10th, Brest was posted as the target for thirty-nine Hampdens in company with sixty-five Wellingtons and Whitleys, which would not have been over the target at the same time. Until the advent of the bomber-stream system introduced by Harris in 1942, groups, squadrons, and even, sometimes, crews, could determine for themselves the details of an operation with regard to timings, routes and attacking height, and, the likelihood is, that each group on this night attacked individually. The Scharnhorst and Gneisenau had been joined at Brest by Bismarck's former consort, Prinz Eugen, which had spent the previous two weeks since the mighty battleship's loss, evading British attempts to locate her and bestow upon her a similar fate. 50 Squadron was not involved in the attack, during which many bombs fell into the docks area without hitting the German cruisers, but, at least, no aircraft were lost. 5 Group also sent nine Hampdens on gardening sorties on this night, to plant their vegetables in Quiberon Bay, between Lorient and St Nazaire on the Biscay coast.

Düsseldorf and Duisburg were the primary targets posted on the 11th, for which forces of ninety-eight and eighty aircraft respectively were made ready. 5 Group supported the latter with thirty-five Hampdens, seventeen of them departing Lindholme between 23.00 and 23.40 led by W/C Walker and S/Ls Burrough and Mulford. P/O Christophers and crew discovered a faulty T.R.9 on take-off, and landed as soon as the others had cleared the circuit. The others flew out over Skegness, climbing through five tenths ice-bearing cloud in a layer between 5,000 and 9,000 feet, and, once over enemy territory, found themselves racing a sheet of ten-tenths low cloud to reach the target first. Those ahead of the eastern edge of the front enjoyed the benefits of good visibility and bright moonlight to assist their map-reading, and found the target with ease by the fires already burning. The others, beaten to the target by the cloud, bombed on estimated positions, and fourteen loads went down from between 10,000 and 17,000 feet, while two others were dropped on the railway station and the Rhine bridge at Wesel. Returning crews reported fires, and that the 2,000 pounders carried by five aircraft had exploded with a large orange flash. There was no information from Duisburg, but Cologne reported extensive damage to its main railway station, the docks area and 173 houses.

The following night was devoted predominantly to attacks on railway yards at four locations in Germany to the east and north of the Ruhr, and most of the available Hampden force, amounting to ninety-one aircraft, was detailed to attack the important hub at Soest. 50 Squadron made ready ten aircraft at Lindholme, and they took off between 23.10 and 23.25 with a W/C Lynch-Staunton named as the senior pilot on duty. They were routed out over

Skegness, where large stretches of medium cloud would be encountered, extending from 5,000 to 12,000 feet over the North Sea. P/O Cooke and crew returned almost immediately, to be followed home by Sgt Ford and crew, who had run into severe icing at 11,000 feet over the Lincolnshire coast, and fallen out of the sky until being recovered at 5,000 feet. The remaining eight crews reached the target area, some pinpointing on the Möhne Lake a few miles to the south, but only three positively identified the target in poor visibility, Sgts Hughes and Quinton and their crews bombing from 1,500 and 4,000 feet respectively, from where the town and marshalling yards were clearly visible. After bombing, the Hughes crew descended to 500 feet to strafe the main roads through the towns of Körbecke, Vollinghausen and Arnsberg. Some of the others attacked on estimated positions, while three crews selected alternative targets at Hamm, Essen and Wesel, and bombed them from between 8,000 and 20,000 feet.

There was a return to Brest for 110 aircraft, including thirty-seven Hampdens, on the night of the 13/14th, but haze and an effective smokescreen prevented the vessels from being hit. 50 Squadron did not participate, but prepared nine Hampdens for a 5 Group effort by twenty-nine aircraft for the first of four raids on consecutive nights against Cologne, a city that would continue to be a popular destination throughout the month. They departed Lindholme between 23.25 and 23.50, led again by W/C Lynch-Staunton, and ran into ten-tenths low cloud with broken medium cloud up to 9,000 feet over the entire route. Not one crew was able to positively identify the target, which was probably one of the marshalling yards, and bombing took place from between 5,000 and 15,000 feet on estimated positions based largely on searchlight and flak activity.

Düsseldorf seemed to be equally attractive as a target, and would be raided simultaneously with Cologne on no fewer than eight nights during the second half of the month, beginning on the 15th. There were no 50 Squadron representatives among the forty-two Hampdens attempting to hit railway targets in Cologne on this night, and only around four of the ninety-one aircraft taking part managed to drop their load within the city. Cologne and Düsseldorf were the principal targets again on the following night, for which Lindholme put up ten Hampdens among the forty-seven provided by 5 Group in an overall force of 105 bound for the former. They took off between 23.25 and 23.50 with F/L Fox the senior pilot on duty, and set course for Brussels, some meeting intense searchlights and flak at the Belgian coast, while others remained unmolested until near the target. The ground was obscured by thick haze and perhaps fog, despite which, a few crews were able to establish their position and home in on the aiming-point on the eastern side of the Rhine, probably the Kalk marshalling yards. Others would attack on estimated positions or e.t.a., and bombs were delivered from between 8,000 and 18,000 feet, after which, Sgt Hughes and crew descended to below 1,000 feet to seek out military objectives in the Euskirchen area. On return, Sgt Maries and crew reported that they had been hit by flak when crossing the enemy coast outbound at 11,500 feet, some ten miles north-east of Ostend. The starboard engine was damaged and threatened to burst into flames, and the IFF system was employed to successfully confuse the searchlights until it shorted, shocking the wireless operator and leaving him incapacitated for the next two hours. The bombs were jettisoned onto the offending batteries at Ostend, and a safe return made to base. Other crews reported fires and many explosions, while the local authorities claimed scattered damage but nothing of significance.

Forty-three Hampdens and thirty-three Whitleys took off to return to Cologne on the 17th, while fifty-seven Wellingtons were dispatched to Düsseldorf and 50 Squadron remained at home. Poor visibility, caused by thick ground haze, prevented most crews from locating their respective targets, and neither operation was effective. An unspecified aiming-point in Bremen was posted as the target for a hundred aircraft on the 18th, for which 5 Group made a contribution of thirty-nine Hampdens, nine of them representing 50 Squadron. Perhaps in preparation, Sgt Hinde took P4389 for an air-test, and was joined by one crewman and three members of ground crew. Sadly, the Hampden crashed into a field almost immediately after take-off at 18.50, and all on board lost their lives. It was four hours later when the squadron element took off for north-western Germany, led by S/L Mulford, and briefed to follow the familiar route via Enkhuizen on the eastern side of the Den Helder peninsular. P/O Cooke and crew returned at midnight after the starboard engine began to vibrate violently, and this left eight crews to continue on over thick ground haze and three-tenths cloud at 2,000 feet, with tops over the target at 8,000 feet. This, inevitably, hindered navigation, and constant harassment from clusters of searchlight and flak batteries added to the difficulties. In the target area, intense and accurate flak was experienced at 10,000 feet and beyond, and F/L Potts' aircraft was hit in the port air-intake. Bombing took place from between 12,000 and 18,000 feet, and a number of bursts were observed but no detail. Sgt Maries and crew were unable to locate the briefed target in the conditions, and found an alternative in the form of a blast furnace at Verden, situated south-east of Bremen, which they bombed from 19,000 feet. Returning crews reported a ring of dummy fires up to twenty miles outside of Bremen, and the employment also of dummy flares.

The country was now basking in a spell of very hot weather, which began on the 19th, and would continue through the 23rd. 115 aircraft set off for Kiel on the 20th in search of the Tirpitz, and among them were twenty-four Hampdens, although none representing 50 Squadron. Poor visibility prevented the location of the battleship from being identified, and this led to an attack being directed at the general area of the town. It was not until the 21st that the Manchester was once more declared fit for operations after almost five weeks on the side lines. During the course of the day, a record number of eighteen was made ready to target the docks at Boulogne, and this figure included a contribution from 61 Squadron, which would be blooding the type for the first time.

The main operations on this night were against Cologne and Düsseldorf, the former the target for sixty-eight Wellingtons, while twenty-eight Hampdens and an equal number of Whitleys attended to the latter. Eight 50 Squadron crews were briefed for an unspecified aiming-point, and took off from Lindholme between 23.00 and 23.15 with no senior pilots on duty. Some adopted a northern route from Skegness to the Den Helder peninsular, while others preferred Orfordness to the Scheldt Estuary, and, among the latter was the crew of Sgt Quinton, who were at 10,000 feet near Great Yarmouth when the rear gunner's door blew open and had to be jettisoned. In the process, the wireless operator sustained a painful injury to a number of fingers, and the sortie had to be abandoned. Sgt Broderick and crew dropped their wing bombs onto a concentration of searchlights on the island of Schouwen after excessive flames from their starboard exhaust advertised their whereabouts, and they also turned back. Sgt Maries and crew reached the enemy coast with their port engine running rough, and, spotting a large fire in the area of Ostend, decided to attack the port as a last-resort target. They observed a large fire with a cloud of black smoke rising into the air as the bombs went down from 13,000 feet, and were seen to burst to the north of the main dock. The remaining crews reached the target area after flying through the protective belt of searchlights and flak, but experienced difficulty in establishing their position, and even the Rhine proved to be elusive. Fires provided the best reference, and bombing was carried out with the aid of flares from between 12,000 and 18,000 feet, without observing the results in the hazy conditions.

Bremen was the destination for twenty-five Hampdens in company with Wellingtons on the night of the 22/23rd, and this operation was another abject failure. Kiel, Cologne and Düsseldorf were the destinations for modest forces on the following night, the last-mentioned an inconclusive 5 Group effort against railway yards involving thirty Hampdens and eleven Manchesters. 50 Squadron returned to action with nine Hampdens on the 24th as part of a 5 Group force of twenty-five of the type assigned to the docks at Kiel, while the Manchester brigade tried its hand at Düsseldorf. All but one of the Lindholme element took off between 22.20 and 22.35 with F/Ls Fox and Potts the senior pilots on duty, leaving P/O Christophers and crew behind until 23.00. On approaching the Danish coast, the last-mentioned crew lost their W/T, and, as they were already behind schedule, bombed the island of Sylt from 16,000 feet before turning back. The others reported some cloud over the North Sea at 6,000 feet, but clear skies over the target, where Sgt Dawson and crew ran into a cone of searchlights and three Me110s, two with a searchlight in the nose. They were providing illumination for the other one, which carried out an attack with cannon and machine-gun fire from 500 to 600 yards without scoring any hits. The rear gunner responded with 150 rounds, after which, the night-fighters were lost to sight, but the Hampden remained coned and under flak-fire as the bomb load was delivered from 14,000 feet. The others carried out their attacks from between 12,000 and 19,000 feet, but saw little of the results through the dense haze extending upwards to around 10,000 feet. Returning crews reported an aircraft being shot down from 16,000 feet over the target, and this would have been a 57 Squadron Wellington.

Thirty Hampdens were made ready to return to Kiel twenty-four hours later to target the Deutsche Werke shipyard, for which the 50 Squadron element of five departed Lindholme between 22.25 and 22.55 with no senior pilots on duty. They exited the English coast at Flamborough Head before setting course for Rømø island to approach the target from the north, and, despite thick haze, four found it without major difficulty. Sgt Austin and crew were the exception, spending twenty-five minutes searching in vain on e.t.a., before eventually returning their bombs to store after failing to find an alternative target. Sgt Quinton managed to coax his Hampden to 15,000 feet as the target drew near, and made a glide approach from the north-east to deliver the bombs from 12,000 feet, while being bombarded by flak. Immediately afterwards, twenty searchlights held them for three minutes as they were chased out of the target area in a long dive that took them down to 6,000 feet. P/O Vivian and crew crossed the Danish coast at 16,500 feet, and shed two thousand feet in a glide to the point of bomb release. P/O Pexton and Sgt Ford also favoured a glide attack after pinpointing on the estuary, and released their loads respectively from 15,000 and 13,000 feet, without observing the outcome.

The target awaiting eight 50 Squadron crews and twenty others from the group on the 27th was the Vulkan Schiffbau U-Boot construction yards at Vegesack, situated on the East Bank of the River Weser to the north-west of Bremen. A second force of 108 Wellingtons and Whitleys was prepared to carry out a simultaneous attack on the city, which, hopefully, might attract the defences and provide 5 Group with a clear run. The 50 Squadron element departed Lindholme between 22.50 and 23.10 with S/L Burrough the senior pilot on duty, while Sgt

Mudd and P/O Pexton and their crews took off at 23.05 and 23.30 respectively to carry out nuisance raids on Düsseldorf and Cologne. Sgt Mudd and crew encountered nine-tenths cloud over Düsseldorf, and bombed from 17,000 feet onto a concentration of searchlights and flak, and it was a similar story at Cologne, which P/O Pexton attacked first with wing bombs and then the main load, all the time under an intense flak barrage. In the meantime, S/L Burrough had crossed the Dutch coast at 12,000 feet, only for the starboard engine exhaust to emit sparks and a ribbon of flame that threatened to engulf the tail. The aircraft vibrated violently, forcing the pilot to reduce power to a level at which height could not be maintained, and the bombs had to be jettisoned. Sgt Dawson and crew also turned back from the Dutch coast after experiencing engine trouble. The others carried out their attacks through seven-tenths cloud from between 15,000 and 19,000 feet, mostly on estimated positions after pinpointing on the river. On return, numerous searchlight and flak batteries were reported to have been active between the coast and the target, a few fires were observed in the Vegesack area and others in Bremen itself, but there were no details of any damage caused.

Bremen was chosen to be in the firing line again on the 29th, when thirty Hampdens were detailed to join seventy-six other aircraft, while six of the group's Manchesters took part in a small raid on Hamburg. 50 Squadron made ready nine Hampdens, which departed Lindholme between 22.20 and 22.35 with no senior pilots on duty, and flew out over Flamborough Head to make landfall on the enemy coast near Rømø island. Sgt Willett and crew turned back with an oil system issue, and they were followed home by Sgt Maries and crew, whose navigator had been unable to access his oxygen supply, thus restricting them to a relatively low bombing height, which previous experiences at this target suggested would be unwise. P/O Vivian crossed the North Sea in cloud at 1,500 feet, before climbing to 15,000 feet to cross the enemy coast and 19,800 feet for the bombing run. Crews approaching from the west had to pass through a belt of about twenty searchlights accompanied by heavy and light flak, but, once over the target, the visibility was good, even though the ground was partly concealed by five-tenths low cloud. Bombing took place from between 12,000 and 18,000 feet, with flak bursting above and below at between 16,000 and 20,000 feet, but no results were observed. X3133 failed to return home with the crew of Sgt Hughes DFM, after being shot down on the way home by Oblt Reinhold Eckardt of II./NJG1 at 02.55, and crashing some fifteen miles west-north-west of Hamburg without survivors.

Following a spate of engine failures, particularly some afflicting 61 Squadron aircraft, another Manchester grounding order was issued on the 30th. A conference was held at 5 Group HQ on this day, when it was decided that each Manchester squadron would select four aircraft for intensive flight testing. During the course of the month, 50 Squadron carried out twelve operations and dispatched 106 sorties for the loss of three Hampdens, two complete crews and a number of air and ground crew in the crash resulting from the air-test.

July 1941

After the comparatively light losses of the preceding two months, 50 Squadron was now to embark on a testing ten-week period, which would see twenty-one aircraft crash or go missing, and this coincided with a return to Germany's heartland at the conclusion of the U-Boot offensive. Having been prominent during the final few days of June, it fell to Bremen to open the Command's July account on the night of the 2/3rd, while smaller forces targeted Cologne and Duisburg. The last-mentioned was an all-Hampden affair, for which 50

Squadron provided eleven aircraft in an overall force of thirty-nine. They were briefed to aim for the marshalling yards, and were given Cologne and Düsseldorf as alternative targets before departing Lindholme between 23.10 and 23.50, with F/Os Abbott and Collins the senior pilots on duty. The last-mentioned take-off time was that of Sgt Maries and crew, who had been delayed by a broken wireless aerial. The briefed preferred route was to take the squadron out via Skegness and the Den Helder peninsular, but Sgt Ford and crew failed to even reach the coast before turning back because of a problem with the wing flaps. The remainder pressed on towards the Dutch coast, which was some twenty miles ahead, when rising oil temperature forced P/O Smith and crew to re-evaluate their situation. The Hampden was vibrating and unable to climb beyond 13,000 feet as they approached the eastern side of the peninsular, where they dropped their bombs from 12,000 feet onto the aerodrome at Wieringermeer. Already behind schedule, the Maries crew opted to bomb a railway junction in the German frontier town of Emmerich, doing so from 15,000 feet without observing the results. The others encountered thick industrial haze in the target area, lurking beneath the seven-tenths cloud at 6,000 feet, and this left them with no prospect of identifying the briefed aiming-point. Searches were carried out, some aided by flares, but it was a futile exercise, and bombs were released on estimated positions from between 11,000 and 18,000 feet with no clue as to the outcome. Sgt Hunter and crew abandoned the search and headed back towards Holland, where they bombed what they believed to be Eindhoven aerodrome from 13,000 feet.

Scampton and Hemswell combined on the following night to send thirty-nine Hampdens to join Wellingtons in attacking shipyards at Bremen, while ninety Wellingtons and Whitleys attempted to hit the Krupp armaments works and railway installations at Essen. 50 Squadron stayed at home, and, thereby, had rested crews to respond on the 4th to the order to attack the U-Boot pens at Lorient, where construction of the major new concrete structure was well under way on the Keroman peninsular. 5 Group put up twenty-five Hampdens, ten of which were loaded with four 500 and two 250 pounders each at Lindholme, and dispatched between 22.30 and 22.45 with S/L Mulford the senior pilot on duty. They crossed the English coast at Chesil Beach in ideal weather conditions of clear skies and an almost full moon in the south-west, and could identify the Brittany coast from many miles away. F/O Collins and Sgts Willett and Hunter opted for a low-level attack, and went in at between 4,500 and 5,000 feet after gliding down through the barrage balloons tethered at between 4,000 and 8,000 feet. The others bombed from between 9,000 and 15,000 feet while under fire from all calibres of flak, some of which reached 18,000 feet. Returning crews reported bomb bursts along the edge of the docks, but there was no confirmation of damage, and it would have required far heavier bombs to even scratch the U-Boot shelter.

Lindholme sat out a 5 Group attack on marshalling yards at Osnabrück on the night of the 5/6th, and then made ready thirteen Hampdens on the 6th to contribute to a 5 Group force of eighty-eight of the type for a raid on the German warships at Brest. Frustrated by the grounding of the Manchester, a few 207 Squadron crews borrowed Hampdens from fellow Waddington residents, 44 Squadron, to enable them to take part, and, as the situation dragged on, they would be given six Hampdens of their own. The 50 Squadron element took off between 22.15 and 22.35 with W/C Walker and S/L Potts the senior pilots on duty, and followed the same route as for Lorient two nights earlier. The weather conditions continued to favour the bombers with unlimited visibility aided by the full moon, and all found the target without difficulty. The defence, as always, was intense, with searchlights and flak providing a barrier between the attackers and the targets, but, initially at least, the smoke generators were not active, allowing those arriving in the vanguard a clear run. Most chose a glide approach, which enabled them to remain largely unnoticed by the defenders, but a few found themselves held by searchlights and at the mercy of the flak batteries, which forced them to take evasive action during the bombing run. The smoke generators soon blanketed the area, concealing the vessels, and the bomb loads were delivered from between 9,000 and 17,000 feet into the general area of the docks, where many detonations were observed. Four of the squadron's Hampdens had been carrying two 2,000 pounders each, while the remainder had 500 and 250 pounders in their bomb bays, and, in all, 5 Group delivered over three hundred high explosive, armour-piercing and semi-armour piercing bombs into the target area. On return, a number of crews reported an aircraft being hit at around 3,000 feet and crashing into the sea in flames, and this was probably a 144 Squadron Hampden.

Four main targets were posted on stations across the Command on the 7th, Cologne, Osnabrück and Münster for Wellingtons and or Whitleys, while forty Hampdens would target marshalling yards in the town of Mönchengladbach on the south-western rim of the Ruhr. 50 Squadron made ready ten Hampdens as part of a 5 Group force of forty, and sent them on their way between 22.45 and 23.20 with F/Os Collins and Cooke the senior pilots on duty. In accordance with the practice of the day, some adopted the northerly route via Skegness and Enkhuizen, while others preferred Orfordness and the Scheldt. Whichever, the outward flight took place under clear skies with a full moon to aid map-reading in coastal areas, until thick ground haze blotted out detail over land, and only four crews would find the target area. A number of lakes to the north-west of the town were of benefit to those approaching from the north, as were the railway lines running into the town, and it was the main south to north track that was followed by Sgt Hunter and crew right to the aiming-point, which they bombed from 10,000 feet. After searching for some time, Sgts Broderick, Good and Mudd attacked the primary target from 8,000, 10,500 and 13,000 feet respectively, while the others selected Düsseldorf, Neuss and Duisburg and a railway junction at Wesel for attention. Having failed to locate the primary target, Sgt Quinton and crew spent thirty minutes dodging searchlights, flak and night-fighters at 15,000 feet over Düsseldorf, observing the ground on occasions by the light of flares dropped by other aircraft. At one point, they were surrounded by a formation of five enemy fighters and another of seven twin-engine hostiles, which, unaccountably, failed to engage the Hampden. A piece of shrapnel smashed a hole in the pilot's Perspex, hitting him in the chest, apparently without effect, and also cut through the bomb-release circuitry. Despite attempts to dislodge the bombs manually, they remained on board and had to be brought home.

5 Group was handed marshalling yards again on the 8th, when forty-five Hampdens were detailed at Scampton, Waddington and Lindholme to target those at Hamm. 50 Squadron made ready seven aircraft, which took off between 22.40 and 23.00 with S/Ls Mulford and Potts the senior pilots on duty. They set course from Skegness to Enkhuizen, encountering cloud over the North Sea, but Sgt Mudd and crew were already struggling with an engine issue that prevented them from climbing above 7,600 feet. On arrival at the Dutch coast, they spent thirty minutes searching for an enemy ship to attack, but, finding none, they returned to base. S/L Potts and crew encountered a JU88 flying towards England, and engaged it from two hundred yards with both rear guns, without observing any hits. They and the remainder of the 50 Squadron element found the cloud dispersing as they skirted the northern rim of the Ruhr, but thick ground haze rendered target identification something of a challenge. P/O

Owens and crew were aided by the light of flares dropped by others, and ran-in on the aiming-point at 10,000 feet to release their bombs and observe bursts within the yards. Sgt Ford and crew crossed the Dutch coast at 11,000 feet before climbing to 17,000 feet to search for the target. After forty-five minutes, they established their position over the Möhnesee, from where they headed north to the aiming point, reducing altitude to 10,000 feet for the attack. F/L Fox and crew described the haze extending to 8,000 feet, and spent fifty minutes searching, before pinpointing on a river and canal and locating the target to release their bombs from 16,000 feet. On return they reported observing an aircraft crash into the sea halfway between the Dutch and English coasts. S/L Mulford failed to locate the primary target, and selected the town of Wesel to bomb from 11,000 feet, while Sgt Broderick attacked Soest and S/L Potts dropped his wing bombs on a searchlight concentration, before bringing the rest of his load home.

A new Air Ministry directive was issued on the 9th, which alluded to the German transportation system and the morale of its civilian population as the enemy's weakest points. The C-in-C, Sir Richard Peirse, was, consequently, ordered to concentrate his main effort in these areas, which meant that from now on during the moon periods, he was to target the main railway centres ringing the Ruhr, to isolate it from the other regions of Germany, thus preventing the movement in of raw materials and the export of finished goods. On dark nights, the Rhine cities of Cologne, Duisburg and Düsseldorf would be easier to locate for area attacks, and, when unfavourable weather conditions prevailed, operations were to be mounted against more distant urban centres in eastern and southern Germany. 50 Squadron remained at home on that night, while thirty-nine Hampdens joined forces with forty-three Whitleys and Wellingtons to target the Nazi Party HQ at Aachen. This meant that it was, in reality, an area raid, and it resulted in much destruction to housing, particularly in central districts.

P/O John Hopgood arrived at Lindholme on posting from 14 O.T.U on the 10th, and he would make a name for himself as a first-rate pilot until his untimely death during Operation Chastise almost two years hence. That night, 50 Squadron made ready nine Hampdens in a 5 Group force of thirty-two, which were to join ninety-eight Wellingtons in attacking a number of aiming-points in Cologne. One of the 5 Group targets was the Humboldt mechanical engineering works in the Kalk district, situated on the East Bank of the Rhine in the city centre, for which the Lindholme element took off between 22.45 and 22.55 with S/L Burrough the senior pilot on duty. F/O Abbott and crew turned back almost immediately with an engine issue, leaving the others to press on to make landfall over Ostend. Here, P/O Burrows and crew ran into two enemy night-fighters, and, as a result of taking violent evasive action, fell into a spin, during which the bombs were jettisoned, and seven thousand feet were lost. The others found the target largely hidden beneath eight-tenths cloud and thick haze extending up to 12,000 feet, which forced them to search for a pinpoint. P/O Owens and crew came upon the Rhine south of the city, and followed it to the aiming-point, which they attacked from 9,000 feet. S/L Burrough and crew were surprised by an absence of defensive activity on e.t.a., and continued to search until they, too, found the Rhine, which led them to attack the target from 11,500 feet and cause a fire to break out. Sgt Mudd and crew spotted the Rhine south of the target, but could not locate Cologne, and ran-in instead on Bonn, which they attacked from 16,000 feet. Sgt Holme and crew were at 19,000 feet, from where the ground could not be seen, and descended in stages to 6,000 feet, before eventually bombing a railway line near Bonn. Sgt Quinton bombed what he thought was Cologne from 18,000 feet after stooging around for an hour, F/O Collins aimed at a bridge over the Rhine from 10,000 feet, and Sgt Fisher jettisoned his load over Bonn, when the failure of one engine to pick up after violent evasive action threw the Hampden into a spin.

Orders were received at Scampton and Lindholme on the 12th to make ready thirty-three Hampdens to join twenty-eight Wellingtons to target the main railway station in the city of Bremen. The 50 Squadron element of twelve took off between 22.15 and 22.35 with F/L Fox the senior pilot on duty, leading eight crews captained by sergeant pilots. They adopted the familiar outward route from Skegness to the Den Helder peninsular, and Sgt Mudd and crew were fifty miles from making landfall when they were attacked and damaged by an enemy night-fighter at 9,500 feet. The port bomb-bay door was shot away, and the bomb-release gear put out of action, forcing the abandonment of the sortie. The others ran into electrical storms on reaching the enemy coast, which would delay the arrival at the target of all but F/O Abbott and crew, who circumnavigated the towering cloud bank and arrived at the target to find clear skies and visibility at twenty miles. They picked up the River Weser and followed it for three minutes at 16,000 feet right into the heart of the city to release their bombs, at no time under attack from the defences. They concluded that this was the result of being tailed by an enemy fighter, but, eventually, the flak batteries lost patience and opened up, putting the fighter at risk of being hit. The rest of the squadron turned up thirty minutes later after flying through the storms, by which time the conditions over Bremen had deteriorated to leave poor visibility. The defences had become highly active as F/L Fox identified the aiming-point, and released the bombs singly during three passes at 13,500 feet, but they fell into the city rather than onto the railway station. The others bombed on estimated positions from between 12,000 and 16,000 feet, Sgt Ford's AE231 picking up shrapnel damage in the process. Sgt Broderick and crew bombed Wilhelmshaven from 14,000 feet in the face of intense searchlight and flak activity, after failing to locate the primary target, and reached home safely to make their report. Absent from debriefing were two crews, those of P/O Vivian and Sgt Austin in AE226 and AE230 respectively, which had fallen victim to night-fighters on the way home. The former crossed paths with the ace, Oblt Helmut Lent of 4./NJG1, and crashed without survivors at 00.55 at Veendam, close to Holland's north-eastern frontier with Germany. Ten minutes later, the latter was intercepted by Lt Heinz-Martin Hadeball of 7./NJG1, and crashed near Westrup, north-east of Osnabrück, killing three members of the crew outright. It seems likely that Sgt Austin survived, but, according to German records, succumbed to his injuries three day later.

Bremen and Hannover were the targets selected for attention on the 14th, for which 5 Group put up forty-four Hampdens, their crews briefed to attack the railway station in the latter. 50 Squadron did not take part in what returning crews reported to be a successful operation that caused many fires in central districts. When Hamburg was posted as the target for 107 aircraft on the 16th, 50 Squadron responded with the preparation of a dozen Hampdens to contribute to the overall 5 Group force of thirty-two. They departed Lindholme between 22.40 and 23.00 with no senior pilots on duty, and soon lost the services of P/O Burrows and crew to an engine issue. Later on, Sgt Hunter and crew experienced excessive vibration followed by yawing and stalling, and this persuaded them to jettison their load and turn back. The others pushed on towards the enemy coast, some choosing to pinpoint on the estuary end of the River Elbe, while others picked up the distinctive waterway to the south of the target area. Even so, small amounts of low cloud and thick ground haze hampered target location, and few crews were able to positively identify the city. Sgt Quinton picked out the waterways in the docks area with the aid of six flares, and observed his bombs to burst among them, and Sgt Maries and crew also reported bombing within the city. Sgt Fisher and crew were another of the Lindholme contingent to claim bombing in the target area, and Sgt Ford and his crew believed that they had also. The others found alternative targets, including Wilhelmshaven and a built-up area near the town of Itzehoe on the Schleswig-Holstein peninsular, some delivering all of their bombs and others just those attached to the wings. Two bearings were sent to P/O Owens and crew in AD844, and a fix obtained at 01.14, but nothing further was heard, and no trace of the Hampden and crew ever found.

Fifty Wellingtons and twenty-five Hampdens were detailed on the 17th to attack a number of aiming-points in Cologne. Lindholme dispatched ten 50 Squadron Hampdens for the last time between 22.50 and 23.25 with F/L Fox the senior pilot on duty. They flew out over Orfordness on course for Brussels, which Sgt Mudd and crew were approaching when an overheating engine forced them to turn back. Thick haze blotted out most of the ground detail, and it required a persistent search to pick up clues as to the precise location of the Rhineland capital. In the event, most crews found the general area of Cologne, and bombed either on estimated positions or brief glimpses of the Rhine, some observing the burst of their bombs and others not. Sgt Holme and crew were aided by a rising moon, which glinted off something in the city to provide a pinpoint, and they did observe their bombs to fall among buildings. Sgt Good and crew bombed an unidentified aerodrome in Belgium, while P/O Smith and crew jettisoned their wing bombs near Liege and brought the remainder home.

Orders had been received by the squadron to prepare to move to Swinderby, a relatively new station situated some eight miles to the south-east of Lincoln on the A46, seven miles from Newark-on-Trent. Opened in August 1940, the station had been occupied by the Polish bomber squadrons, 300 and 301, and, since June, by the newly-formed 455 Squadron RAAF, but the Poles had moved out on the 18th to create room for 50 Squadron. The aircraft were ferried over from Lindholme in formation on the 19th, and, it is believed, that it was during this procedure that AD897 crashed inverted between Lindholme and Finningley at 11.00. It contained the crew of Sgt Bousfield, who had operated thus far as second pilot to P/O Pexton, and all on board were killed. The squadron did not participate in 5 Group's mining operations in the Frisians and Jade Bay that night, but prepared eleven Hampdens on the 20th for its first operation from its new home. They were among thirty-nine 5 Group Hampdens detailed in an overall force of 113 aircraft to target marshalling yards in Cologne, and took off between 23.00 and 23.20 with F/L Fox the senior pilot on duty. P/O Hopgood was undertaking his first operation with the squadron, flying as second pilot/navigator to P/O Smith, and his first task was to guide the aircraft via Orfordness to a turning point at Namur in Belgium for the approach to the target. Despite poor weather conditions of cloud and haze during the outward flight, all reached the target area to find seven to nine-tenths cloud with tops at 7,000 feet accompanied by haze. Glimpses of the Rhine provided an approximate reference, but there was no possibility of identifying the marshalling yards, and attacks were carried out from between 10,000 and 18,500 feet onto the general area of the city. A number of flashes were observed, followed by fires, and Sgt Quinton thought his bombs fell among a collection of factory buildings. P/O Smith and crew described a huge fire burning around a block of buildings covering a large area, while F/L Fox and crew reported bombing a factory situated some fifteen to twenty miles south-west of Cologne, and observing from their lofty perch at 16,000 feet an exceptionally bright white fire, which covered an area a mile long. The Cologne authorities reported a scattered attack with very minor damage and few casualties.

Frankfurt and Mannheim were named as the targets for a mini-campaign on three consecutive nights from the 21/22nd, and it would be the former's first taste of a major Bomber Command assault. Thirty-seven Wellingtons and thirty-four Hampdens were made ready, while thirty-six Wellingtons and eight Halifaxes were prepared to attack Mannheim city centre some forty-five miles to the south. Neither operation was successful, and the city of Darmstadt, situated fifteen miles south of Frankfurt, sustained greater damage than the intended target. On the following night, thirty-four Hampdens were joined by twenty-nine Whitleys and Wellingtons in a return to Frankfurt, while a small force of Wellingtons attended to Mannheim. 50 Squadron contributed four Hampdens, which departed Swinderby between 22.30 and 22.36 led by S/L Potts, and all made it safely to the turning point at Namur, from where they encountered severe icing conditions that prevented Sgt Fisher and crew from gaining sufficient height to break cloud. The wing bombs were jettisoned in an effort to lighten the aircraft, but this failed to solve the problem, and they turned back from a position within twenty-five miles of the target. The others pressed on, and P/O Grant-Dalton and crew dropped two tins of Razzles from 14,000 feet on the leg from Aachen to Frankfurt between 01.25 and 01.45, before gaining a brief glimpse of the River Main on the southern outskirts of the city. That was as good as it got in the face of eight-tenths cloud, and, with no prospect of identifying the briefed aiming-point, the main post office and telephone exchange, bombing was carried out on an estimated position from 11,000 feet, after which, leaflets were dispensed from 12,000 feet at 02.05. S/L Potts bombed from 11,500 feet, and Sgt Broderick from 14,000 feet, both on estimated positions, and, on his return, the latter would report dropping Razzles on the way out at 01.10, and dispensing six bundles of nickels over the target at 01.42.

50 Squadron made ready nine Hampdens on the 23rd for the final raid of the series on Frankfurt, and they would join forces with twenty-three others from Scampton for the all-5 Group show, while fifty Wellingtons tried their hand at Mannheim. The Swinderby element took off between 22.15 and 22.25 with S/L Mulford the senior pilot on duty, and, it seems, that all reached the target area to encounter a small amount of cloud, but thick haze blotting out ground detail. Bombing had to be carried out on estimated position, and there was some evidence that a few incendiaries and high-explosives fell within the city. P/O Smith and crew failed to identify Frankfurt, and back-tracked to what they believed to be the town of Mayen to the west of Coblenz, where they dropped their wing bombs on a marshalling yard, before releasing the rest of their hardware onto an aerodrome near Adenau. A fix was obtained on AD843, which was returning with the crew of Sgt Holme, and appeared to be off the Norfolk coast. It did not return to Swinderby, and the recovery of the bodies of two crew members off Cromer told its own story.

Preparations had been ongoing for a number of weeks to carry out an audacious attack by daylight on the German warships at Brest under the codename Operation Sunrise. Scheduled for the 24th, it was discovered at the last minute that Scharnhorst had slipped away to La Pallice, some two hundred miles further south, and this required an adjustment to the original complex plan of attack. The intention had been to send three 90 Squadron Fortress Is in to bomb from 30,000 feet to draw up enemy fighters, while 5 Group Hampdens performed a similar function at a less rarefied altitude under the umbrella of a Spitfire escort. While this distraction was in progress, it was hoped that Halifaxes and Wellington from 1, 3 and 4 Groups could sneak in unopposed to target the ships. Now that Scharnhorst had moved, it was decided to send the Halifax element to deal with her, while the rest of the original plan went ahead at Brest. 5 Group detailed six Hampdens each from Waddington, Coningsby and North Luffenham, and they took off at 10.45 to proceed to Predannack in three boxes with Coningsby leading. Over Cornwall they were picked up by the Spitfire escort provided by 10 Group, to be shepherded to the target, which they reached at 14.15, seven minutes after the Fortresses had bombed. The enemy defence was more fierce than anticipated, and ten of the seventy-nine Wellingtons were shot down by flak and fighters, along with two Hampdens, in return for six unconfirmed hits on the Gneisenau. The Halifaxes also suffered heavy losses, but inflicted sufficient damage on the Scharnhorst to necessitate her return to Brest, where superior repair facilities existed.

Kiel's shipyards were posted as the primary target for that night, for which a force of thirty-four Wellingtons and thirty Hampdens was made ready. The favourable conditions allowed ground features to be identified during the bombing run, which had to take place in the face of an intense searchlight and flak barrage. Despite the enthusiastic claims of some crews, the bombing was scattered, and inaccurate, and local authorities reported only a few bombs falling in the shipyards or the town. 50 Squadron was not involved in either operation on the 24th, but orders were received at Swinderby on the 25th to provide six Hampdens to join forces with twenty-four from Scampton and twenty-five Whitleys for an attack on Hannover. The crews were briefed to aim for the main railway station and post office, which meant that it was to be an area raid to target the city centre. The 50 Squadron aircraft departed Swinderby between 22.25 and 22.40, with AE234 the last to leave the ground with the crew of Sgt Montgomery on board. *(The squadron ORB recorded the aircraft as AE184)*. Two minutes later it crashed near Thurlby, seven miles south-south-west of Lincoln, killing the occupants. Sgt Ford and crew no doubt witnessed the incident as they remained in the circuit contending with a failed starboard engine that would force them to abandon their sortie. The others continued on to reach the target area under clear skies, but were denied a sight of the target by the thick industrial haze blotting out all ground detail. Bombing was carried out on estimated positions, and no results observed, but the crews withdrew from the target believing that they had hit the city. On the way home, Sgt Broderick climbed to 19,000 feet to avoid a weather front, but a lack of oxygen and fuel persuaded him to return to a lower level, and, shortly before landing at Driffield, the port engine died through fuel starvation.

It would be left to 5 Group to take care of gardening duties on the succeeding two nights, on the approaches to Lorient and St-Nazaire (Artichoke and Beech gardens) on the 27th, in the absence of 50 Squadron. On the following night the gardens were Radish, Forget-me-not and Quince, (Kiel Harbour, Kiel Bay and the Fehmarn Belt), the last mentioned assigned to a dozen Hampdens from 50 Squadron. They departed Swinderby between 21.50 and 22.25 with F/O Collins the senior pilot on duty, and exited the English coast at Mablethorpe, before setting course for Esbjerg, Rømø or Fanø islands, according to the preference of individual crews. They encountered ten-tenths cloud over the North Sea, extending over the mainland, but a few gaps enabled six crews to establish their position and find the garden area to release their mines into the briefed locations from 600 to 800 feet. Electrical storms and severe icing conditions stalked the returning aircraft, and P/O Christophers and crew, who were intending to return their mine to store, lost the use of their instruments as they froze up. Ice-accretion on the wings became so critical on approach to the Yorkshire coast, that the vegetable had to be jettisoned, and they eventually crash-landed at base at 04.30. AD902 was declared a write-off, while the crew emerged from its wreckage shaken, but not stirred, and fit to fight another day.

Not so for the crew of P/O Burrows, who disappeared without trace in AE159, probably after falling victim to the conditions.

A force of 116 aircraft was made ready to unleash on Cologne on the night of the 30/31st, 5 Group contributing forty-two Hampdens from North Luffenham and Waddington. They headed for the Belgian coast to approach the target from the west, but ran into thunderstorms, heavy rain and icing conditions, which persuaded many crews to seek alternative targets. Aachen, which lay close to the planned track, proved to be popular, but, crews had to base their attacks on searchlights and the flashes from flak batteries, and, like the primary target, it probably avoided most of the bombs. During the course of the month, the squadron undertook fourteen operations, dispatching 136 sorties for the loss of eight Hampdens and seven crews.

August 1941

F/L Lloyd arrived on posting from 16 O.T.U at Upper Heyford on the 1st as flight commander-elect, for which role he would shortly be promoted to squadron leader rank. The Manchester grounding order would remain in place until the 7th, and, in the meantime, 5 Group opened its August account on the night of the 2/3rd, when sending fifty Hampdens to attack the town of Kiel and its shipyards, while larger forces attended to Hamburg and Berlin. An incomplete report from Kiel sources confirmed a failed operation, and mentioned a single house damaged, but did not refer to possible hits in the docks and shipyards. Amid a flurry of postings in and out during the first week of the month, P/O Pexton departed for 16 O.T.U on the 4th at the end of his first tour of operations.

There was no operational activity for Swinderby until the 5th, when orders were received to prepare thirteen Hampdens for that night. The primary targets were posted as Mannheim's main railway station in the Ludwigshafenerstrasse, for which an overall force of ninety-eight aircraft was assembled, and railway workshops at Karlsruhe some thirty miles to the south, involving a force of ninety-seven aircraft. 5 Group detailed thirty-three and fifty Hampdens respectively, and an additional five from Scampton to conduct gardening operations in the western Baltic. 50 Squadron made ready seven aircraft for Mannheim and six for Karlsruhe, and dispatched them from Swinderby in a ten-minute slot from 22.00 with no senior pilots on duty. Both elements were routed out over Orfordness with orders to fly direct to their respective destinations, but P/O Pim and crew, who were operating with the squadron for the first time, were recalled in error when just fifteen miles out over the North Sea. Sgt Ford and crew began to experience excessive vibration from the port engine as they made the sea crossing, and were unable to climb to operational altitude. On reaching the Scheldt estuary, they jettisoned the wing bombs "safe" near Flushing, and returned home. This left five 50 Squadron aircraft continuing on to Mannheim, flying over cloud with a bright, full moon to light their way. Over the target they encountered five to ten-tenths cloud in a band between 14,000 and 18,000 feet, but excellent visibility below, and most identified the city with ease although not necessarily the briefed aiming-point. Sgt Quinton and crew descended to 14,000 feet, just beneath the cloud base, to carry out their attack, while the freshman crews of F/O Banker and P/O Maskell bombed from 2,500 and 7,000 feet respectively, and Sgt Mapp and crew dropped their load between Mühlauhafen and Neckar, north-west of the briefed aiming-point, but still within the built-up area of the city. For some reason, the crew of Sgt Rowney was unable to locate the primary target, and dropped their bombs onto a railway line south of Zell on the way home. Meanwhile, the Karlsruhe element had also found cloud over their target area, and, whilst this prevented them from identifying the railway workshops, they were able to hit the town, most observing bursts and a number of fires. AE137 failed to arrive back at Swinderby, and news eventually came through to confirm that it had crashed at Essen with fatal consequences for Sgt Fothergill and his crew, presumably having strayed too far north on the way home.

It was decided to repeat the Mannheim and Karlsruhe operations on the following night, along with another to a similar target at Frankfurt. A 5 Group force of thirty-eight Hampdens was handed the Karlsruhe job, which was to be launched from North Luffenham in Rutland. 50 Squadron sent F/L Fox and Sgt Mudd and their crews over to that station to take part, and they took off from there at 22.40, each loaded with two 500 and two 250 pounders and 480lbs of incendiaries. Exiting the English coast over the Essex resort of Frinton-on-Sea, they set course for the Mons region of Belgium, but a failing starboard engine forced F/L Fox to jettison his bombs into the sea and turn for home. After landing he reported a near-miss with a Whitley, which, presumably, was returning early from the Frankfurt raid. Sgt Mudd and crew carried on to encounter nine-tenths cloud over the target, which prevented them from identifying the railway workshops. They deposited their bombs and incendiaries on the town, and observed bursts but no detail.

The troublesome operational career of the Manchesters got under way again on the night of the 7/8th, when three from 207 Squadron and fifty-four Hampdens were made ready to join forces with forty-nine other aircraft to attack the mighty Krupp factory at Essen. The operation failed in its purpose, and local authorities reported only the destruction of a bakery. Fifty Hampdens and four Whitleys were detailed on the 8th to attack U-Boot yards in Kiel that night, a number that would have been higher had it not been for an incident at Swinderby. 50 Squadron had prepared fifteen Hampdens for the main operation, and two others for gardening duties in the Frisians, and all took off between 21.55 and 22.25 with S/Ls Potts and Lloyd the senior pilots on duty, the latter undertaking his first sortie with the squadron. AE124 was one of the gardeners, the fourteenth in line to race down the runway, and had just lifted into the air when the port engine cut. P/O Milnes maintained some semblance of control as the Hampden came down just beyond the airfield and was written off, fortunately without damage to the occupants. The three Hampdens awaiting take-off for Kiel were scrubbed, leaving a dozen to represent the squadron at this important target, and the number was reduced further when S/L Potts lost his starboard engine at the mid-point of the North Sea crossing. The others pressed on via Rømø to approach the target from the north, but found cloud increasing as they headed across the Schleswig-Holstein peninsular. Three layers of five-tenths cloud lay over the target, which amounted to a cover of up to nine-tenths, and this allowed some crews to identify the aiming-point through gaps, while others contented themselves with bombing the town, all in the face of a fairly intense searchlight and flak defence. Bombing was carried out from as low as 13,000 feet, but mostly from 16,000 feet, and fires were reported to be taking hold as the aircraft retreated to the west. One very large fire appeared to be oil-related, emitting a column of black smoke, which remained visible for eighty miles into the return flight. 150 miles to the south-west, the freshman crew of Sgt Titcomb encountered five tenths cloud at 2,500 feet, but were well below when releasing their vegetable into the briefed location from 600 feet.

The weather prevented operations on the ensuing two nights, and then North Luffenham was handed the task of preparing twenty Hampdens to target the Uerdingen railway yards at

Krefeld in the Ruhr on the 11th, while thirty-two freshman crews from the other stations targeted the docks at Rotterdam. Four 50 Squadron aircraft departed Swinderby between 00.50 and 01.25, before setting course via Southwold for Overflakkee in the Scheldt estuary. They benefitted from excellent visibility above the tenth-tenths cloud laying over the entire route, and P/O Ferrie and crew found a gap, through which they dropped their four 500 pounders onto the docks from 11,000 feet without observing the results. Sgt Farrow and crew attacked a searchlight concentration near Dordrecht in Holland, leaving the remaining two crews to bring their bombs home. Five hundred bags of tea were also dispensed over Holland.

The night of the 12/13th was to be a busy one for the Command, and, throughout the day, aircraft were made ready for attacks on Berlin, Hannover, Magdeburg and Essen. 5 Group detailed thirteen Hampdens to join sixty-five Wellingtons for Hannover, and thirty-six to operate on their own at Magdeburg, while a force of seventy aircraft assigned to the Capital would include nine Manchesters. Hannover lay on the route to both Magdeburg and Berlin, and the three forces would fly out together until reaching it, at which point the Berlin element would continue straight on for the 150 additional miles, while the Magdeburg element peeled off to the south-east with eighty miles still ahead of them. 50 Squadron made ready eight Hampdens, which took off between 20.45 and 21.10 with W/C Walker the senior pilot on duty. They made landfall at Borken and crossed mainland Holland, and it was shortly after crossing into Germany that Sgt Hunter and crew lost the use of their a.s.i. They were between the towns of Rheine and Nordhorn at the time, and unloaded their bombs from 16,000 feet onto whatever lay below. The others pressed on to the target over cloud and haze, which would prevent some from identifying the target. Magdeburg lay under five to ten-tenths cloud at around 8,000 feet with ground mist, despite which, F/O Banker, W/C Walker and Sgts Mudd and Quinton identified the target and carried out attacks from 6,000, 12,000, 12,500 and 15,000 feet respectively, observing some bursts and a fire. Sgt Dawson and crew conducted an extensive search, but came up short, and dropped their bombs onto a built-up area between Magdeburg and Braunschweig on the way home. Sgt Fisher and crew experienced similar difficulties, and set course for Bremen, which also proved to be elusive, and they finally dropped their load onto what they believed was Wilhelmshaven. As they flew home through icing conditions, one engine failed, and all removeable equipment was jettisoned to lighten the load. The Hampden crashed on landing, fortunately, without injury to the occupants, and AE228 would be returned to service after repair. P/O Smith and crew landed at Digby, and no debriefing report was entered into the squadron ORB.

There would be no further operations from Swinderby for four nights, and even longer for Sgts Broderick and Maries, who were posted to 16 O.T.U later on the 13th at the conclusion of their tours. Orders were received across the Command on the 14th to prepare for operations that night against railway targets in three major cities in northern Germany to the north of the Harz mountains, Hannover the most westerly, Magdeburg the most easterly and Braunschweig (Brunswick) in-between. 5 Group detailed eighty-one Hampdens to operate alone against Braunschweig, while seven Manchester crews were briefed for Magdeburg as part of an overall force of fifty-two aircraft. Despite many claims of bomb bursts and fires from the Braunschweig participants, only half of the force reached the target area, and no reports were forthcoming from local sources to confirm or deny any damage.

F/O Whitecross DFC, who had recently returned from France following his forced landing in April, took off with his new crew on an air-sea-rescue sortie over the North Sea in P4408 on the 15th, and failed to return. A message that the engines were failing was received at 15.30, and no trace of the Hamden and its crew was ever found. Railway objectives featured again on the 16th, when orders went out to stations across the Command to prepare for attacks on installations in the Ruhr cities of Düsseldorf and Duisburg, and Cologne to the south. Düsseldorf was to be a 5 Group show involving fifty-two Hampdens and six Manchesters, three and two respectively of which failed to return. The crews of those that did, reported many fires, but no local report materialized to confirm the outcome.

50 Squadron returned to operations on the 17th, when contributing eleven Hampdens to a 5 Group force of thirty-nine briefed to attack the main goods railway station in Bremen, while twenty 4 Group Whitleys targeted the city's Focke-Wulf factory. The Swinderby element took off between 22.20 and 23.00 with S/L Potts the senior pilot on duty, and they were followed into the air between 00.35 and 00.50 by four freshman crews bound for the Nectarines garden off the Frisians. Some of the bombers set course for Enkhuizen, while others chose to approach the target from the north-west, but two would be prevented by engine issues from even reaching the enemy coast. F/Sgt Mapp and crew were back on the ground after forty-five minutes because of an excessive exhaust flame, while P/O Helmore and crew jettisoned their load fifteen miles out from Texel because of rising oil temperature and an inability to climb. Those reaching the target area found variable amounts of cloud and ground haze that prevented all from identifying the briefed aiming-point, and five of them bombed the general area of the city from between 10,000 and 15,000 feet. Others attacked Wilhelmshaven, Cuxhaven and Norderney aerodrome, and there was no report from P/O Maskell and crew, who failed to return. AE185 had been shot down by Oblt Ludwig Becker of 4./NJG1, and had crashed at 01.44 some five miles south of Groningen in northern Holland. P/O Maskell escaped with his life to fall into enemy hands, but his crew perished in the wreckage of the Hampden. S/L Potts reported a hostile reception over the city, and brought home a flak-damaged aircraft to prove his point. Meanwhile, three of the gardeners reached the target area after Sgt Beaver and crew had turned back with engine failure, and found five to eight-tenths cloud with a base at around 2,000 feet. They planted their vegetables into the briefed location from 600 and 800 feet before returning safely.

Unknown to the crews, the operations during June and July had been monitored in order to provide an assessment for the War Cabinet of the effectiveness of the strategic bombing campaign. The project was initiated by Churchill's chief scientific advisor, Professor Lindemann, Lord Cherwell, who handed the responsibility to David M Bensusan-Butt, a civil-servant assistant to Cherwell working in the War Cabinet Secretariat. What became known as The Butt Report was released on the 18th, and its disclosures sent shock waves reverberating around the Cabinet Room and the Air Ministry. Having studied around four thousand photographs taken during night operations, he concluded that only a small fraction of bombs had fallen within miles of their intended targets. This swept away at a stroke any notion, that the Command was reducing the enemy's capacity and will to continue the fight. It also demonstrated the claims of the crews to be wildly optimistic, and unjustly blighted forever the period of tenure as Commander-in-Chief of Sir Richard Peirse. In his defence, the focus of operations changed frequently, the demands and expectations of his superiors were not realistic and the crews, though doing their best, were ill-equipped for the tasks required of them.

While the report was being digested that evening, 5 Group sent forty-two Hampdens from North Luffenham and Coningsby to attack the West Station at Cologne in company with twenty Whitleys and Wellingtons. Returning crews reported many fires on the western side of the Rhine, but local reports of only superficial damage suggested that a decoy fire site had attracted the main weight of bombs. It was a similar story on the following night, when forty-one Hampdens from Scampton and Waddington joined sixty-seven other aircraft to attempt to hit a railway junction in Kiel. Poor weather conditions prevented forty crews from locating the target, and no bombs were reported by the town authorities. A series of three operations against Mannheim began on the night of the 22/23rd, for which 5 Group provided forty-one Hampdens from Coningsby, Syerston and Waddington, which were to join forces with fifty-six Wellingtons. Three aiming-points included the main railway station, but only a handful of high-explosive bombs landed within the city, as yet another operation failed to find the mark. It was left to Scampton to provide a dozen Hampdens to represent the group at Düsseldorf on the 25th, when 4 Group Whitleys and Halifaxes completed the force of forty-four aircraft. Six additional Hampdens were assigned to searchlight suppression duties in the Wesel defensive belt, their task to attack with small bombs and guns any battery holding a bomber in its beams. This activity turned out to be more effective than the raid on Düsseldorf, and caused the beams either to become erratic or to be extinguished altogether.

50 Squadron had not operated for a week when orders were received at Swinderby on the 25th to prepare fourteen Hampdens for a 5 Group attack on Mannheim by thirty-eight Hampdens and seven Manchesters. The crews were briefed to aim for the main Post Office, which made it an area raid, for which the 50 Squadron crews took off between 20.30 and 21.10 with S/L Mulford the senior pilot on duty. They flew out over Orfordness on a direct course for the target, but Sgt Hunter and crew were forced to turn back soon after crossing the coast, after the engines failed to provide sufficient power to climb above 1,500 feet. The others pressed on to encounter an ice-bearing front midway between the Dutch coast and the target, which left few opportunities to see the ground and establish a pinpoint. Sgt Turner and crew were still short of the target when ice-accretion persuaded them to jettison the wing bombs and seek an alternative target on the way home. In the event, only one wing bomb fell off, and, after the rest of the load hung up over the last-resort target of Ostend, they were returned to store. S/L Mulford attacked the briefed aiming-point through a gap in the five-tenths cloud from 11,000 feet, while F/O Banker and P/O Ferrie glided down to 3,500 feet to obtain a clearer view before releasing their loads. The remaining crews bombed the city area from between 9,000 and 17,000 feet, either visually or on estimated positions on e.t.a., and moderate results were claimed. AE320 failed to return with the crew of Sgt Fisher, and it was established later that all had lost their lives after crashing in Germany.

Cologne was posted as the target on the 26th, and a force of ninety-nine aircraft made ready, which included twenty-nine Hampdens and a single Manchester provided by Scampton, Coningsby and Syerston, while six other Hampdens from Scampton were to carry out flak suppression sorties to the west of the city. 50 Squadron was not involved in what became another highly unsatisfactory performance that deposited no more than 15% of the bomb loads into eastern districts. P/O Leslie Manser was posted in from 14 O.T.U on the 27th, but would not take part in either of that night's activities, a return to Mannheim and mining in the Nectarines garden around the Frisians. A force of ninety-one aircraft was assembled for the former, North Luffenham, Waddington and Swinderby making ready thirty-five Hampdens, six of them representing 50 Squadron. The squadron's gardening element of seven Hampdens departed Swinderby first, between 19.45 and 20.00, led by W/C Walter Cheshire (not to be confused with W/C Leonard Cheshire), who was on a brief attachment to Swinderby, presumably to gain operational experience, although for what reason is unclear. He had served previously as Engineering Officer at Bomber Command HQ, and, would return to Bomber Command HQ after leaving Swinderby on the 2nd of September to serve as Chief Intelligence Officer. In 1942, he would be appointed Air Attaché to Moscow, before returning to England in October 1943 to assume command of the new 5 Group bomber station at Spilsby. At about the time that the gardeners were approaching their target area, the bombing element took off between 22.35 and 22.45, with no senior pilots on duty, and immediately lost X2991, which failed to gain height and crashed beyond the airfield, fortunately, without casualties among the crew of P/O Ferrie.

There were mixed opinions concerning the weather conditions around the Frisians, ranging from low cloud and poor visibility according to W/C Cheshire, and reasonable to good visibility as far as the others were concerned. They were able to pinpoint on the island of Borkum without difficulty, and make timed runs to the drop zone, where the vegetables were planted from between 600 and 900 feet. All were diverted to Horsham-St-Faith on return, a number of them to be kept circling for two hours before being given permission to land. Meanwhile, the Mannheim crews were seeking out the main railway station as their aiming-point, and benefitting from good visibility, which enabled a number of crews to identify it, while the others attacked the general area of the city from between 10,000 and 15,000 feet, and caused a number of fires to break out. This was yet another occasion on which the claims of the crews were not borne out by local reports, which spoke of just thirteen buildings sustaining damage.

50 Squadron sat out the following night's operation to attack marshalling yards in Duisburg, for which 5 Group put up thirty Hampdens and six Manchesters in an overall force of 118 aircraft, and six further Hampdens for searchlight suppression duties. Returning crews claimed a successful raid, but, again, this was disputed by local reports, which suggested that only around a dozen bomb loads had hit the city. The final raid of the Mannheim series was posted on Wellington stations on the 29th, while Frankfurt was notified as the destination for a 4 and 5 Group force of 143 aircraft. 5 Group contributed seventy-three Hampdens and three Manchesters for this largest raid yet on the city, 50 Squadron providing fourteen of the former, which departed Swinderby between 21.30 and 22.45 with S/L Potts the senior pilot on duty. This was the maiden operation for P/O Manser, who was flying as second pilot to P/O Ford, and was responsible for guiding his crew to the briefed aiming-point of the inland docks on the River Main. This was a momentous occasion for fellow Swinderby residents, 455 Squadron RAAF, which sent a single Hampden to launch Australia into the bombing war.

The briefed route was to take the crews from Orfordness to Namur in Belgium, but some opted to fly directly to the target from the English coast, which meant landfall over the Scheldt estuary and skirting northern Belgium to pass south of Cologne. Sgt Beaver and crew were fifty miles out from the English coast, when an overheating starboard engine forced them to turn back, while P/O Carter and crew were thirty miles short of the Dutch coast when T.R 9 failure ended their sortie. Cloud lay over most of the route, and icing became a problem for some, P/O Miller and crew having to jettison the wing bombs in order to climb to a reasonable height. A number of crews were able to pick out the river and docks by attacking from below 10,000 feet, but seven to nine-tenths cloud prevented others from identifying the planned aiming-point. Bombing was carried out from between 4,000 and 14,000 feet, P/O Banker and crew responsible for the lower altitude, from where the gunners fired off eight hundred rounds. S/L Potts and crew lost the use of their intercom, and ended up attacking a built-up area south-east of Frankfurt, possibly Offenbach, while Sgt Dawson and crew had dropped their wing bombs on Aachen to gain height, and released the remainder on Wiesbaden in error for the primary target a few miles further to the east. The last fix on Sgt Turner and crew put them homebound over north-eastern France, and news eventually came through to confirm that AD839 had crashed near Abbeville, close to the coast, killing all on board. On return at 04.30, AE229 crashed on a dummy landing site at Bassingham, situated eight miles south-south-west of Lincoln, and was written off, while F/Sgt Mapp and one of his crew sustained injuries.

The last night of the month brought an attack on railway targets in Cologne involving a force of 103 aircraft. 5 Group put up thirty-nine Hampdens and six 207 Squadron Manchesters for the main event, and five further Manchesters to perform a flak suppression role. The weather proved to be unhelpful, and only two-thirds of the force claimed to have bombed the approximate location of the city. 50 Squadron was not involved, and ended the month with a tally of thirteen operations and ninety-seven sorties for the loss of seven Hampdens and five crews.

September 1941

5 Group was in action on the first night of the new month, when twenty Hampdens joined forces with Wellingtons to attack Cologne in what turned out to be favourable weather conditions. Despite this, few bombs found the mark, and the fires reported by returning crews were probably from decoy sites. Briefings took place across the Command on the 2nd for two operations to be carried out that night, both supported by 5 Group. The main operation would be conducted by 126 aircraft, including eleven Hampdens, against Frankfurt, while a force of forty-nine aircraft was to target the central railway station in Berlin, some 260 miles to the north-east. The bulk of the latter force, thirty-two Hampdens and four Manchesters, was provided by 5 Group, with a handful of 3 Group Stirlings and 4 Group Halifaxes in attendance. 50 Squadron made ready five Hampdens for each operation, and four others to undertake gardening duties in the western Baltic, and it was the last mentioned that took off first, between 19.35 and 19.45. Each was assigned to a different garden, F/L Abbott and crew to Wallflower (Kiel Harbour), P/O Carter to Daffodil (southern Sound), P/O Ferrie to Melon (Eckernförde), and P/O Helmore to Quince (Kiel Bay). The sound of their engines had barely died away before the first of the bombers took off at 19.53, to be followed over the ensuing fifty-two minutes by the others. S/L Lloyd was the senior pilot on duty among the Berlin element, with P/O Manser on board as his second pilot/navigator, and P/O Miller leading the Frankfurt-bound quintet.

The weather conditions would prove to be unfavourable to all participants in the night's activities, and few would complete their sorties as briefed. Sgt Rowney and crew had just crossed the French coast when the port engine and the intercom failed, and they experienced a tense time returning over the Channel on one engine. P/O Miller was fortunate to find a large gap in the cloud right over Frankfurt, through which bright moonlight shone to reveal the ground, enabling him to release the bombs onto the aiming-point in the face of intense flak co-operating with around thirty searchlights. Sgt Beaver and crew, who were on attachment to gain operational experience before re-joining the newly-forming 408 Squadron RCAF, picked up the target by approaching from the north, and also found the briefed aiming-point. Sgt Smith and crew were unable to identify the aiming-point, and bombed the city area instead, and it was a similar story for Sgt Howett and crew, who picked up the River Rhine to the south and followed it to Mannheim to release their load there.

The squadron scribe failed to provide any meaningful detail in the ORB for this night's operations, and stated simply that S/L Lloyd was successful at Berlin, despite five to ten-tenths cloud cover between 6,000 and 8,000 feet over the whole of northern Germany. P/O Waddell, and Sgts Dawson and Mudd let their bombs go over the city generally, the last-mentioned from 12,000 feet, and all reported fires burning as they retreated to the west. F/Sgt Titcomb and crew failed to locate the Capital, and attacked Kiel as an alternative target on the way home. The gardeners, meanwhile, were experiencing similar difficulties, F/L Abbott and crew spending fifty minutes searching in rain-bearing cloud in a band between 800 and 8,000 feet, without once observing the sea or land. It was a similar story for the others, and only P/O Helmore eventually released a mine after coming down to 900 feet, although it was not in the briefed location, but in another defined area eight miles off Copenhagen. P/O Ferrie and crew jettisoned their mine after coming under fire from flak and night-fighters, and were hit several times by ground fire before escaping into cloud. Conditions remained challenging for the homeward flight for all crews, and, with fuel running low, accidents were a distinct possibility. P/O Ferrie and crew landed in AE157 at Waddington at 03.20, and collided with a 44 Squadron Hampden, writing off both aircraft. AE305 crash-landed on the A149 road close to the Norfolk coast at Wells-next-the-Sea, sliding through two hedges before coming to rest. Sgt Titcomb and his crew emerged unscathed from the wreckage, and the two pilots would soon be posted to 408 Squadron RCAF. X2919 had been airborne for almost nine hours, when it crash-landed between Wittering airfield and Wansford in Cambridgeshire at 05.10, injuring Sgt Mudd and one of his crew.

The enemy warships at Brest returned to the spotlight on the 3rd after a respite in recent weeks, and a force of 140 aircraft was made ready. 5 Group contributed thirty Hampdens and two 207 Squadron Manchesters, which took off, only for a recall signal to bring them home shortly afterwards, along with those from 1 and 4 Groups, because of deteriorating weather conditions. In the event, 3 Group and four other aircraft that had failed to pick up the signal, carried on and bombed on estimated positions through a smoke screen. On the 6th, 5 Group detailed eighteen Hampdens from Coningsby to join with sixty-eight other aircraft to attack a chemicals-producing factory at Hüls, a northern district of Krefeld in the Ruhr, which was engaged in the manufacture of synthetic rubber for tyres. While this operation was in progress, thirty-four additional Hampdens were sent to Kinloss and Lossiemouth as forward launching pads for mining operations in the Onions garden off Oslo. Not all arrived in time to take part, and ten sorties would be scrubbed, but the eight aircraft representing 50 Squadron all made it back into the air from Lossiemouth between 21.35 and 22.15 with W/C Walker and S/L Mulford the senior pilots on duty. They flew out in perfect conditions under clear skies and a brilliant moon, and all reached the target area to deliver their vegetables from between 600 and 1,000 feet in the face of considerable amounts of light and heavy flak over Oslo and the north-western bank of the fjord. Afterwards, W/C Walker dropped his wing bombs from 800 feet between two vessels of 5,000 and 3,000 tons in Drammens Fjord, while P/O Smith attacked a three-masted ship in Stavanger Harbour and F/O Collins a 5,000 tonner at the mouth of the fjord. Sgt Howett found Lista aerodrome for his wing bombs, and S/L

Mulford dropped his onto a flare-path at a seaplane base, leaving the others to jettison theirs after failing to find a suitable target.

Berlin was posted as the night's main target on the 7th, for which a force of 197 aircraft was made ready, while the Deutsche Werke U-Boot yards and the town of Kiel would occupy a further fifty-one aircraft. 5 Group supported both operations, with eighteen Hampdens for the latter and forty-three Hampdens and four 207 Squadron Manchesters for the Capital. 50 Squadron made ready just three Hampdens, and they departed Swinderby for Kiel at 21.45 carrying two 500 and two 250 pounders each. The ideal weather conditions continued as they set course from Mablethorpe to Rømø Island, but that was of little consequence to Sgt Rowney and crew, who were forced to turn back with an excessively vibrating engine. P/O Helmore found the target with ease, and ran through the defensive fire at 15,000 feet to drop his bombs, which were seen to detonate and cause two fires. Sgt Good and crew failed to return in AE318, but the good news eventually arrived via the Red Cross that all had survived and were in enemy hands, after being shot down near Oldenburg, west of Bremen. The attack on Kiel caused some damage, but nothing of consequence, while that on Berlin fell upon districts north and east of the centre, and hit a number of war-industry factories and housing.

The first large Bomber Command attack on the city of Kassel, situated some fifty miles to the east of the Ruhr, was briefed to crews of all groups on the 8th, and would involve ninety-five aircraft, including twenty-seven Hampdens. The 5 Group crews were given an armaments factory as the aiming-point, and, although not specified, it was probably one of the Henschel or Fieseler aircraft factories within the city. 50 Squadron dispatched five Hampdens between 19.45 and 20.15 with S/L Potts the senior pilot on duty, and four of them followed the briefed route from Orfordness to Dinant in Belgium, while the fifth skirted the northern rim of the Ruhr. The fine weather continued to aid the crews in their search for the target, and four of them described excellent visibility under clear skies and bright moonlight, while S/L Potts reported considerable amounts of cloud and having to climb to 9,000 feet to use his camera. He and P/O Smith failed to pick up the aiming-point, the former bombing the general city area and the latter the nearby town of Bad Hersfeld to the south, before strafing the railway lines and sidings. P/O Ford and crew attacked the primary target from 10,000 feet, and Sgt Smith from 13,500 feet, while the Rowney crew chose to go in high at 18,000 feet. The last-mentioned were in AD854, which was running on fumes as it passed into Bedfordshire airspace north-west of Luton. Sgt Rowney ordered his crew to bale out, leaving him to attempt a forced-landing near Woburn Abbey at 03.50, which he and his wireless operator, who had remained on board, failed to survive.

Orders were received on the 11th to prepare for an attack on the Neptun shipyards at Rostock, while the rest of the force targeted the nearby Heinkel factory and the town itself. A total force of fifty-six aircraft consisted of thirty-nine Hampdens and five 207 Squadron Manchesters in company with a dozen Wellingtons. This was one of three Baltic coast targets for the night, the others, at Kiel and Warnemünde, being assigned to Wellingtons and Whitleys respectively. 50 Squadron was not involved in the main activity, but sent the single freshman crew of Sgt Taylor to mine the waters of one of the four Rosemary gardens in Heligoland Bight. They took off at 23.40 and returned six hours later to report finding the target area in favourable conditions, and delivering the vegetable into the briefed location from 800 feet. Cloud over the Baltic coast prevented the main operations from identifying the aiming-points and the towns received most of the bombs.

Sgt Bartlett was killed in a flying accident while training at 14.O.T.U at Cottesmore on the 12th, but no further details were recorded. A force of 130 aircraft was assembled on the 12th to target Frankfurt, thirty-one of them Hampdens, and, at Swinderby, eight were loaded with a single 1,000 and two 500 pounders each. They took off between 22.35 and 23.25 with F/L Abbott the senior pilot on duty, and headed out over Orfordness to make landfall at the Scheldt before setting course for Namur in Belgium. They were well on their way to the target when the freshman gardening crews of Sgt Atkinson, Sgt Lord and P/O Laidlaw took to the air between 01.20 and 01.40 bound via Skegness for the Nectarines region off the Frisians. They all encountered cloud over the sea and for most of the outward flight, until it thinned to six-tenths at 6,000 feet in the target area of Frankfurt to allow moonlight to penetrate through and illuminate the ground. Sgt Howett and crew failed to identify the primary target after a long search, and flew back towards the Ruhr, where they ran into intense searchlight and flak activity and dropped their bombs from 11,500 feet onto a built-up area on the southern fringes. F/O Banker and crew were also unsuccessful, and found a suitable alternative in the form of a large factory at Aschaffenburg, which they attacked from 1,000 feet. The others located the target, P/O Smith and crew gliding down from 11,000 to 5,000 feet to release their bombs, before being caught in a cone of forty searchlights and narrowly escaping with themselves and their aircraft intact. P/O Grant-Dalton and crew dodged the defences to bomb the general area of the city, while P/O Helmore and crew ran the gauntlet at 5,000 feet as they released their load onto the main marshalling yards. They were hit in the port engine oil tank and the tailplane, and the engine worked spasmodically thereafter, until seizing up and shedding its propeller near Martlesham, forcing them to land wheels-up at Mildenhall. F/O Collins and F/L Abbott returned to report bombing the target area and the docks respectively, and observing a fire and billowing white smoke. The gardeners, meanwhile, found good visibility beneath the ten-tenths cloud, and delivered their vegetables from between 500 and 700 feet.

It was time for another attempt on the German warships at Brest on the 13th, and a force of 147 aircraft of six different types was assembled across the Command. 5 Group contributed thirty-eight Hampdens and four Manchesters from North Luffenham, Coningsby and Waddington, all of which, like the rest of the participants, were thwarted by the smoke screen that engulfed the vessels and hid them from view. 50 Squadron remained at home on this night and until the 15th, when the focus of the 5 Group crews was to be on the particular job in hand, which, for the Manchester element was a railway junction in Germany's Second City, while fifty Hampdens targeted the Blohm & Voss shipyards in company with more than a hundred other aircraft. Nine 50 Squadron Hampdens were loaded with a mixture of high-explosives and incendiaries and departed Swinderby between 18.15 and 18.50 with S/L Lloyd the senior pilot on duty. They crossed the coast at Mablethorpe and flew out over the North Sea with a layer of ten-tenths stratus cloud beneath them at 5,000 feet. On arrival at the enemy coast shortly before 22.00, the skies had cleared sufficiently to allow sight of the Elbe estuary, from which point the force would have to run the gauntlet of searchlights and flak all the way to the aiming-points. Light flak was reaching 10,000 feet, with searchlights co-operating with night-fighters to create the usual hostile environment for the attackers, and it was the searchlight glare that prevented P/O Waddell and crew from identifying the aiming-point. They turned back towards the west and dropped their bombs from 16,000 feet, leaving the others to target the briefed aiming-point from between 10,000 and 18,000 feet. Many bursts and fires were observed from east to west across the docks, and the residential district of

Wandsbek was also hit and casualties inflicted. Sgt Taylor and crew arrived back short of fuel and joined the Scampton circuit, only to be kept waiting until the starboard engine failed through fuel starvation. AD927 was crash-landed in a field, sustaining considerable, but not terminal damage.

There was more than an element of chaos surrounding the Berlin operation on the night of the 20/21st, when the force of seventy-four aircraft was recalled because of deteriorating weather conditions. 5 Group had sent thirty-six Hampdens to forward bases, but ten of these were cancelled when they could not be refuelled in time. 50 Squadron's eight Hampdens took off from Swanton Morley between 19.40 and 20.20 with S/L Mulford the senior pilot on duty, and were spread from the western coast of Denmark to the eastern side of the Schleswig-Holstein peninsular by the time that the recall came through via W/T. Bombs were dropped on the nearest last-resort targets, and these ranged from Heligoland in the west, Lübeck in the east and Rheine in the south as the crews made their way home to encounter challenging conditions of fog and mist. Aircraft were diverted to a variety of stations in Lincolnshire and Yorkshire, and most made it onto terra-firma with dwindling reserves of fuel. Among the last to land was the crew of P/O Grant-Dalton, who had failed to pick up the recall signal, and had reached Berlin, where the poor visibility prevented them from identifying the Alexanderplatz railway station that had been their briefed aiming-point. The bombs were dropped onto the city from 15,000 feet, and a safe return made to Church Fenton, between Leeds and York, where they reported three aircraft being shot down by flak in the Berlin defence zone.

On the 22nd, W/C Walker attended an investiture at Buckingham Palace to receive his DSO, while the squadron, and, indeed, the group, spent the next week on the ground as the weather rendered operations impracticable. After the cancellation of less-experienced crews and accidents and incidents, thirty Hampdens from Scampton, Coningsby and Waddington took off on the 28th to attack Frankfurt's main railway station. Those reaching the target found it impossible in the conditions to identify the aiming-point, and bombed the general area of the city. The 29th brought briefings for Stettin and Hamburg, the former for all but 5 Group, which contributed thirty-eight Hampdens and four Manchesters to an overall force of ninety-three aircraft bound for Germany's Second City. Their target was the Hamburger Flugzeugbau aircraft factory, a subsidiary of the Blohm & Voss company, situated in the Finkenwerde district on the southern bank of the Elbe to the west of the city centre. 50 Squadron made ready six Hampdens for this, and two more to join eight others from the group to attack the Admiral Scheer pocket battleship moored nearby. S/L Potts and F/L Banker took off first at 18.10 and 18.15 respectively, and they were followed into the air immediately by the main element in a twenty-five-minute slot to 18.40. Sgt Lord and crew were well on their way when the oxygen supply to the rear gunner was found to be absent, and they were forced to turn back. The others found the conditions over Hamburg to be hazy, which made identification something of a challenge, and accurate searchlight and flak activity added to the difficulties. S/L Potts identified the Admiral Scheer with some difficulty, and was only targeted by flak when on a straight-and-level bombing run, but F/L Banker could not locate it and bombed the docks area close to the Blohm & Voss shipyards. They were aided by moonlight, but this was insufficient to enable the main element to find the aircraft factory, and they attacked the general target area from between 10,000 and 17,000 feet. Local reports confirmed nine fires, but no damage worthy of particular mention.

Hamburg was posted as the destination again on the last night of the month, this time for eighty-two aircraft targeting the Blohm & Voss aircraft factory after the previous night's failure. 5 Group put up forty-eight Hampdens from Coningsby, Scampton, North Luffenham, Syerston and Swinderby, six of them representing 50 Squadron, while two of its freshman crews were to bomb the docks at Cherbourg. The main element took off between 18.15 and 18.25 with no senior pilots on duty, but P/O Ford was unable to coax his aircraft beyond 12,000 feet and turned back. The others pressed on to meet the usual reception of intense searchlight and flak, with the light tracer reaching up to 15,000 feet, but visibility, aided by the moonlight, was relatively good and allowed some to identify the briefed aiming-point. Others contented themselves with bombing the general area of the docks from around 15,000 feet, and a number of fires were observed, which were confirmed by local reports. Meanwhile, the freshmen had taken off either side of 20.00, and returned shortly after midnight to report successful sorties and one large fire. During the course of the month the squadron took part in fifteen operations and dispatched seventy-five sorties for the loss of five Hampdens and one-and-a-half crews.

October 1941

The new month began for 5 Group with an operation on the 1st to Karlsruhe in southern Germany, for which forty-five Hampdens were made ready, seven of them belonging to 50 Squadron. They departed Swinderby between 19.14 and 19.28, having been preceded into the air by the freshman crew of P/O Hore, who were bound for the Nectarines garden off the Frisians. S/L Lloyd was the senior pilot among the bombing brigade, with P/O Manser flying now as his second pilot, on a night when doubts about the weather at home would once more intervene to force a recall signal to be sent at 21.00. Unaccountably, none of the 50 Squadron crews picked it up, and all continued on across Belgium, where S/L Lloyd and crew ran into searchlights in the Ardennes, and were attacked from the port quarter and above by a Ju88. The wireless operator was wounded by the first burst, but continued to return fire, as did the rear gunner, and three plumes of fire were seen to emanate from the nose of the assailant. They were then set upon by a single-engine fighter, which scored hits on the port wing, but this, too, was driven off by return fire, and the bombs dropped onto a factory at Chimay on the way home. The others reached the target area over ten-tenths cloud, and spent time searching for a reference on the ground. When this failed to materialize, F/L Banker found a railway junction for his bombs in the upper Rhine Valley, and observed fires break out after straddling the line. While he was circling, admiring his work, a Me109 fired a short burst before being lost in the haze. P/O Helmore and crew were searching for the target, when a diversion signal was received, and they dropped their bombs on an unidentified flare-path north-west of the target. Sgt Lord and crew attacked an unidentified town on the West Bank of the Rhine, Sgt Smith let his wing bombs go on a searchlight concentration, and P/O Waddell released his load over a built-up area, which might have been Karlsruhe. P/O Ford and crew bombed a small town to the west of the Rhine from 11,000 feet, before returning safely with the others. P/O Hore and crew had landed some time earlier after completing a successful maiden gardening sortie.

There were no operations for 5 Group and most other elements of the Command between the 2nd and 9th as the weather took a hand, and this would pave the way for a busy and record-breaking night of operations on the 12th. In the meantime, on the 10th, 5 Group dispatched forty-six Hampdens and ten Manchesters to target the Krupp works at Essen, and a further six to patrol the searchlight belt at Bocholt on the north-western approach to the Ruhr. 50 Squadron was not involved, but detailed four freshman crews to cut their teeth on the docks at Dunkerque, waving them off from Swinderby between 18.46 and 18.50. Sgt Williams and crew spent three hours over enemy territory, but were clearly off track, and saw little in the way of defensive activity. The bombs were jettisoned over the sea, and the English coast crossed near Withernsea with just twenty gallons left in each inboard tank. A belly-landing was carried out a few miles inland near Patrington, and the crew emerged unscathed. The others ran through fairly heavy flak at 10,000 to 12,000 feet to drop their bombs from 8,000 to 18,000 feet, and returned safely.

A largely rested and serviced bomber force allowed a new record number of 373 aircraft to be made ready on stations from Yorkshire to East Anglia on the 12th, 152 of them for an operation against Nuremberg, while ninety-nine others, including twenty Hampdens, were given Bremen as their destination. The bulk of 5 Group, however, was to target the previously mentioned synthetic rubber factory at Hüls in the Ruhr, for which eighty-two Hampdens and fourteen 207 Squadron Manchesters were detailed. There would also be eight Hampdens carrying out searchlight suppression in the Bocholt area as the main body of aircraft passed through. Technical problems forced the withdrawal of three Hampdens and three Manchesters, but fourteen of the former from 50 Squadron departed Swinderby between 00.28 and 01.18 with W/C Walker and S/L Potts the senior pilots on duty. Sgt Atkinson and crew were still over Norfolk when an engine issue curtailed their sortie, leaving the others to begin the North Sea crossing under clear skies and a half moon en-route for Enkhuizen. The element was further reduced when P/O Carter and crew turned back after thirty minutes, to be followed fifteen minutes later by Sgt Taylor and crew, both with communications issues. The others pressed on to the enemy coast to find nine to ten-tenths cloud at 7,000 to 10,000 feet, which extended all the way to the target and tested the crews' ability to establish their positions. Sgt Lord and crew turned back at Enkhuizen, another victim of communications problems, while the others reached the target area to find it obscured by cloud. Balloons were found to be tethered at 5,000 to 6,000 feet to create hazards for aircraft descending through the cloud, and P/O Helmore and crew severed a cable with the starboard wing as they carried out their bombing run in the face of a spirited flak defence. They were hit a number of times, but escaped into cloud and failed to observe the results of their efforts. P/O Ferrie also hit a cable, which broke at 3,000 feet after he had put the Hampden into a flat spin, only then to become entangled in another cable, from which they broke free at 1,000 feet, while under intense and accurate anti-aircraft fire. One bomb door was smashed, which prevented the 1,900lb bomb from being released, and ten other hits were sustained. Having noted the balloons, W/C Walker ran in on the aiming-point at 8,000 feet, surrounded by searchlight beams and exploding light and medium calibre flak, and watched his four SBCs of incendiaries fall on the factory buildings and start fires. Other crews attacked from 2,200, 4,000 and 11,000 feet, and one bombed a searchlight concentration as an alternative. Only one aircraft failed to return from the entire force, and that was the squadron's AE367, which came down somewhere in the target area, killing P/O Waddell RNZAF and his crew.

Thirty Hampdens and nine Manchesters eventually made their way to take-off from 5 Group stations in the early hours of the 13th, after a number had been withdrawn for technical reasons. The target for this 5 Group operation was the main railway station in Cologne, situated in the shadow of the cathedral, while twenty miles to the north, elements of 1 and 3 Groups would be attending to Düsseldorf, the close proximity of the two operations guaranteeing an intense searchlight and flak response. The eight 50 Squadron participants departed Swinderby between 00.37 and 01.30 with F/L Abbott the senior pilot on duty, and made for the Scheldt estuary in good weather conditions. These held firm all the way to Cologne, but haze and searchlight glare over the city combined with accurate flak to make identification of the aiming-point impossible. Sgt Taylor and crew claimed to be among the first to arrive, before the defences became ultra-hostile, and made two runs to deliver the bombs from 15,000 feet. P/O Cooper and crew picked up the Rhine, and their bombs went down onto the docks, according to their report, on the southern side of the river, but more likely on the East Bank of an S-bend near the city centre. Three other crews reported bombing the general area of the city, and observing bursts in various districts, on the industrialized East Bank, in the centre and to the south, but no details were determined through the haze and the defensive activity. P/O Miller and crew failed to locate the primary target after running into intense searchlight and flak activity on the western approaches, and were forced down to 6,000 feet, from where they strafed factory buildings. They ended up over what they believed to be Düsseldorf, and emptied the contents of the bomb bay there, while Sgt Norris and crew bombed Aachen as an alternative target. A number of 5 Group crews reported observing an aircraft falling in flames near the target, and this was almost certainly the 50 Squadron Hampden, AE251, which was shot down by flak. This was one of those happy but rare occasions when an entire crew survived, and news eventually arrived to confirm that F/L Abbott DFM and the others were PoWs. Shortly afterwards, the award of a DSO to F/L Abbott appeared in the London Gazette.

5 Group contributed twenty-six Hampdens from Scampton and Syerston to a force of eighty-one aircraft sent to attack railway yards at Duisburg on the night of the 16/17th, when cloud cover forced all to bomb on estimated positions. The weather intervened to keep the bomber force on the ground on the following three nights, until orders came through at all but 4 Group stations on the 20th to prepare for a major raid on Bremen that night. The force of 153 aircraft included a 5 Group contribution of eighty-two Hampdens and eight Manchesters, fifteen of the former representing 50 Squadron. S/L Oxley had re-joined the squadron at this time, and, with W/C Walker on leave and about to be posted, was appointed commanding officer on this day, and granted the acting rank of wing commander. "Beetle" Oxley had a reputation as a "Hun Hater", and would do his best to engender similar sentiments among his crews. While this operation was in progress, smaller forces would be raiding the ports of Wilhelmshaven, Emden and Antwerp, and a 5 Group element would be attending to gardening duties in northern waters. The 50 Squadron crews departed Swinderby between 18.00 and 18.58 with no pilots above the rank of pilot officer, and made their way across the North Sea under relatively clear skies, but, in the absence of a moon, extreme darkness. P/O Peace and crew turned back from sixty miles out because of a persistent swing, and P/O Miller abandoned his sortie because of an engine issue after two hours. Those reaching the target found six to seven-tenths cloud along with intense searchlight activity and light tracer reaching 10,000 feet, while the heavier calibre shells were climbing to 16,000 feet. The briefed aiming-point of a railway junction could not be located, and bombing was carried out by most on the general area of the city, although Wilhelmshaven and Rotenburg were attacked as alternative targets. AE383 came down somewhere in north-western Germany, and there were no survivors from the crew of P/O Laidlaw.

50 Squadron sat out a raid on Mannheim on the night of the 22/23rd, for which a force of 123 aircraft had been dispatched, forty-five of them Hampdens. Thick cloud and icing conditions

prevented an effective attack from taking place, and the local authorities reported a light raid. Briefings took place at Swinderby and Coningsby on the 23rd to prepare crews for that night's operation against the Germania shipyard at Kiel, for which a force of 114 aircraft was assembled. 5 Group contributed thirty-eight Hampdens and six Manchesters, sixteen of the former provided by 50 Squadron. They took off between 23.50 and 00.50 with F/L Banker the senior pilot on duty, but Sgt Atkinson and crew turned back at the English coast with a port engine issue, leaving the rest to cross the enemy coast over ten-tenths cloud that denied them sight of the ground. On spotting a flare-path through a gap, Sgt Taylor and crew decided to attack it as an alternative target, while the others pushed through pockets of flak to find the cloud diminishing to leave five to six-tenths and favourable conditions over the primary objective. A number of aircraft were held in a blue master-searchlight, but the flak proved to be less accurate and intense than anticipated, and bombing was carried out from between 7,000 and 14,000 feet, the lower altitudes after a glide approach. P/O Cooper and his crew failed to return in AE256 after being brought down by flak in the target area, and there were no survivors.

On the 24th, S/L Jeffs joined the squadron on attachment from 16 O.T.U at Upper Heyford, and, on the 26th, W/C Walker officially concluded his lengthy term as commanding officer. On promotion to group captain rank, he was posted to command the bomber station at North Luffenham in Rutland. "Gus" Walker would become one of the best-known figures and characters in Bomber Command, and, while station commander at Syerston in December 1942, he would lose his right arm to a 4,000 pounder, which detonated under a 106 Squadron Lancaster as he was rushing towards it to offer assistance. This man of small stature and enormous heart recovered and returned to duty, and at just thirty-one, became the youngest Air Commodore ever and a leading light in 4 Group as 42 Base commander, with responsibility for Pocklington, Melbourne and Elvington.

Later on the 26th, W/C Oxley presided over his first operation as the squadron's official commanding officer, taking part in the briefing of nine crews for an attack on the Blohm & Voss shipyards in Hamburg, and three others for gardening duties in the Forget-me-not region of Kiel harbour. A force of 115 aircraft was assembled for the main operation, with 5 Group's six Manchesters assigned to the main railway station, and the two 50 Squadron elements took off between 17.55 and 18.30 with no senior pilots on duty. Sgt Norris and crew turned back when an hour out after the rear gunner developed severe cramp, and, shortly afterwards, F/Sgt Mapp and crew abandoned their sortie because of a port engine problem. P/O King and crew were close to or even over the enemy coast when they gave up on trying to fix a persistent radio issue, while P/O Hore and crew bombed Wilhelmshaven as a last-resort target after the intercom failed. P/O Helmore and crew reached the target to find what they described as a "genuine" fire already burning in the docks area, and they employed this as an aiming-point as the only 50 Squadron crew to attack the primary objective. The others bombed the general vicinity of the city after failing to locate the briefed aiming-point through the haze and defensive activity. Meanwhile, the gardeners were enjoying clear skies and visibility of ten to fifteen miles over the western Baltic, and delivered their vegetables into the briefed locations. Sgt Howett and crew came under fire from a flak-ship at Eckernförde, which shot away the hydraulics and prevented the wing bombs from being released, but P/O Smith and Sgt Redfearn each managed to find a suitable target for theirs.

Following two nights on the ground because of continuing adverse weather conditions, 5 Group detailed forty Hampdens and five Manchesters on the 29th to target the aerodrome at Schiphol, situated to the south-west of Amsterdam. 50 Squadron loaded a record nineteen Hampdens with 500 and 250lb bombs, and dispatched them between 21.48 and 22.27 with S/L Lloyd the senior pilot on duty. Sgts Howett and Norris and P/O Carter returned early with technical failures, leaving the remainder to press on in the most difficult conditions of ten-tenths thick cloud and rain, and only six crews would report locating and bombing the primary target. Sgt Smith and crew jettisoned their bombs "live" from 500 feet after a shell from the airfield defences passed through the port aileron. As they broke cloud in an attempt to observe the results, they were met by a barrage of flak and searchlights, which they evaded by returning to the cloud. F/L Banker and crew were among a very few to gain a clear view of the ground, and watched their bombs fall from 800 feet among barrack buildings. The others tried gallantly to locate the target, some making repeated runs, and P/O Ferrie and crew even flew back out to sea to find a different approach and, perhaps, a clear path through the cloud. When they returned to Schiphol, they found that the cloud base had sunk to 400 feet, and, to make matters worse, a large hole suddenly appeared in the port wing. They turned for home in what was now an unstable aircraft, and jettisoning the bombs into the sea, ultimately arriving home safely to make their report. The most successful aspect of the operation was the delivery of boxes of precious tea to the residents of The Hague.

The month ended with a return to the Blohm & Voss shipyards at Hamburg on the 31st, for which a force of 123 aircraft was assembled. 5 Group called upon the services of Syerston, Coningsby and Swinderby to prepare forty-two Hampdens and five Manchesters, and, at the last-mentioned, 50 Squadron obliged with fifteen Hampdens, while 455 Squadron RAAF managed two. A further eighteen Hampdens and a single Manchester were assigned to gardening duties in northern waters, and 50 Squadron supported this endeavour with three aircraft for the Forget-me-not garden in Kiel Harbour and one for Nectarines, off the Frisians. The two elements took off together between 17.40 and 18.47 with no senior pilots on duty, but F/Sgt Mapp, Sgt Williams and Sgt Lloyd were forced to curtail their sorties because of technical difficulties. The others pressed on to the target area, where, as often was the case, opinions differed as to the weather conditions. Some crew described good visibility, and even the presence of moonlight, while others reported up to ten-tenths cloud at between 5,000 and 8,000 feet, and great difficulty in identifying the briefed aiming-point. However, all were in agreement about the intensity of the searchlight and flak defences, and all did their best to, at least, land their bombs within the city area. A few were unable to locate Hamburg and bombed alternatives, including Kiel and Cuxhaven, and all returned safely. The gardeners encountered up to seven-tenths cloud and moonlight, and exploited the favourable conditions beneath the cloud base to deliver their vegetables into the briefed locations. P/O Grant-Dalton and crew came under heavy ground fire and were held in searchlights off Kiel, but jettisoned their wing bombs to increase manoeuvrability and managed to avoid being hit.

During the course of the month, the squadron took part in twelve operations, and dispatched 115 sorties for the loss of four Hampdens and crews.

November 1941

The new month began with preparations to send a force of 132 aircraft to attack harbour installations at Kiel on the 1st. Thirty-two Hampdens were detailed from Scampton, North

Luffenham and Waddington, while nine further Hampdens and two Manchesters conducted mining and anti-shipping sorties. Swinderby remained inactive until the night of the 3/4th, when ten 50 Squadron Hampdens were dispatched to Swanton Morley as a forward launching pad for mining duties in the Daffodil and Nasturtium gardens at each end of Oresund (The Sound) between Denmark and Sweden. They took off between 23.06 and 23.59, five assigned to each garden, and, apart from a little icing on the outward flight, all but one reached their respective target areas in good conditions with excellent visibility. F/Sgt Mapp and crew turned back at the Jutland coast after ice-accretion became too severe to continue. Four crews planted successfully in Nasturtium in the north, and two in Daffodil in the south, while two others selected alternative, previously visited locations. Heading for Daffodil, Sgt Smith and crew were hit by flak at Esbjerg on Denmark's western coast, and the rear gunner sustained wounds to the leg and arm. This persuaded them to deliver the vegetable into the nearby Hawthorn garden, before returning safely with the others. Debriefing confirmed that one crew had failed to locate its assigned or alternative target area, while nine mines had been planted, and thirteen 250lb wing bombs had been dropped onto appropriate targets on land and at sea.

On the following night, the group sent six Hampdens from Coningsby to continue the anti-shipping patrols, and twenty-four others and four Manchesters for gardening duties in the Frisians and Kiel Bay. 50 Squadron handed three crews a "roving commission" to conduct individual sorties against targets of opportunity with a load each of a single 2,000 pounder and two 250 pounders. The 5 Group ORB as described these sorties as "sneakers", for which P/O Smith and crew took off three minutes after midnight, before proceeding via Skegness and Texel to Emden. They were followed off the ground seven minutes later by W/C Oxley, and at 00.20 by F/L Banker, bound for Bremen and Bremerhaven respectively. W/C Oxley ran into intense and accurate heavy flak on e.t.a over Bremen, and was hit in the starboard wing as he dropped his bombs through cloud. It was much quieter over Bremerhaven, but no results were observed, and a little light flak attended the Smith crew's inconclusive efforts at Emden.

A busy night awaited 5 Group on the 5th, the programme of operations involving six Hampden "sneakers", five on anti-shipping sorties, twenty-four gardeners and twenty-two to bomb the docks at Cherbourg. 50 Squadron briefed three freshman crews for the last-mentioned, and they departed Swinderby in a fourteen-minute slot either side of 04.00. They found between five and nine-tenths low cloud, but good visibility, and all unloaded their bomb bays while over the port, P/O Peace and crew observing bursts in the Bassin Napoleon III dock. Orders were received at Swinderby on the 6th to send fifteen Hampdens up to Wick in the north of Scotland to carry out a mining operation in the Onions garden in Oslo Harbour. They took off from the forward base between 01.15 and 02.30, and headed almost due east to the target with the newly-promoted F/L Grant-Dalton the senior pilot on duty. Shortly after taking-off, Sgt Smith and crew lost the doors of the lower rear-gun position, and had no choice but to abandon their sortie. Sgt Lord and crew were approaching the Norwegian coast at 19,000 feet, when severe icing persuaded them to jettison their ordnance and turn for home. At about the same time, with the enemy coastline in sight, Sgt Norris turned back after complaints from the rear gunner of extreme cold that a change of position could not alleviate. The others reached the target area, where four planted their vegetables into the briefed locations, and five others found alternatives. In all, four crews returned their mines to store, and one, that of Sgt Howett, was absent from debriefing. It was learned later that AE427 had been hit by flak and had crashed without survivors into Oslo Fjord.

No doubt frustrated by his inability to deliver a telling blow on Germany during the extended period of unfavourable weather, and almost certainly eager to rescue the besmirched reputation of the Command after the damning Butt Report, Peirse planned a major night of operations for the night of the 7/8th. The original intention was to send over two hundred aircraft to Berlin, but, continuing doubts about the weather prompted the 5 Group A-O-C, AVM Slessor, to question the wisdom of going ahead, and he was allowed to withdraw his force and send it instead to Cologne. A third operation, involving fifty-three Wellingtons and two Stirlings from 1 and 3 Groups was also to take place with Mannheim as the target. 169 aircraft eventually took off for the Capital, while sixty-one Hampdens and fourteen Manchesters set off for the Rhineland Capital. In addition to these operations, a further thirty-four Hampdens and four Manchesters were to carry out mining, intruder and small-scale bombing sorties. At Swinderby, 50 Squadron made ready just two Hampdens, one for Cologne and the other for an intruder role in the searchlight belt on the south-western approaches. P/O Peace and crew had been briefed to aim for the Deutz railway station on the East Bank of the Rhine in the city centre, while F/L Smith and crew were to take care of the defences in company with two 455 Squadron crews, and they all took off at around 19.30. Cologne lay under thick haze and six to eight-tenths cloud in a band between 6,000 and 11,000 feet, which prevented all but a handful of crews from identifying their briefed aiming-point and left them with the rest of the giant city to drop their bombs into. The Peace crew bombed the general city area, and had little to report on their return. Other returning crews reported observing the flashes as their bombs hit home and many fires, but local reports mentioned just eight high-explosive bombs and sixty incendiaries falling into the city, causing minor housing and no industrial damage. The only positive from this was the absence of casualties from among the 5 Group participants on a night when a new record of losses would be established. F/L Smith and crew enjoyed a successful sortie, finding five tenths cloud at 2,500 to 8,000 feet and plenty of searchlights to occupy their attention. The bombs were dropped near Maastricht and searchlight batteries strafed, before they strayed too close to Antwerp on the way home, and were holed in the port engine and fuel tanks. They were, perhaps, fortunate, as the two 455 Squadron Hampdens failed to return.

There was a similar story of failure at Mannheim, where local authorities recorded no bombs falling on this night, at a cost to the attackers of seven Wellingtons. Fewer than half of the Berlin crews reported bombing within the target area, and twenty-one aircraft failed to return, which, when added to the losses from the night's minor operations, provided an overall casualty figure of thirty-seven aircraft, more than twice the previous highest for a single night. This was the final straw for the War Cabinet and the Air Ministry, and AM Peirse was summoned to an uncomfortable meeting with Churchill to make his explanations. On the 13th, he would be ordered to restrict further operational activity, while the future of an independent bomber force was considered at the highest level, and this shackle would remain in place for the next three months. With loud voices calling for the redeployment of bomber aircraft to combat U-Boots in the Atlantic and to redress reversals in the Middle East, the very existence of an independent bomber force hung in the balance.

In the meantime, 5 Group detailed twenty Hampdens on the 8th for an attack on the Krupp works at Essen in company with thirty-four other aircraft, and ten Hampdens and five Manchesters for freshman sorties over Dunkerque. 50 Squadron made ready nine Hampdens for the main operation and two for Dunkerque, and they took off between 17.52 and 19.01

with no senior pilots on duty. It would turn into another night of under-achievement as, first, P/O Miller and crew turned back because of intercom failure, and only one of the squadron's remaining Essen-bound crews actually attacked the Krupp works. P/O Hore and crew reported three bursts in the neighbourhood of machine shop N°4, while the others failed to identify the aiming-point and bombed either the general area of the city or alternative targets at Düsseldorf and an unidentified aerodrome. At Dunkerque, Sgt Crampton and crew dropped their bombs from 11,000 feet, and watched them fall into the sea, blaming intercom problems for poor communications between the pilot and navigator/bomb-aimer. Sgt Baddeley and crew were unable to climb sufficiently to fly over the target, and bombed nearby Mardyck aerodrome from 8,500 feet as an alternative.

The following night brought a raid on Hamburg for which 5 Group contributed thirty Hampdens and six Manchesters to an overall force of 103. Swinderby was not involved in this operation, which, according to crew reports, caused fires in the docks and city. Thereafter, the weather kept the Command on the ground until the 15th, when 5 Group contributed eleven Hampdens and six Manchesters to a force of forty-nine aircraft targeting the port of Emden. 50 Squadron briefed two crews for this operation, and three others for mining duties in the Nectarines garden off the Frisians. They took off during a two-hour period between 18.30 and 20.32 with S/L Jeffs the senior pilot on duty and assigned to gardening activities. Despite the presence of five to ten-tenths cloud with a base at 500 to 1,000 feet and very poor visibility, he and P/O Southgate and crew managed to pinpoint on Juist and make timed runs to release their mines over the briefed locations. Sgt Young and crew flew out at 1,500 feet, encountering icing conditions, and failed to locate the garden. They turned back, and, unable to establish a pinpoint at the English coast, despite being aided by searchlights, turned towards Swinderby, only to fly into a hill at Guisborough, four miles south-east of Middlesborough. Veteran Hampden, P1152, was wrecked, and the rear gunner was killed, while the rest of the crew sustained injuries. Of the Emden pair, Sgt Gruber and crew were back on the ground within twenty-five minutes with an unserviceable intercom, and Sgt Crampton and crew failed to locate the target in the unfavourable conditions.

After another seven-night intervention by the weather, 5 Group detailed fifty-one Hampdens and two Manchesters on the 23rd to attack the U-Boot base at Lorient that night. 50 Squadron made ready four Hampdens, which took off between 16.45 and 17.15 with S/L Jeffs the senior pilot on duty. On reaching the English coast, two crews misinterpreted a recall signal and turned back, leaving S/L Jeffs and Sgt Gruber and their crews to continue on, for a change, in excellent weather conditions and good visibility. A cone of red tracer was seen to be bursting at between 12,000 and 14,000 feet, but this proved to be no impediment to bombing, and bursts were observed in the docks area, followed by a yellow fire. On the 26th, the squadron moved to a new home at Skellingthorpe, situated on the south-western edge of Lincoln. Originally intended to act as a satellite for Waddington, it was upgraded with the construction of concrete runways in 1941, and 50 Squadron would be its first resident unit, shortly to be joined by 455 Squadron RAAF. The move exempted the squadron from participation in that night's raid on the docks at Emden, for which Scampton and Coningsby put up twenty Hampdens.

The squadron was still settling in at its new home on the 27th, when other 5 Group stations were alerted to make ready for a raid that night on Düsseldorf. Thirty-four Hampdens and six Manchesters took off to join forty-six 3 Group aircraft, and, despite claims of large fires in the railway yards, local reports detailed only light damage, while Cologne recorded damage to 119 houses. 50 Squadron was ready to go to war again by the last night of the month, when a major raid was planned for Hamburg. A force of 181 aircraft included forty-eight Hampdens and four Manchesters, whose crews had been briefed to aim for the Blohm & Voss shipyards. 50 Squadron prepared eleven Hampdens for the main operation, and four others for mining duties in the Forget-me-not, Nasturtium and Jasmine gardens, respectively in Kiel Harbour and off Warnemünde in the western Baltic. They took off between 16.57 and 17.54 with S/Ls Jeffs and Potts the senior pilots among the bombing brigade, and S/L Lloyd leading the gardeners having taken over W/C Walker's crew. Sgt Baddeley and crew turned back early with an engine issue, while P/Os Helmore and Southgate became lost and overshot the target area, arriving eventually over the western Baltic, before turning back to bomb Kiel.

The 5 Group ORB recorded that the weather conditions over Hamburg were most favourable, with little or no cloud and bright moonlight, while the 5 Group ORB described much cloud and poor visibility that prevented all but one crew from identifying the shipyards. The individual crew reports range from one extreme to the other, but most bombed the city centre from between 5,800 and 14,000 feet, guided by the prominent landmarks of the Binnen and Aussen-Alster Lakes. On his return, S/L Potts reported observing a new kind of shell, which exploded with great force and caused a violent disturbance of the surrounding air. Later in the war, crews would begin to report "scarecrows", which, they were told, was a German shell designed to simulate the destruction of a bomber with a full bomb load, the purpose of which was to demoralize witnesses. Scarecrows actually never existed, and were, in realty, bombers exploding with a full bomb load on board. 120 returning crews claimed to have reached and bombed the primary target, and reported many fires, local reports confirming twenty-two fires, two of them large, and 2,500 people bombed out of their homes. P1202 arrived back short of fuel, and was force-landed at 01.20 by Sgt Williams between the airfield and the outskirts of Lincoln. The Hampden was written off, but the crew clambered from the wreckage with just one injury to report.

While the above was in progress, the gardeners had encountered ten-tenths cloud with bright moonlight above, but mist and poor visibility below. S/L Lloyd was unable to locate his drop zone in the Jasmine garden, and jettisoned the mine "safe", while F/L Banker found his Nasturtium garden in The Sound near Helsingør, and delivered his vegetable from 600 feet. Sgt Norris and P/O Miller also succeeded in fulfilling their briefs in the Forget-me-not and Jasmine gardens respectively. During the course of the month the squadron undertook thirteen operations, dispatching sixty-eight sorties for the loss of three Hampdens, one complete crew and a rear gunner.

December 1941

The dominant theme during December would be the continuing presence at Brest of Scharnhorst, Gneisenau and, sometimes, Prinz Eugen, and no less than fifteen operations of varying sizes would be mounted against the port and its guests during the month, some by daylight. 455 Squadron RAAF joined 50 Squadron at Skellingthorpe during the first week, and F/L Banker was posted across the tarmac to add his experience. The weather kept the entire Command on the ground for the first six nights of the new month, and it was not until the 7th that a planned operation actually got off the ground. The target for a force of 130 aircraft was Aachen, Germany's most westerly city, perched on the frontiers with both

Holland and Belgium. The briefed aiming-point was the Nazi Party HQ, which had no special significance other than the fact that it was situated in the city centre, at a time when it was not yet admitted publicly that population centres were being bombed. 5 Group detailed fifty Hampdens and a dozen Manchesters, six of the former made ready by 50 Squadron at Skellingthorpe, and they would have to wait until after midnight before getting away. In the meantime, the freshman crew of Sgt Young took off at 18.19 to bomb the docks at Boulogne, but landed at Marham sixty-eight minutes later with I.F.F failure. The main element departed Skellingthorpe between 01.57 and 02.09 with F/L Smith the senior pilot on duty, and reached the target area to find challenging cloud conditions and modest visibility. P/O Bartley and crew were running in on the aiming-point, when a direct flak hit caused a loss of control, which forced the bombs to be jettisoned "live" from 7,000 feet some two miles north-west of the city. P/O Carter and crew experienced no difficulty in carrying out their attack from 9,000 feet, and they reported observing bursts. F/L Smith and crew took advantage of the slight and inaccurate defence to attack from 5,000 feet, while P/O Hore let his load go from 9,500 feet. Sgt Redfearn and crew searched for twenty minutes before bombing what they thought was Aachen from 8,000 feet, only to realise later that it had probably been Liege. Sgt Smith and crew brought their bombs home after failing to locate the target because of cloud, poor visibility and snow-covered ground.

Daylight operations were a matter of course for 2 Group squadrons, and some, known as "Circus", had a purpose, to tempt enemy fighters into the air to face RAF Spitfires in a war of attrition. These were, however, very different from the unescorted daylight operations known as "moling", conducted by the other groups, which relied on cloud and surprise to protect the crews. It was utter madness to put crews' lives at risk for a very small potential gain, but 5 Group ordered six crews into the air on the 10th to target ports and aerodromes in Germany and Holland. S/L Potts and crew took off at 12.18 for the Luftwaffe base at Soesterberg in south-central Holland, to be followed thirty minutes later by S/L Jeffs and crew bound for a similar objective at Gilze-Rijen further south. The Potts crew flew out beneath the cloud at 700 feet, making landfall at Texel, before hitting a bank of cloud that touched the surface of the Zuider Zee. It lifted to 300 feet, thereafter, allowing them to map-read along the railway line to the target, during which leg, the trailing aerial hit high-tension wires and caused a large flash. On reaching the aerodrome, they bombed buildings on the south-eastern corner from 350 to 400 feet, noting that the defences were very slow to swing into action. The Jeffs crew found the conditions to be so poor that, having located the target at 14.30, they lost it immediately, and, having searched for an hour, went back to the coast to re-establish their bearings. Returning to the target, they were able to identify it and deliver their bombs from 250 feet, before, on crossing the Dutch coast homebound, being waved at enthusiastically by local fishermen.

Skellingthorpe was not involved in a totally ineffective raid on Cologne on the night of the 11/12th, in which fifteen Hampdens participated, but provided two of sixteen Hampdens on this night to bomb the docks at Le Havre. Sgt Young and P/O Milnes and their crews took off at 18.50, and ran into ten-tenths cloud between 1,500 and 6,000 feet in the target area, that prevented the former from locating the aiming-point despite a twenty-minute search. They brought their bombs home, while the Milnes crew braved the intense and accurate light flak to deliver their load from 2,000 feet, and pick up some damage to the tail-plane for their troubles. The same two crews continued their operational education on the 15th, as part of a force of twelve Hampdens targeting the docks at Ostend. Taking off shortly before 18.00, P/O

Milnes and crew returned before reaching the coast because of starboard engine problems, and Sgt Young and crew failed to return in AE380. The pilot's body was recovered from the sea off the Belgian coast, but no trace of the Hampden and the rest of the crew was ever found. In between these two operations, 5 Group sent six 408 Squadron Hampdens to bomb Brest in daylight on the 13th, but they turned back because of insufficient cloud cover. Twenty-two Hampdens were sent back on the night of the 14/15th, when all but one crew were thwarted by ten-tenths cloud and icing conditions. Earlier on the 14th, a dozen 50 Squadron Hampdens and ground crews had proceeded to Wick to prepare for a combined forces operation planned for the near future.

Scampton and Coningsby represented the group on the night of the 16/17th, the former dispatching fourteen Hampdens to attack the main railway station at Wilhelmshaven, while eighteen from the latter took care of gardening duties. P/O Milnes and crew were on duty again on the 17th as the sole 50 Squadron crew among three to target the docks at Le Havre, while twenty-five other Hampdens tried again at Brest as part of an overall force of 121 aircraft. Taking off at 16.57, the Milnes crew were over Northamptonshire, when the port engine cut at 2,000 feet, and forced them to jettison the bombs and return to base. Eleven Manchesters took part in the next attempt on Brest, by daylight on the 18th, when claims were made of at least one hit on Gneisenau. A dozen daylight intruder sorties by Hampdens over north-western Germany on the 21st came to nothing, after insufficient cloud presented itself to protect them. A force of sixty-eight aircraft, including twenty Hampdens, set off for Cologne on the night of the 23rd, but fewer than half claimed to have bombed the city, which, according to local reports, recorded no bombs. The third wartime Christmas passed with the country in sombre mood and seeking a silver lining in the ominously dark clouds. What few knew, was that 44 Squadron had taken delivery during the month of a new weapon, that, once produced in large numbers, would transform and dominate the bombing war.

The Lancaster lay in the future for 50 Squadron, and, in the meantime, the crews at Wick were notified of a daylight operation to be mounted on the 27th, in support of a landing by commandos on the Norwegian islands of Vågsøy and Måløy. The main purpose of Operation Archery was to drive out German forces and destroy the fish-oil factories that produced ingredients for high explosives, but a secondary objective was to persuade the enemy to reinforce its Norwegian strongholds with forces which might otherwise be employed on the Eastern Front. The combined assault by Naval and commando units was to begin at first light, and was to be preceded by an attack by nineteen Blenheims of 2 Group. Five 50 Squadron Hampdens were to drop special smoke-bombs on Måløy to screen the landings, while two others performed a similar function on Rugsundsøy island to the south, and three more attacked the latter's gun batteries with eight 250lb bombs each and machine guns. They took off from Wick between 05.15 and 05.55 with W/C Oxley the senior pilot on duty, but lost the services of Sgt Atkinson and crew after they were unable to maintain altitude. The others pressed on, and arrived in the target area to find perfect weather conditions and unlimited visibility. S/L Potts and crew were the first on the scene at Måløy, dropping their smoke containers from 100 feet at 08.50, to be followed at 08.59 by P/O Miller at a perilously low 30 feet. W/C Oxley, who, on his return, would describe the operation as going exactly as planned, delivered his smoke containers from 100 feet at 09.00, while taking four or five hits from a flak-ship. The remaining two members of this section, Sgts Smith and Redfearn and their crews, in AE428 and AE369 respectively, were shot down by flak and crashed into the sea off Måløy. The sole survivor was Sgt Smith, who was picked up from the water by HMS

Kenya. At Rugsundsøy, P/O Hore dropped his smoke containers in a dive attack at 08.57, before the gunners strafed a machine gun nest and silenced it. P/O King's smoke bombs overshot and fell into the water, but a strafing pass at 30 feet scattered the crew of a shore battery and stopped it from firing. By this time, P/O Goldsmith and crew had bombed another gun emplacement from 150 feet at 08.30, but the navigator had been seriously wounded by flak, despite which, he gave the pilot a course for home before lapsing into unconsciousness. First aid was administered by the wireless operator and rear gunner, and a landing was made at the first available airfield, which was Sumborough in the Shetlands. F/Sgt Norris attacked a gun position from 800 feet, and the wireless operator fired off four hundred rounds at the battery and adjacent observation hut. Operation Archery was an outstanding success that achieved it aims at a cost of seventeen commandos and four sailors killed and fifty-three soldiers wounded. Six Blenheims and two Hampdens failed to return, and the above-mentioned 50 Squadron pilot was the only survivor among the twenty-six airmen.

This was the day on which Sgt Harlo "Terry" Taerum of the RCAF arrived on posting from 16 O.T.U to begin a career as a navigator, initially with P/O Goldsmith and crew, but later, as a member of Gibson's Dams crew in May 1943, and, ultimately, an untimely death four months later. Operations were not yet done for the 27th, and the force of 132 aircraft assembled for a major attack that night on Düsseldorf included thirty Hampden and seven Manchesters. The 5 Group crews were given the main marshalling yards as their aiming-point, for which the 50 Squadron quartet departed Skellingthorpe between 17.07 and 17.36 with no senior pilots involved. They had been preceded into the air between 16.12 and 16.21 by five gardeners bound for the Forget-me-not region in Kiel Harbour led by F/L Grant-Dalton. The bombers arrived in the target area to find three-tenths cloud at 5,000 feet and good visibility, despite which, only Sgt Baddeley and crew of the 50 Squadron contingent managed to identify the briefed aiming-point, bombing it from 13,000 feet. Sgt Gruber and crew attacked the city from 12,000 feet after gliding down, and Sgt Williams and crew followed suit from 11,000 feet, before returning home to almost collide head-on with an RAF night-fighter near Lowestoft. P/O Southgate and crew failed to locate Düsseldorf, and selected a bridge over the Rhine near Bonn as a last-resort objective, claiming a near-miss from 14,000 feet. Four of the gardeners, meanwhile, had reached the eastern side of the Schleswig-Holstein peninsular to encounter six-tenths cloud in a band between 500 and 2,500 feet, but, otherwise, good visibility and moonlight. P/O Helmore and crew were the absentees, after losing their way and overshooting the turning point on the Danish coast. Having established their position off the western coast of North Jutland after four-and-a-half hours of flying, they had insufficient time and fuel to continue, and jettisoned the vegetable. The others delivered their stores into the briefed location from between 400 and 800 feet, some facing a little opposition, and all returned safely to report largely uneventful sorties.

The two main operations posted on the 28th involved eighty-six Wellingtons at Wilhelmshaven, while eighty-one Hampdens returned to the synthetic rubber factory at Hüls in the Ruhr. 50 Squadron made ready seven Hampdens, which departed Skellingthorpe between 17.51 and 18.26 with S/Ls Jeffs, Lloyd and Potts the senior pilots on duty. P/O Bartley's sorted lasted twenty-five minutes and was brought to an end by port engine failure. The others arrived in the target area under bright moonlight that provided excellent visibility, and five carried out their attacks from between 6,500 and 10,000 feet. S/L Potts found the flak at high level to be very accurate, and, after watching two loads of incendiaries from other aircraft fall near the aiming-point, went in at 1,100 feet to deliver his own bombs. A huge explosion rocked the Hampden and threw debris into the air, and then it was time to hit the deck and empty the .303 ammunition racks on buildings, a train and searchlights. Returning crews claimed good bombing results, but no report came out of the target to confirm or deny. During the course of the month the squadron participated in nine operations and dispatched thirty-nine sorties for the loss of three Hampdens and crews.

It had been a disappointing year for the Command, and despite the best efforts of the crews, one of under-achievement, with little to show in terms of an advance on the performance of 1940. The new aircraft types, the Stirling, Halifax and Manchester, introduced into operational service early in the year, had each failed to meet the requirements expected of them, and had undergone long periods of grounding while essential modifications were carried out. 1942 would bring changes, however, chief among which were the arrival on the operational scene of a war-winning aircraft, and a new Commander-in-Chief, who would know how to exploit it.

W/C Gus Walker (2nd right) and his Hampden crew with Sgt Richard Trevor-Roper (extreme right) at RAF Lindholme 1941. F/L Trevor-Roper was the rear gunner in W/C Gibson's Dams Crew 16/17th of May 1943. He lost his life with 97 Squadron on the Nuremburg raid on the 30/31st of March 1944.

A distinguished crew pose on the fuselage of 50 Squadron Hampden VN-U. From left to right: Sgt Brown, W/C Oxley, S/L Lloyd and F/L Grose.

Pilot, Sgt John Gordon Procter was killed in action on the 30th of August 1941 aged 26 years. Hampden AD839 took off from RAF Swinderby at 21.45 hours on the night of 29/30th of August 1941 to bomb Frankfurt. The aircraft was last heard in contact with Sealand D/F Station, but it failed to return. Sgt.Procter is buried in Abbeville Cemetery, N. France.

S/L Denis "Dusty" Miller RNZAF DSO DFC
S/L Miller was a New Zealander who flew on the 'thousand bomber' raids in the summer of 1942. Denis 'Dusty' Miller came to Britain in 1941 to serve in Bomber Command, gaining the DSO and DFC for his bravery and leadership in two tours of operations against heavily defended targets.

Sgt "Wally" Layne arrived at RAF Lindholme on the 3rd of July 1941, and undertook his first operation with F/L Fox against the Scharnhorst and Gneisenau at Brest on the night of the 6/7th of July.

F/O Walter Henry Layne (Wally) DFC

Hampden AE116 of 50 Squadron being recovered at Waddington. Wally Layne was a crew member. All photos on this page from www.wallyswar.wordpress.com (David Layne)

Wally at his sister's house in Grantham

RAF Skellingthorpe 1942 just before his wedding

On 15th of February 1942, Walter Layne married Joan Maunders of Grantham. As the bride was about to enter Grantham Church, 3 Hampden Bombers buzzed the Church. Joan was so excited that she threw her bouquet up in the air. Actually, the trio had buzzed every church in Grantham to make sure they found the correct one. All photos on this page are from www.wallyswar.wordpress.com.

Skellingthorpe. Wally is under the right (aircraft's left) propeller hub.

Friends Doug and Maurice with Syd on Right, during training at RAF Weeton January 1941.

*LAC Sydney James Arthur King
50 Squadron 1940 -1945*

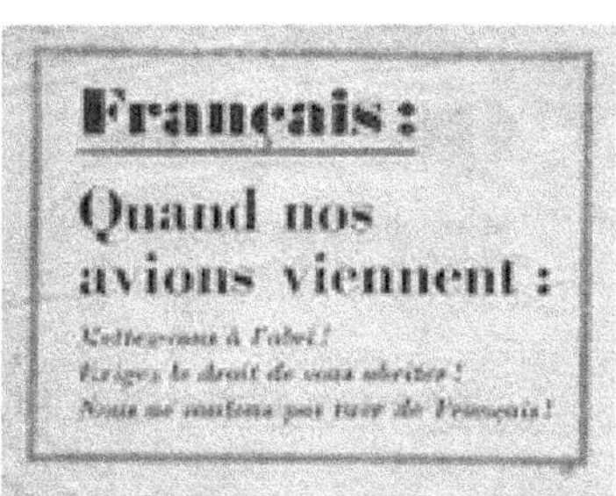

The above items are propaganda Leaflets collected by Syd King from the early days of the war.

P/O, later F/L John Hopgood, who lost his life attacking the Möhne Dam 16/17th of May 1943.

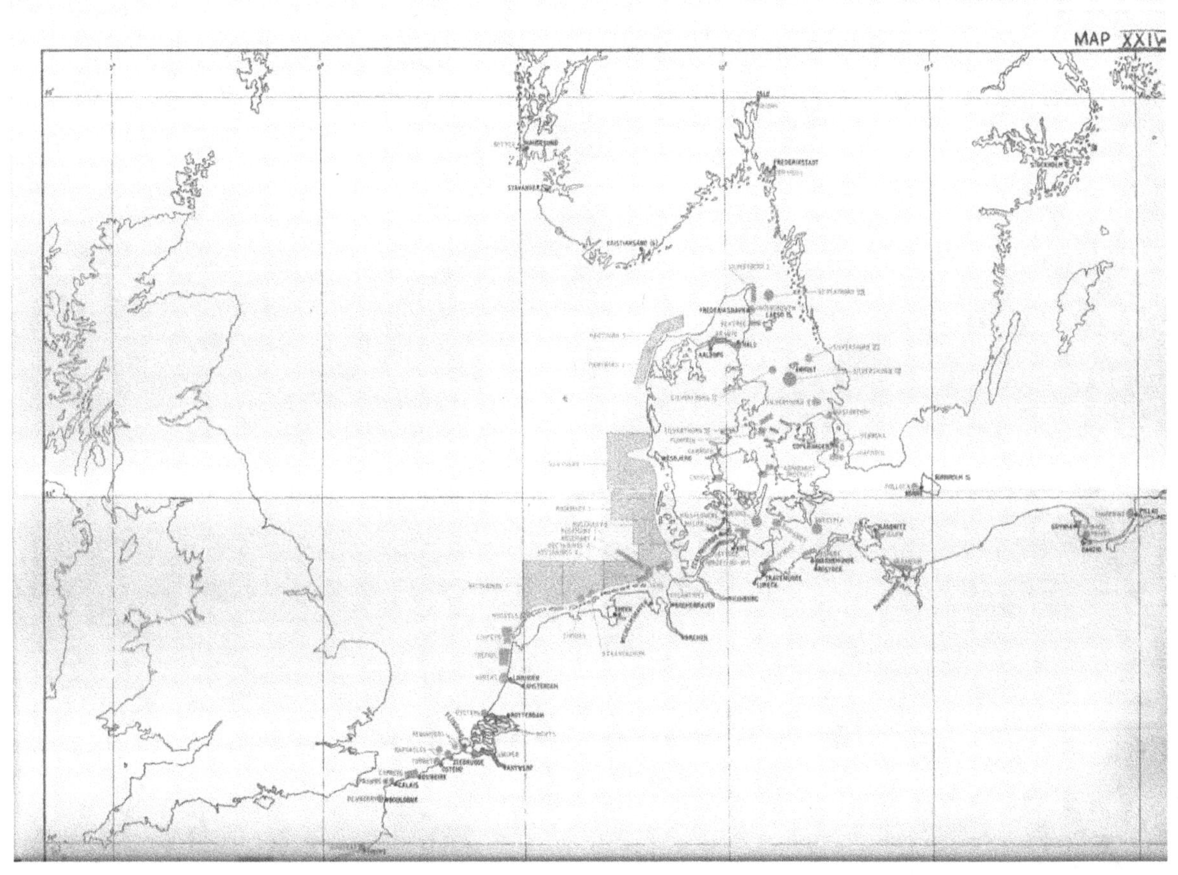

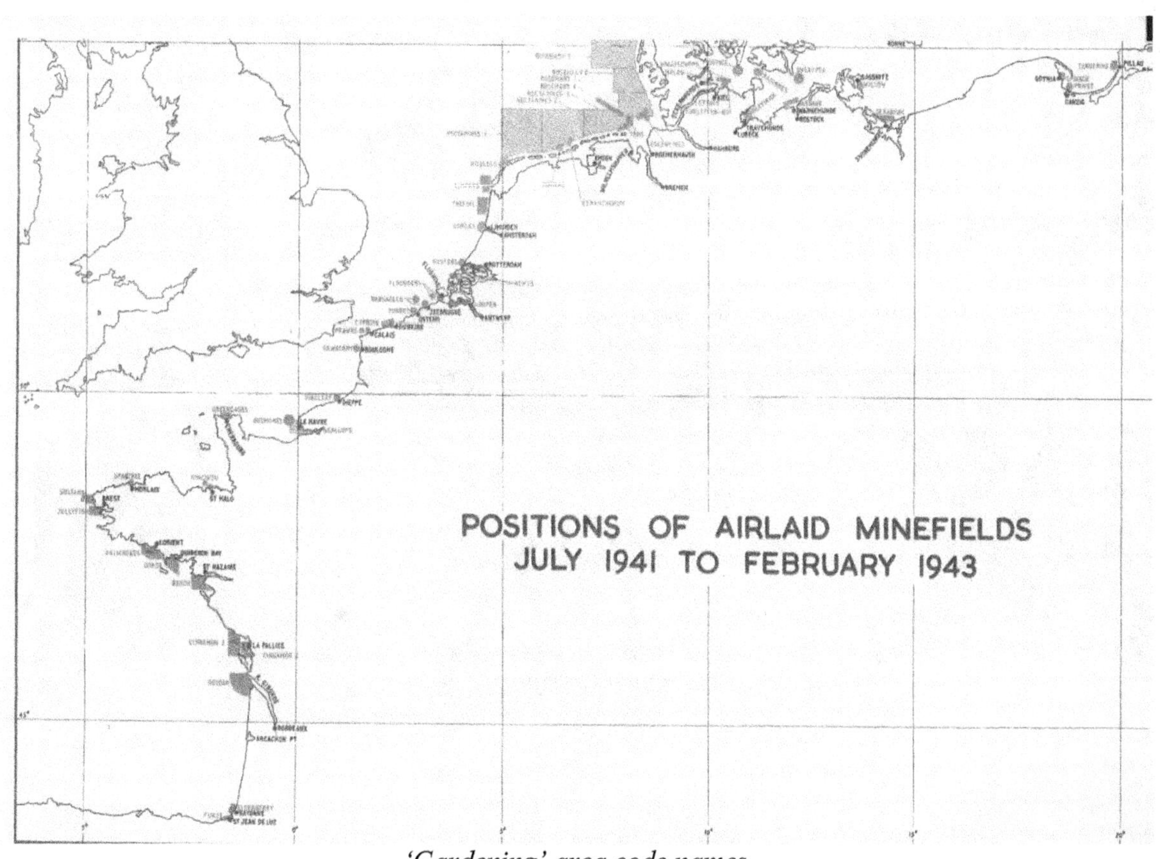

'Gardening' area code names

Hampden Cockpit

Hampden rear gunner. The template is fitted to stop him shooting the tail off.

Believed to be P/O Ford with air and ground crew.

As far as the crews were concerned, the New Year would look and feel exactly like the outgoing one, and, still under the restrictions of the November directive, the Command's activities reflected the continuing obsession with the German raiders at Brest, and a further eleven operations against the port would take place during January. 5 Group detailed a dozen Manchesters for a raid on St-Nazaire on the 2nd, and thirty-six Hampdens for gardening duties off the Biscay ports and the Frisians. 50 Squadron made ready eleven horticultural Hampdens and briefed six crews for the Beech garden off the port of St-Nazaire, four for Deodars at the mouth of the Gironde further south along the French coast, and one for Nectarines off the Frisians. They took off between 17.03 and 17.42 with F/L King the senior pilot on duty, and P/O Peace and crew had reached Chesil Beach on their way to the Beech garden, when the artificial horizon collapsed and terminated their interest in proceedings. While their colleagues headed south, P/O Milnes and crew crossed the Lincolnshire coast on an easterly course, running into exceptionally bad visibility in the target area of the Frisians, despite which, they established a pinpoint and delivered their vegetable from 400 feet. The wing bombs were dropped onto a searchlight on Ameland, and they had the satisfaction of seeing it doused.

Sgts Atkinson and Gruber and their crews were early arrivals on the approaches to St-Nazaire, when the visibility was good, and they experienced no difficulty in establishing their positions and dropping their mines from 600 feet. The others assigned to this garden found up to ten-tenths cloud down to sea level, but F/Sgt Lord and P/O Carter managed to establish their position and deliver their mines from 600 and 850 feet respectively. Sgt Crampton and crew were defeated by the conditions, and jettisoned their vegetable "safe". Conditions were better in the area of the Gironde estuary, with bright moonlight to illuminate ground features, and three crews dropped their mines into the briefed locations from 400, 700 and 800 feet. Unaccountably, Sgt Norris and crew found poor conditions, and failed to locate the drop zone after carrying out a square search, and they were another to jettison their mine "safe".

Acting F/L Smith was posted to 16 O.T.U at Upper Heyford for instructional duties on the 3rd, after completing his first tour of operations. Small-scale mining operations occupied elements of the group that night, and daylight "moling" operations on the 4th. Twenty-seven Hampdens and twelve Manchesters took off on the evening of the 5th as part of a force of 154 aircraft targeting the Scharnhorst and Gneisenau at Brest and the naval docks area. An effective smoke screen prevented accurate bombing, but many fires were claimed. 50 Squadron remained on the ground on this night, but detailed nine Hampdens on the 6th to join ten others in "scuttle" sorties over northern Germany. These were roving commissions against targets of opportunity at specific locations, and appear to differ from "moling", only by relying on the cover of darkness rather than cloud. They departed Skellingthorpe between 03.03 and 03.48 with S/L Lloyd the senior pilot on duty, and set course in threes for Münster, Essen and Cologne. The Münster trio found ten-tenths cloud at between 7,000 and 10,000 feet, and P/O Helmore and S/L Lloyd bombed on estimated positions from 7,000 and 10,000 feet respectively. Sgt Atkinson and crew flew around the target until finding a gap in the cloud, through which they descended to 8,000 feet, spotting and bombing a railway station without observing results. The Essen crews found similar conditions and carried out their attacks on estimated positions from 10,000 to 12,000 feet, P/O Bartley and crew reporting on return that they had actually bombed a built-up area to the north of Essen. Bound for Cologne, Sgt Norris and crew descended through cloud at the enemy coast, and immediately iced-up to the extent that the starboard engine cut and threw the Hampden into a spin from 10,000 down to 4,000 feet. Control was eventually regained, and the engine restarted, but the sortie was abandoned. P/O Goldsmith and F/L Grant-Dalton bombed through cloud from 10,000 and 11,500 feet respectively, and had little of interest to pass on at debriefing.

Brest was posted as the target for a force of 151 aircraft on the 8th, reconnaissance having revealed that Scharnhorst and Gneisenau had been joined by Prinz Eugen. 5 Group contributed thirty-seven Hampdens and ten Manchesters for this early-morning attack, and it was actually during the early hours of the 9th when they got away, the fifteen 50 Squadron crews becoming airborne between 02.44 and 03.34 with S/L Potts the senior pilot on duty. F/Sgt Lord turned back at the English coast after failing to pick up a navigation pinpoint, leaving the others to fly out over varying amounts of cloud, to establish their positions by dead-reckoning (DR), and on e.t.a at the target. On arrival, they were met by seven to ten-tenths low cloud, with good visibility above and haze below, and Sgts Baddeley and Smith were able to identify the briefed aiming-point through gaps in the cloud, aided by fires already burning. They bombed from 12,000 and 13,000 feet respectively, while most of the others relied on estimated positions from between 9,500 and 14,000 feet, all the time under fire from intense and accurate flak. Sgt Gruber and crew were preparing for the bombing run when engine trouble forced them to turn back, and they jettisoned the bombs into the sea. P/O Goldsmith and crew circled the target for ten minutes at 8,000 feet, but saw nothing through the cloud, and found no improvement even after descending to 2,000 feet. Eventually, after seventy-five minutes in the target area, they let their load go over the general area of the docks.

A force of eighty-two aircraft was assembled on the 9th for a return to Brest, but there was no contribution from Skellingthorpe among the twenty-seven Hampdens and six Manchesters provided by 5 Group. It turned into another inconclusive raid, from which eleven Hampden crews brought their bombs home after failing to identify the target. Thirty-four Hampdens and nine Manchesters were detailed by 5 Group on the 10th to contribute to an overall force of 124 aircraft bound for Wilhelmshaven that night. 50 Squadron prepared fifteen Hampdens for the night's activities, ten loaded with high-explosives and incendiaries intended for the main railway station, and five carrying a vegetable cach for delivery to the Yams garden on the approaches to Wilhelmshaven and the Weser estuary at Bremerhaven on the eastern side of the bay, in an area known at the time as the Schillig Roads. They departed Skellingthorpe between 16.32 and 17.05 with S/L Jeffs the senior pilot on duty, but soon lost the services of P/O Bartley and crew to engine problems. The others found the target area under ten-tenths low cloud, and, with the exception of P/O Peace and crew, failed to locate the briefed aiming-point, bombing the town instead from between 7,500 and 15,000 feet. P/O Peace and crew described the conditions as good, and attacked the railway station from 9,000 feet, observing bursts in the general area of the aiming-point. On return, AE250 strayed off track and ran very low on fuel over northern England, forcing Sgt Williams to attempt an emergency landing some nine miles north-east of Carlisle. It resulted in a crash at midnight, which killed the pilot and navigator outright, and fatally injured one of the gunners, who succumbed on the 12th. The gardeners, meanwhile, had located their target area after completing timed runs, and four of them delivered their vegetables as briefed from around 500 and 600 feet. Sgt Baddeley and crew were forced to evade the attentions of a flak ship, and dropped their mine in an alternative location close by.

The focus remained on north-western Germany for the next two operations, both of which were to be directed at Hamburg. Eleven 50 Squadron Hampdens were made ready on the 14th, and their crews briefed to attack the Blohm & Voss shipyards, situated on the Kuhwerder Island opposite the Sankt Pauli district to the west of the city centre. They were to be part of an overall force of ninety-five aircraft, which included a further contribution from 5 Group of twenty-one Hampdens and eleven Manchesters. They took off between 16.35 and 17.19 with F/L King the senior pilot on duty, and lost P/O Bartley and crew immediately to an intercom issue. The remainder reached north-western Germany, although P/O Peace and crew had to contend also with a failed intercom, which persuaded them to bomb a flak concentration at Baden to the south-west of Hamburg. At the target, extreme darkness and thick ground haze created challenging conditions for aiming-point identification, but crews could always rely on the searchlight and flak batteries lining the Elbe to guide them into the heart of the city. Large ground features like the Binnen and Aussen-Alster Lakes on the north-western edge of the centre were a good guide for non-precision bombing, and, those from the squadron unable to locate the briefed aiming-point, attacked the built-up area generally from 12,000 and 15,000 feet. F/L King and crew described clear skies and good visibility, which enabled them to make a positive identification of the shipyards, and attack them from 10,000 feet. P/O Miller and crew established a pinpoint fifteen miles out, and carried out a timed run, also at 10,000 feet, which brought them to where they wanted to be. F/O Carter and crew overshot the aiming-point on the first run, and were then aided by a flare from another aircraft as they approached a second time to hit the shipyards from 9,500 feet. P/O Ferrie and crew identified the target by the Altona-Basin and a fork in the Elbe to the north, and released their bombs from 9,000 feet, before taking violent evasive action that prevented observation of the results. Among four aircraft missing from this operation were two 50 Squadron Hampdens, AE420 and AE431, both of which were both lost without trace with the crews of Sgt Baddeley and P/O Hore respectively. Half of the crews involved in this operation claimed to have bombed within the city, and local authorities confirmed damage to the Altona railway station, situated on the North Bank of the Elbe to the west of Sankt Pauli.

Hamburg was "on" again twenty-four hours later, for which a force of ninety-six aircraft was assembled. 5 Group's contribution amounted to twenty-seven Hampdens and ten Manchesters, with 50 Squadron's four participants departing Skellingthorpe between 16.43 and 17.03. The crews had been briefed to attack the city centre, but P/O Southgate and F/Sgt Lord turned back as the latest to be afflicted by intercom failures. P/O Bartley and crew were flying over ten-tenths cloud at 12,000 feet with the Schleswig-Holstein peninsular beneath them, when the oxygen supply to the navigator failed. The wing bombs were dropped onto a flak concentration, and the incendiaries somehow fell out at the same time, but the remaining bombs were returned to store. This left just Sgt Crampton and crew to represent the squadron at the target, which they identified by a bend in the river and bombed from 11,000 feet, while held in a searchlight cone and bombarded by flak. Hamburg reported thirty-six fires, only three of them large, and no major incidents.

50 Squadron would spend the next six nights on the ground, while other elements of the group participated in operations against Bremen on the night of the 17/18th, and Emden on the 20/21st. Sgt Heron RAAF and his crew had been among a batch of new arrivals from 14 O.T.U at Cottesmore on New Year's Day, and were on a training flight on the 21st, attempting to land at Ringway near Manchester in poor weather conditions and bad visibility. At 20.38,

AE381 flew into high ground on Kinder Scout in the Derbyshire Peak District, and all on board lost their lives. The garrison town of Münster was posted as the destination for forty-seven aircraft on the 22nd, for what would be the first attack on a target in inland Germany since late December. 5 Group detailed twenty-two Hampdens from Skellingthorpe, eleven from each squadron, and five Manchesters, but confusing records suggest that only eight from 50 Squadron took off, along with two others for mining duties in the Yams garden off Wilhelmshaven and the Weser estuary. They took off together between 17.10 and 17.37 with F/L King and the newly promoted F/L Helmore the senior pilots on duty, but lost P/O Miller and F/O Carter and their crews to technical problems immediately after taking off. The others found the many canals and rivers in this region of Germany, north of the Ruhr, standing out as dark lines in the snow-covered landscape, and this made navigation a simple task in cloud-free skies and bright moonlight. F/L King followed the course of the Dortmund-Ems Canal and railway lines right to the aiming-point, the main railway station, and bombed it from 7,000 feet, while the defences were focussing their attention at a higher level. Sgt Crampton and crew also went in at 7,000 feet, before diving to rooftop height to escape, and shooting up searchlights and targets of opportunity as they raced westwards to the Dutch frontier. F/Sgt Mapp and crew attacked from 12,000 feet, where they were found by the defences and surrounded by exploding flak shells, which they managed to avoid. F/L Helmore and crew made two runs on the aiming-point at a little under 8,000 feet, while Sgt Gruber did likewise from 9,000 feet to bomb the town centre after failing to identify the station. The recently promoted F/O Peace and crew completed the operation, but AT142 crashed near Oakham in Rutland at 22.20, while trying to land at Cottesmore, and all on board lost their lives. Meanwhile, the gardeners, Sgt Dampier-Crossley and P/O Goldsmith, had completed their sorties successfully, the former without difficulty from 600 feet, while the latter experienced intercom failure and problems identifying the drop zone, before having to evade the attentions of a Ju88.

On the 25th, the squadron took delivery of its first example of the troublesome Manchester, R5778, an ex 207 Squadron aircraft, and this made 50 Squadron the sixth recipient of the type. Thankfully, its association with this aircraft would be brief, and it would be some months yet before it would be used operationally. In the meantime, the seemingly interminable campaign against the enemy warships at Brest continued on the night of the 25/26th, for which a force of sixty-one aircraft was made ready. 5 Group put up thirty-five Hampdens and fifteen Manchesters, but 50 squadron was not represented. The force made its way to the Cornish coast, where small amounts of cloud were encountered, but this increased during the Channel crossing to three to eight-tenths in the target area. The crews had a clear view of the coastline as they approached, and were also guided to the aiming-point by searchlights, flares and the heavy and accurate flak defence. Another inconclusive and frustrating raid ensued, from which returning crews were unable to offer any indication of the results.

Hannover was posted as the primary target on the following night, for which a force of seventy-one aircraft was dispatched, nine of them Hampdens belonging to 50 Squadron as the entire 5 Group contribution. They departed Skellingthorpe between 17.09 and 17.48 with F/Ls Grant-Dalton and King the senior pilots on duty, and each carrying a single 1,000 and two 500 pounders. On what was destined to be an inauspicious night for the squadron, they lost a third of their number to technical failures before the Dutch coast was reached. P/O Milnes and crew were back on the ground within thirty minutes with intercom failure, and a similar malfunction brought Sgt Gruber and crew back to base two hours later. Five minutes after they touched down, a shivering F/L King and crew landed to complain of losing their heating system a few miles short of the Dutch coast. The others pressed on, but P/O Bartley and crew failed to establish a pinpoint as they crossed the enemy coast, and continued on for thirty-five minutes expecting to find a built-up area to tell them where they were. When nothing appeared below them, they turned back and brought their bombs home. Conditions in the target area could not have been better, with clear skies and bright moonlight providing excellent visibility, despite which, P/O Ferrie and crew failed to locate Hannover during a forty-minute search. They overshot the city by many miles, and bombed a railway junction at what they believed to be Stendal, situated closer to Berlin than Hannover. Unaccountably, Sgt Atkinson and crew failed to locate the target because of ten-tenths cloud that prevented them from finding the alternative or a last-resort objective, and they bombed on e.t.a from 12,000 feet. Contrast this with the reports of F/L Grant-Dalton, F/O Carter and P/O Goldsmith, who each found Hannover without difficulty in the "excellent" conditions, and were only deflected from the briefed aiming-point, the main railway station, by the ferocity of the searchlight and flak defences. They bombed the city from 8,000, 11,000 and 7,500 feet respectively, but, in their haste to get away intact, failed to observe any bursts. Returning crews described many fires, but reports rarely came out of this city to confirm or deny, and the likelihood is that decoy sites were operating.

The next attack on Brest was mounted on the 27th, and involved thirty-two Hampdens and three Manchesters from Scampton, Syerston, North Luffenham and Bottesford. *(The Bomber Command War Diaries does not record any operations taking place on this night)*. It was reported that Prinz Eugen was also "in town" as an added attraction for the force that arrived in the target area under a half moon and two to ten-tenths cloud with a base at 3,000 feet. Haze, or a smoke-screen, further obscured the docks area, and it was not possible to identify the warships, which escaped damage yet again. 50 Squadron was not called into action, and its crews were fully rested, therefore, when orders came through on the 28th to prepare for a raid that night on the town of Münster. A force of fifty-five Wellingtons and twenty-nine Hampdens was prepared for this operation, while a second force consisting of four Hampdens, seven Manchesters and thirty-seven other aircraft was assembled for a freshman operation against the docks at Boulogne. The ten 50 Squadron participants departed Skellingthorpe between 17.52 and 18.21 with W/C Oxley and S/L Jeffs the senior pilots on duty, and headed into the most appalling conditions of ten-tenths snow and ice-bearing cloud and blizzards, which stretched all the way into Germany. Not one 50 Squadron crew would locate the target area, and bombs were either released on e.t.a., and on flak concentrations, or were simply jettisoned to reduce weight as ice built up on wings and propellers. P/O Milnes and crew endured a torrid time over Germany after all of the instruments froze and the Hamden stalled twice. On return to English air space, they had no clue as to their whereabouts, not only in relation to the ground, but also air speed, altitude, and, indeed, attitude, having lost the artificial horizon. A beacon was spotted, which they decided to circle, only to fall out of the sky, at which point the pilot ordered his crew to abandon ship. Unfortunately, in the absence of a working intercom system, no-one heard, and all were still on board as the pilot braced his feet against the instrument panel and pulled back on the yoke with all his might. The G-Force was sufficient to break the cohesion of the ice, and the Hampden pulled out at a bare fifty feet, heading straight for a line of wireless masts. Narrowly avoiding these, P/O Milnes decided upon a belly-landing, and passed beneath unseen grid wires, before pulling off a gentle touchdown in a field near Norwich. AE373 would soon be returned to duty, and was the only 50 Squadron casualty on a night that cost 106 Squadron four Hampdens and crews.

50 Squadron had now concluded operations for the month, and sat out another tilt at Brest on the last night of the month, for which a force of seventy-one aircraft was made ready. 5 Group supported the operation with forty-one Hampdens and eleven Manchesters, whose crews found the coastline to be clearly visible in the bright moonlight, and were guided to the docks area by the intense flak and searchlight activity. This made the run-in to bomb an uncomfortable experience, and another inconclusive raid cost the group three 61 Squadron Manchesters and two 144 Squadron Hampdens. During the course of the month the squadron took part in eleven operations and dispatched ninety-four sorties for the loss of five Hampdens and crews.

February 1942

There were no operations for 5 Group during the first few days of the new month, and all available personnel were press-ganged into snow-clearing duties. Although the impending breakout from Brest by the three enemy warships would take the Royal Navy and the RAF by complete surprise in what would be a most humiliating episode for the government and the nation, there was clearly some advance warning, as three Manchesters were put on stand-by for daylight operations at Bottesford on the 4th in preparation for precisely that event, and six more on the 5th. 50 Squadron was notified on the 6th to make ready seven Hampdens for a daylight mining operation in the Nectarines garden off the Frisians. They were to be part of an all-5 Group force of thirty-three Hampdens and thirteen Manchesters, and took off between 11.41 and 12.02 with S/L Jeffs the senior pilot on duty. Conditions were generally favourable, and the drop zone, off the island of Terschelling, was easily located, mostly by an approach from the south via Vlieland, some finding cloud to mask their approach and others not. Those finding cloud cover were able to make timed runs to their briefed release points, while the remainder planted their vegetables as close as possible in known sea-lanes. All seven mines were deployed from between 650 and 1,000 feet, but wing bombs were brought home in the absence of suitable targets. That night, 3 Group sent fifty-seven Wellingtons and three Stirlings to continue the assault on Brest, and only a third of crews reported bombing through thick cloud.

The daylight gardening operation in the Frisians was repeated on the following day employing thirty-two Hampdens, six of which were 50 Squadron aircraft, which took off between 11.52 and 12.11 with S/L Lloyd the senior pilot on duty. The target area on this occasion was further north, off the island of Wangerooge in the Waddensee, where cloud was very thin and provided little cover. P/O Southgate and crew would not risk proceeding to the briefed drop zone, and found an alternative location for their mine, which they released from 1,000 feet. P/O Miller ran out of cloud before reaching his briefed drop zone, and deployed his mine from 1,000 feet between Schiermonnikoog and the Dutch mainland. The others carried out timed runs from Wangerooge and let their mines go as briefed from either side of 1,000 feet, S/L Lloyd attracting some moderately accurate heavy flak from the western end of the island. German fighters were seen to be operating, and three Hampdens failed to return home, among them the squadron's AE306, which was shot down west of Terschelling by the Me109 of Ofw Detlef Luth of II./JG1. Rhodesian-born F/Sgt Smith perished with his crew, a mere six weeks after being plucked from the sea as the sole survivor of his crew during the Vågsøy raid at the end of December.

S/L Jeffs and F/L King were sent on attachment to Waddington on the 8th to learn the ways of the Manchester, and P/O Milnes was posted on the same day to 44 Squadron, where he would get his hands on a Lancaster. 5 Group was not called into action again until the 10th, when nineteen Hampdens and a handful of Manchesters were assigned to attack the main railway station in Bremen. It became another shambles of an operation, carried out by a few crews through complete cloud cover, while most attacked alternative targets, jettisoned their bombs or returned them to store. 50 Squadron did not take part, and received orders on the 11th to prepared three Hampdens for an operation that night against a railway station at Mannheim, and another for a freshman crew to take to Cherbourg for a nickelling sortie. The bombing element was part of a 5 Group contribution of a dozen Hampdens and six Manchesters in company with thirty-one other aircraft, and departed Skellingthorpe between 18.12 and 18.19, having been preceded into the air at 17.50 by the freshman crew of P/O Davidson. The last-mention returned to Chipping Norton after three hours and twenty minutes to a report a successful sortie carried out in excellent visibility. The bombers also enjoyed favourable conditions, which enabled them to identify the target and release their bombs unopposed by flak from 9,500 to 11,500 feet in the vicinity of the briefed aiming-point.

Among other small-scale operations on this night was one against Brest by eighteen Wellingtons, the crews of which would have been unaware that they were the last to engage in this seemingly endless saga. As the sound of their engines receded into the eastern cloud-filled skies, Vice-Admiral Otto Cilliax, the Brest Group commander, whose flag was on Scharnhorst, put Operation Cerberus into action at 21.14, and Scharnhorst, Gneisenau and Prinz Eugen slipping anchor, before heading into the English Channel under an escort of destroyers and E-Boats. It was an audacious bid for freedom, covered by bad weather, widespread jamming and meticulously planned support by the Kriegsmarine and the Luftwaffe, all of which had been practiced extensively during January. The planning, and a little good fortune, allowed the fleet to make undetected progress until spotted off Le Touquet by two Spitfires piloted by G/C Victor Beamish, the commanding officer of Kenley, and W/C Finlay Boyd, both of whom maintained radio silence, and did not report their find until landing at 10.42 on the morning of the 12th.

The British authorities had prepared a plan in advance for precisely this eventuality, under the Codename, Operation Fuller, but so secret was it, that few either new of its full requirements or even of its existence. Once the enemy fleet was spotted in the late morning, frantic efforts were made to get Coastal and Bomber Command aircraft away, but only 5 Group was standing by at four hours readiness. It was 13.30 hours before the first sorties were launched, and the 5 Group stations worked frantically to get sixty-four Hampdens and fifteen Manchesters into the air. Eight 50 Squadron Hampdens took off between 14.38 and 15.12 with F/O Carter the senior pilot on duty. They were part of the largest commitment of aircraft by daylight in the war to date, amounting to 242 sorties, and were given a search area off the Hague, where rainstorms compounded the difficult conditions, and prevented most crews from locating the enemy fleet. Amidst universal reports of low cloud, P/O Miller and crew turned back because of an apparent absence of cloud below 14,000 feet, while Sgts Gruber and Crampton and F/Sgt Norris cited visibility of two to three hundred yards as their reason for abandoning the search. F/Sgt Mapp and crew established a pin-point on the Dutch coast, from where a number of runs were made, and a destroyer observed, at which they fired 350 rounds. However, breaking cloud threatened to rob them of their cover, and, after spending seventy-five minutes in the target area, they turned for home. Sgt Atkinson and crew spotted vessels below, but lost them while taking evasive action to defend against two attacks by an enemy fighter. It took some time to re-establish contact, and the largest ship was bombed from 1,200 feet in the face of heavy flak, which drove them to seek cloud cover before the results could be observed. P/O Goldsmith and crew carried out a square search, resulting in the location of an enemy ship, which was bombed inconclusively from 800 feet. AT177 failed to return home with the crew of F/O Carter, and no trace of the aircraft and crew was ever found.

Despite the heroic effort and sacrifice of the Bomber Command, Coastal Command and Fleet Air Arm crews, the enemy fleet made good its escape into open sea, although, its own trials and tribulations were not yet over. Scharnhorst struck a mine in the late afternoon and began to fall back, and, at 19.55, a magnetic mine detonated close enough to Gneisenau, when off Teschelling, to open a small hole in the starboard side, and, temporarily, slow her progress also. Later still, at 21.34, when passing through the same stretch of water, Scharnhorst hit another mine which stopped both engines and damaged steering and fire control. The vessel got under way again at 22.23 using its starboard engines and making twelve knots, while carrying an additional one thousand tons of seawater. The day's activities were not yet over for 5 Group, and the crews of twelve Hampdens and nine Manchesters were briefed to lay mines in the Nectarines garden off the Frisians through which the enemy fleet would have to pass to reach safety. S/L Lloyd and P/O Miller and their crews departed Skellingthorpe at 23.06 and 23.20 respectively to mine the waters off Wangerooge, and, having reached the estimated position of the target area, the former suffered an engine problem and had to jettison the mine and wing bombs "safe". The latter were able to release their mine over the briefed location and observe the parachute to deploy.

Gneisenau and Prinz Eugen reached the Elbe Estuary at 07.00 on the 13th, and, tied up at Brunsbüttel North Locks at 09.30, while Scharnhorst arrived at Wilhelmshaven at 10.00 with three months-worth of damage to repair. The mines had been laid almost certainly by 5 Group Hampdens over the preceding nights, and demonstrated the remarkable effectiveness of this war-long campaign. The entire episode was a major embarrassment to the government and the nation, but, worse still, cost the Command a further fifteen aircraft and crews on top of all of those sacrificed to this endeavour over the past eleven months. 5 Group alone posted missing nine Hampdens and crews, all lost in the North Sea, six of them without trace. On a positive note, this annoying and distracting itch had been scratched for the last time, and the Command could now concentrate its forces against the strategic targets for which it was best suited.

S/L Jeffs and F/L King returned from Waddington on the 13th, and, on the 14th, acting F/Ls Grant-Dalton and Helmore were posted to Upavon pending their postings as instructors to 16 and 14 O.T.Us respectively. A new Air Ministry directive, issued on the 14th, was to change the emphasis of bomber operations from that point until the end of the war. Lengthy consideration having been given to the Butt Report and the future of an independent bomber force, the new policy authorized the blatant area bombing of Germany's industrial towns and cities in a direct assault on the morale of the civilian population, particularly its workers. This had, of course, been going on since 1940, but no longer would there be the pretence of claiming to be attacking industrial and military targets. Waiting in the wings, in fact, at this very moment, four days into his voyage from the United States in the armed merchantman, Alcantara, was a new leader, a man well-known to 5 Group, who would not only pursue this policy with a will, but also possessed the self-belief, arrogance and stubbornness to fight his corner against all-comers on behalf of his beleaguered Bomber Command.

That night, a force of ninety-eight aircraft took off to employ the main post office and railway station as the aiming-points for an area attack on Mannheim, to which 5 Group contributed twenty-five Hampdens and nine Manchesters. Crews were guided to the city by the searchlight and flak activity, and encountered four to ten-tenths cloud at between 2,000 and 12,000 feet, with fair visibility above and ground haze below. Such weather conditions proved to be unhelpful, and, despite the claims of sixty-seven crews to have bombed the city, local reports spoke of two buildings destroyed and fifteen damaged. On the 15th, the now commissioned P/O Trevor-Roper was sent on a two-week gun turret training course at the Parnall aircraft factory at Yate in Gloucestershire, to prepare him for life as a "Tail-end Charlie" in a Manchester.

Gardening duties in the Nectarines region occupied thirty-seven Hampdens and twelve Manchesters on the night of the 16/17th, 50 Squadron providing a single participant, and two freshman crews to drop leaflets over the Cherbourg area. They took off together between 18.14 and 18.20, and P/O Davidson and crew made their way directly towards the target area, which encompassed the Frisian islands of Terschelling, Wangerooge, Juist and Borkum. They encountered a variety of cloud conditions, and remained beneath them until fifty miles from their destination. The sight of flak ahead, which appeared to be from Borkum, persuaded them to climb above the cloud, and the mine was delivered on e.t.a after a timed run. At the French coast, Sgt Wiseman and P/O Stone ran into nine to ten-tenths cloud at around 5,000 feet, and identified Cherbourg by the searchlight and flak activity emanating from the ground on e.t.a. They delivered between them 164 bundles of reading matter from 10,000 feet, and returned safely after sorties lasting under five hours. On the following night, three 50 Squadron leafleteers were the only crews from 5 Group operating, and departed Skellingthorpe between 17.59 and 18.32, Sgt Wiseman and crew bound for the Paris area, and those of Sgt Gray and P/O Fair for Cherbourg. The coastal region lay under a blanket of ten-tenths cloud, while only three-tenths sat over Paris, leaving haze and extreme darkness to do their best to conceal its massive sprawl. Each crew delivered forty-eight bundles of leaflets, but none found a suitable target for their wing bombs. Skellingthorpe remained inactive on the night of the 18/19th, when twenty-five Hampdens were sent gardening off the Frisians, in Heligoland Bight (Rosemary) and the Schillig Roads approaches to Jade Bay and the Weser estuary (Yams).

Following a few nights at home, 50 Squadron briefed six crews on the 21st, who would be among twenty detailed by 5 Group to carry out "roving commission" sorties over Germany, along with twenty-two Wellingtons. The Skellingthorpe crews were assigned to the Rhine Valley, which covers a region south of Cologne, and took off between 18.24 and 18.40 with F/Ls Ferrie and King the senior pilots on duty. They reached the target area to be greeted by clear skies and moonlight with ground haze, and Coblenz was identified easily by topographical features, and bombed from 11,500 feet by P/O Goldsmith and crew, who observed three bursts in the town. F/L King and crew spent thirty minutes cruising up and down the Rhine between Cologne and Coblenz, enjoying the conditions and lack of opposition, and dropped their wing bombs on Coblenz from 9,000 feet, before aiming the heavy stuff at a factory situated somewhere to the west. P/O Miller and crew thought that they had emptied their bomb bay over Coblenz, but discovered on return that the bombs had hung-up and had been brought home. On e.t.a at Coblenz, Sgt Norris and crew found themselves over ten-tenths cloud, which suggested that they were not where they thought they were. They bombed blindly from 10,000 feet, and, at some time while over enemy territory, were attacked three times by a night-fighter. Observing a searchlight, which they took to be at the English coast, they switched on navigation lights and sought assistance to establish their position. It was then that they realized they were still over enemy territory, and headed back into cloud to regroup, only to suffer severe icing, which caused their instruments to fail. Five S.O.S fixes were obtained to help them regain the English coast, and they eventually landed at Desford, near Leicester, after descending through snowstorms and poor visibility. This caused them to overshoot the flare-path and sustain some repairable damage. F/L Ferrie and crew dropped their bombs from 7,000 feet on e.t.a over Aachen, and then stirred up the defences as they leafleted the region between the German frontier and Coblenz, collecting a number of flak hits for their troubles. W/O Mapp and crew bombed a railway junction west of Coblenz from 10,000 feet, and, shortly afterwards, the navigator passed out through lack of oxygen. He came round later to resume his duties, and guided them towards the English coast, just short of which an engine cut out, and that problem was compounded by severe icing. They had crossed the Yorkshire coast by the time that fuel starvation left them without power, and the order was given to abandon aircraft. W/O Mapp arrived safely on the ground, but AE394 crashed at 02.18 near the Rowntree's theatre in York, with the remaining crew members still on board. It seems that the lower escape hatch may have jammed to prevent them from escaping.

Air Chief Marshal Sir Arthur Harris took up his post as the new Commander-in-Chief of Bomber Command on the 22nd. He was a man well-known to 5 Group, having served as its A-O-C until November 1940, when he became second deputy to Sir Charles Portal, the Chief-of-the-Air-Staff. Harris arrived at the helm with firm ideas already in place on how to win the war by bombing alone, a pre-war theory, which no commander had yet had an opportunity to put into practice. It was obvious to him, that the small-scale raids on multiple targets favoured by his predecessor, served only to dilute the effort, and that such pin-prick attacks could not hurt Germany's war effort. He recognized the need to overwhelm the defences and emergency services, by pushing the maximum number of aircraft across the aiming-point in the shortest possible time, and this would signal the birth of the bomber stream, and an end to the former practice, whereby squadrons or even crews determined for themselves the details of their sorties. He knew also that urban areas are most efficiently destroyed by fire, rather than blast, and it would not be long before the bomb loads carried in his aircraft reflected this thinking. In the meantime, while he developed his ideas, he would continue with the fairly small-scale attacks on German ports favoured by his predecessor, and, later on the evening of his appointment, sent thirty-one Wellingtons and nineteen Hampdens to Wilhelmshaven to attack the floating dock likely to be employed during repairs to Scharnhorst and Gneisenau. Sadly, the target area was covered by dense cloud and the bombing that took place on estimated positions missed the target altogether.

On the 23rd, 5 Group detailed twenty-three Hampdens for gardening duties in the Rosemary and Yams regions in the Heligoland Bight and Schillig Roads respectively, 50 Squadron dividing its eight crews equally between them. They had to wait until the early hours of the 24th before departing Skellingthorpe between 02.55 and 03.40 with W/C Oxley the senior pilot on duty, and Sgt Atkinson and crew last away after ice had to be cleared from the wings.

The delay resulted in a change of garden for this crew to the nearer one at Nectarines off the Frisians, where ground mist prevented the establishing of a pin-point, and the sortie was abandoned. By this time, F/O Miller and crew had returned with a failing engine, leaving F/Ls Ferrie and King as the squadron's only representatives in the Schillig Roads. They planted their vegetables from 600 and 900 feet respectively in conditions of poor visibility in the grey light of dawn, the former then attacking a small convoy with his wing bombs. Meanwhile, to the north, P/O Bartley and crew alone of the Rosemary section planted their vegetable into the briefed location, doing so, also in poor visibility, from 1,000 feet. W/C Oxley, P/O Goldsmith and F/Sgt Lord all decided on the alternative target area in the Frisians, and their mines went down from 500, 800 and 900 feet respectively.

5 Group detailed forty-two Hampdens and nine Manchesters on the 24th to return that night to the same three gardens, the nine 50 Squadron participants departing Swinderby in two sections almost five hours apart. The first element of four Hampdens took off between 18.03 and 18.15, to be followed within ten minutes by two freshman crews bound for the Paris area on nickelling sorties. The second element of five aircraft took off between 22.53 and 00.02, but the ORB does not make clear to which garden each was assigned. It does, however, make clear that adverse weather conditions were likely to prevail, and crews were instructed at briefing not to fight the elements, and to bring the mines back if accurate delivery was not guaranteed. As matters turned out, four mines were planted in the allotted locations, three in alternative gardens and two were returned to store. The leafleting duo released their forty-eight bundles each of propaganda on e.t.a in the Paris area in fair visibility, and, thereby, gained a little more experience in their quest to survive their tours.

5 Group detailed a dozen Manchesters on the 25th to target the Gneisenau at Kiel, while eighteen Hampdens and a Manchester took care of gardening duties in the Nectarines I and II, Yams and Rosemary gardens. 50 Squadron made ready nine Hampdens for mining in the waters off the Frisians, Heligoland, Schillig Roads/Weser estuary and Terschelling, and two others for P/O Cole and Sgt Wilkie and their crews to take on nickelling trips to Paris. Departures of the various elements would again be separated by some hours, with the first section of four taking off between 18.03 and 18.15, to be followed at 18.23 and 18.26 by the leafleteers, and, finally, by the final five between 22.53 and 00.02. All would encounter ten-tenths cloud with poor visibility below, despite which, F/O Miller, and P/Os Bartley and Goldsmith delivered their vegetables into the allocated positions in the Schillig Roads and Weser estuary region. P/O Stone was also successful in the Nectarines garden, returning fire after a convoy opened up with machine-guns, and P/O Roblin also managed to find his briefed drop zone. The others sought out alternative locations close to the allotted gardens, delivering their stores from between 600 and 1,000 feet, and only F/Sgt Lord and crew brought their mine home. Meanwhile, Sgt Wilkie and crew dropped forty-eight bundles of leaflets from 8,000 feet on e.t.a at Paris, while P/O Cole delivered his over an area some twenty-five miles further to the north-north-west.

Skellingthorpe remained inactive on the evening of the 26th, when Scampton and North-Luffenham dispatched ten Hampdens between them to join Wellingtons and Halifaxes in targeting the floating dock at Kiel, at which Gneisenau was thought to be at berth. The operation took place under clear skies, and threw up one of the war's great ironies, after a high explosive bomb struck the bows of Gneisenau, now supposedly in a safe haven, having endured eleven months of constant bombardment at Brest. This killed 116 of her crew and ended her sea-going career for good, after which, her main armament was removed for use in coastal defence, and she was towed to Gdynia to remain unrepaired.

Kiel was the destination once more on the following night, when a force of sixty-eight aircraft included eighteen Hampdens and seventeen Manchesters, whose crews were briefed to aim for the floating dock. 50 Squadron detailed eight for the main operation, and seven for mining duties in the Nectarines garden. The bombing brigade departed Skellingthorpe first between 17.40 and 17.57 with S/L Lloyd the senior pilot on duty, and they were followed into the air between 18.18 and 18.38 by the gardeners. P/O Stone and crew set course for Teschelling, until their intercom failed and forced them to turn back, and it was the same problem that afflicted F/Sgt Lord and crew, and persuaded them to abandon their sortie after around two hours. Shortly after they landed, F/O Miller and crew touched down having been defeated by the icing conditions. P/O Bartley and crew were also contending with icing conditions, and dropped their bombs through the cloud onto a flak position as they turned for home. The others pressed on to reach their respective target areas and encounter bright moonlight above the ten-tenths cloud, but poor visibility below. There was no chance of identifying the floating dock, and the remaining bombers attacked the general area of the town from between 11,000 and 13,000 feet, guided by the flashes of searchlights and flak. The six remaining gardeners enjoyed greater success, each planting a vegetable into the briefed location from between 500 and 800 feet. F/Sgt Johnson and crew were on final approach to Skellingthorpe, flying on fumes, when the engines cut, and AE218 flopped onto the ground at 02.20, writing itself off but not damaging the crew, who walked away. During the course of the month the squadron participated in seventeen bombing, mining and nickelling operations, and dispatched eighty-four sorties for the loss of four Hampdens, two complete crews and three members of another.

March 1942

Adverse weather conditions welcomed in the new month and kept the bomber force on the ground on the 1st. It was the same on the 2nd, and it was the 3rd before orders were received across the Command to prepare for an operation, which, in its bold conception, was a clear indication of what was to come. Bomber Command's evolution to war-winning capability was to be long, arduous and gradual, but the first signs of a new hand on the tiller came early on in Harris's reign with this meticulously planned attack on the Renault lorry factory, which was located in a loop of the Seine in the district of Billancourt to the south-west of central Paris. The plant was capable of producing 18,000 lorries per year, which was a massive boon to the German war effort, and the attempt to destroy it came in response to an Air Ministry request. The operation would be conducted in three waves, led by experienced crews, and would involve extensive use of flares to provide illumination. In the face of what was expected to be scant defence, crews were also briefed to attack from as low a level as practicable, both for the sake of accuracy, and in an attempt to avoid civilian casualties. In time, such operations would be led by Gee-equipped aircraft, but the 3 Group squadrons already employing the device were forbidden from taking part on this occasion, lest one be lost over enemy territory and its secrets revealed. A force of 235 aircraft was assembled, a new record for a single target, and 50 Squadron was called upon to contribute nine Hampdens to the forty-eight of the type and twenty-six Manchesters representing 5 Group. S/L Lloyd led them off the ground at 17.58, and all were safely airborne by 18.12 with W/C Oxley the senior pilot on duty. Each Skellingthorpe Hampden was carrying a single 1,900 and two 500 pounders along with flares, all of which would reach the target area on a night of good serviceability. For the first time, crews were given strict time-on-target slots, those in the vanguard between 20.45 and 21.00, the main force, which included most of the 5 Group element, 21.00 to 22.00, and the rear guard 22.00 to 22.15. Bright moonlight aided target location, and most picked up the River Seine in good time to enable them to plan their bombing runs. A number of 50 Squadron crews were able to identify the diesel engine test shed, and added their flares to the many others floating down to reveal the city in detail. The belief in the absence of a flak defence proved to be well-founded, and many crews felt confident to make multiple passes across the target before releasing their bombs. The 50 Squadron element carried out their attacks from between 2,100 and 3,000 feet, and reported the factory buildings to be well alight as they turned away. They were among 223 crews who reported successful sorties, and post-raid reconnaissance would confirm the operation as an outstanding success for the loss of just one aircraft. 40% of the factory's buildings had been destroyed, and production was halted for four weeks, costing the Germans around 2,300 lorries, although, sadly, not all of the bombs had fallen precisely where intended. Inevitably, adjacent workers' housing had been hit by stray bombs, killing 367 French civilians and severely injuring 341 others, some of whom would die. At the time, this was more than twice the heaviest death toll inflicted on a German target. It was somewhat paradoxical, that, as a champion of area bombing, Harris should gain his first major victory by way of a precision target.

Earlier in the day, the now crewless P/O Mapp had been posted to 1506 Beam Approach Training (B.A.T.) Flight. It rained all day on the 4th, and snowed all day on the 5th, and it was the 7th before orders came through from 5 Group to make ready seventeen Hampdens for gardening duties in the Artichoke garden, in the approaches to the port of Lorient, an operation not recorded in the 5 Group ORB. While preparations were in hand, AE387 began to take off at 16.30 either for a training flight, or, more likely, an air test, but swung in the gusty wind and crashed before being consumed by fire. P/O Nock sustained injury, and the other occupant, a member of ground crew, lost his life. The eight operational crews had to wait until the early hours of the 8th before departing Skellingthorpe between 01.58 and 02.30 with F/L King the senior pilot on duty. They were heading south for the Dorset coast when Sgt Gray and crew turned back from a position south-west of Oxford after an engine problem arose. The others continued on to find favourable conditions and good visibility in the target area, where F/L King, P/O Goldsmith and Sgt Atkinson delivered their mines from between 600 and 1,000 feet, and F/Sgt Lord dropped his close to the briefed location also from 600 feet, after searching for thirty-five minutes. F/Sgt Johnson and crew jettisoned their mine and wing bombs "safe", after deciding that they could not complete the sorties before the advent of daylight. P/O Bartley and crew were thrown off course by a navigational error, and returned their mine and bombs to store, while F/O Davidson and crew failed to return after AE400 disappeared into the sea off the Brittany coast.

Essen was to feature prominently in Harris's future plans, and a series of raids was planned against this massively important industrial powerhouse of a city, beginning with the first of three on consecutive nights from the 8/9th. A force of 211 aircraft was put together during the course of the 8th, of which thirty-seven Hampdens and twenty-two Manchesters were to represent 5 Group. The leading aircraft, belonging to 3 Group, would be those equipped with the new Gee navigation device, which carried the great hope that it could solve the problem of target locating. 50 Squadron made ready nine Hampdens for the main operation and four others for mining duties in the Nectarines region off the Frisians. The bombers departed Skellingthorpe first, between 01.02 and 01.34, with S/Ls Jeffs and Lloyd the senior pilots on duty, and they were followed into the air by the all-NCO gardening crews between 03.17 and 03.34. Sgt Wiseman and crew abandoned their sortie immediately because of intercom failure, and this reduced the bombing brigade to eight aircraft, which arrived over the Ruhr to find fine weather conditions, and, also, the ever-present industrial haze, which obscured ground detail. They had been assigned to aiming-point "B", which was the Krupp works, but only the crews of S/Ls Jeffs and Lloyd and F/O Miller were able to make a positive identification after pinpointing on the Rhine, and they carried out their attacks from 6,000, 10,000 and 11,000 feet respectively. The remaining crews bombed the general city area from around 10,000 to 12,000 feet, some observing bursts and others not, and, while few of them had useful information to pass on at debriefing, local reports described a light raid with a little housing damage in southern districts. Meanwhile, some 150 miles to the north-north-west, three of the gardeners had managed to plant their vegetables in the briefed location off Terschelling from 500 and 600 feet, and one had brought theirs home after failing to find it.

The Krupp works was back on twenty-four hours later as one of two aiming-points at Essen, and a force of 187 aircraft made ready, which included a 5 Group contribution of fifteen Hampdens and ten Manchesters. This figure had originally been higher, but adverse weather conditions, technical difficulties and one unidentified Manchester becoming bogged down on the way to take-off at Bottesford, reduced the numbers significantly. 50 Squadron briefed just two crews, those of F/Sgt Johnson and P/O Goldsmith departing Skellingthorpe at 20.23 and 20.27 respectively. The Goldsmith crew claimed to be able to see the flares over Essen even before reaching the Dutch coast, which confirmed that the horizontal visibility was reasonable, while vertical visibility at the target would be compromised by industrial haze. They and the Johnson crew had been briefed to aim for the city's main square, but this was better interpreted as ordering them to continue the assault on the morale of the civilian population, particularly its work force, in line with the February 14th Directive. Three minutes from the aiming-point, the Johnson crew observed many fires burning, and added their high explosives and incendiaries from 12,000 feet, a thousand feet higher than their squadron colleagues. The rest of the force scattered their bombs over twenty-four other Ruhr towns and cities, with Hamborn and Duisburg the chief beneficiaries, and the Essen authorities reported the destruction of two buildings, with seventy-two others damaged.

Essen was posted as the target again on the 10th, for which a force of 126 aircraft was made ready, almost half of them provided by 5 Group. Forty-three Hampdens, thirteen Manchesters and, for the first time over Germany, two Lancasters, took to the air, the eight 50 Squadron participants, led by F/L Ferrie, departing Skellingthorpe between 19.10 and 20.02, at the same time as three freshman crews bound for the docks at Boulogne. Last away, and first to return seventeen minutes later with engine failure, was the crew of Sgt Atkinson, reducing the Essen-bound element by one. They all reached the target to find extreme darkness and poor visibility, made worse by the glare from searchlights and flares. They also had to contend with intense and accurate flak, which managed to puncture the skins of a number of the Skellingthorpe Hampdens. Unable to identify the main square, they bombed the built-up area from between 5,000 and 12,000 feet, before turning for home to report observing some bursts and fires. P/O Stone and crew had difficulty maintaining height after running into icing conditions on the way home, and were running short of fuel as they crossed the Essex coast at Harwich. Here, thick fog denied them the opportunity to land, and the decision was taken at 02.25 to abandon AT173 to its fate. The crew floated down to a safe landing, leaving the Hampden to crash into the fenlands of East Anglia. The three freshman crews of Sgt Gray,

Sgt Weber and F/Sgt Morgan had encountered low cloud and poor visibility at the French coast, persuading each to abandon their sorties and return the bombs to store.

The ports of Kiel and Emden were the main targets on the night of the 12/13th, and were assigned mostly to Wellingtons, with assistance from 4 Group Whitleys at the latter. 5 Group committed twenty-six Hampdens and a lone Manchester to gardening duties in the Yams, Hawthorn and Rosemary regions off Germany's North Sea coast. The 50 Squadron crews of F/Sgt Morgan and Sgt Weber departed Skellingthorpe at 01.47 and 02.02 respectively, bound for Yams, in the Schillig Roads approaches to Jade Bay and the Weser estuary. Both reached the target area to find contradictory conditions, the latter reporting low cloud that prevented an identification of the briefed release point, and the planting of the vegetable in an alternative location, while the former enjoyed good visibility, and dropped the mine from 500 feet into the correct spot.

Orders were received on stations across the Command on the 13th to prepare for an operation against Cologne that night, which would employ six aircraft types. A force of 135 aircraft was assembled, which would be led by an element from 3 Group, equipped with Gee and carrying flares and all-incendiary bomb loads. Their job was to locate the target and create a beacon of fires to draw on the other participants, on what would be a dark, moonless night. 5 Group supported the operation with twenty-two Hampdens, sixteen Manchesters and a single Lancaster, ten of the Hampdens provided by 50 Squadron. They took off from Skellingthorpe between 19.02 and 19.13 with S/L Jeffs the senior pilot on duty, and among them were two additional Hampdens containing the freshman crews of F/O Seeley-King and P/O Crombie, who were bound for Paris to deliver "toilet paper". F/O Miller and crew were soon back on the ground as a result of technical difficulties, and F/O Seeley-King turned back also when two hours out, after encountering poor weather conditions. The others pressed on into Germany, where visibility was good through the partial cover of three to five-tenths cloud that lay over the Rhineland Capital between 8,000 and 12,000 feet. The bombers had to run the gauntlet of intense searchlight and flak to reach the aiming-point, where flares provided effective illumination, and the 50 Squadron crews delivered their attacks from 4,500 to 13,000 feet, observing at least six fires to develop in the city centre. A later assessment revealed that some useful industrial damage had resulted, mainly in the Nippes district, to the north of the city centre, west of the river, which was also the location of a major marshalling yards with railway workshops. In addition to this, 1,500 houses had also been hit in what proved to be the first genuinely successful Gee-led raid. Meanwhile, at Paris, P/O Crombie had delivered forty-eight bundles of leaflets through ten-tenths cloud from 10,500 feet.

During the following week operations were posted and cancelled, and it was the 20th before 5 Group next stirred into action to send nineteen Manchesters and Lancasters to mine the waters off the Frisians. S/L Potts was rested from operations and posted to 14 O.T.U on the 22nd. On the 23rd, twelve Hampdens and two Manchesters were detailed for gardening duties in the Artichokes region off the port of Lorient. P/O Crombie and crew departed Skellingthorpe that evening to take part, but returned some two-and-a-half hours later because of technical problems. On the following night, twenty-three Hampdens three Manchesters and two Lancasters were sent back to Lorient, the 50 Squadron element of five Hampdens departing Skellingthorpe between 19.02 and 19.20 with S/L Jeffs the senior pilot on duty. P/O Stone and crew decided to drop their wing bombs onto Lannion aerodrome from 5,000 feet as they crossed the Brest peninsular outbound, but the vegetable fell out at the same time and ended their interest in the proceedings. Three of the others took advantage of the moonlight and good visibility to pinpoint on Quiberon and the Ile-de-Croix, before making a timed run to deliver their mines into the briefed locations from around 600 feet. AE429 failed to return with the others, and news was received eventually to confirm that it had crashed in the vicinity of Brest with no survivors from the crew of P/O Fair.

Harris resumed his campaign against Essen on the night of the 25/26th, when sending the largest force yet to a single target of 254 aircraft. 5 Group played its part by contributing twenty Manchesters, nine Hampdens and seven Lancasters, 50 Squadron providing just two Hampdens and four others for gardening and nickelling duties. P/O Seeley-King and crew started the ball rolling when taking off for their nickelling trip to Rouen in northern France at 19.05, to be followed into the air by F/Sgt Morgan, P/O Crombie and Sgt Gray between 19.06 and 19.12, all bound for the Artichokes garden. Before the departure of the Essen duo, Sgt Atkinson and crew returned from a training sortie in Manchester L7486 at 19.15, bounced heavily, stalled and burst into flames on impacting the ground, fortunately, without injuring the occupants. F/Sgt Johnson and P/O Roblin and their crews took off for the main event at 19.34 and 19.40 respectively, the latter never to be seen again after AT151 disappeared without trace. Despite clear skies and good visibility, thick industrial haze thwarted the Johnson crew's attempts to identify Essen, and a single 1,000 pounder was dropped from 11,000 feet onto a built-up area on the western fringe of the Ruhr, possibly Duisburg, the 500 pounders having been jettisoned after the starboard engine began to overheat. The promise shown in the recent attack on Cologne was not repeated, and much of the effort was wasted on a decoy site at Rheinberg, some eighteen miles away. It was a bad night for 5 Group, which posted missing six aircraft, two-thirds of the overall casualty figure, and among them were five of the twenty Manchesters dispatched, a loss rate of 25%. Two of the gardeners returned safely after delivering their vegetables into the briefed locations under moonlight, but AT158 had crashed in the target area with fatal consequences for P/O Crombie and his crew.

Later, on the 26th, S/L Jeffs and crew set off in AT118 to conduct a sea-search in the hope of spotting the Crombie crew in a dinghy. While flying at 150 feet over the sea, an engine seized, and they barely maintained height as they struggled to reach the Cornish coast, before crash-landing at 15.20 in a ploughed field five miles north of Penzance. There were no crew casualties, but a flare ignited, and the Hampden was consumed in the subsequent fire.

On the following night, while a force of 115 Wellingtons and Stirlings returned to Essen, 5 Group detailed thirty Hampdens and fifteen Manchesters to conduct mining operations in the Yams, Nectarines and Deodars gardens, respectively in Jade Bay/Weser estuary, off the Frisians and the Gironde estuary. 50 Squadron made ready five Hampdens, four for Deodars and one for Nectarines, and dispatched them between 19.08 and 19.35 with F/O Seeley-King the senior pilot on duty. All reached their respective target areas, on the Biscay coast to find clear skies and good visibility, and off the Frisians, high cloud but also favourable conditions. F/O Seeley-King and crew dropped their mine into the allotted location from 400 feet after pinpointing on Terschelling, while their colleagues were equally successful some 640 miles to the south, and all returned safely. Skellingthorpe remained inactive on the 27th when eighteen Hampdens were sent mining in the Yams, Nectarines and Rosemary (Heligoland Bight) gardens.

These operations preceded another foretaste of things to come, when Harris launched a major assault on the historic Hansastadt (free-trade) city of Lübeck on the north German coast, believing, that, if he could provide his crews with the means to locate a target, they would hit it. Coastlines offered the most distinctive features for the purpose of identification, hence, Lübeck, which not only lay on the Baltic coast to the east of Kiel, but also represented the perfect target for destruction by fire because of the narrow streets and half-timbered buildings in its old centre. The operation was to be conducted along the same lines as the highly successful attack on the Renault factory at the start of the month, and a force of 234 aircraft was assembled, 5 Group represented by forty-one Hampdens and twenty-one Manchesters. 50 Squadron made ready six Hampdens, which departed Skellingthorpe between 20.06 and 20.44 with P/O Stone the senior pilot on duty. Sgt Gray and crew returned to the circuit within the hour because of a technical problem, leaving the others to reach the target area in excellent visibility that allowed them to map-read across the Schleswig-Holstein peninsular. Four of the 50 Squadron crews bombed from between 800 and 8,800 feet, aiming at the city centre, where many fires were seen to develop, but Sgt Weber and crew arrived an hour behind schedule after becoming confused by the frozen surface of the Baltic, and they bombed from 10,000 feet. On return they reported the burning city to be visible from seventy miles away, and F/Sgt Johnson and crew described firing seven hundred rounds at buildings. The operation was a major success, which destroyed almost fifteen hundred houses and seriously damaged almost two thousand more, in a 190-acre area of devastation representing some 30% of the city's built-up area. It was the first major success for area bombing, and another sign of what was in store for the residents of Germany's towns and cities. There was an outcry following this unexpected attack on Lübeck, which was a vital port for the Red Cross, and an agreement was struck that ensured its future protection from bombing.

Eighteen Hampdens and eight Manchesters were made ready for further gardening operations on the 29th, all but two assigned to the Nectarines garden, while two of the Manchesters ventured as far as the Bottle garden, off Haugesund on Norway's western coast. F/O Seeley-King and crew took off at 19.26 as the lone 50 Squadron gardeners, while F/Sgt Packard and Sgt Dickenson and their crews headed off a few minutes later to dispense sixty bundles of nickels each in the general area of Lille. All fulfilled their briefs and returned home safely from uneventful sorties. A daylight "moling" cloud cover operation on the 31st involved eleven Hampdens and six Wellingtons, the two of the former belonging to 50 Squadron departing Skellingthorpe at 12.00 and 12.07 for railway targets in north-western Germany. P/O Stone and Sgt Dampier-Crossley and their crews flew out over Skegness over ten-tenths cloud, which, according to the Stone crew, began to disperse as they crossed Holland to within ten miles of the German frontier, where it ran out altogether, forcing them to turn back. The other crew, unaccountably, found cloud cover all the way to the briefed target area, where a railway line was attacked, the eight 250lb bombs falling short of a goods train. They fired five hundred rounds at an aerodrome, and sustained flak damage to the starboard rudder for their trouble, but made it home safely. During the course of the month, the squadron took part in twenty operations, and dispatched eighty-four sorties, losing seven Hampdens and one Manchester along with four complete crews and a pilot.

April 1942

The new month began for 5 Group with operations on the 1st in company with Wellingtons, although not operating together. Twenty-two Hampden crews were briefed to take part in a raid on the docks area and shipping at Le Havre, while fourteen others were to be sent to carry out low-level attacks on railway targets in north-western Germany in the Meppen and Lingen region just over the frontier from Holland. 50 Squadron would support both operations, F/Sgt Packard and crew departing Skellingthorpe for the French coast at 19.30, to be followed two minutes later by F/Sgt McKenzie and crew bound for Paris to deliver reading material. Sgts Weber and Wiseman and their crews set off for north-western Germany at 20.09 and 20.12 respectively, but engine problems forced the former to turn back when thirty minutes from the enemy coast. Sgt Wiseman and crew were also experiencing technical problems, in their case with the intercom system, as a result of which the crew members were unable to communicate with the pilot to tell him of a tempting target in the form of a train in Leer station. The bombs were aimed at a bridge on the line between Emden and Lingen, but it missed by twenty yards. The gunners expended seven hundred rounds in defending the Hampden against the attentions of a night-fighter, but no claims were forthcoming. Meanwhile, F/Sgt Packard and crew were enjoying the perfect conditions over Le Havre, and bombed the docks from 7,000 feet, observing three bursts. The McKenzie crew benefitted from similar conditions over the moonlit French Capital, and delivered their bundles of leaflets along with twenty-five rounds intended for a searchlight. It turned into a disastrous night for 3 Group, whose railway targets were at Hanau and Lohr to the east of Frankfurt, from which five out of twelve 57 Squadron Wellingtons failed to return and seven of fourteen belonging to 214 Squadron. This caused a rethink by those responsible for planning operations, despite which, a similar disaster awaited 5 Group in December.

On the following night, twenty-three Hampdens were detailed for mining duties in the Gorse garden in Quiberon Bay, situated on the western coast of Brittany, north-west of St-Nazaire. 50 Squadron made ready five Hampdens, which took off between 19.08 and 19.16 with S/L Jeffs the senior pilot on duty, only for F/O Seeley-King and crew to turn back early. The others pressed on in ideal moonlight conditions to establish their positions without difficulty to pinpoint on Quiberon Point or Ile-d'Houat, from where they carried out their timed runs to deliver the vegetables into the allotted locations from between 400 and 850 feet. A daylight mining operation in the Nectarines garden was planned for the late afternoon of the fourth, and the seven 50 Squadron participants departed Skellingthorpe between 15.45 and 15.06 with S/L Jeffs the senior pilot on duty. They were relying on cloud cover over the Frisians to provide protection, and, when this failed to materialize, the operation was abandoned, and all returned home with their stores.

The first major operation of the new month was to be directed at Cologne on the night of the 5/6th, and involved a new record force of 263 aircraft, including a 5 Group contribution of forty-four Hampdens and eleven Manchesters. The aiming point was the Humboldt engineering works in the Deutz district on the East Bank of the Rhine in the city centre, for which the squadron dispatched just two crews at 00.29 and 00.45 respectively. At 00.34, AT216 crashed at Thorpe-on-the-Hill, six miles south-west of Lincoln, killing F/O Seeley-King and his crew, who would be the last 50 Squadron airmen to lose their lives on Hampdens. Sgt Gray and crew continued on to reach the target, where bright moonlight penetrated the nine-tenths cloud to glint off an S-bend in the Rhine to the south of the city centre and assist with establishing their position. The bombs were dropped from 10,000 feet, and one large burst was observed, but many others involved in the attack scattered their loads right across the built-up area, destroying or seriously damaging ninety houses but no important industrial buildings.

Harris turned his attention back upon Essen on the night of the 6/7th for the first of three raids on the city in the space of six nights. 5 Group contributed eighteen Hampdens and ten Manchesters, with just one of the former provided by 50 Squadron. Sgt Dampier-Crossley and crew took off at 00.10, briefed to aim their single 1,900 and two 250 pounders at the main square, and managed to cover most of the distance before port engine failure forced them to jettison their load "live" and turn for home. Only a third of the crews reported bombing the target, which escaped with minor damage at a cost to the Command of five aircraft, three of them belonging to 5 Group.

Hamburg was posted as the target on the 8th, and yet another record force, this time of 272 aircraft, was made ready. 5 Group stepped up with thirty-two Hampdens and thirteen Manchesters assigned to the Blohm & Voss shipyards located to the west of the city centre, while the Lancasters and nine further Hampdens were to attack aiming-point C. They had to fly through or round one of the frequent electrical storms with icing conditions that built up over the North Sea, and only 188 crews reported bombing at the primary target. The result was another poor performance, which deposited no more than the equivalent of fourteen bomb loads in the city and caused eight fires. 50 Squadron was not involved, but was in action elsewhere to deliver mines or leaflets, some, for the first time, in Manchesters. Four Hampdens and three Manchesters departed Skellingthorpe between 20.53 and 21.12, three of the former, captained by F/Sgts McKenzie and Packard and Sgt Dickenson, to head for the Rosemary garden in the Heligoland Bight, while F/O Wilkins, P/O Southgate and Sgt Crampton and their crews set course for Paris in Manchesters L7432, L7489 and L7455 respectively, accompanied by P/O Manser and crew in another Hampden. They all reached their respective target areas, the gardeners finding extreme darkness under starlit skies, two of them observing no cloud and good visibility, and the other, unaccountably, eight tenths cloud and poor visibility. They pinpointed on Westerhever or Pellworm, the island to the north, and carried out timed runs to the release point, where the vegetables went down into the allotted positions from 500 to 700 feet. Conditions in the Paris region were favourable, with partial cloud cover and good visibility that enabled the crews to pick out ground features like the River Seine. F/O Wilkins and crew dispensed eighty-three bundles of nickels from 4,500 feet over the south-western suburbs, while P/O Southgate and crew dropped seventy bundles from 6,000 feet onto an area twenty-five miles south-west of the French Capital. Sgt Crampton and crew delivered 106 bundles from 5,000 feet five miles to the west, and P/O Manser and crew let theirs go from 10,000 feet fifteen miles further out from the same compass point. A seagull strike caused a little damage to the Perspex of L7432, but all returned safely from what had been a gentle introduction to Manchester operations.

It was back to Essen for 254 aircraft on the 10th, an operation supported by 5 Group with forty-three Hampdens, ten Manchesters and eight Lancasters. 50 Squadron briefed three Hampden crews to attack the main square, but was not yet ready to commit its fledgling Manchester crews to the cauldron of the Ruhr, and would send two to bomb the docks at Le Havre and another to maintain the stock of reading matter for the residents of Paris. P/O Southgate and crew were first to depart Skellingthorpe, at 20.52, bound for Le Havre, where they identified the Seine estuary in good visibility, before running in on the target at 10,000 feet and delivering their load in the vicinity of docks N[o]s 7 and 11. F/O Wilkins and crew were only two minutes behind, and carried out their attack from 6,000 feet, observing eight bursts on the docks. P/O Baker and crew were handed Paris for their maiden Manchester sortie, and found clear skies from which to scatter their nickels from 8,000 feet. The Essen-bound trio took off either side of 22.00, and reached the target area, where clear skies had been forecast. However, a layer of eight-tenths cloud between 5,000 and 8,000 feet lay across the central Ruhr to prevent them from locating the main square and forcing them to bomb the general city area instead. Local reports confirmed the operation to have been a dismal failure, which destroyed only twelve houses and caused no industrial damage.

Orders were received across the Command on the 12th to prepare another large force to return to Essen, and 251 aircraft were made ready accordingly. 5 Group responded with thirty-one Hampdens and nine Manchesters, just one of the former representing 50 Squadron, while two others would mine the sea-lanes in the Rosemary garden and two Manchesters in Hawthorn, off western Jutland, leaving three further Manchesters to carry nickels to Paris. These would be the final sorties by Hampdens in 50 Squadron service. They took off for their respective destinations and assignments between 20.54 and 22.23, F/Sgt Packard and crew reaching Essen to find industrial haze blotting out ground detail and dummy fires to distract them. They also encountered intense searchlight activity, and were coned for a time as they dropped their bombs into the general built-up area from 3,000 feet. Two hundred miles to the north, P/O Manser and F/Sgt McKenzie and their crews pinpointed on Westerhever and delivered their vegetables into the briefed location in good visibility, the latter dropping their wing bombs onto a flak position. Even further north, P/O Baker and Sgt Crampton and their crews established their positions on Thyborøn, before carrying out timed runs to deliver their stores into the briefed locations from 500 and 700 feet respectively. This left just the nickelling brigade to fulfil their briefs over a poorly blacked-out Paris, which F/L Ferrie, P/O Goldsmith and Sgt Atkinson and their crews accomplished under clear skies from 4,000 to 8,000 feet. The Essen raid had been another disappointing affair, which had caused a fire and some useful damage at the Krupp works, and destroyed or seriously damaged eighty houses, but it was a poor return for the size of the force. Harris took stock, thereafter, and the statistics made uncomfortable reading. During eight heavy attacks on the city since the 8/9th of March, 1,555 sorties had been launched, of which 1,006 crews had claimed to have bombed, at a cost to the Command of sixty-four aircraft. Only twenty-two bombing photos had shown ground detail within five miles of Essen, demonstrating in the eyes of the critics, that there had been no improvement in the effectiveness of operations since the Butt Report.

Dortmund was posted as the target for a force of 208 aircraft on the 14th, by far the largest effort against this industrial giant situated at the eastern end of the Ruhr. This would provide 50 Squadron with the opportunity to blood two of its Manchesters over Germany as part of a 5 Group contribution to the operation of thirty-four Hampdens and four Manchesters. F/O Wilkins and P/O Southgate and their crews departed Skellingthorpe at 22.20 and 22.28 respectively, and had to run the gauntlet of intense searchlight and flak activity as they traversed the most heavily defended region of Germany. Clear skies enabled them to map-read their way by river and railway features to the aiming-point, where they dropped their loads from around 8,000 feet, while attempting to dodge some eighty searchlights in cones. It would be established later that the bombing had been scattered over a forty-mile stretch of the region, with no significant damage to the intended target.

A reduced force of 152 aircraft was assembled for the same target twenty-four hours later, this time supported by 5 Group with nineteen Hampdens and seven Manchesters. 50 Squadron would provide two Manchesters, but first, four others set off between 21.16 and 21.20, two bound for the Beech garden off St-Nazaire, and two for Rennes in north-western France to deliver nickels. F/L Ferrie and P/O Goldsmith and their crews pinpointed on Belle Isle in good visibility, before delivering their mines into the allotted locations from 800 feet. Over to the east, F/Sgt Willett and Sgt Gruber and their crews had arrived at Rennes, after picking up the Selune estuary in the Gulf of St-Malo, and they dispensed their bundles of nickels from 6,000 and 5,000 feet respectively. The two Manchesters assigned to Dortmund departed Skellingthorpe either side of midnight with the crews of P/O Baker and Sgt Crampton on board, and, like most of the participants, had to contend with severe icing conditions on the southern approaches to the Ruhr. P/O Baker and crew decided not to push on through, and bombed a built-up area believed to be north-west of Bonn, which might have been the south-western suburbs of Cologne. Sgt Crampton and crew made it through the icing only to run into intense searchlight and flak activity over the Ruhr, but fought their way to the target area to deliver their bombs through two-tenths low cloud from 12,000 feet. This raid was another dismal failure that scattered bombs over a wide area, and caused only the slightest damage in the target city.

Minor operations occupied the night of the 16/17th, for which 5 Group contributed ten Hampdens and two Manchesters for gardening duties and five Hampdens and two Manchesters for nickelling activities over Lille in north-eastern France. 50 Squadron was invited to provide two crews for the latter, and dispatched those of Sgt Atkinson and S/L Lloyd at 21.30 and 22.00 respectively. They located the target by means of its poor black-out, and, in excellent visibility, dispensed between them 228 bundles of printed paper from 8,000 feet.

On the 17th, The Lancaster was announced to the enemy in an audacious daylight attack on the M.A.N. diesel engine works at distant Augsburg in southern Germany, conducted by six aircraft each from 44 and 97 Squadrons. While flying at very low level over France, the 44 Squadron element was pounced upon by BF109s, which shot down four Lancasters, and a fifth was lost at the target. The 97 Squadron element arrived intact, but lost two Lancasters during the attack, and S/L Nettleton and crew were the sole returnees from 44 Squadron. Nettleton would be rewarded with a VC, but, sadly, would not survive the war. While Operation Margin was in progress, 173 aircraft were being prepared for an operation that night against Hamburg, for which 5 Group contributed five Manchesters. 50 Squadron put up three of them and two others for mining duties in one of the Rosemary gardens in the Heligoland Bight. The Hamburg-bound trio of P/O Southgate, Sgt Crampton and P/O Baker and their crews took off first between 23.31 and 23.40, to be followed by the gardeners, captained by F/Sgt Willett and Sgt Gruber, at 00.07 and 00.13. Hamburg was found to be under clear skies, but shrouded in haze and protected by the usual intense searchlight and flak barrage from both banks of the Elbe. The city-centre aiming-point could not be identified, and the Skellingthorpe crews bombed the built-up area from 9,000 to 10,000 feet, observing several fires. R5782 was heading home, when shot down to crash near Tangstedt, some ten miles north-north-west of Hamburg, and, while five members of the crew survived in enemy hands, P/O Baker and his rear gunner died in the wreckage. The operation was modestly successful and caused seventy-five fires, thirty-three of them classed as large, but, even so, fewer than a third of the bomb loads had actually found the mark. While these events were taking place, F/Sgt Willett and crew were some fifty to seventy miles to the north-west conducting a search for their drop zone, which they failed to locate in the hazy conditions, and, after forty-three minutes, turned for home. In contrast, Sgt Gruber and crew pinpointed on Westerhever, and delivered their vegetable into the allotted location from 700 feet.

On the 19th, 5 Group detailed twenty-five Hampdens, ten Manchesters and two Lancasters for gardening duties in the Nectarines region around the Frisians. 50 Squadron made ready six Manchesters, which departed Skellingthorpe between 21.28 and 21.45 with P/Os Goldsmith and Southgate the senior pilots on duty. The latter turned back early on because of a technical problem, leaving the others to press on to the target area to find extreme darkness, visibility ranging from poor to good and ten-tenths cloud with a base at 2,000 feet. Sgt Gruber and crew were unable to establish a pinpoint and brought their mine home, while the remainder located the eastern side of Terschelling from which to make their timed runs, and successfully delivered their stores into the briefed locations from 700 to 1,000 feet.

The first attempt to employ Gee as a blind bombing aid took place on the night of the 22/23rd, when Cologne was the target for a 3 Group force of sixty-four Wellingtons and five Stirlings. Fewer than 20% of the bomb loads fell into the city, and some landed up to ten miles away, proving that Gee was capable of guiding a force to a general area, but lacked the precision necessary to deliver a telling blow on an urban target. While this operation was in progress, 5 Group dispatched twenty-two Hampdens and a dozen Manchesters on gardening duties in Forget-me-nots (Kiel Harbour), Quinces (Kiel Bay), Radishes (Fehmarn Belt) and Rosemary (Heligoland Bight). 50 Squadron provided six Manchesters for the first-mentioned, and they took off between 20.23 and 20.50 with S/L Lloyd the senior pilot on duty. All reached the western Baltic to encounter clear skies and good visibility, and pinpointed on the southern tip of Denmark's Langeland Island and on the German mainland north-east of Kiel, before making their timed runs and dropping their mines into the briefed locations from between 600 and 900 feet.

In an attempt to repeat the success gained at Lübeck, Rostock, also on the Baltic coast, was earmarked for a series of four raids on consecutive nights from the 23/24th, with the old town and the Heinkel aircraft factory on its southern outskirts the specific aiming-points. A force of 161 aircraft was assembled, 143 of them assigned to the town and eighteen to the factory, and 5 Group managed to put up eleven Hampdens, six Manchesters and a single Lancaster. 50 Squadron was not invited to take part in this first operation, which, despite favourable weather conditions and good visibility, failed to find the mark at either aiming-point. S/L Lloyd was posted to 24 O.T.U on the 24th at the conclusion of his tour, while activity continued at Skellingthorpe to make ready five Manchesters for round two at Rostock and two for nickelling duties in the Rennes area of France. The 5 Group element of thirty-four aircraft was assigned to the Heinkel factory and included four Lancasters from the newly-converted 207 Squadron at Bottesford, while ninety-one aircraft from the other groups focussed on the old town. The two freshman nickelling crews of Sgt Wilkie and P/O Cole took off from Skellingthorpe either side of 21.30, leaving the quintet for the main event to become airborne between 21.36 and 22.30 with P/Os Goldsmith and Southgate the senior pilots on duty. They all reached the target area, drawn on from many miles away by the fires already burning. Bright moonlight illuminated the Unterwarnow River running south from the coast to the heart of the town, and provided excellent visibility for the low-level attacks. The town seemed to be ablaze as they crossed over it to reach the Heinkel factory, which they attacked from 2,500 to 5,000 feet, mostly on existing fires. Many searchlights were co-operating with light flak, and Sgt Gruber and crew were ensnared by a cone of fifteen as they pulled out of their dive-attack, whereupon the gunners shot out four of them. According to the observations of returning crews, the Heinkel factory and adjacent aerodrome had been hit by many bombs and were left burning, and, while post-raid reconnaissance revealed extensive damage within the town, the factory buildings remained intact, demonstrating that the impressions gained by crews in the heat of battle could be somewhat unreliable. Meanwhile, the nickelling duo had also enjoyed ideal conditions and had delivered their reading matter to the residents of the Rennes region from 8,000 and 8,500 feet.

50 Squadron was not involved in the third raid on the night of the 25/26th, when 110 aircraft were assigned to the town and eighteen from 5 Group to the Heinkel factory, led by 106 Squadron's commanding officer, W/C Guy Gibson. Ideal weather conditions again prevailed, and post-raid reconnaissance revealed that the factory had, at last, been hit, and that the town had suffered severe damage, without loss to the attackers. Earlier in the day, S/L Moore had been posted in from 455 Squadron RAAF, which was about to join Coastal Command, and he would fill the vacancy for a flight commander created by the departure of S/L Lloyd. A force of 106 aircraft was detailed for the final raid of the series on the 26th, 50 Squadron putting up four Manchesters in an overall contribution by 5 Group force of nineteen Hampdens, nine Manchesters and a single Lancaster. The Skellingthorpe quartet took off between 21.53 and 22.15 with P/O Southgate the senior pilot on duty, and all reached the target area, where moonlight, excellent visibility and existing fires aided target location. Sgt Crampton and crew went in at 1,000 feet and observed six bursts, as did P/O Southgate and crew from a thousand feet higher, while F/Sgt Willett and crew chose a height of 5,000 feet, but all had to dodge the intense light flak hosing up at them. L7432 was buffeted by near misses and damaged, but arrived home safely in the hands of P/O Southgate and crew. Two hundred miles to the west, having taken off at 00.16 and 00.32, P/O Cole and Sgt Wilkie and their crews were delivering their mines into the briefed region of the Waddenzee after pinpointing on Ording on the western coast of the Schleswig-Holstein peninsular. An analysis of the Rostock campaign revealed it to have been highly successful, destroying 1,765 buildings and seriously damaging five hundred more, which represented 60% of the town's built-up area. In his diaries, Propaganda Minister Goebbels used the phrase "Terrorangriff", terror raid, for the first time.

On the 27th, 5 Group sent a dozen Lancasters from 44 and 97 Squadrons to join forces with 4 Group Halifaxes to attack the Tirpitz at its mooring in Trondheim Fjord. The operation was repeated on the following night with eleven Lancasters this time, but neither attack produced confirmed hits. On the latter occasion, ten Hampdens took part in a raid on the shipyards at Kiel, and contributed to damage to three of them. 50 Squadron operated for the final time during the month on the 29th, when sending five Manchesters to four gardens in the western Baltic. They departed Skellingthorpe between 21.42 and 22.17, Sgts Gruber and Wilkie bound for Quince, F/Sgt Willett for Forget-me-not, P/O Cole for Radish and F/L Wilkins for Endive (Little Belt). F/L Wilkins and crew turned back immediately because of a buffeting of the rudder bar, and L7516 was attacked by the night-fighter of Oblt Günter Köberich of II./NJG3, before crashing on a sandbank off Rantum on the island of Sylt. Both gunners failed to survive, probably having been killed during the engagement, but F/Sgt Willett DFM and four of his crew were rescued by the enemy and taken into captivity. The three remaining crews completed their sorties as briefed and returned safely. During the course of the month, the squadron took part in twenty-five bombing, mining and leafleting operations, dispatching nineteen Hampden and fifty-four Manchester sorties for the loss of one Hampden and two Manchesters.

May 1942

Ninety-six aircraft from 3 and 5 Groups were detailed for mining operations on the 2nd, 5 Group providing twenty-one Lancasters, eight Manchesters and twelve Hampdens for gardens in the Baltic and off the Biscay coast, and nine Manchesters for nickelling duties in the Rennes area. 50 Squadron made ready four Manchesters for the delivery of propaganda material, and they departed Skellingthorpe between 21.51 and 22.07 with P/O Stone the senior pilot on duty. They returned safely five hours later having fulfilled their briefs from between 5,000 and 8,000 feet, describing their sorties as uneventful and enjoyable. Hamburg was posted as the primary target for a force of eighty-one aircraft on the 3rd, the numbers somewhat reduced in the face of a forecast of poor weather conditions. 5 Group contributed just five Hampdens from 420 Squadron RCAF, while other elements from the group were occupied by minor endeavours elsewhere. 50 Squadron dispatched F/O Heaton and crew at 21.58 to continue supporting the morale of French civilians in the Rennes region, and good weather conditions and visibility enabled them to map-read their way to their destination in north-western France. They dispensed 110 bundles of leaflets from 9,000 feet, before returning safely from another uneventful sortie. The Hamburg raid was unusually effective, causing more than a hundred fires, fifty-seven of them large, and eleven blocks of flats were destroyed by the blast from a single cookie.

Orders were received on the 4th to make ready for the first of what would be a "Rostock-style" sustained assault on the important industrial city of Stuttgart over three consecutive nights. A force of 121 aircraft included a contribution from 5 Group of nineteen Hampdens and fourteen Lancasters, the crews of the former briefed to aim for the highly important Robert Bosch factory, which was engaged in the manufacture of dynamos, injection pumps and magnetos. The Lancaster crews were briefed to attack military barracks, but all intentions were thwarted by ten-tenths cloud over the series of deep valleys occupied by the sprawling city, and the bombing was scattered over a wide area. 5 Group contributed four 97 Squadron Lancasters to the same target on the following night, and they again bombed the town rather than the Bosch factory to which they had been assigned. Despite clear skies, ground detail was obscured by haze, and no bombs fell in the city. It was Stuttgart again on the 6th, for which 5 Group detailed ten Hampdens and ten Lancasters in an overall force of ninety-seven aircraft. They flew out across Belgium, and, after an outward flight lasting almost three hours, reached the target area to find largely clear skies, but haze again making target identification difficult. Most picked out a built-up area on e.t.a., backed up by evidence of searchlights, flak and burning incendiaries from other aircraft, and scattered their bombs over a wide area. This operation was another massively ineffective affair, which again failed to land a single bomb in Stuttgart, but did hit 150 buildings in Heilbronn, a large town situated five miles from the Lauffen decoy site and twenty miles from Stuttgart. 50 Squadron was also in limited action on this night, launching two Manchesters to bomb the Loire docks at Nantes and another to continue the leafleting of the Rennes region. F/O Heaton and Sgt Dampier-Crossley took off at 21.40 carrying a dozen 500 pounders each, and established their positions on the river running through the city from east to west. The former approached from the west and the latter from the east at around 8,000 feet, and the bomb bursts were followed by a number of fires. Meanwhile, some sixty miles to the north, P/O Manser and crew were dropping nickels from 5,000 feet over Rennes, having pinpointed on Avranches on the north Brittany coast.

P/O Drew Wyness was posted in from 10 O.T.U on the 7th to begin his first tour, in a career that would end tragically more than two years hence at the hands of a German war criminal. The night of the 7/8th was devoted to mine-laying operations in the western Baltic and Heligoland Bight conducted by eighty-one aircraft drawn from 3 and 5 Groups, the latter providing fourteen Hampdens, twelve Lancasters and ten Manchesters, although none representing 50 Squadron. The recent successes at Lübeck and Rostock prompted the posting of another Baltic coast target on the 8th, this time Warnemünde, situated on the Left Bank of the estuary ten miles north of Rostock, where a Heinkel aircraft factory was an added attraction. A force of 193 aircraft was assembled, among which 5 Group put up twenty-one Lancasters, nine Manchesters and nineteen Hampdens, the last-mentioned representing the two Canadian squadrons, 408 and 420, the only units still equipped with the type. 50 Squadron detailed three crews for the main event, Sgts Gruber and Wilkie and P/O Cole departing Skellingthorpe between 21.46 and 21.48, and reaching the target area to find clear skies and good visibility along with a ferocious searchlight and flak defence. R5778 was hit in the port engine at the start of the bombing run, forcing Sgt Wilkie to jettison the bombs and turn for home, where the Manchester would be deemed to be beyond economical repair. L7489 was hit by flak over the target, and, knowing that England was out of reach, Sgt Gruber decided to head towards Sweden, some one hundred miles to the north. A message was received that the crew was having to bale out over Denmark, and the Manchester crashed at 02.20 into a forest near Stege on Denmark's Møn island, killing Sgt Gruber, while his crew benefitted from his sacrifice to all survive in enemy hands. P/O Cole and crew successfully negotiated the gauntlet of flak and delivered their six 1,000 pounders from 2,000 feet, observing all to burst. Meanwhile, F/Sgt Morgan and P/O Manser and their crews had taken off at 00.19 and 00.32 respectively for gardening sorties in the Rosemary region of the Heligoland Bight, and both fulfilled their briefs without incident. The Warnemünde operation proved to be very expensive, costing nineteen aircraft, eight of them belonging to 5 Group, and it was a particular disaster for 44 Squadron, which lost four Lancasters, including that of the recently appointed commanding officer, W/C Lynch-Blosse.

The career of the Manchester as a front-line aircraft was now effectively over, and Lancasters began to arrive on 50 Squadron dispersals during the first week of the month, making it the sixth operational squadron in the Command to receive the type. It would be some time before the crews were fully converted, however, and Manchesters would remain on charge for almost two more months. While training on the 13th, Manchester L7519 was observed by witnesses to nose down into a dive while flying at around 800 feet, and fail to recover, crashing at 16.45 at North Farm near Thurlby, between Alford and the Lincolnshire coast. F/Sgt Blake and the four other occupants, two of whom were ground crew, lost their lives. 50 Squadron was not called into action again until the 16th, when contributing four Manchesters to a 5 Group mining effort by seven Lancasters and seven Manchesters in gardens on either side of the Schleswig-Holstein peninsular. The Skellingthorpe quartet was assigned to Rosemary, in the Heligoland Bight, and took off between 23.58 and 00.17 with P/O Southgate the senior pilot on duty. F/Sgt Morgan and crew returned early with wireless failure, leaving the others to deliver their five vegetables each as briefed from between 600 and 900 feet.

Mannheim was posted as the primary target on the 19th, and a force of 193 aircraft was made ready, of which fifteen Hampdens, thirteen Lancasters and four Manchesters were provided by 5 Group. The three Manchesters belonging to 50 Squadron took off from Skellingthorpe at 22.15, shortly before two freshman crews departed for nickelling duties in the Le-Mans area of north-western France. Sgt Gray and crew turned back for an undisclosed technical reason, leaving P/O Roy Calvert and crew to take care of the postal activities, which they did from 8,000 feet after pinpointing on the coast north of Caen and navigating their way without difficulty to the drop zone. Those bound for Mannheim reached the target area under clear skies, and, after running the gauntlet of masses of searchlights that required evasive action, identified the city by means of a Gee-fix and the River Rhine. However, extreme darkness and ground haze prevented any chance of identifying the city centre aiming-point, the main Post Office, despite which, Sgt Wilkie and crew claimed to have found and bombed it from 6,000 feet, while P/O Manser and F/Sgt Morgan and their crews failed to locate it and bombed the general built-up area instead from 3,500 and 9,000 feet respectively. Returning crews were optimistic about the effectiveness of the raid, but local reports claimed that only around ten bomb loads landed in the city, and this was after the force was heard overhead for an extended period, as if searching for it.

There now followed another lull in major operations as Harris prepared for his master stroke. At the time of his appointment as C-in-C, the figure of four thousand bombers had been bandied around as the number required to wrap up the war. Whilst there was not the slightest chance of procuring them, Harris, with a dark cloud still hanging over the existence of an independent bomber force, needed to ensure that those earmarked for him were not spirited away to what he considered to be less-deserving causes. The Command had not yet achieved sufficient success to silence the detractors, and the Admiralty was still calling for bomber aircraft to be diverted to the U-Boot campaign, while reverses in the Middle East also needed to be redressed. Harris was in need of a major victory, and, perhaps, a dose of symbolism to make his point, and, out of this was born the Thousand Plan, Operation Millennium, the launching of a thousand aircraft in one night against a major German city, for which Hamburg had been pencilled in. Harris did not have a thousand front-line aircraft, and required the support of other Commands to make up the numbers. This was forthcoming from Coastal and Flying Training Commands, and, in the case of the former, a letter to Harris on the 22nd promised 250 aircraft. However, following an intervention from the Admiralty, the offer was withdrawn, and most of the Flying Training Command aircraft were found to be not up to the task, leaving the Millennium force well short of the magic figure. Undaunted, Harris, or more probably his able deputy, AM Sir Robert Saundby, scraped together every airframe capable of controlled flight, or something resembling it, and pulled in the screened crews from their instructional duties. He also pressed into service aircraft and crews from within the Command's own training establishment, 91 Group. Come the night, not only would the thousand mark be achieved, it would be comfortably surpassed.

During the final week of the month, the arrival on bomber stations from Yorkshire to East Anglia of a motley collection of aircraft from training units gave rise to much speculation among crews and ground staff alike, but, as usual, only the NAAFI staff and the local civilians knew what was really afoot. The most pressing remaining question was the weather, and, as the days ticked by inexorably towards the end of May, this was showing no signs of complying. Harris was aware of the genuine danger, that the giant force might draw attention to itself, and thereby compromise security, and the point was fast approaching when the operation would have to take place or be abandoned for the time being. Harris released some of the pressure by sanctioning operations on the night of the 29/30th, for which the Gnome & Rhone aero-engine and Goodrich tyre factories at Gennevilliers in Paris were the main targets. A force of seventy-seven aircraft included a contribution from 5 Group of fourteen Lancasters and three Hampdens, and, in spite of claims of a successful operation, the only damage caused was to eighty-seven houses, in which thirty-four people were killed and 167 injured. S/L Jeffs was posted to 207 Squadron on the 28th, and would take up his appointment as commanding officer on promotion to acting wing commander rank on the 1st of June.

It was in an atmosphere of frustration and hopeful expectation, that "morning prayers" began at Harris's High Wycombe HQ on the 30th, with all eyes turned upon the civilian chief meteorological adviser, Magnus Spence. After careful deliberation, he was able to give a qualified assurance of clear skies over the Rhineland, while north-western Germany and Hamburg would be concealed under buckets of cloud. Thus, did the fickle fates decree that Cologne would bear the dubious honour of hosting the first one thousand bomber raid in history. At briefings, crews were told that the enormous force was to be pushed across the aiming-point in just ninety minutes. This was unprecedented and gave rise to the question of collisions as hundreds of aircraft funnelled towards the aiming-point. The answer, according to the experts, was to observe timings and flight levels, and they calculated also that just two aircraft would collide over the target. It is said that a wag in every briefing room asked, "do they know which two?"

5 Group had seventy-three Lancasters, forty-six Manchesters and thirty-four Hampdens bombed up and ready to go, and, at Skellingthorpe, sixteen Manchesters and a single Lancaster awaited the arrival of their crews. The crews had been briefed to attack aiming-point Y, one of three areas spanning the city centre from north to south, and bordering the western and southern extremities of the city centre on the West Bank. Late that evening, the first of an eventual 1,047 aircraft took off to deliver the now familiar three-wave-format attack on the Rhineland Capital, the older training hacks struggling somewhat reluctantly into the air, lifted more by the enthusiasm of their crews than by the power of their engines, and some of these, unable to climb to a respectable height, would fall easy prey to the defences, or would simply drop from the sky through mechanical breakdown. The 50 Squadron element, which included two hacks, L7301 and L7456, borrowed from 106 Squadron and containing the crews of P/O Manser and Sgt Wilkie, departed Skellingthorpe between 22.57 and 23.48 as part of the third and final wave, with F/Ls Stone and Wilkins the senior pilots on duty, the latter in the Lancaster, and S/L Moore flying as second pilot with F/O Southgate and crew. Sgt Weber and crew turned back at the Dutch coast having lost their intercom, but the others, from as far away as the Den Helder peninsular, were able to see the glow from the burning city a hundred miles ahead, and were drawn on by the sight without having to worry about accurate navigation. On arrival, the conditions were found to be precisely as predicted by Magnus Spence, even to the presence of moonlight, and fires were burning across the city, sending columns of smoke drifting up through 10,000 feet. Bombing was carried out by the 50 Squadron crews mostly from 9,000 feet, with a low height of 5,000 feet by Sgt Dampier-Crossley and crew, and a top height of 12,000 feet by the Lancaster.

Two Manchesters failed to return to Skellingthorpe, and, as coincidence would have it, they were the ones borrowed from 106 Squadron. L7301 had been hit by flak during the bombing run, but P/O Manser pressed on to release the bombs before setting a course that would, hopefully get them home. As they reached the Dutch/Belgian frontier, it became clear that England was beyond the Manchester's capability, and the crew was ordered to bale out, while P/O Leslie Manser held it steady. He was unable to save himself before the aircraft came down at 02.00 in a dyke at Bree on the Belgian side, and he lost his life. All but one of the crew evaded capture, and would eventually return home through the magnificent and courageous Resistance escape organisations. Their testimony would ultimately lead to the posthumous award to Manser of the Victoria Cross, the only such decoration to be earned by a Manchester crewman. The bomb-aimer, P/O Horsley, would re-muster as a pilot, and, in 1944, join the, by-then, much vaunted 617 Squadron. L7456 refused to climb above 8,000 feet, and, while trying to escape from searchlights and flak, lost the use of its port engine and had to be crash-landed on Lohausen aerodrome in Düsseldorf (now Düsseldorf Airport). Sgt Wilkie and three of his crew survived to be taken into captivity, but three others lost their lives. Returning crews described a city on fire from end to end, and scenes which had never before been witnessed. Post-raid reconnaissance confirmed that the operation had, by any standards, been an outstanding success, and had destroyed more than 3,300 buildings, while inflicting serious damage to two thousand others. Although the losses, at forty-one aircraft, represented a new record high, the conditions had favoured both attackers and defenders alike, and, in the context of the scale of success and the numbers despatched, it could not be considered an inordinately high figure. 5 Group registered a loss of four Manchesters, one Lancaster and one Hampden, but it was the training units that sustained the greatest losses amounting to twenty-one aircraft. During the course of the month the squadron took part in ten operations, and dispatched thirty-eight Manchester sorties and one by a Lancaster for the loss of four Manchesters and crews.

June 1942

While the Millennium force remained assembled, Harris wanted to exploit its potential again immediately, and, was no doubt excited about the prospect of visiting upon the old enemy of Essen a similar ordeal to that just experienced by Cologne. A force of 956 aircraft was the best that could be achieved during the 1st, 5 Group managing seventy-three Lancasters, thirty-three Manchesters and twenty-six Hampdens, with 50 Squadron contributing ten Manchesters, including two borrowed from 44 Squadron's conversion flight, and another from 106 Squadron's. They departed Skellingthorpe between 23.02 and 23.15 with F/O Southgate the senior pilot on duty, all carrying incendiary bomb loads, and reached the target area to seek out the Krupp works as their aiming-point. They ran into a thin layer of seven to ten-tenths cloud over the target, with a band of industrial haze below at between 2,000 and 4,000 feet and moonlight above. These were typical conditions for a Ruhr target, and most crews established their position by Gee-fix, although the searchlight and flak activity helped, while flares illuminated the general area and incendiaries were burning on the ground as the 50 Squadron crews began their bombing runs. The Skellingthorpe crews delivered the contents of their bomb bays from between 7,000 and 10,000 feet, L7476 sustaining flak damage, which wounded the navigator in the crew of P/O Cole. At debriefing, some crews commented on a lack of defence from the ground, and, for many, it had been a quiet trip, but few could offer a meaningful assessment of the outcome. A total of thirty-one aircraft failed to return, a dozen of them from the training units, and, sadly, there would be no major success to mitigate the scale of the loss as this raid followed the pattern for this and other Ruhr targets. Local reports confirmed that only eleven houses had been destroyed in Essen, and fewer that two hundred others damaged, mostly in southern districts, and more bomb loads had actually fallen on Oberhausen, Duisburg and Mülheim an der Ruhr.

A follow-up raid was planned for the following night, and a much-reduced force of 197 aircraft made ready, with 5 Group providing twenty-seven Lancasters and a dozen Hampdens.

50 Squadron remained on the ground on a night of cloudless skies over the Ruhr, with the usual industrial haze and a low moon providing some illumination. Most crews would describe the visibility as good, and reported being further aided by flares, which highlighted the Rhine over to the west. Those equipped with Gee confirmed their positions over what they believed to be the Krupp works aiming-point, and, despite the apparent confidence of the crews that they had attacked Essen, local authorities reported just three high explosive bombs and three hundred incendiaries falling in the city to cause only minor damage. Such was the density of the Ruhr, with overlapping town and city boundaries, that it was difficult not to hit something urban, but concentration was the key to success, and the scattering of bombs over a wide area was never going to achieve a knock-out blow. Harris was stubborn and would keep trying, but it would be a further nine months before the means were to hand to make a genuine impact.

For the next operation, on the 3rd, Harris turned his attention upon Bremen, which, along with Essen and Emden would share the Command's attention for the remainder of the month. A force of 170 aircraft was made ready for the first major attack on the port-city since the previous October, and a force of 170 aircraft was assembled, fifteen Lancasters, nine Hampdens and six Manchesters provided by 5 Group. 50 Squadron made ready four Manchesters for the main event, which departed Skellingthorpe between 23.01 and 23.05 with F/O Heaton the senior pilot on duty, and they were followed at 00.53 and 00.56 by P/O Garland and Sgt Roy and their crews bound for nickelling duties in the area of Le-Mans. The bombing quartet had been briefed to attack an unspecified aiming-point located six hundred yards from aiming-point "A", but P/O Beatty and crew made it only thirty miles into the sea crossing before overheating engines persuaded them to turn back. Sgt Dampier-Crossley and F/Sgt Weber and their crews found clear skies over north-western Germany, with ground haze in the target area, and the former carried out their attack from 9,000 feet having identified the aiming-point. The latter was unable to pick out the briefed objective, and let their all-incendiary load go over the general built-up area. L7432 failed to return with the crew of F/O Heaton, who were on their way home over Holland when crossing paths with the night-fighter of Oblt Viktor Bauer of III./NJG1. The Manchester crashed at 02.33, three miles south of Apeldoorn, killing the pilot and three others and delivering the three survivors into enemy hands. Returning crews lacked confidence in the effectiveness of the raid, but local reports told a story of heavy damage to housing in six streets and to harbour installations, and there were also hits on U-Boot construction yards and the Focke-Wulf aircraft factory, although, any loss of production was slight. While this operation was in progress, the leafleteers had attracted a surprising amount of flak, but dispensed their cargo and made it home with slight damage to one of them.

180 aircraft were prepared for the next intended assault on Essen on the 5th, for which 5 Group put up thirteen Lancasters and eleven Hampdens. 50 Squadron would not take part, but made ready three Manchesters for one of the night's mining operations, and dispatched them from Skellingthorpe between 22.25 and 22.30. They were bound for the Gorse garden in Quiberon Bay off the Brittany coast, where pin-points were aplenty from which to make a timed run to the drop zone. Sgt Roy and crew thought that they had pinpointed on the Ile-de-Groix, and dropped their vegetables from 700 feet, only to discover too late that they were over the wrong location. Sgt Wiseman and crew established their position by Pointe-de-Congual and Ile-de-Quiberon before delivering their stores into the allotted location, and both of these crews returned safely. R5833, which was still on loan from 44 Squadron's conversion

flight, failed to return after crashing into the sea, killing P/O Garland and all but one crew member, who fell into enemy hands.

The first of four attacks during the month on the naval port of Emden was posted on the 6th, and a force of 233 aircraft made ready. 5 Group contributed twenty Lancaster, fifteen Hampdens and seven Manchesters, two of the last-mentioned provided by 50 Squadron. P/Os Beatty and Atkinson and their crews departed Skellingthorpe at 23.16 and 23.22 respectively, and the latter reached the target area after flying over the Dollart Sea and the Ems estuary located to the south of the port. They had already dumped 180 x 4lb incendiaries to gain additional height, and dropped the remaining 1,080 onto the target from 8,000 feet, before returning home to report witnessing a bomber being shot down by a night-fighter. An S.O.S signal was received from L7471 at 01.40, and this was the last contact with the all-Australian crew of P/O Beatty. News came through eventually from the Red Cross that one member of the crew had been killed, and that the others were in enemy hands. P/O Beatty had sustained serious injury, to which he would succumb on the 10th of September. Photographic reconnaissance and local reports confirmed that the raid had been responsible for the destruction of some three hundred houses, with a further two hundred severely damaged, in return for the loss of nine aircraft.

The squadron would now remain off the Order of Battle for three weeks while the conversion to Lancasters gathered pace, and the Command as a whole entered a period of gardening and minor operations, punctuated by two further attacks on Essen. The first of these by an initial force of 170 aircraft, took place on the night of the 8/9th, and was supported by 5 Group with thirteen Lancasters and nine Hampdens. It was another disappointing and widely scattered raid, which caused only minor housing damage. Earlier in the day, S/L Everitt DFC had returned to the squadron from 25 O.T.U on the 8th, to start a second tour, this time in the role of flight commander. Another new recruit was Australian P/O H B "Mickey" Martin, who had been at 455 Squadron RAAF at the time of its departure to Coastal Command, and he brought with him his former Hampden crew, fellow Australians, navigator P/O Jack Leggo and gunners Sgt Tammy Simpson and Toby Foxlee. After spending four nights on the ground because of adverse weather conditions, the Command stirred itself again on the 16th to prepare a force of 106 aircraft for yet another tilt at Essen. 5 Group put up fifteen Lancasters, a type which, until the start of 1 Group's conversion in the autumn, would remain exclusive to 5 Group. The 61 and 207 Squadron crews had been briefed to employ TR (Gee) to locate the target and bomb blindly based on that. Returning crews reported both real and dummy fires, and it emerged at debriefing that only sixteen crews claimed to have bombed the primary target, while fifty-six others had found alternatives, mostly the city of Bonn. This concluded a series of five raids on Essen in sixteen nights, during which 1,607 sorties had been dispatched and eighty-four aircraft lost. The city had sustained no industrial damage, and a few wrecked houses was all that Bomber Command had to show for the massive effort expended.

Emden would be targeted three more times over a four-night period beginning on the 19/20th, when 5 Group contributed nine Lancasters and eleven Hampdens to an overall force of 194 aircraft. The 5 Group crews were instructed to bomb Osnabrück if the weather created difficult conditions at Emden, and seven crews complied, while the remainder tried and almost entirely failed to bomb the primary target. With the squadron in the process of converting to Lancasters, Skellingthorpe required a runway extension to cope with the heavier aircraft and the increase in bomb-carrying capacity. As a result, 50 Squadron moved back temporarily to Swinderby on the 20th, which was, perhaps, a surprise to the person entrusted with writing up the 5 Group ORB, according to whom, it had never left! Swinderby was falling out of favour as an operational station, partly because of its inability to cope with protracted periods of wet weather, but it would perform adequately during the dry summer months until Skellingthorpe could be returned to service in the autumn. That night, 185 aircraft set off to return to Emden, among them twenty-four Lancasters and a dozen Hampdens. The docks were the briefed aiming-point and the town the alternative for those arriving to find five to eight tenths cloud with generally poor visibility, and positions were established by TR-fix and glimpses of the coastline. Local reports confirmed that only a proportion of the force had located the target, and around a hundred houses had been damaged in return for the loss of eight aircraft. A force of 227 aircraft took off on the 22nd to conclude the series against Emden, and among them were eleven Lancasters and eight Hampdens. Returning crews were largely enthusiastic about the outcome, citing many fires, but a good proportion of these were decoys that drew off much of the effort, and a modest fifty houses were destroyed and a hundred damaged.

The time had now arrived for the final employment of the Thousand Force, and, indeed, for the Manchester in operational service. A force of 960 aircraft was assembled, 142 provided by 5 Group in the form of ninety-six Lancasters, twenty-six Hampdens and twenty Manchesters. It was an indication of the failure of the Manchester, that the aircraft it had been intended to replace, the Hampden, would continue to serve 5 Group in small numbers until mid-September. To the above numbers were added five aircraft from Army Co-operation Command and 102 aircraft from Coastal Command, which had been ordered by Churchill himself to take part, although, its contribution was to be deemed a separate operation. However, the 1,067 aircraft from all sources would represent a larger combined force than that sent to Cologne at the end of May. The Swinderby gang of twelve Manchesters and two Lancasters took off between 23.07 and 23.52 with F/Ls Stone and Wilkie the senior pilots on duty, the last-mentioned and F/O Goldsmith and their crews in the Lancasters. F/L Wilkins and crew were back home after an hour having lost their starboard-outer engine, and F/Sgt Taylor and crew were an hour out when the rear turret became unserviceable, and they had the presence of mind to fly north for four minutes rather than turn back into the oncoming stream. The others pressed on, and, above the ten-tenths cloud that persisted all the way from the English coast to the target area, the sky was extremely bright, courtesy of a full moon and the Northern Lights. P/O Martin lost intercom contact with the rear turret as he and his crew approached the Dutch coast, and dropped their bombs on Alkmaar aerodrome as a last resort target. A band of nine to ten-tenths cloud lay over Bremen at between 3,000 and 5,000 feet, completely obscuring ground detail, which precluded any chance of picking up the briefed aiming-point of the Focke-Wulf aircraft factory. Positions were established by TR-fix, the glow of fires on the ground and the volume of flak coming up through the cloud, and the loads of a cookie and 720 x 4lb incendiaries for the Lancaster and all-incendiaries for the Manchesters were delivered by the Swinderby crews onto the built-up area generally from a variety of altitudes from between 6,000 and 10,500 feet. F/O Southgate and crew braved the defences to come down to the cloud base at 2,500 feet to try to locate the factory, and were rewarded for their audacity by being the only crew from the squadron to claim to have attacked the primary target, reporting a large fire on the adjacent aerodrome.

Returning crews could only estimate that they had hit the city, and reported several areas of fire, but none of the 696 crews claiming to have attacked the primary target had any real clue as to the outcome. Local sources confirmed a number of hits on the Focke-Wulf aircraft factory and some shipyards, along with the destruction of 572 houses, and damage to more than six thousand others, mostly in southern and eastern districts, but estimated the size of the bomber force to be around eighty. The level of success fell well short of that achieved at Cologne, but surpassed by far the failure at Essen, albeit at a new record loss of forty-eight aircraft, which represented 5% of those dispatched. The O.T.Us of 91 Group suffered the highest casualty rate of 11.6%, largely because they were employing tired, old Whitleys, Wellingtons and Hampdens, which were not up to the task, while 5 Group lost one Lancaster and one Manchester.

50 Squadron had now concluded its operational activity for the month, and waved farewell to the Manchesters, which moved on to non-operational duties. Meanwhile, follow-up operations against Bremen were mounted on the 27/28th and 29/30th employing forces of 144 and 253 aircraft respectively, including twenty-four and sixty-four Lancasters. Both resulted in useful damage to important war-industry factories and shipyards, and also to housing, at a combined cost to the Command of twenty aircraft. During the course of the month the squadron undertook six operations and dispatched thirty-two Manchester and thee Lancaster sorties for the loss of three Manchesters and crews.

July 1942

A gentle start to the new month had 5 Group operating alone on the night of the 1/2nd, when sending two Lancasters each from 97 and 106 Squadrons to mine the waters of the Great Belt in the western Baltic. 50 Squadron remained at home to work towards operational status on the Lancaster, and, over at Bottesford, the former flight commander, W/C Jeffs, now commanding officer of 207 Squadron, carried out a ten-hour cross-country flight as he also sought to become qualified on the type. The campaign against Bremen continued on the 2nd, with the preparation of a force of 325 aircraft, more than half of which were Wellingtons. 5 Group squadrons contributed fifty-three Lancasters and twenty-eight Hampdens, and those reaching the target found favourable weather conditions, with excellent visibility, no low cloud, high cirrus at around 22,000 feet, and only a little haze to spoil the view below. Positions were established by TR-fix confirmed by a visual check, but searchlight glare created great difficulty for the bomb-aimers trying to identify the Focke-Wulf aircraft factory aiming-point, and most would settle for estimating the fall of their bombs. A large fire was reported on the aerodrome attached to the Focke-Wulf factory, and another at Delmenhorst to the south-west, and the consensus of returning crews was of an effective operation. Local reports spoke of a thousand houses damaged, along with four small industrial premises, while three cranes and seven ships were hit in the port, one of the vessels sinking and becoming a danger to navigation. The likelihood is, however, that much of the effort was wasted beyond the city's southern boundary.

The remainder of the first half of the month would be low-key, with mining operations occupying much of the night-time activity. 5 Group sent six Lancasters to lay mines in the Great Belt on the 3rd, and fifty-two Lancasters and twenty-four Hampdens on the 8th to attack Wilhelmshaven as part of an overall force of 285 aircraft. Thin cloud at 10,000 feet and haze made it almost impossible for most to identify ground detail, including the docks aiming-point, and positions were established on e.t.a., and by TR-fix, some backed up through a visual check assisted by the use of flares. Local reports confirmed some damage in

Wilhelmshaven, but post-raid reconnaissance revealed that much of the bombing had missed the town to the west.

The first daylight foray deep into enemy territory by Lancasters, the previously mentioned raid on the M.A.N diesel engine factory at Augsburg in April, had cost seven of the twelve aircraft dispatched, and Harris, never an enthusiast of such operations, particularly at low level, had not been eager to repeat the exercise. Despite this, he sanctioned a similar plan by 5 Group for an attack on the U-Boot construction yards in the distant port of Danzig by forty-four Lancasters on the 11th. They were to fly out in formation at low level, before splitting up to cross Denmark and the Baltic independently, and then climb to bombing altitude and make their own individual approaches to the target. The attack was to be carried out in the fading light, to allow a withdrawal to take place under the cover of darkness, and the 1,500-mile round-trip would be the longest yet attempted by the Command. An unanticipated band of ten-tenths ice-bearing cloud was encountered over the North Sea extending from 1,000 to 14,000 feet, and this ruined the plan as aircraft lost contact with each other, forcing the individual crews to break formation and make their way independently to the target. This would have a detrimental effect on the raid, and cause some crews to abandon their sorties or arrive late, when darkness had already settled over the area to make identification a challenge. Twenty-six aircraft bombed either the ship-building wharfs or the town, and two of them were shot down by flak.

5 Group joined others in mining operations on the night of the 12/13th, dispatching fifteen Lancasters to the Nectarines garden off the east Frisians. The first of a series of five operations over a four-week period against Duisburg was mounted on the night of the 13/14th, and involved 194 aircraft, including thirteen Lancasters of 5 Group. The operation failed to find the mark in adverse weather conditions consisting of electrical storms and heavy cloud, and the bombing became widely scattered and ineffective. A force of ninety-nine four-engine types was assembled on the 19th to send against the Vulkan U-Boot construction yards at Vegesack, situated on the River Weser a few miles to the north-west of Bremen city centre. 5 Group contributed twenty-eight Lancasters to the attack, which was delivered on Gee-fix over ten-tenths cloud with tops at 10,000 to 12,000 feet, and completely missed the target, confirming the fact that Gee was useful as a guide to navigation, but was not precise enough to employ as a blind-bombing device. A force of 291 aircraft was assembled on the 21st for the second raid of the series on Duisburg, and this number included twenty-nine Lancasters and seventeen Hampdens representing 5 Group. It was a moonless night with clear skies over the target and the usual industrial haze, the effects of which, it was hoped, would be negated by flares dropped from the leading aircraft by TR and used as a guide by the following aircraft. However, these proved to be not entirely inaccurate, and some illuminated an area of open country on the West Bank of the Rhine. Returning crews could offer no useful information to the intelligence section at debriefing, but local reports confirmed extensive damage in residential districts, with ninety-four apartment buildings destroyed and 256 seriously damaged, and there was also mention of damage to the Thyssen steel works and to two other important war-industry factories.

A reduced force of 215 aircraft was made ready to continue the assault on Duisburg on the 23rd, and forty-five of these were Lancasters. Those reaching the target encountered seven to ten-tenths cloud with tops as high as 12,000 feet in places, and a large gap that afforded some crews a sight of the ground. Despite that, for many, there was little chance of locating the briefed aiming-point, which was probably the Thyssen steel works. The Gee-based (TR) flares were again scattered and largely ineffective, leaving most crews to carry out their attacks on their own TR-fix. The outcome of the raid was similar to the previous one, with residential property sustaining the bulk of the damage. While this operation was in progress, 50 Squadron announced itself as a fully-fledged Lancaster squadron, when sending six aircraft to lay mines in the Trefoil garden off the southern end of the Dutch Frisian island of Texel. They took off between 01.50 and 02.08 with S/Ls Everitt and Moore the senior pilots on duty, each carrying six parachute mines, and all reached the target area to find extreme darkness, but, good visibility. The mines were delivered unopposed into the briefed locations from between 500 and 1,000 feet, and all returned safely to make their reports. P/O Martin was alarmed by the magnitude and extent of the exhaust flame, and suggested modification to the exhaust dampers.

The fourth raid on Duisburg was posted on the 25th, for which the largest force yet of the series was assembled. Among the 313 aircraft were 177 Wellingtons and fourteen Hampdens, with the four-engine types making up the numbers. The thirty-three Lancasters included five representing 50 Squadron, each of them loaded with a cookie, six 500 and two 250 pounders as they departed Swinderby between 00.22 and 00.35 with P/Os Bunbury and Calvert the senior pilots on duty. F/Sgt Weber and crew climbed to 18,000 feet, but, on reaching the Dutch coast, found the rear gunner to be in a state of distress caused by oxygen starvation, and they abandoned their sortie. The others pushed on to find around seven-tenths cloud over the target, with fair visibility, which enable a visual confirmation of the TR-based approach, but not the briefed aiming-point "D". F/Sgt Morgan and crew identified the inland docks, and used them as a guide to bomb the built-up area generally from 17,000 feet, while his colleagues carried out their attacks from well below at between 8,000 and 14,000 feet. A number of bursts and fires were observed, but it was left to local reports to confirm further damage to residential property, but less extensive than in the two previous attacks.

A maximum effort was planned on the 26th for the annual last-week-of-July attack on Germany's Second City, Hamburg. 404 aircraft answered the call, among them seventy-seven Lancasters and thirty-three Hampdens. 50 Squadron made ready eight Lancasters, which departed Swinderby between 22.25 and 23.12 with S/Ls Everitt and Moore the senior pilots on duty, and other experienced crews captained by F/Ls Stone and Wilkins and P/O Martin. The petrol cock for the port-inner tank on R5728 became unserviceable, leaving S/L Everitt uncertain as to whether or not he would have sufficient available fuel to complete the round trip. On this basis he decided to attack Emden as an alternative target, and did so under bright moonlight from 12,000 feet, sadly, overshooting to the west. This left seven crews to press on to the target, which they reached after flying though the frequently-met conditions on this route of towering cloud and icing conditions. The skies over the target were clear and the visibility excellent, however, which allowed crews to confirm their positions by visual reference, with the docks area standing out particularly clearly in the bright moonlight. The 50 Squadron crews had been handed aiming-point "D", which was probably the shipbuilding yards to the west of the city centre, but smoke was already drifting across the city to obscure some ground detail. The Swinderby crews bombed the central area generally from between 8,000 and 18,600 feet, S/L Moore aiming for a railway junction to the west of the Aussen-Alster lake. Returning crews reported bomb bursts and thirty to forty fires seeming to merge into one single conflagration. This was borne out by local reports, which spoke of eight hundred fires, more than five hundred of which were classed as large, and it seems that the residential and semi-commercial districts bore the brunt of the raid. When the flames had died down and the smoke cleared, 823 houses were found to have been reduced to ruins, with five thousand others damaged to some extent. It was a highly successful raid for the period, which the Command hoped to build on forty-eight hours later until the weather took a hand to reduce the number of aircraft available.

Another maximum effort was called for on the 28th, and a force well in excess of four hundred aircraft was assembled for the return to Hamburg that night, 256 of them provided by 3 Group and the operational training units. In the event, these would take off alone, after the weather conditions over the 1, 4 and 5 Group stations prompted the withdrawal of their contributions to the operation, and, as conditions worsened over the North Sea, the O.T.U aircraft were recalled. Many of the 3 Group crews turned back also, and only sixty-eight would claim to have attacked the primary target, where fifteen large fires and forty smaller ones were reported. This modicum of success was gained at the high cost of twenty-five aircraft, 15% of those dispatched, and four O.T.U Wellingtons also failed to return, while a fifth, a Whitley, ditched, and its crew was picked up safely.

Saarbrücken was posted as the target on the 29th, and a force of 291 aircraft assembled, which would be the largest raid by far on this major industrial and coal-producing Saarland Capital city, situated right on the frontier with France in south-western Germany. 5 Group contributed sixty-nine Lancasters and seventeen Hampdens, fourteen of the former representing 50 Squadron, and they took off between 23.37 and 00.11 with S/Ls Everitt and Moore the senior pilots on duty. They had been briefed to attack aiming-point "C", and, in the expected absence of a strong searchlight and flak defence, the intention was to attack from a lower level than customary for the period. P/O Cole and crew experienced port-engine problems immediately after taking off, and remained in the circuit until it was clear for them to land. Faulty fuel cocks persuaded F/L Wilkins and crew to turn back after an hour, and this left a dozen Swinderby crews to press on across France to the target, where they encountered a layer of four to eight-tenths low cloud between 2,000 and 7,000 feet. The visibility below the cloud base was good, and this enabled F/O Southgate and crew to deliver their bombs from 5,500 feet into a factory, which disintegrated before their eyes. The others carried out their attacks from between 3,600 and 12,000 feet, but mostly below 6,000 feet, and observed many fires, some large and emitting black smoke, and returning crews were confident that their bombs had found the mark. This was confirmed by local reports of severe damage in central and north-western districts, where almost four hundred buildings had been destroyed. Nine aircraft failed to return, among them the inevitable first loss of a 50 Squadron Lancaster, R5728, which must have been on its way home when shot down by the night-fighter of Oblt Reinhold Eckardt of 7./NJG3. It crashed at 03.30 at Braine-le-Comte, some twenty miles south-west of Brussels, killing Sgt Foster RCAF and his crew. According to Bill Chorley in Bomber Command Losses, Eckardt was himself shot down minutes later when attacking a Halifax.

The month ended with a major assault on the Ruhr city of Düsseldorf, for which a force of 630 aircraft was assembled, the numbers bolstered by a large contribution from the training units. 5 Group offered 113 Lancasters, the first time that the one hundred figure had been reached, and they would be accompanied by twenty-four Hampdens belonging to the two Canadian squadrons, 408 and 420. The sixteen Swinderby Lancasters took off between 00.21 and 01.07 with S/Ls Everitt and Moore the senior pilots on duty, and P/O Wyness and crew undertaking their first operation with the squadron. Each Lancaster was carrying a cookie and a mixture of other high-explosives and incendiaries, which all arrived in the target area, where bright moonlight and good visibility enable the crews to confirm their TR-fixed positions visually by an S-bend in the Rhine. They carried out their attacks from between a suicidally low 6,500 and a slightly more sensible 16,000 feet, but still mostly below their 5 Group colleagues from other squadrons. The searchlight and flak defence was intense and accurate, and P/O Crampton and crew became ensnared in a cone of forty to fifty searchlights as they withdrew from the target. They lost part of their hydraulics system to flak, and both starboard engines were damaged and cut out at the Dutch coast, causing the port engines to overheat and the Lancaster to shed height. An attempt to land at Bircham Newton without brakes and with two burst tyres caused the undercarriage to collapse and R5788 to come to a halt about half a mile beyond the airfield. More than nine hundred tons of bombs had been delivered, some wasted in open country, but the remainder had been scattered across all parts of the city and neighbouring Neuss, resulting in the destruction of 453 buildings, damage to fifteen thousand more, the majority of them only slightly afflicted, and sixty-seven large fires. The success came at the cost of twenty-nine aircraft, including five Hampdens and two Lancasters, and the O.T.Us were again hit disproportionately hard, losing fifteen of their number.

P/O Tytherleigh had been posted to 1654 Conversion Unit on the 23rd, and he would become a founder member of 617 Squadron in March 1943, and find a seat in the Lancaster of flight commander, S/L Henry Maudslay. By coincidence, in the coming month, flight engineer, Sgt Jack Marriott, and navigator, P/O Robert Urquhart, would be posted to 50 Squadron to begin their tours, and they, too, would end up at Scampton to join Maudslay's crew for Operation Chastise, and, sadly, lose their lives. During the course of the month the squadron took part in five operations, and dispatched forty-nine sorties for the loss of a single Lancaster and crew.

August 1942

A gentle start to the new month saw the heavy brigade remain at home because of unfavourable weather on the first two nights. 5 Group sent out orders to Swinderby and Woodhall Spa on the 3rd to prepare small numbers of Lancasters for mining duties in the Forget-me-not and Radish gardens, respectively Kiel Harbour and the Fehmarnbelt in the western Baltic. 50 Squadron briefed two crews for the former and three for the latter, and sent them off between 23.45 and 00.12 with F/L Wilkins the senior pilot on duty. All reached their respective target areas, where three to eight-tenths cloud extended down to a base at 2,000 feet, where visibility was fair. F/Sgt Weber and crew cited poor weather conditions for their failure to locate the drop zone, and they brought their stores home. P/O Bunbury and crew experienced no such difficulties, and delivered their five vegetables into the allotted locations while firing on two flak ships and silencing them. Some forty miles to the east, P/O Dampier-Crossley, P/O Calvert and F/L Wilkins were able to establish pinpoints on Ærø island and Markelsdorfer Huk, and drop their mines largely unopposed from 600 to 800 feet.

On the following night, 5 Group contributed a handful of Lancasters and Hampdens for mining duties around the Frisians and off the Biscay coast. The 50 Squadron freshman crew of Sgt Howie took off at 21.55 bound for the Deodars garden in the mouth of the Gironde, and successfully fulfilled their brief before returning safely after more than seven hours aloft. Meanwhile, ten Lancasters from 44 and 97 Squadrons had been sent to join twenty-eight other aircraft in a blind attack on Essen employing Gee, but towering, ice-bearing cloud with tops at 22,000 feet prevented all but eighteen from bombing in the target area, and it was decided to try again twenty-four hours later. Consequently, eight Lancasters were detailed on the 5th, one of them made ready at Swinderby, along with four others for gardening duties in the Gironde estuary. P/O Dampier-Crossley and crew took off at 23.43, and reached Essen on this moonless night to find clear skies and a blanket of industrial haze. They bombed from 13,500 feet, picking up a little flak damage for their trouble, but were denied by the vertical visibility any observation of the outcome. The gardeners departed Swinderby between 23.48 and 00.01 with F/O Southgate the senior pilot, and established a pinpoint on Ile-de-Re as they skirted the Biscay coast towards the target area, where they found extreme darkness and thick ground haze. They pinpointed on Pointe-de-Coubre, from where they carried out timed runs to deliver their five vegetables each from 800 to 1,000 feet, and all parachutes were seen to deploy.

5 Group's contribution to the fifth and final operation of the three-week campaign against the Ruhr industrial giant of Duisburg amounted to forty-seven Lancasters and ten Hampdens, which were part of an overall force of 216 aircraft assembled on the 6th. 50 Squadron loaded nine Lancasters with a cookie and ten SBCs of 4lb incendiaries and another with five mines to be taken by Sgt Howie and crew to the Nectarines garden off the Frisians. The latter departed Swinderby first, at 22.23, and pinpointed on the eastern rim of Juist, before releasing the mines into the briefed location by visual reference from 2,000 feet, after the Gee signal became too weak to rely on. The bombing brigade took off between 00.38 and 01.10 with S/Ls Everitt and Moore the senior pilots on duty, and all reached the target area, where cloud was reported at between zero and ten-tenths with tops at 10,000 feet and barrage balloons tethered as high as 12,000 feet. Positions had to be established by TR-fix confirmed by visual reference aided by fires, flak and flares, and the bombs were delivered from between 7,000 and 16,000 feet without their fall being plotted. According to local reports, eighteen buildings were destroyed and sixty-six seriously damaged, giving a sum total over the five raids of 212 houses destroyed, 741 seriously damaged, and significant industrial damage resulting from just one raid. In return for this modest gain, Bomber Command had lost forty-three aircraft.

The garrison town of Osnabrück was posted as the target on the 9th, and a force of 192 aircraft assembled accordingly. 5 Group contributed forty-two Lancasters, eight of them made ready by 50 Squadron, with another three for freshman crews to take to Le Havre to target the docks. The crews bound for northern France took off first, between 21.29 and 21.37, and they were followed into the air by those participating in the main event between 00.25 and 00.51, led by F/Ls Stone and Wilkins. By this time, the freshmen were almost back home, Sgt Howie and crew having been misled by a navigation error, which prevented them from locating Le Havre. F/Sgt Taylor and Sgt Rees-Jones had delivered their loads onto the target from 9,000 and 8,500 feet respectively, some two thousand feet above the three-tenths cloud tops, through which they observed bursts across the docks. There were clear skies over the Münsterland region of Germany to the north of the Ruhr, but haze contributed to the poor visibility that awaited the approaching bombers. They all found that they were unable to establish their positions by TR after it was jammed by the enemy on crossing the Dutch coast. Flares were dropped to illuminate the area, and some crews picked out railway lines and the River Hase, but it was mainly the fires, searchlights and flak that pointed the way to what was described in the ORB as a "special" aiming-point. Bombing was carried out from between 6,000 and 10,000 feet, and some observed the burst of their cookie. The resulting fires remained visible for eighty to a hundred miles into the return flight, and TR functioned again once the Dutch coast had been crossed homebound.

The night of the 10/11th was devoted to mining operations in northern waters, and would occupy fifty-two aircraft, including a contribution from 5 Group of seventeen Lancasters. Seven of these were made ready at Swinderby, six for one of the Silverthorn gardens in the Kattegat region of the western Baltic between Jutland and Sweden, and one for Forget-me-not in Kiel Harbour. They took off between 22.03 and 22.27 with F/Ls Stone and Wilkins the senior pilots on duty, and P/O Bunbury and crew bound for the Kiel area. They pinpointed on the southern tip of Langeland island, before running south-west to the drop zone, where the five vegetables were delivered through a layer of ten-tenths rain-cloud from 2,000 feet. Meanwhile, some 150 miles to the north, the Silverthorne area was also covered by low cloud, with squalls producing poor visibility as the Swinderby crews pinpointed on Anholt island and delivered their vegetables unopposed into the briefed locations from between 800 and 2,000 feet.

The main operation on the night of the 11/12th was the first of two on consecutive nights against the city of Mainz, situated to the south-west of Frankfurt-am-Main, for which 154 aircraft were made ready. The number included a contribution from 5 Group of thirty-three Lancasters, for what would be the first large-scale raid on this target. 50 Squadron would not take part, but loaded two Lancasters with fourteen 500 pounders each for delivery by freshman crews to the docks at Le Havre. Sgt Rees-Jones and Sgt Gray and their crews took off at 02.03 and 02.13 respectively, and only the former returned three hours later to report bombing the docks from 7,000 feet and observing bursts. The return of R5746 was awaited in vain, and news reached the station eventually that the Lancaster had crashed in the target area with no survivors from the mixed RAAF, RAF and RCAF crew of P/O Gray RAAF. The raid on Mainz was highly successful, and caused major destruction in the central districts, where many historic and cultural buildings were damaged or destroyed. In the excellent tome, Bomber Command War Diaries by Martin Middlebrook and Chris Everitt, the losses from this operation are put at six aircraft, but the actual number failing to return was fourteen, while four others were lost in crashes at home.

The ordeal was not yet over for Mainz, which was posted as the primary target again on the following day, and a force of 138 aircraft made ready, to which 5 Group contributed thirty-three Lancasters and ten Hampdens. This time eight Lancasters of 50 Squadron were included on the Order of Battle, and they departed Swinderby between 22.29 and 22.45 with S/L Everitt the senior pilot on duty. They all reached the target area, where they found eight to ten-tenths cloud between 5,000 and 12,000 feet, but still managed to identify the aiming-point visually by islands in the River Rhine north and north-west of the city centre, and the fires already burning. The cookies, 2,000 pounders and incendiaries were released unopposed from between 4,400 and 9,000 feet onto the centre of the built-up area, and many fires were reported by returning crews. Post-raid reconnaissance and local reports confirmed further heavy damage in central and industrial areas, and the main railway station was also a casualty.

On the 13th, 5 Group issued orders to Waddington and Swinderby to prepare a dozen Lancasters between them for gardening duties in the Geranium, Willow and Radish gardens in the Baltic. 50 Squadron made ready six Lancasters for Geranium, situated off the port of Swinemünde, which, as the crow flies, was eight hundred miles away and one of the more distant targets attempted by the Command. Of course, a route would rarely be direct, and a track over the Danish half of the Schleswig-Holstein peninsular would add at least another one hundred miles to the round-trip. The Lancaster bound for Radish (Fehmarnbelt) with the crew of Sgt Rees-Jones on board, had, in contrast, a mere 1,150 miles to cover, if it flew directly there and back. Those with the greatest distance to cover departed Swinderby between 21.16 and 22.23, the latter time that of P/O Bunbury and crew, who had been delayed for an undisclosed reason, and would elect to seek out an alternative location for their stores. The Rees-Jones crew took off at 22.46, and reached the target area to find challenging weather conditions, which thwarted their attempts to locate their briefed drop zone, and they, too, would find an unnamed alternative location for their vegetables. F/O Abercrombie and crew crossed the Danish coast north of track, and, on e.t.a., found themselves near Copenhagen with no chance of reaching their briefed destination. They then found themselves under fire from light flak, which threw them further off course and persuaded them to abandon their sortie and return their mines to store. P/O Martin pinpointed on the Stettiner Haff, the body of water separated from the Baltic by the narrow bridge of land linking Swinemünde with Usedom Island, on which was located the highly secret Peenemünde rocket research facility. Other crews established their positions on the Achterwasser and Jasmund peninsular, and carried out timed runs to the garden to deliver their vegetables from 500 to 800 feet, before returning safely from largely uneventful trips of between seven and a half and eight hours.

A new era for Bomber Command began on the 15th, with the formation of the Pathfinder Force, although it would be two days later before the four founder heavy squadrons arrived on their stations in Huntingdonshire and Cambridgeshire. 83 Squadron moved into Wyton, the Pathfinder HQ, as the 5 Group representative operating Lancasters, and it would be the responsibility of 5 Group's front-line units to provide a steady supply of their most promising crews. The other founder members were 35 Squadron, which took up residence at Graveley with Halifaxes to represent 4 Group, while 156 Squadron retained its Wellingtons for the time-being at Warboys, drawing fresh crews from 1 Group, and 3 Group would be represented by the Stirling-equipped 7 Squadron at Oakington. In addition to the above, 109 Squadron was posted in to Wyton, where it would spend the next six months developing the Oboe blind-bombing device and marrying it to the Mosquito under the command of W/C Hal Bufton. The new force would occupy 3 Group stations, falling nominally under 3 Group administrative control and receiving its orders through that group, which was commanded by AVM Baldwin, whose tenure, which had lasted since just before the outbreak of war, was shortly to come to an end.

A "Pathfinder" force was the brainchild of the former 10 Squadron commanding officer, G/C Sid Bufton, Hal's brother, and now Director of Bomber Operations at the Air Ministry. He had used his best crews at 10 Squadron to find targets by the light of flares and attract other crews by firing off a coloured Verey light, and, it could be said, that the concept of target-finding and marking was born at 10 Squadron. Once at the Air Ministry, Bufton promoted his ideas with vigour, and gained support among the other staff officers, culminating with the idea being put to Harris soon after his enthronement as Bomber Command C-in-C. Harris rejected the principle of establishing an elite target-finding and marking force, a view shared by the other group commanders with the exception of 4 Group's AVM Roddy Carr. However, once overruled by higher authority, Harris gave it his unstinting support, and his choice of the former 10 Squadron commanding officer, and still somewhat junior, G/C Don Bennett, as its commander, was both controversial and inspired, and ruffled more than a few feathers among more senior officers. Australian, Bennett, was among the most experienced aviators in the RAF, a pilot and a Master Navigator of unparalleled experience, with many thousands of hours to his credit. He also had the recent and relevant experience as a bomber pilot through his commands of 77 and 10 Squadrons, and had demonstrated his strong character when evading capture and returning from Norway after being shot down while attacking the Tirpitz in April. Despite his reserve, total lack of humour and his impatience with those whose brains operated on a lower plane than his, he would inspire in his men great affection and loyalty, along with an enormous pride in wearing the Pathfinder badge. He would forge the new force into a highly effective weapon, although this would not immediately be apparent.

There is some confusion surrounding 5 Group operations on the night of the 15/16th, the group ORB recording no operations because of the weather conditions, while the 50 and 207 Squadron ORBs each record four of their Lancasters operating from Swinderby against Düsseldorf, along with nine others from 106 Squadron at Coningsby. A force of 131 aircraft was assembled, the 50 Squadron quartet taking off between 00.25 and 00.57 with F/L Stone the senior pilot on duty and "Mick" Martin now elevated to the rank of flying officer. Each Lancaster carried a cookie and mixture of 4lb and 30lb incendiaries, and all reached the target area to encounter six to nine-tenths cloud at 10,000 feet and poor to modest visibility. They established their position by TR-fix confirmed by a visual confirmation on the River Rhine, or simply relied on e.t.a., and F/L Stone spent twenty minutes searching, before bombing a built-up area from 10,000 feet. F/O Southgate delivered his load from 13,000 feet, while F/O Martin, who was renowned for his enjoyment of flying at low-level, braved the intense light flak by going in at 6,000 feet, and lost his port-inner engine as a result. On return, he would hand R5687 back to the ground crew with twelve areas of damage to be repaired. R5735 was absent from its dispersal, and the crew of Sgt Rees-Jones RAAF was posted missing. The Red Cross would eventually provide notification that the navigator and bomb-aimer were safe in enemy hands as the only survivors of the crash, which had occurred somewhere in the general target area. At debriefing, a number of bursts and flashes were reported, and the abiding impression was of a scattered attack, which was confirmed by local reports from Düsseldorf and its neighbour across the Rhine, Neuss, which described a light raid and no damage of note.

The night of the 16/17th was to be devoted to mining operations involving fifty-six aircraft, some representing 5 Group, despite the fact that the 5 Group ORB again denied any operational activity on its stations. Six Lancasters each were made ready by 106 and 207 Squadrons to mine the Willows, Geranium and Spinach gardens, located respectively off the Baltic ports of Sassnitz on the island of Rügen, Swinemünde, further east along the coast, and Spinach, even further to the east off the port of Danzig (Gdansk), which, at the time, was a German city, rather than Polish as it is today. 50 Squadron did not take part, but received orders on the 17th to prepare seven Lancasters for a return to Osnabrück that night as part of a 5 Group effort of thirty-two Lancasters and ten Hampdens in an overall force of 139 aircraft. During the course of the day, the founder squadrons of the Pathfinder Force moved into their new homes with an expectation of operating in their new role that very night, however, their commanding officers decided they were not ready, and their debut would be delayed by twenty-four hours. The Swinderby element took off between 21.32 and 21.48 with S/L Everitt the senior pilot on duty, and reached the target area after making a timed run from the Dümmer Sea, a large lake situated some twenty miles to the north-east. The visibility was not particularly good, but some were able to identify the river and railway lines, and bombing took place from between 6,000 and 8,000 feet. S/L Everitt was unable to establish his position because of thick ground haze, and attempted to release his bombs on estimated position, only to have them hang up and have to be brought home. R5639 failed to return with the crew of F/O Bunbury, and no clue to their fate ever emerged. Local reports confirmed a moderately destructive raid, which fell mainly into northern and north-western districts, and, thereby, built on the damage inflicted eight nights earlier.

The Pathfinders took to the air in anger for the first time on the 18th, when contributing thirty-one aircraft to an overall force of 118, of which twenty Lancasters and sixteen Hampdens were provided by 5 Group. They were bound for the naval port of Flensburg, situated on the eastern coast of the Schleswig-Holstein peninsular close to the border with Denmark, where the U-Boot pens were the briefed aiming-point. It had been selected as a worthwhile and easy-to-locate target, but the planners had not factored in an incorrect wind forecast, which pushed the bomber stream north of the intended track and over southern Denmark. The Pathfinders failed to notice, and, as a result, illuminated an area of similar coastal terrain, which led to a scattering of bombs across Danish territory up to twenty-five miles north of the frontier, and into the towns of Abenra and Sønderborg. Flensburg escaped being hit in this inauspicious operational debut of a force, which, in time, would become a highly efficient, successful and vital component in Bomber Command's armoury.

On the 19th, 5 Group was handed the task of locating and bombing a German tanker and support vessel of the Altmark class, which was reported to be off northern Spain. Seven 50 Squadron Lancasters departed Swinderby between 02.37 and 02.54 on the 20th, led by S/L Everitt, and with W/C Oxley making a rare operational appearance as a member of the crew of F/L Wilkins. In the event, they were unable to locate the vessel, and all returned safely after at least eight hours aloft, all but one bringing their five 1,000 pounders home. That night, an element from 44 Squadron tried and failed also to locate the vessel.

Frankfurt was selected on the 24th to host the second Pathfinder-led operation, for which a force of 226 aircraft was assembled. 5 Group contributed forty-seven Lancasters, seven of them made ready at Swinderby, along with three others for lone attacks on specific targets in the towns of Mayen, Bad Kreuznach and Bingen-am-Rhein, all situated on the western approaches to Frankfurt. All participants in the night's activities departed Swinderby between 21.06 and 21.34 with S/L Moore the senior pilot on duty for the main event, and S/L Everitt, F/O Southgate and F/O Martin the lone wolves respectively. Five to nine-tenths cloud lay over the target area at between 6,000 and 9,000 feet, and ground haze added to the difficulties experienced by the pathfinders in locating the aiming-point. The 50 Squadron crews bombed from between 5,000 and 10,000 feet, having located the target themselves by ground features and timed runs rather than by the guidance of the Pathfinders. Meanwhile, S/L Everitt had carried out a timed run from the Laacher Sea, a lake to the north of Mayen, and delivered his cookie from 6,000 feet onto the western edge of the town. The blockbuster was seen to detonate before impacting the ground, and started fires in what was not a densely built-up area. F/O Southgate and crew map-read their way down the Rhine, and identified Bad Kreuznach by railway tracks and the river. Their cookie went down from 8,000 feet to be followed by a white flash and a pall of smoke. This kind of sortie was meat and drink to F/O Martin, who revelled in the opportunity to remain almost at ground level for all but the bombing run, which was conducted at Bingen-am-Rhein at 7,800 feet. The target was identified by the junction of rivers and three bridges, and the cookie aimed at a church in the town centre. A local report described the detonation near the famous Ehrenfels mountain overlooking the Rhine, and the resultant blast damage to 225 houses. Opinions at debriefing concerning the Frankfurt raid would be mixed, some satisfied with the results and others not. Certainly, a number of fires were observed across the built-up area, but no detailed assessment was possible. No mention was made of the Pathfinder contribution, which, at this early stage of its development, restricted crews to identifying and then illuminating the target. Sixteen aircraft failed to return, 7.1% of those dispatched, and among them were five Pathfinders

The third Pathfinder-led operation was to be against the city of Kassel, situated some fifty miles to the east of the Ruhr, where it was home to three Henschel aircraft factories and other important war-industry concerns, as well as being the HQ for the military's Wehrkreis IX, and the site of a subcamp of the Dachau concentration camp, which supplied slave labour to the factories. A force of 306 aircraft was assembled on the 27th, 5 Group detailing seventy-five Lancasters and a dozen Hampdens, twelve of the former made ready at Swinderby. They took off between 20.50 and 21.22 with F/Ls Stone and Wilkins the senior pilots on duty, and all made it to the target, where they were greeted by minimal cloud and good visibility, with only ground haze between them and the aiming-point. The Pathfinder flares assisted greatly in enabling the crews to pick out ground detail, like a bend in the River Fulda and lakes to the south-west, and the Swinderby crews took advantage to deliver their cookies, 2,000 and 500 pounders and incendiaries from between 5,000 and 11,000 feet, the low height, predictably, that of F/O Martin and crew. Local reports confirmed the effectiveness of the raid, which was spread across the city and destroyed 144 buildings, while causing serious damage to over three hundred others. Among those afflicted to some extent were all three Henschel aircraft factories and a number of military establishments, and the fire services had to deal with seventy-three large blazes. However, the success was gained at the high cost of thirty-one aircraft, twenty-one of them Wellingtons, of which fifteen belonged to 1 Group.

A force of 159 aircraft was assembled on the 28th to send to the city of Nuremberg, deep in southern Germany, and the scene of massive Nazi Party rallies during and after Hitler's rise to power during the thirties. The Pathfinders were to employ target indicators (TIs) for the first time in adapted 250lb bomb casings. 5 Group detailed sixty-three Lancasters, while also contributing seventeen Hampdens to a simultaneous raid on Saarbrücken by a force of 113 "oddments", which included 4 Group Halifaxes and new crews from other groups, but no Pathfinders. 50 Squadron made ready a dozen Lancasters for the main operation, and they took off between 20.59 and 20.32 with S/L Moore the senior pilot on duty. On a night of poor serviceability for the squadron, P/O Wyness and crew turned back after an hour because of an engine problem, and they were followed home first by F/O Abercromby and crew and then Sgt Crampton and crew, both as a result of technical problems. Sgt Heinrich and crew had entered enemy territory when excessive exhaust flame persuaded them to turn back also, and a brief skirmish with a night-fighter just short of the French coast resulted in a "damaged" claim by the Lancaster crew. The others pushed on across France to southern Germany, where clear skies, good visibility and a four-fifths moon aided a visual identification of the city, and enabled the Pathfinder element to exploit the conditions to deliver their TIs with great accuracy. Some of the Swinderby crews pinpointed on the Autobahns leading into the city, and bombed from between 5,000 and 11,500 feet, observing many bursts and fires. There was no question in their minds as they withdrew, that they had hit the target, a belief confirmed by fires remaining visible for some seventy miles into the return flight. Local reports suggested that about a third of the force had landed bombs within the city, causing damage to the Altstadt, but that others had wasted their effort on communities up to ten miles to the north.

Twenty-three aircraft failed to return, 14.5% of the force, and the Wellingtons were hit particularly hard again, losing a third of their number. During the course of the month the squadron took part in eighteen operations and dispatched 108 sorties for the loss of three Lancasters and crews.

September 1942

The first half of the new month would distinguish itself through an unprecedented series of effective operations, although, it would begin ignominiously for the Pathfinder Force, when posting a "black" on the night of the 1/2nd by marking the wrong town. Saarbrücken had been briefed out to 231 crews, of which sixty-nine represented 5 Group, sixty-two to fly Lancasters and seven in Hampdens, a type with just two more weeks of front-line service ahead of it. 50 Squadron made ready a dozen Lancasters, which departed Swinderby between 23.38 and 00.01 with S/L Everitt the senior pilot on duty. Eight of them were carrying a cookie and the others 2,000 pounders, all loads supplemented with small bomb containers (SBCs) of 30lb and 4lb incendiaries. All reached south-western Germany to find the target under clear skies with good visibility, and established their positions by TR, confirmed by visual identification of the River Saar and Pathfinder flares. The 50 Squadron crews bombed from between 4,400 and 11,500 feet, with F/O Martin and crew responsible for the lowest attack, which hit the town centre. They described the town as being smothered in incendiaries and fires welding into one vast red glow visible from eighty miles away. S/L Everitt, whose crew included future Dambusters, P/O Bob Hay RAAF and Sgt "Spam" Spafford RCAF, was another to select a low bombing height of 5,600 feet, from where the bombs were seen to burst among factory buildings. There was no question in the minds of the crews as they retreated to the west, that this had been an outstandingly accurate attack, and some claimed to be able to see the glow from up to 140 miles into the return flight. It was only later that the truth emerged, that the Pathfinders had not marked Saarbrücken, but the non-industrial town of Saarlouis, situated thirteen miles to the north-west. Much to the chagrin of its inhabitants, and those in surrounding communities, the main force bombing was accurate, and heavy damage was inflicted.

This could have been an ill-omen for the month's efforts, but, in fact, the Command now embarked on the unprecedented run of effective operations mentioned above. It began at Karlsruhe on the night of the 2/3rd, for which a force of two hundred aircraft was made ready, the 4 Group Halifax brigade having now returned to operations following intensive training to restore confidence in the type after a period of above average losses and a series of design-flaw accidents. 5 Group put up sixty Lancasters and five Hampdens, of which nine of the former were provided by 50 Squadron. They departed Swinderby between 23.06 and 23.50 with S/L Moore the senior pilot on duty, and headed out over Suffolk on their way to the Belgian coast. Again, there were no early returns to reduce the squadron's impact, and they found the target under clear skies, basking in moonlight and naked to the eyes of the bomb-aimers high above. The Rhine and its docks stood out clearly as a guide to the aiming-point and bombing took place from between 8,000 and 15,000 feet, from where the city appeared to be swallowed by a sea of flames, before becoming obscured by smoke. Returning crews reported as many as two hundred fires burning, the glow from which remained visible for a hundred miles into the homeward journey. Post-raid reconnaissance confirmed much residential and some industrial damage, and local reports mentioned seventy-three fatalities.

When Bremen was posted as the target on the 4th, 5 Group responded with a contribution of forty-six Lancasters in an overall force of 251 aircraft. Crews were told at briefing that the Pathfinders would be rolling out a new three-phase technique of illumination, visual marking and backing-up, which, if successful, would form the basis of Pathfinder operations for the remainder of the war. Eleven 50 Squadron Lancasters lined up at Swinderby, seven of the crews briefed to attack the city and four the Focke-Wulf aircraft factory, and took off between 23.51 and 00.21 with S/Ls Everitt and Moore the senior pilots on duty. They reached the target area to find cloudless skies and good visibility, although ground haze and smoke created challenging conditions for target identification. F/O Calvert and crew searched for the Focke-Wulf factory for twenty-five minutes before finding it already on fire, and F/O Abercromby spotted it in the light of flares. S/L Everitt and F/O Martin were unable to make a positive identification, and bombed on its estimated position after pinpointing on the river. The bombing of the factory was carried out from between 6,000 and 7,500 feet, and the town area from 8,000 to 13,300 feet, all in the face of an intense flak defence, which caused a little damage to F/O Martin's port-outer engine. Twelve aircraft failed to return from this successful operation, and debriefing reports of fires in the central districts were confirmed by a local assessment, which listed 460 dwelling houses, six large/medium industrial premises and fifteen small ones destroyed, and a further fourteen hundred buildings seriously damaged.

The Ruhr city of Duisburg came next for a force of 207 aircraft, which included fifty-four Lancasters and four Hampdens representing 5 Group. 50 Squadron made ready ten Lancasters, which took off between 00.53 and 01.24 with S/L Everitt the senior pilot on duty, and all reached the target area to find it partially concealed by cloud, below which the usual industrial haze rendered ground detail indistinct. Positions were established by TR and confirmed as far as possible by visual reference, and bombing took place from between 6,000 and 11,000 feet, consistently below the altitude of other 5 Group squadrons. The defences performed to their usual high standard, and S/L Everitt's R5689 took a hit in the port-inner engine, which caused a drop in oil pressure and the loss of the hydraulics system. Even so, the Duisburg authorities reported the heaviest raid to date, which destroyed 114 buildings and seriously damaged more than three hundred others, and, while this was only modest, it still represented something of a victory at this notoriously elusive target.

There was no pattern to the choice of targets thus far in the month, southern and north-western Germany and the Ruhr all featuring during the busy first week, and Frankfurt in south-central Germany was posted as the latest target on the 8th, for which a force of 249 aircraft was assembled. 5 Group contributed sixty-two Lancasters and nine Hampdens, the eleven participants from 50 Squadron departing Swinderby between 20.35 and 21.01 with S/Ls Everitt and Moore the senior pilots on duty. Sgt Eyres and crew observed Mainz over to port while flying at 17,000 feet, at which point, both starboard engines cut, and they unloaded their bombs onto a railway line south-west of the town. The others reached the target, where, according to some, the skies were clear of cloud and the visibility good, while others reported up to eight-tenths cloud at 2,000 feet and poor to moderate visibility. Another factor was the intensity of the searchlight and flak activity, which should, perhaps, have helped to guide the Pathfinders to the aiming-point, but, surprisingly, they failed to locate the city. Pathfinder flares were in evidence, but scattered over a wide area, and it was clear that they were by no means certain as to their proximity to Frankfurt. 50 Squadron crews established their own positions by what they could glimpse on the ground, and bombed from between 6,000 and 10,000 feet, observing fires in what appeared to be the built-up area. However, according to local reports, only a handful of bomb loads hit the intended target, and this halted the run of successes thus far in the month. The majority of bombs appeared to have fallen to the south-west of Frankfurt as far as Rüsselsheim, fifteen miles away. The Rüsselsheim authorities confirmed damage to the Opel tank works and a Michelin tyre factory, which compensated in small measure for the failure to hit the primary target.

The Pathfinder Force was constantly evolving in tactics and equipment, and had a new weapon in its armoury for the next operation, which was to be against the Ruhr city of Düsseldorf on the 10th. "The Pink Pansy", which weighed in at 2,800lbs, was the latest attempt to produce a genuine target indicator, and used converted 4,000lb cookie casings. A force of 479 aircraft included a contribution from the training units of 91, 92 and 93 Groups, and eighty-one Lancasters and eight Hampdens from 5 Group. 50 Squadron made ready thirteen Lancasters, which were launched off the end of the Swinderby runway between 20.29 and 21.04 with S/L Moore the senior pilot on duty. Sgt Heinrich and crew had reported a problem with the rear turret before take-off, but went anyway, only for the guns to fail while being tested over the sea, and bring their sortie to an end. The others reached the target area to encounter clear skies with the usual industrial haze muddying the vertical visibility, but fires were already burning to help them identify the target visually, and pick out major features like a bend in the Rhine and the docks complex. They bombed from between 8,000 and 12,000 feet, still well below what must have been the briefed bombing height, and observed fires to develop. They turned away believing the attack to have been successful, and, on return, made complimentary comments about the performance of the Pathfinders. Post-raid reconnaissance and local reports confirmed this operation to have been probably the most successful since Operation Millennium at the end of May. Other than the northern districts, all parts of the city and its neighbour, Neuss, had been hit, and 911 houses had been destroyed with a further fifteen hundred seriously damaged. In addition to the destruction also of eight public buildings, fifty-two industrial firms in the two cities sustained damage sufficient to cause a total shut down of production for varying periods. It had been an expensive victory for the Command, however, with thirty-three failures to return, of which sixteen were from the training units. 50 Squadron was also represented in the form of R5725, which came down in the target area, killing the navigator and both gunners. Sgt Blaskey was on his third sortie as crew captain, and was taken into captivity with the three other survivors.

F/L Stone was posted to 1654 Conversion Unit on the 12th at the conclusion of his tour, leaving twelve of his pilot colleagues and their crews to attend briefing on the 13th to learn that Bremen was to be their target for that night, and for the second time during the month. A force of 446 aircraft was made ready, again bolstered by aircraft and crews from the training groups, and there was a contribution from 5 Group of ninety-eight Lancasters and seven Hampdens. The 50 Squadron element departed Swinderby between 23.00 and 23.23 with S/L Moore the senior pilot on duty, and all reached the target area to find clear skies but considerable ground haze, which made pinpointing something of a challenge. Some major ground features, like the docks, could be identified visually, otherwise it was down to flares and fires to point the way, and the 50 Squadron crews did their best from between 6,000 and 11,500 feet, while, as an example, the 207 Squadron element attacked from 16,000 to 19,000 feet and 106 Squadron from around 15,000 feet. The 5 Group ORB described the Pathfinder performance as unhelpful, but the successes of the operation suggested otherwise, and by far exceeded the destruction resulting from June's Thousand Bomber raid. A total of 848 houses was destroyed, and much damage was inflicted on the city's industry, including to the Lloyd

Dynamo works, where two weeks production was lost, and parts of the Focke-Wulf factory were put out of action for between two and eight days. Of the twenty-one aircraft lost, fifteen belonged to the training units.

The end of the Hampden era arrived on the following night, when the naval port of Wilhelmshaven was posted as the target for 202 aircraft. Sixty-two Lancasters and four Hampdens were made ready as the 5 Group contribution, the latter from Syerston's 408 (Goose) Squadron RCAF. The 50 Squadron element of eleven departed Swinderby between 20.04 and 20.34 with S/L Moore the senior pilot on duty, each Lancaster loaded with a cookie and SBCs of 4lb and 30lb incendiaries. A burst oil-pressure line in Sgt Howie's rear turret covered the occupant and the Perspex with hydraulics fluid, leaving them with no choice but to abandon their sortie, leaving the others to press on to Germany's north-western coastal region, where clear skies awaited, as did extreme darkness and ground haze to impede vertical visibility. The waterline and the docks provided an adequate pinpoint for the Pathfinders to establish their position and mark accurately, and the 50 Squadron crews carried out their part in the plan mostly from between 7,200 and 11,000 feet, although Sgt Morley and crew felt more comfortable at 18,000 feet. It was difficult to distinguish individual bomb bursts, but the consensus was of a successful outcome, which was confirmed by local reports that this was the port's most destructive raid to date.

After such a run of successes, Harris had to have another go at Essen, and a force of 369 aircraft was assembled on the 16th, which again called upon the training units to supply aircraft and crews. Ninety-three Lancasters represented 5 Group, and the eleven provided by 50 Squadron departed Swinderby between 20.06 and 20.29 with S/L Moore the senior pilot on duty. They all reached the target area to encounter between three and eight-tenths cloud, but generally good visibility, and the industrial haze could be penetrated sufficiently for some ground detail to be identified visually by the light of Pathfinder flares. Even so, the overlapping boundaries of the Ruhr towns and cities made it difficult to establish positions with absolute certainty, and some of the crews dropping their bombs on e.t.a would find, from the evidence of their bombing photos, that they had been over Bochum, Oberhausen or some other built-up expanse. Some of the pathfinder flares were estimated to be falling some twenty miles to the east of Essen, which would have put them over Dortmund and Hagen. The 50 Squadron element carried out their attacks from between 6,000 and 13,000 feet over what they believed to be Essen, doing so in the face of an intense searchlight and flak response. Local reports would confirm this to be Essen's worst night of the war to date, with much housing damage and more than a hundred medium and large fires. In addition, fifteen high-explosive bombs found their way onto the Krupp complex, as did a crashing bomber loaded with incendiaries. A post-raid analysis revealed that bombs had been scattered across a large part of the Ruhr, with Bochum, Wuppertal and Herne among the hardest hit, and, until the advent of Oboe in the coming spring, such inaccuracies were a fact of life. It was far from a one-sided affair, and cost the Command a massive thirty-nine aircraft, 10.6% of those dispatched, nineteen of them from the training units.

If any period in the Command's gradual evolution to war-winning capability could be seen as a turning point, then, perhaps, the first half of September 1942 qualified. It can be no coincidence, that the Pathfinder Force was emerging from its hesitant start, as the crews got to grips with the complexities of their demanding role, and new tactics and aids were being brought to bear against the enemy. It would be no overnight transformation, and failures would still outnumber victories for some time to come, but the encouraging signs were there, and it boded ill for Germany's industrial towns and cities.

Extensive mining operations occupied 115 aircraft on the night of the 18/19th, 5 Group supporting the effort with forty-nine Lancasters, eleven of them representing 50 Squadron. The Swinderby crews were assigned to six separate gardens, five in the Baltic and one located off south-western France, and they took off for their respective destinations between 10.09 and 20.01, with F/L Wilkins the senior pilot on duty. He and P/O Dampier-Crossley and their crews were the last to depart, bound for the Elderberry garden located off Bayonne, some fifteen miles north of the Franco-Spanish frontier, and a straight-line distance from home of 620 miles. Sgts Howie and Morley and their crews had around 550 miles to travel to reach their target area of Nasturtium, the northern reaches of The Sound (Oresund) between Denmark and Sweden, while, some miles to the south, Sgt Heinrich and F/Sgt Taylor and their crews had Daffodil (the southern Sound) as their garden. F/O Abercromby and P/O Wiseman and their crews had, perhaps, the longest round trip on this night to reach and return from Pollock, situated off the island of Bornholm, twenty-five miles south of the Swedish mainland. The crews of P/O Wyness and Sgt Crampton headed for the island of Rügen to the Willows garden off the port of Sassnitz, and this left just Sgt Eyres and crew for the Quince garden in Kiel Bay. All would find favourable weather conditions in which to complete their tasks, with visibility described as good to excellent. F/L Wilkins had the frustration of being unable to open his bomb doors when trying to release the mines, and he had to bring them home, but the others all fulfilled their briefs and delivered their vegetables into the allotted locations from between 400 and 900 feet before returning safely to home airspace. It was here that both port engines failed on R5689 shortly after it crossed the Lincolnshire coast, causing it to crash at Thurlby, killing one of the occupants. There is considerable confusion surrounding the outcome of this incident involving the crew of Sgt Morley RAAF, the immediate report in the squadron and group ORBs stating four and five fatalities respectively, while Bill Chorley's superb Bomber Command Losses has the rear gunner as the sole fatality. However, in the postings summary of the squadron ORB, completed at the end of the month, the second pilot, P/O Harrison, was recorded as the sole fatality on the 19th, just four days after arriving from 1654 Conversion Unit.

Munich was posted as one of two targets on the 19th, and would involve sixty-one 5 Group Lancasters, seven Lancasters from 83 Squadron of the Pathfinders and twenty-one Stirlings from 3 Group, some of them also Pathfinders from 7 Squadron. A simultaneous operation by 118 aircraft would target Saarbrücken. 50 Squadron made ready five Lancasters, loading two with a cookie and three with a 2,000 pounder, all supplemented by SBCs of 30lb incendiaries. They departed Swinderby between 20.04 and 20.14 with S/L Everitt the senior pilot on duty, but lost the services of P/O Wyness and crew to an electrical fault within minutes of taking off. The others pressed on across France into southern Germany, where they were greeted by clear skies and good visibility, which enabled them to identify the lakes to the south-west of the city. Most crews adopted a time-and-distance run from Lake Constance to bring them to the aiming-point, which had been well-illuminated by Pathfinder flares. Three of the Swinderby crews bombed from 9,000 feet and one from a thousand feet higher, although Sgt Howie couldn't release the cookie because of a faulty plug. Bomb bursts were observed in the city centre, along with a large explosion to the north and numerous fires, including a large one to the south-west. Saarbrücken was reported to be well-alight by crews passing by on the way home. Bombing photos revealed that the main weight of the attack had fallen into western, southern and eastern suburbs of Munich, but there was no confirmation from local reports. Saarbrücken had largely escaped damage after the bombing became widely scattered.

F/O "Mick" Martin was posted to the squadron's Conversion Flight at the end of his tour on the 20th, his navigator, P/O Jack Leggo having departed a few days earlier for 92 Group. Other future Dambusters, navigator, P/O Hobday, and bomb-aimer, P/O Edward Johnson, were posted out to 1654 Conversion unit on the 23rd, the day on which the squadron was notified that it would be operating that night against the Baltic coastal town of Wismar and the nearby Dornier aircraft factory, as part of an all-5 Group affair involving eighty-three Lancasters. 50 Squadron made ready eleven of its own, loading them with 1,000 pounders and a mixture of 4lb and 30lb incendiaries, before sending them off between 22.45 and 23.06 with S/Ls Everitt and Moore the senior pilots on duty. Two-thirds of the force were assigned to the town, situated some thirty miles east of Lübeck and a third to the factory, the 50 Squadron crews allotted eight and three respectively. S/L Moore lost an exhaust muff over the North Sea and had to turn back, leaving ten to press on and run into a violent electrical storm when around a hundred miles short of Denmark's western coast. This caused many to turn back, and added to a total of twenty-one early returns from all causes. Those reaching the target found ten-tenths cloud with tops at 8,000 feet and a base at 800 feet, with intense and accurate searchlight and flak activity awaiting any brave enough to venture so low. Three Swinderby aircraft sustained flak damage, including that of Sgt Crampton and crew, who lost the use of their rear turret and jettisoned their load. P/O Wiseman and crew were unable to identify the target and brought their bombs home, leaving six 50 Squadron crews to bomb from between 1,200 and 3,000 feet without observing any results. F/L Wilkins and crew pinpointed on Samso Island off the Baltic coast of Jutland, before arriving at the target to be ensnared by searchlights and having to take evasive action. A slightly confusing account from this crew suggested that they bombed the harbour at Århus on the Jutland coast from 11,000 feet on the way home, and observed a large explosion. Returning crews reported fires in the town and at the Dornier factory, while local reports listed thirty-two houses and eight industrial buildings seriously damaged. Four Lancasters failed to return, and among them was R5909, which exploded and crashed into the sea off Lolland Island in southern Denmark, killing the crew of F/Sgt Dickenson, four of whom were members of the RAAF.

The squadron did not take part in the 5 Group's mining operations on the nights of the 24/25th and 29/30th, and completed the month with a record of participating in twelve operations, during which, 127 sorties had been dispatched for the loss of three Lancasters and two crews.

October 1942

5 Group's October account opened on the 1st with news of a return to Wismar that night, for which a force of seventy-eight Lancasters was prepared, ten of them at Swinderby. The plan called for three-quarters of the force, including seven of the 50 Squadron element, to attack the town and the remainder the Dornier aircraft factory. They took off between 18.24 and 18.34 with S/L Everitt leading the way and Sgt "Les" Knight RAAF and his crew operating for the first time, and all reached the target area to encounter three to ten-tenths cloud with a base at between 1,500 and 7,000 feet, and poor visibility over the town caused by heavy ground haze. Brief glimpses of the coastline provided a scant reference by which to establish position, and bombing runs on the town were carried out largely on DR with bomb release on e.t.a. The attacks were carried out from between 5,000 and a more conservative 9,000 feet in

the face of an intense flak barrage, some crews gaining a glimpse of a built up area, and P/O Wiseman and crew searching for twenty minutes, during which they passed through the heaviest flak twice. Sgt Howie and crew actually found the visibility to be reasonable, and even spotted a decoy fire some two to three miles north of the town. Of those seeking out the Dornier factory, only the newly promoted F/L Abercromby and crew claimed to identify it, and they bombed from 7,000 feet, observing bursts among buildings followed by two fires emitting large volumes of smoke. Returning crews reported a few large fires, and some viewed their sorties as successful, while others were less confident in the effectiveness of their work, and three admitted that they had probably bombed Rostock, thirty miles to the east, in error.

The Ruhr town of Krefeld was posted as the target for a force of 188 aircraft on the 2nd, 5 Group contributing twenty-four Lancasters from Waddington, Coningsby and Syerston, while the rest of the group stood down. Dense industrial haze thwarted the Pathfinders' best efforts, and the attack failed to produce damage commensurate with the size of the force. P/O Dampier-Crossley RAAF, who was actually a Kiwi, was posted to 61 Squadron's Conversion Flight on the 4th, to lend his experience to the training of new crews arriving from training establishments. He would return to the operational scene with 619 Squadron in the rank of flight lieutenant, and he and his crew are remembered by W/C John Bell, who was bomb-aimer to Bob Knights at 619 Squadron, and, later, at 617 Squadron. Knights undertook his first two sorties as second pilot to Dampier-Crossley, who imparted to him many valuable tips, which helped to see him and his crew survive the war. Sadly, the Dampier-Crossley crew failed to return from Nuremberg on the 10th of August 1943, and all lost their lives. In memory of them, the Knights crew adopted Dampier-Crossley's nose-art on their Lancaster, a depiction of the rabbit, Thumper.

The Swinderby crews remained operationally inactive until being alerted on the 5th to an operation that night against the city of Aachen. A force of 257 aircraft was put together, of which sixty-nine Lancasters were provided by 5 Group, ten of them at Swinderby, and they took off between 19.13 and 19.46 with S/Ls Everitt and Moore the senior pilots on duty. While negotiating thunderstorms over the Channel on the way out, S/L Everitt's R5733 was struck by lightning, which knocked out the intercom. They elected to press on, and ran into searchlights and heavy cloud at the French coast, which forced them to descend from 12,000 to 4,000 feet for the rest of the journey. On arrival in the target area, flares were visible, but up to nine-tenths cloud and poor visibility created challenging conditions, and S/L Everitt was preparing to deliver his cookie and incendiaries on e.t.a., when a flak shell exploded beneath the starboard wing and punctured a fuel tank. The bombs were dropped, and a course set for home, and, on reaching the Belgian coast, it became necessary to feather both starboard engines. The navigator guided the Lancaster to West Malling, which they found under a 700-foot cloud base with only forty-five minutes fuel remaining and the flare-path not visible. Further time was wasted requesting floodlights and gooseneck flares to be lit, and, after twice overshooting, it was decided to carry out a belly-landing, which was accomplished expertly with no crew casualties and little damage to the Lancaster. Meanwhile, the remaining Swinderby crews had experience extreme difficulty in establishing their positions, and observed Pathfinder flares falling on the Dutch side of the frontier. Loads were delivered blindly and mostly missed the target, although black smoke was seen to be rising through 4,000 feet as they turned away and local sources would report that the southern district of Burtscheid had suffered quite extensive damage to housing and industry, and five large fires had required attention. Even so, they estimated the attack to have involved only around ten aircraft. Some bombs fell seventeen miles away onto the small Dutch town of Lutterade, and this would have consequences for the trials of the Oboe blind-bombing device in late December.

Osnabrück was posted as the target on the 6th, for which 237 aircraft were made ready, including fifty-nine Lancasters of 5 Group. 50 Squadron loaded nine of its aircraft with a cookie each and twelve SBCs of either 30lb or 4lb incendiaries, and dispatched them between 19.25 and 19.58 with S/L Moore the senior pilot on duty. The Pathfinders dropped flares over Makkum in Holland and the Dümmer See to the north-east of the target as route markers, and these proved to be very effective in guiding the main force in, although, inevitably, some bomb loads were released early during the twenty-mile leg between the Dümmer See and the town. Four to eight-tenths cloud lay over the town at 8,000 feet, and provided challenging conditions for accurate bombing, although opinions varied as to the quality of the visibility. The current 50 Squadron scribe was not given to providing bombing heights, but other squadrons carried out their attacks from between 11,000 and 16,500 feet, and much of the effort fell into the central and southern districts. Returning crew described many fires and a glow visible by some from the Dutch coast homebound, and were confident in the effectiveness of the raid. According to local reports, 149 houses and six industrial buildings were destroyed, 530 houses seriously damaged and more than 2,700 others slightly damaged.

The following week was devoted exclusively to mining operations, until 5 Group launched another shot at Wismar with fifty-nine Lancasters on the night of the 12/13th. 50 Squadron made ready eleven Lancasters, with seven crews briefed to attack the town and four the Dornier aircraft factory. They departed Swinderby between 17.53 and 18.07 with S/L Everitt the senior pilot on duty, but lost the services of Sgt Howie and crew after an hour because of rear turret failure. The others continued on to find difficult weather conditions over the sea, that prevented many from establishing a pinpoint on the enemy coast and forced them to navigate by DR. F/L Abercromby and crew arrived at the target five minutes ahead of e.t.a., and, somehow, pinpointed on a road that confirmed their position on the western side of the bay, from where they ran in and delivered their load. The town lay under six to ten-tenths cloud in a band between 1,000 and 7,000 feet, and the lack of pinpoints forced some crews to search for up to thirty minutes before bombing on estimated positions. This inevitably led to a scattered and probably ineffective attack, and Sgt Knight and crew reported bombing in the Lübeck area after a fruitless search for the primary target. Despite the challenges, the squadron ORB reported that the factory had been left burning furiously and the flames had remained visible for seventy miles into the homeward journey. R5902 failed to return to Swinderby with the freshman crew of Sgt Rawlins, the navigator surviving in enemy hands, while only the remains of the pilot and one other were recovered for burial.

On the 13th, the naval port of Kiel was posted as the target for a force of 288 aircraft, of which sixty-nine Lancasters represented 5 Group, nine of them made ready by 50 Squadron at Swinderby. They were loaded with a cookie and SBCs of 4lb and 30lb incendiaries, and dispatched between 18.37 and 19.03 with S/L Moore the senior pilot on duty. They all reached the target area to find almost clear skies and good visibility, and red and white flares marking out the Selenter Lake some ten miles to the east. Illuminator flares were also deployed over the town, revealing a built-up area, which the Swinderby crews bombed after pinpointing on the docks and railway installations. Few observed the results of their efforts, but bomb bursts and fires were evident, and the impression was of a successful operation. Local sources reported that around half of the crews had been deceived by a decoy fire site, but the rest had hit the town and caused an appropriate amount of damage.

P/O Wiseman was posted to 14 O.T.U on the 14th, and he would eventually graduate to become a member of 5 Group's Master Bomber fraternity after it gained independence in 1944. A force of 289 aircraft was assembled on the 15th to send against Cologne, which had been left in peace for a considerable time, and the operation was supported by sixty-two Lancasters of 5 Group, although none representing 50 Squadron. Inaccurately forecast winds and a large, effective decoy fire site combined to attract the main force away from the target, and damage within the city was slight and superficial.

On the 17th, the squadron began the process of returning to Skellingthorpe, where it would remain for the rest of the war, while, in 5 Group's briefing rooms, crews learned of the purpose behind the formation-flying training flights that had involved them since the start of the month. Operation Robinson was a daylight attack on the Schneider armaments works at Le Creusot, deep in eastern France, and the nearby Montchanin transformer station, which provided its power. Often referred to as the French "Krupp", the company belonged to the Schneider family, which had donated the famous aviation trophy bearing its name. The Schneider Trophy was initially a prize to encourage technical advances in civil aviation, but, eventually, became a speed contest for float and seaplanes competed for biannually by Britain, France, Italy and the USA. It was a massively prestigious and popular spectator event that drew crowds of 200,000 people. Britain claimed it outright after three consecutive wins culminating in 1931, when the revolutionary Supermarine S6B triumphed. Ninety-four Lancasters were to take part in the operation, which required an outward flight at low level by daylight, the attack at dusk, and a return under the cover of darkness. It was a bold plan to commit such a large force, which would be difficult to conceal, and it was only six months since six 44 Squadron Lancasters had been caught by German fighters over France while on their way to Augsburg, and four had been shot down in a matter of minutes.

The plan called for eighty-eight aircraft to bomb the factory complex from as low as practicable, led by W/C Len Slee of 49 Squadron, while six others, two each from 106, 61 and 97 Squadrons, led by W/C Gibson, went for the power station in a line-astern attack. The 50 Squadron contribution amounted to twelve Lancasters, which departed Swinderby in anger for the last time between 11.56 and 12.07 with S/Ls Everitt and Moore the senior pilots on duty. They would join up with the rest of the force over Upper Heyford, before heading for Land's End at under 1,000 feet, and, once over the sea, aim for a point just south of the Ile d'Yeu to cross the French coast midway between St Nazaire and La Rochelle at around 100 feet. Shortly before the sea crossing began, Coastal Command Whitleys had carried out a sweep to force enemy U-Boots beneath the surface and prevent them from spotting the force and transmitting a warning. For most, the three-hundred-mile low-level dash across France would be relatively uneventful, but bird strikes became a constant threat, causing injury to a number of crewmen as they smashed Perspex, while others became ingested in engines. F/L Wilkins complained that the lead section was too low, which placed upon him an exhausting physical strain as he wrestled with slipstream turbulence, and others commented on bunching-up and occasional congestion, despite which, this middle leg terminated successfully at the predetermined point some forty-five miles from the target. It was at this juncture that the main force broke up to form into a fan and climb to a bombing height of between 5,000 and 7,000 feet. The target was reached at dusk under clear skies and in good visibility, and crews were able to follow a railway line directly to the heart of the factory complex and bomb as briefed between around 18.10 and 18.30. Not all were able to plot the fall of their bombs, but Sgt Knight observed his four 1,000 pounders and incendiaries hit a rolling-mill, and others would report strikes on the buildings or at least straddling them. F/Sgt Taylor and crew had the misfortune to lose their hydraulics system at the start of the bombing run, and the bomb doors refused to open. They continued on over the aiming-point in the vain hope that they could jettison them, but it was not to be, and they had to bring them home. All returned safely home after a round-trip of ten hours, and reported what they believed to be a highly successful operation, which had cost just a single 61 Squadron Lancaster from the Montchanin element. It was discovered later that the damage had been less severe than first thought, and production was soon back to normal. Another raid would be mounted eight months hence.

The 20th brought a number of significant postings in and out, beginning with the arrival from 1654 Conversion Unit of W/C Russell to succeed W/C Oxley, who went to command 1660 Conversion Unit after a year at the helm of 50 Squadron. It will be recalled, that the then F/O Russell had been a mainstay of the squadron in 1940 and 1941, completing a first tour of operations before being screened. The Australian, F/O Bob Hay, was posted to 5 Group HQ on this day, and, in March of the following year, would find himself appointed Bombing Leader of the newly forming 617 Squadron at Scampton, and a member of the crew of F/L "Mickey" Martin. Other future Dambusters arriving during the month to begin their operational careers were flight engineer, Sgt Ray Grayston and wireless operator, Sgt Alden Cottam.

W/C Russell took up his appointment in time for him to preside over the squadron's involvement in a campaign against Italian cities, in support of land operations in North Africa under Operation Torch. The first of the series would be mounted on the night of the 22/23rd against the city of Genoa and the naval dockyard, where part of the Italian fleet was sheltering. It was the eve of the opening of the Battle of Alamein, which, after twelve days' fighting, would see Montgomery push Rommel's forces all the way back to Tunisia and out of the war. Ten 5 Group squadrons mustered between them 101 Lancasters, eleven of them made ready in the familiar surroundings of an upgraded Skellingthorpe, while 83 Squadron of the Pathfinders contributed eleven more to take care of target marking. The 50 Squadron element took off between 17.15 and 17.35 with S/Ls Everitt and Moore the senior pilots on duty, and each carrying two 1,000 pounders and six SBCs of incendiaries. Sgt Cumberland and crew were passing some fifty miles to the south-west of Paris when the port-outer engine cut at 19.45, and soon burst into flames, leaving them with no option but to jettison a small part of their load and return safely on three engines. The others pushed on across France to traverse the Alps under clear skies and an almost full moon, and the clear air and perfect visibility over Italy was a joy to behold after contending with the industrial haze at German targets. The Pathfinder flares could be seen by approaching main force crews from sixty miles away, and, on arriving over the city, they found the flak defence to be wildly inaccurate, and a smoke screen proved ineffective as the wind blew it straight out to sea. The 50 Squadron crews were able to establish their positions visually on the layout of the docks and the city, and carried out their attacks, based on the bombing heights of other squadrons, from between 9,000 and 17,000 feet either side of 22.00. Most were able to observe the fall of their bombs, which post-raid reconnaissance confirmed had fallen predominantly into central and eastern districts, causing extensive damage to the city and to the morale of its civilian population. It was a highly successful demonstration of what could be achieved by a relatively small force with just 180 tons of bombs, and it had been loss-free.

Twenty-four hours later, a force made up of elements of 3 and 4 Groups and the Pathfinders attempted to follow up at Genoa, but, in cloudy conditions, attacked in error the town of Savona, thirty miles to the west. Eighty-eight 5 Group crews attended briefings on the morning of the 24th to learn that they would be undertaking the first daylight crossing of the Alps to attack the city of Milan. This would require an even longer flight over fighter-defended territory than the Le Creusot operation a week earlier, but it was forecast, that cloud would protect them for most of the way. Nine 50 Squadron Lancasters took off between 12.20 and 12.35 with S/Ls Everitt and Moore the senior pilots on duty, and headed for Selsey Bill, from where they would cross the Channel at very low level with the rest of the loose formation under a Spitfire escort. They had been briefed to expect the cloud of a warm front awaiting them at the Normandy coast, however, to their discomfort, they saw that it had formed further inland, and they had to run the gauntlet of anti-aircraft fire as they raced over the clifftops with three hours to go to the Alps. A bank of cloud could be seen in the distance, to which the force climbed as rapidly as possible, and, once reached, the crews had to plot their own individual course until rendezvousing over Lake Annecy, sixty miles short of the target. From there they formed a loose formation and lost height, until reaching the target to find eight to nine-tenths cloud with a base at 3,000 feet, but sufficient gaps through which to establish their positions visually. The marshalling yards, a seaplane base and an aerodrome were among ground features identified as the Skellingthorpe crews delivered their payloads from a variety of heights from around 17.00. Some squadrons had loaded their Lancasters with a cookie, which required a minimum of 4,000 feet of clearance, despite which, a few crews, including that of F/O Calvert, dived down to a few hundred feet to strafe factories and other targets of opportunity. The Calvert crew shot up a locomotive and two factories to the west of the target, and would regard their sortie as a complete success.

F/L Abercromby and crew broke cloud for the bombing run and followed a railway line, descending all the time to low level to avoid the flak. They were hit by machine-gun fire from the rooftops, which severely wounded the rear gunner and put the mid-upper turret out of action. The bombs were dropped onto a factory or warehouse and seen to penetrate the roof, while the rear gunner was removed and his turret repaired by the mid-upper gunner, who then occupied it. He and the wireless operator in the front turret shot up two trains on the way home, while the flight engineer tended to the rear gunner and calculated the maximum at which the engines could be run to get him home for treatment as quickly as possible. The sun was setting ahead of them as they crossed the Alps homebound, and France passed beneath them unseen in darkness, with enemy night-fighters waiting over the coastal region as the returning bombers passed through. Three Lancasters failed to return, all after being shot down into the Channel, and this was the fate of 50 Squadron's R5691, containing the crew of Sgt Cumberland RAAF, whose time with the squadron had been brief and none of whom survived. After F/L Abercromby landed the badly damaged W4135 at Boscombe Down, F/Sgt MacDonald demonstrated great courage by assisting himself from the aircraft, before being transported to Salisbury Hospital, where he succumbed to his wounds on the following day. Post-raid reconnaissance revealed that the 135 tons of bombs had caused extensive damage to housing, public buildings and a number of war-industry factories, including the Caproni aircraft works, and had also seriously affected railway communications between Italy and

Germany. Local reports confirmed a figure of 441 houses destroyed or seriously damaged along with nine public buildings.

Mining operations would occupy the remainder of the month for most squadrons after a 1 and 3 Group follow-up at Milan on the night of the 24/25th failed to create much impact. During the course of the month, the squadron took part in eight operations, and dispatched eighty-one sorties for the loss of two Lancasters and crews and a rear gunner.

November 1942

The squadron's first operation in the new month would not be posted until the 6th, when Genoa was to be the target, and, in the meantime, P/O Cole was posted to 1654 Conversion Unit on the 4th at the conclusion of his tour. Fifty-seven Lancasters of 5 Group and fifteen belonging to 83 Squadron of the Pathfinders were detailed for the next round of the Italian campaign, and five Lancasters presented themselves for take-off at Skellingthorpe, becoming airborne between 21.27 and 21.45 with W/C Russell and S/L Moore the senior pilots on duty, the former, in contrast to his predecessor, demonstrating a style of leading from the front. They all reached the target after an uneventful outward flight of four hours in favourable weather conditions, and the excellent visibility enabled them to locate the aiming-point visually after identifying ground features like the breakwater, harbour and town. S/L Moore and crew arrived some six minutes early, and, having obtained their bearings, stooged around off the coast while the Pathfinder element illuminated the area. The Squadron's all-incendiary bomb loads went down accurately, adding to the many fires breaking out, and, by the time that F/O Wyness arrived late after a delayed departure, a colossal fire was burning on a hill near the city centre, and the effectiveness of the attack was laid out before them. One Lancaster was seen to be shot down over the target, and this would have been one of two missing aircraft from 83 Squadron.

On the 7th, acting F/L Wilkins was posted to N°1 A.A.S at Manby after completing his tour of operations. A follow-up raid on Genoa was called for that night, and a force of 175 aircraft made ready, which involved Halifaxes, Stirlings and a handful of Wellingtons to join eighty-one Lancasters of 5 Group. The twelve Lancasters of 50 Squadron took off between 17.36 and 17.57 with W/C Russell and S/L Moore the senior pilots on duty, and experienced the same ideal conditions as on the previous night, particularly on the far side of the Alps. They were able to make a visual identification of the aiming-point, and W/C Russell and F/L Abercromby praised the performance of the Pathfinders for arriving bang on time and effectively illuminating the target. A smoke screen failed to shield the city, and the flak defence seemed to give up once the bombing began, although light flak from rooftops continued to fire, even if inaccurately. S/L Moore's R5687 was damaged, and lost an engine on the way home, and, with another displaying signs of stress, the Lancaster was nursed home to a safe landing. Returning crew reported bombs exploding in the built-up area causing numerous fires, and many brought home an aiming-point photograph to add to those from reconnaissance flights, which confirmed the operation to have been highly successful.

Future Dambuster, P/O Ken Earnshaw RCAF, arrived from 9 Squadron's Conversion Flight on the 9th, the day on which, in a break from Italy, Hamburg was posted as the target. No mention was made by the "met boys" during briefing of strong winds and ice-bearing cloud of the type that often lay in wait across the bombers' path to Germany's Second City. 213

aircraft were made ready, of which sixty-seven Lancasters were provided by 5 Group, eight of them at Skellingthorpe, where they were loaded with a cookie and twelve SBCs containing ninety 4lb incendiaries. They took off between 18.02 and 18.29 with S/L Everitt the senior pilot on duty, but lost the services of Sgt Knight and crew at the first turning point after they experienced a problem with the starboard-outer engine. This would have been as they were about to enter the troublesome cumulo-nimbus cloud over the North Sea, which the others negotiated successfully to reach the target area. However, on arrival they found it to be completely hidden by ten-tenths cloud, which forced them to bomb on e.t.a in the absence of Pathfinder flares, but in the presence of heavy flak, particularly from naval guns, the shells from which were detonating above the bombing height. It was impossible to assess what was happening beneath the cloud, but, a strong wind from the north almost certainly pushed the bombing south of the intended aiming-point, and this seemed to be confirmed by local reports, that many bombs had fallen into the River Elbe or into open country, and only three large fires had required attention. Fifteen aircraft failed to return, five of them belonging to 5 Group, and among these was the squadron's W4194, which crashed somewhere on the Schleswig-Holstein peninsular, north of the target, without survivors from the crew of Sgt Jones. It was a bad night generally for 5 Group, which also registered nine early returns.

Mine-laying would occupy the ensuing two nights, and 5 Group detailed a dozen Lancasters on the 10th to send that night to the Biscay coast, 50 Squadron's Sgts Dennis and Knight taking off at 17.30 and 17.38 bound for the Elderberry and Furze gardens respectively, located off Bayonne and a dozen miles further south at St-Jean-de-Luz, right down on the border between France and Spain. Sgt Dennis and crew were more than two hours out when the starboard-inner engine failed and persuaded them to turn back and return their vegetables to store. Sgt Knight and crew flew out at 5,000 feet, until about fifteen minutes from the target, when they broke through the ten-tenths cloud base at 2,500 feet to establish a pinpoint on the coastline. The mines were dropped into the briefed location and a safe return completed after more than seven hours aloft.

The Italian campaigned continued at Genoa on the 13th, with a relatively small-scale operation by sixty-one 5 Group Lancasters acting as the main force, supported by a Pathfinder element comprising six Lancasters of 83 Squadron and nine Stirlings of 7 Squadron. Nineteen of the 5 Group element were to attack the Ansaldo engineering works, which could be viewed as the Italian "Krupp", while the remainder had their own aiming-point in the town. 50 Squadron made ready seven Lancasters, which departed Skellingthorpe between 18.15 and 18.27 with W/C Russell the senior pilot on duty, three carrying all-incendiary loads and the others either a cookie or two 1,000 pounders plus incendiaries. Sgt Heinrich and crew turned back when over the Channel, after the intercom to the mid-upper turret failed and a hydraulics pipe burst in the rear turret. The remainder pushed on across France to cross the Alps in good weather conditions that allowed the target to be identified visually from cloudless skies. The bombing was carried out in the face of a "beefed-up" searchlight and flak defence, and high explosive and incendiary bursts were observed across the target area. Those plotted were found to be at least a thousand yards from the aiming-point, but there was no attempt to assess the outcome through reconnaissance. Some returning crews reported the glow of fires to be visible for 130 miles into the return flight, and confidence was high that the loss-free raid had been successful.

Two days later a force of seventy-eight aircraft was made ready to continue the assault on Genoa, and twenty-one of twenty-seven Lancasters were provided by 5 Group. 50 Squadron contributed just three crews led by S/L Moore. They took off between 18.02 and 18.15, to enjoy an uneventful outward flight across France, and the ten-tenths cloud to the south of the Alps stopped just short of the target to provide clear skies and moonlight. The Pathfinders performed well to illuminate the aiming-point, allowing it to be identified visually, and the Skellingthorpe trio delivered their attacks largely untroubled by the defences, observing six large fires in the built-up area, that were still visible from up to a hundred miles into the return journey.

Sgts Kitching and Dennis took off at 17.05 and 17.14 respectively on the 16th as part of 5 Group's small contribution to mining operations from the Baltic to the Biscay coast. Both were assigned to the Geranium garden off the distant Baltic port of Swinemünde, but turned back early after the former's navigator reported to be too ill to continue and the latter's compass failed. On the following day, Sgt Kitching and crew took R5753 on a training sortie, and crashed while landing at Skellingthorpe, emerging unscathed from the wreckage before it was consumed by fire. S/L Birch was posted in from 1660 Conversion Unit on the 14th to succeed the tour expired S/L Everitt as a flight commanded on the latter's posting in the opposite direction. Arriving at the same time from the same source for his second tour with the squadron was the larger-than-life P/O Richard Algernon Dacre Trevor-Roper, who would find himself occupying S/L Birch's rear turret.

Attention shifted from Genoa to Turin on the 18th, when a force of seventy-seven aircraft was made ready to attack the Fiat motor works. The force had originally been significantly larger, but forty-two 5 Group Lancasters were withdrawn because of doubts about the weather over their stations, and the 50 Squadron element was among these. This left twenty-five to represent the group, and they arrived at the target some three-and-at-half hours later to find clear skies that left the city naked to the eyes of the bomb-aimers, who were able to ensure that the aiming-point was squarely in their bomb-sights as they ran in. Many fires broke out in the city centre, and the Fiat works sustained an unspecified degree of damage, which was confirmed by bombing photos.

Following the recent run of relatively small-scale operations to Italy, the 20th brought a return to Turin with greater numbers, amounting this time to 232 aircraft, of which seventy-eight Lancasters were provided by 5 Group. 50 Squadron made ready seven of its own, and dispatched them between 18.26 and 18.35 with S/L Birch the senior pilot on duty for the first time. It would take almost four hours to reach the target, but, in the meantime, S/L Birch and crew were soon back home with engine trouble and an intact bomb load, and they were followed in twenty minutes later by Sgt Dennis and crew, also with an engine issue. By the time that the Skellingthorpe crews arrived over the city, smoke was already drifting across it, and ground features appeared fleetingly, creating challenging conditions for target identification. Ground haze added to the difficulties, but, even so, by running in at low to medium level, some crews were able to identify the factory visually, and deliver the bombs with some degree of accuracy. The 50 Squadron quintet attacked from 7,000 to 12,000 feet, aiming for the town, and contributed to massive fires raging in the city centre. F/L Abercromby reported smoke rising through 6,000 feet as he turned away, and this would continue to climb considerably higher over the ensuing hours.

Sixty-four 5 Group crews attended briefings on the 22nd, to learn that their destination that night was to be Stuttgart as part of an overall force of 222 aircraft. 50 Squadron made ready nine Lancasters, which departed Skellingthorpe between 18.35 and 19.00 with S/L Birch the senior pilot on duty. Seven were carrying all-incendiary loads and two had a cookie on board supplemented by 4lb incendiaries, but Sgt Kitching and crew turned back early on with intercom and oxygen supply issues, and they were followed home much later by F/O Wyness and crew, who had taken off in a spare aircraft with an existing failed intercom connection to the front turret. They could live with this, but when the DR and P4 compasses were found to be fifteen degrees off and the mid-upper turret became unserviceable, it was time to call it a day. Three hours and fifteen minutes after take-off, the others had Pathfinder flares in their sights, and F/L Abercromby, when still ten miles away, counted eighteen fires already burning. The flares illuminated the target area to enable a visual identification of the aiming-point, and the marshalling yards, a station and the River Po stood out clearly as the crews began their bombing runs. The 50 Squadron crews dropped their bombs from 6,600 to 10,500 feet, and observed bursts, before returning safely from what most described as a quiet trip with a satisfactory result. F/L Abercromby and crew reported shooting up trains on the way home over France, and some crews witnessed three bombers being shot down during the outward journey. A post-raid analysis revealed that a thin layer of cloud and ground haze had prevented the Pathfinders from identifying the centre of the city, and much of the bombing had fallen onto south-western and southern districts and outlying communities up to five miles from the centre, something which F/O Goldsmith and crew had spotted. Local reports confirmed that a modest eighty-eight houses had been destroyed, and described two bombers attacking the city centre at low level and causing extensive damage to the main railway station.

Skellingthorpe was not involved in gardening operations on the night of the 23/24th, and the madness of "moling" on the 25th, and it was not until the 28th that orders came through to prepare its crews for operations that night. The target was Turin, and, during the course of the day, a force of 228 aircraft was made ready, ninety-one of the Lancasters on 5 Group stations. 50 Squadron loaded four aircraft with a cookie each and two with incendiaries, and launched them from Skellingthorpe between 19.00 and 19.10 with W/C Russell the senior pilot on duty. All reached the target area to find clear skies and a little ground haze, and were able to establish their positions by visual reference of the River Po assisted by Pathfinder flares. W/C Russell ran down the river from north to south, before performing a right-hand turn to bring him over the centre of the city, where he identified the racetrack. The bombs were delivered into the middle of the built-up area, but their detonation was not observed. F/L Atkinson and crew made three runs across the target trying to persuade their cookie to release, and the bomb-aimer managed to get rid of it manually on the fourth run. F/O Wyness counted thirty-five fires, but could not attribute any specifically to his incendiaries, while Sgt Heinrich confirmed that the city was a mass of flames as he bombed from 7,000 feet, and commented on a particularly large blaze in the city centre. W/C Gibson and F/L Whamond of 106 Squadron dropped the first two 8,000 pounders to fall on Italy, and all indications were that the operation had been entirely successful.

During the course of the month the squadron carried out ten operations, and dispatched sixty-one sorties for the loss of two Lancasters and one crew.

The weather at the start of the new month restricted operations, and an unsuccessful raid on Frankfurt involving 112 aircraft on the 2nd did not include a contribution from 5 Group. Squadrons were warned of operations daily between the 2nd and 5th, but each was cancelled, and it was the 6th before an operation was posted at Skellingthorpe that would actually go ahead. 50 Squadron made ready ten Lancasters, while six of their crews were informed at briefing that Mannheim was to be their target in company with sixty-eight other Lancasters of 5 Group in an overall force of 272 aircraft. Four others were briefed for gardening duties in the Nectarines area off the Frisians, and they took off first between 17.23 and 17.40, followed immediately by those involved in the main event, and all were safely airborne by 17.51 with no senior pilots on duty. Sgt Dennis and crew were an hour out bound for Mannheim, when the mid-upper gunner collapsed, and a lack of oxygen was found not to be the cause. A reduction in altitude to 5,000 feet also failed to revive him, and the sortie was abandoned. The gardeners found three to six-tenths cloud with a base at 1,000 feet, and carried out their runs from Schiermonnikoog to deliver their vegetables into the briefed locations. The remaining five crews in the Mannheim element reached the target, where they encountered eight to ten-tenths cloud between 4,000 and 12,000 feet, which rendered ineffective the Pathfinders' efforts to mark the city with flares. A decoy site was also operating some twenty miles to the south, and this, inevitably, attracted a proportion of the bombing. The Skellingthorpe crews could only bomb blindly on DR through the cloud, and did so from between 8,000 and 11,000 feet, observing bursts and fires, but nothing of use to the intelligence section.

On the following night, 5 Group called for nine crews to carry out gardening duties in the Elderberry and Furze gardens off the south-western coast of France. 50 Squadron was asked to provide one crew for each, and, always eager to get at the enemy, W/C Russell put himself up for the job and invited S/L Birch and crew to be the other. They took off at 16.53 and 17.00 respectively, but S/L Birch experienced a series of communications issues and turned back. W/C Russell and crew pressed on to find up to three-tenths cloud and good visibility in the target area off Bayonne, and lights from the notoriously poor blackout at Biarritz to provide a solid reference. Lights were blazing in Spain, and a steel works at Bilboa appeared to be in full production. The vegetables were delivered as briefed from 900 feet, and the parachutes were seento open, after which they had to contend with poor weather to get home.

Notification was received on 5 Group stations on the 8th that Turin was to be the target for that night, in an operation to be conducted by a 5 Group main force of ninety-eight Lancasters, supported by thirty-five Pathfinder aircraft of all types. The Skellingthorpe element of ten took off between 17.42 and 18.05 with S/L Birch the senior pilot on duty, eight of the bomb bays containing an all-incendiary load and two a cookie and incendiaries. Sgt Yates and crew must have been outbound for almost three hours when intercom failure forced them to turn back and jettison their incendiaries. The others reached the target area to find clear skies and good visibility, and the city visible to the south as they approached the final turning point. Swinging towards the start of their bombing run, over to port to the east of the city, a large bend in the River Po provided a strong reference, which enabled the Pathfinders to identify the aiming point and deliver their flares right on the mark. The 50 Squadron crews followed in their wake, and Sgt Dennis and crew described the aiming-point as being well-defined by two arcs of Pathfinder flares, and one massive explosion a mile-and-a-half to the south-west. The bombing was carried out by the main force generally from 5,000 to 13,000 feet, but these were the extremes, and most settled for a bombing height of 6,500 to 9,500 feet, from where the city could be seen to be well-alight. F/O Wyness and crew arrived a little late when smoke was drifting across the aiming-point, and they counted thirty to forty sizeable fires burning across the city. A huge pall of smoke was rising through 8,000 feet as the force retreated towards the Alps, and the fires would still be burning when the next bomber force arrived twenty-four hours later.

Orders came through on the 9th to prepare for another assault on Turin that night, and nine crews attended the briefing at Skellingthorpe to learn that they would be part of a 5 Group effort of eighty-two Lancasters in an overall force of 227 aircraft. S/L Birch was the senior pilot on duty as they took off between 17.40 and 18.00, and enjoyed an uneventful outward flight. They were guided the final few miles to the target by the fires still burning from the previous night, but the smoke from these created challenging conditions for the Pathfinders, who failed to deliver as strong a performance this time. The raid was spread out over more than thirty minutes and bombing took place from medium level, creating many more fires and producing even larger volumes of smoke, which obscured much of the ground from those arriving at the tail end of proceedings. Returning crews reported explosions and fires, but the consensus was of a less effective raid than that of the previous night.

For the third night in succession the torment of Turin continued, although at the hands of a reduced force of eighty-two aircraft drawn from 1 and 4 Groups and the Pathfinders. They had to fight their way through severe icing conditions over France, and more than half of the force turned back before reaching the Alps. Those completing their sorties failed to inflict more than the slightest damage on the city, in what proved to be the final raid of this first Italian campaign. F/L Abercromby was posted to 1660 Conversion unit on the 10th at the conclusion of his tour, but he would return to the squadron for a second tour in mid-July 1943, this time as a flight commander. W4117 crash-landed at Skellingthorpe on return from night-flying training on the 11th, and was written off, but there were no casualties among the crew of Sgt Murray. Seven 50 Squadron freshman crews were among sixty-eight sent mining on the night of the 14/15th, and took off between 17.10 and 17.26 bound for the Nectarines garden off the Frisians in company with sixteen others from the group. The 5 Group element was recalled after about an hour, presumably because of concern over the effect of challenging weather conditions on inexperienced crews.

No further major operations would take place during what remained of the year, but 5 Group dispatched twenty-seven Lancasters to eight small German towns on the night of the 17/18th. One wonders if, in the cold light of dawn, anyone in raid planning recalled the disaster that had afflicted 57 and 214 Squadrons of 3 Group as a result of similar operations on the first night of April. Five 50 Squadron Lancasters departed Skellingthorpe at 17.00 with S/L Birch the senior pilot on duty, and set course for the town of Soltau, situated some forty miles to the east of Bremen. They flew out in moonlight, until cloud slid across the sky and map-reading became impossible. Sgt Knight and crew bombed from 2,000 feet on DR without making a positive identification, and observed bursts in the built-up area and two fires. F/O Davies and crew managed to avoid the cloud, but complained later that that had been an advantage for the searchlight and flak crews, who followed their progress in the bright moonlight. Constant evasive action brought them to a point to the west of Hannover, where, what they believed to be the town of Wunstorf, was bombed from 1,600 feet. S/L Birch followed the Nienburg to Soltau road, and bombed from 1,500 feet, observing bursts across the marshalling yards, which set fire to an adjacent large building and produced a sizeable blue explosion five minutes later. They crossed paths with a night-fighter on the way home, but arrived safely to report, what for them, was a successful night's work. Nine Lancasters failed to return, and two of them were conspicuous by their absence from Skellingthorpe. W4266 was hit by flak and then finished off by the night-fighter of Oblt Herbert Lütje of III./NJG1, and crashed at 21.10 some two miles north-east of Zwolle in Holland. The experienced F/O Goldsmith DFC lost his life along with three members of his crew, and the three survivors were taken into captivity. W4382 was lost without trace with the equally experienced crew of F/L Atkinson DFM, which included four members of the RAAF. While this carnage was in progress, sixteen Stirlings and six Wellingtons of 3 Group targeted the Opel works at Fallersleben, a little further east. Six Stirlings and two Wellingtons failed to return from this operation, thus making a total of seventeen aircraft and crews sacrificed for little or no return.

Apart from isolated "moling" daylight operations, the Ruhr had been left in peace since Krefeld at the start of October, while attention had been focussed on Italian targets. Now, on the 20th, Duisburg was posted as the target, and would mask another operation of great significance for the Command that was taking place at the same time over Holland. Although, in the event, not all would proceed according to plan, it would be a mere blip in the development of the Oboe blind-bombing device. A force of 232 aircraft was assembled for the main event, of which seventy-five were Lancasters of 5 Group, while 50 Squadron remained at home. Favourable weather conditions and bright moonlight afforded good visibility with slight ground haze, through which the River Rhine and the Ruhrort docks stood out to provide a visual reference. Bombing was carried out from around 14,000 to 16,000 feet either side of 20.00, and at least fifteen fires were observed, many of them large. Meanwhile, six 109 Squadron Oboe-equipped Mosquitos had targeted a power station at Lutterade in Holland, in a test to gauge the device's margin of error, believing the target to be free of bomb craters to impair the data. Unfortunately, three of the Mosquitos suffered Oboe failure, and went on to bomb Duisburg instead, leaving W/C Hal Bufton and two other crews to deliver the bombs. What they hadn't bargained for was a whole carpet of bomb craters left over from the attack on Aachen, seventeen miles away, in October, and it proved impossible to identify those aimed by Oboe. The calibration tests would continue, however, and, come the spring, Oboe would be ready to unleash with devastating results against the Ruhr.

A force of 137 aircraft was made ready on the 21st for an operation that night against Munich, deep in southern Germany. A number of 1 Group squadrons had begun to receive Lancasters during the autumn, and would contribute in small numbers, but eighty-two of the 119 of the type made available for this operation were provided by 5 Group, and some others by the Pathfinders. 50 Squadron briefed seven crews, who were in their aircraft and lined up for take-off by 17.40, and were all safely on their way by 17.57 with the recently arrived F/O Johanson the senior pilot on duty. They pushed on across France for the long trek to the target area, which they reached after a three-and-a-half-hour outward journey, only to find it concealed beneath ten-tenths cloud. The Pathfinders illuminated the Ammersee to the south-west of the city, and crews carried out a time-and-distance run from there to the aiming-point, the Skellingthorpe crews bombing from between 4,000 and 12,000 feet. There were plenty of flashes below the cloud, together with the glow of fires to convince the crews that they had found the mark, but, it is likely, that these came from a decoy site, as most bombing photos would reveal open country. Twelve aircraft failed to return, six of them belonging to 5 Group, but all from 50 Squadron came home safely.

The squadron remained away from the operational scene from then until almost the end of the month, celebrating in between the fourth wartime Christmas. On the 29th, 5 Group ordered fourteen Lancasters to mine the waters at the mouth of the Gironde River, that led to the port and U-Boot haven of Bordeaux in what was the Deodars garden. The five 50 Squadron participants departed Skellingthorpe between 01.25 and 01.48 with F/Os Calvert and Johanson the senior pilots on duty, and all arrived in the target area to find ten-tenths cloud with a base at around 1,000 feet. There were pinpoints aplenty from which to establish a position, Ile-d'Oleron, Pointe-de-la-Coubre and the lighthouse at Cordouan, from where timed-runs were carried out to the drop zones and the mines delivered into the briefed locations from below 1,000 feet.

During the course of the month, the squadron undertook nine operations, and dispatched fifty-five sorties for the loss of three Lancasters and two crews. The year had seen the Command stop the rot, and begin to emerge as an effective force under a single-minded and resolute leader. Technological development was about to bear fruit in the form of the Oboe blind bombing device, thanks to the dedicated pioneering work of W/C Hal Bufton and his crews at 109 Squadron since the summer. The device would be ready for use early in the coming year, and would be perfected by the summer, by which time, it would already have played the major role in laying bare Germany's industrial heartland.

S/L Alistair Douglas Atkinson
Sgt 'Johnny' Atkinson, 1942, alongside his Hampden

F/Sgt Welford (WO/AG) Sgt Bailey (Nav), Sgt Atkinson (Pilot), F/O Tytherleigh (AG)
Welford, Bailey and Atkinson survived the war. Tytherleigh was lost on the Dams raid.

One of the 50 Squadron Hampdens used by Atkinson

UNIT	DATES FROM	TO
No 6 E.F.T.S Sywell	16.11.40	14/1/41.
No 14 S.F.T.S Cranfield	15.1.41	16.5.41
No 25 O.T.U. Finningley	17.5.41	26.6.41
Attached Bauldeston	26.6.41.	4.7.41
No 25 O.T.U. Finningley	4.7.41	20.8.41
No 50 Sqn. Swinderby	21.8.41	22.11.41
No 50 Sqn. Skellingthorpe.	23.11.41	19.6.42
No 29 O.T.U. North Luffenham.	20.6.42	29.9.42
No 3 F.I.S. Castle Combe	30.9.42	31.10.42
No 29 O.T.U North Luffenham	1.11.42	8.11.42
No 29 O.T.U. Bruntingthorpe	9.11.42	8.12.42
92 G.I.F. Upper Heyford	9.12.42	20.3.43
No 29 O.T.U. North Luffenham	21.3.43	1.6.43
No 29 O.T.U. Bitteswell	2.6.43	

AIRCRAFT FLOWN

AIRCRAFT	ENGINE	AIRCRAFT	ENGINE	AIRCRAFT	ENGINE
D.H. 82 Tiger Moth	Gipsy Major	Boulton Paul Defiant	RR Merlin		
Airspeed Oxford	Cheetah IX				
Vickers Armstrong Wellington Ic	Pegasus XVIII				
Handley Page Hampden	Pegasus XVIII				
Avro Manchester I	Vulture R				
Avro Lancaster	Merlin XX				
Vickers Armstrong Wellington	Merlin				
Short Stirling	Hercules				
Miles Master II	Mercury				
Miles Magister	Gipsy				

Atkinson's Logbook

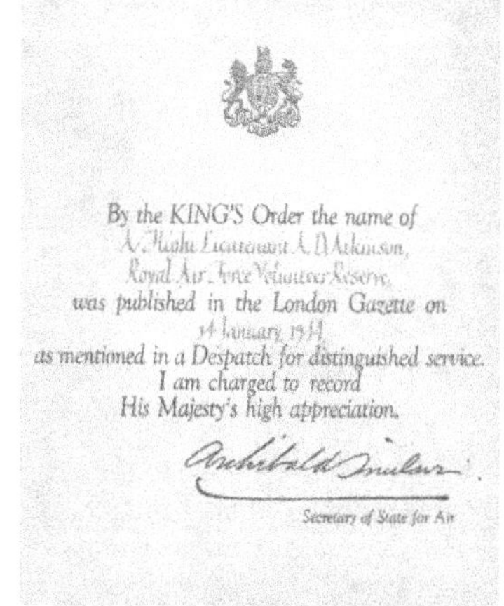

Wedding of P/O Atkinson and Marion Martin, 12th of September 1942

Wally Layne, "Woof" Welford, "Johnnie" Tytherleigh (with pipe) and F/Sgt Stuart Hobson. www.wallyswar.wordpress.com

F/O George Alexander Phillips DFM.

P/O Ivor Owen Davies (P/O Fair's crew)
Lost 25th March 1942 while mining off Brest.
The Crew: P/O D R Fair (Pilot), P/O I O Davies
(Obs), Sgt J Hudson, Sgt J H Parson

"B Flight" 50 Squadron, April 1942. The Hampden in the background, according to the writing on the
back of the photo, was the last Hampden to leave 50 Squadron.

50 Squadron Manchester of the type before the tailplane modifications.

50 Squadron Manchester R5784 P/O T B "King" Cole and crew. May 1942

P/O Leslie Manser VC

50 Squadron Lancaster

Lancaster R5691 VN-K Sgt R.L. Cumberland & crew all KIA 24th of October 1942

F/L Russell Cumberland (Pilot)   Sgt S A Gregg (WO/AG)
Lancaster R 5691 VN-K of 50 Squadron took off from RAF Skellingthorpe, Lincolnshire, at 12.32
on 24th of October 1942 for a daytime attack on Milan, and was shot down off the coast of France.
All are commemorated on the Runnymede Memorial.

Gunner, F/O Gordon Cruickshanks DFM

*Sgt Francis Reginald Law of
Sgt Ivor Mapp's crew*

*Gordon Cruickshanks and surviving members of the crew of P/O Calvert after crash landing at
Bradwell Bay on return from Hamburg on the 10th of November 1942.*

Sgt Gordon Cruickshanks DFM (rear gunner) and some of his crew after crash landing on return from Hamburg 9/10th of November 1942. The uninjured members of the crew of Lancaster R5702 "S" 'Taipo' sit in one of the holes caused by enemy action. Left to right are P/O Power (2nd Pilot), Sgt Cruickshank (RG), Sgt Wilson (BA) and Sgt Alan Connor RAAF (WO/AG).

"Taipo's" cockpit, showing the damage inflicted by flak that had injured pilot Roy Calvert and killed wireless operator, Sgt Lewis Herbert Austin RAAF, instantly.

50 Squadron Lancaster R5702 VN-S which came down at Bradwell Bay November 1942

Lancaster R5702, coded VN-S, Nickname "Taipo", after being badly shot up during the fateful Hamburg raid on the night of 9/10th of November 1942 and crash-landing back in the UK at Bradwell Bay. The aircraft was repaired and sent back on operations, only to be shot down over Denmark two years later by Oberleutnant Gerhardt Raht of 4./NJG 3

Lancaster R5702 VN-S of 50 Squadron was lost as CF-Y with 625 Squadron Sgt. W. Ashurst and five crew KIA. One PoW, Berlin, 15th of February 1944.

F/L Jack Abercrombie,(standing left), S/L Moore RAAF, S/L Hugh Everitt, standing right), P/O Drew Wyness kneeling left and P/O Roy Calvert kneeling right). W/C Abercromby was killed on his way to Berlin on the 1/2nd of January 1944 when commanding officer of 83 Squadron. S/L Drew Wyness joined 617 (Dambusters) Squadron in 1944, and was murdered with his crew by a Nazi official on the 7th of October 1944. (By kind permission of the Calvert family via Dave Homewood).

Roy Calvert 's 50 Squadron Commander had a little thing going where any crew that had received damage to their aircraft during a raid would receive a token souvenir. This took the form of a post card sized cartoon, with details of the raid on it. It seems that Roy received at least eight of these cards, in two different designs. Two of them are shown below.

A card received following a raid on Bremen on the night of the 13/14th of September 1942, depicting Hitler and Goering inspecting the damage they had made.

Another card design depicting a 50 Squadron Lancaster dropping bombs, this time on Bremen. (By kind permission of the Calvert family via Dave Homewood).

Lancaster R5689 VN-N crashed on the 19th of September 1942

Lancaster R5689 VN-N.

Lancaster R5689 VN-N

Lancaster R5689 VN-N

Lancaster R5689 VN-N

50 Squadron Lancaster 1942, piloted by S/L Hugh Everitt

50 Squadron Lancaster VN-Q

Lancasters of 50 Squadron in August 1942

50 Squadron Armourers at Skellingthorpe on the 22nd of April 1942 (IBCC)

Posed shot of a returning crew at Swinderby in 1942.

50 Squadron Lancaster VN-R at Swinderby in 1942

P/O E Dampier-Crossley & WAAF Section Officer J Bentley at the time of his DFC award.
F/L E Dampier-Crossley was killed while serving with 619 Squadron in 1943

F/Sgt Ron Eyres (Pilot)

T McMerrow and another member of Sgt Eyre's crew

Sgt Jim Philpot (Navigator)

Sgt Frank Adey (Rear Gunner)

50 Squadron Lancaster crew

January 1943

The year began with the official formation on New Year's Day of the Canadian 6 Group, and the handing over to it of the former 4 Group stations in North Yorkshire on which its squadrons had been lodging. Eventually, all Canadian squadrons would find a home in the group, which was financed by Canada and controlled by Harris, but, initially, there were eight founder members, including 408 and 420 Squadron, which had left 5 Group during the autumn. Further south, a continuation of the Oboe trials would occupy the first two weeks, during which 109 Squadron marked for small forces of 1 and 5 Group Lancasters at Essen on seven occasions and Duisburg once. For the first time, the cloud cover and ever-present blanket of industrial haze would have no bearing on the outcome of the raid as reliance on e.t.a, DR and Gee was cast aside in favour of Oboe, at least, that is, at targets within the device's range. Until the advent of mobile transmitter stations late in the war, Oboe would be restricted by the curvature of the earth and the altitude at which Mosquitos could fly, but this meant that the entire Ruhr lay within range of Harris's bombers.

The year began for 50 Squadron with the arrival from 1654 Conversion Unit of F/L Henry Maudslay, who had completed a tour with 44 Squadron in 1941. Thereafter, he had been involved in test flying, before passing on his skills at a training unit and taking part in the Thousand Bomber raids in May and June 1942. Going in the opposite direction at the conclusion of his tour was F/O Drew Wyness, who would return to the operational scene as a flight commander with 57 Squadron in 1944, before joining 617 Squadron as a flight commander late in August 1944. In October, he would ditch his Lancaster in the River Rhine during an attack on the Kembs Barrage on the German/Swiss frontier, and he and his crew would become victims of an horrendous war crime at the hands of a Nazi official.

In a gentle start to operations on the 2nd, 50 Squadron briefed six crews for gardening duties in the Deodars garden and one in Furze off south-western France. They departed Skellingthorpe between 17.03 and 17.16 with W/C Russell and S/L Birch the senior pilots on duty at the head of the Deodars element bound for the mouth of the Gironde, and F/O Calvert and crew for Furze off St-Jean-de-Luz. F/O Power and crew were back home within an hour after the failure of their starboard-inner engine, and Sgt Dennis and crew followed them in two hours later because of an indisposed rear gunner. The others reached their respective gardens, where opinions differed widely concerning the weather conditions in the Gironde estuary. W/C Russell reported eight-tenths cloud with a base at 800 feet and poor visibility, and he spent fifty minutes searching for pinpoints on Ile-de-Grave and Pointe-de-Cordouan, before delivering his vegetables from 1,000 feet. In contrast, S/L Birch and crew found no cloud, but some haze, and identified their pinpoints without difficulty, while the others described conditions between the two extremes and delivered their stores from between 500 and 700 feet. Meanwhile, some 170 miles to the south, F/O Calvert and crew encountered seven-tenths cloud, but picked out Fort Socoa with ease, and delivered their mines as briefed during an uneventful sortie.

The squadron was not invited to take part in the first two of the forays against Essen mounted on the 3rd and 4th, which involved nineteen and twenty-nine Lancasters respectively. However, when the next one was posted, on the 7th, the squadron loaded three of its Lancasters with a cookie each and SBCs of incendiaries, and dispatched them from Skellingthorpe between 03.45 and 04.01 on the 8th as part of an overall heavy force of nineteen. They found five to nine-tenths cloud in the target area with tops at around 5,000 feet, and aimed their loads at Pathfinder flares, which Sgt Dennis and crew described as very useful, even though a double-edged sword, in that it assisted the accuracy of the bombing but attracted the flak, which, on this night was quite intense and accurate. Sgt Knight and crew, which now included Sgt Ray Grayston as the established flight engineer, attacked from 19,000 feet, the height at which flak shells were bursting, and they saw nothing of the results of their efforts. Later that day, the Pathfinder Force was granted group status as 8 Group, and, for the purpose of this book, the titles Pathfinders and 8 Group are interchangeable.

Duisburg was to host the Oboe trial on the 8th, for which thirty-eight Lancasters were made ready, five of them by 50 Squadron, and they departed Skellingthorpe between 17.21 and 17.40 with S/L Birch the senior pilot on duty, accompanied as a passenger by F/L Maudslay. Taking off at the same time were three freshman crews bound for the Nectarines garden off the Frisians, but F/O Gilmour turned back early on because of starboard-outer engine failure. Sgts Yates and Richardson and their crews found ten-tenths cloud and poor visibility, but pinpoints aplenty on the various islands, and delivered their vegetables as briefed from 800 and 900 feet respectively. Meanwhile, some 170 miles to the south, the bombing element had reached the western edge of the Ruhr to encounter ten-tenths cloud with tops at around 10,000 feet, S/L Birch and crew having already evaded the attentions of a night-fighter over the eastern shore of the Ijsselmeer. The ground was completely obscured, and the crews focussed purely on the Pathfinders' red and green parachute flares to establish the position of the target, bombing from 21,000 to 22,000 feet in the face of intense and accurate flak bursting around them. S/L Birch also described a rocket projectile bursting like the hub of a Catherine wheel with white stars and a three-to-four-hundred-yard radius. Three Lancasters failed to return, and among them was 50 Squadron's W4800, which crashed near Düsseldorf, killing Sgt Kiernan and his crew.

Later, during the 9th, ED394 crashed at 23.37 while trying to land at Crosby-on-Eden aerodrome in Cumberland during night-flying training, and four members of Sgt Smith's crew lost their lives, while he and two others escaped with injuries. The squadron did not take part in the Oboe-trials raid on Essen by 50 Lancasters that night, when the main activity involved 120 aircraft in mining operations in northern waters. S/L Moore was posted to 25 O.T.U on the 10th at the conclusion of his outstanding tour, and his crew would be taken over by F/L Maudslay. The squadron made ready five Lancasters on the 11th for the largest Oboe trial yet involving seventy-two Lancasters and four Mosquitos at Essen. They departed Skellingthorpe between 17.17 and 17.35, but F/O Power and crew turned back ninety minutes later after the guns in the rear turret failed. The others encountered ten-tenths cloud with tops at 8,000 feet, dimly illuminated by a quarter moon, and carried out their attacks from 20,000 feet on either a Pathfinder red warning flare or white release-point flare if they could see it. No results were observed, and no local report was forthcoming.

It was similar fare for four 50 Squadron crews at the same target on the following night as part of a Lancaster force of fifty-five, with four Oboe Mosquitos to carry out the marking. They departed Skellingthorpe between 03.31 and 03.47, but lost the services of F/O Johanson and crew when the rear gunner's electrically-heated suit stopped working. The first Oboe Mosquito suffered equipment failure, and the others were late on target, leading to some Lancaster crews bombing on DR over the ten-tenths cloud that topped out at around 12,000 feet. The Skellingthorpe crews arrived a little later, when the release-point marker flares were visible, and these were used as the reference to bomb from 20,000 to 22,000 feet in the face of intense and accurate flak. The flashes from bursting cookies were observed, and returning crews were enthusiastic about the performance of the Pathfinder crews, and also commented on the ferocity of the flak in the Cologne corridor on the southern approach to the Ruhr.

The final Oboe trial in the current series was posted on the 13th, for which the squadron detailed four Lancasters as part of a force of sixty-six. They took off between 16.58 and 17.17 with the recently promoted F/L Davies the senior pilot on duty, but their number was reduced within an hour or so by the return of Sgt Kitching and crew after their guns froze. The remaining three crews continued on to the Ruhr, where Essen lay beneath seven to ten-tenths cloud with tops at 7,000 to 10,000 feet, above which, the moon had waxed to half-size. When Sgt Huntley and crew arrived about fifteen minutes early, all was eerily quiet, until others started to bomb on DR seven or eight minutes before H-Hour, bringing the flak batteries to life. The Oboe Mosquitos again experienced technical difficulties, two returning without marking, and the flares of the third failed to ignite, which meant that the only flares over the target were those delivered by night-fighters to illuminate the bombers. It seems that the Skellingthorpe crews assumed them to be legitimate Pathfinder release-point flares, and bombed by their reference from around 20,000 feet, all the time under fire from a box-barrage. They returned with nothing of interest to report at debriefing and photos showing only cloud, and it was left to local sources to report that more than a hundred buildings had been either destroyed or seriously damaged.

A new Air Ministry directive was issued on the 14th, which authorized the area bombing of the French ports providing a home for U-Boots with concrete bunkers and support facilities. A list was drawn up accordingly, headed by Lorient, and, that night, the port received the first of what would be a nine-raid series over the ensuing four weeks, five of which would take place during the second half of January. As mentioned earlier, between February 1941 and January 1942, the Germans had built three giant concrete structures K1, K2 and K3 on the southernmost point of the Keroman Peninsular. They were capable of housing and servicing thirty U-Boots and providing accommodation for their crews, and were impregnable to the bombs available to Bomber Command at the time. The purpose of this new campaign, therefore, was to render the town and port uninhabitable, and block or sever all road and rail communications to them. The first of the series of attacks on the port took place that very night at the hands of a force of 122 aircraft, and, despite accurate marking by the Pathfinder element, the main force bombing was scattered and destroyed a modest 120 buildings. Also, on this night, 5 Group contributed to gardening activities along the Biscay coastline, to which 50 Squadron contributed three Lancasters containing freshman crews. P/O Evans and Sgts Schofield and Murray took off between 17.37 and 17.42 bound for the Deodars garden in the Gironde estuary, and successfully delivered their vegetables into the briefed locations from 500 to 800 feet. Flying as bomb-aimer in the Schofield crew was Sgt John Fraser RCAF, who was another destined to be a founder member of 617 Squadron. An improvement was achieved at Lorient on the following night by a larger initial force of 157 aircraft, which destroyed eight hundred buildings in what was now a largely evacuated town.

5 Group's involvement with Lorient would come in February, and, in the meantime, Harris planned two operations against the "Big City", Berlin, beginning on the 16th, for which a force of 201 aircraft was made ready. This would be the first raid on Germany's capital for fourteen months, and would bring with it the first use of custom-designed target indicators (TIs). The

main force would be made up predominantly of 5 Group Lancasters, with others from 1 Group, while eleven Halifaxes would be included in the Pathfinder element. 50 Squadron detailed eight Lancasters, which took off between 16.48 and 17.03 with W/C Russell the senior pilot on duty, but, F/O Johanson and crew turned back with an engine issue when a little more than an hour out. P/O Heinrich had reached Mandø Island off the west coast of Jutland, before turning back at 18.51 after the intercom to the rear turret failed. Heading for home over Sylt, the contents of the bomb bay were dropped from 19,000 feet onto a searchlight and flak position on the island's northern tip. Those reaching the target reported a half moon, good visibility and six-tenths cloud at 10,000 feet, through which the built-up area could be seen clearly. W/C Russell orbited the Strausberg Wood, some twenty miles east-north east of Berlin, waiting for the TIs to go down, but ran out of patience and homed in on a large fire in a built-up area, whereupon the Pathfinders dropped their markers across the same area. Black smoke was rising through 5,000 feet as W/C Russell turned away, and he was left unconvinced by the effectiveness of the raid. Most crews reported having observed the Pathfinder TIs, but the bombing was concentrated around the southern fringe of the city, particularly in the Tempelhof district, and damage was less than might have been hoped. R5631 was hit by flak at 19,500 feet over the target, which left a two-foot-square hole in the bomb doors, and it was attacked by a Ju88 at 18,000 feet sixty-five miles into the return flight. The rear turret and tail control surfaces sustained damage, as did the rear gunner in the arm and foot, and Sgt Schofield had to work hard to maintain control of the Lancaster. The hydraulics system failed completely, leaving all turrets inoperable, and the landing gear had to be blown down, but good crew co-operation saw them home to a safe landing. Sgt Kitching and crew also made it safely home, where they reported being blown onto their back by a flak explosion at 21,000 feet over Berlin. One notable scalp was the ten-thousand-seater Deutschlandhalle, the largest covered venue in Europe, which was hosting the annual circus as the bombers approached, and was efficiently emptied of people and animals with only minor injuries to a few people. Shortly afterwards, incendiaries set fire to the building and reduced it to ruins. Remarkably, only a single Lancaster failed to return from this operation, but the balance would be redressed somewhat twenty-four hours later.

Eight 50 Squadron crews were called to briefing at Skellingthorpe on the 17th to learn of their part in that night's return to Berlin. 170 Lancasters and seventeen Halifaxes were made ready on 1, 4, 5 and 8 Group stations, and those reaching the target would be sharing the airspace over it with the broadcaster, Richard Dimbleby, who would be in a 106 Squadron Lancaster captained by W/C Guy Gibson. The Skellingthorpe element took to the air between 16.54 and 17.27 with S/L Birch the senior pilot on duty, each Lancaster carrying an all-incendiary bomb load. On a night of poor serviceability for the squadron, Sgt Dennis returned early with an indisposed rear gunner, Sgt Huntley and crew with a failed port-outer engine and F/O Johanson, also with a dead port-outer engine, which had actually caught fire before being shut down. The others, by this time, were well into their three-and-half hour outward flight across Denmark and Germany's Baltic coast, where they were stalked by night-fighters, S/L Birch and crew twice being forced into violent evasive action, during which the incendiaries were jettisoned. They turned for home, descended to ground level and adopted a course thirty miles north of track to avoid further contact with the enemy. The others reached the target to be greeted by eight to ten-tenths cloud with tops at between 10,000 and 14,000 feet, and it was possible for most to pick out the Müggelsee to the south-east of the Capital, from where a timed run was carried out to the target. Some crews failed to see any Pathfinder flares and bombed on e.t.a or DR, while others did benefit from target marking, which, sadly, was once more concentrated over the southern fringes of the city rather than over the centre. Sgt Knight bombed on markers from 18,000 feet and F/O Power from 16,000 feet, while F/L Davies just let his load go after flak damaged his Lancaster in a number of places and wounded the bomb-aimer, preventing him from seeking out the aiming-point. Little was seen of the results of the bombing, and local reports confirmed that the operation had not been successful, and no significant damage had occurred. The disappointment was compounded by the loss of twenty-two bombers, 11.8% of those dispatched, and many of these disappeared without trace in the Baltic or North Sea. Among the missing was 50 Squadron's ED471, which crashed somewhere near the Baltic coast with no survivors from the crew of P/O Heinrich RAAF, which contained three members of the RCAF.

A force of seventy-nine Lancasters and three Mosquitos was detailed to resume the Oboe trials programme at Essen on the 21st, for which six crews were briefed at Skellingthorpe. They took off between 17.15 and 17.36 with F/L Maudslay the senior pilot on duty, and two future Dambusters, navigator, F/O Robert Urquhart, and gunner, Sgt Norman Burrows, in his crew. Other founder members of the future 617 Squadron, navigator, F/O Ken Earnshaw, bomb-aimer, F/Sgt John Fraser and gunner, Sgt Brian Jagger, were members of the crew of Sgt Schofield. It was to be another night to forget for 50 Squadron, after P/O Evans, F/O Gilmour, F/O Power and Sgt Kitching all returned early because of a variety of technical problems, mostly affecting rear turrets and guns. This left just the Maudslay and Schofield crews to continue on to the target, with condensation trails forming at 18,000 feet to advertise their presence to the German defences. There was a question as to the cloud conditions, some reporting clear skies, others ten-tenths cloud, neither of which would have mattered if the Oboe marking had worked and been visible to all. In the event, the entire Ruhr was concealed beneath thick industrial haze, which proved to be impenetrable, and, as far as the 50 Squadron duo was concerned, there were no Pathfinder markers to point the way. F/L Maudslay hung around for thirty minutes, with an intense flak barrage all around, before bombing what appeared to be a fire, and collecting a little flak damage in the process. Sgt Schofield and crew spotted a stick of incendiaries burning near Duisburg, and bombed these from 19,000 feet at 19.45. Four Lancasters failed to return, and the outcome of the raid remained undetermined.

Gunner, P/O Bill Tytherleigh, returned to the squadron for a second tour on the 23rd, and would join the crew of F/L Maudslay. This was the day on which the Oboe trials programme moved to Düsseldorf, situated some fifteen miles south-south-east of Essen. 1, 5 and 8 Groups assembled a force of eighty Lancasters and three Mosquitos, of which six Lancasters belonging to 50 Squadron were loaded with a cookie each and a dozen SBCs of 4lb incendiaries. They lifted off the end of the Skellingthorpe runway between 17.09 and 17.23 with F/Os Gilmour and Power the senior pilots on duty. F/O Power and crew turned back early after the guns in the front and rear turrets failed to fire on being tested, and P/O Evans and crew were over Holland when their guns froze, and they bombed a flak position near Roermond as a last resort target. F/O Gilmour and crew saw warning flares as they approached the southern Ruhr, but, with no release-point flares in evidence, bombed an alternative target, believed to be Krefeld, from 20,000 feet, in the face of an intense flak barrage. Sgt Kitching and crew arrived early on target, and were cruising around waiting for the marker flares to appear, when the flight engineer and rear gunner collapsed with oxygen starvation. The bombs were jettisoned, and, immediately, thereafter, the marker flares appeared ahead, but too late for this crew, who returned home without further incident. P/O Townsend and crew found ten-tenths cloud with good visibility above, and spotted warning flares ahead at the appointed time, but no release-point flares. They carried out a DR run from the second warning flare, and dropped their load slightly north of the intended release-point, before returning home to report intense and accurate predicted and barrage flak. Sgt Schofield and crew were waiting for the marker flares, which were late, when they were hit by flak, and released their bombs on estimated position, only to see the markers three minutes later. They were attacked by a night-fighter seventy-five minutes into the return flight, but shook it off after sustaining a little damage, and landed safely at base.

Düsseldorf was selected again as the primary target on the 27th, when the Pathfinders were to use ground marking for the first time, rather than skymarking. Ground markers, which were TIs fused to burst and cascade just above the ground, could be seen through thin or partial cloud and industrial haze, and were much more reliable than the previously-employed parachute flares, that drifted in the wind. However, skymarkers would remain an indispensable part of target marking techniques on nights of heavy cloud or to use in combination with ground markers. From this night onwards, Pathfinder heavy aircraft would back-up the Mosquito-laid Oboe markers, to ensure that the aiming-point remained marked throughout the operation. A heavy force of 124 Lancasters and thirty-three Halifaxes was made ready on 1, 4, 5 and 8 Group stations, 50 Squadron providing ten of the Lancasters, which took off between 17.51 and 18.22 with F/Ls Davies and Maudslay the senior pilots on duty. Maudslay was flying with the crew of Sgt McGrath RCAF, who had joined the squadron a few days after Christmas, and for whom this was their maiden operation. ED486 was seen to climb away normally and enter cloud, before re-emerging in a steep dive from which it did not recover, and there were no survivors from the crew of Sgt Kitching. Sgt Schofield and crew returned early for an unspecified reason, and P/O Evans and crew because of the failure of the oxygen system, leaving the others to reach the target to find a thin layer of five to ten-tenths cloud at 10,000 feet, through which the red and green TIs could be seen burning on the aiming-point. The 50 Squadron crews carried out their part in the proceedings, and returned safely, impressed by the potential of ground marking, and confident that they had hit the aiming-point. This was confirmed by local reports, which spoke of widespread destruction in southern districts, amounting to 456 houses, ten industrial premises and nine public buildings destroyed or seriously damaged, and many others affected to a lesser extent. Such conditions before the advent of ground markers would have led to the kind of scattered and ineffective raid that had characterized attempts at Ruhr targets in the past.

Another new blind-bombing device, the ground-mapping H2S radar, was to be employed operationally for the first time at Hamburg on the 30th, for which a force of 135 Lancasters of 1, 5 and 8 Groups would be joined by thirteen H2S-equipped Pathfinder Stirlings and Halifaxes of 7 and 35 Squadrons respectively. The H2S equipment was housed in a cupola aft of the bomb bay, and projected an image of the terrain onto a cathode-ray tube in the navigator's compartment. It was the job of the operator to interpret what he was seeing, and guide the pilot to the aiming-point, but this was no easy task, particularly with the Mk I set, and it proved difficult to distinguish particular ground features in the jumble of images presented to him. It would take much practice and experience to master the device, but, in time, and once the Mk III set became available, it would become an indispensable tool, which, ultimately, would become standard equipment for main force as well as Pathfinder aircraft.

50 Squadron made ready eight Lancasters, which departed Skellingthorpe between 00.20 and 00.35 with F/Ls Davies and Maudslay the senior pilots on duty, only for the weather

conditions to reduce the squadron's impact. As mentioned frequently before, north-western Germany had a "gatekeeper" in the form of weather fronts, which, on this night, contained severe icing conditions and electrical storms for the bombers to negotiate as they made their way across the North Sea, and this persuaded F/O Power and Sgt Yates and their crews to turn back with frozen guns. P/O Evans and crew were among a number to misinterpret a recall signal meant for other aircraft, and turned back when within striking distance of the target. This left six crews to fly the 50 Squadron flag over Germany's Second City, where they encountered between zero and nine-tenths cloud, according to which crew report one reads, with tops as high as 15,000 feet. They bombed onto flares or TIs, and saw the reflections of explosions in the cloud, which led to a consensus that the operation had been effective. This was partially confirmed by local reports that mentioned seventy-one large fires, but much of the bombing fell either into the Elbe or into marshland outside of the city. This would have been disappointing to the raid planners, as Hamburg, with the nearby coastline and wide River Elbe, was an ideal target for H2S, and should have been easy to identify on the cathode-ray tubes. During the course of the month the squadron carried out fourteen operations, dispatching seventy-nine sorties for the loss of four Lancasters, three complete crews and four other crew members.

February 1943

It was a time of honing and refining for the Command, in preparation for the launching of a major campaign a month hence, and S/L Street arrived with his crew from 1654 Conversion Unit on the 1st to assume the duties of flight commander and add his experience. Among his crew was bomb-aimer, Sgt Les Rutherford, to whom this book is jointly dedicated with W/O Frank McGrath. Les had joined the army in 1940 as a dispatch rider, and escaped from Dunkerque by floating out to sea on the remains of a barn door, from which he was rescued by a French trawler. On return to England he joined the RAF, and began a colourful career, eventually joining 50 Squadron, where he would fly with some of the most experienced crews.

February opened with the posting of Cologne as the target for an experimental operation on the 2nd, in which two marking methods were to be employed. Situated just to the south of the Ruhr, the Rhineland's capital city was within range of Oboe Mosquitos, and these were to be supplemented by Pathfinder heavies relying on H2S. A force of 159 heavies included seventy-four 5 Group Lancasters, eight of them provided by 50 Squadron, while two Pathfinder Mosquitos of 109 Squadron carried the Oboe markers. The Skellingthorpe element took off between 18.20 and 18.27 with S/L Birch the senior pilot on duty, but lost the services of F/Sgt Stitt and crew to the rear turret gremlin that had been stalking the squadron over recent operations. The others pressed on through severe cold, which caused almost all of the guns to freeze solid, but reached the target to find a layer of two to five tenths thin cloud up to 8,000 feet and patches above. This afforded good vertical visibility and a clear sight of the markers, even from some distance on approach to the bombing run. There was some debate as to the accuracy and concentration of the markers, which a few crews from other squadrons would report as five to ten miles to the north-west of the city, while others described them as scattered. Most of the 50 Squadron crews had markers in the bomb sight as they delivered their loads from between 12,000 and 19,000 feet, and, although few were able to observe their own bombs burst, many scattered fires were evident, the glow from which could be seen from a hundred miles into the return journey. Local reports confirmed bombs falling all over the city, but nowhere with concentration, and damage was, consequently, not commensurate with the size of the force. 50 Squadron's ED488 was one of only five aircraft missing, and fell to a night-fighter on the way home. It crashed at 21.27 at Hamont, on the Belgian side of the frontier with Holland, killing F/O Power RCAF and both gunners, including F/L Bousefield DFC, and delivering the four survivors into enemy hands.

Hamburg was posted as the target on the 3rd, for which a force of 263 aircraft was made ready, unusually, with Halifaxes representing the most populous type followed by Stirlings. 5 Group contributed forty of the sixty-two Lancasters, five of them belonging to 50 Squadron, and they departed Skellingthorpe between 18.00 and 18.20 with W/C Russell the senior pilot on duty, flying with the McGrath crew. Fifteen of the 5 Group crews turned back on encountering the towering cloud and severe icing conditions common to this route over the North Sea, and among them were those of F/Sgt Stitt, Sgt Murray and F/O Johanson, all of whom cited frozen guns for not pressing on. W/C Russell and F/L Davies and their crews arrived in the target area to find nine to ten-tenths cloud, which they estimated topped out at between 7,000 and 8,000 feet, while 207 Squadron crews reported the cloud to be at 17,000 to 20,000 feet. Scattered red and green Pathfinder H2S-laid skymarker flares were in the bomb sights as the 50 Squadron pair bombed from 17,000 feet, but no results were observed, and the impression was of an ineffective attack. This was confirmed by local reports, which mentioned forty-five large fires but no concentration or significant damage, and this disappointing outcome cost the Command sixteen aircraft. The losses by type made interesting reading, and would reflect the trend for the remainder of the year, with the Stirlings suffering the highest numerical and percentage casualties, followed by the Halifaxes and Wellingtons, with the Lancasters clearly at the top of the food chain.

Turin was posted as the main target on the 4th for which 188 aircraft were made ready, while 128 others, mostly Wellingtons, were prepared to continue the assault on Lorient. 5 Group contributed forty-eight Lancasters to the former and eight with freshman crews to the latter, 50 Squadron putting up five Lancasters for Italy and two for France. Those bound for Italy took off first between 18.17 and 18.35 with S/L Birch the senior pilot on duty, and they were followed into the air at 18.39 and 18.47 by Sgts Ward and Thomas respectively. The freshmen reached the target area under cloudless skies and in good visibility, which enabled them to make a visual identification of the port, before bombing from 10,000 feet and observing bursts, explosions and fires. After crossing the Alps in cloud at 21,000 feet, the Turin-bound crews found conditions on the Italian side much improved, with clear skies and excellent visibility, which facilitated a visual confirmation of the accuracy of the Pathfinder TIs. An estimated one hundred searchlights were active, and the flak defence had also been "beefed-up", but was still inaccurate and in keeping with expectations at an Italian target. Following a raid on a German target, a bomb symbol would be painted on the forward fuselage of a bomber, but after a raid on an Italian target, the symbol would be an ice-cream cone. Red TIs were much in evidence in the city centre as the Skellingthorpe crews attacked from between 8,000 and 14,000 feet, the low height recorded by F/L Maudslay and crew, who had aimed at two factory chimneys, and watched their cookie fall into a built-up area. Returning crews were enthusiastic about the effectiveness of their work, and it was confirmed later that serious and widespread damage had resulted. A signal was received from ED527 at approximately 22.30 to the effect that the operation had been completed and the crew of F/O Johanson RNZAF was making for Gibraltar. Another signal at 23.05 mentioned a forced landing and gave a position between the Spanish and Moroccan coasts. News came through later from Bomber Command HQ, that the Lancaster had crashed in Morocco, killing all on board.

The seventh raid in the series on Lorient was posted on the 7th, and was by far the largest to date, employing 323 aircraft, of which forty-three of eighty Lancasters were provided by 5 Group. It was to be conducted in two waves, 50 Squadron detailing six Lancasters, those of Sgts Murray and McGrath departing Skellingthorpe first at 18.06, to be followed into the air by four others between 19.26 and 19.42 led by F/O Taylor. This would be the first time that Sgt McGrath was operating as captain of his crew, and they could see fires already burning as they closed on the target under clear skies and in ideal bombing conditions, which they exploited after making a visual identification of the aiming-point confirmed by Pathfinder TIs. They delivered their cookie and incendiaries from 13,000 feet, and returned to report an outstandingly destructive raid which left fires raging across the town. F/Sgt Stitt and crew returned within an hour after experiencing starboard-inner engine issues, leaving the three remaining second-phase crews of F/O Taylor and Sgts Thomas and Ward to continue to the target, drawn on by the glow. The docks stood out clearly, although a pall of smoke rising through 8,000 feet threatened to obscure the ground as they began their bombing runs at around 12,000 feet, with a modest amount of heavy flak bursting three thousand feet above them. They returned safely, the freshman crews full of enthusiasm and reporting too many fires to count.

Before the penultimate raid on Lorient took place, attention was switched to the important naval port of Wilhelmshaven, situated on the north-western coast of Jade Bay, some sixty miles to the west of Hamburg. A force of 177 aircraft was put together on the 11th, of which 129 were Lancasters, sixty-eight of them representing 5 Group. Ten Lancasters were made ready at Skellingthorpe, and they took off between 17.41 and 17.52 with S/L Birch the senior pilot on duty. The serviceability gremlins struck the squadron again, forcing Sgt Yates, F/Sgt Stitt and F/O Gilmour to turn for home and jettison their bombs on the way. The others reached the target area to find ten-tenths cloud with tops at 7,000 feet, and the least reliable H2S skymarking method in progress. On the credit side, at a smaller, more compact urban target it was easier to interpret the images on the cathode-ray screens, and, on this night, great accuracy was achieved. The flares were right over the aiming-point as the Skellingthorpe crews delivered their cookies and incendiaries from between 11,000 and 14,500 feet, but it was impossible to assess what was happening beneath the cloud, until an enormous explosion took place, the glow from which lingered for ten minutes. All crews commented on this at debriefing at Skellingthorpe, and there must have been much speculation about the source, which turned out to be the naval ammunition depot at Mariensiel, situated to the south of the town. It blew itself into oblivion, devastating 120 acres and causing widespread damage in the dockyard and town.

It was back to Lorient for eight 50 Squadron crews on the 13th, who learned at briefing that they were to be part of the largest force yet sent to the port. 466 aircraft were made ready, 103 of them 5 Group Lancasters, and the Skellingthorpe element took off between 19.01 and 19.32 with S/L Birch the senior pilot on duty. There were no early returns to deplete the squadron's impact, and they located the target with ease in excellent visibility under clear skies, which allowed them to make a visual identification of both aiming-points, the U-Boot pens on the Keroman peninsular and the town. Bombing by the 50 Squadron element took place from between 6,000 and 13,000 feet, with F/L Maudslay and crew responsible for the low height. The rear gunner shot out three searchlights on the French coast on the way home, and they joined with the others at debriefing to describe observing many bursts and a town consumed by fire. F/L Davies and crew were absent from debriefing, and it was established later that ED484 had crashed into the sea, and none of the eight occupants had survived. Just three bodies were recovered for burial from this experienced crew, and their presence at Skellingthorpe would be missed.

F/L Calvert was posted to 1660 Conversion Unit on the 14th at the conclusion of his tour, as orders came through from 5 Group to make ready for a return to Italy that night for a crack this time at Milan. A force of 142 Lancasters of 1, 5 and 8 Groups was assembled to carry out the attack, while 243 Halifaxes, Stirlings and Wellingtons were prepared to try their hand at Cologne. Among the eighty-nine 5 Group Lancasters were nine representing 50 Squadron, which took off between 18.35 and 18.47 with W/C Russell the senior pilot on duty. Sgt Dennis and crew were defeated by what they described as a navigational failure, but, whether this referred to equipment or human is unclear. They reached the target area after a trouble-free outward flight, and were guided to the aiming-point by green and red Pathfinder route-marker flares. They were able to identify the aiming-point visually, and W/C Russell made his bombing run at 9,000 feet, one of three from the squadron with a cookie on board, and that was seen to burst slightly to the south-east of the aiming-point at 22.44. The rest attacked from 8,000 to 12,000 feet, five with all incendiary loads, between 22.36 and 22.46, with F/L Maudslay again responsible for the low height, having picked out the railway and built-up area in the light of Pathfinder flares. The glow of fires remained visible for at least a hundred miles into the return journey, and the operation was deemed successful, although no local confirmation was forthcoming.

The final raid of the series on Lorient was posted on the 16th, for which another large force was made ready, this time of 377 aircraft. Of seventy-five Lancasters offered by 5 Group, eight were made ready at Skellingthorpe, and took off between 18.52 and 19.13 with F/O Taylor the senior pilot on duty, but his starboard-inner engine failed after about ninety minutes, and he was forced to abandon his sortie. The others found clear conditions over the target, aided by an almost full moon, and delivered their cookies and SBCs of incendiaries on red TIs onto the Keroman peninsular from 8,000 to 12,000 feet between 20.49 and 20.59. The majority of the force dropped incendiaries into the town, which, after nine attacks, 1,926 sorties and four thousand tons of bombs, was now a desolate and deserted ruin.

Preparations were put in hand on the 18th to make ready 195 aircraft for the second of four raids on Wilhelmshaven during the month. 5 Group contributed seventy-nine Lancasters, including ten belonging to 50 Squadron, which departed Skellingthorpe between 18.32 and 18.45 with F/Os Gilmour and Taylor the senior pilots on duty. F/Sgt Stitt and crew were again unable to complete their sortie after their oxygen system let them down when about ninety minutes out, and they left the others to push on to reach the target area, which was identified visually in excellent conditions. Red TIs could be seen clearly and were in the bomb sights as the Skellingthorpe bomb bays were emptied from 10,000 to 20,000 feet between 20.33 and 20.44. Bombs were observed to burst and fires to spring up, and returning crews were confident that an accurate and concentrated attack had taken place. However, bombing photos revealed that the operation had been a failure, after the main weight of bombs had fallen into open country to the west of the town, and this demonstrated how easy it was to be misled by what the eye saw. Local reports admitted to a number of bombs hitting the town, causing no serious damage or casualties.

Twenty-four hours later a force of 338 aircraft set off to return to Wilhelmshaven, with Wellingtons and Halifaxes accounting for 230 of the number and Stirlings and Lancasters the rest. 5 Group dispatched thirty-three Lancasters, but none from Skellingthorpe, and, once again, the conditions provided excellent visibility that enabled crews to identify the coastline and line themselves up on the target, which was being marked by green TIs. Bomb bursts and fires were observed in the docks area and the town to leave the crews with the impression that another successful raid had taken place, but, again, bombing photos told a different story, and revealed that the Pathfinder marking had fallen to the north of the built-up area, partly through reliance upon outdated maps, which would now be replaced. Of the twelve missing aircraft five were Stirlings and represented 8.9% of those dispatched, thus confirming the type's vulnerability compared with the Lancaster and Halifax. The four missing Lancasters represented a 7.7% loss rate, while no Halifaxes failed to return, but this would prove to be a blip. During the course of the year, the food chain would become established with Lancasters firmly at the top, Halifaxes in the middle and Stirlings at the bottom, when all types operated together.

An all-Lancaster main force from 1 and 5 Groups was made ready to attack the U-Boot construction yards at Vegesack in Bremen on the 21st, with Pathfinder Lancasters, Halifaxes and Stirlings to provide the marking in an overall force of 143 aircraft. Seventy-four of the Lancasters were put up by 5 Group, and eight of these departed Skellingthorpe between 18.29 and 18.55 with F/Os Gilmour and Taylor the senior pilots on duty. Sgt Thomas began to experience engine trouble soon after take-off, and eventually turned back, to be followed in a few minutes later by F/O Taylor, also with an engine issue. Those reaching the target were met by ten-tenths cloud at 3,000 feet, above which, marker flares drifted down to join the TIs dimly visible to some crews burning on the ground. The 50 Squadron crews bombed from 12,500 to 16,000 feet between 20.47 and 20.55, and a considerable glow from beneath the clouds suggested a successful outcome. Bombing photos depicted only cloud, and no local report was available to provide details of damage.

115 aircraft of 6 and 8 Groups concluded the current series of raids on Wilhelmshaven on the night of the 24/25th, with indeterminate results, and the port would now be left in peace until October 1944. A major operation against Nuremberg was posted on stations across the Command on the 25th, and 5 Group responded with a maximum effort of 101 Lancasters, seven of them made ready at Skellingthorpe. They took off between 19.52 and 20.09 with F/Os Gilmour and Taylor the senior pilots on duty, and each Lancaster carrying a cookie and SBCs of 4lb and 30lb incendiaries. Sgt Thomas and crew ran into flak as they closed on the target area, and were some twenty miles short when hit by shrapnel, which wounded the bomb-aimer. The bombs were jettisoned immediately, and a return made at all possible speed. The others pressed on to reach the target area under cloudless skies, and had to wait for the Pathfinder element to turn up, some sixteen to twenty minutes after the raid was due to begin. They dropped marker flares on the approach, and the 5 Group crews carried out a time-and-distance run to the aiming-point, which was marked by red and green TIs. The Skellingthorpe element bombed from 11,000 to 13,000 feet shortly before 23.30, and all of the indications, including what looked like an oil-depot exploding, suggested a concentrated attack predominantly in northern and western districts. This was confirmed by local reports, which

mentioned damage to three hundred buildings, but also revealed that bombs had fallen onto other communities and open country up to seven miles to the north. Nine aircraft failed to return, and among them was 50 Squadron's ED387, which crashed somewhere in southern Germany, killing Sgt Yates and two of his crew, and delivering the four survivors into enemy hands. Sadly, the navigator would die while in captivity almost two years to the day later, and shortly before liberation.

When Cologne was posted as the target on the 26th, 5 Group responded with ninety Lancasters, six of which were made ready at Skellingthorpe as part of an overall force of 427 aircraft. They took off between 18.53 and 19.07 with W/C Russell the senior pilot on duty, and all reached the Cologne area on a night of almost perfect serviceability for the group and good visibility. It seems from some comments that a proportion of the force bombed before the Pathfinders had a chance to mark, but, once the red and green TIs were seen on the ground, the 50 Squadron crews bombed them from 12,000 to 18,000 feet between 21.26 and 21.30. Fires were reported in the city centre, as were decoys to the west of the city, and bombing photos showed fire tracks and smoke that suggested an effective raid. In fact, a large proportion of the effort had fallen to the south-west of the city, and, perhaps, only a quarter had landed in the built-up area, causing much damage to housing, minor industry and public buildings.

Having dealt with Lorient under the January Directive, attention now turned upon St-Nazaire, situated further south along the Biscay coast. A force of 437 aircraft included a contribution from 5 Group of eighty-nine Lancasters, of which nine represented 50 Squadron. They departed Skellingthorpe between 18.38 and 18.53 with F/Os Gilmour, Taylor and Townsend the senior pilots on duty, and, after F/O Taylor and crew had turned back with an engine failure, the others reached the target area to find clear skies and good visibility, with only a little ground haze to contend with. They bombed on red TIs from 11,000 to 15,500 feet between 21.10 and 21.37, and it was clear from the many explosions and at least forty fires burning in the docks that the port was undergoing an ordeal of destruction. Post-raid reconnaissance revealed that the marking had been concentrated and the bombing accurate, and local reports confirmed that 60% of the town had been destroyed. This concluded operations for a month in which the squadron had taken part in fourteen, and had dispatched 101 sorties for the loss of four Lancasters and crews.

March 1943

March would bring with it the opening rounds of the Ruhr campaign, the first for which the Command was adequately equipped and genuinely prepared, with a predominantly four-engine bomber force to carry an increasing weight of bombs and Oboe to provide accuracy. First, however, the crews would have to negotiate operations to Germany's Capital and Second Cities, and it was the "Big City" itself, Berlin, that opened the month's account on the 1st. A force of 302 aircraft was assembled, made up of 156 Lancasters, eighty-six Halifaxes and sixty Stirlings, 5 Group putting up a maximum effort of ninety-eight Lancasters, of which eight represented 50 Squadron. They departed Skellingthorpe between 18.57 and 19.13 with F/Os Gilmour, Taylor and Townsend the senior pilots on duty, and they had reached the western Baltic before ED472 was hit by flak when five miles south of Rostock. The bombs were jettisoned immediately, but F/Sgt Murray decided to remain with the bomber stream rather than risk a collision by turning back across it. The target area was found to be under clear skies with only haze to impair the vertical visibility, but, reliant on H2S, the Pathfinder navigators experienced great difficulty in establishing their positions based on the images on their cathode-ray tubes over such a massive urban sprawl. This led to scattered marking, and the main weight of the attack falling into south-western districts. The Skellingthorpe crews bombed from 15,000 to 18,000 feet on red and green TIs between 22.12 and 22.16, and many fires were reported, the glow from which, according to some, could be seen from two hundred miles away on the return flight. Seventeen aircraft failed to return, two of them belonging to 50 Squadron, and both crashed in Holland on the way home. ED592 was shot down by a night-fighter, and crashed at 23.47 near Tiel, some twenty-five miles east of the Hague, while ED423 came down six miles south-east of the centre of Rotterdam at 00.44, and neither produced a survivor from the crews of P/O Townsend and Sgt Thomas respectively. A post-raid analysis based on bombing photos revealed the attack to have been spread over an area of a hundred square miles, but, because of the increasing bomb tonnage being carried, more damage was inflicted on the city than on any previous raid. 875 buildings, mostly houses, were destroyed, and twenty factories seriously damaged, along with railway workshops in the Tempelhof district.

A force of 417 aircraft was assembled to send against Hamburg on the 3rd, and eighty-nine of 149 Lancasters were provided by 5 Group, eight of them at Skellingthorpe, where each had a cookie and twelve SBCs of incendiaries winched into its cavernous thirty-three-foot-long bomb bay. They took off between 18.53 and 19.13 with F/L Maudslay the senior pilot on duty, but lost the services of F/O Gilmour and crew to an undisclosed issue, leaving the others to continue on to find the target basking under clear skies and in good visibility. They carried out their attacks from 15,000 to 18,000 feet between 21.26 and 21.33, aided by the H2S-laid Pathfinder TIs, and numerous fires were observed in the docks area along with black smoke rising to meet the bombers as they turned away. What was not appreciated, was the fact that some markers had fallen onto the town of Wedel, situated some thirteen miles downstream of the Elbe, and they had attracted perhaps the bulk of the bombs, while those hitting the primary target had caused a hundred fires that needed to be dealt with before the fire services could go to the aid of their neighbour. Ten aircraft failed to return, but there were no empty dispersals at Skellingthorpe.

The decks were now cleared for the opening of the Ruhr offensive, which, over the ensuing months, would change the face of bombing and provide for the enemy an indication of the burgeoning power of the Command. This was a momentous occasion, a culmination of all that had gone before during three and a half years of Bomber Command operations. The backs-to-the-wall desperation of 1940, the tentative almost token offensives of 1941, the treading water and gradual metamorphosis under Harris in 1942, when failures still far outnumbered successes, had all been leading to this night, from which point would begin the calculated and systematic dismantling of Germany's industrial and population centres. The only shining light during these dark years had been the quality and spirit of the aircrew, and this had never faltered. It would begin on the 5th at Essen, Harris's nemesis thus far and the home of the giant armaments-producing Krupp works, and, for the first time since the war began, the Command would have at its disposal a device which would negate the industrial haze protecting this city and its neighbours. The magnificent pioneering work on Oboe by W/C Hal Bufton and his crews at 109 Squadron was about to bear fruit in spectacular fashion, and the towns and cities of Germany's arsenal would suffer destruction on an unprecedented scale.

A force of 442 aircraft included ninety-seven Lancasters representing 5 Group, 50 Squadron contributing seven Lancasters and crews, those of F/Sgt Knight in ED478, F/L Gilmour in ED483, P/O Evans in ED470, and Sgts Huntley, Richardson, Schofield and Ward in ED491, ED693, ED648 and ED712. They departed Skellingthorpe between 19.00 and 19.32, and were not involved in the unusually high number of early returns, only seven from 5 Group, which, together with those bombing alternative targets, would reduce the size of the force reaching Essen and bombing as briefed to 362 aircraft. 5 Group favoured a time-and-distance approach to the aiming-point, and the 50 Squadron crews used the Pathfinders' yellow route markers as the initial reference point, before exploiting the good visibility to bomb through the industrial haze onto red and green TIs from 14,500 to 18,500 feet between 21.11 and 21.23. The overwhelming impression was of a concentrated attack, which left many fires burning, and a glow in the sky reported by some to be visible from the North Sea homebound. Post-raid reconnaissance revealed 160 acres of devastation and damage to fifty-three buildings within the Krupp factory complex, and the success of the operation was confirmed by local reports of 3,018 houses destroyed and more than two thousand others seriously damaged. The operation cost the Command an acceptable fourteen aircraft, and it was a most encouraging start to what would become a five month long offensive.

It would be a further week before round two of the Ruhr offensive was mounted, and, in the meantime, Harris turned his attention upon southern Germany, beginning with Nuremberg on the 8th. A force of 338 aircraft included 105 Lancasters of 5 Group, of which ten represented 50 Squadron, and they departed Skellingthorpe between 19.37 and 19.56 with S/L Birch the senior pilot on duty. Again, there was none from the squadron among 5 Group's eight early returns, and the others reached the target to find clear skies but ground haze and extreme darkness. This seemed to impede the Pathfinders' ability to locate the city centre blind by H2S, and the main force crews experienced the same difficulty in identifying ground detail, allowing themselves to be guided to the aiming-point by red and green TIs, which appeared to lack concentration. Just one of the Skellingthorpe crews bombed on the reds, and the rest on the greens or by visual identification of the built-up area, and they carried out their attacks from 14,000 to 18,000 feet between 23.29 and 23.58. The initial impression was of a scattered raid, but a greater concentration of fires developed, and the glow from these was reported by some to be visible for two hundred miles into the return journey. Local reports confirmed the marking and bombing to have been spread along a ten-mile stretch, half of it falling short of the city boundaries, while the rest destroyed six hundred buildings and damaged fourteen hundred others, including a number of important war-industry factories.

On the following day, preparations were put in hand to return to southern Germany to attack the city of Munich, situated deep in the Bavarian mountains of south-eastern Germany, a round-trip of more than 1,200 miles. A force of 264 aircraft included eighty-one Lancasters of 5 Group, of which nine at Skellingthorpe were loaded with a cookie each and SBCs of incendiaries. They took off between 20.36 and 20.50, with F/L Maudslay the senior pilot on duty, but lost Sgt Schofield and W/O Stevens and their crews to undisclosed issues, and they were back home within three hours. The others reached the target area, where clear skies and good visibility prevailed, and the Pathfinder green and white TIs could be seen to have fallen within the built-up area. An enormous orange explosion was witnessed at 00.17, just as the first Skellingthorpe arrivals were running in on the aiming-point, and these had the TIs in the bomb sights as they released their loads from 12,500 to 18,000 feet between 00.19 and 00.43. Another huge explosion at 00.25 was described by Sgt Huntley as the largest he had experienced in his nineteen sorties, and another particularly large one occurred at 00.43. Fires were taking hold and sending a large pall of smoke rising above the city as the bomber force withdrew to the west. A relatively modest eight aircraft failed to return, and only two of these were from 5 Group. A post-raid analysis concluded that a strong wind had pushed the attack into the western half of the city, where 291 buildings had been destroyed and 660 severely damaged. The aero-engine assembly shop at the B.M.W factory was put out of action for six weeks, and many other industrial concerns also lost vital production.

The trio of operations to destinations in southern Germany concluded with the highly industrial city of Stuttgart, situated in a series of valleys which made it difficult to identify. A force of 314 aircraft was assembled on the 11th, 5 Group contributing ninety-six of 152 Lancasters, and nine of these were made ready at Skellingthorpe, where take-off was accomplished safely between 20.05 and 20.22 with F/Ls Elderfield and Gilmour the senior pilots on duty, the former with Sgt Fuller as bomb-aimer before his transfer to the crew of F/L Maudslay. Sgt Pickens and crew turned back after thirty minutes with a dead port-outer engine, leaving the others to press on across France to the target. Visibility was excellent as the main force element arrived late to find Pathfinder TIs burning out on the ground, leaving the way clear for dummy TIs to lure the bombing away from the city centre. In this endeavour they were largely successful, although, to the bomb-aimers high above, the green TIs appeared to be legitimate, and were bombed by the Skellingthorpe crews from 12,000 to 19,000 feet between 23.16 and 23.26. Most of the effort was wasted in open country, but the south-western suburbs of Vaihingen and Kaltental were hit and 118 buildings, mostly houses, were destroyed. It was a disappointing outcome, which cost eleven aircraft, only one of which was from 5 Group.

Round two of the Ruhr campaign was posted on the 12th, when 457 crews learned at briefing that Essen was once more to be their destination. 5 Group detailed ninety-five Lancasters, of which ten were made ready at Skellingthorpe and took off between 19.29 and 19.43 with F/L Maudslay the senior pilot on duty. P/O Evans and crew had reached enemy territory when let down by their intercom system and had to turn back, and Sgt Ward RCAF and crew were approaching the German frontier within forty miles of the target, when intercepted by a night-fighter, which shot down ED449 to crash five miles east-north-east of Venray at 21.25, killing all on board. The others found the target well marked by red and green Pathfinder TIs, with only smoke to mar the visibility, and attacked from 15,000 to 19,000 feet between 21.32 and 21.40. It was clear that the bombing was accurate and mostly concentrated around the Oboe-laid TIs, and, this time, the Krupp complex found itself in the centre of the area of destruction. The defences fought back to claim twenty-three bombers, in return for which, post-raid reconnaissance confirmed another highly successful assault on this centre of war production, which, although destroying substantially fewer buildings, achieved greater concentration, and inflicted 30% more damage on Krupp than the raid of a week earlier.

On the 13th, 5 Group sent seventeen Lancasters to mine the waters in one of the seven Silverthorn gardens of the Kattegat, between northern Denmark and Sweden, for which the sole 50 Squadron participant, F/O Day and crew, took off at 20.02. They arrived in the target area some three-and-a-quarter hours later to find good visibility and establish a pinpoint on Anholt Island, before delivering their stores into the briefed location from 4,000 feet at 23.26. Thereafter, the weather caused a lull in operations, and, on the 15th, while at least three of the squadron's aircraft were at Scampton for an undisclosed reason, the bomb load of 57

Squadron's W4834 went up, and wrote off W4112, W4196 and W4823, happily, without crew casualties.

It was the 22nd before orders came through to prepare for the second attack under the January directive on St-Nazaire, for which a force of 357 aircraft was assembled, including a contribution from 5 Group of 120 Lancasters. 50 Squadron made ready a dozen Lancasters, which departed Skellingthorpe between 18.55 and 19.18 with S/Ls Birch and Street the senior pilots on duty, the latter for his first sortie with the squadron. F/Sgt Dennis and crew lost the use of their intercom and turned back at 21.00, when within about thirty minutes of the target. The others reached the target area to find good visibility impeded only by ground haze, which did not prevent a visual identification of ground features. Red and green Pathfinder TIs confirmed the location of the aiming-point, and the 50 Squadron crews released their mix of high-explosives and incendiaries from 11,500 to 15,000 feet between 21.37 and 21.43. Fires were taking hold as they turned away, and, despite the recall of the Stirling element, to which fifty-five crews responded, the town and its port facilities sustained massive damage. All from Skellingthorpe were diverted to one of eight stations on return, after mist descended on the Lincoln area.

A mass posting-out to the newly-formed 617 Squadron at Scampton took place on the 25th, and involved two complete crews. F/L Maudslay's consisted of flight engineer, Sgt Jack Marriott, navigator, F/O Robert Urquhart, bomb-aimer, P/O Mike Fuller, wireless operator, W/O Alden Cottam and gunners F/O Bill Tytherleigh and Sgt Norman Burrows. The newly-commissioned P/O Les Knight took with him flight engineer, Sgt Ray Grayston, navigator, F/O Harold (known as Sydney) Hobday, bomb-aimer, F/O Edward Johnson, wireless operator, F/Sgt Bob Kellow and gunners, Sgt Fred Sutherland and Harry "Obie" O'Brien. Three others would follow them to Scampton late in April, but in time to participate in what would become the most celebrated feat of arms in the history of military aviation.

Duisburg was selected as the host for the third operation of the Ruhr offensive, to be launched on the 26th and involve 455 aircraft. 5 Group detailed ninety-four Lancasters, of which eleven were made ready at Skellingthorpe and took off between 18.51 and 19.13 with S/Ls Birch and Street the senior pilots on duty. They had learned at briefing that marking would be by "Musical Wanganui", the code for Oboe skymarking, to be carried out by nine Mosquitos of 109 Squadron. F/O Elderfield and crew were ninety minutes out, when starboard-outer engine failure ended their interest in proceedings, and they returned home to find Sgt Murray and crew already there after the failure of their oxygen system. The others pressed on to the target area, where they found ten-tenths cloud with tops at 10,000 feet and good visibility above. They were greeted by the Oboe release-point parachute flares, which were in the bomb sights as they dropped their loads from 18,000 to 20,000 feet between 21.41 and 21.56, and a large explosion was witnessed at 21.53. What the crews couldn't know, was that five of the Oboe Mosquitos had returned early with equipment failure and a sixth had been shot down, leaving just three to deliver what could only be sparse marking. This was insufficient, and led to a scattered and ineffective attack, which, according to local reports, caused only minor damage. Fortunately, the failure cost a modest six aircraft, none of them belonging to 5 Group.

Orders were received on stations across the Command on the 27th to prepare for a trip to the "Big City" that night, and a force of 396 aircraft was duly assembled, which included 111 Lancasters from 5 Group. A dozen of these were made ready at Skellingthorpe, and they took off between 20.12 and 20.26 with W/C Russell accompanying the crew of W/O Stevens, and once again leading from the front for what was always a challenging target. For the second operation running, Sgt Murray and crew were involved in an early return, this time because of an intercom issue, leaving the others to continue on to approach the city from the south-west, each carrying a cookie and eleven or twelve SBCs of incendiaries. The Pathfinders were again reliant upon H2S to locate the city-centre aiming-point, but failed to establish their positions accurately, and marked two areas at least five miles short. The Skellingthorpe crews reported three-tenths cloud at 13,000 feet and five tenths stratus at 19,000 feet with moderate to good visibility, and bombed on red and green TIs from 14,000 to 18,000 feet between 23.05 and 23.20. ED478 was hit by flak in the port-inner engine, but W/C Russell and his adopted crew brought it home safely. From bombing altitude, the attack appeared to be effective, but local reports confirmed that the main weight of bombs had fallen between seven and seventeen miles short of the target, and 25% of those hitting the city had failed to detonate.

There would be a chance to rectify the failure two nights hence, but, in the meantime, St-Nazaire would face its third heavy assault under the January Directive, for which a force of 323 aircraft was made ready on the 28th. 5 Group detailed twenty-one freshman crews, of which six belonged to 50 Squadron, and they departed Skellingthorpe between 19.51 and 20.03 with S/Ls Birch and Street the senior pilots on duty, the former flying with an adopted crew. All reached the target area to encounter good visibility and red and green Oboe-laid TIs marking out the aiming-point, and these were in the bomb sights as the attacks were carried out from 12,000 to 17,000 feet between 22.15 and 22.23. Returning crews reported concentrated fires, and post-raid reconnaissance confirmed the accuracy and effectiveness of the raid.

On the following day, a force of 329 aircraft was assembled for the return to Berlin that night, night, for which 50 Squadron made ready eight of the 106 Lancasters provided by 5 Group. They departed Skellingthorpe between 21.54 and 22.08 with F/O Taylor the senior pilot on duty, but lost F/Sgt Richardson and crew to severe icing that prevented them from climbing above 11,000 feet. F/O Nichols and crew also turned back after their starboard-outer engine overheated, and they were followed home by Sgt Pickens and crew for an undisclosed reason. These were just three of an alarming eighteen 5 Group crews to abandon their sorties for a variety of causes. The others reached Berlin, although did so behind schedule with the rest of the main force because of inaccurately forecast winds. Visibility was described by most as good, which enabled them to identify the target visually, aided by red TIs burning on the ground. Bombing was carried out by the 50 Squadron crews from 15,000 to 19,000 feet between 01.00 and 01.17, and appeared to be scattered. This was confirmed later, when bombing photos revealed that most of the effort had fallen into open country south of the city, a disappointment compounded by the loss of twenty-one aircraft. During the course of the month the squadron took part in thirteen operations, and dispatched 111 sorties for the loss of three Lancasters and crews.

April 1943

April would be the least rewarding month during the Ruhr offensive, principally, because of the number of operations directed at targets in regions of Germany beyond the range of Oboe. It began for two 5 Group squadrons with the preparation of eight Lancasters on the 2nd, to carry out the final raid on St-Nazaire, while forty-seven aircraft from other groups dealt with

Lorient to bring down the curtain on the January Directive. 50 Squadron, meanwhile, loaded nine Lancasters with six mines each for delivery to the Deodars garden in the Gironde estuary on the approaches to the port of Bordeaux, and dispatched them from Skellingthorpe between 20.02 and 20.28 with S/L Street the senior pilot on duty. For most, it would be an uneventful trip, reaching the target area after an outward flight of around three-and-a-half hours, before obtaining firm pin-points and dropping the mines as briefed from 500 to 1,000 feet between 22.51 and 23.49. ED842 failed to return with the crew of F/O Nichols, and no trace of the Lancaster and crew was ever found.

The Lancaster and Halifax stations received orders on the 3rd to prepare for an operation against Essen that night, for which the Krupp works was designated as the aiming-point. They responded with forces of 225 and 113 aircraft respectively, 5 Group contributing 123 of the Lancasters, and this would be the first time that more than two hundred of the type had operated together. 50 Squadron loaded its twelve participating aircraft with a cookie and twelve SBCs of incendiaries each, and dispatched them between 19.32 and 19.57 with S/L Birch the senior pilot on duty. Accompanying him was W/C Edmund "Ronnie" Baxter, who was beginning a short spell with the squadron in order to gain experience before being appointed to command 106 Squadron a month hence. Sgt Duncan and crew returned early for an undisclosed reason, leaving the remaining Skellingthorpe crews to press on to the target, where almost clear skies prevailed. Because of uncertainty by the Command's meteorological section of the likely weather conditions over the Ruhr, the Pathfinders had prepared both sky and ground marking plans, which led to a degree of confusion among the main force crews as they decided at which they should aim their bombs. The 50 Squadron crews mostly responded to red and green release-point flares before observing the TIs on the ground, and bombed from 15,000 to 18,000 feet between 22.11 and 22.21. Returning crews reported many explosions, with fires emitting large volumes of smoke, and the consensus was of a successful raid. This was confirmed by bombing photographs and local reports, which spoke of widespread destruction in central and western districts, where 635 buildings had been reduced to rubble and many more seriously damaged. The defence was intense, and F/O Day and crew reported being coned by thirty to forty searchlights for the entirety of their bombing run. It was an expensive night for the Command, which registered the loss of a dozen Halifaxes and nine Lancasters, 6% of those dispatched, but it was the respective loss rates of the types that was most telling, with the Halifaxes suffering 10.62% compared with 4% for the Lancasters.

The largest non-1,000 force to date of 577 aircraft was made ready on the 4th for an attack that night on the naval port of Kiel, for which 5 Group put up 112 Lancasters, thirteen of them representing 50 Squadron. They departed Skellingthorpe between 20.59 and 21.15 with W/C Russell the senior pilot on duty, and all reached the target area, where they were guided towards the aiming-point by yellow route marker flares, released by the Pathfinder heavy brigade either side of 23.00. On arrival, Kiel was found to be concealed beneath ten-tenths cloud with good visibility above, and bombs were released onto the glow of fires below the cloud from 15,000 to 19,000 feet between 23.21 and 23.35. It was not possible to assess the outcome, and bombing photos would reveal only cloud. A post-raid analysis concluded that decoy fires were operating, and probably lured away a proportion of the effort, while the strong wind caused the markers to drift, leading the remainder astray and resulting in most of the bombs missing the target altogether. According to local reports, only eleven houses were destroyed, and this was a major disappointment in view of the size of the force involved.

50 and 467 RAAF Squadrons put up two and three Lancasters respectively on the 6th to mine the sea lanes off south-western France. The Skellingthorpe pair of Sgts McGrath and Wilkie took off at 20.34 and 20.38 bound for the Furze garden off St-Jean-de-Luz, but encountered visibility so poor that it prevented them from locating the target area. The Ruhr offensive continued at Duisburg on the 8th, for which a mixed force of 379 Lancasters, Wellingtons, Halifaxes and Stirlings was assembled as the heavy element, while ten Oboe Mosquitos would provide the initial marking. 5 Group was responsible for eighty-four of the Lancasters, nine of them belonging to 50 Squadron, which departed Skellingthorpe between 20.59 and 21.10 with S/L Street the senior pilot on duty. Sgt Pickens and crew turned back early after experiencing intercom and oxygen system problems, and the failure of navigational equipment curtailed F/O Elderfield's sortie and created difficulties in getting home. Those reaching the western Ruhr encountered ten-tenths cloud with tops in places as high as 20,000 feet, and the conditions completely nullified the Pathfinders' attempts to mark either the route or the target. The bombing was carried out on e.t.a, some crews embarking on a time-and-distance run from as far away as the Dutch coast as the last visual reference. The 50 Squadron crews attacked from 17,000 to 22,500 feet between 23.24 and 23.45, and had nothing of value to pass on to the intelligence section at debriefing. Local reports confirmed a widely scattered raid, which hit at least fifteen other Ruhr locations, and destroyed just forty buildings in Duisburg.

Not content with the outcome, Harris ordered another raid twenty-four hours later, only this time, employing a much-reduced force of 104 Lancasters and five Mosquitos. 5 Group detailed seventy Lancasters, of which nine represented 50 Squadron, and they departed Skellingthorpe between 20.17 and 20.38 with F/Ls Gilmour and Taylor the senior pilots on duty. There were no early returns, and they were guided to the target by red route-marker flares, and then red and green skymarkers over the aiming-point, which was hidden by ten-tenths cloud with tops at 5,000 to 15,000 feet. They delivered their cookie and twelve SBCs each from 14,000 to 21,000 feet between 23.05 and 23.12, some observing a large red glow reflected in the clouds. Local reports confirmed that this was another highly scattered raid, which spread bombs over a wide area of the Ruhr and destroyed only fifty houses in Duisburg.

Frankfurt was posted as the destination for 502 aircraft on the 10th, on a night when Wellingtons would represent the most populous type, demonstrating that this trusty old warhorse still had an important part to play in Bomber Command operations. 5 Group provided sixty-six of 136 Lancasters, six of them from Skellingthorpe, and they took off between 00.15 and 00.24 with F/L Taylor the senior pilot on duty. At 01.35, Waddington received a message from Sgt McGrath RCAF and crew to the effect that they were turning back with a technical problem. At 02.38, permission was sought to jettison the bombs off Skegness, and instructions were issued to do so some sixty miles out over the North Sea. This signal was acknowledged at 02.57, and, at 03.10, the Royal Observer Corps reported ED478 crossing the Lincolnshire coast heading inland. However, a feint W/T signal was picked up at 04.45, which was plotted some sixty miles off Skegness, and this was the last confirmed contact. An air-sea rescue launch would find small pieces of wreckage in the search area on the following morning, but no trace of the crew was ever found. This was Sgt McGrath's fifth sortie, and, in 1946, he would be promoted posthumously to the rank of warrant officer. The others had pressed on across France over ten-tenths cloud, and carried out time-and-distance runs from green route marker flares to deliver their loads from 15,000 to 19,000 feet between

02.55 and 03.16. No one saw anything other than an apparent glow of fires beneath the cloud, and bombing photos would reveal nothing, while local reports suggested that most of the bombing had missed the city altogether.

208 Lancaster crews were notified on the 13th of a change of scenery for their next operation, which was to be against the docks at La Spezia on Italy's northern coast some forty miles south-east of Genoa. 5 Group detailed 124 of the Lancasters, with the remainder provided by 1 and 8 Groups, the latter also sending three Halifaxes as part of the marker force. 50 Squadron loaded nine of its aircraft with 1,000 pounders and SBCs of incendiaries, and five others with mines for delivery to the Mullett garden, on the approaches to the port. They were sent on their way between 20.36 and 20.58 with W/C Russell and S/L Birch the senior pilots on duty among the bombing brigade, and F/L Gilmour leading the gardeners. There were no early returns, and all arrived on the Italian side of the Alps to find almost cloudless skies and only haze and smoke to mar the vertical visibility. Despite this, S/L Birch and crew were unable to locate the target, and bombed two searchlights as a last resort. The others established their positions by visual reference of ground detail, such as rivers and the docks, confirmed by Pathfinder flares, and bombing took place from 8,000 to 10,500 feet between 01.43 and 02.18, by which time many fires had added to the smoke obscuring the town. A number of large explosions were reported, and the operation was revealed later to have caused extensive damage. Three aircraft from other squadrons landed on recently captured airfields in North Africa, and were the first to do so before so-called "shuttle-raids" became a feature of operations to the Mediterranean region. While this operation was in progress, three of the gardeners had fulfilled their brief by delivering their vegetables accurately from 3,000 to 4,000 feet between 01.42 and 02.08, despite challenging conditions of poor visibility, and two others had aborted their sorties because of technical issues.

The busy round of non-Ruhr operations would continue at Stuttgart, for which a force of 462 aircraft was made ready on the 14th. 5 Group detailed fifty-seven Lancasters, and six of these were made ready at Skellingthorpe and loaded with a cookie and twelve SBCs of incendiaries. They took off between 22.13 and 22.22 with S/L Birch the senior pilot on duty, and, there were no early returns to reduce the squadron's presence for the attack. They approached the city from the north-east to find an absence of cloud, but haze, aggravated by smoke, made ground detail indistinct. The aiming-point was established by the green and red Pathfinder TIs, and bombing was carried out by five of the Skellingthorpe crews from 15,000 to 16,000 feet between 01.23 and 01.29. Few crews were able to make out the impact of their own bombs, and noted only a concentration of fires and considerable amounts of smoke. Sgt Pickens and crew suffered a hang-up on the first pass, but, according to an "all-bombs-gone" light-indicator, it seemed that the bombs had released on the second run. A visual inspection revealed them to be still in the bomb bay, however, and the cookie was released manually over an aerodrome in the Reims area on the way home, and caused a large red fire on the end of the runway. Post-raid reconnaissance revealed that the Pathfinders had marked the centre of the city, but that a "creep-back" had developed, which had spread back along the line of approach. Creep-back was a feature of many large raids, and was caused by crews bombing the first fires they came upon, rather than pushing through to the planned aiming-point. It could work for or against the effectiveness of the attack, and, on this night, worked in the Command's favour by falling across the industrial district of Bad-Canstatt, before spreading further back along the line of approach onto the residential suburbs of Münster and

Mühlhausen. It was here that the majority of the 393 buildings were destroyed and more than nine hundred others severely damaged.

Two major operations were planned for the 16th, the main one employing 327 Lancasters and Halifaxes to target the Skoda armaments factory at distant Pilsen in Czechoslovakia, while a force of 271 aircraft, consisting predominantly of Wellingtons and Stirlings, created a large-scale diversion at Mannheim some 240 miles to the west. 197 Lancasters and 130 Halifaxes were detailed, of which 102 of the former were provided by 5 Group. The plan of attack at Pilsen called for the Pathfinders to drop route markers at the final turning point, seven miles from the target, which the crews were to then locate visually in the anticipated bright moonlight, and bomb from as low a level as practicable. It was a complicated plan that invited confusion and failure, and the outcome would question the quality of some of the briefings. 50 Squadron made ready ten Lancasters, loading six with a cookie and incendiaries and the remainder with all-incendiary loads, before dispatching them from Skellingthorpe between 21.30 and 21.43 with S/L Birch the senior pilot on duty. Ahead of them lay a round-trip of some 1,500 miles, which four of the 50 Squadron crews would fail to negotiate, F/Sgt Weber falling ill and turning back after two-and-a-half hours.

The remaining nine 50 Squadron participants arrived in the target area to find the forecast favourable weather conditions, with a layer of eight-tenths cloud at between 9,000 and 15,000 feet, below which, visibility was good and ground features could be made out clearly. The briefings should have made clear that the bombing was to be carried out visually from below the cloud base after making a timed run from the turning-point, which had been marked by TIs. Many 5 Group crews reported bombing from 7,000 to 9,000 feet visually and on TIs between 01.42 and 01.55, proving that they had failed to comply with the instructions at briefing, and had bombed the turning point. The 50 Squadron crews, on the other hand, made no reference to TIs, but all described difficulty in locating and identifying the factory buildings, some after spending time searching, while having to dodge searchlights and flak. The bombing was carried out from 7,000 to 8,000 feet between 01.43 and 02.01, the latter timing that of S/L Birch, who circled the area for twenty-five minutes until bombing a last-resort objective in the vicinity of the Skoda works. He also reported many cookies bursting in open country, and intense night-fighter activity in the Mannheim area on the way home. F/L Gilmour and crew returned at low-level over France, attacking locomotives and an aerodrome on the way. The details of the crew reports across the group demonstrated that they could not have related to the Skoda works. Post-raid reconnaissance revealed the truth, that, despite the claims of returning crews, no bombs had fallen within miles of the factory, and had been concentrated instead around an asylum at Dobrany, some seven miles to the south-west. This failure was compounded by the loss of thirty-six aircraft, split equally between the two types, and eighteen aircraft were also missing from the Mannheim contingent, which had, at least, achieved the destruction of 130 buildings and damage to some degree to three thousand others.

The total casualty figure for the night, of fifty-four aircraft, represented a new record, and, among them were three from Skellingthorpe. ED691 crashed at Épense, some forty miles south-east of Reims, killing F/O Day. It seems that he remained at the controls to allow his crew and a second pilot to save themselves, the six members of his crew falling into enemy hands, while the second pilot evaded a similar fate. ED800 was shot down by the night-fighter of Hptm Alfred Haesler of I./NJG4, and crashed at 04.00 about four miles north-north-west of

Philippeville in Belgium, before sinking into marshy ground and descending beyond reach into old mine galleries, where the crew of Sgt J G Duncan remain. (This was one of two Sgts Duncan serving as pilots with the squadron at this time.) The pilot and two others were Scottish, while both gunners were Welsh and two came from Lancashire. ED784 reached as far as Saarbrücken outbound, before being attacked by two Me110 night-fighters and further damaged by flak. F/O Elderfield flew it back over the French coast, where he ditched about six miles out at 04.00, and two of the crew drowned, one of them, an additional member flying as second pilot. The remaining six managed to gain the safety of the dinghy, but, at some point, F/O Elderfield decided to attempt to swim ashore to summon assistance. He was not seen again, and, at 02.00 on the 18th, some twenty-two hours after ditching, they were located and rescued by a motor torpedo boat and delivered to Dover Hospital at 04.55. The good news was passed on to Skellingthorpe at 08.30.

A return to the docks at La Spezia was notified to the Lancaster squadrons of 1, 5 and 8 Groups on the 18th, and 8 Group would also contribute five Halifaxes to the overall force of 178 aircraft. The eighty-nine 5 Group Lancasters included five representing 50 Squadron, which also loaded mines into four others for delivery to the nearby Mullett garden. They departed Skellingthorpe together between 21.08 and 21.19 with W/C Baxter the senior pilot on duty among the bombing brigade. Operating with the squadron for the first time were F/L Stone and crew, who had arrived from 1654 Conversion Unit only three days earlier. F/L Gilmour and crew were back on the ground with their mines within three hours after a plethora of technical problems forced them to curtail their sortie. The other members of the squadron continued on across France, and F/L Stone and crew had reached the foothills of the Alps, still an hour short of their destination, when the starboard-outer engine failed. They turned back at 00.45, jettisoning their bombs from 10,000 feet in Lake Bourget. The others found the weather to be ideal and visibility good in the target area, apart from an effective smokescreen over the town and docks. The aiming-point was identified visually after a timed run from Palmaria Island to the south, and confirmed by red Pathfinder TIs, on which they bombed from 6,000 to 9,000 feet between 01.51 and 02.05. The gardeners, F/Ls Evans and Taylor, and Sgt D A Duncan, delivered their vegetables as briefed from 2,000 to 2,500 feet between 01.58 and 02.02, and both sections noted that the fires were becoming concentrated as they turned away and set course for home, completely satisfied with their night's work. Photographic reconnaissance revealed that the marking and bombing had missed the dockyards to the north-west, but had caused extensive damage to the railway station and public buildings in the town centre.

F/Sgt John Fraser RCAF was posted to 617 Squadron on the 20th, where he would join the crew of F/L John Hopgood for Operation Chastise. Orders were received on that day to prepare for another long-range operation that night, this one against the port of Stettin, situated 640 miles away as the crow flies at the midpoint of Germany's wartime Baltic coast. 5 Group contributed ninety-one Lancasters to the force of 339 aircraft, eight of them belonging to 50 Squadron, whose crews learned at briefing that the route would take the bomber stream across the North Sea to a point north of Esbjerg on the Danish coast, before traversing Jutland to then head south-east towards the target. The distance, which was similar to that for Pilsen, dictated a slightly reduced bomb load of a cookie and SBCs of 4lb and 30lb incendiaries each, and these were lifted into the air at Skellingthorpe between 21.38 and 21.58 with S/L Street the senior pilot on duty. There were targets, like Duisburg, that seemed to enjoy something of a charmed life, and managed to dodge the worst ravages of a Bomber

Command attack, but Stettin was not among them, perhaps because of its location near an easily identifiable coastline. Sgt Huntley and crew were outbound at 23.31 when approached by at least two Ju88s, initially on the port quarter and port beam, and it may have been these or others, which appeared then on the starboard beam and astern. The rear gunner fired five hundred rounds into the face of the last-mentioned, which was seen to fall in flames and impact the ground. The bombs had been jettisoned in preparation for the engagement, during which the Lancaster sustained damage to the rear turret, and its occupant some bruising. On this night, clear skies and good visibility paved the way for the Pathfinders to deliver a perfect marking performance, which was exploited by the main force crews to devastating effect. The Skellingthorpe element arrived to find the city laid out before them with the river, built-up area and the docks clearly defined, and the aiming-point marked by green TIs. They carried out their attacks from 12,000 to 13,500 feet between 01.09 and 01.20, and, on return, reported fires raging across the built-up area and the glow of fires visible for ninety miles into the return journey. It was thirty-six hours before a reconnaissance aircraft captured photographs of the still-burning city, and these revealed an area of one hundred acres of devastation across the centre. Local reports confirmed that thirteen industrial premises and 380 houses had been destroyed at a cost to the Command of twenty-one aircraft, four of them 5 Group Lancasters.

F/L Taylor was posted to the newly-forming 619 Squadron at Woodhall Spa on the 22nd, where his experience would prove to be invaluable, and he would meet up again with F/O Dampier-Crossley. Orders on the 26th signalled a return to the Ruhr and Duisburg, for which a large force of 561 aircraft was assembled, the numbers bolstered by the inclusion of 135 Wellingtons, while 215 Lancasters represented the largest contribution by type. 5 Group was responsible for 105 of them, and 50 Squadron nine, which departed Skellingthorpe between 00.18 and 00.40 with F/Ls Evans and Gilmour the senior pilots on duty. They set course for the Dutch coast for the northern approach to the Ruhr, and reached the target area after approaching from the north-east. They found largely clear skies and good visibility, and were guided to the aiming-point by red and green TIs. Bombing by the Skellingthorpe element was carried out from 17,000 to 21,000 feet between 02.33 and 02.41, and gave rise to many fires, although opinions were divided as to the degree of concentration achieved. A large orange explosion was witnessed to the east of the aiming-point at 02.34, but fires had not gained a hold by the time they withdrew, although black smoke was rising through 7,000 feet. Seventeen aircraft failed to return, but only one of these was from 5 Group. Post-raid reconnaissance revealed that the attack had fallen short of the city centre and had been focussed around the north-eastern districts under the line of approach, thus sparing Duisburg again from the full weight of a Bomber Command heavy raid. Even so, local reports confirmed the destruction of more than three hundred buildings, which represented something of a telling blow upon this target.

The 27th was devoted to the largest mining operation of the war to date, which involved 160 aircraft targeting the waters off the Brittany and Biscay coasts and the Frisians. Twenty-eight 5 Group Lancasters were detailed, four of them, captained by W/C Baxter, F/Ls Evans and Stone and Sgt Saxton, departing Skellingthorpe between 02.00 and 02.09 bound for the Nectarines II garden off the Frisians. They found seven to ten-tenths cloud in the target area, and delivered their six vegetables each unopposed into the briefed locations from 1,100 to 1,500 feet between 03.32 and 03.56, before returning home safely from uneventful sorties. The following night brought an even larger gardening effort involving 207 aircraft, of which forty-one Lancasters were provided by 5 Group, four of them by 50 Squadron. The

Skellingthorpe quartet took off between 20.53 and 21.02 with FO Hollis and W/O Dennis and their crews bound for the Daffodil garden at the southern end of The Sound (Øresund) between Copenhagen and Malmo, while Sgts Hendry and Saxton headed further north to Silverthorn 5 in the Kattegat. They all reached the western Baltic, where clear skies and good visibility prevailed, and they fulfilled their briefs from 1,000 to 2,000 feet between 00.01 and 00.13 with only W/O Dennis and crew running into a little light flak, which holed the starboard side of the fuselage and severed a feed pipe to the mid-upper turret. Elsewhere, where low cloud was encountered, the flak proved to be more troublesome, and twenty-two aircraft failed to return, only one of them from 5 Group, and this would be the largest-ever loss to result in a single night from mining. The number of mines delivered, 593, was also a record for one night, and would not be surpassed.

On the 29th, navigator, F/O Ken Earnshaw RCAF, was posted to 617 Squadron, where he would find a seat in the Dams Lancaster of F/L John Hopgood with fatal consequences, and he was accompanied to Scampton by gunner, Sgt Brian Jagger, who would protect F/L Shannon and crew on Operation Chastise from the front turret. He would survive his operational career as a valued member of Shannon's crew, but lose his life in a tragic accident, while flying with the Bombing Development Unit a year and a day after leaving Skellingthorpe.

Essen was posted as the target on the 30th, as attention swung once more towards the Ruhr, and would remain upon it almost exclusively now until well into July. A force of 305 aircraft included 101 Lancasters of 5 Group, of which eleven were loaded with a cookie and twelve SBCs each at Skellingthorpe and dispatched between 00.25 and 00.45 with W/C Baxter the senior pilot on duty. A layer of ice-bearing cloud lay across the bomber stream's path over the North Sea, and, when W/O Dennis found his windscreen and turrets glazed over and the guns frozen and inoperable, he turned back. On landing, he found Sgt Wilkie and crew already on the ground after the failure of their Gee-box. The others continued on to the target area, where they were greeted by ten-tenths cloud with tops in places as high as 21,000 feet, and red and green Oboe-laid Wanganui flares (skymarkers) identifying the aiming-point. Some crews carried out a time-and-distance run from green tracking markers, and all had some kind of flare in the bomb sight, or, at least the glow of one, as they released their loads from 19,000 to 23,000 feet between 02.58 and 03.06. Returning crews reported the glow of fires beneath the cloud and a number of large explosions, but it was impossible to determine whether or not concentration had been achieved, particularly as bombing photos showed only cloud. Post-raid reconnaissance and local reports confirmed a lack of concentration and the liberal distribution of bombs onto ten other Ruhr locations, particularly Bottrop to the north, but 189 buildings were destroyed and 237 severely damaged in Essen, and, importantly, the Krupp works sustained further damage.

During the course of an extremely busy month, the squadron was involved in eighteen operations and dispatched 135 sorties for the loss of five Lancasters, four complete crews and three crew members.

May 1943

May would bring a return to winning ways, with a number of outstanding successes and new records as the Ruhr offensive expanded its horizons to include targets other than Essen and

Duisburg. The first of these "new" targets was Dortmund, which had been attacked many times before, but not on the scale that it was about to face on the 4th, when a force of 596 aircraft was assembled, which represented the largest non-1,000 effort to date. 5 Group made available 125 Lancasters, of which nine were prepared at Skellingthorpe and loaded with a cookie and twelve SBCs each. They took off between 21.56 and 22.34 with W/C Baxter the senior pilot on duty, but would soon lose the services of four crews as technical gremlins took their toll. F/L Evans and crew were the first to return early, after some ninety minutes, because of the failure of the a.s.i., and they were joined by Sgt Saxton, F/O Chopping and F/L Stone between 01.03 and 01.33 with Gee, rear turret and oxygen supply issues. The others pushed on across Holland to the target, situated at the eastern end of the Ruhr, and found clear skies, good visibility and only industrial and smoke haze to spoil the vertical view. The defences responded with many searchlight cones and intense heavy flak, and much evasive action would be required after bombing to vacate the target area intact. The initial Pathfinder marking was accurately placed around the city centre, but some of the backing-up fell short, and a decoy site was also successful in luring away a proportion of the bombing. The 50 Squadron crews bombed on red or green TIs from an average of 20,000 feet shortly after 01.30, and, on return, reported many explosions, some large, and developing fires, the glow from which could be seen, according to some, from 150 miles into the return flight. F/Sgt Burnett and crew had just come out of a corkscrew when attacked by an unseen night-fighter, which scored hits around the starboard-inner engine, but they shook it off in time to complete a perfect bombing run, thirty seconds after which, an enormous explosion threw flame to a height of 2,000 feet, and burned for ten seconds. Post-raid reconnaissance revealed that approximately half of the force had bombed within three miles of the aiming-point, and had destroyed 1,218 buildings and seriously damaged more than two thousand others. Local reports confirmed a death toll of 693 people, which was a record from a Bomber Command attack. It was not a one-sided affair, however, and the loss of thirty-one aircraft was a foretaste of what was in store for the bomber crews operating to "Happy Valley".

A break from major operations took the Command through to the 12th, when Duisburg was posted as the target for a bombing force of 562 aircraft with ten Oboe Mosquitos to take care of the initial marking. 5 Group was responsible for 119 of the 238 Lancasters, and they would be accompanied by 142 Halifaxes, 112 Wellingtons and seventy Stirlings. Ten 50 Squadron Lancasters departed Skellingthorpe between 23.56 and 00.27 with S/L Birch the senior pilot on duty, and there was one early return, which could, so easily, have been a failure to return. F/O Hollis and crew were cruising at 19,500 feet over the Dutch coast at Egmond, when they collided at 01.47 with another Lancaster approaching from the south, which was almost certainly ahead of schedule and orbiting to lose time. The contact was almost head on, and there was no time for evasive action other than a slight pull to port, which, clearly saved them from damage immeasurably worse than the several feet of the starboard wing that fell away with a section of aileron. The bombs were jettisoned, and a safe return made. The identity of the other aircraft has never been established, and it may also have remained airborne, or, if lost, recorded as a victim of either flak or a night-fighter. The others reached the target area guided by yellow tracking flares, and found ideal bombing conditions with no cloud and good visibility, which helped the Pathfinders to mark with great accuracy and focus. The main force crews exploited the opportunity by producing a display of concentrated bombing, the Skellingthorpe element releasing their loads onto red TIs, but the author of the squadron ORB during this month failed to record the details. For once, the attack proceeded according to plan, and this elusive target finally succumbed to a devastating assault. Returning crews described a large explosion at 02.30, streets outlined by fire and a highly successful outcome, the best yet witnessed by some, and their impressions were confirmed by photo-reconnaissance, which revealed extensive damage in the city centre and the Ruhrort Rhine docks, the largest inland port in Germany. 1,596 buildings were totally destroyed and the Thyssen steelworks damaged, while dozens of barges and ships were sunk or damaged. However, many crews were absent from debriefing at stations across the Command, and it soon became clear that the success had been gained at a cost of thirty-four aircraft. The loss rates by type made interesting reading and confirmed the established food chain, the Lancasters sustaining a 4.2% loss, compared with 8.9% for Wellingtons, 7.1% for Stirlings and 6.3% for Halifaxes. W7462 was the 50 Squadron representative among the missing, after being shot down into the Ijsselmeer by a night-fighter on the way home at 03.32. There were no survivors from the crew of P/O Huntley DFM, which included a second pilot gaining experience before captaining his own crew. Such was the level of destruction that Duisburg would now be left in peace for a year.

On the following night, the squadron contributed a dozen aircraft to a 5 Group force of 124 Lancasters, which were detailed with thirty-two other Lancasters and twelve Halifaxes of 8 Group to attempt to rectify the recent failure at the Skoda armaments works at Pilsen. A simultaneous raid on the Ruhr city of Bochum was planned, and would involve 442 aircraft from the other groups, and, perhaps, split the defences. The Skellingthorpe element took off between 21.53 and 22.09 with S/L Birch the senior pilot on duty, and had crossed the Dutch/German frontier near Lingen, when ED693 was intercepted by Lt Hans-Heinz Augustein of III./NJG1, and shot down to crash at 23.57 four miles east-south-east of the town. Sgt Pickens RCAF and four members of his crew parachuted into the hands of the enemy, but both gunners perished, and may well have been killed during the engagement. The others reached the target to find clear skies and good visibility, but with ground haze and a smokescreen to impair the vertical visibility. The Pathfinders dropped red TIs with a fairly good concentration that would have been perfectly adequate over a built-up area, but was too scattered at a precision target like the Skoda works. Bombing took place from around 10,000 feet, and the impression was that most of it fell among the TIs. Sadly, these were found to have missed the target, and most of the bombs had fallen into open country to the north of the factory. Some compensation was gained at Bochum, where almost four hundred buildings were destroyed and seven hundred seriously damaged at a cost of twenty-four aircraft, and these were added to the nine Lancasters missing from Pilsen.

The above operations proved to be the last major outings for the Pathfinders and main force squadrons for nine days, and, it was during this lull, that 617 Squadron entered bomber folklore with its epic attack on the Dams under Operation Chastise on the night of the 16/17th. Among those taking part were the former 50 Squadron crews of "Mick" Martin, "Les" Knight and Henry Maudslay, who had been promoted at Scampton to squadron leader rank and appointed B Flight commander. He and his crew were all killed when shot down at Emmerich on the way home, and losing his life also was Ken Earnshaw of Hopgood's crew, which crashed after attacking the Möhne Dam, and from which bomb-aimer, John Fraser, was one of only three to survive being shot down. Martin and Knight returned safely, and all but Bob Hay of Martin's crew would survive the war. Les Knight had four months to live, but his crew would make it through to the end of hostilities, largely because of his sacrifice. Gibson's Canadian navigator, P/O "Terry" Taerum, had flown twenty-eight operations with 50 Squadron before being posted to 1654 Conversion Unit in February, and Australian P/O

"Spam" Spafford was Gibson's bomb-aimer, having been posted to 617 Squadron from 1660 Conversion Unit after completing a tour with 50 Squadron in January. Gibson's rear gunner, the irrepressible F/L Trevor-Roper, had completed two tours with 50 Squadron, amounting to fifty-one operations, and they all returned safely, but the first two-mentioned would lose their lives on the same operation to the Dortmund-Ems Canal as Knight, and Trevor-Roper would be killed during the Command's blackest night of the entire war, during the infamous Nuremberg operation at the end of March 1944. Gunner, Brian Jagger, as already mentioned, would come home as a member of Shannon's crew, but not survive the war.

By the time that the next major operation was launched on the 23rd, the main force squadrons had undergone an expansion with the addition to many units of a third or C Flight, which, in most cases, would eventually be hived off to form the nucleus of a brand-new squadron. The giant force of 826 aircraft was the largest non-1,000 force to date, and surpassed the previous record set three weeks earlier by a clear 230 aircraft. The number of available Lancasters had leapt by eighty-eight, Halifaxes by forty-eight, Stirlings by forty, and Wellingtons by forty-one, and their destination for the second time in the month was to be Dortmund. The entire Command was rested and replenished, and ready to resume the Ruhr offensive, and activity on all participating stations was hectic. 5 Group detailed a record 154 Lancasters, and fifteen of them were made ready at Skellingthorpe, where they were loaded with the standard Ruhr load of a cookie and twelve SBCs of incendiaries. They took off between 22.43 and 23.21 with S/L Street the senior pilot on duty, and all reached the target area to find clear skies but considerable industrial haze. Before the advent of Oboe, this would have rendered the attack a lottery, but, now, the thirteen Pathfinder Mosquitos marked the centre of the city accurately, and the Pathfinder heavy brigade backed-up to maintain the aiming-point with red and green TIs. These could be seen from twenty miles away on approach, but the yellow track markers assisting the early 5 Group arrivals for their time-and-distance runs, were no longer in evidence, and bombing took place largely on the greens from an average height of 20,000 feet. Many explosions and fires were observed, which were merging into a large area of conflagration with large columns of smoke rising up through 18,000 feet as the bombers turned away. Returning crews reported fierce night-fighter activity over the target and on the way home, and this was reflected in the high casualty rate of thirty-eight aircraft, the largest loss of the campaign to date. Almost half of these were Halifaxes and eight were Lancasters, 5 Group posting missing just four crews. Post-raid reconnaissance revealed the operation to have been an outstanding success, which had hit mainly central, northern and eastern districts, where almost two thousand buildings had been destroyed, and some important war industry factories had suffered severe damage and loss of production. The scale of the success was such, that, like Duisburg, this city would remain unmolested by the heavy brigade for a year.

The Ruhr offensive continued with the posting of Düsseldorf as the target on the 25th, for which a force of 759 aircraft was assembled. 5 Group contributed 139 Lancasters, of which thirteen would represent 50 Squadron, and they departed Skellingthorpe between 23.36 and 00.06 with F/L Evans the senior pilot on duty. Sgt Saxton and crew returned early with a number of issues, including the failure of the rear gunner's electrically-heated suit, leaving the others to press on and observe feverish activity at the target from the Dutch coast, when still thirty minutes away. All reached the target to encounter two layers of thin cloud and poor visibility, which impacted the Pathfinders' ability to back up the Mosquito-laid TIs. There were also decoy markers and dummy fire sites operating, which succeeded in causing confusion and prevented a concentration of bombing. The 5 Group crews carried out time-

and-distant runs from yellow track markers, before identifying the target visually and by red and green TIs, and bombing from an average of 20,000 feet either side of 02.00. Post-raid reconnaissance and local reports confirmed that the raid had failed to achieve concentration, and had developed into an "old-style" scattering of bombs across a wide area, leading to the destruction in Düsseldorf of fewer than a hundred buildings.

Harris was not yet done with Essen, and the fifth visitation by the bomber force during the campaign was notified to stations on the 27th, and 518 aircraft made ready. 5 Group put up 133 Lancasters, fourteen of them from Skellingthorpe, and they were safely airborne between 22.17 and 22.58 with F/Ls Evans and Stone the senior pilots on duty. Sgt Duncan and crew returned in a little after two hours with an unserviceable rear turret, and it was a further seventy minutes before F/Sgt Weber and crew touched down having lost their oxygen system. The others continued on to reach the target and find six to eight-tenths cloud with tops at 12,000 feet, with tracking flares to guide them in and Wanganui skymarkers gently descending into the cloud tops over the aiming-point. The 5 Group crews carried out time-and-distance runs and bombed on white flares and red parachute markers with green stars from an average height of 20,000 feet at around 01.30. Post-raid reconnaissance revealed that much of the bombing had fallen short, but 488 buildings had been destroyed, mostly in central and northern districts, and ten nearby towns reported themselves to be victims of collateral damage. Twenty-three aircraft failed to return, and the Halifaxes again represented almost half of the casualties.

A force of 719 aircraft, including a 5 Group contribution of 129 Lancasters, was assembled on the 29th, to pitch against a new Ruhr target, the conurbation known as Wuppertal, perched on the southern rim of the Ruhr Valley east of Düsseldorf. It consisted of the towns of Barmen and Elberfeld, which were built on the proceeds of the rich coal deposits upon which they sat. The aiming-point for this night's attack was the Barmen half at the eastern end, for which the 50 Squadron element of eleven Lancasters departed Skellingthorpe between 22.37 and 23.05 with S/L Street the senior pilot on duty. There were no early returns as they made their way across Belgium, employing the southern approach to the Ruhr, and having to run the gauntlet of searchlights and flak in the Cologne and Düsseldorf corridor. They were greeted by clear skies over the southern Ruhr, with the usual industrial haze stretching up to 10,000 feet, but the yellow tracking flares clearly identified the final turning-point, and, first, concentrated green and then red TIs marked out the aiming-point. The 50 Squadron crews bombed from an average height of 20,000 feet either side of 01.30, and it was clear to all that something extraordinary was taking place as the built-up area beneath them became a sea of explosions and flames with smoke rising very quickly through 15,000 feet as the force withdrew. On return, Sgt McCrossan and crew reported flak hits to both outer engines during the bombing run, and the one on the starboard side had to be shut down. The bomb doors and hydraulics also sustained damage, and six thousand feet of altitude was lost before the bombs were released. The lack of hydraulic fluid prevented the bomb doors from closing, and the port-outer engine began to misfire, causing a further reduction in height and the dumping overboard of all non-essential equipment. The return flight as far as the night-fighter belt was undertaken at 1,500 feet, and 1,000 feet or below, thereafter, all the way home. Post-raid reconnaissance revealed this to be the most awesomely destructive raid of the campaign thus far, which devastated by fire a thousand acres, or around 80% of the built-up area, and destroyed almost four thousand houses, five of the six largest factories and more than two hundred other industrial buildings. It would be some time before the human cost could be established, but it is now accepted that 3,400 people lost their lives during this savage Saturday night. The defenders had their say also, and fought back to claim thirty-three bombers, only seven of which were Lancasters.

During the course of a much less hectic month, the squadron participated in seven operations, and dispatched eighty-four sorties for the loss of two Lancasters and crews.

June 1943

There were no major operations at the start of June because of the moon period, and, although Skellingthorpe was alerted on each of the first ten days, operations were cancelled. This kept the Pathfinder and main force crews kicking their heels on the ground until the 11th, when Düsseldorf was briefed out to 783 crews. 5 Group was responsible for 162 of the 326 Lancasters, and fourteen of them were loaded with a cookie, four 500 pounders and ten SBCs each at Skellingthorpe, and dispatched between 22.30 and 23.21 with F/Ls Evans and Southgate the senior pilots on duty. F/O Crawford and crew lost the use of their Gee-box and reflector sights in the mid-upper and rear turrets, and turned back after ninety minutes, leaving the others to press on over ten-tenths cloud, which dissipated to leave just small amounts at 2,000, 5,000 and 10,000 feet, dependent upon their time of arrival on final approach to the target. Those in the vanguard of the main force were drawn on by yellow tracking flares from 01.05, and red skymarkers with green stars at 01.16, while those a little further back in the bomber stream were guided on by red and green skymarkers at around 01.24. These carried out time-and-distance runs to the aiming-point five minutes away, noting that fires were beginning to build and join together. The Paramatta marking (ground-marking TIs) did not seem to appear until these crews were turning away, but they were clearly visible to the crews in the rear-guard, who described a sea of flames covering a massive area and columns of smoke rising through 21,000 feet. The 50 Squadron effort seemed to be spread throughout the bomber stream, and bombing took place from an average of 20,000 feet right through until around 02.15, and all returned home to pass on their impressions to the intelligence section at debriefing. When all aircraft had been accounted for, thirty-eight were found to be missing, a figure that equalled the heaviest loss of the offensive to date. Post-raid reconnaissance revealed an area of fire across central districts measuring eight by five kilometres, and local reports confirmed 8,882 individual fire incidents. More than seventy war-industry factories suffered a complete or partial loss of production, 140,000 people were bombed out of their homes and 1,292 lost their lives. Had it not been for an errant Oboe marker attracting a proportion of the bombing onto open country some fourteen miles to the north-east, the destruction would have been greater.

Bochum would face its second heavy visitation of the campaign on the 12th, and a force of 503 aircraft was made ready for the purpose. 5 Group contributed 165 Lancasters, of which sixteen were provided by 50 Squadron. They departed Skellingthorpe between 22.40 and 23.12 with F/Ls Southgate and Stone the senior pilots on duty, but F/Sgt Saxton and crew had to turn back after the navigator became ill. The remaining 50 Squadron crews carried on to the target, passing over central Holland and entering Germany to the west of Münster, before turning south for a direct run on Bochum, situated between Essen to the west and Dortmund to the east. It is believed that night-fighters were waiting over Dutch airspace and the frontier region, and it was here that ED472 was intercepted and shot down by Oblt Dietrich Schmidt of III./NJG1 and crashed at 01.30 at Ahaus, killing F/Sgt Weber and his crew. The likelihood is that ED828 met its fate at the hands of another night-fighter at about the same time some twenty-five miles to the north-west near Almelo on the Dutch side of the frontier. F/L Stone DFC perished with four members of his crew, all but two of whom were commissioned, and only the navigator and bomb-aimer, P/Os Glenn DFM and Batson DFM respectively, survived to be taken prisoner. According to the superb book, the Bomber Command War Diaries, by Martin Middlebrook and Chris Everitt, Bochum was completely covered by ten-tenths cloud, but, according to many 5 Group crew reports, they encountered three to six-tenths patchy cloud, and many described almost clear skies and good visibility. The 5 Group crews carried out time-and-distance runs from yellow markers, and had green or red TIs in the bombsights as they let their loads go from 15,000 to 21,000 feet between 01.20 and 02.00. Returning crews reported concentrated fires, the glow from which was visible for up to a hundred miles into the return flight. Photo-reconnaissance revealed 130 acres of devastation, backed up by local reports that 449 buildings had been destroyed and more than nine hundred severely damaged at a cost to the Command of twenty-four aircraft, at least nine of which had been dispatched by night-fighters. A third empty dispersal at Skellingthorpe should have been occupied by ED429, which, it was established later, had blown up in the air near Castrop-Rauxel, some eight miles north-east of the target, and only the bomb-aimer escaped with his life from the crew of Sgt McCrossan DFM.

Following a night's rest, the Ruhr offensive continued at Oberhausen, the oil town situated between Duisburg to the west and Essen to the east. An all-Lancaster heavy force numbering 197 aircraft contained 108 provided by 5 Group, of which seven represented 50 Squadron. They departed Skellingthorpe between 23.02 and 23.11 with W/C Russell the senior pilot on duty, with Les Rutherford as his bomb-aimer, and set course for the Scheldt estuary to bypass Antwerp on their way to the Belgian/German frontier. ED810 crossed paths with Uffz Rudolf Frank of II./NJG3, and was shot down to crash at 01.24 at Ekeren on the northern outskirts of the port, and there were no survivors from the crew of F/O Crawford. The others reached the target area to find three to ten-tenths cloud with tops in places at 18,000 feet, and tracking flares drifting above from which to make time-and-distance runs. The Skellingthorpe crews bombed from an average of 19,000 feet from around 01.30 onwards after aiming at red and green stars and white skymarkers dropped by the six Oboe Mosquitos and the backing-up 8 Group heavies. They had to run the gauntlet of heavy flak both in and out, and the combined ground and night-fighter defences accounted for seventeen Lancasters, 8.4% of the force. Local reports confirmed that the Wanganui flares had been right over the city centre, where 267 buildings were destroyed and 584 seriously damaged.

On the 16th, 1, 5 and 8 Group stations were notified that Cologne was to be the target for that night, for which a force of 202 Lancasters and ten Halifaxes was made ready. They learned at briefings that there would be no Oboe Mosquitos on hand to mark the target, as that role was to be undertaken by the Pathfinder Halifax element and six Lancasters employing H2S. 5 Group detailed eighty Lancasters, of which five at Skellingthorpe were loaded with the usual mix of high explosives and incendiaries and dispatched between 22.31 and 22.46 with F/L Southgate the senior pilot on duty. F/O Parks and crew were back in the circuit within three hours because of an oxygen supply issue, but the remaining four arrived in the target area to find six to ten-tenths cloud, and green tracking flares from which to make a time-and-distance run to the aiming-point. The Pathfinders were late on target, and problems with some of the H2S sets led to sparse and scattered marking with solid white flares and reds with green stars. The 50 Squadron crews bombed from an average of 20,000 feet between 01.06 and 01.21, and a number witnessed a large orange explosion at 01.08, although, generally, they were unable to assess the outcome. The impression was that a proportion of the bombing had been concentrated where intended, but that some crews had been lured away by dummy markers, and local reports, which suggested that only around a hundred aircraft had been involved, tended to support this view. Residential districts bore the brunt of the raid, and 401 houses were destroyed, with 13,000 others sustaining damage to some extent, mostly lightly, while sixteen industrial premises were hit and nine railway stations along with public and utility buildings.

A rare training accident claimed the lives of Sgt Hill and his crew during a night bombing exercise on the 18/19th, when W4932 crashed two miles south-east of Dunholme Lodge airfield and within sight of Lincoln Cathedral at 01.56, killing all on board, three of whom were members of the RCAF. The recent successes in the Ruhr had been aided by the sheer size of the urban areas below, which all but guaranteed that the bombs would hit something useful, even after smoke had obscured the aiming-point TIs. It was a different matter at a small or precision target, however, which would rapidly be enveloped in smoke from the first bombs before the rest of the attacking force had a chance to draw a bead on the aiming-point. When, on the 20th, therefore, an attack was mounted under the codename Operation Bellicose against the production site of the Würzburg radar sets, which the enemy was employing very successfully to warn of and intercept Bomber Command raids, a plan was already in place to combat the problem by adopting the oft-used and still-under-development 5 Group time-and-distance method. Briefings actually took place on the day before, when crews learned that the factory was housed in the old Zeppelin sheds at Friedrichshafen, situated on the shore of Lake Constance (Bodensee) on the frontier with Switzerland, and represented a very small target. The plan was to use a designated "Master of Ceremonies" to direct the bombing, much in the manner of Gibson at the Dams, and the officer chosen was the highly experienced G/C Len Slee, the former 49 Squadron commanding officer, with the popular W/C Cosme Gomm, commanding officer of 467 Squadron RAAF, as his deputy. 5 Group was to provide the main force element of fifty-six Lancasters, five of them from 50 Squadron, with four others from 8 Group's 97 Squadron to provide the marking for the selected crews at the head of the stream. The plan called for the Channel to be crossed at a standard altitude, before descending gradually to 10,000 feet by the time that Orleans was reached, and, thereafter, to fly at between 2,500 and 3,000 feet all the way to the Rhine. After crossing the Rhine, they were to climb to their briefed bombing height of between 5,000 and 10,000 feet for the rendezvous over the north-western shore of Lake Constance, and then circle until receiving the start signal.

The Skellingthorpe quintet took off between 21.47 and 22.03 with F/L Hollis the senior pilot on duty, and all would make it to the target on a rare night when not a single aircraft from the entire force turned back, despite encountering electrical storms on the route and having to adjust the briefed course. That said, G/C Slee lost an engine over France, and was forced to drop back into the formation and hand over the lead to W/C Gomm, who, on arrival at the target under clear skies and in bright moonlight, became concerned about the hostility of the searchlight and light flak defences. In order to reduce the very real risk of heavy casualties, he decided to add five thousand feet to the bombing height, where, unknown to him, the wind was stronger and would push the bombing towards the north-east. The Pathfinder element also had little time to climb to the new height, and this caused a slight delay in the opening of the attack. The first TI fell wide of the aiming-point, but the second one was assessed by W/C

Gomm to be accurate, upon which he called in the first crews, whose high explosives and incendiaries created the expected smoke and obscured the target. He decided that another TI on the aiming-point might still provide a reference for some crews, but the Pathfinders were driven off by the searchlights and light flak and abandoned the attempt. They were then ordered to drop flares along the shore of Lake Constance, to enable the remaining crews to begin their runs from a pre-determined landmark, fly across the Lake to the opposite shore, pick up another landmark 2,000 yards from the target, and continue at a constant speed for the requisite number of seconds to cover the distance to bomb release. P/O Dennis and crew had been thrown off by the weather outbound, and had not been able to regain track, but still arrived in the general target area, where they became ensnared and held in a cone of thirty-to forty searchlights for three-and-a-half minutes. The bombs were jettisoned live from 7,000 feet onto an unidentified town at 02.36, which, in view of the number of searchlights and the time, may have been Friedrichshafen. The other Skellingthorpe crews carried out their attacks from around 12,500 feet between 02.45 and 02.50, and observed explosions and fires, some of which remained visible for eighty miles into the onward flight to landing grounds in North Africa, in what was the first shuttle operation of the war. Post-raid reconnaissance revealed that a proportion of the bombs had hit the target, causing extensive damage, and there had been no losses among the attacking force.

While these crews were absent from England, a hectic round of four major operations to the Ruhr in the space of five nights began at Krefeld on the 21st, for which a force of 705 aircraft was assembled. 5 Group contributed ninety-two Lancasters, of which eight represented 50 Squadron, and they departed Skellingthorpe between 22.50 and 23.13 with F/L Southgate the senior pilot on duty. There were no early returns, and all reached the target, situated a short distance to the south-west of Duisburg, and on the opposite side of the Rhine. Conditions in the target area were ideal, with small amounts of thin cloud between 6,000 and 10,000 feet and bright moonlight, which would benefit attacker and defender alike. The Pathfinders delivered a near-perfect marking performance, red TIs falling in concentrated fashion to clearly identify the city centre aiming-point for the main force crews. Those from Skellingthorpe carried out their attacks from 19,000 to 21,500 feet between 01.35 and 02.11, and described a sea of red fire giving off masses of smoke, with one particular jet-black column rising through 18,000 feet as they turned away. All were convinced of the success of the operation, and one crew likened it to the Wuppertal-Barmen raid. There was no hint of troublesome flak or night-fighters, and yet, forty-four aircraft failed to return, the heaviest casualties of the campaign to date, and many of these were lost to the Nachtjagd. Remarkably, only three 5 Group Lancasters were among the missing, while the Pathfinders' 35 Squadron lost six of its nineteen Halifaxes. Three-quarters of the bombing photos were plotted within three miles of the aiming-point, and the 2,306 tons of bombs wiped out by fire an estimated 47% of the built-up area. 5,517 houses were destroyed, the largest number to date at a single target, and more than a thousand people lost their lives.

The medium-sized town of Mülheim-an-der-Ruhr, a close neighbour of Duisburg, Oberhausen and Essen, lies around a dozen miles to the north-east of Krefeld, and it was here that the red ribbon terminated on the target maps at briefings across the Command on the 22nd. A force of 557 aircraft was prepared, of which ninety of the Lancasters were provided by 5 Group, eight of them representing 50 Squadron. They departed Skellingthorpe between 22.46 and 23.19 with F/L Southgate the senior pilot on duty, but, on a night of poor serviceability for the squadron, F/O Parks and crew turned back with a dead starboard-outer engine, and he was followed home by F/Sgt Thompson and crew with overheating engines and Sgt Brock and crew, who had been let down by their navigational equipment. The others pressed on via the southern route to the Ruhr through the Cologne corridor, and arrived at the target to find small amounts of cumulo-stratus cloud at between 5,000 and 10,000 feet, with red and green TIs clearly visible and defining the aiming-point. The 50 Squadron crews bombed from 18,000 to 20,500 feet between 01.23 and 01.50, and witnessed the development of a concentrated area of fire, which was visible from the Dutch coast homebound. Returning crews commented on the intense searchlight and flak response, and the number of night-fighters, and reported that Krefeld was still burning from the night before. Local reports confirmed that the town had suffered severe damage, particularly in the northern districts, where 1,135 houses were destroyed and more than 12,000 others damaged to some extent, and road and telephone communications to Oberhausen had been cut, preventing any passage out of the town other than on foot. In fact, some of the bombing had spilled into the eastern districts of Oberhausen, which was linked to Mülheim for air-raid purposes. It was another expensive night for the Command, however, which registered the loss of thirty-five aircraft, with the Halifaxes and Stirlings representing two-thirds of them, and suffering a respective loss rate of 7.7% and 11.8%.

While the Pathfinder and main force units were enjoying a night off and girding their loins for the next round of the Ruhr offensive, fifty of the 5 Group Lancasters that had landed in North Africa following the Friedrichshafen raid, took off with two 97 Squadron Pathfinder aircraft to bomb the docks at La Spezia on the way home to England. The five 50 Squadron crews of Sgts Duncan and Mason, P/O Dennis, F/O Chopping and F/L Hollis took off from Blida in Algeria between 19.29 and 19.45, and arrived in the target area to find clear skies but hazy conditions made worse by a smoke-screen. There appeared to be a degree of confusion in getting the raid started, but a lucky hit on an oil storage facility resulted in a large explosion at 23.41 while the main force was running-in, and most crews were able to identify the target visually, thereafter, and by red, green and white Pathfinder flares. Bombing was carried out by the Skellingthorpe quintet on instructions from a Master Bomber from 8,250 to 15,000 feet between 23.38 and 00.09, and all returned safely home to moan about the length of time it had taken for the raid to develop, and the poor communications with the raid controller. The authorities seemed happy to claim the destruction of the oil depot and an armaments store, and declared the operation to be a success.

F/L Gilmour was posted to 1654 Conversion Unit on the 24th for a well-earned rest at the conclusion of his tour. Having destroyed the Barmen half of Wuppertal at the end of May in one of the most devastating attacks to date, it was time to visit the same catastrophe on the western half, Elberfeld, for which a force of 630 aircraft was made ready on the 24th. 5 Group managed to support the operation with 103 Lancasters, nine of which were provided by 50 Squadron, and they departed Skellingthorpe between 22.34 and 23.14 with W/C Russell the senior pilot on duty. They ran the usual gauntlet of searchlights and flak from the Cologne and Düsseldorf defence zones, and P/O Hendry and Sgt Lees were coned and decided to jettison their bombs live over the latter, before turning for home. The defences were aided by the formation of condensation trails at between 18,000 and 21,000 feet to advertise the presence of the bomber stream, but fewer guns seemed to be firing at them over the target, where small amounts of cloud with tops at 17,000 feet were insufficient to obscure the ground. The 5 Group crews carried out time-and-distant runs from yellow tracking flares until observing cascading red and green TIs, the 50 Squadron element bombing from 17,500 to 22,000 feet between 01.08 and 01.33. Those arriving at the tail end of the attack, when the built-up area was well-alight, described thick columns of smoke already passing through 19,000 feet and the glow of fires visible from the Dutch coast. Post-raid reconnaissance revealed another massively concentrated and accurate attack, which had reduced to rubble an estimated 90% of Elberfeld's built-up area, including three thousand houses and 171 industrial premises. It had also severely damaged 2,500 houses and dozens of important factory buildings, and the fact that more buildings were destroyed than damaged, provides a telling commentary on the conditions on the ground. The number of fatalities stood at around eighteen hundred, and some of the survivors might have been cheered to know that thirty-four bombers, containing 240 of their tormentors, would not be returning to England that night. Remarkably, only two of these belonged to 5 Group, and one of them was 50 Squadron's ED712, which crashed outbound at 01.30, six miles south-east of Bad Münstereifel, and twenty-five miles south-west of Cologne. It contained the crew of Sgt Brock RAAF, and there were no survivors.

114 Lancasters were made ready on 5 Group stations on the 25th as part of an overall force of 473 aircraft, which were to attack the Ruhr city of Gelsenkirchen, where a number of synthetic oil refineries were supporting the German war effort. At Skellingthorpe, eleven Lancasters were loaded with a cookie, four 500 pounders and thirteen SBCs of incendiaries each, and were dispatched between 22.51 and 23.33 with F/Ls Hollis and Parks the senior pilots on duty. Sgt Wilkie's rear turret failed and covered its occupant in hydraulic fluid, forcing them to turn back, but the others all reached the target area to find ten-tenths stratus lying over the region with tops at 10,000 to 15,000 feet, which would not have been a problem for Oboe, had five of the twelve participating Mosquitos not suffered equipment failures. This caused tracking flares to be late and to drop in the wrong order in a somewhat scattered manner, at a time when the crews were contending by an intense flak barrage. Searchlights illuminated the cloud as those from Skellingthorpe bombed on red flares with green stars from 18,000 to 20,400 feet between 01.23 and 01.50. A large explosion was witnessed at 01.43, and the glow from the target was visible from the Dutch coast, to which the returning bombers were chased by a large deployment of enemy night-fighters. Post-raid reconnaissance and local reports confirmed that the operation had failed to achieve accuracy and concentration, and, in an echo of the past, bombs had been sprayed all over the Ruhr, leaving Gelsenkirchen largely untouched. Thirty aircraft failed to return, and, this time, eight of them were from 5 Group, four alone from 106 Squadron.

F/L Evans was posted to 81 O.T.U at the conclusion of his tour on the 28th, the day on which P/O Edward and crew arrived from 1660 Conversion Unit to begin theirs. A series of three operations against Cologne would span the turn of the month, and began on the night of the 28/29th, when 608 aircraft took off in the late evening to deliver what would be the Rhineland Capital's greatest ordeal of the war to date. 5 Group contributed 131 Lancasters, the eleven belonging to 50 Squadron departing Skellingthorpe between 23.01 and 23.43 with F/Ls Hollis and Parks the senior pilots on duty. The services of P/Os Hendry and Mason and their crews were soon lost to an indisposed front gunner and Gee-box failure respectively, but the remaining nine pressed on to the target area, where they encountered ten-tenths cloud below them at 8,000 to 10,000 feet, with good visibility above. The main force crews were unaware that five of the Oboe Mosquitos had turned back and a sixth was unable to drop its skymarkers, leaving just six to do so, and these were behind schedule by seven minutes and could manage only intermittent flares. The omens for a successful attack were not good, particularly as skymarking was the least reliable method because of drift, but, by the time the

Skellingthorpe crews arrived, red and white flares greeted them, and bombing was carried out from 17,300 to 24,000 feet between 01.40 and 02.17. The glow from beneath the clouds and the presence of smoke rising through them gave the impression of a successful operation, and this was confirmed by post-raid reconnaissance and local reports, which provided details of forty-three industrial buildings and 6,374 others completely destroyed, and a further fifteen thousand sustaining damage to some extent. The death toll was put at 4,377, the greatest by far from a Bomber Command attack, and 230,000 others had lost their homes for varying periods. By recent standards, the figure of twenty-five missing aircraft could be considered moderate, and the Halifax and Stirling brigades again represented the highest percentage loss rates. During the course of the month the squadron participated in eleven operations, and dispatched ninety-nine sorties for the loss of six Lancasters and crews.

July 1943

5 Group began the new month by sending a dozen Lancasters to mine the waters around the Frisians on the 1st. As a reward for a promising level of performance to date, Sgt Saxton and crew were posted to 97 Squadron of the Pathfinders on the 3rd, which would guarantee them at least one step up in rank, as well as the coveted winged badge. 50 Squadron was not called upon until the 3rd, when ten Lancasters were detailed as part of 5 Group's contribution of 141 of the type to the 653-strong force assembled for the second of the raids on Cologne. The Skellingthorpe element took off between 22.43 and 23.23 with S/L Street the senior pilot on duty, but F/Sgt Thompson, F/O Bolton and, finally, P/O Hendry and their crews turned back with engine issues. The others pressed on in favourable conditions to reach the target, which they found clearly visible under two to three-tenths cloud at 8,000 feet, and protected by many searchlight cones and a moderate flak defence. Tracking flares guided the first wave crews to the aiming-point, which the Pathfinders marked with great accuracy and concentration, while later crews were drawn on for the final one hundred miles by the sight of the city already burning fiercely. The Skellingthorpe crews bombed on red TIs from 19,000 to 21,000 feet between 01.17 and 01.55, and reported the city to be a mass of flames, the glow from which remained visible for 170 miles into the return journey.

Some crews commented on the presence of day fighters over the target, and this was clear evidence of a new tactic being employed by the Luftwaffe. The newly-formed JG300 was operating for the first time, employing the Wilde Sau (Wild Boar) tactics, which was the brainchild of former bomber pilot, Major Hans-Joachim (Hajo) Herrmann. The unit had been formed in June with borrowed standard BF109 and FW190 single-engine day fighters to operate directly over a target, seeking out bombers silhouetted against the fires and TIs. On this night, the unit would claim twelve victories, but would have to share them with the flak batteries, which claimed them also. Unaccustomed to being pursued by fighters over a target, it would take time for the bomber crews to work out what was happening, and, until they did, friendly-fire would often be blamed for damage incurred by unseen causes. Post-raid reconnaissance and local reports confirmed another stunningly accurate and concentrated attack, in which twenty industrial premises and 2,200 houses had been destroyed, and 72,000 people bombed out of their homes at a cost to the Command of thirty aircraft.

The series against Cologne would be completed on the 8th by an all-Lancaster heavy force of 282 aircraft drawn from 1, 5 and 8 Groups, with six Oboe Mosquitos to carry out the initial marking. 5 Group provided 151 Lancasters, of which eleven were made ready at

Skellingthorpe, and they took off between 22.37 and 22.56 with S/L Street the senior pilot on duty. F/Sgt Cole and crew were forced to turn back when the mid-upper gunner reported sick, and the bombs were jettisoned live at 00.16, when still an hour from the target. Sgt Duncan and crew were a mere twenty minutes from the target, when their intercom system failed, and ended any chance of their carrying out a co-ordinated attack. Conscious of his position in the middle of the bomber stream, Sgt Duncan ordered the bombs to be jettisoned from 22,500 feet in order to gain further height to avoid any risk of collision when turning back. *(After careful consideration, his magnanimous commanding officer would deem the sortie completed.)* His squadron colleagues flew through the tops of towering cumulo-nimbus as they made their way to the target, where ten-tenths cloud at around 10,000 feet concealed the ground from view. Tracking flares guided the main force crews to the aiming-point, but the release-point flares were late, and some crews bombed on e.t.a before they were deployed. The 50 Squadron crews carried out their attacks from 21,000 to 24,000 feet between 01.12 and 01.22 in the face of an intense flak barrage, and a very large orange explosion was witnessed at 01.23. Post-raid reconnaissance and local reports revealed another highly successful operation, which had caused extensive damage in north-western and south-western districts, where nineteen industrial premises and 2,381 houses had been destroyed. The success cost a modest seven Lancasters, five of them from 5 Group. When the dust had settled over Cologne, the local authorities catalogued the destruction over the three raids of more than eleven thousand buildings, and a death toll of almost 5,500 people, with a further 350,000 rendered homeless.

The Ruhr campaign was winding down by the time that Gelsenkirchen was posted across Lancaster and Halifax stations as the target on the 9th, for which a heavy force of 408 aircraft was made ready supported by ten Oboe Mosquitos. Eleven 50 Squadron Lancasters were among the 112 representing 5 Group, and they departed Skellingthorpe between 22.30 and 23.05 with F/Ls Chopping, Hunt and Southgate the senior pilots on duty. F/Sgt Thomson and crew turned back after some ninety minutes when the rear gunners electrically-heated suit failed him, but the others made their way to the target above ten-tenths cloud, which stretched over the Ruhr at around 16,000 feet, with tops in places as high as 20,000 feet. The Pathfinder skymarkers were several minutes late, partly as a result of a 50% failure rate of the Oboe equipment, while a sixth Mosquito dropped its markers ten miles to the north. The Skellingthorpe crews timed their runs from red and green tracking flares, and were over the aiming-point between 01.13 and 01.41 delivering their bombs from 20,000 to 22,500 feet onto the Wanganui markers as they drifted into the cloud. Some explosions were reflected in the cloud, but the impression was that the raid had fallen short of the recent outstanding successes, and this was confirmed by local reports. To those on the ground, it appeared that the attack had been meant for Bochum and Wattenscheid, which received more bombs than Gelsenkirchen, where limited damage occurred in southern districts. Among a dozen failures to return was 50 Squadron's ED617, which was homebound and only some fifteen miles from the coast and safety, when crashing near Oisemont in north-eastern France with total loss of life among the crew of P/O Hendry. ED475 had sustained flak damage to three engines over the target, and had struggled as far as the French coast, when the starboard-inner burst into flames, inflicting superficial burns to the face of the pilot, Sgt Clifford. He immediately gave the order to abandon ship, and the mid-upper gunner complied, before it was realised that they were now over the sea. The order was rescinded, and the fire abated when the engine was shut down. A ditching was inevitable, and this took place at 03.50 some four miles off the Sussex coast at Hastings, after which it took eight minutes to get the dinghy to inflate. The Lancaster remained afloat for twenty-five minutes, and the dinghy was boarded from the starboard wing before it sank from sight. An air-sea-rescue launch arrived on scene at 05.20, and the six crew members were taken ashore, the flight engineer with severe burns. Sadly, the Australian mid-upper gunner was never seen again.

Although two more operations to the region would be launched late in the month, Harris was already planning his next attempt to shorten the war by bombing, and was buoyed by the success of the spring offensive. He could look back on the past four and a half months with genuine satisfaction at the performance of his squadrons, and, as a champion of technological innovation, take particular pride in the performance of Oboe, which had been the decisive factor. Although losses had been grievously high, and the Ruhr's reputation as "Happy Valley" well earned, its most important towns and cities had suffered catastrophic destruction. In Britain, the aircraft factories had more than kept pace with the rate of attrition, while the training units both at home and overseas were pouring eager new crews into the fray to fill the gaps. With confidence high in the ability of his Command to destroy almost any target at will, Harris prepared for his next major campaign, the erasure from the map of a prominent German city in a short, sharp series of maximum effort raids to be launched during the final week of the month.

In the meantime, 1, 5 and 8 Groups were alerted to prepared for a trip to Italy to attack the city of Turin, for which 295 Lancasters were made ready on the 12th. 5 Group put up 130 aircraft, a dozen of them representing 50 Squadron, and they departed Skellingthorpe between 22.28 and 22.44 with S/L Street the senior pilot on duty. There were no early returns, despite having to negotiate poor weather conditions, which included icing, and clear skies and good visibility awaited them over the target, where the defences up to their usual poor standard of ineffective searchlights and inaccurate light flak rising to 15,000 feet. The marking was punctual, accurate and concentrated, inviting the bombing by the 50 Squadron crews to be carried out from 15,800 to 19,000 feet between 01.50 and 02.14, and a column of black smoke was observed rising through 12,000 feet as they withdrew. The return route involved a low-level circumnavigation of the Brest peninsular, and many of the thirteen missing Lancasters disappeared without trace into the sea after running into enemy night-fighters. DV156 failed to return to Skellingthorpe with the crew of P/O Burnett, which contained an additional pilot, and no trace of the Lancaster and crew was ever found. Also, among the missing was W/C John Nettleton VC, the commanding officer of 44 Squadron, who had earned his award for the daylight Augsburg raid of April 1942.

On the 15th, acting S/L Birch dropped back to flight lieutenant rank on posting to Station HQ at Waddington, and he was succeeded as flight commander by S/L Abercromby, who was returning for a second tour having served his stint at 1660 Conversion Unit. Orders were received on a number of 5 Group stations on that day to prepare a total of eighteen Lancasters to be sent against two transformer stations in Italy. 50 Squadron loaded three aircraft with a 1,000 pounder each, supplemented with 500 pounders, while the crews were briefed on the details of the target, located at Reggio nell'Emilia, situated some twenty miles north-west of Milan and within sight of the Swiss frontier. F/Ls Southgate, and Hunt and S/L Street and their crews took off between 22.23 and 22.27, and all reached the target area after an outward flight of more than five hours, finding on arrival clear skies and moderate visibility with just some ground haze to spoil the view. S/L Street spent an hour making dummy runs before confirming a positive visual identification of the aiming-point, and bombed it from 1,500 feet at 04.00, observing three vivid, yellow flashes. F/L Southgate followed up twenty-four minutes later from 2,600 feet, and observed tell-tale blue flashes from something electrical. Aircraft from other squadrons had already attacked by this time, and black smoke had climbed past their flight levels. Crews arriving earlier had strafed the site, but orders were received from the leader for the later crews to head south to the landing ground in North Africa and to await further instructions. DV167 did not make it, having crashed near Traversetolo on approach to the target, a dozen or so miles south-south-east of Parma, and there were no survivors among the crew of F/L Hunt.

Germany's Second City, Hamburg, had been a regular target for the Command throughout the war to date, and had been attacked, amongst other occasions, during the final week of July in 1940, 1941 and 1942. It had been spared by the weather from hosting the first "One Thousand" bomber raid at the end of May 1942, but Harris now identified it as the ideal candidate for destruction under Operation Gomorrah, the intention of which was to cause the maximum impact to the enemy's morale in a short, sharp campaign, employing ten thousand tons of bombs. Hamburg's political status was second only to Berlin, and its value to the war effort in terms of U-Boot construction and other war production was undeniable, but, it suited Harris's criteria also in other respects. Its location close to a coastline aided navigation and made it accessible from the North Sea without the need to spend time over hostile territory, and its relatively short distance from the bomber stations enabled a force to approach and retreat during the few hours of darkness afforded by mid-summer. Finally, lying beyond the range of Oboe, which had proved so decisive at the Ruhr, Hamburg had the wide River Elbe to provide a solid H2S signature for the navigators high above.

The campaign would begin on the night of the 24/25th, for which a force of 791 aircraft was assembled, 143 of the Lancasters provided by 5 Group, and fourteen of these by 50 Squadron. The crews would be aided by the first operational use of "Window", tinfoil-backed strips of paper of precise length, which, when released in bundles into the airstream at a predetermined point, would drift down slowly in vast clouds to swamp the enemy night-fighter, searchlight and gun-laying radar with false returns and render it blind. The device had actually been available for a year, but its use had been vetoed in case the enemy copied it for use against Britain. It was not realized that Germany had, in fact, already developed its own version called Düppel, which it had withheld for the same reason. The Skellingthorpe crews took off between 22.33 and 23.20 with S/L Abercromby the senior pilot on duty, but lost the services of Sgt Smith and P/O Shortt to engine failures and F/L Chopping and crew to an intercom breakdown. Meanwhile, some 1,150 miles away, the two surviving crews from the Reggio nell'Emilia operation had taken off from Blida in Algeria shortly before 21.00 to target the docks at Leghorn on their way home. They encountered thin, hazy cloud with tops at around 7,000 feet, and carried out timed runs from Cape Cross, before bombing on e.t.a and flak and searchlight activity from either side of 18,000 feet between 00.23 and 00.34. They arrived home safely after a flight lasting more than eight hours.

At a predetermined point over the North Sea, the Hamburg force began to dispense Window, beginning shortly after 00.30, and the effects appeared to be immediate as few fighters rose to meet the approaching bombers. A number of aircraft were shot down over the sea during the outward flight, two of them 103 Squadron Lancasters, but these were off course, and outside of the protection of the bomber stream, and may well have been returning early with technical difficulties. The efficacy of Window was made more apparent in the target area, where the crews noticed an absence of the usually efficient co-ordination between the searchlights and flak batteries, and defence was random and sporadic. This offered the Pathfinders the opportunity to mark the target by visual reference and H2S virtually unmolested, and, although the red and green TIs were a little misplaced and scattered, they landed in sufficient numbers close to the city centre to provide the main force crews with ample opportunity to deliver a massive blow. The 50 Squadron crews delivered their loads of a cookie, four 500 pounders and thirteen SBCs of incendiaries from 18,200 to 21,500 feet between 01.06 and 01.48, before returning home to report a successful operation that had left part of the city ablaze with a column of smoke rising through 20,000 feet. Post-raid reconnaissance revealed that a six-mile long creep-back had developed, which cut a swathe of destruction from the city centre along the line of approach, out across the north-western districts, and into open country, where a proportion of the bombing had been wasted. In fact, less than half of the force had bombed within three miles of the city centre during the fifty-minute-long raid, in which 2,284 tons of bombs had been delivered, but, despite that, the city had suffered a telling blow, and fifteen hundred of its inhabitants lay dead. For the Command it was an encouraging start to the campaign, particularly in the light of just twelve missing aircraft, for which Window was largely responsible.

On the following night, Harris switched his force to Essen, to take advantage of the body blow dealt to the enemy defensive system by Window. A force of 705 aircraft included 136 Lancasters of 5 Group, the nine at Skellingthorpe taking off between 21.40 and 22.13 with F/Ls Chopping and Hollis the senior pilots on duty. There were seventeen early returns from the 5 Group contingent, and two of these were from among the 50 Squadron participants, P/O Lees and crew progressing as far as seventy miles out from the Lincolnshire coast before their starboard-inner engine failed, and it was the port-inner that let down the crew F/Sgt Castells. Those arriving in the target area found clear skies, with just the usual ground haze to spoil the vertical visibility, and yellow tracking flares to guide them to the aiming-point, which was marked by red and green TIs. They bombed from 19,000 to 21,500 feet between 01.13 and 01.46, and reported observing concentrated fires around the aiming-point in the heavily-industrialized eastern half of the city. Two large, red explosions were witnessed at 00.36 and 00.39, and a column of smoke was rising through 20,000 feet as they withdrew to the west. Post-raid reconnaissance confirmed the raid to be another outstanding success against this important war materials producing city, with more than 2,800 houses destroyed, while the Krupp works suffered its heaviest damage of the war to date. Twenty-six aircraft failed to return, just two of them from 5 Group, and 50 Squadron was represented by ED753, which was shot down by the night-fighter of Hptm Hans-Dieter Frank of I./NJG1, and crashed at 00.55 some four miles west-south-west of Nijmegen in Holland. P/O Dennis RAAF was killed along with four of his crew, but the second pilot, navigator and rear gunner escaped with their lives to fall into enemy hands.

After a night's rest, a force of 787 aircraft was made ready for round two of Operation Gomorrah, for which 50 Squadron bombed-up and fuelled twelve Lancasters as part of 5 Group's contribution of 155. They departed Skellingthorpe between 22.18 and 23.08 with F/L Chopping the senior pilot on duty, but lost F/Sgt Code and crew to starboard-outer engine failure, and F/Sgt Cole and crew to a W/T issue. The remainder pushed on towards Hansastadt Hamburg, crossing the coast over the Schleswig-Holstein peninsular to the north, none of them having any concept of the events that were to follow their arrival. A previously unknown and terrible phenomenon was about to present itself to the world, and introduce a new word "Firestorm" into the English language. A number of factors would conspire on this night to seal the fate of this great city and its hapless inhabitants in an orgy of destruction quite unprecedented in air warfare. An uncharacteristically hot and dry spell of weather had left the city a tinderbox, and the spark to ignite it came with the Pathfinders' H2S-laid red and green TIs, which fell with almost total concentration some two miles to the east of the intended city-centre aiming-point, and into the densely populated working-class residential districts of Hamm, Hammerbrook and Borgfeld. To compound this, the main force, which had been drawn on to the target by yellow release-point flares, bombed with rare precision and almost no creep-back, and deposited much of its 2,300 tons of bombs into this relatively compact area. The 50 Squadron crews carried out their attacks from 16,500 to 22,000 feet between 01.02 and 01.34, and observed many explosions and a sea of flames developing below. Those bombing towards the later stages of the raid observed a pall of smoke rising through 20,000 feet, and the glow of fires was reported to remain visible for 190 miles into the return journey.

On the ground, individual fires began to join together to form one giant conflagration, which sucked in oxygen from surrounding areas at hurricane speeds to feed its voracious appetite. Trees were uprooted and flung bodily into the inferno, along with debris and people, and temperatures at the seat of the flames exceeded one thousand degrees Celcius. The defences were overwhelmed, and the fire service unable to pass through the rubble-strewn streets to gain access to the worst-affected areas. Even had they done so, they could not have entered the firestorm area, and, only after all of the combustible material had been consumed, did the flames subside. By this time, there was no-one alive to rescue, and an estimated forty thousand people died on this one night alone. A mass exodus from the city, which would ultimately exceed one million people, began on the following morning, and this undoubtedly saved many from the ravages of the next raid, which would come two nights later. Seventeen aircraft failed to return, reflecting the enemy's developing response to the advantage gained by the Command through Window. No gain was ever permanent, and the balance of power would continue to shift from one side to the other for the next year. For a change, it was the Lancaster brigade that sustained the highest numerical casualties on this night, and among them was 50 Squadron's veteran Lancaster R5687, which was brought down by flak over Bremerhaven on the way home, and there were no survivors from the crew of F/Sgt Castells.

Bomber Command's heavy brigade stayed at home on the following night, while four Mosquitos carried out a nuisance raid on Hamburg, to ensure that the residents' sleep was disturbed. A force of 777 aircraft was put together to continue Hamburg's torment on the 29th, and, this time, 5 Group contributed 148 Lancasters, of which eleven would represent 50 Squadron. They departed Skellingthorpe between 22.24 and 22.59 with F/Ls Hollis and Southgate the senior pilots on duty, and, for the third operation running, 50 Squadron suffered a casualty, only this time much closer to home. ED468 failed to climb away and crashed, before bursting into flames and being totally consumed, but, happily, not before the crew of Sgt Clarke had scrambled away to safety, shocked but unhurt. F/Sgt Thomson and crew turned back at 23.00 from a position sixty miles out over the North Sea because of an engine failure, but the others continued on to reach the target, which they found under clear skies and protected only by slight ground haze. The plan was to approach from due north to hit the northern and north-eastern districts, which had, thus far, escaped serious damage, but the Pathfinders strayed two miles to the east of the intended track, and dropped their markers just to the south of the already devastated firestorm area. A four-mile creep-back rescued the situation for the Command, by spreading along the line of approach into the residential districts of Wandsbek and Barmbek, and parts of Uhlenhorst and Winterhude. The 50 Squadron crews bombed on yellow and green TIs from 17,800 to 21,400 feet between 00.55 and 01.21, and reported smoke rising through 17,000 feet and fires visible for two hundred miles into the return journey. It was another massive blow against this proud city, but, as the defenders began to recover from the effects of Window, so the bomber losses began to creep up, and twenty-eight aircraft failed to return home on this night, five of them from 5 Group.

Before the final round of Operation Gomorrah took place, the curtain on the Ruhr offensive was brought down for the last time with a raid on the town of Remscheid, situated on the southern edge of the region, about six miles south of Wuppertal, where the main industries were mechanical engineering and tool-making. Up until this point, only twenty-six people had lost their lives in this town as a result of stray bombs, but it was now to face a modest force of 273 aircraft consisting of roughly equal numbers of Lancasters, Halifaxes and Stirlings with nine Oboe Mosquitos to mark out the aiming-point. 5 Group put up thirty-nine Lancasters, three of which were loaded with a cookie and seventeen SBCs of various incendiaries at Skellingthorpe, and took off containing the crews of F/Sgts Cole and Thomson and P/O Ruskell between 21.58 and 22.11. The last-mentioned turned back when over the North Sea because of an engine issue, leaving the others to find clear skies and good visibility in the target area, and bomb on red TIs from 16,500 and 20,200 feet between 01.02 and 01.10, observing the burst of many cookies and a pall of smoke rising through 5,000 feet. DV197 was coned by searchlights as it left the target, and was weaved violently by F/Sgt Cole in an attempt to break free. Bombarded by flak, the Lancaster sustained severe damage to the control surfaces of the tailplane and the hydraulics system, rendering all turrets inoperable, and killing the rear gunner instantly. The gyro toppled, and they found themselves upside down at 3,000 feet hurtling towards the ground at 400 m.p.h, and it was only through a combined effort by the pilot and flight engineer that some semblance of control was recovered. It was necessary to use the pilot's belt to strap the rudder back to maintain that control, but, the Gee-box was still working, which enabled the navigator to set a course for home, and they crossed the Dutch coast at 4,000 feet with little more than two hundred gallons of fuel in the tanks. By the time the English coast was sighted, they were down to 2,000 feet, with all crew members performing their tasks magnificently, prompting the captain to record later how proud he was to be a member of that crew. He made special mention of the wireless operator, who had been backwards and forwards within the fuselage, first to establish the fate of the rear gunner, and then to tend to the mid-upper gunner, who had been unconscious for twenty minutes before making a full recovery. They landed at 03.00 at Kings Cliffe after mistaking it for Wittering, and careered off the end of the runway to cross a railway line and come to a halt in a field. The Lancaster was a write-off, but the crew unhurt, and F/Sgt Cole's conduct was recognised by the immediate award of the DFM. The rest of the force had flown home confident that another Ruhr town had been left devastated, and with a red glow behind them that remained visible as they crossed the enemy coast homebound. It would be left to a post-war bombing survey to establish that a mere 871 tons of bombs had laid waste to around 83% of the town's built-up area, destroying 107 industrial buildings and 3,117 houses. Three months war production was lost, and the town's industry never recovered fully. Fifteen aircraft failed to return, and the Stirling brigade suffered 10% casualties.

During the course of the month the squadron participated in ten operations and dispatched eighty-seven sorties for the loss of eight Lancasters, five complete crews and two gunners.

August 1943

Briefings for the final act of Operation Gomorrah took place on the 2nd, and a force of 740 aircraft was made ready, 128 of the Lancasters provided by 5 Group. 50 Squadron detailed ten Lancasters, which took off between 23.41 and 00.25 with S/L Abercromby the senior pilot on duty, but he was forced to shut down his starboard-outer engine over the North Sea, and, although continuing on, was unable to maintain height, and altered course to bomb Cuxhaven as an alternative target. After landing, he found F/Sgts Nelson and Thomson and their crews already on the ground, having abandoned their sorties respectively because of oxygen-supply failure and an unserviceable rear gunner's heated suit. The weather conditions for the remainder were good initially, until fifty miles out over the North Sea when a towering bank of ice-bearing cloud was encountered, which could not be circumnavigated, and, upon entering it, aircraft were thrown around by violent electrical storms. It was a hugely terrifying experience beyond anything that most crews had ever experienced, with enormous flashes of lightning, thunder, electrical discharges and instruments going haywire. Many crews simply abandoned their sorties and jettisoned their bombs over Germany or into the sea, but, to their great credit, this was not the attitude of the Skellingthorpe participants. They were among the proportion of the force that battled through the conditions to reach the target area, which was concealed beneath seven to ten-tenths cloud, and, while some caught a glimpse of the Elbe and isolated yellow and green Pathfinder flares, the majority bombed on e.t.a and on the glow of fires beneath the cloud and the smoke rising through it. The Skellingthorpe crews bombed from 12,000 to 21,000 feet between 02.12 and 02.41, before returning to unanimously report an unsuccessful operation, described by some from other units as "pure hell". F/L Chopping reported four aircraft shot down on the way in to the target, and ascribed their loss to night-fighters. Little fresh damage occurred in Hamburg as bombs were sprayed over an area of a hundred miles, but that was of little consequence in view of what had gone before. The Command suffered the relatively heavy loss of thirty aircraft, and some of these had fallen victim to the weather conditions. During the four-raid campaign, 50 Squadron despatched forty-seven sorties, thirty-seven of which bombed the target, one aircraft failed to return, and one crashed on take-off. (The Battle of Hamburg. Martin Middlebrook).

Italy was now teetering on the brink of capitulation, and Bomber Command was invited to help nudge it over the edge with a short offensive against its major cities. It began with elements of 1, 5 and 8 Groups making ready to attack Genoa, Milan and Turin on the 7th, and, with preparations already in hand for, perhaps, the most important operation of the war to date to be launched in ten days' time, the Turin raid was to be used to test the merits of employing a raid controller, or Master of Ceremonies, in the Manner of W/C Gibson during Operation Chastise. The man selected for the job was Group Captain John Searby, currently serving as commanding officer of 83 Squadron of the Pathfinders, and, before that, Gibson's successor as commanding officer of 106 Squadron. 5 Group detailed seventy-eight Lancasters divided between Genoa and Milan, with the ten 50 Squadron crews briefed for the latter, and they departed Skellingthorpe between 21.09 and 21.22 with F/Ls Parks and Southgate the senior pilots on duty. It is believed that all 197 aircraft reached their respective targets, after flying out in excellent weather conditions, and, from under clear skies, those at Milan were able to pick out the river, before bombing on green TIs from around 16,000 to 18,000 feet. P/O Lees and crew were approaching the city, when the port-outer engine caught fire and had to be shut down. They let their bombs go onto the eastern outskirts, and, with little chance of reaching England with the others, they set course for Maison Blanche in North Africa. On landing at

06.20, DV223 crashed and ran into another Lancaster, damaging both aircraft and breaking the arm of the bomb-aimer, who would remain in hospital when his crew mates returned home. Although the Master Bomber experiment at Turin was not entirely successful, experience was gained which would prove useful for the forthcoming Operation Hydra.

S/L Street had now concluded his tour of operations, and was posted to 81 O.T.U on the 8th. The rest of the heavy brigade remained inactive until the 9th, when a force of 457 Lancasters and Halifaxes was made ready for an operation that night against Mannheim. 50 Squadron prepared eleven Lancasters as part of a 5 Group contribution of 143, and they departed Skellingthorpe between 23.05 and 23.32 with F/Ls Chopping and Parks the senior pilots on duty. After climbing out, they headed for the rendezvous point over Reading, before exiting England via Beachy Head on course for the French coast at Boulogne. P/O Duncan and crew turned back with oxygen supply failure, leaving the others to press on across Belgium on a direct track to the target, where the crews were greeted by a five-tenths layer of broken cloud at 4,000 feet and eight-tenths at 10,000 feet. Despite this, the visibility was fair, and the yellow skymarkers and green TIs were sufficient to provide a reference for the bomb-aimers. The Skellingthorpe participants carried out their attacks from 17,500 to 19,600 feet between 01.37 and 02.01, and returned home to report a number of very large fires but a generally scattered raid. In fact, according to local reports, 1,316 buildings had been destroyed, forty-two industrial concerns had lost production, and more than fifteen hundred fires of varying sizes had required attention. Six Halifaxes and three Lancasters failed to return, two of the latter belonging to 5 Group.

Nuremberg was posted as the target on the 10th, for which a force of 653 aircraft was assembled, 128 of the Lancasters provided by 5 Group. 50 Squadron briefed ten crews while their Lancasters were being loaded with a cookie and up to twelve SBCs of incendiaries and sufficient fuel and reserves for the 1,300-mile round-trip. Take-off was safely accomplished between 21.51 and 22.25 with P/O Duncan the only commissioned pilot on duty, and, after climbing out and forming-up, they set course for Beachy Head on the Sussex coast to follow a route similar to that of the previous night. There were no early returns to deplete the squadron's effort, and all arrived in the target area, where conditions also reflected those of twenty-four hours earlier with eight to ten-tenths cloud at 12,000 feet. The Pathfinders had prepared a ground-marking plan, and there were no release-point flares to draw the head of the main force on, but the green TIs were visible to most, as were the fires for those arriving later. The Skellingthorpe crews delivered their bombs from 17,200 to 21.500 feet between 01.04 and 01.37, and returned safely to report a good concentration of fires, the glow from which remained visible for 150 miles into the return journey. Post-raid reconnaissance and local reports confirmed that the city had sustained much housing and industrial damage in mostly central and southern districts, and a death toll of 577 people was evidence of the intensity of the bombing.

On the 11th, W/C Russell concluded his long and successful tour as commanding officer and was posted to 1654 Conversion Unit, where he would remain until the 18th of February 1944, at which point, he joined the highly secret 138 Squadron. This was one of two units in 3 Group, 138 and 161 Squadrons, stationed at Tempsford in Bedfordshire, which operated on behalf of the Special Operations Executive (SOE) and the Special Intelligence Service (SIS) to deliver agents into the Occupied Countries and arms and equipment to the Resistance organisations. He would have to drop rank to squadron leader to remain on operations, but this irrepressible officer was determined to take the fight to the enemy at any cost and in any way. He would be rewarded with a return to wing commander rank and command of the squadron on the 1st of May 1944, only to lose his life on operations six days later. He was succeeded at 50 Squadron by W/C McFarlane DFC, who arrived on promotion from his flight commander role with 9 Squadron.

During the course of the 12th, two forces were prepared for a return to Italy that night, one of 504 Lancasters and Halifaxes to attack Milan, and the other of 152 Stirlings, Halifaxes and Lancasters to target Turin. 5 Group contributed 130 Lancasters to the former, of which ten represented 50 Squadron, and they departed Skellingthorpe between 21.26 and 21.56 with W/C McFarlane, on his first sortie with the squadron, and S/L Abercromby the senior pilots on duty. The route was to take the bomber stream via Selsey Bill to Cabourg on the Normandy coast, and then south-east in a straight leg across central France to the northern tip of Lake Bourget, to cross the Alps and skirt southern Switzerland before the final run-in on the target. This represented a round-trip of some sixteen hundred miles, which not all from 50 Squadron would complete. W/C McFarlane lost his starboard-inner engine over the sea and turned back, as did F/Sgt Thomson and crew with an oxygen-supply issue. The others completed the outward leg to arrive at the target under clear skies with just ground mist to spoil the view. They bombed visually or on yellow flares and green TIs from 16,000 to 20,200 feet between 01.17 and 01.40, and observed large fires in the city centre, which could be seen for a hundred miles into the return flight. Local reports, though short on detail, confirmed that four important war-industry factories had sustained serious damage during August, and most of it probably occurred on this night, as did the majority of the 1,174 fatalities in the city in 1943.

Milan would face two further attacks before the Command's interest in Italy ceased for good, and the first of these was posted on the 14th, for which 1, 5 and 8 Groups put together a force of 140 Lancasters. Fifty-nine of them represented 5 Group, with 50 Squadron providing five, which took off between 21.30 and 21.38 with F/Ls Chopping and Parks the senior pilots on duty. They all reached the target under clear skies and in good visibility aided by moonlight and Pathfinder route markers. The Pathfinder target marking with green TIs was accurate and concentrated, and was exploited by the Skellingthorpe crews from 15,550 to 18,000 feet between 01.17 and 01.26. Many fires were seen to take hold as the force turned away, and the glow remained visible for a considerable distance into the return flight.

There was to be no respite for Milan as a force of 199 Lancasters was made ready later on the 15th for a return that night for what would be the last time over Italy for main force Lancasters. 50 Squadron provided eight of the eighty-five 5 Group Lancasters, and they took off from Skellingthorpe between 20.28 and 20.38 with F/L Hollis the senior pilot on duty. All reached the target to find clear skies, but haze and smoke from the previous night spoiling the vertical visibility. The Pathfinders marked the city-centre aiming-point with green TIs, and these were bombed to good effect by the 50 Squadron crews from 15,000 to 17,000 feet between 00.06 and 00.19. Enemy night-fighters were waiting over France to catch the bombers as they returned home, and, among the seven missing aircraft was that of 467 Squadron's popular commanding officer, W/C Gomm DSO, DFC, who died with all but one of his crew. The consensus of returning crews was of a concentrated attack, but no local report was forthcoming to confirm or deny.

The final raid of the war against an Italian city was carried out by 154 aircraft of 3 and 8 Groups against Turin on the following night. A successful raid was claimed at the modest cost of four aircraft, but many of the participating Stirlings were diverted on return, and did not reach their home stations in time to be made ready for the night's highly important operation, for which a maximum effort had been planned. This would deplete the available number of Stirlings by sixty, and heap an even greater responsibility upon the rest of the force to complete the job.

Since the very beginning of the war, intelligence had suggested that Germany was researching into and developing rocket technology, and, although scant regard was given to the reports, photographic reconnaissance had confirmed the existence of an establishment at Peenemünde at the northern tip of the island of Usedom on the Baltic coast. The activities there were monitored through Ultra intercepts and surreptitious reconnaissance flights, and the V-1, known to the photographic interpreters at Medmenham because of its wingspan as the "Peenemünde 20", was captured on a photograph. The brilliant scientist, Dr R V Jones, had been able to gain vital information concerning the V-1's range, which would ultimately be used to feed disinformation to the enemy, largely through the double agent "Zigzag", otherwise known as Eddie Chapman. Unfortunately, Churchill's chief scientific adviser, Professor Lindemann, or Lord Cherwell as he became, steadfastly refused to give credence to the existence and feasibility of rocket weapons, and held stubbornly to his viewpoint even when presented with a photograph of a V-2 on a trailer, taken by a PRU Mosquito in June 1943. It required the combined urgings of Duncan Sandys and Dr Jones to persuade Churchill of the urgency to act, and Operation Hydra was planned for the first available opportunity, which occurred on the night of the 17/18th. Earlier in the day, the USAAF 8th Air Force had carried out its first deep-penetration raids into Germany to attack ball-bearing production at Schweinfurt and the Messerschmidt aircraft plant at Regensburg, and, to the shock of its leaders, had learned the harsh lesson that unescorted daylight raids in 1943 were not viable. The folks at home would not be told that sixty B17s had failed to return. It was vital that the Peenemünde installation be destroyed, ideally, at the first attempt, and a force of 596 aircraft and crews answered the call. 5 Group contributed 117 of the 324 Lancasters, with Skellingthorpe making ready eleven, and the rest of the force was comprised of 218 Halifaxes and fifty-four Stirlings.

The operation had been meticulously planned to account for the three vital components of Peenemünde, the housing estate, where the scientific and technical staff lived, the factory buildings and the experimental site. Each was assigned to a specific wave of aircraft, which would attack from medium level, with the Pathfinders bearing the huge responsibility of shifting the point of aim accordingly. After last minute alterations, 3 and 4 Groups were given the first mentioned, 1 Group the second, and 5 and 6 Groups the third. The whole operation was to be overseen by a Master of Ceremonies (referred to hereafter as Master Bomber), and the officer selected for this hazardous and demanding role was G/C Searby of 83 Squadron, who, as already mentioned, had stepped into Gibson's shoes at 106 Squadron after Gibson was posted out to form 617 Squadron. Searby's role was to direct the marking and bombing by VHF, and to encourage the crews to press on to the aiming-point, a task requiring him to remain in the target area and within range of the defences throughout the attack. In an attempt to protect the bombers from the attentions of enemy night-fighters for as long as possible, eight Mosquitos of 139 Squadron were to carry out a spoof raid on Berlin, led by the highly experienced, and former 49 Squadron commander, G/C Len Slee. In the expectation of encountering drifting smoke as the last wave on target, the 5 Group crews were instructed to employ their oft-used time-and-distance approach to the aiming-point, and had practiced this over a stretch of coast near the Wainfleet bombing range at the mouth of the Wash in Lincolnshire, progressively cutting the margin of error from one thousand to three hundred yards.

The 50 Squadron element took off between 21.38 and 21.51 with S/L Abercromby the senior pilot on duty in EE189, on a night when many squadron commanders elected to fly, in some cases, with fatal consequences. The other 50 Squadron aircraft and crews were; F/Ls Chopping and Parks in ED755 and JA961, P/Os Duncan and Mason in ED588 and DV217, F/Sgts Code, Nelson, Smith, Thompson and Thomson in W5004, ED415, EE124, DV227 and ED470, and Sgt Weatherstone in ED393. There were no early returns to Skellingthorpe, and the overall early-return rate was lower than normal, suggesting that crews had taken to heart the importance of the operation. The various groups made their way individually to a rendezvous point some ninety minutes flying time or three hundred miles from the English coast and sixty miles from Denmark's western coast, where they became a stream. Darkness had fallen as they crossed the North Sea, and, twenty miles short of landfall over the southern tip of Fanø island, south of Esbjerg, Windowing began, in order to simulate a standard raid on a northern or north-eastern city. Southern Denmark was traversed by the Lancaster brigade at 18,000 feet, twice the altitude required for the attack, but, worryingly, in a band of cloudless sky under a bright moon. They adopted an east-south-easterly course and began to shed altitude gradually during the 240-mile run to the target a little over an hour away, and, at the rear of the stream, the 5 Group crews focussed on the island of Rügen, the ideal starting point for their timed run to Peenemünde, which lay some fifteen miles beyond to the south-east.

The initial marking of the housing estate went awry, and some target indicators fell onto the forced workers camp at Trassenheide, more than a mile south of the intended aiming-point. Many of the 3 and 4 Group bombs fell here, inflicting grievous casualties on friendly foreign nationals, who were trapped inside their wooden barracks. Once rectified, however, the attack proceeded according to plan, and a number of important members of the technical staff were killed. The 1 Group second-wave crews encountered strong crosswinds over the narrow section of the island where the construction sheds were located, but this phase of the operation largely achieved its aims, and they were on their way home before the night-fighters arrived from Berlin, having been attracted by the glow of fires well to the north. On their arrival at Rügen, the 5 Group crews began their timed run, and reached the experimental site to encounter the expected smoke, and bomb on green TIs, in the case of the 50 Squadron element, from 6,000 to 9,850 feet between 00.35 and 00.54. They and the 6 Group Halifaxes and Lancasters then ran into the night-fighters, which proceeded to take a heavy toll of bombers, both in the skies over the target, and on the route home towards Denmark. Twenty-nine of the forty missing aircraft came from this third wave, seventeen of them belonging to 5 Group and twelve to 6 Group, which represented a loss rate for the Canadians of 19.7%. 50 Squadron was one of a number of 5 Group units to operate without loss, and most crews brought home aiming-point photographs, although, the time-and-distance method was found not to have been entirely effective. Returning crews praised the work of the Pathfinders and the Master Bomber, and post-raid reconnaissance revealed the raid to have been sufficiently effective to delay the V-2 development programme by a number of weeks, and, ultimately, to force the manufacture of secret weapons underground. The flight testing of the V-2 was eventually withdrawn eastwards into Poland, beyond the range of Harris's bombers, and, thus Peenemünde had been nullified as a threat.

On the following day, S/L Abercromby found himself assuming command of 619 Squadron, to replace W/C McGhie, who had failed to return, while F/L Pullen moved in the opposite direction on promotion to succeed him as a flight commander at 50 Squadron. Sadly, Scotsman, W/C Abercromby, would also not survive the war. He would be given command of 83 Squadron of the Pathfinders (8 Group) in early December 1943, and would take with him his somewhat arrogant 5 Group attitudes of superiority. He criticised the practice of weaving as a protection from night-fighter attack, and banned it, thereby, ruffling a few feathers, most notably and appropriately those of F/L Chick, whose flying he apparently described as cowardly. Chick refused to abandon a policy that had seen him through more than forty operations, and predicted that Abercromby would survive no more than three weeks if he continued to fly straight and level. It is highly likely, although unrecorded, that the other crews shared Chick's opinion, and Chick would complete his tour on forty-eight operations shortly afterwards, having seen his prophecy fulfilled. On the night of the 1/2nd of January 1944, the thirty-three-year-old Abercromby would die in an exploding Lancaster on his way to Berlin.

Before the next campaign began, Leverkusen was posted on the 22nd as the target for a heavy force of 449 Lancasters and Halifaxes with 8 Group Oboe-Mosquito to provide the initial marking. The aiming-point was to be a factory belonging to the infamous I.G. Farben chemicals company, which was engaged in the development and production of synthetic oil, and employed slave labour at all of its factories across Germany, including 30,000 from the Auschwitz concentration camp, where it had built a plant. One of the company's subsidiaries manufactured the Zyklon B gas used during the Holocaust to murder millions of Jewish victims. 50 Squadron made ready eleven Lancasters in a 5 Group contribution of 108, and they departed Skellingthorpe between 21.13 and 21.37 with W/C McFarlane the senior pilot on duty. After climbing out they headed for the Belgian coast at Knokke, to follow a well-worn route to the southern Ruhr, which would require them to pass through the searchlight and flak belt near Cologne, which always provided a hot welcome. All made it safely through the narrow corridor to reach the target, where ten-tenths cloud blanketed the area. Oboe-equipment failures forced most crews to bomb on e.t.a in the absence of markers, until the glow of fires came to their aid as the raid developed, although a small number of crews spotted green TIs on the ground and aimed for them. Bombing was carried out by the Skellingthorpe crews in the face of intense flak from 18,000 to 20,200 feet between 00.03 and 00.36, and the glow of fires and the flash of explosions was initially the only confirmation of something happening under the cloud, until a column of smoke was observed to be rising through 12,000 feet. Local reports would reveal that up to a dozen neighbouring towns had been hit, Düsseldorf suffering the destruction of 132 buildings.

Harris had long believed that the key to ultimate victory lay in the destruction of Berlin, the seat of the Nazi government and the symbol of its power. On the 23rd, orders were received on stations across the Command to prepare for a maximum effort that night against Germany's Capital City, which had not been visited by the heavy brigade since the end of March. The crews, of course, could not know that this was to be the first of an eventual nineteen raids on the "Big City", in a campaign which, with an autumn break, would drag on until the following spring. It was a campaign that would test the resolve of the crews to the absolute limit, whilst also sealing the fate of the Stirlings and the Mk II and V Halifaxes as front-line bombers. There are varying opinions concerning the true start date of what became known as the Berlin offensive or the Battle of Berlin, some commentators believing these first three operations in August and September to be the start, while others point to the sixteen raids from mid-November. However, there was little doubt in Bomber Command circles that this was it, a fact demonstrated by the comments in numerous squadron ORBs, which speak of the "long-awaiting Berlin campaign" and similar sentiments. There would be a Master Bomber on hand for this operation, and the officer chosen was Canadian W/C "Johnny" Fauquier, the tough, grizzled and popular onetime bush pilot and frequent brawler, who was enjoying his second spell as the commanding officer of 405 (Vancouver) Squadron, now of the Pathfinders, and formerly of 4 Group. The route had been planned to take the bomber stream to a rendezvous point over the North Sea, before crossing the Dutch coast near Haarlem and setting a course to pass between Bremen and Hannover to bypass the southern rim of Berlin. The intention was then to turn back to approach the city from the south-east, and, after bombing, to pass out over the Baltic coast and make for the Schleswig-Holstein peninsular. Finally, seventeen Mosquitos were to precede the Pathfinder and main force elements to drop route markers at key points in an attempt to keep the bomber stream on track.

A force of 727 aircraft was assembled, of which 124 Lancasters represented 5 Group, twelve of them belonging to 50 Squadron, and they departed Skellingthorpe between 20.22 and 21.02 with no senior pilots on duty. The route was to take the bomber stream over northern Holland to enter Germany between Meppen to the north and Osnabrück to the south, and pass to the south of Hannover to reach a position south-east of Berlin, before turning sharply to adopt a north-westerly course across the city centre. F/Sgt Cole and crew were the first of three early returns, in their case because of an indisposed mid-upper gunner, while P/O Lees and crew had just entered Germany, when their starboard-inner engine burst into flames at 23.05, and they had to turn back. Fifteen minutes later, Sgt Litherland's rear gunner reported his turret to be unserviceable, and they, too, had to abandon their sortie. Those reaching the target area found clear skies, but the Pathfinders were unable to identify the aiming-point in the centre of the city, a result of the inherent difficulties of interpreting the H2S images over such a massive urban sprawl, and marked the southern outskirts instead. Many main force crews then cut the corner to approach the city from the south-west rather than south-east, and this would result in the wastage of many bomb loads in open country and on outlying communities. The 50 Squadron crews each delivered their cookie and incendiaries visually and on red and green TIs from 15,100 to 20,100 feet between 23.56 and 00.24, doing so in the face of intense searchlight activity with moderate flak. Returning crews reported large explosions and many fires, the glow from which was visible for at least 140 miles, and a pall of smoke had already risen to meet them as they turned towards the north-east. Curiously, only a few crews commented on hearing the Master Bomber, and finding his instructions helpful. A new record of fifty-six aircraft failed to return, twenty-three Halifaxes, seventeen Lancasters and sixteen Stirlings, representing a percentage loss rate respectively of 9.1, 5.1 and 12.9, which perfectly reflected the food chain when all three types operated together. Berlin experienced a scattered raid, but, because of the numbers attacking, extensive damage was caused, a little in or near the centre, but mostly in south-western residential districts and industrialized areas a little further east. 2,611 buildings were reported to have been destroyed or seriously damaged, and the death toll of 854 people was surprisingly high, caused largely, perhaps, by a failure to heed the alarms and go to the assigned shelters.

Orders were received on the 27th to prepare for an operation that night against Nuremberg, for which a force of 674 aircraft ultimately lined up for take-off in mid-evening. 5 Group contributed 140 Lancasters, the thirteen at Skellingthorpe taking to the air between 21.01 and 21.34 with S/L Pullen the senior pilot on duty for the first time. After climbing out, they headed for the French coast, and, once there, followed the line of the frontier with Belgium until crossing into Germany south of Luxembourg on course for the target, where clear skies and intense darkness prevailed. The Pathfinders had been briefed to check their H2S equipment by dropping a 1,000 pounder on Heilbronn, and some crews complied, while others, it seems, experienced technical difficulties. The initial marking was accurate, but a creep-back developed, which the backers-up and the Master Bomber could not correct, and this resulted in many bomb loads falling into open country, while others hit south-eastern and eastern districts. The 50 Squadron crews aimed at green TIs from 17,000 to 20,500 feet between 00.36 and 01.06, and gained an impression of a fairly concentrated and accurate attack, which produced many fires. Searchlights and night-fighters were described as numerous, and thirty-three aircraft failed to return, eleven of each type, which again confirmed the vulnerability of the Stirlings and Halifaxes when operating alongside Lancasters. The loss rate on this night was 3.1% for the Lancaster, 5% for the Halifax and 10.6% for the Stirlings.

The twin towns of Mönchengladbach and Rheydt were posted as the targets for a two-phase operation on the 30th, and it would be the first major attack for both of them. Situated some ten miles west of the centre of Düsseldorf in the south-western Ruhr, they would face an initial force of 660 aircraft of four types, in what, for the crews, was a short-penetration trip across the Dutch frontier, which would be a welcome change from the recent long slogs to eastern and southern Germany. The plan called for the first wave to hit Mönchengladbach, before a two-minute pause in the bombing allowed the Pathfinders to head south to mark Rheydt. 50 Squadron made ready thirteen Lancasters as part of a 5 Group contribution of 138, the Skellingthorpe crews having been briefed to bomb in the second wave, and they took off between 00.02 and 00.41 with F/L Chopping the senior pilot on duty. He and his crew were back on the ground after seventy-five minutes because of low oil pressure in the port-inner engine, but the others all reached the target to find good visibility above the seven to ten-tenths cloud at 8,000 feet. A near perfect display of target-marking by Oboe delivered red and green flares to draw on the main force to bomb with scarcely any creep-back, the 50 Squadron element doing so from 15,500 to 20,000 feet between 02.04 and 02.42. On return, they would report many fires, the glow from which could be seen from the Dutch coast homebound. Photo-reconnaissance confirmed a highly accurate and concentrated attack, which destroyed more than 2,300 buildings in the two towns, 171 of them of an industrial nature, along with 869 residential properties. Twenty-five aircraft failed to return, and Halifaxes narrowly sustained the highest numerical casualties.

The month ended with preparations for the second of the Berlin operations on the night of the 31st, for which 622 aircraft were made ready, more than half of them Lancasters, 129 of these provided by 5 Group. 50 Squadron loaded eleven of theirs with a cookie and nine SBCs of incendiaries each, and dispatched them between 20.10 and 20.34 with F/L Chopping the senior pilot on duty. F/Sgt Thomson's navigator "lost" his protractor while they were climbing out, but it was decided to carry on, hoping that Gee would provide the necessary guidance. On reaching the mid-point of the North Sea, the futility of their cause hit home, and they turned back, possibly for the navigator to face the wrath of the squadron commander.

The route on this night took the bomber stream on an east-south-easterly heading across Texel to a position between Hannover and Leipzig, before turning to pass to the south-east of Berlin and approach the city-centre aiming-point on a north-westerly track. The return leg would involve a south-westerly course to a position south of Cologne for an exit over the French coast, but despite the attempts to outwit the enemy night-fighter controller, he was able to predict to some extent where to concentrate his fighters. This would be the first occasion on which the Command registered the German use of "fighter flares" to mark out the path of the bombers to and from the target. The Pathfinders encountered five to six-tenths cloud in the target area, and this combined with H2S equipment failure and a spirited night-fighter response to cause the markers to be dropped well to the south of the planned aiming-point. The main force crews became involved in an extensive creep-back, which would stretch some thirty miles into open country and outlying communities. The 50 Squadron crews reported up to eight-tenths thin cloud, and bombed on red and green TIs from 17,100 to 20,800 feet between 23.32 and 00.01, observing many fires over a wide area. It was noted by some that two groups of green TIs were ten miles apart, and both attracted attention from the main force. The outcome was a major disappointment, brought about by woefully short marking and a pronounced creep-back, and resulted in the destruction of just eighty-five houses, a figure in no way commensurate with the effort expended and the loss of forty-seven heavy bombers. The percentage loss rates made alarming reading at Bomber Command HQ, the Lancasters with an acceptable and sustainable 3%, the Halifaxes with 11.3% and the Stirlings with 16%.

During the course of the month the squadron participated in thirteen operations, and dispatched 135 sorties for the loss of a single Lancaster in the landing crash at Maison Blanche, and there had been no missing crews or fatalities.

September 1943

The new month began operationally for 50 Squadron with the departure at 20.18 of the crew of P/O Duncan, who were bound for the Nectarines I garden, situated a fraction north of due east on the other side of the North Sea. They homed-in on the drop zone by Gee-fix, and delivered their vegetables from 6,000 feet at 21.50, before returning home safely to land exactly three hours after taking off. Probably as a result of the heavy losses recently incurred by the Halifaxes and Stirlings, an all-Lancaster force was to conclude the current series of operations against the "Big City". 316 aircraft were made ready on the 3rd, of which 121 were provided by 5 Group, including ten by 50 Squadron, which departed Skellingthorpe between 20.11 and 20.22 led by three pilots of flying officer rank. P/O Wilkie and crew had been outbound for less than an hour when the bomb-aimer reported sick and forced the abandonment of their sortie. After rendezvousing over the North Sea, the bomber stream crossed the Dutch coast over the Den Helder peninsular, and adopted a direct course of 350 miles, which took them north of Hannover to Brandenburg, some thirty-five miles short of the target. Long, straight legs were rarely employed because of the risk of interception by the Luftwaffe, but the forecast heavy cloud with tops at 18,000 feet accompanied the stream all the way from the Dutch coast to the target area, and helped to keep the enemy at bay. The Pathfinders had been briefed to use H2S to navigate their way via the region's lakes to the city centre aiming-point, but the cloud miraculously dispersed in time to leave clear skies and allow the Pathfinders to drop ground-marking TIs rather than the less reliable skymarkers. The first TIs fell right over the aiming-point, before others crept back for between two and five miles along the line of approach from the west. Fortunately, the backers up maintained the marking as the main force Lancasters came in in a single wave, and, although much of the bombing fell short of the city centre, most of it landed within the city boundaries, principally into the largely residential districts of Tiergarten, Wedding, Moabit and Charlottenburg, and the industrial Siemensstadt, where much useful damage occurred and caused loss of war production. The 50 Squadron crews carried out a time-and-distance run from yellow track markers and bombed on red and green TIs from 16,000 to 21,000 feet between 23.23 and 23.41. Many fires were observed, which appeared to be merging as the bombers turned towards the north for a return route that would intentionally violate Swedish airspace. Four Mosquitos laid spoof route marker flares well away from the actual track to mislead the night-fighters, but, in the absence of the poorer performing Halifaxes and Stirlings, twenty-two Lancasters failed to return, almost 7% of those dispatched. among them the squadron's ED755, which crashed nine miles east-north-east of Neuruppin shortly after leaving the target, killing F/O Coates RCAF and his crew. Whether by design, or as a result of the losses sustained, Berlin was now shelved for the next ten weeks, while Harris sought other suitable targets, of which there were many.

He would shortly begin a four-raid series against Hanover stretching over a four-week period, but first he focussed on southern Germany, beginning on the 5th with the twin cities of Mannheim and Ludwigshafen, which face each other from the East and West Banks respectively of the Rhine. The plan was to exploit the creep-back phenomenon that attended most large operations, by approaching the target from the west, and marking the eastern half of Mannheim, with the expectation that the bombing would spread back along the line of approach across western Mannheim and into Ludwigshafen. A force of 605 aircraft was assembled, which included 108 Lancasters of 5 Group, a dozen of them at Skellingthorpe loaded with a cookie each and a variety of incendiaries packed into thirteen to eighteen SBCs. They took off between 19.43 and 20.25 with F/Ls Bolton and Chopping the senior pilots on duty, and, after climbing out, set course for Beachy Head and the Channel crossing. P/O Edward had to turn back after the mid-upper gunner complained of problems with his electrically-heated suit. They others made it all the way in favourable weather conditions to find clear skies over the target, where the Pathfinders performed at their absolute best. After first observing red and yellow markers, the 50 Squadron crews had green TIs in their bomb sights as they let their loads go from 15,800 to 20,500 feet between 23.02 and 23.36, and all reported hitting them. Those arriving towards the later stages of the raid were drawn on by the burgeoning fires fifty miles ahead, and a number of large, red explosions were observed at 23.12, 23.23 and 23.27, the last of which was followed by a purplish-red mushroom of fire. Searchlights were numerous, but the flak negligible, and it was the abundance of night-fighters that posed the greatest risk to life and limb, although the Skellingthorpe crews appeared to avoid any contact. Black smoke was rising through 15,000 feet as the bombers withdrew to the west, and the glow from the burning cities was visible for 150 miles into the return journey, which thirty-four aircraft would fail to complete. Thirteen Lancasters, an equal number of Halifaxes and eight Stirlings were missing, and the percentage loss rates continued to tell the same story. Local reports confirmed that both Mannheim and Ludwigshafen had suffered catastrophic destruction, with almost two thousand fires in the latter alone, 986 of them classed as large. Mannheim's reporting system broke down completely, and little detail emerged of this raid, although it would recover in time for the next assault in less than three weeks' time.

Munich was posted as the target on the 6th, for which the squadron made ready ten Lancasters as part of the ninety-two-strong 5 Group element in an overall force of 257 Lancasters and 147 Halifaxes, the Stirling brigade made conspicuous by its absence. The Skellingthorpe crews were airborne between 19.54 and 20.15 with the newly-promoted S/L Parks the senior pilot on duty, each carrying a similar bomb load and adopting the same route as for the previous night. Conditions in the target area on this night were not ideal, with cloud varying between five and nine-tenths, although some ground features, like the River Isar, could be identified and the red, yellow and green TIs observed. The 50 Squadron crews were among those carrying out a timed run from the Ammersee, located twenty-one miles away to the south-west, and bombed from 18,300 to 22,000 feet between 23.34 and 23.46. A large number of fires were observed to be grouped around the markers, but an accurate assessment was not possible, and local reports would suggest that the attack had been scattered across southern and western districts. The searchlights were ineffective because of the cloud, but large numbers of night-fighters were again evident, and sixteen aircraft failed to return, thirteen of them Halifaxes, a percentage loss rate of 8.8, compared with 1.2 for the Lancasters.

5 Group largely left the war to the other groups for the ensuing two weeks, during which period only elements of 617 and 619 Squadrons were in action. On the night of the 15/16th, 617 Squadron sent eight Lancasters to attack the raised earthen banks of the Dortmund-Ems Canal at a point south of the twin aqueduct section near Ladbergen. Five failed to return home, including the one containing the former 50 Squadron crew of F/L Les Knight DSO, MiD. Seven men baled out near the Dutch town of Den Ham, leaving Knight to attempt a forced-landing in what was an uncontrollable Lancaster, but he hit trees and died in the ensuing crash. Ray Grayston and "Obie" O'Brien RCAF were captured, but the others were assisted by the Dutch Resistance, and retained their freedom. Also lost as members of W/C Holden's crew were the former 50 Squadron navigator and bomb-aimer, F/L Taerum RCAF and F/O Spafford RAAF.

It was not until the commencement of the series of raids on Hannover that 5 Group, as a whole, was roused from its slumber. The irony of such long layoffs was that airmen, despite occupying the most dangerous jobs in the fighting services, grew listless and bored when left to kick their heels, attend lectures and take part in PT, and, no doubt, cheered when the tannoys called them to briefing on the 22nd. At briefing, the crews learned that they were to be part of a force of 711 aircraft to attack the ancient city of Hannover, situated in northern Germany midway between the Dutch frontier and Berlin. They were told that it was home to much industry, with oil, rubber and tank production of particular significance to the raid planners of Bomber Command, and was also the location of seven Nazi concentration camps. According to Martin Middlebrook and Chris Everitt in Bomber Command War Diaries, the first two operations produced concentrated bombing, but mostly outside of the target, while only the third one succeeded in causing extensive damage, which, if the figures are to be believed, seem to be massively out of proportion. The author contends that the reports of the crews after the first two operations suggest strongly that the damage to Hannover was accumulative over the first three raids and did not result from just one, as will be explained in the following narrative. The telling feature is, perhaps, that no reports came out of Hannover to corroborate the testimony of the crews on the first two raids, although post-raid reconnaissance by the RAF after the second one did show that some of the bombing had fallen into open country, and the Pathfinders did admit to at least one poor performance.

50 Squadron prepared sixteen Lancasters, which took off between 18.58 and 19.25 with W/C McFarlane and S/L Pullen the senior pilots on duty, before climbing out and joining up with the other 135 participants from 5 Group for the 430-mile outward leg. There were no early returns to Skellingthorpe, and all reached the target area, where good visibility prevailed, but stronger-than-forecast winds would play their part in pushing the marking and bombing towards the south-east. The 50 Squadron crews carried out their bombing runs from 16,800 to 20,800 feet between 21.30 and 21.51, aiming at red and green TIs and dodging the intense searchlights and heavy flak, which was bursting at around 18,000 feet. Some returning crews observed a line of fires developing from west to east, with smoke rising through 14,000 feet, while others claimed that fires ran from the aiming-point in a north-north-westerly direction across the city, but all were unanimous, that the raid had been highly successful, and that the glow of fires was still visible from the Dutch coast, a distance of two hundred miles. Twenty-six aircraft failed to return, twelve of them Halifaxes, which, again, sustained the highest numerical losses, and, this time, at 5.3%, even exceeded the Stirling's loss rate.

Now let us examine the claim that the main weight of bombs fell two to five miles south-south-east from the city centre, and that the operation largely failed. Firstly, two to five miles in any city means that the bombing fell within the boundaries, and, therefore, within the built-up area. Secondly, the majority of crews, if not all, reported a highly successful raid with fires right across the city, smoke rising to 14,000 feet as they left the scene and the glow visible from the Dutch coast. It is true that crews were very frequently mistaken in their belief that an attack had been successful, but the evidence on this occasion would seem to confirm their testimony. Decoy fire-sites do not produce a glow visible from a distance of two hundred miles, or sufficient volumes of smoke to reach bombing height during the short duration of a raid, and be dense enough to be visible at night.

On the 23rd, and for the second time in the month, Mannheim was posted as the target for that night, and would face a force, which, at take-off, numbered 628 aircraft, 139 of them 5 Group Lancasters. Fifteen of these were made ready at Skellingthorpe, and took off between 18.47 and 19.16 with F/Ls Bolton, Chopping and McLeod the senior pilots on duty. There were no early returns to Skellingthorpe as the bomber stream pushed on across France and into southern Germany, where they encountered largely clear skies and good visibility. At the head of the stream, the Pathfinders had marked out the northern districts, which had not been hit so severely during the previous operation. The marking was accurate and concentrated, allowing the Skellingthorpe crews to attack on red, green and yellow TIs from 17,800 to 20,100 feet between 21.47 and 22.09. Later bombing spilled over into the northern fringe of Ludwigshafen and out into the nearby towns of Oppau and Frankenthal, where much damage resulted. P/O Litherland and crew had a narrow escape after being hit by flak at 19,000 feet at 22.11, and losing their starboard fin, rudder and elevator, but managed and overcame the challenging control situation, and reached home without further incident. Returning crews reported that smoke had reached around 6,000 feet as they turned away, and that the glow of fires remained visible for 150 miles into the return journey. Thirty-two crews were absent from debriefing, and, this time, eighteen of them were in Lancasters, compared with seven each for the Halifaxes and Stirlings. This provided a somewhat topsy-turvy and unusual loss-rate of 5.7%, 3.6% and 6% respectively. 50 Squadron's ED415 was intercepted shortly after bombing, and shot down by the night-fighter of Lt Bock of III./NJG1 to crash at 22.55 some six miles west of Ludwigshafen. The timing suggests that P/O Nelson RAAF and his crew were late on target, or had, perhaps, sustained damage that slowed them, and all died in the wreckage of their Lancaster. Post-raid reconnaissance and local reports revealed that 927 houses and twenty industrial premises had been destroyed in Mannheim, and that the I.G Farben factory in Ludwigshafen had sustained serious damage.

Hannover was posted as the target again on the 27th, and a force of 678 aircraft made ready. 50 Squadron answered the call with fifteen Lancasters in a 5 Group contribution of 141, and they departed Skellingthorpe between 19.12 and 19.35 with F/Os Brown and Shortt the senior pilots on duty. Poor weather conditions were encountered over the North Sea, and it was at this stage, that F/O Taylor's a.s.i failed, forcing him to turn back, when twenty-five miles short of the Dutch coast. The others pressed on in the wake of the Pathfinders, who were unaware that the weather forecasts on which their performance would be based, were incorrect. The result of that would be to push the marking some five miles from the city centre towards the north of the city, but, at least, the weather improved markedly over Germany to present the crews with clear skies at the target. The 50 Squadron crews delivered their cookie and 4lb and 30lb incendiaries mostly on green TIs from 17,800 to 22,500 feet between 21.59 and 22.21, and observed many fires with smoke rising to 15,000 feet. Returning crews again reported the glow of fires visible from the Dutch coast, and confidence in the success of the operation was unanimous across the Command, giving lie to the claim that little damage resulted. Post-raid photos did reveal many bomb craters in open country, but the fire and smoke evidence did not support decoy fire-sites, and no local report was forthcoming. The loss of thirty-eight aircraft was probably something of a shock, but, at least, common sense returned to the statistics to re-establish the status-quo after the topsy-turvy outcome of the Mannheim raid. Seventeen Halifaxes, ten Lancasters, ten Stirlings and one Wellington failed to return, giving loss-rates for the four-engine types of 9% for the Stirling, 7.3% for the Halifax and 3.2% for the Lancaster. 50 Squadron's EE189 crashed four miles north-north-west of Hildesheim on the way out of the target area, and only the Australian mid-upper gunner survived from the crew of P/O Banks RAAF.

The month ended with an operation to Bochum in the central Ruhr on the 29th, for which 50 Squadron made ready twelve Lancasters in a 5 Group effort of 111, and they were part of an overall heavy force of 343 aircraft. They departed Skellingthorpe between 18.31 and 19.02 with S/L Parks the senior pilot on duty, having been preceded into the air at 18.09 and 18.24 by F/Sgt Thompson and P/O Code, who were bound for the distant Spinach I garden located off the Baltic port of Gdynia, now in Poland. The bombing element proceeded to the target, kept on track by two route-marker flares at 20,000 feet, and arrived in a little over two-and-a-half hours to find good visibility, which enabled them to establish their positions visually. The Pathfinders marked the aiming-point with green TIs, and the bombing was carried out from 17,500 to 21,000 feet between 20.46 and 21.06 in the face of a strong searchlight and moderate flak defence. Some returning crews described the target as a mass of flames, with smoke rising rapidly to meet them, while local reports confirmed the destruction of 527 houses, with 742 others seriously damaged. Meanwhile, it had taken three-and-a-half hours for F/Sgt Thompson and crew to reach a pinpoint on the Baltic coast, from which they made a timed run of 102 seconds to release their mines from 6,000 feet. Satisfied with the results, they returned safely from their eight-and-a-half-hour round-trip. The arrival of JB143 was awaited in vain, and, later, on the afternoon of the 30th, P/O Mason and F/L Chopping carried out a four-hour sea-search for the P/O Code and crew, but found nothing. News was eventually received that the Lancaster had been ditched off Denmark's eastern coast following a brush with a night-fighter, and P/O Code RCAF and five of his crew had begun a period of extended leave in a prison camp. Sadly, the navigator had been carried away by a wave, and was lost.

During the course of the month the squadron took part in nine operations, dispatching eighty-four sorties for the loss of four Lancasters and crews.

October 1943

The start of October was a busy time for the Lancaster squadrons, which would be called upon to participate in six major operations in the first eight nights. The month's account was opened at Hagen, at the eastern end of the Ruhr on the 1st, for which a moderately sized heavy force of 243 Lancasters was drawn from 1, 5 and 8 Groups. 5 Group contributed 125 aircraft, eleven of them representing 50 Squadron, and they were loaded with a cookie and up to sixteen SBCs of incendiaries each, before departing Skellingthorpe between 18.28 and 18.44 with F/Os Brown and Ruskell the senior pilots on duty. P/O Medley and crew turned back from twenty miles off Lowestoft because of an indisposed wireless operator, leaving the others to arrive in the target area to find ten-tenths cloud with tops at 8,000 feet and red and green Oboe-laid skymarkers to aim at. Bombing took place from 16,700 to 20,000 feet between 21.00 and 21.10, and all returned safely to report a large bluish-green explosion at 21.03, an effective Pathfinder performance, and the glow of fires beneath the cloud. In addition to the usual housing damage, local reports confirmed the destruction of forty-six industrial firms, among them a manufacturer of accumulator batteries vital to U-Boot construction, and this had an impact on U-Boot production.

294 crews from 1, 5 and 8 Groups were called to briefings on the 2nd to learn that Munich was to be their target for that night. 5 Group detailed 113 Lancasters, whose crews were to adopt the time-and-distance method of bombing, and the eleven at Skellingthorpe were loaded with a cookie and ten SBCs each before taxiing to take-off in the minutes after 18.30, with F/Os Brown, Ruskell and Wilson the senior pilots on duty. F/O Ruskell was the first to roll at 18.48, and take-offs were completed by 18.59, before a course was set to the south coast and the Channel crossing. P/O Adams and crew were within fifteen miles of Dunkerque when the port-outer engine failed and ended their interest in proceedings. The others reached the target area some three-and-a-half hours later to encounter cloud over the Wörthsee, situated some fifteen miles west-south-west of the centre of Munich, and the starting point for the time-and-distance run. The skies over the city were clear of cloud, but the marking was scattered and led to most of the early bombing falling into southern and south-eastern districts. The 5 Group crews were unable to establish a firm fix on the Wörthsee, and this would lead to a creep-back of up to fifteen miles along the line of approach. The 50 Squadron crews bombed on red and green TIs from 18,000 to 21,000 feet between 22.32 and 22.38, but it was not all plain-sailing. Returning crews suggested that the raid appeared to be concentrated on the eastern side of the city, and local authorities reported that 339 buildings had been destroyed.

Kassel, an industrial city located some eighty miles to the east of the Ruhr, would receive two visits from the Command during the month, the first on the 3rd, for which a force of 547 aircraft was assembled consisting of 223 Halifaxes, 204 Lancasters and 113 Stirlings. 5 Group supported the operation with ninety-two Lancasters, of which ten were made ready at Skellingthorpe, and they took off between 18.21 and 18.51 with W/C McFarlane and S/L Parks the senior pilots on duty. There were no early returns, and all reached the target area to find largely clear skies but thick ground haze. The Pathfinder H2S "blind" markers overshot the planned aiming-point, and, because of the haze, and, possibly, decoy markers, the backers-up, whose job was to confirm their accuracy by visual means, were unable to correct the error. The 50 Squadron crews identified the target visually and by green TIs, and bombed from 17,800 to 21,000 feet between 21.15 and 21.33, reporting on their return what appeared to be a good concentration of fires and a pall of smoke rising to meet them. In fact, the main weight of the attack had fallen onto the western suburbs, where the Henschel and Fieseler aircraft factories were hit, but a stray bomb load had also detonated an ammunition dump at Ihringshausen, situated close to the north-eastern suburb of Wolfsanger, which was left devastated by the blast. Twenty-four aircraft failed to return, fourteen Halifaxes, six Stirlings and four Lancasters, which gave a loss-rate of 6.3%, 3.2% and 2.9% respectively.

The busy schedule of operations was to continue at Frankfurt on the 4th, for which a force of 406 aircraft was made ready. The American confidence in the ability of its forces to deliver daylight attacks on military and war production targets in Germany had been shaken by the high loss rates, which were not sustainable. Since the first Hannover raid, a small number of 8th Air Force B17s had been flirting with night raids alongside their RAF colleagues, and this night would bring their final involvement. 5 Group detailed ninety-five Lancasters, of which ten would represent 50 Squadron, and they departed Skellingthorpe between 18.25 and 19.02 with F/L Bolton the senior pilot on duty. They had to follow a somewhat circuitous route, which departed England over the Sussex coast and tracked across Belgium as if heading for southern Germany, before swinging to the north-east and passing to the west of Frankfurt for the final run-in of around eighty miles. This added significantly to the mileage, but avoided the flak hotspots from the Dutch coast and north of the Ruhr. There were no early returns to Langar, and the target was reached after a four-hour outward flight, although an hour of that was generally accounted for in climbing-out and gaining height before setting course. Frankfurt was found to be clear of cloud, and the Pathfinders produced a masterful marking performance to leave the city at the mercy of the main force. The 50 Squadron crews bombed on red and green TIs from 18,000 to 20,700 feet between 21.34 and 21.52, and witnessed a highly-concentrated attack taking place that left the eastern half of the city and the docks area a sea of flames. A large red explosion was observed at 21.37, which threw flames up to 3,000 feet, and smoke was rising through 8,000 feet as the bombers turned away, some crews returning to report the glow from the burning city to be visible for 120 miles into the homeward leg. The success was gained at the modest cost of ten aircraft, half of which were Halifaxes. The squadron's veteran Lancaster, W4905, failed to return with the experienced crew of P/O Wilkie CGM, who died with his crew in the wreckage in the southern outskirts of the target. The rear gunner was Sgt Brant of the USAAF and a native of Illinois.

The busy first week of the month concluded with an operation against Stuttgart, for which a force of 343 Lancasters was drawn from 1, 3, 5, 6 and 8 Groups on the 7th. A new weapon in the Command's armoury was introduced for the first time in numbers on this night with the participation of a night-fighter-communications-jamming device called "Jostle". It required a specialist operator in addition to the standard crew of seven, who, though not necessarily a German speaker, could recognise the language, and, on hearing it, jam the signals on up to three frequencies by broadcasting engine noise over them. At 101 Squadron the device was referred to as ABC or Airborne Cigar, and, once proved to be effective, ABC Lancasters would be spread through the bomber stream for all major operations, whether or not 1 Group was otherwise involved. The Lancaster would also carry a full bomb load reduced by 1,000lbs to compensate for the weight of the equipment and its operator. 5 Group put up 128 Lancasters, of which thirteen were made ready at Skellingthorpe, and they took off between 20.27 and 20.57 with F/L McLeod the senior pilot on duty. P/O Weatherstone and crew were back on the ground within ninety minutes because of an issue with both outer engines, but the others all reached the target area, where ten-tenths cloud at 10,000 feet concealed the ground from view. The Pathfinders employed H2S and established two areas of marking, which led to bombs falling in many parts of the city from the centre to the south-west. The 50 Squadron crews bombed from 19,000 to 21,800 feet between 00.08 and 00.22, before returning safely to report their impressions of a scattered attack, which cost a remarkably modest four aircraft. Whether or not the presence of the radio-countermeasures Lancasters was responsible could not be certain, but it was a promising start, and, would lead, ultimately, to the formation of a dedicated RCM group, 100 Group, in November.

The third raid of the series on Hannover was posted on the 8th, and a force of 504 aircraft duly assembled. 5 Group contributed eighty-four Lancasters, nine of them made ready at Skellingthorpe, and they took off between 22.51 and 23.07 with S/Ls Parks and Pullen the senior pilots on duty. After climbing out, they set course for the northern tip of Texel, and all reached the target area to find largely clear skies and red and green TIs marking out the city-centre aiming-point. The Skellingthorpe crews bombed from 18,600 to 21,200 feet between 01.33 and 01.49, and, having arrived in the early stages of the attack, saw fires just beginning to take hold. It became clear, as they retreated westwards, that the fires were developing into a serious conflagration, but, curiously, despite the claim by some commentators that this was the one successful raid of the series, there was no mention of the glow being visible from a considerable distance, as had been the case with the first two operations. This time a local report did emerge, which described heavy damage in all districts except for those in the west, with a large area of fire engulfing the central districts. A total of 3,932 buildings was destroyed, and thirty thousand others damaged to some extent, with a death toll of 1,200 people. These statistics seem somewhat excessive for a single operation by fewer than five hundred aircraft, particularly in the absence of the kind of crew reports common to the first two raids, and this adds weight to the author's contention, that the damage was accumulative over the three operations. Twenty-seven aircraft failed to return, and another 50 Squadron Lancaster was among them. DV324 was hit by flak shortly after bombing, and went in near the target, killing two of P/O Taylor's crew, while he and four others escaped by parachute to become PoWs.

The Pathfinder and main force squadrons would effectively stand down now for a period of ten days, while Mosquitos of 8 Group's Light Night Striking Force took the war to Germany. F/L Chopping and P/O Mason were posted to 1668 Conversion Unit at Balderton, Newark on the 18th at the conclusion of their tours. It was also on this day, that the fourth and final raid of the series on Hannover was posted, crews learning at briefings that this was to be an all-Lancaster affair involving 360 aircraft. 5 Group provided 143 of them, thirteen made ready by 50 Squadron, and they departed Skellingthorpe between 17.10 and 18.06 with F/L McLeod the senior pilot on duty. They crossed Holland, seemingly unmolested, but appear to have run into a nest of night-fighters on crossing the frontier into Germany, and at least thirteen aircraft were brought down during the ensuing forty-five minutes that encompassed the approach and withdrawal phases. A layer of eight to ten-tenths cloud hung over Hannover with tops at 12,000 to 15,000 feet, and these conditions made it difficult for the Pathfinders to establish the aiming-point. It resulted in them dropping both sky and ground markers that lacked concentration, which would lead to a scattering of the effort. The Skellingthorpe crews bombed mostly on red and green TIs or on release-point flares from 18,400 to 20,500 feet between 20.15 and 20.32, and a colossal explosion was observed at around 20.19. The strong night-fighter presence dissuaded crews from hanging around to assess the outcome further, and the impression of those returning was of a scattered attack. It was established later that most of the bombs had fallen into open country, a disappointment compounded by the loss of eighteen Lancasters. The four raids on Hannover had cost the Command 110 aircraft from 2,253 sorties, a loss rate of 4.9%, but much of the city now lay in ruins. The close proximity of the Misburg synthetic oil plant to the east, would keep the region in the firing line a year hence.

The first major attack of the war on the eastern city of Leipzig was planned for the 20th, and an all-Lancaster force of 358 aircraft 1, 5, 6 and 8 Groups assembled. 5 Group was responsible for 140 Lancasters, and 50 Squadron thirteen, which took off from Skellingthorpe between 17.20 and 17.40 with S/L Pullen the senior pilot on duty. Atrocious weather conditions were encountered outbound, and it was icing that presented the greatest difficulties and persuaded many crews to turn back. To their credit, all but one of the 50 Squadron crews pushed on through the front to reach the target after a three-and-a-half-hour outward flight, to then encounter seven to ten-tenths cloud with tops as high as 14,000 feet. P/O Heckendorf, clearly a man of German descent, lost his rear turret to technical gremlins shortly after crossing the Dutch coast, but continued on until losing his starboard-inner engine, a situation made worse by icing. As they began to sink, an attempt was made to jettison the cookie to save weight and enable them to reach the target, but the bomb-release gear was frozen, and they had to jettison the whole content of the bomb bay from 14,000 feet over Calvörde, a town some thirty miles west-north-west of Brauschweig. The Pathfinders had been unable in the conditions to establish and mark the aiming-point, leaving crews to bomb on e.t.a., on fires glimpsed through the cloud or on scattered skymarkers, the 50 Squadron element doing so from 14,500 to 23,000 feet between 21.02 and 21.15. Sixteen Lancasters failed to return, and those crews that did make it home were unable to offer any useful details at debriefing.

The final major operation of the month was the second one against Kassel, for which preparations were put in hand on the 22nd. A force of 569 aircraft ultimately stood ready to take off in the early evening, 133 of them 5 Group Lancasters, ten of them provided by 50 Squadron. They became airborne from Skellingthorpe between 18.10 and 18.22 with F/L Brown the senior pilot on duty, but F/O Ruskell and crew turned back early after the a.s.i froze. The others pressed on across Belgium in unfavourable weather conditions, which miraculously improved in the target area to leave clear skies between the bombers and the target, but ten-tenths cloud above them at 24,000 feet. At the opening of the raid the H2S "blind" markers overshot the city-centre aiming-point, leaving the success of the operation reliant upon the visual marker crews backing up, and they did not disappoint. The red and green TIs were concentrated right on the aiming-point, and the main force followed up with accurate and concentrated bombing with scarcely any creep-back. The 50 Squadron crews carried out their attacks from 18,000 to 20,500 feet between 21.01 and 21.27, and observed the fires just beginning to take hold as they turned away. It was after the sound of their engines had receded that the fires joined together to engulf the city in what, in some areas, was a firestorm, though not one as fierce as that experienced in Hamburg. The massively successful operation was achieved at a high cost of forty-three bombers, twenty-five of them Halifaxes, and among the eighteen missing Lancasters was 50 Squadron's ED483, which crashed near Höxter, some thirty-five miles north of Kassel, killing P/O Broadbent, while his crew all escaped with their lives to fall into enemy hands. In Kassel, the shell-shocked inhabitants emerged from their shelters to find their city devastated and unrecognizable. After 3,600 fires had been dealt with, it would be established eventually that more than 4,300 apartment blocks containing 53,000 dwelling units had been destroyed or damaged, leaving up to 120,000 people without homes, and in excess of six thousand others killed. 155 industrial buildings had also been destroyed or severely damaged, along with numerous schools, hospitals, churches and public buildings.

F/O Michael Beetham and crew arrived from 1654 Conversion Unit on the 25th to begin their tour of operations. During the course of the month the squadron participated in nine operations, and dispatched one hundred sorties for the loss of three Lancasters and crews.

November 1943

In a minute to Churchill on the 3rd of November, Harris stated, that with the participation of the American 8th Air Force, he could "wreck Berlin from end to end". He estimated that the campaign would cost the two forces between four and five hundred aircraft, but that it would cost Germany the war. This would remove the need for the kind of bloody, expensive and protracted land campaign, which he had personally witnessed during the Great War, and had prompted him to "get into the air". It should be remembered that this was the first time in the history of air warfare, that an opportunity had existed to prove the theory, that an enemy could be defeated by bombing alone. It is only in the light of more recent experiences, that we have learned of the need, in a conventional conflict at least, to occupy the enemy's territory to secure submission. The Americans, however, were committed to victory on land, where film cameras could capture the glory, and would not accompany Harris to Berlin. It was also on this day that F/L Brown and crew were posted from 50 Squadron to the Pathfinders to join 97 Squadron at Bourn.

Düsseldorf was selected to open the month's operational account that very night, and, no doubt, while the Prime Minister was digesting Harris's epistle, a force of 589 Lancasters and Halifaxes was being prepared for action. 5 Group's contribution amounted to 147 Lancasters, of which a dozen represented 50 Squadron, and they were each loaded with a cookie and up to eighteen SBCs of various incendiaries before taking off between 17.11 and 17.31 with F/Ls Bolton, Shortt and the newly-promoted Edward the senior pilots on duty. P/O Adam and crew's sortie was cut short abruptly, as it became clear almost immediately that their a.s.i was unserviceable, and they were back on the ground forty-six minutes after leaving it. The others remained with the bomber stream, and, as they approached the south-western Ruhr after flying out over Belgium, small patches of cloud were encountered at 12,000 feet and smoke was beginning to drift across the target. Having, shortly before, traversed the narrow neck of southern Holland to enter Germany, P/O Litherland and crew ran into a concentration of fifty to sixty searchlights in the Mönchengladbach-Cologne corridor, some fifteen miles from the target, and were latched onto by a Ju88, which attacked from astern. The Lancaster was thrown into a corkscrew, but not before hits knocked out the hydraulics system, causing the bomb doors to flop open. The bombs were jettisoned "live" onto the searchlights as they turned for home and a distress signal sent from the Dutch coast. Happily, they were able to reach an airfield at Hardwick in Cambridgeshire, where DV227 was damaged further in a ground-loop. Meanwhile, the visibility at the target was generally good, and the Pathfinders employed both sky and ground markers to good effect to identify the aiming-point in the city centre. Bombing took place by the 50 Squadron crews on red and green TIs and skymarkers from 19,000 to 21,100 feet between 19.46 and 19.57, and fires were observed to be developing on both sides of the Rhine with black smoke rising through 6,000 feet as they turned away. Eighteen aircraft failed to return, and, unusually, eleven were Lancasters and only seven Halifaxes. It was on this night, that 61 Squadron's F/L Bill Reid earned the award of a Victoria Cross for pressing on to bomb the target after his Lancaster, LM360, was severely damaged, and a number of his crew either killed or wounded. On return, the aircraft was crash-landed on the American base at Shipdham, and following repair, would eventually find its way to 50 Squadron for further service. Post-raid reconnaissance revealed that central and southern districts had sustained widespread damage to industry and housing, but no report came out of Düsseldorf to provide detail.

The only serious activity for 50 Squadron thereafter, until the resumption of the Berlin campaign, was as part of a 5 and 8 Group force of 313 Lancasters, which was sent to destroy railway yards at Modane, situated in the foothills of the Alps in south-eastern France on the night of the 10/11th. 5 Group supported the operation with 136 Lancasters, of which a record eighteen representing 50 Squadron departed Skellingthorpe between 20.45 and 21.25 with F/Ls McLeod and Shortt the senior pilots on duty. Ahead of them lay an outward flight of more than 650 miles, which they covered in around four-and-a-quarter hours to be rewarded by the presence of a full moon shining brightly from a cloudless sky. They pinpointed on Lake Bissorte before making a time-and-distance run to the target, which they identified visually and by red and green TIs, before bombing from 12,000 to 16,400 feet between 01.00 and 01.13. The attack seemed to be concentrated around the markers, and fires appeared to be taking hold, while a large explosion was observed at 01.13. Returning crews were fairly confident in the quality of their night's efforts, and two hundred bombing photos revealed detonations within one mile of the aiming-point, which had caused extensive damage to track and installations without loss. On the 15th, 61 Squadron arrived at Skellingthorpe after moving from Syerston, and would remain, during this spell, for two-and-a-half months.

Undaunted by the American response to his invitation to join the Berlin party, Harris would return alone, and the rocky road to the Capital was re-joined by an all-Lancaster heavy force on the night of the 18/19th, while a predominantly Halifax and Stirling contingent of 395 aircraft acted as a diversion by raiding Mannheim and Ludwigshafen three hundred miles to the south-west. The Berlin-bound crews would benefit from four Mosquitos dropping dummy fighter flares, while other Mosquitos carried out a spoof raid on Frankfurt to protect the Mannheim force. The two forces would cross the enemy coast simultaneously some 250 miles apart to confuse the enemy night-fighter controllers, and the route chosen for the Berlin brigade was via the Frisian island of Texel to a point north of Hannover, and thence to the target to pass over the centre on an east-north-easterly heading. After bombing they would return south of Berlin and Cologne, before crossing central Belgium to gain the English Channel via the French coast. An innovation for this operation was a shortening of the bomber stream to reduce the time over the target to sixteen minutes. When the first Thousand Bomber raid had taken place in May 1942, with an unprecedented twelve aircraft per minute crossing the aiming-point, there was considered to be a high risk of collisions. The number had since been increased to sixteen per minute, with large raids lasting up to forty-five minutes, but, on this night, twenty-seven aircraft per minute were to pass over the aiming-point.

50 Squadron made ready a new record number of twenty-one Lancasters as part of a 5 Group force of 182, and take-off from Skellingthorpe was accomplished without incident between 17.09 and 18.07 with S/L Pullen the senior pilot on duty. The departure of F/O Keith and crew had been delayed by sixteen minutes, and theirs was the later time recorded above. As they crossed the North Sea towards Texel, they had clawed back four minutes, but were too far behind schedule at Point A to continue to the primary target, and bombed gun flashes on Texel from 20,000 feet at 19.27 as a last resort. When they landed at base at 20.55, they found W/O Saxton and P/O Weatherstone and their crews already there, having abandoned their sorties because of a failed starboard engine and an indisposed bomb-aimer respectively. P/O Heckendorf and crew were the last of the "boomerangs", and touched down at 21.00, also with an ailing bomb-aimer. This left seventeen others from the squadron to continue the journey to Germany's Capital, over a blanket of cloud covering northern Germany. It persisted all the way to the target, where the tops reached 6,000 feet and the marking and bombing had to be carried out blindly. The 50 Squadron participants delivered their loads from 18,000 to 23,000 feet on red and green sky-markers between 20.57 and 21.12, and all returned home with nothing useful to pass on to the intelligence section at debriefing. The diversion at Mannheim was deemed to have been successful in its purpose, and caused some useful industrial damage, most seriously to the Daimler-Benz motor factory, which suffered a 90% loss of production for an unknown period. In addition to this, more than three hundred buildings were destroyed at a cost of twenty-three aircraft, while the losses from Berlin were encouragingly low at just nine aircraft.

The Lancasters stayed at home on the 19th, while 3, 4, 6 and 8 Groups combined to put 170 Halifaxes, eighty-six Stirlings and 10 Mosquitos into the air for Leverkusen. They were greeted in the target area by ten-tenths cloud and an absence of marking, which was caused by equipment failure among the Oboe Mosquitos. A few green TIs were spotted some five to ten miles to the north-west of the target during the approach, but the crews were left to establish their positions on the basis of their own H2S, which, over a region as densely built-up as the Ruhr, was a challenge. As a result, the operation was a complete failure, which sprayed bombs over twenty-seven towns in the Ruhr, mostly to the north of Leverkusen.

Harris called for a maximum effort on Berlin on the 22nd, and 764 aircraft were made available, of which nineteen of the 166 Lancasters contributed by 5 Group were provided by 50 Squadron. They departed Skellingthorpe between 16.30 and 16.59 with F/Ls Bolton and Burtt the senior pilots on duty, and, after climbing out, adopted an outward route similar to that employed by the all-Lancaster force four nights earlier. This took them from Texel to a point north-west of Hannover, where a slight dogleg to port would put them on a due-easterly heading directly to the target. Unlike the previous raid, however, rather than the circuitous return south of Cologne and out over the French coast, they would come home via a reciprocal route. This was based on a forecast of low cloud and fog over Germany, which would inhibit the night-fighter effort, while broken, medium-level cloud over Berlin would facilitate ground marking. An additional bonus was the availability to the Pathfinders of five new H2S Mk III sets, while a new record of thirty-four aircraft per minute passing over the aiming-point would be achieved by abandoning the long-standing practice of allocating aircraft types to specific waves. On this night, aircraft of all types would be spread through the bomber stream, and this was bad news for the Stirlings, which, by the very nature of their design, would be below the Lancaster and Halifax elements, and in danger of being hit by friendly bombs.

P/O Dennis Lundy and crew were back home within ninety minutes after losing their starboard-inner engine, leaving the others to discover that the meteorological forecast had been inaccurate, and that the city was hidden under a blanket of ten-tenths cloud with tops at around 12,000 feet. This meant that ground marking would be largely ineffective, and that the least reliable Wanganui (skymarking) method would have to be employed. Crews ran into intense predicted flak and a mass of searchlights as they began their bombing runs, and those from 50 Squadron aimed at red and green TIs and release-point flares from 19,000 to 23,000 feet between 20.00 and 20.26. The glow of fires was observed beneath the clouds, and a very large explosion lit up the sky at 20.10. The impression was of a successful operation, but an assessment through the clouds was impossible. Post-raid reconnaissance and local reports confirmed that this attack on Berlin had been the most effective of the war to date, and had caused a swathe of destruction from the city centre through the western residential districts of Tiergarten and Charlottenburg as far as the suburb town of Spandau. A number of firestorm areas were reported, and the catalogue of destruction included three thousand houses and twenty-three industrial premises. Many thousands more sustained varying degrees of damage, costing 175,000 people their homes and an estimated two thousand their lives, and, by daylight on the 23rd, the smoke had risen to almost 19,000 feet.

50 Squadron suffered its first failure to return for a month, after DV366 crashed in the target area, killing W/O Saxton and his crew, who had recently returned to the squadron for a second tour. This was one of twenty-six aircraft to be lost, eleven of which were Lancasters, ten Halifaxes, and five Stirlings, which amounted to a loss-rate among the types respectively of 2.3%, 4.2% and 10.0%. This proved to be the final straw for Harris as far as the Stirling was concerned, which, because of its short wing design, was restricted to a low service ceiling, and by the configuration of its bomb bay to small calibre bombs. Unlike the Lancaster and Halifax, it lacked development potential, and was immediately withdrawn from future operations over Germany. It would still have an important role to play on secondary duties, however, bombing over occupied territory, mining, and, in 1944, it would replace the Halifax to become the aircraft of choice for the two SOE squadrons, 138 and 161, at Tempsford. Many of those released from Bomber Command service would find their way to 38 Group, where they would give valuable service as transports and glider-tugs for airborne landings.

A heavy force of 365 Lancasters and ten Halifaxes was made ready with some difficulty on the 23rd for a return to Berlin. Back-to-back long-range operations put a strain on those charged with the responsibility of getting the aircraft off the ground, and the Ludford Magna armourers were unable to load all nineteen 101 Squadron Lancasters with the intended weight of bombs, sending them off 2,000lb short. 5 Group detailed 141 Lancasters, of which the sixteen belonging to 50 Squadron were each loaded with a cookie, and some had a 1,000 pounder along with their SBCs of incendiaries. They took off between 16.42 and 17.30 with F/Ls Burtt, McLeod and Ruskell the senior pilots on duty, and not one of them was among the eighteen 5 Group early returns among forty-six from the force as a whole. This was a further indication of the strain of back-to-back long-range operations, and another was the dumping of bombs over the North Sea by crews intending to push on to the target, but wanting to gain more height. It involved largely those from 1 Group, who were shedding their cookies in protest at their A-O-C's policy of loading each Lancaster to its maximum all-up weight at the expense of altitude. The slogan "H-E-I-G-H-T spells safety" could be found on the walls of most bomber station briefing rooms at the time. The target was reached by way of the same route adopted on the previous night, and was found to be covered by ten-tenths cloud with tops at between 10,000 and 15,000 feet. Guided by the glow of fires still burning beneath the clouds from the night before, and the presence of red and green TIs, the 50 Squadron crews bombed from 17,500 to 23,000 feet between 20.02 and 20.19 to contribute to another stunning blow. Returning crews described a column of smoke reaching 20,000 feet, and the glow of fires visible again from the Hannover area some 150 miles from the target. It was on this night that fake broadcasts from England caused annoyance to the night-fighter force by ordering them to land because of fog over their bases, despite which, they still had a major hand in the bringing-down of twenty Lancasters. Post-raid reconnaissance and local reports confirmed that this operation had destroyed a further two thousand buildings, and killed around fifteen hundred people. This would be one of the few Berlin operations negotiated by the squadron without loss.

After a three-night rest for most of the Lancaster crews, 443 of them were briefed on the 26th for a return to the "Big City" for the fourth attack on it since the resumption of the campaign. 5 Group detailed 161 Lancasters, fourteen of them made ready by 50 Squadron, and they departed Skellingthorpe between 17.00 and 17.30 with F/Ls Bolton, Burtt, McLeod and Ruskell the senior pilots on duty. A diversionary raid on Stuttgart by a predominantly Halifax force followed the same route as those bound for Berlin, which involved an outward leg across the French coast and Belgium to a point north of Frankfurt, where they separated. An indication of the beneficial effects of the three-day lay-off was a 44% reduction in early returns by 5 Group crews compared with the previous Berlin raid. The 50 Squadron element remained intact and found Berlin under clear skies, despite which, the Pathfinders overshot the city centre aiming-point by six or seven miles, and marked an area well to the north-west, which happened to contain many war-industry factories. The 50 Squadron crews bombed on red and green TIs from 18,000 and 23,000 feet between 21.15 and 21.28, and returning crews spoke of a mass of fires and thick smoke rising to 15,000 feet. It was learned later that thirty-eight war-industry factories had been destroyed and many others damaged, in return for the loss of twenty-eight Lancasters, many of which had fallen victim to night-fighters on the return flight.

It was during this return phase of the operation, that 50 Squadron's problems arose. DV377 landed at the 4 Group station at Melbourne, and collided with a motor vehicle and JA961, also of 50 Squadron, and both Lancasters were burned out, although neither of the eight man crews of the recently commissioned P/O Weatherstone and P/O Toovey sustained casualties. Also attempting to land in Yorkshire, in their case at Pocklington, were F/Sgt Thompson and his crew in ED393, and, sadly, while awaiting their turn in the circuit, they crashed onto a farmhouse at Hayton, four miles north-west of Market Weighton, killing the pilot and four others, along with two ladies in the building. The wireless operator and rear gunner survived with injuries. DV178 failed to return, having been involved in a mid-air collision with another Lancaster and losing at least one engine. A message was received at 22.30 confirming that the target had been attacked, and that the Lancaster was losing height, after which, nothing more was heard. It was eventually established through the Red Cross that it had been ditched near Wilhelmshaven, and that P/O Adams RAAF and five of his eight-man crew had been rescued by the enemy, while two had drowned. These last three operations against Berlin undoubtedly represented the best phase of the entire campaign, and, according to local reports, the total death toll on the ground resulting from them amounted to 4,330 people, while the destruction of 8,700 apartment buildings containing more than 104,500 flats, and damage to several times that number, robbed 450,000 residents of their homes for varying lengths of time. However, Berlin was not Hamburg, where narrow streets had aided the spread of fire. Berlin was a modern city of concrete and steel with wide thoroughfares and wide-open spaces to create natural firebreaks, and each building destroyed added to these, so that the campaign would become a bitter struggle of ever decreasing returns. During the course of the month the squadron took part in five operations, and dispatched eighty-six sorties for the loss of five Lancasters and three crews.

December 1943

Berlin would continue to be the dominant theme during December, and, as November had ended, so December would begin. In the meantime, F/L McAlpine and crew arrived from 1661 Conversion Unit on the 1st, as one of a number of new crews arriving during the month. A heavy force of 443 aircraft stood ready to take off in the late afternoon of the 2nd, all but fifteen of them Lancasters, after the main Halifax element had been withdrawn because of fog over their Yorkshire stations. 5 Group contributed 145 Lancasters, of which ten would represent 50 Squadron, and they departed Skellingthorpe between 16.27 and 17.07 with F/Ls Bolton, Burtt and Shortt the senior pilots on duty. After climbing out, they headed for the Lincolnshire coast to rendezvous over the North Sea with the rest of the force for a straight-in-straight-out route across Holland and northern Germany with no feints or diversions. First, however, the crews had to negotiate a towering front of ice-bearing cloud over the North Sea, which would contribute to a 10% rate of early returns. 50 Squadron's Sgt Taylor and crew lost their starboard-outer engine shortly after take-off, before reaching the front, and were back on the ground seventy-eight minutes after leaving it. The others pushed through the challenging conditions, and made it to the target area, although mostly south of track after variable winds had thrown them off course and dispersed the bomber stream. They also had to contend with large numbers of enemy night-fighters that would harass the bombers all the way to the target, which the controller had been able correctly to predict. The Pathfinders were using H2S to establish their position at Stendal, but had strayed some fifteen miles south of track and mistakenly used the town of Genthin as their reference for the run-in. The 50 Squadron crews found good visibility, and were drawn by release-point flares to the aiming-point, where they encountered a thin layer of two to three-tenths cloud at around 5,000 feet, but up to nine-tenths between 10,000 and 12,000 feet, which the searchlights were able to pierce. They bombed on skymarkers and red and green TIs, and, where possible, ground detail, like burning streets, doing so from 19,000 to 21,000 feet between 20.08 and 20.34. They reported observing scattered fires and a number of large explosions, and some claimed the glow to be visible from 120 miles into the homeward leg. Bombing photographs suggested that the raid was only partially successful, causing useful damage in industrial districts in the west and east, but scattering the main weight of bombs over the southern districts and outlying communities to the south. It was a bad night for the bomber force, which lost forty aircraft, mostly in the target area and on the way home, and a night-fighter caused the demise of 50 Squadron's DV325 in the target area. F/L Bolton, four of his crew and a Daily Express war correspondent, Mr L L Bennett, managed to vacate the stricken Lancaster before it crashed, killing the remaining two crew members, and all were taken into captivity, from where, it is believed, Mr Bennett escaped.

Having been spared by the weather from experiencing an effective visitation from the Command in October, and exploiting the enemy expectation that Berlin would be the target again, Leipzig found itself at the end of the red tape on briefing-room wall-maps from County Durham to Cambridgeshire on the 3rd. A force of 527 aircraft was made ready, which included 103 Lancasters of 5 Group, nine of them belonging to 50 Squadron, and they departed Skellingthorpe between 00.21 and 00.39 with F/Ls Burtt and Shortt the senior pilots on duty. P/O Lloyd and crew returned to the circuit after three hours with an unserviceable rear turret, and, as the bomber stream headed for Berlin as a feint, passing north of Hannover and Braunschweig, Sgt Taylor and crew lost their port-outer engine. They turned towards Hannover, and delivered their cookie and incendiaries onto it through ten-tenths cloud from 18,000 feet at 03.08, before heading home. The others still had an hour's journey ahead of them to reach Leipzig, and, as they turned towards the south-east, the Mosquito element continued on to carry out a diversion at the Capital. Night-fighters had already infiltrated the stream at the Dutch coast, but the feint had the desired effect, and few night-fighters were encountered in the target area, where two layers of ten-tenths cloud prevailed with tops at around 7,000 and 15,000 feet. The Pathfinders marked by H2S with green skymarkers, and the 50 Squadron crews bombed on these from 16,000 to 21,000 feet in a six-minute slot to 04.11, observing explosions and a strong glow beneath the clouds. The emergence through the cloud tops of black smoke suggested that an accurate and concentrated attack had taken place, and the smoke remained visible for a hundred miles into the return journey south-east towards the French frontier. Had many aircraft not then strayed into the Frankfurt defence zone, the losses may have been fewer, but twenty-four aircraft failed to return, fifteen of them Halifaxes. Local reports confirmed this as a highly successful operation, which had hit residential and industrial areas, and was the most destructive raid visited upon this eastern city during the war. Sadly, for the Command, it would take its revenge in time.

On the 6th, W/C McFarlane was posted out to 51 Base at Swinderby, to be succeeded as commanding officer from within, through the promotion of S/L Pullen to wing commander rank, and S/L Parks left on the same day for Scampton. Thereafter, minor operations carried the Command through to mid-month, when, on the 16th, the Lancaster stations were roused to prepare 483 of the type for that night's operation to Berlin for the sixth time since the resumption of the campaign. 5 Group put up 165 aircraft, thirteen of them representing 50 Squadron, which took off between 16.20 and 16.49 with F/Ls Burtt, Edward and McAlpine the senior pilots on duty. They were to cross the Dutch coast in the region of Castricum-aan-Zee, and then head due east all the way to the target with no deviations. A three-quarter moon would rise during the long return leg over the Baltic and Denmark, but it was hoped that the very early take-off and the expectation of fog, to keep the enemy night-fighters on the ground, would reduce the risk of interception. Night-fighters were sent to meet the bomber stream at the Dutch coast, but the 50 Squadron crews remained unmolested, and pressed on to find Berlin obscured by ten-tenths cloud with tops at around 5,000 feet. However, it could be identified by red and green sky-markers, which were bombed from 17,500 to 22,000 feet between 19.59 and 20.14. The return over Denmark passed largely without major incident, but the greatest difficulties awaited the 1, 6 and 8 Group crews as they arrived home to find their airfields covered by a blanket of dense fog. With little reserves of fuel, the tired crews began a frantic search to find somewhere to land, stumbling blindly through the murk to catch a glimpse of the ground. For many, this proved fatal, while others gave up any hope of landing, and abandoned their aircraft. Twenty-nine Lancasters and a mine-laying Stirling were thus lost, and more than 150 airmen killed in these most tragic of circumstances. To this number was added the twenty-five Lancasters failing to return from the raid, many of which were accounted for by night-fighters over Holland and Germany while outbound. At debriefing some crews reported the glow of fires, while others saw nothing through the cloud, and it was a local report that confirmed a moderately effective raid, which had fallen principally onto central and eastern districts, where housing suffered most.

A three-day stand-down allowed the crews to recover from the Berlin operation, and it was the 20th when all stations were notified of an operation that night to Frankfurt, for which a force of 390 Lancasters and 257 Halifaxes was assembled. 5 Group made ready 168 Lancasters, and, at Skellingthorpe, fourteen 50 Squadron Lancasters were loaded with the requisite amount of fuel and a cookie and sixteen SBCs of incendiaries each, and dispatched between 16.55 and 17.26 with W/C Pullen the senior pilot on duty. While the main operation was in progress, forty-four Lancasters and ten Mosquitos of 1 and 8 Groups were to carry out a diversion at Mannheim, some forty miles to the south. After climbing out, the crews set course for Southwold and the North Sea-crossing to the Scheldt estuary, before passing north of Antwerp and flying the length of Belgium to the German frontier north of Luxembourg. The German night-fighter controller had picked up transmissions from the bomber stream as soon as it left the English coast, and was able to track it all the way to the target and vector his fighters into position. Many combats took place during the outward flight, and the diversion failed to draw fighters away from the main action. DV234 was brought down by a combination of flak and a night-fighter while outbound at 20,000 feet, and crashed five miles west-north-west of Leinefelde, some fifteen miles south-east of the university city of Göttingen, killing W/C Pullen and three others, and leaving the four survivors to be rounded up by the enemy. The problems continued at the primary target, where the forecast clear skies failed to materialize, and the crews were greeted by four to nine-tenths cloud at between 5,000 and 10,000 feet. This allowed some of them to pick out ground features, while others fixed their positions by H2S, if so equipped, and the main force Lancaster crews simply waited for TIs on e.t.a. The Pathfinders had prepared a ground-marking plan in expectation of good vertical visibility, and dropped red, green and yellow TIs, while the Germans lit a decoy fire-site five miles to the south-east of the city. Some crews described the marking as late and erratic, and those from 50 Squadron bombed on red and green TIs from 19,000 to 22,000 feet between 19.41 and 19.48. Most thought the attack to be scattered in the early stages, becoming more concentrated as it progressed, and many commented on the new cookies detonating with a brighter flash than the old ones. A dozen 50 Squadron Lancasters returned safely to Skellingthorpe, having contributed to a moderately successful raid, and at least one crew reported the glow of fires remaining visible for 150 miles into the return journey. Any success was achieved largely as the result of the creep-back from the decoy site falling across the suburbs of Offenbach and Sachsenhausen, situated on the southern bank of the River Main. 466 houses were destroyed and more than nineteen hundred seriously damaged, despite which, the operation fell well short of its aims, and the loss of forty-one aircraft was a high price to pay. The Halifaxes suffered heavily, losing twenty-seven of their number, a loss-rate of 10.5%, compared with the Lancaster's 3.6%.

Unusually for 50 Squadron, a second of its aircraft was among the missing, DV217 reportedly having been hit by flak at 20,000 feet, before blowing up in the air, and throwing clear two members of the crew. They were the only survivors from the experienced crew of P/O Heckendorf RAAF and four others were killed in the crash at Kelsterbach, five miles south-west of Frankfurt. The bomb-aimer was F/O Les Rutherford, who was on his twenty-fourth operation and was rendered unconscious as he was catapulted into space, but came-to in time to deploy his parachute. Both survivors were captured, and F/O Rutherford soon found himself at Stalag Luft III, where unknown to the camp staff, escape tunnels were being dug, one of which would be used for the famed "Great Escape" on the 24th of March 1944. Les was not involved in this endeavour, and he remained at Stalag Luft III until being force-marched to Lückenwalde, thirty miles south of Berlin, in early February 1945, in what became known as "The Long March", as the Russians advanced westwards. He would be liberated by the Russians on the 22nd of April. The book, My War, Wartime Memoirs of Flight Lieutenant Les Rutherford, is available from the IBCC.

Just two more operations remained before the year ended, and both were to be directed against Germany's capital city. The first was posted on the 23rd, and would involve an all-Lancaster heavy force with seven Halifaxes among the Pathfinder element, and eight Mosquitos to provide a diversion. The 130 Lancasters of 5 Group included eleven from 50 Squadron, which were loaded with a cookie and eleven SBCs each, and launched into the cold night air between 23.35 and 00.32 with F/Ls Edward and Shortt the senior pilots on duty. The route to the target was somewhat circuitous, and took the bomber stream in a south-easterly direction to the Scheldt estuary, before hugging the Belgian/Dutch frontier to cross into Germany south of Aachen, as if threatening Frankfurt. When a point was reached south of Leipzig, the route turned sharply towards the north and Berlin, while the Mosquito feint threatened Leipzig as the target. F/L Edward's rear gunner suffered frostbite because of the failure of his electrically-heated suit, and this forced them to return early, while F/O Keith and crew turned back with an engine issue. The remaining 50 Squadron crews pressed on, and ED445 was brought down to crash near Lauterbach, fifty miles north-east of Frankfurt, with no survivors from the crew of F/O Herbert. The others reached the target to find it enveloped in up to eight-tenths cloud between 5,000 and 10,000 feet. This might not have been critical had the Pathfinders not suffered an unusually high failure rate of their H2S equipment, which resulted in scattered and sparse sky-marking. P/O Toovey and crew lost their port-outer engine with Berlin a short distance ahead, and jettisoned their bombs "live" onto the outskirts at 03.45 as they sank down to 13,000 feet. The other 50 Squadron crews found red and green marker flares at which to aim their bombs from 19,000 to 23,000 feet between 04.05 and 04.13, and observed well-concentrated fires and at least four large explosions, one described as being orange and red and lasting for thirty seconds. A relatively modest sixteen Lancasters failed to return, in exchange for which a local report named the south-eastern suburbs of Köpenick and Treptow as the ones to sustain the most damage, with 287 houses and other buildings suffering complete destruction.

The fifth wartime Christmas period passed in peace and traditional style, and S/L Chadwick and crew arrived from 1660 Conversion Unit on the 28th, before the "Big City" was posted as the target again on the 29th, for what, for the Lancaster operators, would be the first of three raids on it in five nights spanning the turn of the year. A force of 712 aircraft included 163 Lancasters of 5 Group, of which fifteen represented 50 Squadron, and they departed Skellingthorpe between 16.42 and 17.26 with F/Ls Burtt, Edward, McAlpine and Russell the senior pilots on duty. It was from this juncture that the intolerable strain on the crews of successive long-range flights in difficult weather conditions would begin to become manifest in some squadrons through the rate of early returns, which on this night reached forty-five or 6.3%. The bomber stream was routed out over the Dutch Frisian islands pointing directly for Leipzig, and, having reached a point just to the north of that city, was to turn to the north towards Berlin, while Mosquitos carried out spoof raids on Leipzig and Magdeburg. 50 Squadron was exempt from early returns, and its crews reached the target area to find ten-tenths cloud with tops at anywhere between 7,000 and 18,000 feet. Red and green Pathfinder release-point flares could be seen hanging over the city, upon which they aimed their bombs from 18,500 to 22,000 feet between 20.04 and 20.23. At debriefing crews reported a considerable red glow beneath the clouds, which remained visible for a hundred miles, and gave the impression of a concentrated and successful assault. This was not entirely borne out by local reports, which revealed that the main weight of the raid had fallen onto southern and south-eastern districts, and also into outlying communities to the east. 388 buildings were destroyed, although none of significance, and ten thousand people were bombed out of their homes. Eleven Lancasters and nine Halifaxes failed to return, a loss-rate of 2.4% for the former and 3.5% for the latter. 50 Squadron's DV375 was plotted by a Gee-fix to be at the mid-point of the North Sea at 23.00, and news came through shortly afterwards that the rear gunner had been picked up by a destroyer with slight injuries to both arms caused by shrapnel. One other member of the crew eventually washed ashore on the German coast, but no trace of F/L McAlpine and the four others was ever found.

During the course of the month the squadron participated in six operations and dispatched seventy-two sorties for the loss of five Lancasters and crews. It had been a testing end to a year which had brought major successes and advances in tactics, but it had also been a year of high losses, particularly among the Stirling and Halifax squadrons, Whilst Window had been an instant success, it had also caused the Luftwaffe to rethink and reorganise, and the night-fighter force which emerged from the ruins of the old system, was a leaner, more efficient and altogether more lethal beast than that of before. As far as the crews of Bomber Command were concerned, the New Year offered the same fare as the old one, and few would view that with relish.

50 Squadron Lancaster ED810 VN-Z. Night shot with crew.

Armourers of 50 and 61 Squadrons at Skellingthorpe in 1943.

Lancaster ED592 before delivery to 50 Squadron as VN-B

Memorial Stone at Hamont, Belgium for Lancaster ED488 VN-M, lost on the 2nd of February 1943.

F/O David Allan Power RCAF, who was killed in action on the 2nd of February 1943 in 50 Squadron Lancaster ED488.

Debris from Lancaster ED394 VN-R near Brampton, Cumbria, 9th of January 1943.

Lancaster ED394 VN-R crashed on The Kirby Moor House in Brampton on 9th of January 1943.

The wreckage of ED394 VN-R on The Kirby Moor House in Brampton, Cumbria on 9th of January 1943

The scar on the ground left by ED394 at Brampton on the 9th of January 1943

50 Squadron Lancaster R5687 VN-D (nearest).
F/Sgt N.P.I. Castells & crew all KIA on the 28th of July 1943.

50 Squadron Lancaster DV375 VN-E ditched in the North Sea on the 30th of December 1943.

W/O Leonard C Green

Photo taken by Pathé following a raid to Berlin. Len is 4th from right. Early October 1943 he was posted to 50 Squadron having crewed up with the now P/O Lundy. The full crew was: P/O D Lundy, Sgt M Stevens, Sgt A E Jordan, Sgt W M Rundle, P/O A H Bignell, F/Sgt F Wilding, Sgt L C Green.

After completing his 30 operations, F/L Lundy went to No.5 Lancaster Finishing School on the 12th of May 1944, as an instructor. His posting there finished on 30th of March 1945, and his logbook shows his assessment as a pilot instructor as "Above the average".

He arrived back at 50 Squadron at the beginning of April 1945, as an instructor, moving to Sturgate with them in July 1945. His C.O at that time was W/C "Jimmy" Flint DFM, GM. In June 1946 he took part in a Victory Parade fly-past over Buckingham Palace. Because of bad weather the full fly past was cancelled and Dennis volunteered to fly Richard Dimbleby and Raymond Glendenning over the palace while they did the commentary.

F/L Dennis Lundy DFC
50 Squadron September 1943 to April 1944
and April 1945 to August 1945

From:-   No.50 Squadron, Skellingthorpe.

To:-   Headquarters, No.5 Group.

Date:-   8th October, 1943.

Ref:-   50S/430/Arm.

NIGHT

Lancaster "T" V/IG E/A

<u>COMBAT REPORT.</u>

On the night of the 7th October, 1943, Lancaster "T" of No.50 Squadron was detailed to attack Stuttgart. At 22.10 hours on the outward journey, position 50.40 N. 06.25 E., height 20,000', speed, 160 Ind., course 140 mag., the Rear Gunner saw a single engine aircraft on the port quarter at 400 yards closing in. Lancaster dived port and Rear Gunner fired three long bursts and M.U. Gunner fired two long bursts. Enemy aircraft broke away to starboard without opening fire.

Four minutes later, M.U. Gunner saw a single engine aircraft on port quarter down at 300 yards closing in. Lancaster corkscrewed port and Rear Gunner fired three long bursts and M.U. Gunner two long bursts. Enemy aircraft broke away to starboard without opening fire. Monica did not indicate.   Enemy aircraft carried no lights and there was no unusual phenomena. No claim.

Captain. -	P/O.	Lundy.
Flt/Eng. -	Sgt.	Stevens.
Navigator.-	Sgt.	Jordan.
A/Bomber. -	P/O.	Bignell.
WOP/AG. -	Sgt.	Green.
MU. A/G. -	Sgt.	Rundle. No.5 A.F.U. No.29 OTU.
Rear A/G. -	P/O.	Denny. No.1 B & GS.No.29 OTU.

Flying Officer, for
<u>No.50 Squadron Gunnery Leader.</u>

This combat report for the night of the 7th of October 1943 details an attack by an enemy fighter, which was driven off and no claim made. This operation was, in fact, Dennis's first.

From:- No.50 Squadron, R.A.F. Station, Skellingthorpe.

To:- Headquarters, No.5 Group,

Date:- 3rd December, 1943.

Ref:- 50S/430.Air.

<u>COMBAT REPORT</u>

On the night of 2nd December, 1943, Lancaster "P"
of No.50 Squadron, was detailed to attack BERLIN. At 20.25
hours in the target area, height 19,600 feet, speed 165
ind, on a course of 097 mag. a twin engined aircraft was
observed on port quarter up at 700 yards. The R/G ordered
a corkscrew to port and opened fire immediately. The e/a
returned the fire and pressed home his attack to 300 yards
before breaking across the stern to the starboard quarter.
Both M/U and R/G continued to fire throughout attack and
got in some good shots in the break away. The e/a, now
identified as a JU.88 attacked from the starboard quarter
both gunners returned fire and e/a closed to 250 yards
and pulled up into an apparent stall dead astern giving
the gunners a belly shot. Both gunners took full
advantage of this point blank shot and fired long bursts
into the JU.88 and saw tracer hit.   E/a then dropped out of
sight apparently out of control. This aircraft is claimed
as probably destroyed. Monica did not indicate as it was
m/s.

<pre>
Captain.............P/O Lundy.   NIGHT
F/Eng..............Sgt. Stevens.   Lanc   V   JU.88
Nav................F/S Jordan.
A/Bomber...........P/O Bignall.
W/AG...............Sgt. Green.
MU/G...............Sgt. Rundle.   20 A.T.U.   No.29 O.T.U.
R/G................F/S Wilding.   5 BADS (sin)No.24 O.T.U.
</pre>

Flight Lieutenant,
No.50 Squadron, Gunnery Leader

Wing Commander, Commanding,
50 Squadron, Skellingthorpe.

99

*This combat report refers to his operation on the 2nd of December 1943 flying in VN-P. It refers to
actions taken and the result when attacked by a JU88, which was claimed as destroyed.*

(Above and below) Lancaster ED588 VN-G in March 1943 after 128 sorties.. Lost August 1944.

ED 588 VN-G George
Her first operation with 50 Squadron was a trip to Berlin on the 27/28th of March 1943.

Sgt (posthumous W/O) Francis (Frank) Gerard McGrath RCAF.
December 16, 1921 - April 11, 1943.

Frank McGrath's Graduation of basic training in Canada. (He is 3rd from right, top row.)

Picture of 50 Squadron Lancaster VN-N, kept by Frank McGrath

Service details of Sgt McGrath (Signed by F/L H Maudslay)

To Mrs. William McGrath

This commemorates the gratitude of the Government and people of Canada for the life of a brave man freely given in the service of his Country.

Sergeant Pilot
Francis Gerard McGrath, R.C.A.F.

His name will ever be held in proud remembrance.

April 11, 1943.

Charles G. Power
Minister of National Defence for Air

Recognition and sympathy from Canada and King George VI

The Queen and I offer you our heartfelt sympathy in your great sorrow.

We pray that your country's gratitude for a life so nobly given in its service may bring you some measure of consolation.

George R.I.

S/L Street and crew, with which P/O Les Rutherford served for a time as bomb-aimer

P/O Rutherford on left

P/O Les Rutherford

50 Squadron Lancaster ED585 VN-G

F/L Les Knight and his crew taken while with 617 Squadron.

F/Sgt John Fraser RCAF
(Hopgood's Dams Crew)

F/O Ken Earnshaw RC
(Hopgood's Dams Crew)

P/O H T Taerum RCAF
(Gibson's navigator on Dams Raid)

P/O F M Spafford DFM
(Gibson's bomb-aimer on Dams Raid)

F/L "Micky" Martin and his crew

L-R: Jack Leggo, Mick Martin, Tammy Simpson, Bob Hay and Toby Foxlee in London after being decorated at Buckingham Palace, June 1943. (Australian War Memorial)

Sgt Brian Jagger
(F/L Shannon's front gunner on Dams Raid)

Sgt Jack Marriott
(S/L Maudslay's flight engineer on Dams Raid)

F/O Robert Urquhart DFC RCAF
(S/L Maudslay's navigator on Dams Raid)

W/O Alden Cottam
(S/L Maudslay's wireless operator on Dams Raid)

P/O Mike Fuller
(S/L Maudslay's bomb aimer on Dams Raid)

Sgt Norman Burrows
(S/L Maudslay's rear gunner on Dams Raid)

<h1 style="text-align:center">January 1944</h1>

The change of year was not destined to bring a change in the emphasis of operations, and this was, no doubt, a disappointment, not only to the hard-pressed crews of Bomber Command, but also to the beleaguered residents of Germany's Capital City. Proud of their status as Berliners first and Germans second, they were a hardy breed, and just like their counterparts in London during the Blitz of 1940, they would bear their trials with fortitude and humour, and would not buckle under the constant onslaught from above. "You may break our walls", proclaimed banners in the streets, "but not out hearts", and the most popular song of the day, "Nach jedem Dezember kommt immer ein Mai", "After every December comes always a May", was played endlessly over the airwaves, its sentiments hinting at a change in fortunes with the onset of spring. Harris allowed the Berliners little time to enjoy New Year, and, as New Year's Day dawned, plans were already in hand to continue the onslaught. Before it ended, the first of 421 Lancasters, 161 representing 5 Group, would be taking off and heading eastwards to arrive over the city as the clock showed 03.00 hours on the 2nd.

Earlier in the day, W/C Heward, an exacting man, had been appointed as the new commanding officer on posting from his flight commander role with 57 Squadron at East Kirkby. He had previously served as a flying instructor at home and overseas, but 57 Squadron had given him his first taste of action. Take-off had actually been delayed because of doubts over the weather, and this meant that insufficient hours of daylight remained to allow the planned outward route over Denmark and the Baltic. Instead, the bomber stream would adopt the previously used almost direct route across Holland and northern Germany, but return, as originally planned, more circuitously, passing east of Leipzig, before racing across Germany between the Ruhr and Frankfurt and traversing Belgium to reach the Channel near the French port of Boulogne. 50 Squadron's fourteen participants took off between 23.24 and 00.24 with F/Ls Burtt and Shortt the senior pilots on duty, each carrying a cookie and ten SBCs of incendiaries. The force was gradually depleted by twenty-nine early returns, two of them, P/Os Litherland and Jennings and their crews, arriving back at Skellingthorpe at 03.08 and 03.19 respectively, the former after the bomb-aimer's parachute became accidentally deployed and the latter because of a starboard-inner engine fire. The bomber stream covered the four hundred mile leg from the Dutch coast to Berlin in ninety minutes without once catching a glimpse of the ground through the dense cloud, and it was no different at the target, which was completely obscured by a layer of ten-tenths cloud with tops in places as high as 19,000 feet. The Pathfinders had to employ skymarking (Wanganui), which was somewhat scattered, and the 50 Squadron crews aimed for these parachute flares from 15,000 (F/L Shortt) and 22,000 feet between 03.06 and 03.18, observing the glow of fires and smoke rising through the cloud tops, but no detail. The operation was a failure, which scattered bombs across the southern fringes of the city, causing only minor damage, while the main weight of the attack fell beyond the city boundaries into wooded and open country. The disappointment was compounded by the loss of twenty-eight Lancasters, and, although none represented 50 Squadron, one did contain the former flight commander, W/C Abercromby DFC & Bar. As already mentioned, he was now commanding 83 Squadron and was killed while mentoring a rookie crew.

During the course of the 2nd, a heavy force of 362 Lancasters and nine of the new Mk III Hercules-powered Halifaxes was made ready for a return to Berlin that night. There was snow on the ground, and many of the crews called to briefing were still tired from being late to bed following the almost-eight-hour round trip the night before. Some of these were in a mutinous frame of mind at being on the Order of Battle again so soon. 5 Group cancelled twenty-five of its intended contribution, leaving 119 to take part, thirteen of which belonged to 50 Squadron. The outward route crossed the Dutch coast near Castricum and took the bomber stream to a point south-east of Bremen, followed by a dogleg to the north-west and, finally, a ninety degree change of course to the south-east in the Parchim area to leave a ninety-mile run to the target. The 50 Squadron element departed Skellingthorpe between 23.13 and 23.47 with F/Ls Burtt, Ruskell and Shortt the senior pilots on duty, and only one crew was among a massive sixty early returns, 15.7% of those dispatched. Many of them were defeated by severe icing conditions, while others abandoned their sorties because of minor problems that might have seen them carry on had they been fully rested. F/L Ruskell and crew were entirely justified in turning back because of a defective rear turret and failing oxygen supply system. The route changes worked well to throw off the night-fighters, but they would congregate in the target area after the controller correctly identified the Capital as the target forty minutes before zero-hour. Ten-tenths cloud with tops at 16,000 feet forced the bombing to take place on the red skymarkers with green stars or on the glow of fires, the 50 Squadron crews carrying out their attacks from 20,000 to 22,000 feet between 02.46 and 02.56. They reported smoke rising to 20,000 feet as they turned away, but it was not possible to make an accurate assessment of the outcome, and the impression was of an effective attack, when, in fact, it had been another failure. Bombs had been scattered across the city and destroyed just eighty-two houses for the loss of twenty-seven Lancasters, most of which had fallen victim to night-fighters in the target area.

After three trips there in five nights, Berlin would now be left to the Mosquitos of 8 Group's Light Night Striking Force until the final third of the month, allowing Harris to turn his attention on the 5th upon the Baltic port-city of Stettin, which had not been attacked in numbers since September 1941. It was to be another predominantly Lancaster affair, involving 348 of the type accompanied by ten Halifaxes, 5 Group putting up 120 aircraft and 50 Squadron thirteen. They took off from Skellingthorpe between 23.40 and 00.10 with S/L Chadwick the senior pilot on duty for the first time. In contrast to the seventeen early returns by 5 Group crews during the last Berlin operation, only one came home early on this night, and those continuing on found themselves in thick cloud at cruising altitude, some struggling to find a clear lane even when as high as 23,000 feet. On the plus side, they all benefitted from a Mosquito diversion at Berlin, which kept the night-fighters off the scent. Stettin was found to be partially visible through five-tenths thin cloud with tops at around 10,000 feet, and crews were able to identify some ground features before focussing on H2S-laid flares and green TIs, which the 50 Squadron crews bombed from 20,000 to 22,500 feet between 03.47 and 03.59. All returned home to provide the intelligence section with accounts of a highly accurate and concentrated attack, which seemed to leave the entire city on fire. Fourteen Lancasters and two Halifaxes failed to return, in exchange for which, post-raid reconnaissance and local reports confirmed heavy damage in central and western districts, where 504 houses and twenty industrial buildings had been destroyed, a further 1,148 houses and twenty-nine industrial buildings seriously damaged, and eight ships had been sunk in the harbour.

Following this operation, the crews of the heavy squadrons were rested until mid-month, and when briefings took place on the 14th, there was doubtless some relief to see the red tape on the wall maps terminate some way short of Berlin. It led, in fact, to Braunschweig (Brunswick), an historic and culturally significant city situated some thirty-five miles to the east of Hannover. It had not been attacked by the Command in numbers before, and, on this night, would face a force, which, at take-off, numbered 496 Lancasters and two Halifaxes. 5 Group supported the operation with 153 Lancasters, of which sixteen represented 50 Squadron, and they took off between 16.37 and 17.16 with F/Ls Edward and Ruskell the senior pilots on duty. After climbing out they headed towards Germany's north-western coast, where they were met by part of the enemy night-fighter response, which would harass the bomber stream all the way to the target and back. Complete cloud cover, in places, up to around 15,000 feet, dictated the use of red skymarkers with green stars, which the 50 Squadron crews bombed from 19,500 and 22,800 feet between 19.10 and 19.29. The enemy fighters scored consistently, and accounted for the majority of the thirty-eight missing Lancasters, many of which came down around Hannover. The attack almost entirely missed the city, falling mostly onto outlying communities to the south, and was reported locally as a light raid. This would be a continuing theme in future attacks up to the autumn, as Braunschweig enjoyed something of a charmed life, leading to a belief among the populace that the surrounding villages were being targeted intentionally, in an attempt to drive the residents into the city, before a major operation destroyed it with them in it!

The Pathfinders, in particular, had been taking a beating since the turn of the year, with 156 Squadron alone losing fourteen Lancasters and crews in just three operations, four and five on Berlin, and five again on Braunschweig. This was creating something of a crisis in Pathfinder manpower, particularly with regard to experienced crews, and a number of sideways postings took place between the squadrons to ensure a leavening of experience in each one. One of the solutions was to take the cream from among the crews emerging from the training units, rather than wait for them to gain experience at a main force squadron.

Another lull in operations kept the crews on the ground until the 20th, when orders were received to assemble a maximum effort force for the next round of the Berlin offensive. The Halifax squadrons, which had appeared to be in hibernation since late December, were roused from their slumber, and 264 of them joined 495 Lancasters to constitute the Pathfinder and main force elements, while two small Mosquito sections carried out spoof raids on Kiel and Hannover. 5 Group weighed in with 155 Lancasters, of which sixteen were made ready by 50 Squadron, and they took off between 16.28 and 16.46 with S/L McLeod the senior pilot on duty. It was a rare pleasure for them to be taking off in daylight, and they circled as they climbed out above Skellingthorpe before setting course, while observing the dozens of Lancasters rising up into the dusk to join them from the neighbouring stations. They turned their snouts towards the west coast of the Schleswig-Holstein peninsular at a point opposite Kiel, rendezvousing with the other groups over the North Sea and all the time shedding individual aircraft as a hefty seventy-five crews abandoned their sorties and turned back. P/O Cole's navigator became ill as they approached the enemy coast, and they diverted to Heligoland, identified by the flak penetrating the cloud tops two thousand feet below them, and bombed it from 20,000 feet at 18.21. The others made landfall, before turning to the south-east on a more-or-less direct course for Berlin, and soon found themselves being hounded by night-fighters. The enemy controller had fed a proportion of his resources into the bomber stream east of Hamburg, and they would remain in contact until a point between Leipzig and Hannover on the way home, although, curiously, the 5 Group brigade saw nothing of this and would lose just a single 57 Squadron Lancaster. The two Mosquito diversions had been completely ignored by the Luftwaffe controller, who knew well in advance that Berlin was to be the target. The Pathfinders arrived over the Müritzsee to the north of Berlin with a sixty-mile run-in to the aiming-point, and they found this to be concealed beneath the same ten-tenths cloud that had accompanied them for the entire outward leg. The tops of the cloud lay beneath the bombers at up to 15,000 feet as the main force crews carried out their attacks on red skymarkers with green stars, those from 50 Squadron doing so from 18,000 to 22,500 feet between 19.34 and 19.54. On return, the crews commented on the lack of flak activity over Berlin, and reported the glow of large fires under the cloud and smoke rising through the tops. Thirty-five aircraft failed to return, twenty-two of them Halifaxes, which represented an 8.3% casualty rate compared with 2.6% for the Lancasters. It took a little time for an assessment of the operation to be made because of continuing cloud over north-eastern Germany, by which time four further raids had been carried out. It seems from local reports that the eastern districts had received the heaviest weight of bombs in an eight-mile stretch from Weissesee in the north to Neukölln in the south, although no details of destruction emerged.

On the following day, the city of Magdeburg was posted to host its first major attack of the war. Situated some fifty miles from Braunschweig and slightly to the south of east, it was on an increasingly familiar route as far as the enemy night-fighter controllers were concerned, and within easy striking distance of the night-fighter assembly beacons. In an attempt to deceive the enemy, a small-scale diversion was planned at Berlin involving twenty-two Lancaster of 5 Group and twelve Mosquitos of 8 Group. 5 Group contributed 122 Lancasters to the main event, fourteen of them made ready by 50 Squadron, which were loaded with a cookie and thirteen SBCs of incendiaries each, while F/O Beetham and P/O Dobbyn and their crews would take part in the diversion and carry a cookie and a few 1,000 and 500 pounders. They took off together between 19.51 and 20.37 with S/L Chadwick the senior pilot on duty, and flew out over the North Sea to a point some one hundred miles off the west coast of the Schleswig-Holstein peninsular, before turning to the south-east to pass between Hamburg and Hannover. Enemy radar was able to detect H2S transmissions during night-flying tests and equipment checks, and the night-fighter controller was, thereby, always aware of an imminent heavy raid. On this night, the night-fighters were able to infiltrate the bomber stream even before the German coast was crossed, and the recently-introduced "Tame Boar" night-fighter system provided a running commentary on the bomber stream's progress, enabling the fighters to latch onto the bombers and remain in contact. The final turning-point was twenty-five miles north-east of the target, and this was identified both by Pathfinder markers and the bombing of twenty-seven main force aircraft. These had been driven by stronger-than-forecast winds to arrive ahead of schedule, and contained crews anxious to get the job done and get out of the target area as soon as possible. They bombed using their own H2S without waiting for the TIs to go down, and, together with dummy fires, were blamed by the Pathfinders as the reason for their failure to produce concentrated marking.

The conditions over Magdeburg varied according to the time of arrival, the early birds encountering seven to nine-tenths thin cloud at around 6,000 feet, while those turning up towards the end of the raid found the northern half of the city completely clear with cloud over the southern half only. The 50 Squadron crews experienced a mixture of eight-tenths cloud and relatively clear skies, and, in the face of fairly modest opposition, bombed on green TIs from 16,000 to 22,000 feet between 22.58 and 23.13, all gaining the impression that the attack was concentrated around the markers. Returning crews from other groups reported observing explosions and fires or their glow, and smoke beginning to rise as they turned away. A number reported a flash some twelve minutes after bombing, that lit up the clouds for seven seconds, and two large explosions at 23.15. Fires that initially seemed to be scattered, appeared to become more concentrated as the crews headed for home, and the impression was of a successful operation. While all of this was in progress, the diversionary force arrived at Berlin, some seventy miles away to the north-east, where the 50 Squadron duo found a layer of eight to ten-tenths cloud at 10,000 feet, through which they bombed from 22,000 and 22,500 feet at 22.55. The 5 Group ORB expressed the opinion that the diversion had succeeded in the early stages in reducing the impact of the Nachtjagd, although this was not borne out by the figures. In the absence of post-raid reconnaissance and a local report, the outcome at Magdeburg was not confirmed, and it is generally believed now that most of the bombing fell outside of the city boundaries. A record fifty-seven aircraft failed to return, thirty-five of them Halifaxes, and this provided another alarming statistic of a 15.6% loss-rate compared with 5.2% for the Lancasters.

The end of the month was to bring the final concerted effort to destroy Berlin, and would involve three trips to this destination in the space of an unprecedented four nights. This hectic round of operations began on the 27th, after five nights of rest since the bruising experience of Magdeburg, and involve an all-Lancaster heavy force of 515 aircraft. 5 Group put up a record 172, eighteen of them belonging to 50 Squadron, which departed Skellingthorpe between 17.27 and 17.44 with W/C Heward the senior pilot on duty for the first time. After climbing out and rendezvousing with the rest of the group, they set course on a complex route that would take the bomber stream towards the north German coast, before swinging to the south-east to enter enemy territory over the Frisians and northern Holland. Having then feinted towards central Germany, suggesting Leipzig as the target, the force was to turn north-east to a point west of Berlin, from where the final run-in would commence. The long return route passed to the west of Leipzig before turning due east to miss Frankfurt on its northern side and traverse Belgium to gain the Channel south of Boulogne. P/O Toovey and crew turned back after both starboard engines failed, leaving the others to press on towards the target, while a mining diversion off Heligoland, combined with dummy fighter flares and route-markers, partially succeeded in reducing the numbers of enemy night-fighters making contact. It was, therefore, a relatively intact bomber force that approached the target over ten-tenths cloud with tops at 15,000 feet, which required the Pathfinders to use sky-marking, and it was the red Wanganui flares with green stars that led the 50 Squadron crews to the aiming-point, where all but one bombed from 19,000 to 22,000 feet between 20.31 and 20.45. ME567 was set on fire by a night-fighter during the bombing run at 21,000 feet, and the bombs were dropped by F/L Keith and crew from two thousand feet lower two minutes short of the markers. The mid-upper turret fairing had been shot away, and the underside of the fuselage and port wing holed, while part of the electrical system was knocked out and the fire in the starboard wing had to be dealt with. Excellent crew co-operation and coolness under extreme pressure facilitated a safe return to debriefing, when crews reported the glow of fires and the appearance of a successful raid, but no detailed assessment. Of course, not all would make it back to tell their stories at debriefing, and thirty-three Lancaster dispersals stood empty in dawn's early light. Reports from Berlin described bombs falling over a wide area, more so in the south than the north, and damage to fifty industrial premises, a number of them engaged in important war work, while twenty thousand people were bombed out of their homes. A feature of the campaign was the number of outlying communities suffering collateral damage, and, on this night, sixty-one such hamlets recorded bombs falling.

The early time-on-target had allowed crews to get a full night in bed, and they were, hopefully, fully rested, when news came through on the 28th that many of them would be returning to the "Big City" that night. A heavy force of 673 aircraft was assembled, of which 432 were Lancasters and 241 Halifaxes, 155 of the former provided by 5 Group. 50 Squadron made ready sixteen Lancasters, which departed Skellingthorpe between 00.10 and 00.50 with S/L McLeod the senior pilot on duty. They were routed out over southern Denmark before turning south-east on a direct course for the target, with an almost reciprocal return and various diversionary measures to distract the night-fighter controller. Sixty-six crews turned back early, suggesting some adverse reaction to the back-to-back operations. Those reaching the target area encountered ten-tenths cloud, and a mixture of sky and ground-marking to aim at. The 50 Squadron crews delivered their bombs on red and green release-point flares from 20,000 to 22,000 feet between 03.14 and 03.33, some crews reporting two huge explosions at 03.18 and 03.25, the earlier one described by a 10 Squadron crew as lighting up the sky over a radius of fifty miles. Forty-six aircraft failed to return, twenty-six of them Halifaxes, as the defenders fought back to exact another heavy toll of bombers. Remarkably, 50 Squadron had not posted missing a single crew since the end of December, despite the nature and frequency of operations, but this superb record had to come to an end, and did so on this night. LM428 crashed somewhere in the general area of Berlin, killing the highly experienced crew of F/L Burtt, an officer well above the average age for operational flying, and someone whose presence would be missed. The impression gained from returning crews at debriefing was of a concentrated and effective attack, and this was partly borne-out by local reports of heavy damage in western and southern districts, where 180,000 people were bombed out of their homes. However, as had been the pattern throughout the campaign against Berlin, seventy-seven outlying communities had also been afflicted.

After a night's rest a force of 534 aircraft was made ready on the 30th for the final operation of this concerted effort against Berlin. 5 Group offered 156 Lancasters, of which sixteen were made ready by 50 Squadron, and they took off between 16.49 and 17.31 with S/Ls Chadwick and McLeod the senior pilots on duty. After climbing out, they joined with the rest of the group to follow a route similar to that adopted two nights earlier. P/O Lloyd and crew had reached the west coast of the Schleswig-Holstein peninsular when their starboard-outer engine failed and ended their interest in the proceedings. The bomber stream remained relatively free of harassment until approaching the target, where it was greeted by ten-tenths cloud at around 8,000 feet and the sight of Pathfinder sky-marking in progress. The 50 Squadron crews bombed on these from 19,000 and 23,300 feet between 20.18 and 20.31, and all commented on the smoke rising through 12,000 feet and the glow of fires beneath the cloud, which, according to some, was still visible from a hundred miles into the return flight. Thirty-two Lancasters and a single Halifax failed to make it home, in return for which, according to local reports, central and south-western districts suffered heavy damage and serious areas of fire. Other parts of the city were also hit, while many bomb loads were again scattered liberally onto outlying communities, and at least a thousand people lost their lives. 112 heavy bombers and their crews had been lost to the Command as a result of these three operations, and with the introduction of the enemy's highly efficient Tame Boar night-fighter system based on running commentaries, the advantage had swung back in the defenders' favour.

Two further heavy raids would be directed at Berlin before the end of the winter offensive, one in February and the other in March, but they would be almost in isolation. There is no question that Germany's Capital had been sorely afflicted by the three latest operations, but it remained a functioning city, and showed no signs of imminent collapse. During the course of the month the squadron participated in ten operations, and dispatched 138 sorties for the loss of a single Lancaster and crew.

February 1944

Bad weather during the first two weeks of February allowed the crews to draw breath and the squadrons to replenish. Harris had intended to maintain the pressure on Berlin, and would have launched a further attack, had he not been thwarted by the conditions, and as a result, the time was filled with training and mining operations. On the 1st, 61 Squadron moved out of Skellingthorpe temporarily to take up residence at Coningsby, but would return after the conclusion of the winter campaign. On the 12th, veteran Lancaster W4119, which had originally served with 207 Squadron and a conversion unit, was engaged in fighter affiliation with ten souls on board, when the port-outer engine burst into flames, and F/L Beetham gave the order to bale out. He and five others were able to comply, before a section of the port wing broke away, sending the Lancaster into a spin that ended with a crash at 15.55 near East Kirkby airfield, the home of 57 and 630 Squadrons, and the four remaining occupants died. On the 13th, according to the squadron ORB, F/L Edward and crew were posted to 617 Squadron at Woodhall Spa, a move which would have fatal consequences for the pilot and four others, while attacking a V-Weapon site at Wizernes in France on the 24th of June.

When the Pathfinder and main force squadrons next took to the air, it would be for a record-breaking effort to Berlin on the 15th, and would also be the penultimate operation of the campaign, and, indeed, of the war by Bomber Command's heavy brigade, against Germany's Capital City. The force of 891 aircraft represented the largest non-1,000 force to date, and, therefore, the greatest-ever to be sent against the Capital, and it would be the first time that more than five hundred Lancasters and three hundred Halifaxes had operated together. 5 Group would surpass its previous best effort by fifty Lancasters when putting 226 of them into the air, and eighteen of them would be representing 50 Squadron. The bomb bays of this huge armada would convey to Berlin the greatest-ever tonnage of bombs to any target to date, and 50 Squadron's contribution would be eighteen cookies and 1,050 x 30lb and 16,350 x 4lb incendiaries. They departed Skellingthorpe between 17.25and 17.41 with S/L Chadwick the senior pilot on duty, and, surprisingly, F/L Edward and crew named among the participants, having, apparently, not yet joined 617 Squadron. After joining up with the rest of the 5 Group squadrons, they set course for the western coast of Denmark, before crossing Jutland and entering Germany via the Baltic coast between Rostock and Stralsund, with a direct heading, thereafter, for the target. The return route required the bombers to pass south of Hannover and Bremen, and cross Holland to the North Sea via Castricum. Extensive diversionary measures included a mining operation in Kiel Bay ahead of the arrival of the bombers, a raid on Frankfurt-an-Oder to the east of Berlin by a small force of 8 Group Lancasters, and Oboe Mosquitos attacking five night-fighter airfields in Holland. The force had been depleted by seventy-five early returns by the time the remainder homed in on the target, where ten-tenths cloud at around 10,000 feet concealed it from their view, but those with H2S were able to confirm their positions, while the others relied on the Pathfinders' red release-point flares with green stars and red and green TIs on the ground. The 50 Squadron crews bombed on these from 18,500 to 22,500 feet between 21.16 and 21.36, and, on return, reported the markers to be highly effective and well-concentrated, and the burgeoning glow beneath the clouds convinced them that they had taken part in a successful operation. This was borne out by local reports, which confirmed that the 2,642 tons of bombs had caused extensive damage in central and south-western districts, but had also spilled out into surrounding communities. A thousand houses and more than five hundred temporary wooden barracks were destroyed, and important war-industry factories in the Siemensstadt district were damaged in return for the loss to the Command of forty-three aircraft, twenty-six Lancasters, (4.6%) and seventeen Halifaxes, (5.4%). Perhaps slightly disturbing was the fact that eight of the missing Halifaxes were Mk IIIs, only one fewer than the nine Mk II/Vs. The squadron posted missing another highly experienced crew, that of F/O Litherland DFC & Bar, who were all killed when DV376 came down somewhere in the general area of Berlin.

Despite the recent heavy losses, when orders were received on the 19th to prepare for another major assault that night, this time on Leipzig, the heavy squadrons were able offer 816 aircraft, 561 Lancasters and 255 Halifaxes. 5 Group managed 209 Lancasters and 50 Squadron sixteen, which departed Skellingthorpe between 23.50 and 00.31 with S/L McLeod the senior pilot on duty. After climbing out over the station, they joined up with the others heading for the Dutch coast, where a proportion of the Luftwaffe Nachtjagd was waiting for them, while others had been drawn away by a mining diversion off Kiel. F/Sgt Berry and crew were unable to maintain height because of an engine issue, and diverted to Bremen, which they identified by searchlights and flak, before bombing the outskirts and turning for home. The remainder continued on, some to become embroiled in a running battle with night-fighters all the way into eastern Germany, where inaccurately forecast winds caused some aircraft to arrive at the target early. They were forced to orbit, while they waited for the Pathfinders to arrive to mark the target, and the local flak batteries accounted for around twenty of these, while four others were lost through collisions. The 50 Squadron crews arrived to find ten-tenths cloud with tops at around 10,000 feet, and bombed on green Wanganui flares and red and green TIs from 21,000 to 22,500 feet between 03.57 and 04.13. It seems that there was a brief period during the attack when skymarking stopped and led to some scattering of bombs, but the marker-flares were soon replenished with the arrival of more backers-up, and a considerable glow beneath the cloud remained visible for some fifty minutes into the return journey, giving the impression of a successful assault. When all of those aircraft returning home had been accounted for, there was a massive shortfall of seventy-eight, a record loss by a clear twenty-one aircraft. Forty-four Lancasters and thirty-four Halifaxes had failed to return, with a loss-rate of 7.8% and 13.3% respectively, and this prompted Harris to immediately withdraw the Mk II and V Halifaxes from further operations over Germany, which, at a stroke, removed a proportion of 4 Group's fire-power from the front line until they could be re-equipped with the Mk III Halifax. In the meantime, the Mk II and V operators would focus their energies for the remainder of the month on gardening duties.

Despite this depletion of available numbers, a force of 598 aircraft was made ready on the 20th for an operation that night against Stuttgart, which would be the first of three against the city over a three-week period. 5 Group contributed 176 Lancasters, thirteen of them belonging to 50 Squadron and they were each loaded with a cookie and eleven SBCs, before being dispatched between 23.57 and 00.22 with F/L Keith the senior pilot on duty. P/O Wort and crew were over the Channel and some twenty miles north-west of Dieppe, when the pilot became ill, and had to turn back, and they were followed by P/O Botha and crew, whose W/T had broken down. The others made their way across the Channel to the French coast, from where the cloud remained at ten-tenths with tops at 8,000 feet all the way into southern

Germany. A North Sea sweep and a diversionary raid on Munich two hours ahead of the main activity had caused the Luftwaffe to deploy its forces early, and this allowed the bomber stream to push on unmolested to the target. By the time it hove into view, the cloud had thinned to five to eight-tenths at around 6,000 feet, and the excellent visibility enabled the crews to draw a bead on the Pathfinder red and green sky-markers and similar-coloured TIs on the ground. The 50 Squadron crews bombed from 22,000 to 23,000 feet between 04.01 and 04.16, observing many large fires, and, on return, there were reports that the glow from the burning city was still visible from 250 miles into the return flight. Despite some scattering of bombs, local reports described central districts and those in a quadrant from north-west to north-east, suffering extensive damage, and a Bosch factory was one of the important war industry concerns to be hard-hit. In contrast to twenty-four hours earlier, a modest nine aircraft failed to return.

In an attempt to reduce the prohibitive losses of recent weeks, a new tactic was introduced for the next two operations. A force of 734 aircraft was assembled on the 24th for an operation to the centre of Germany's ball-bearing production, Schweinfurt, situated some sixty miles to the east of Frankfurt in southern Germany. The plan called for 392 aircraft to depart their stations between 18.00 and 19.00, and to be followed into the air two hours later by 342 others in the hope of catching the night-fighters on the ground refuelling and re-arming as the second wave passed through. While this operation was in progress, extensive diversionary measures would be put in hand that involved more than three hundred other aircraft, including 179 from the training units conducting a North Sea sweep, and 110 Halifaxes and Stirlings mining in northern waters. 5 Group contributed 204 Lancasters, of which fifteen were made ready by 50 Squadron, four assigned to the first phase, and taking-off between 18.35 and 18.43 with W/C Heward the senior pilot on duty, and eleven departing between 20.30 and 20.44 to join the second phase. F/O Weatherstone's rear turret failed as he closed on the French coast, depleting the first phase element by one, but the others reached the target to find three-tenths cloud at 3,000 to 4,000 feet, with haze spoiling the vertical visibility. The aiming-point was identified by red and green TIs, and F/L Keith and crew found fires already established, but on the south-western edge of the town as they bombed from 22,500 feet at 23.17. W/C Heward saw no cloud, and described the visibility as excellent, enabling him to pick out the River Main as he ran in to bomb on a single red TI from 22,000 feet at 23.19. He reported two columns of black smoke rising through 5,000 feet as he turned away, and considered the attack to be effective, if a little scattered. F/L Shortt's assessment of the conditions mirrored that of his commanding officer, and he attacked from 21,000 feet at 23.13.

Meanwhile, the second phase crews were well on their way, but, for the second operation running, P/O Wort fell ill, and had to abandon his participation in the operation. The remainder pressed on, and picked up the glow of fires from the earlier raid at a distance of two hundred miles. The visibility in the target area remained good, despite the rising smoke, and bombing by the 50 Squadron crews took place out of almost cloudless skies onto red and green TIs from 21,000 to 22,500 feet between 01.03 and 01.37. All indications suggested an effective raid, but, unfortunately, both phases of the operation had suffered from undershooting after some Pathfinder backers-up failed to press on to the aiming-point. In that regard it was a disappointing night, but an interesting feature was the loss of 50% fewer aircraft from the second wave in comparison with the first, in an overall casualty figure of thirty-three, and this suggested some merit in the tactic. Since the turn of the year a wind-finder system had been in use, in which selected crews monitored wind speed and direction, and passed their findings back to HQ, where the figures were collated, and any changes from the briefed conditions could be re-broadcast to the bomber stream. This had been found to be extremely useful, but, as would be discovered in the ensuing weeks, the system had its limitations.

The main operation on the following night was directed at the beautiful and culturally significant southern city of Augsburg, situated around thirty miles north-west of Munich. It was home to a major Maschinenfabrik Augsburg Nuremberg (M.A.N) diesel engine factory, which had been the target for the previously-mentioned epic low-level daylight raid by 5 Group Lancasters in April 1942. On this night, 594 aircraft were divided into two waves, and among them were 164 Lancasters of 5 Group, including fourteen representing 50 Squadron. Ten of these were assigned to the first phase, taking-off between 18.26 and 18.41 with S/L McLeod the senior pilot on duty, and four to the second, departing Skellingthorpe between 21.23 and 21.38 with no senior pilots to take the lead. The first wave bomber stream flew out over Belgium with ten-tenths cloud beneath them, but that had dissipated by the time the target drew near, and, on arrival, it was possible for crews to gain a visual reference. The Pathfinders' red and green TIs were in the bomb sights as the 50 Squadron crews carried out their attacks from 20,500 to 22,000 feet between 22.38 and 22.55, and fires were beginning to take hold as they turned away. The second wave crews were drawn on by the glow in the sky from a hundred miles away, and arrived to find visibility still good despite copious amounts of smoke rising through 10,000 feet, and they bombed on existing fires and red and green Wanganui flares and TIs from 21,000 to 22,500 feet between 01.15 and 01.17. The loss of twenty-one aircraft seemed to confirm the benefits of splitting the forces, and this tactic would remain an important part of Bomber Command planning for the remainder of the war. 50 Squadron posted missing P/O Taylor and his crew in LL791, which had been intercepted by a pair of night-fighters over France while outbound, and shot down to crash some forty-five miles west of Strasbourg. The navigator was the only fatality, while five were taken into captivity and the flight engineer evaded a similar fate. It had been a devastatingly destructive operation, in which all facets of the plan had come together in near perfect harmony, spelling disaster for this lightly-defended treasure trove of culture. Its heart was torn out by blast and fire that destroyed almost three thousand houses along with buildings of outstanding historical significance, and centuries of irreplaceable culture was lost forever. There was also some industrial damage, and around ninety-thousand people were bombed out of their homes.

During the course of the month the squadron carried out five operations, and dispatched seventy-six sorties for the loss of three Lancasters, two crews and four other airmen.

March 1944

March would bring an end to the winter campaign, but a long and bitter month would have to be endured first before any respite came from long-range forays into Germany. The crews had enjoyed a few nights off when the second raid of the series on Stuttgart was posted on the 1st, for which a force of 557 aircraft was made ready. This number included 178 Lancasters representing 5 Group, fourteen of which were provided by 50 Squadron. Take-off from Skellingthorpe was accomplished without incident between 20.07 and 23.44 with S/L Chadwick the senior pilot on duty, and there would be no early returns. They flew out over ten-tenths cloud with tops at between 12,000 and 17,000 feet, and encountered similar conditions in the target area, where the Pathfinders employed a combination of sky and ground-marking. This, unfortunately, became scattered, and the bombing was directed between two main concentrations, the 207 Squadron crews carrying out their attacks on Wanganui red markers with green stars from 20,000 to 22,200 feet between 02.58 and 03.19. It was not possible to assess the accuracy of the attack, although a column of smoke had reached 25,000 feet by the end of the raid, and large fires were evident from the glow in the sky visible from up to 150 miles away. The presence of thick cloud all the way there and back made conditions difficult for enemy night-fighters, and a remarkably modest four aircraft failed to return. It was eventually established that the raid had been an outstanding success, which had caused extensive damage in central, western and northern districts, where a number of important war-industry factories, including those belonging to Bosch and Daimler-Benz, sustained damage.

At the end of the first week, the Halifax brigade, particularly those withdrawn from operations over Germany, fired the opening salvoes of the pre-invasion campaign, the purpose of which was to dismantle by bombing thirty-seven railway centres in France, Belgium and western Germany. It began on the night of the 6/7th at Trappes marshalling yards, situated some ten miles west-south-west of Paris, and continued at Le Mans in north-western France on the following night. For most of the heavy crews, however, there was no employment following Stuttgart, until a return there in mid-month, but, in the meantime, matters were afoot at 5 Group, and had been ever since a frustrating series of operations against flying bomb launching sites conducted by 617 Squadron since December had failed to achieve the desired results. The problem had been pinpoint accuracy, which was vital to destroy small, precision targets, but could not be achieved by reliance upon Oboe. Accurate though Oboe undoubtedly was at an urban target, where a margin of error of 400 to 600 yards was nothing, precision targets required more. 617 Squadron had obliterated the Oboe markers, only for bombing photos to show that the targets, situated only a matter of yards away, had remained intact. W/C Cheshire and S/L Martin had experimented with a dive-bombing technique, which had proved to be successful, but impracticable in a Lancaster, and Cheshire had borrowed a Mosquito for further trials. These were so promising, that the 5 Group A-O-C, AVM Cochrane, authorized a number of operations by the squadron against factory targets in France, before taking the idea to Harris. Harris approved, paving the way for 5 Group to become effectively independent of the main bomber force and begin larger-scale trials.

Orders were received at Skellingthorpe on the 9th to prepare eleven Lancasters for a forty-four-strong 5 Group force for an attack that night against the Lioré et Olivier aircraft factory at Marignane, situated a few miles to the north of Marseilles in southern France. The area was the main pre-war hub for commercial flying boat operations, particularly for the Pan American Clipper Class flights, and the factory had been engaged in the manufacture of the LeO 45 twin-engine medium bomber for the French Air Force. They took off between 20.35 and 20.50 with W/C Heward the senior pilot on duty, and a round-trip ahead of them of some 1,350 miles if they flew direct. There were no early returns among the 50 Squadron element, and they arrived in the target area under clear skies and bright moonlight, which facilitated an easy identification of the factory buildings, which had been marked by red spotfires. The bombing was carried out from 8,000 to 10,250 feet between 01.27 and 01.35, and the high-explosives were seen to fall among the buildings, while the incendiaries appeared to be a little scattered. A large explosion was witnessed at 01.24 and a huge pall of smoke was rising through 6,000 feet as they turned away. All arrived home safely, most having spent more than nine hours aloft.

5 Group received orders on the 10th to prepare 102 Lancasters to form four small forces, each to attack a specific factory in France that night. 50 Squadron was not involved in these moonlit operations against the Michelin tyre factory at Clermont-Ferrand, the Bloch aircraft factory at Châteauroux, which was the first to be set up by the famed designer, Marcel Dassault, in 1935, the Morane Saulnier aircraft plant at Ossun, just north of the Pyrenese and the Ricamerie needle-bearing works at St-Etienne, the last-mentioned, the objective for sixteen Lancasters from 617 Squadron. All were successfully bombed for the loss of a single Lancaster occupied by the crew of a 207 Squadron flight commander.

Now that the Mk III Halifax was becoming available in larger numbers, the Command was quickly returning to full strength, and it was a force of 863 aircraft that set out for Stuttgart in the early-evening of the 15th. This number included 206 Lancasters provided by 5 Group, eighteen of them departing Skellingthorpe between 19.15 and 19.35 with S/Ls Chadwick and McLeod the senior pilots on duty. They rendezvoused with the rest of the force as they passed over Reading on their way to the south coast, and it was after this that P/O Jennings and crew turned back with an engine issue. The bomber stream crossed the French coast at 20,000 feet over broken cloud with clear conditions above, and made its way parallel with the frontiers of Belgium, Luxembourg and Germany as if heading for Switzerland, before turning towards the north-east for the run-in to the target. It was during this final leg that the night-fighters managed to infiltrate a section of the stream and score heavily, although, this was not apparent to the 50 Squadron crews. Adverse winds were responsible for the Pathfinders arriving up to six minutes late to open the attack, when they employed both sky and ground-markers in the face of seven to ten-tenths cloud at between 8,000 and 15,000 feet. The Wanganui flares drifted in the wind, marking an area to the north-east of the River Neckar, while the TIs landed far apart in the north and south of the city. The 50 Squadron crews bombed on whatever markers presented themselves, mostly red TIs, and did so from 19,000 to 22,500 feet between 23.08 and 23.31, observing a spread of fires, including two large ones ten miles apart, and smoke rising to bombing altitude. It would be established later that some of the early bombing had been accurate, but, that most of the loads had undershot and fallen into open country, a disappointment compounded by the loss, mostly to night-fighters, of thirty-seven aircraft.

Many operations had been mounted against Frankfurt during the preceding two years, only a small number of which had been really effective. This state of affairs was about to be rectified, however, and the first of two raids against this southern powerhouse of industry was posted on the 18th, for which a force of 846 aircraft was made ready. 5 Group supported the operation with 212 Lancasters, eighteen of which belonged to 50 Squadron, and they were loaded at Skellingthorpe with a cookie each and a variety of incendiaries, before taking off between 18.56 and 19.18 with S/L Chadwick the senior pilot on duty. F/O Botha and crew reached the French coast before their starboard-outer engine failed, and they unloaded the contents of their bomb bay on the docks at Ostend as a last resort target. The others pressed on across France and into south-central Germany in good weather conditions, where they encountered a layer of haze 20,000 feet thick over the target, and, according to most, no more than three-tenths cloud. This allowed the Pathfinders to employ the Newhaven ground marking technique (blind marking by H2S, followed by visual backing-up), which the 50

Squadron crews exploited when carrying out their attacks on red and green TIs from 20,100 to 22,000 feet between 22.00 and 22.12. A large explosion was witnessed at 22.05, and they flew home confident that their efforts had been worthwhile. They had, indeed, contributed to an outstandingly successful raid, during which 5 Group alone dropped more than one thousand tons of bombs for the first time at a single target. Local reports calculated that six thousand buildings had been destroyed or seriously damaged in predominantly eastern, central and western districts, and this was in return for the loss of twenty-two aircraft, five of which were from 5 Group. 50 Squadron's ED308 crashed somewhere in the general target area killing three members of the crew, after P/O Miller and three others had parachuted into the arms of their captors.

F/L Ruskell was posted to 5 Lancaster Finishing School (5 LFS) at the conclusion of his tour on the 20th, during a three-day period of minor operations, until Frankfurt was named again on the 22nd as the target for that night. 217 crews of 5 Group learned that they were to be part of another huge force of 816 aircraft, and the eighteen participants from Skellingthorpe took off between 18.52 to 19.14 with S/L McLeod the senior pilot on duty. After climbing out above their stations and forming up, they adopted an unusual route for a target south of the Ruhr, crossing the enemy coast over Vlieland and Teschelling, before passing to the east of Osnabrück on a direct course due south for the target. There were no early returns from the 50 Squadron element, and they arrived at the target to find five to six-tenths thin, low cloud at around 4,000 feet, and Paramatta marking (blind marking by H2S) in progress. They focussed their attention on the release-point flares and red and green TIs marking out the aiming-point, before bombing from 21,000 to 23,000 feet, between 21.51 and 22.04. The exception was F/O Botha and crew, who lost the use of their port-inner engine immediately after take-off, but pressed on to reach the target late, when red Wanganui flares with yellow stars appeared ahead and they bombed from 10,000 feet at 22.23. A massive rectangular area of unbroken fire was observed across the centre of the city, the glow from which could be seen for at least a hundred miles into the return flight. Returning crews reported numerous searchlights lighting up the cloud, and moderate to intense flak that reached up to the bombers' flight level. Local reports confirmed the enormity of the devastation, which was particularly severe in western districts and left this half of the city without electricity, gas and water for an extended period. More than nine hundred people lost their lives and a further 120,000 were bombed out of their homes, at a cost to the Command of twenty-six Lancasters and seven Halifaxes, a loss-rate of 4.2% and 3.8% respectively. 50 Squadron was represented among the missing by DV384 and ME578, both of which crashed outbound shortly after bypassing the eastern edge of the Ruhr. The former came down two miles north-north-east of Grevenbrück with no survivors from the crew of F/O Dobbyn DFC, RCAF, and just two escaped with their lives from the eight-man crew of P/O Thornton DFC in the latter. It was a bad night for senior officers, 207 and 7 Squadrons losing their commanding officers, while Bardney's station commander, G/C Norman Pleasance, failed to return in a 9 Squadron Lancaster. What was about to happen over the next week and a half, however, would overshadow anything that had gone before, and would certainly not fall within what might be considered acceptable.

It was more than five weeks since the main force had last visited the Capital, and 811 aircraft were made ready on the 24th for what would be the final raid of the war by RAF heavy bombers on the "Big City". 5 Group put up 193 Lancasters, of which sixteen were made ready by 50 Squadron, and they departed Skellingthorpe between 18.55 and 19.14 with S/L Chadwick the senior pilot on duty. They had a long flight ahead of them, which would take them across the North Sea to the Danish coast near Ringkøbing and then to a point on the German Baltic coast near Rostock. When north-east of Berlin they were to adopt a south-westerly course for the bombing run, and, once clear of the defence zone homebound, dogleg to the west and then north-west to pass around Hannover on its southern and western sides, before heading for Holland and an exit via the Castricum coast. The extended outward leg provided a time-on-target of around 22.30, but an unexpected difficulty would be encountered, which would render void all of the meticulous planning. The existence of what we now know as "Jetstream" winds was unknown at the time, and the one blowing from the north with unprecedented strength on this night pushed the bomber stream south of its intended track. Navigators, who were expecting to see the northern tip of Sylt on their H2S screens, were horrified to find the southern end, which meant that they were thirty miles south of track, and about to fly over Germany rather than Denmark. The previously-mentioned "wind-finder" system had been set up for precisely this eventuality, but the problem on this night was that the wind-finders refused to believe what their instruments were telling them. Winds in excess of one hundred m.p.h had never been encountered before, and, fearing that they would be disbelieved, many modified the figures downward. The same thing happened at raid control, where the figures were modified again, so that the information rebroadcast to the bomber stream bore no resemblance to the reality of the situation.

P/O Jennings and crew lost their starboard-outer engine, and diverted to northern Holland, where they bombed a cone of three searchlights believed to be located on the infamous "Wespennest" (wasps' nest) fighter aerodrome at Leeuwarden. P/O Durham and crew were also beaten by an engine issue, in their case port-inner failure, and bombed the island of Sylt as a last resort target. By the time the others had reached Westerhever on the west coast of the Schleswig-Holstein peninsular, most realized that they were some distance south of track, and set course for the north to try to regain the planned route and avoid the defences that would be met if they turned east over Germany. Many commented on the inaccurate wind information that they had received during the outward journey, and, having arrived in the target area, some were convinced that the Pathfinders were up to ten minutes late in opening the raid. This was confirmed to some by the voice of the Master Bomber exhorting them to hurry up. Crews reported a variety of cloud conditions, from three to ten-tenths at between 6,000 and 14,000 feet, but most were able to pick out the red and green TIs on the ground, and, if not, found red Wanganui flares with green stars to guide them to the aiming-point. The 50 Squadron crews confirmed their positions by H2S before bombing from 20,250 to 23,000 feet between 22.32 and 22.59, and observed what appeared to be a scattered attack in the early stages, until fires began to become more concentrated in three distinct areas, and large explosions were witnessed at 22.42 and 22.54. The defences were very active with moderate flak bursting at up to 24,000 feet, and light flak attempting to shoot out the skymarkers, but night-fighter activity was described by the 5 Group ORB as unusually quiet. There was a shock awaiting the Command as the returning aircraft landed to leave a shortfall of seventy-two, and, it would be established later that two-thirds of them had fallen victim to the Ruhr flak batteries after being driven into that region's defence zone by the wind on the way home. Post-raid analysis revealed that the wind had also played havoc with the marking and bombing, and had pushed the attack towards the south-western districts of the Capital, where most of the damage occurred, while 126 outlying communities also received bombs. 50 Squadron had been present on each of the nineteen main raids to the Capital, and the diversion there on the night of the Magdeburg debacle in January, and had despatched 281 sorties, the equal second highest in 5 Group by one sortie to 57 Squadron. Eight of its Lancasters failed to return, and another crashed to give a loss rate of 2.8%, which was bettered in the whole Command only by fellow 5 Group, 49 Squadron. (The Berlin Raids. Martin Middlebrook.)

A small number of 5 Group Lancasters were invited to take part in an attack on the extensive railway yards at Aulnoye in north-eastern France to be carried out on the evening of the 25th. Just three Lancasters were detailed at Skellingthorpe, and they took off between 19.15 and 19.19 containing freshman crews, all of which reached the target to find clear skies and ground haze, through which a bend in the River Sambre provided a useful pinpoint, although the aiming-point had been clearly marked by concentrated red and green TIs. They bombed from 8,000 to 8,500 feet between 21.46 and 21.51, and observed fires and a large explosion at 22.03 as they retreated.

Although Berlin was now consigned to the past, the winter campaign still had a week to run, and two more major operations for the crews to negotiate. The first of these was posted on the 26th, and would bring a return to the old enemy of Essen that night, for which a force of 705 aircraft was made ready. 5 Group contributed 172 of the 476 Lancasters, seventeen of them provided by 50 Squadron, which took off between 19.50 and 20.07 with W/C Heward displaying good leadership from the front as the senior pilot on duty. They climbed out over Skellingthorpe and set course for the Dutch coast to pass north of Haarlem and Amsterdam, before swinging to the south-east on a direct run to the target. There were no early returns, and all reached the target to find it under eight to ten-tenths cloud with tops in places as high as 14,000 feet. Oboe performed well and enabled the Pathfinders to mark the city with red and green TIs and Wanganui flares, which the 50 Squadron crews bombed from 18,500 and 22,250 feet between 22.00 and 22.16, before returning safely, having been unable to assess the results of their efforts. The impression was of a successful raid, and this was based on a considerable glow beneath the clouds as they withdrew. Post-raid reconnaissance soon confirmed another outstandingly destructive operation against this once elusive target, thus continuing the remarkable run of successes here since the introduction of Oboe to main force operations a year earlier. Over seventeen hundred houses were destroyed in the attack, with dozens of war industry factories sustaining serious damage, and, on a night when the night-fighter controllers were caught off guard by the switch to the Ruhr, the success was gained for the modest loss of nine aircraft.

The period known as the Battle of Berlin, but which was better referred to as the winter campaign, was to be brought to an end on the night of the 30/31st, with a standard maximum-effort raid on Nuremberg, the birthplace of Nazism. The plan of operation departed from normal practice in only one important respect, and this was to prove critical. It had become standard routine over the winter to employ diversions and feints to confuse the enemy night-fighter controllers. Sometimes they were successful and sometimes not, but with the night-fighter force having clearly gained the upper hand with its "Tame Boar" running commentary system, all possible means had to be adopted to protect the bomber stream. During a conference held early on the 30th, the Lancaster Group A-O-Cs expressed a preference for a 5 Group-inspired route, which would require the bomber stream to fly a long straight leg across Belgium and Germany, to a point about fifty miles north of Nuremberg, from where the final run-in would commence. The Halifax A-O-Cs were less convinced of the benefits, and AVM Bennett, the Pathfinder chief, was positively overcome by the potential dangers and predicted a disaster, only to be overruled. A force of 795 aircraft was made ready, of which 201 Lancasters were to be provided by 5 Group, twenty of them representing 50 Squadron, and the crews attended briefings to be told of the route, wind conditions and the belief that a layer of cloud would conceal them from enemy night-fighters. Before take-off, a Meteorological Flight Mosquito crew radioed in to cast doubts upon the weather conditions, which they could see differed markedly from those that had been forecast. This also went unheeded, and, from around 21.45 for the next hour or so, the crews took off for the rendezvous area, and headed into a conspiracy of circumstances, which would inflict upon Bomber Command its heaviest defeat of the war.

At Skellingthorpe, take-off began at 21.57, and proceeded smoothly until the fifteenth aircraft, veteran Lancaster, W4933, burst a tyre at 22.15, and careered off the runway, with the crew of F/Sgt Bucknell RAAF inside. They emerged unscathed, but it was the end of the road for the Lancaster, which was declared to be beyond economical repair. The remaining four crews lifted off between 22.25 and 22.35, unaware that this loss of an aircraft was to be the first in a record number to afflict the Command on what would be its blackest night of the war. They climbed away to gain height over the station with F/Ls Beetham, Keith, Robinson and Shortt the senior pilots on duty, and it was not long into the flight before they and the other crews began to notice some unusual features in the conditions, which included uncommonly bright moonlight, and a crystal clarity of visibility that allowed them the rare sight of other aircraft in the stream. On most nights, crews would feel themselves to be completely alone in the sky all the way to the target, until, bang on schedule, TIs would be seen to fall and other aircraft would make their presence known by the turbulence of their slipstreams as they funnelled towards the aiming-point. Once at cruising altitude on this night, they were alarmed to note that the forecast cloud was conspicuous by its absence, and, instead, lay beneath them as a white tablecloth, against which they were silhouetted like flies. Condensation trails began to form in the cold, clear air to further advertise their presence to the enemy, and the Jetstream winds, which had so adversely affected the Berlin raid a week earlier, were also present, only this time from the south. As then, the wind-finder system would be unable to cope, and this would have a serious impact on the outcome of the operation. The final insult on this sad night was, that the route into Germany passed close to two night-fighter beacons, which the enemy aircraft were orbiting while they awaited their instructions, unaware initially that they were about to have the cream of Bomber Command handed to them on a plate. P/O Dobson and crew were spared what was to follow by the indisposition of their navigator, and they bombed the docks at Ostend before heading for home.

The carnage began over Charleroi in Belgium, and from there to the target, the route was sign-posted by the burning wreckage on the ground of eighty Bomber Command aircraft. Among these were three from 50 Squadron, the first of them, veteran Lancaster, R5546, was torn asunder after being hit by fire from a night-fighter, and crashed east of Sinzig, between Bonn and Coblenz. F/Sgt Gray and two of his crew were flung into space as the only survivors, and they soon found themselves in enemy hands. Some fifty miles due east and just west of Giessen, LM394 suffered a similar fate at the hands of a night-fighter, and there were no survivors from the eight-man crew captained by F/L Robinson RNZAF. Finally, EE174 also fell to a night-fighter and crashed just south of Ebern, some forty miles north of the target, delivering F/Sgt Waugh and three of his crew into captivity as the only survivors. The wind-finder system broke down again, and those crews who either failed to detect the strength of the wind, or simply refused to believe the evidence, were driven up to fifty miles north of their intended track, and, consequently, turned towards Nuremberg from a false position. This led to more than a hundred aircraft bombing at Schweinfurt in error, which combined with the massive losses sustained before the target was reached to reduce considerably the numbers arriving at the primary target. The remaining fifteen 50 Squadron crews arrived over Nuremberg to encounter eight to nine-tenths cloud with tops as high as 16,000 feet, and bombed from 19,000 to 22,800 feet between 01.15 and 01.30, aiming at red and green TIs and sky-markers after confirming their positions by H2S. Many fires were observed, the glow from which, according to some reports, remained visible for 120 miles into the return journey. Ninety-five aircraft failed to return home, twenty-one of them from 5 Group, and many others were written off in landing crashes or with battle damage too severe to repair. The shock and disappointment were compounded by the fact that the strong wind had driven the marking beyond the city to the east, and Nuremberg had, consequently, escaped serious damage.

During the course of the month, the squadron participated in nine operations, and dispatched 135 sorties for the loss of seven Lancasters and six crews.

April 1944

The winter campaign had brought the Command to its low point of the war, and was the only time when the morale of the crews was in question. What now lay before the hard-pressed men of Bomber Command was in marked contrast to that which had been endured over the seemingly interminable winter months. In place of the long slog to Germany on dark, often dirty nights, shorter range hops to France and Belgium in improving weather conditions would become the order of the day. However, these operations would be equally demanding in their way, and would require of the crews a greater commitment to accuracy, to avoid casualties among friendly civilians. Despite this, a decree from on high insisted that such operations were worthy of counting as just one third of a sortie towards the completion of a tour, and, until this flawed policy was rescinded, an air of mutiny would pervade the crew rooms. Despite the horrendous losses of the winter campaign, the Command was in remarkably fine fettle to face its new challenge, with 3 Group gradually changing to Lancasters, and the much-improved Hercules powered Halifaxes equipping 4 Group and most of 6 Group. Harris was now in the enviable position of being able to achieve what had eluded his predecessor, namely, to attack multiple targets simultaneously with enough strength to be effective. Such was the hitting-power now at his disposal, he could assign targets to individual groups, to groups in tandem, or to the Command as a whole, as dictated by operational requirements. Although invasion considerations would come first, while Harris was at the helm, his favoured policy of city-busting would never be entirely shelved.

On the 2nd, the squadron was notified of the award of the DFC to W/C Heward and P/O Lloyd. 5 Group returned to operations on the 5th, with an operation involving 144 Lancasters and a Mosquito flown by W/C Cheshire of 617 Squadron. The target was the former Dewoitine aircraft factory at Toulouse in south-western France, which, under a nationalization plan in 1936 involving six aircraft companies, including Lioré et Olivier and Potez, was now operating under the name SNCASE, or Sud Est for short. Cheshire was to mark it with spotfires from low level, using the system that he was instrumental in developing, and one which would become an integral part of 5 Group operations, with refinements, from this point on. This would be Cheshire's first operational flight in a Mosquito, and the first time that he marked a target for the group, rather than just 617 Squadron. Much depended upon its success if Harris were to become sold on the idea of the low-level visual marking technique and give it his backing. At Skellingthorpe, eight Lancasters were bombed up, two with a cookie each, and the rest with six 1,000 and six 500 pounders and assorted incendiaries. They took off between 20.27 and 20.40 with W/C Heward the senior pilot on duty, supported by seven of the more senior crews including that of S/L McLeod, who had with him the station commander, G/C Jefferson. Ahead lay an outward flight of more than four hours, which all from Skellingthorpe completed, and they arrived in time to watch Cheshire lob two red spotfires onto the roof of the factory at 00.17 during his third pass. So accurate were they, that the two 617 Squadron Lancaster backers-up were not required, and bombing took place in bright moonlight, the 50 Squadron crews delivering their loads from 8,500 to 10,250 feet between 00.19 and 00.34, and observing large fires with smoke rising through 7,000 feet. One 207 Squadron Lancaster was hit by flak over the target at 00.30 and exploded, killing all on board, and this was the only loss from an outstandingly successful operation. Within hours, Harris gave the go ahead for 5 Group to take on its own marking force, and become, in effect, an independent entity.

It would be almost two weeks before the necessary moves took place, and, in the meantime, the pre-invasion campaign got into full swing with the posting of two operations on the 9th. The Lille-Delivrance goods station in north-eastern France was assigned to 239 aircraft from 3, 4, 6 and 8 Groups, while the marshalling yards at Villeneuve-St-Georges, on the southern outskirts of Paris, were to be targeted by 225 aircraft drawn from all groups. The weather conditions were excellent, and clear skies greeted the latter force as it crossed the French coast at around 14,000 feet. The target could be identified visually, but crews aimed for the red and green TIs that had been accurately placed by the Pathfinders, delivering their hardware from between 13,000 and 14,500 feet in the face of little opposition. Many bomb bursts were observed along with orange explosions, and, to those high above, the raid appeared to be highly successful. In fact, many bomb loads had fallen into adjacent residential districts, where four hundred houses had been destroyed or seriously damaged, and ninety-three people killed. This was far fewer than had died in the simultaneous operation at Lille, many miles to the north-east, where over two thousand items of rolling stock had been destroyed, and buildings and installations seriously damaged, but at a collateral cost of 456 French civilian lives. Civilian casualties would prove to be an unavoidable by-product of the campaign.

50 Squadron did not take part in the above operation, or in that night's large minelaying effort to the Baltic area involving 103 Lancasters from 1 and 5 Groups. Nine Lancasters failed to return, having been intercepted by night-fighters on the route home over the western coast of Denmark, and it was a reminder, that this most productive of enterprises could be as dangerous as operating over a city.

On the following day, Monday the 10th, a further five railway yards, four in France and one in Belgium, were posted as the targets and assigned to individual groups. 5 Group was handed those at Tours in the Loire region of western France, for which 180 Lancasters were made ready, eleven of them at Skellingthorpe. They took off between 22.45 and 23.36 with S/L Chadwick the senior pilot on duty, and set course for the south coast and the Channel crossing. There were no early returns, and all arrived at the target to find bright moonlight and red spotfires marking the aiming-point. Master Bombers were on hand to direct the two phases of the attack, the first against the western side of the yards and the second against the eastern side, the 50 Squadron crews attacking the latter from 8,000 to 9,800 feet between 02.14 and 02.49. The later stages of the second phase bombing was affected by smoke drifting across the target area and rising through 6,000 feet, persuading the Master Bomber to call a halt to bombing at 02.48, and send home any crews with bombs still on board. F/O Oram and P/O Berry jettisoned their loads, while S/L Chadwick dropped his on Caen aerodrome from 11,000 feet at 03.35, from where he could see the town of Tours burning seventy miles to the south. His impression was that the eastern half of the yards had not been touched, but others claimed the attack to have been accurate and concentrated within the yards, and two large fires were observed. Post-raid reconnaissance confirmed the effectiveness of the attack, but the Germans would round up local civilians and force them into repairing the damage to get the yards working again before long.

Aachen was a major railway centre with marshalling yards at both the western and eastern ends, but the attack planned for the night of the 11/12th was clearly designed as a city-busting exercise for which a force of 341 heavy aircraft was drawn from 1, 3, 5 and 8 Groups. 50 Squadron detailed fifteen Lancasters, which took off between 20.30 and 20.44 with F/Ls Beetham, Blackham and Keith the senior pilots on duty. The bomber stream climbed to between 18,000 and 20,000 feet by the time it reached the Belgian coast at 3 degrees east, and maintained that altitude all the way to the target, where six to ten-tenths thin cloud was encountered at 7,000 to 8,000 feet. Red and green TIs identified the aiming-point, which, for the 50 Squadron crews, was a road bridge, and they bombed from 19,100 to 20,000 feet between 22.42 and 22.58, observing many bomb bursts and fires, which suggested that the attack was accurate. The crews maintained height on the way home until fifty miles from the coast, at which position they began a gentle descent to exit enemy territory at 15,000 feet or above. Reports coming out of Aachen revealed this to be the city's worst experience of the war to date, with extensive damage in central and southern districts, disruption of its transport infrastructure and a death toll of 1,525 people. However, the railway yards had not been destroyed and would require further attention. The operation cost nine Lancasters, ME572 representing 50 Squadron and disappearing without trace with the crew of P/O Skillen RAAF.

On the 14th, the Command became officially subject to the orders coming from the Supreme Headquarters of the Allied Expeditionary Force (SHAEF), under General Dwight D Eisenhower, and would remain thus shackled until the Allied armies were sweeping towards the German frontier at the end of the summer. On the 18th, 83 and 97 Squadrons were loaned to 5 Group from the Pathfinders, on what amounted to a permanent detachment, along with the Mosquito unit, 627 Squadron. The Lancaster units were to become the 5 Group heavy markers, while the Mosquitos would eventually take over the low-level marking role currently in the hands of 617 Squadron. This was a major coup for AVM Cochrane and 5 Group and a bitter blow to AVM Bennett, the Pathfinder Chief. Relations between Cochrane and Bennett had never been cordial, but this plunged them to new depths. Both were brilliant men, Bennett, an Australian, in particular, a man of the greatest intellect, who, despite his total lack of humour, commanded the deepest respect and loyalty from his men. He and Cochrane possessed vastly different opinions on the subject of target marking, Bennett believing that a low-level method exposed the crews to unnecessary danger, while Cochrane insisted that the risks in a fast-flying Mosquito were negligible and would produce greater accuracy. Though 83 and 97 Squadrons were formerly of 5 Group, and, at that time, had undoubtedly considered themselves part of the elite, most of the current crop of crews had come to see 8 Group as the pinnacle, and were upset at being removed from what they considered to be an elevated status. They were fiercely proud to wear the Pathfinder badge and enjoyed the one step-up in rank, but, happily for them, as the squadrons were only officially on loan to 5 Group, these were privileges that they would retain. Any resentment might have been smoothed over had their reception at Coningsby been handled better, but, as the newly arrived crews tumbled out of their transports, they were summoned immediately to the briefing room, to be lectured by the 54 Base commander, Air Commodore "Bobby" Sharp. Rather than welcoming them as brothers-in-arms, he harangued them over their bad 8 Group habits, and ordered them to buckle down to learning 5 Group ways. This was an insult to experienced airmen, for whom the task of illuminating targets for 5 Group would be a piece of cake compared with the complexities of their 8 Group duties. The fact that the insult was being delivered by a pompous, self-important man with no relevant operational experience, made it doubly unpalatable. From this point on, 5 Group would be known in 8 Group circles somewhat disparagingly as the "Independent Air Force", or " The Lincolnshire Poachers".

61 Squadron had returned to Skellingthorpe on the 15th, to make room at Coningsby for the new arrivals, and this would, inevitably, extend the time needed to get both squadrons into the air. The 5 Group target on the 18th was the marshalling yards at Juvisy, situated on the West Bank of the Seine south of Paris, which was one of four similar targets for the night. The intention had been for the new arrivals to participate, but the disgruntled commanding officers, G/C Deane of 83 Squadron and W/C Jimmy Carter of 97 Squadron, announced that they were not yet ready, and the operation would have to go ahead without them. 202 Lancasters and four Mosquitos were made ready, the latter belonging to 617 Squadron, and 8 Group would provide three Oboe Mosquitos to deliver the initial marking. 50 Squadron bombed up eighteen Lancasters with fourteen 1,000 pounders each, and dispatched them from Skellingthorpe between 20.34 and 21.16 with S/L McLeod the senior pilot on duty. All reached the target to find clear skies and ideal bombing conditions, in which they observed W/C Cheshire's red spotfires become backed up by green TIs. Despite black smoke drifting across the aiming-point and upwards from the destruction of a fuel dump at 23.32, the 50 Squadron crews were able to hit the markers from 7,000 to 11,000 between 23.30 and 23.46, and returning crews were enthusiastic about the success of the operation. This was confirmed by post-raid reconnaissance, and prompted the crews to make the valid comment that, to count this operation as just one-third of a sortie, was undervaluing it, a sentiment shared by all whose job involved putting their lives on the line.

Briefings on 5 Group stations for the first operation to include the three newly-transferred squadrons took place on the 20th, when the crews learned that Cologne would host the main operation by elements of 1, 3, 6 and 8 Groups, while they would be involved in a two-phase attack on railway yards at La Chapelle, situated just to the north of Paris. There would be an hour between waves, each with its own specific aiming-point, and 83 Squadron's W/C Deane was to be the Master Bomber with S/L Sparks his deputy. The plan called for 8 Group Mosquitos to drop cascading flares by Oboe to provide an initial reference, and for a Mosquito element from 627 Squadron to lay a Window screen ahead of the main force Lancasters. Once the target had been identified, the first members of the 83 Squadron flare force were to provide illumination for the low-level marker Mosquitos of 617 Squadron, which would mark the first aiming point with red spot fires for the main force element to aim at. The whole procedure would then be repeated at the second aiming point. At Coningsby, W/C Deane conducted the briefing, and, at its conclusion, wished the assembled throng good luck, before dismissing them, whereupon a voice from the back declared that the briefing wasn't over, and that the base and station commanders wanted their say. This had not been standard practice in 8 Group, and left Deane mystified and a little humiliated. The senior officers had only waffle to offer, but it made them feel important, while confirming the first impressions of the crews, that A/C Sharp was a self-important and irrelevant link in the chain of command.

50 Squadron made ready eighteen Lancasters as part of the overall force of 247 Lancasters of 5 Group and twenty-two Mosquitos of 5 and 8 Groups, and departed Skellingthorpe between 22.43 and 23.33 with S/L Chadwick the senior pilot on duty. They were assigned to the second aiming-point, each loaded with a mix of 1,000 and 500 pounders, and, as they made their way to the target, the first-phase element arrived to find largely clear skies, good visibility and only some ground haze to mar the view. Zero hour for the opening phase was set for 00.05, but the Oboe Mosquitos were two minutes late, and some communications problems had to be ironed out before matters began to run smoothly. A large orange explosion at 00.28 sent a column of black smoke skyward, which impaired visibility to some extent, but, the crews were able to identify a red spotfire and bomb it, observing large explosions and fires that were visible to the second phase crews as they approached. Not among these was the crew of F/Sgt Milne, who had lost both starboard engines seven minutes after take-off, and had returned home with their load intact. The others reached the target, where the conditions remained favourable, and red spotfires marked out their aiming-point, which they bombed from 7,300 and 11,000 between 01.20 and 01.37. The fires were still visible for a hundred miles into the return flight, and returning crews expressed confidence that they had contributed to a successful operation. Post-raid reconnaissance confirmed the success of both phases of the operation, which had left the yards severely damaged for the loss of six Lancasters. P/O Lundy and crew concluded their tour with this operation, the effectiveness of which drew a congratulatory message from Cochrane.

The real test for the 5 Group low-level marking system would come at a heavily defended German target, for which Braunschweig was selected on the 22nd, while the rest of the Command targeted the Ruhr city of Düsseldorf. 5 Group put together a force of 238 Lancasters and seventeen Mosquitos, with ten ABC Lancasters of 1 Group's 101 Squadron to provide radio countermeasures. 50 Squadron contributed eighteen Lancasters, which took off between 22.58 and 23.43 with W/C Heward the senior pilot on duty. All of them reached the target area after being guided by route-markers, and found six to eight-tenths thin cloud at between 8,000 and 10,000 feet, and accurate marking by the 617 Squadron Mosquito element. Despite this, the main force crews were unable to properly identify the target, a situation again compounded by communications problems between various controllers, caused by the failure of VHF and the consequent need to pass on instructions instead by W/T. This led to confusion, and many crews were forced to orbit for up to fifteen minutes before bombing. The 50 Squadron crews carried out their attacks on green TIs and red spotfires from 15,000 to 19,000 feet between 01.55 and 02.07, and returned safely to report what appeared to be a successful operation, while also complaining about the dangers of orbiting a target with aircraft heading in a variety of directions. Although some bombs did fall in the city centre, most were directed at reserve H2S-laid TIs to the south of the city, and damage was less severe than might otherwise have been.

When Munich was posted across 5 Group as the target on the 24th for another live test of the low-level visual marking method, it might have been seen as somewhat ambitious to select such a major city, that was protected by two hundred flak guns. The main operation on this night was to be conducted by a force of 637 aircraft against Karlsruhe, 150 miles to the north-west, which would help to distract the night-fighters. 234 Lancasters were made ready by 5 Group, and added to by ten of the ABC variety from 101 Squadron, while four Mosquitos of 617 Squadron were loaded with spotfires to carry out the marking, and twelve of 627 Squadron with Window to dispense during the final approach to the target. 50 Squadron's eighteen Lancasters took to the air between 20.43 and 21.17 with S/L McLeod the senior pilot on duty, and headed for the south coast before setting course across France towards the south-east and feinting towards Italy. The 617 and 627 Squadron Mosquitos took off three hours after the heavy brigade and adopted a direct route, the latter laying a Window screen from high level six minutes from the target, masking the arrival of the flare force that was to provide seven minutes of illumination for the 617 marker Mosquitos. 50 Squadron's excellent record of serviceability continued, as all reached the target area to encounter clear skies and good visibility. W/C Cheshire dived onto the aiming-point in the face of murderous light flak, before racing away across the rooftops to safety. The main force followed hard on his heels, the 50 Squadron crews bombing on the red spotfires and green TIs from 15,000 (S/L McLeod) to 22,000 feet between 01.50 and 02.02 in the face of intense searchlight and flak activity. Many fires were seen to take hold, and, as the bombers pointed their snouts back towards France to eventually pass to the north of Paris, Karlsruhe could be seen burning over to starboard. Post-raid reconnaissance and local reports confirmed the success of the raid, which left 1,104 buildings in ruins and a further thirteen hundred severely damaged. It was probably this operation that sealed the award to Cheshire of the Victoria Cross at the conclusion of his operational career of one hundred sorties. ND876 was the 50 Squadron representative among the nine missing Lancasters, and was brought down by flak over the target, killing F/O Durham and his crew.

At briefing on the 26th, seventeen 50 Squadron crews were told, that Schweinfurt was to be their target that night, after the failure of the RAF to destroy it in February and the American 8th Air Force just two weeks ago. The tone was very much, "leave it to RAF Bomber Command", and, with the satisfaction of Munich still fresh in the mind, and the natural rivalry between the two forces, such attitudes were to be expected. They learned that, for this operation, 627 Squadron would act as the low-level marker force for the first time, and for a main force of 215 Lancasters, including nine from 101 Squadron to provide RCM protection. This was just one of three major operations taking place, the main event being at Essen, while the railway yards at Villeneuve-St-Georges were being attended to by a predominantly Halifax main force. The 50 Squadron crews took off between 21.18 and 21.47, with S/L Chadwick the senior pilot on duty, but lost the services of P/O Wort and crew over Reading when the pilot became unwell. The others encountered stronger-than-forecast head winds, which delayed the arrival in the target area of the heavy brigade. They found generally clear skies and good visibility, which the 627 Squadron crews failed to exploit, as their debut marking effort proved to be inaccurate. The 83 Squadron crews remarked on the lack of illumination, and those carrying hooded flares were called in a number of times to back-up. The 50 Squadron crews bombed from 14,250 to 21,000 between 02.26 and 02.55, aiming at red spotfires and green TIs, some following the instructions of the Master Bomber to overshoot by a thousand yards. A large white explosion was witnessed at 02.29, and many fires were reported, but, once again at this target, most of the hardware fell outside of the target area, leaving this centre of ball-bearing production more or less unscathed. Night-fighters got amongst the heavy force, and twenty-one Lancasters were shot down, a hefty 9.3%,

5 Group made preparations on the 28th to send a force of eighty-eight Lancasters and four Mosquitos to attack the Alfred Nobel Dynamit A.G explosives works at St-Médard-en-Jalles, situated in a wood on the north-western outskirts of Bordeaux in south-western France. Sixteen 50 Squadron Lancasters departed Skellingthorpe between 22.46 and 23.25 with W/C Heward the senior pilot on duty, each loaded with a mix of 1,000 and 500 pounders, some of the former of American manufacture. They all arrived in the target area to find clear skies, but some flares had landed in a nearby wood, causing volumes of smoke to drift across the factory and obscure it from view. F/L Blackham, F/Os Botha and Mouat and P/O Berry delivered their bombs from 4,250 to 5,000 feet between 02.59 and 03.28, along with twenty-two aircraft from other squadrons, before the Master Bomber called a halt at 03.30, and instructed the remaining crews to take their bombs home. Despite that last instruction, W/C Heward jettisoned his load, while most of the others complied and returned all or most of their bombs to store.

The operation was rescheduled for the following night, when the Michelin tyre factory at Clermont-Ferrand was added to the target list. Sixty-eight Lancasters were assigned to the explosives works and fifty-four to the tyre factory, with five 627 Squadron Mosquitos at each to provide the low-level marking. The 50 Squadron element of thirteen took off for the former between 22.30 and 22.56 with F/Ls Beetham and Blackham the senior pilots on duty, and all reached the target area to be met by clear skies and haze. The aiming-point was identified both visually and by red spotfires and red and green TIs, which could be seen burning between factory buildings, and the 50 Squadron crews bombed them from 4,250 to 5,750 feet between 02.25 and 02.33, in accordance with instructions from the Master Bomber. P/O Mouat and crew suffered the frustration of a hang-up, and had to bring the entire load home. All returned safely to Skellingthorpe, filled with enthusiasm at the explosions that had ripped the site apart, and some crews commented that it was the most destructive attack they had taken part in. Post-raid reconnaissance confirmed that both targets had been severely damaged with a massive loss of production. During the course of the month the squadron participated in ten operations, and dispatched 152 sorties for the loss of two Lancasters and crews.

May 1944

Eleven 50 Squadron crews were called to briefing at Skellingthorpe on the 1st, to learn that they would be going to southern France that night to attack a SNCASE aircraft assembly factory at Saint-Martin-du-Touch, a western suburb of Toulouse. They would be part of two 5 Group forces totalling 131 Lancasters and eight Mosquitos sent to the city, the other to target the Proudrerie explosives works, while a third 5 Group force of forty-six Lancasters and four Mosquitos went for an aircraft repair workshop at Tours in western France. The 50 Squadron crews took off between 21.31 and 21.50 with F/Ls Beetham and Blackham the senior pilots on duty, and all reached the target to find moonlight, clear skies and excellent visibility. They were able to identify the target visually, aided by the illumination of flares and confirmed by red spotfires on the aiming-point, and carried out their attacks from 5,000 to 7,000 feet between 01.30 and 01.55 in accordance with the instructions of the Master Bomber. The attack was clearly focussed on the aiming-point, where the main assembly shop and the boiler house were observed to be hit, and a large explosion occurred, although the fire was less extensive than anticipated as they withdrew to the north. All crews returned to their respective stations confident of a successful outcome, and post-raid reconnaissance revealed all three factories to have been heavily damaged.

Briefings took place on 1 and 5 Group stations on the 3rd, for what would become a highly contentious operation that night against a Panzer training camp and transport depot at Mailly-le-Camp, situated some seventy-five miles east of Paris in north-eastern France. The units based there posed a potential threat to Allied forces as the invasion unfolded, and needed to be eliminated. The events of the operation proved to be so controversial, that recriminations abound to this day concerning the 5 Group leadership provided by W/Cs Cheshire and Deane. Although the grudges by 1 Group aircrew against them can be understood in the light of what happened, they are unjust, and based on emotion and incorrect information, and it is worthwhile to examine the conduct of the operation in some detail. W/C Cheshire was appointed as marker leader, and was piloting one of four 617 Squadron Mosquitos, while 83 Squadron's commanding officer, W/C Deane, was overall raid controller, with S/L Sparks as Deputy. Deane and Cheshire attended separate briefings, and neither seemed aware of the complete plan, particularly the role of the 1 Group Special Duties Flight from Binbrook, which was assigned to mark its own specific aiming point for an element of the 1 Group force.

The eleven 50 Squadron participants became airborne between 21.47 and 22.07 with F/L Blackham the senior pilot on duty, and all reached the target area to find clear skies, moonlight and excellent bombing conditions, but confusion already beginning to influence events. 617 Squadron's W/C Cheshire and S/L Shannon were in position before midnight, and as the first flares from the 83 and 97 Squadron Lancasters illuminated the target below, Cheshire released his two red spot fires onto the first aiming point at 00.00½ from 1,500 feet. Shannon backed them up from 400 feet five and a half minutes later, and, as far as Cheshire was concerned, the operation was bang on schedule at this stage. A 97 Squadron Lancaster also laid markers accurately, to ensure a constant focal point, and Cheshire passed instructions to Deane to call the bombers in. It was at this stage of the operation, that matters began to go awry. A communications problem arose, when a commercial radio station, believed to be an American forces network, jammed the VHF frequencies in use. Deane called in the 5 Group element, elated that everything was proceeding according to plan, but nothing happened. He checked with his wireless operator that the instructions had been transmitted, and called up S/L Sparks, who was also mystified by the lack of bombing. A few crews from 9, 207 and 467 Squadrons had heard the call to bomb, and did so, but, for most, the instructions were swamped by the interference. 50 Squadron's F/Sgt Laidlaw reported an American news broadcast jamming the signal, but he, W/O Mason and P/O Bucknell received instructions and bombed at 00.10, 00.12 and 00.13 respectively from 8,000 to 7,750 and 5,750 feet as W/C Deane attempted to control the operation by W/T, which also failed. The remaining 50 Squadron crews bombed from 5,250 to 7,500 feet between 00.29 and 00.33, by which time, palls of smoke were drifting across the site. S/L Blome-Jones of 207 Squadron described the situation as a complete shambles and chaos, the controller as inefficient and the discipline of some crews as bad. Others voiced the opinion that this was a trip worthy of more than one-third of a sortie.

Post raid reports are contradictory, and it is impossible to establish an accurate course of events, particularly when Deane and Cheshire's understanding of the exact time of zero hour differed by five minutes. Remarkably, it also seems, that Deane was unaware that there were two marking points, or three, if one includes 1 Group's Special Duties Flight. Cheshire, initially at least, appeared happy with the early stages of the attack, and described the bombing as concentrated and accurate. It seems certain, however, that many minutes had passed between the dropping of Cheshire's markers and the first main force bombs falling, during which period, Deane was coming to terms with the fact, that his instructions were not getting through. A plausible scenario is, that in the absence of instructions, and with red spot fires clearly visible in the target, some crews opted to bomb, and others followed suit. These would have been predominantly from 5 Group, but as the 1 Group crews became increasingly agitated at having to wait in bright moonlight, with evidence of enemy night fighters all around, some of them inevitably joined in.

Now a new problem was arising. Smoke from these first salvoes was obliterating the entire camp, and Cheshire had to decide whether or not to send in Fawke and Kearns to mark the second aiming point. His feeling, and that of Deane, as it later transpired, was, that it was unnecessary. The volume of bombs still to fall into the relatively compact area of the target, would ensure destruction of the entire site. By 00.16, the first phase of bombing should have been completed, leaving a clear run for Fawke and Kearns across the target. In the event, the majority of 5 Group crews were still on their bombing run, a fact unknown to Cheshire, who asked Deane for a pause in the bombing, while the two Mosquitos went in. As far as Cheshire was concerned, there was no response from Deane, who would, anyway, have been confused by mention of a second aiming point. In the event, Deane's deputy, S/L Sparks, eventually found a channel free of interference, and did, in fact, transmit an instruction to halt the bombing, both by W/T and R/T, and some crews reported hearing something. While utter chaos reigned, Kearns and Fawke dived in among the falling cookies at 00.23 and 00.25 respectively, to mark the second aiming point on the western edge of the camp. At 2,000 feet, they were lucky to survive the turbulence created by the exploding 4,000 pounders, when 4,000 feet was considered to be a minimum safe height. They were not entirely happy with their work, but F/O Edwards of 97 Squadron dropped a stick of markers precisely on the mark, and S/L Sparks was then able to call the 1 Group main force in. Meanwhile, the night fighters continued to create havoc among the Lancasters, as they milled around in the target area, and, as burning aircraft were seen to fall all around, some 1 Group crews succumbed to their anxiety and frustration. In a rare breakdown of R/T discipline, let fly with comments of an uncomplimentary nature, many of which were intended for, and, indeed, heard by Deane.

Despite everything, the operation was a major success, which destroyed 80% of the camp's buildings, and 102 vehicles, of which thirty-seven were tanks, while over two hundred men were killed. Forty-two Lancasters failed to return, however, two thirds of them from 1 Group, and 50 Squadron was 5 Group's most afflicted unit with four Lancasters and crews unaccounted for. It would be learned in time that ND953 had been an early victim, intercepted as it passed some twenty miles north-east of Paris outbound, and shot down to crash at Marigny-en-Orxois with four crew members still on board. P/O Dobson, his flight engineer and navigator survived, and soon found themselves in enemy hands. ED870 was bearing down on the aiming-point from the north-east, when shot down to crash at Poivres, killing the eight occupants captained by P/O Handley. LM437 and just released its bombs when brought down at Trouan-le-Petit, killing P/O Hanson and all but the wireless operator, who evaded capture. Finally, LM480 was homebound with the eight-man crew of F/L Blackham DFC, when shot down to crash between Troyes and Romilly-sur-Seine, south-east of Paris, killing six of the occupants. The pilot and bomb-aimer survived, and both managed to evade capture, the latter joining up with a Resistance group only to lose his life in June during an attack by the Wehrmacht on their camp. F/L Blackham was captured eventually, and ended up at the infamous Buchenwald concentration camp. On the following day, an inquest into the conduct of the raid revealed that the wireless transmitter in Deane's Lancaster had been sufficiently off frequency to allow the interference from the American network to mask the transmission of instructions and prevent the call to bomb from reaching the main force crews. The 1 Group A-O-C, AVM Rice, decided he would not participate in further operations organized by 5 Group, which was probably not a blow to Cochrane, who was confident that his group did not need back-up.

On the 6th, 1 and 5 Groups were invited to send a modest force each to attack ammunition dumps in France, 5 Group detailing sixty-four Lancasters and four Mosquitos for a site at Louailles, situated some four miles south-east of the town of Sable-sur-Sarthe, south west of Le-Mans. 50 Squadron put up eleven Lancasters, each loaded with eleven 1,000 pounders and four 500 pounders, which departed Skellingthorpe between 00.31 and 01.14 on the 7th with W/C Heward the senior pilot on duty. All reached the target to find clear skies and excellent visibility, and a Master Bomber on hand to direct the attack once the red spotfires had been delivered by the low-level Mosquitos. His assessment was that the markers had fallen fifty yards north of the aiming-point, and his instruction was to bomb fifty yards to the south on a northerly heading. The crews complied from 3,250 to 7,000 feet between 02.47 and 02.54, and observed numerous bomb flashes that lit up long sheds, and two enormous explosions that each resulted in a large mushroom of smoke rising through 3,000 feet as the force withdrew.

Five small-scale operations were mounted on the night of the 7/8th, against airfields, ammunition dumps and a coastal battery, all in support of the coming invasion. 5 Group was involved in two raids, the airfield at Tours and an ammunition dump at Salbris, some sixty miles to the east. 50 Squadron was not called upon to take part, on what turned out to be another night of perfect conditions, and both targets were bombed accurately and effectively to leave them severely damaged. Another small-scale operation was mounted by the group on the 8th against the airfield and seaplane base at Lanveoc-Poulmic, located on the northern side of the peninsular forming the southern boundary of the L'Elorn estuary opposite Brest. A force of fifty-eight Lancasters and six Mosquitos included eleven of the former provided by 50 Squadron, and they took off between 21.22 and 21.40 with S/L Chadwick the senior pilot on duty. Each carried a cookie and sixteen 500 pounders, which all reached the destination, where the target was easily identified by the coastline and hangars. Bombing was carried out from 7,000 to 9,500 feet between 23.59 and 00.08, and hangars and other buildings were seen to be on fire and enveloped in smoke at the conclusion of the attack.

The night of the 9/10th brought attacks on seven coastal batteries in the Pas-de-Calais by four hundred aircraft. The purpose of these operations was to confirm in the mind of the enemy the belief that the Allied invasion forces would land at Calais, and right up to D-Day itself, the coastal region between Gravelines to the east of the port and Berck-sur-Mer to the south-west, would be subjected to constant bombardment. 5 Group, meanwhile, prepared fifty-six Lancasters and eight Mosquitos to attack two factories, the Gnome & Rhône aero-engine works and another unspecified one at Gennevilliers in northern Paris, while a second force of thirty-nine Lancasters and four Mosquitos targeted a small ball-bearing factory at Annecy, situated in south-eastern France close to the frontiers with Switzerland and Italy. 50 Squadron was not called into action on this night, but those entrusted with the responsibility claimed to have produced accurate bombing at both sites, and post-raid reconnaissance confirmed the Annecy site to have been severely damaged.

Five railway targets were selected for attention on the 10/11th, among them the marshalling yards at Lille for 5 Group, for which 50 Squadron contributed fifteen Lancasters. They departed Skellingthorpe between 21.42 and 22.16 with W/C Heward the senior pilot on duty, but lost the services of P/O Slywchuk to rear-turret failure before crossing the coast. The others found the target area to be under clear skies, with the aiming-point slightly obscured by ground haze, but this was a situation easily negated by red spotfires and green TIs, and bombing took place in the light of flares from 8,000 to 10,000 feet between 23.54 and 00.07. Bomb bursts were seen across the tracks, and two large explosions were observed to confirm a successful assault on this important hub linking north-eastern France with Belgium. Night-fighters were out in force, and most of the night's casualties resulted from the attack at Lille, from which a dozen Lancasters failed to return. 50 Squadron was represented by NN694, which crashed with great force five miles east of Lille, right on the frontier, and LM429, which came down on the Belgian side ten miles north-west of Ypres, with no survivors from the crews of W/O Mason DFC and P/O McFarlin respectively.

5 Group put together a force of 190 Lancasters and eight Mosquitos on the 11th, to target a military camp at Bourg-Leopold in north-eastern Belgium, for which 50 Squadron made ready fifteen Lancasters, dispatching them between 22.04 and 22.36 with S/L Chadwick the senior pilot on duty. There were no early returns, and all from the squadron reached the target to find hazy conditions and a little thin cloud at around 10,000 feet, despite which, they would be able to identify ground detail in the form of buildings and huts in the light of illuminating flares. Three Oboe Mosquitos were on hand to deliver the initial marking, but wrongly-forecast winds caused the 83 Squadron element to arrive late, by which time the main force crews had begun to orbit to await instructions. A communications problem prevented some crews from hearing the Master Bomber's broadcasts, but the aiming-point could be seen to be marked by red spotfires and green TIs. From the Master Bomber's perspective, the initial Oboe marker had been visible only to a few crews, and quickly burned out, and so he called for another Mosquito to drop a red spot fire onto the aiming point. Before this was accomplished, however, the main force began to bomb, and nine 50 Squadron crews were among ninety-four to release their loads, doing so from 14,500 and 17,000 feet between 00.15 and 00.33. As smoke began to obscure the ground, the Master Bomber, S/L Mitchell, quickly became uncomfortable about the close proximity of civilian residential property, and called a halt to the bombing at 00.35, before sending the rest of the force home, some of them after circling for more than twenty minutes.

The station teleprinters were working overtime on the 19th, as orders came through for five operations against marshalling yards, two against coastal batteries and one against a radar station. 5 Group detailed 225 Lancasters, 112 to be sent to Amiens with eight Mosquitos, and 113 for Tours with four Mosquitos, the 50 Squadron element of nineteen assigned to the latter. A previous attack by 5 Group had targeted the installations on the outskirts of the town, while this night's effort was directed at those in the central district between the rivers Loire to the north and La Cher to the south. They departed Skellingthorpe between 23.08 and 23.28 with S/L McLeod the senior pilot on duty, and set course for north-western France, where they found clear skies and visibility good enough to identify ground detail. The aiming-point was marked by red spotfires, and, in view of the close proximity of civilian housing, the

Master Bomber took great care and much time before issuing the order to bomb. This would extend the time on target, but, fortunately, the Luftwaffe was absent, and the bombing by the 50 Squadron element was carried out from 5,000 to 7,250 feet between 00.47 to 00.56 in accordance with instructions. F/L Keith and P/O Berry failed to receive the W/T broadcasts and withheld their loads, but the accuracy of the bombing by the others was sufficient to cause massive damage to the target, with only a little collateral damage. There were no losses, but while attempting to land at Benson in Oxfordshire on return, ND989 hit a barn and crashed at 04.20 crashed on the east-south-eastern side of Wallingford, killing P/O Irving and two of his crew and injuring the others. At Amiens, the target was found to be shrouded in a layer of eight to ten-tenths cloud between 6,000 and 11,000 feet, and only thirty-seven aircraft had bombed when instructions came through by W/T at 01.25 to terminate the attack and return home.

For the first time in a year, Duisburg was posted as the target for a heavy raid on the 21st, for which a force of 510 Lancasters was drawn from 1, 3, 5 and 8 Groups. They would be supported by twenty-two Mosquitos, and, while this operation was in progress, seventy Lancasters, including some from 5 Group, and thirty-seven Halifaxes would undertake gardening duties in the Nectarines and Rosemary gardens of the North Sea around the Frisians and off Heligoland, and in the Silverthorn and Quince gardens in the Kattegat and Kiel Bay regions of the Baltic. 50 Squadron would support only the main event, for which seventeen Lancasters were made ready and dispatched from Skellingthorpe between 22.14 and 22.47 with S/L Chadwick the senior pilot on duty. Crews had been told at briefing to adhere to the plan for the outward route, which involved a few aircraft from 3 Group gaining height as they adopted a north-westerly course as far as Sleaford, so as not to cross into enemy radar cover earlier than necessary. The groups would rendezvous at 18,000 feet over the North Sea at 3 degrees east to cross the enemy coast at 20,000 feet and climb to 22,000 or 23,000 feet, before increasing speed for the run across the target. All of the 50 Squadron participants reached the Ruhr, which they found to be concealed beneath ten-tenths cloud with tops at between 11,000 and 20,000 feet, into which the red-with-yellow-stars Wanganui markers fell almost before they could be seen. A number of crews commented on the data provided by the windfinder system to be inaccurate, and this made it a challenge to establish positions. The 50 Squadron crews used the explosion of cookies, the glow of fires and the evidence of intense flak as references, and bombed from 18,250 to 22,000 feet between 01.10 and 01.30, before returning home with little useful information to report. The loss of twenty-nine Lancasters was a reminder to the Command that the Ruhr remained a dangerous destination, although most of the missing had come down onto Dutch and Belgian soil or into the sea homebound, after falling victim to night-fighters. Martin Drewes of III./NJG1 alone accounted for at least three Lancasters. 50 Squadron's ME979, was brought down by flak, and crashed west-south-west of Krefeld on the way home, and there were no survivors from the crew of F/O Amphlett. Returning crews were not enthusiastic about the outcome, and post-raid reconnaissance confirmed that a modest 350 buildings had been destroyed in the southern half of Duisburg, and 665 others had been seriously damaged.

Just like Duisburg, Dortmund was posted on the 22nd to host its first large-scale visit from the Command for a year, and would face an all-Lancaster heavy force of 361 aircraft drawn from 1, 3, 6 and 8 Groups. While this operation was in progress, 220 Lancasters of 5 Group and five from 101 Squadron were to target Braunschweig, which, thus far, had evaded severe damage at the hands of the Command. 50 Squadron made ready sixteen Lancasters, which departed Skellingthorpe between 22.12 and 22.47 with F/Ls Botha, Keith and Startin the senior pilots on duty. P/O Wood and crew were over northern Holland, approaching the German frontier, when a starboard-outer engine issue ended their sortie, while F/L Botha and crew were experiencing navigation difficulties, and identified the Münster area by its defensive activity, before unloading the contents of their bomb bay onto it. The others pressed on through the clearly evident night-fighter activity from the Dutch coast all the way to the target, and negotiated the patches of ten-tenths cloud over northern Germany, and intense searchlight activity as they passed between Bremen and Osnabrück. The forecast at briefings had suggested clear skies over Braunschweig, but, in fact, the marker force encountered four to seven-tenths drifting cloud with tops up to 7,000 feet. Although highly effective in the right weather conditions, the 5 Group low-level visual marking method could easily be rendered ineffective by cloud cover. The blind heavy markers dropped skymarkers by H2S, while the 627 Squadron Mosquito element went in at low level to release red spotfires. Some crews described "hopeless confusion" with flares and incendiaries spread over a distance, and many had to rely on their own H2S to establish their position. Some found a complete absence of marking, and orbited for up to fifteen minutes until a few green TIs appeared, and bombing by the 50 Squadron element took place on these or on incendiary fires from 19,000 to 21,500 feet between 01.10 and 01.37. Considerable interference over R/T communications added to the problems, and, although the Master Bomber could be heard in discussions with his Deputies, no instructions were received from him, and the attack lacked cohesion. Post-raid reconnaissance confirmed that most of the bombing had fallen onto outlying communities, confirming in the minds of the residents that this was an intentional ploy by the Command. It was a relatively expensive failure that cost thirteen Lancasters, and among them was 50 Squadron's LL744, which is presumed to have crashed into the North Sea on the way home, taking with it the crew of F/L Startin RAAF.

The main operation on the 24th would involve 442 aircraft in an attack on two marshalling yards at Aachen, Aachen-West and Rothe-Erde in the east. As the most westerly city in Germany, sitting on the frontiers of both Holland and Belgium, it was a major link in the railway network that would be a route for reinforcements to the Normandy battle front. Other operations on this night would be directed at coastal batteries in the Pas-de-Calais and war-industry factories in Holland and Belgium. 5 Group detailed forty-four Lancasters to attack the Ford motor works in Antwerp, and fifty-nine for the Philips electronics factory at Eindhoven in southern Holland, and it was for the latter that 50 Squadron made ready nine Lancasters and dispatched them from Skellingthorpe between 22.54 and 23.14 with S/L McLeod the senior pilot on duty. They were more than an hour into the outward journey when the Master Bomber sent them home by W/T, presumably after a Met Flight Mosquito crew had found poor visibility in the target area. There were no such difficulties at Antwerp, where the target was identified by illuminating flares, a yellow TI and red spotfires, despite which, post-raid reconnaissance revealed the factory to be intact.

The night of the 26/27th was devoted to minor operations, including mining off the Occupied coasts by forty-two aircraft including some representing 5 Group, but none from 50 Squadron, which stayed at home. The night of the 27/28th was to be one of feverish activity, which would generate more than eleven hundred sorties and reflected the close proximity of the invasion, now just ten days away. The largest operation would bring a return to the military camp at Bourg Leopold in Belgium, the previous attack on which, two weeks earlier, had been abandoned part-way through. There was also a repeat of the Aachen attack of the 24th, which had failed to destroy the Rothe-Erde marshalling yards at the eastern end of the city and needed further attention. 5 Group was not involved in either of the above, and, instead, prepared forces of 100 Lancasters and four Mosquitos and seventy-eight Lancasters and five Mosquitos respectively to target marshalling yards and workshops at Nantes and the aerodrome at Rennes, situated some fifty miles apart in north-western France. The group would also support operations against coastal batteries, of which there were five on this night, but it was for Nantes that fifteen 50 Squadron Lancasters departed Skellingthorpe between 22.22 and 22.59 with S/L McLeod the senior pilot on duty. They all reached the target area to find clear skies and good visibility, and the aiming-point marked by red spotfires, and the first fifty aircraft bombed so accurately, that the Master Bomber was satisfied and called a halt to proceedings. Seven of the 50 Squadron element were among those delivering their bombs, doing so from 8,000 to 10,000 feet between 01.37 and 01.53.

On the 28th, 181 Lancasters and twenty Mosquitos were made ready to attack three coastal batteries overlooking the Normandy beaches, which, a week hence, would be the scene of Operation Overlord. The target for the eleven Lancasters of 50 Squadron was at Sainte-Martin-de-Varrevilles, situated close to what would be Utah Beach, the landing ground for the American 1st Division. They departed Skellingthorpe between 22.32 and 22.51 with no senior pilots on duty, and each carrying fifteen SAP and GP 1,000 pounders of American manufacture, all of which reached the target under clear skies and in excellent visibility. The aiming-point was marked by red spotfires backed up by green TIs, and bombing took place from 6,500 to 9,000 feet between 00.24 and 00.41 in accordance with the instructions of a Master Bomber. Bomb bursts were observed close to the markers, and a large explosion occurred at 00.29, which suggested a successful conclusion to the operation, as far as that was possible at such difficult-to-eliminate targets.

On the 31st, S/L McLeod and crew were posted to 97 Squadron to join the ranks of the Pathfinders, but still within 5 Group. That night, 5 Group sent a force of eighty-two Lancasters and four Mosquitos to attack a railway junction at Saumur in the Loire Valley, and another of sixty-eight Lancasters to a coastal battery at Maisy, overlooking Omaha Beach. It was for the former that 50 Squadron prepared seventeen Lancasters, and they took off between 23.13 and 23.47 with S/L Chadwick the senior pilot on duty. They had to fly through a belt of storm-bearing clouds as they passed over Norfolk, heading south, during which, P/O Balance and crew were thrown off course and turned back, as did F/L Botha and crew for a similar reason. They were joined on the ground by F/O Long and crew, whose bomb-sight had become unserviceable. The others managed to negotiate the violent thunderstorm, and reached the target to find clear skies and good visibility, and orbited to await the instructions of the Master Bomber. P/Os Davis, Milne and Gilmour and F/L Keith carried out their attacks from 7,250 and 8,250 between 02.31 and 02.34, before a "stand-by" order was received, followed a few minutes later by "return to base". This operation was deemed to be a success, but cloud over the Maisy site caused the abandonment of the attack after just six crews had bombed. During the course of the month the squadron carried out thirteen operations, and dispatched 178 sorties for the loss of nine Lancasters, eight crews, a pilot and two airmen.

June 1944

June was to be a hectic month which would make great demands on the crews. The bombing of coastal batteries was to be the priority during the first few days of June leading up to D-

Day, but 5 Group would open its account by returning to Saumur to attack a second railway junction on the 1st. The day dawned cloudy and cold, and these conditions would persist throughout the first week of the month, causing concern among the invasion planners. 50 Squadron remained at home, while fifty-eight Lancasters took off in the late evening to find ten-tenths cloud covering the route out to within twenty miles of the town, where it dispersed completely to leave clear skies and good visibility under a three-quarter moon. The flare force was almost superfluous in the conditions, but the first wave was called in by the Master Bomber, W/C Jeudwine, to release from 15,000 feet at 01.08, and the first red spot fire from an Oboe Mosquito fell bang on the aiming-point two minutes later. Smoke became a problem as it drifted across the area to obscure the spotfire that was still burning, and a green TI was dropped to maintain the aiming-point. Apart from a few scattered sticks to the north, and on an island in the Loire to the south, the attack seemed to be accurate. Returning crews reported little opposition, fires in the yards and a large explosion at 01.35, and the success of the raid was confirmed by photo-reconnaissance, which showed severe damage to the track.

S/L Cole arrived from 5 LFS on the 3rd to fulfil the role of flight commander, while fifteen 50 Squadron crews were among those called to briefing at Skellingthorpe. They were told that they would be joining eighty-six other Lancasters of the group in an attack on a listening station at Ferme-d'Urville, situated on the Cherbourg peninsular to the west of the port, which had escaped damage when attacked by Halifaxes two nights earlier. They took off between 22.42 and 23.18 with F/L Botha the senior pilot on duty, and all reached the target area to find clear skies and good visibility apart from ground haze. The first of three Oboe Mosquitos dropped a red TI at 00.50, and this was followed by a second one seven minutes later, and these were supplemented shortly afterwards by green TIs from the heavy marker aircraft. The 50 Squadron crews carried out their bombing from 6,000 and 9,250 feet between 01.02 and 01.08, and returned to report a successful attack that had been focussed in a five-hundred-yard radius of the aiming-point. Photographic reconnaissance confirmed that the listening station had ceased to exist.

Orders came through on the 4th to prepare for attacks that night on coastal batteries, three in the Pas-de-Calais to maintain the deception, and the one at Maisy, overlooking the Utah and Omaha beaches. 259 aircraft of 1, 4, 5, 6 and 8 Groups were made ready, the majority for the deception targets, while fifty-two of the Lancasters, all representing 5 Group, were assigned to Maisy. 50 Squadron was not involved in these pre-dawn attacks, which took place through ten-tenths cloud with a base at around 4,000 feet. This necessitated the use of Oboe skymarkers, and positions were confirmed by Gee-fix and a faint red glow, before the bombing was carried out from just above the cloud tops. It was impossible to assess the outcome, and similar cloudy conditions had thwarted two of the three attempts in the Pas-de-Calais.

The night of the 5/6th was D-Day Eve, and, during the course of the night, a record number of 1,211 sorties would be flown against coastal defences and in support and diversionary operations. Sixteen 50 Squadron crews attended briefing at Skellingthorpe, where no direct reference was made to the invasion, but, unusually, they were given strict altitudes at which to fly, and were told not to jettison bombs over the sea. They also learned, that they would be among more than a thousand aircraft targeting ten heavy gun batteries along the Normandy coast, and that their specific objective was at Sainte-Pierre-du-Mont, which, although not disclosed to them, was the closest to Omaha Beach. The plan called for 5 Group to provide

115 Lancasters and four Mosquitos, among which would be a 97 Squadron presence of seventeen Lancasters, led by W/C Carter, to provide the illumination and marking. 50 Squadron loaded its Lancasters with a mixture of 1,000 and 500 pounders, and launched them from Skellingthorpe between 02.25 and 03.02 with no senior pilots on duty. They all arrived in the target area to find a layer of ten-tenths cloud with a base at around 7,000 feet and tops at 12,000 feet, with broken cloud below. The first Oboe marker was late and landed just off the shore, but others were accurate and were backed up by red and green TIs, before the 50 Squadron crews bombed from 6,000 to 12,000 feet between 04.48 and 05.00. Any homeward-bound crews looking down through the occasional gaps in the clouds were rewarded by the incredible sight of the greatest armada in history, ploughing its way sedately southwards towards the French coast. A total of five thousand tons of bombs was dropped during the night, and this was a new record. Those returning to Skellingthorpe reported that the bombing appeared to be concentrated around the markers, but there was little else to say. Only seven aircraft failed to return from these operations, three of them from Sainte-Pierre, two from 97 Squadron, including the one containing W/C "Jimmy" Carter and seven highly experienced others, all but one of whom held either a DFC or DFM. 50 Squadron's ND874 was among the missing, and almost certainly came down in the sea. P/O Ward and five of his crew perished, while the mid-upper gunner was reported to have been rescued and brought home to recover in hospital.

As the beachheads were being established during the course of the 6th, preparations were put in hand to support the ground forces by attacking nine road and railway communications centres through which the enemy could bring reinforcements. 5 Group was assigned to two targets, Argentan supply depot and railway centre located some thirty miles south-east of Caen, and a road bridge in Caen itself, for which forces of 112 Lancasters and six Mosquitos and 120 Lancasters and four Mosquitos respectively were assembled. 50 Squadron made ready seventeen Lancasters for the former, and they departed Skellingthorpe between 23.20 and 23.54 with S/L Chadwick the senior pilot on duty. All reached the target area to find ten-tenths cloud with a base at 5,000 to 6,000 feet, below which, red spotfires and red TIs could be seen marking out the aiming-point. The 50 Squadron crews bombed from 3,000 to 6,000 feet between 01.28 and 01.43, in accordance with the Master Bomber's instructions, and observed a large explosion at 01.33, other bomb bursts and a number of fires. Six Lancasters failed to return from the Caen raid, and this resulted largely from the need for the force to orbit while the markers were assessed. Post-raid reconnaissance confirmed severe damage to the railway installations and the town at Argentan.

Four railway targets were earmarked for attention by a force of 337 aircraft on the 7th, while elements of 5 Group were being prepared to join forces with 1 and 8 Groups to attack a six-way road junction at Balleroy, situated fifteen miles west of Caen on the approach to the Foret-de-Cerisy, where it was believed the enemy was concealing a fuel dump and tank units. 50 Squadron was not involved in the operation, which took place in conditions of ten-tenths cloud with a base at 8,000 to 10,000 feet and haze below. The initial Oboe markers appeared to be accurate and on time, but another marker fell simultaneously some five miles to the south-west and attracted some bomb loads. The Master Bomber quickly gained control of the situation and directed the bombing to the correct marker, which was pounded by concentrated bombing. Dense clouds of black smoke and one particularly large explosion were evidence of a successful outcome, during which the gunners in the crew of the 207 Squadron commanding officer shot down three enemy fighters in a twenty-minute period.

The night of the 8/9th was devoted to the disruption of railway communications, for which 483 aircraft were detailed and assigned to five centres. Orders were received at Skellingthorpe for 50 Squadron to prepare seventeen Lancasters as part of a 5 Group force of ninety-seven Lancasters and four Mosquitos to attack railway installations at Rennes in Brittany, while a second force of fifty-four Lancasters and four Mosquitos went for a similar target at Pontabault, thirty miles to the north-east. 617 Squadron would also operate on this night to deliver the very first Barnes Wallis-designed 12,000lb Tallboy earthquake bombs against the railway tunnel at Saumur. The 50 Squadron element took off between 22.39 and 23.21 with F/L Keith the senior pilot on duty, and all reached the target area to encounter ten-tenths thin cloud with a base at 6,000 to 7,000 feet. F/O Long and crew must have been within sight of the French coast when their compasses let them down, and they had to turn back. The aiming-point was marked by red spotfires and red and green TIs, and bombed by the rest of the squadron from 4,500 to 10,000 feet between 01.34 and 01.52. Returning crews reported concentrated bombing on or near the markers, and the target area becoming obscured by smoke and dust as they withdrew. Not at debriefing was the crew of P/O Gilmour, who all lost their lives when LL841 crashed in the general target area.

401 aircraft from 1, 4, 6 and 8 Groups were detailed on the 9th to target airfields in the battle area, while 5 Group concentrated on a railway junction at Etampes, south of Paris. 108 Lancasters and four Mosquitos took part, while 50 Squadron stayed at home. Those reaching the target found eight to ten-tenths cloud with a base at 8,000 feet, and patches of two to three-tenths lower down at 4,000 feet, but this had had no effect on the marking with red spotfires, backed up with green and yellow TIs and illumination flares. Some crews thought that they had picked up a recall signal, and others a message at around midnight to orbit, until being called in to bomb. The Master Bomber called an end to bombing at 00.17, after what appeared to be a successful operation for the loss of six Lancasters. Photo-reconnaissance confirmed that all tracks had been cut for a distance of four hundred yards to the north-east of the junction, but it revealed also that the town had sustained collateral damage, which caused many civilian casualties.

5 Group detailed 108 Lancasters and four Mosquitos on the 10th, and briefed the crews for an attack on a railway junction at Orleans, situated some thirty miles south-west of Paris. 50 Squadron made ready sixteen Lancasters, which departed Skellingthorpe between 22.14 and 22.44 with S/L Cole first away and the senior pilot on duty for the first time. P/O Peters and crew were over Cambridgeshire when a number of instruments on the pilot's panel began to play up and bring an end to their sortie. The others reached northern France to find clear skies and good visibility, and the aiming-point marked by red spotfires and green TIs, which they bombed from 4,000 to 7,750 feet between 00.42 and 00.54. P/O Davis was about to start his bombing run at 00.54, when the Master Bomber called a halt and sent them home to return their bombs to store. The consensus was, that, as long as the markers had been on the intended aiming-point, it no longer existed, but there were no post-raid reports to confirm the outcome.

The campaign against communications targets continued on the 12th at six locations, including Caen and Poitiers, for which 5 Group detailed forces of 109 Lancasters and four Mosquitos and 112 Lancasters and four Mosquitos respectively. 50 Squadron made ready sixteen Lancasters to take part at the latter, situated in west-central France, and they departed Skellingthorpe between 22.12 and 22.57 with F/L Mouat RNZAF the senior pilot on duty. All reached the target area, where they encountered clear skies with good visibility, conditions which they exploited to deliver their four 1,000 and twelve 500 pounders each onto the red spotfires and red and green TIs. A number of large explosions were witnessed, and the fires remained visible for fifty miles into the return journey. Photo-reconnaissance revealed the Paris to Bordeaux line to have been cut in seven places. A new oil campaign began on this night, prosecuted by 286 Lancasters and seventeen Mosquitos of 1, 3 and 8 Groups, whose target was the Nordstern (Gelsenberg A.G.) plant at Gelsenkirchen. Such was the accuracy of the attack, that all production of vital aviation fuel was halted for a number of weeks at a cost to the Germans of a thousand tons per day.

The immediate award of DFC to F/L Botha was approved on the 13th, while plans for the group to operate that night were cancelled. F/L Beetham was posted to 5 LFS on the 14th at the conclusion of his tour, and he would not return to operational duties until after the war. However, a glittering RAF career lay ahead of him, which included a Knighthood and becoming Air ADC to Her Majesty Queen Elizabeth II between 1977 and 1982. He was appointed Chief of the Air Staff at the same time, and was the last to occupy this position having served in WWII. W/C Heward also left the squadron on this day to fill the vacancy at 97 Squadron created by the loss of W/C Carter, and S/L Chadwick would step temporarily into the breach at Skellingthorpe. The 14th also brought the Command's first daylight operation since the departure of 2 Group twelve months earlier. The target was Le Havre, from where the enemy's E-Boats and other fast, light marine craft were posing a threat to Allied shipping supplying the Normandy beaches. The two-phase operation was conducted by predominantly 1 and 3 Groups with 617 Squadron representing 5 Group, and took place in the evening under the umbrella of a fighter escort. The attack was highly successful, and few craft survived the onslaught.

Other operations on this night were directed against railway installations at three locations in France, while elements of 4, 5 and 8 Groups attended to enemy troop and vehicle concentrations at Aunay-sur-Odon and Évrecy near Caen. 5 Group assembled a force of 214 Lancasters and five Mosquitos for the former, of which seventeen of 50 Squadron departed Skellingthorpe between 22.13 and 22.47, with S/L Cole the senior pilot on duty. The weather was generally clear with some low cloud, but this did not hamper the marking process, which proceeded punctually and accurately. W/C Jeudwine was the Master Bomber, with 83 Squadron's W/C Northrop as Deputy, and the latter made four passes over the target, at 00.30 at 8,000 feet, 00.41 at 10,000 feet, and at 00.54 and 01.00 at 11,000 feet, dropping clusters of flares on the first two, green TIs on the third and red TIs on the fourth. The 50 Squadron crews bombed the above-mentioned TIs from 6,000 to 10,000 feet between 00.35 and 01.05, observing what appeared to be a concentrated attack that produced numerous fires and much smoke.

A force of 297 aircraft from 1, 4, 5, 6 and 8 Groups was assembled on the 15th to try to do to Boulogne what had been done to Le Havre twenty-four hours earlier. It was again left to 617 Squadron to represent 5 Group, and the operation was concluded with equal success. While this was in progress, 5 Group dispatched 110 Lancasters and four Mosquitos to deal with a fuel dump at Châtellerault, situated between Tours and Poitiers in western France. 50 Squadron loaded fifteen Lancasters with two 1,000 and fourteen 500 pounders each, and dispatched them from Skellingthorpe between 21.05 and 21.44 with F/Ls Botha and Mouat the senior pilots on duty. Clear skies and good visibility greeted their arrival in the target area, and red spotfires and green TIs marked out the aiming-point for the 50 Squadron crews to bomb from 7,000 to 10,000 feet between 00.35 and 01.09. Post-raid reconnaissance confirmed that eight out of thirty-five individual fuel storage sites within the target had been destroyed.

50 Squadron remained at home on the 16th, while plans were put in hand to launch 829 sorties that night against a number of targets. Just three days earlier, the first V-1 flying bombs had landed on London, and this prompted a response in the form of a second new campaign to open during the month, this one against the revolutionary weapon's launching and storage sites in the Pas-de-Calais. Four targets were earmarked for attention, 5 Group being handed a storage site at Beauvoir, located some twenty miles inland from Berck-sur-Mer. Such sites were referred to in Bomber Command parlance as "constructional works", and many were, indeed, large concrete structures in various stages of completion. 112 Lancasters were detailed, all but one of which reached the target area to find nine to ten-tenths cloud with tops at 6,000 to 8,000 feet. The Oboe markers went down on time, but few crews were able to see them through the cloud, and resorted to bombing on the reflected glow, which left them with little to pass on to the intelligence section at debriefing.

The oil campaign continued on this night in the hands of 1, 4, 6 and 8 Groups at Sterkrade-Holten, a district of Oberhausen in the Ruhr, but cloudy conditions caused the bombing to be scattered, and there was little impact on production. With the exception of 617 Squadron, 5 Group remained inactive until the 21st, leaving the "specialists" to attack constructional works at Watten and Wizernes with Tallboys in daylight on the 19th and 20th. Cloudy conditions affected accuracy at the former and caused the latter to be aborted, so as not to waste the precious and inordinately expensive Tallboys. 50 Squadron had actually dispatched seventeen Lancasters to Watten between 22.19 and 22.54, led by F/Ls Botha and Keith, but they were recalled after about ninety minutes, and almost the entire load of ninety-eight 1,000 and sixty-four 500 pounders ended up on the seabed.

5 Group had to wait until then, Mid-Summer's Night, the 21st, before becoming involved in the oil offensive, and was handed two targets to attack simultaneously. A force of 120 Lancasters and six Mosquitos was assembled for the refinery at Wesseling, south of Cologne, and 120 Lancasters and four Mosquitos for the Scholven-Buer plant in Gelsenkirchen, both with a sprinkling of ABC Lancasters of 101 Squadron for RCM duties, and the latter including a number of Oboe Mosquitos. 50 Squadron made ready seventeen Lancasters for Scholven-Buer, and they departed Skellingthorpe between 22.55 and 23.31 with S/L Cole the senior pilot on duty. Five early returns reduced the force, but none of these was from 50 Squadron, and all arrived in the target area expecting to find clear skies, instead of which they encountered ten-tenths cloud. This was the only flaw in the highly-effective 5 Group low-level marking method, and nothing could be done in the face of complete low-level cloud cover. The preliminary Oboe markers were backed up by red and green TIs, the glow from which could be observed only dimly through the cloud, and the crews had to aim for these, the 50 Squadron element from 16,000 to 20,000 feet between 01.39 and 01.59. It was impossible to assess the outcome, and to compound any sense of disappointment at Skellingthorpe, S/L Cole and crew were one of eight from the group to fail to return from this operation. Night-fighters had been waiting to greet them as they crossed Holland outbound, and LL840 was one of at least six to fall victim in this way, crashing three miles east of Epe, thirty-five miles east of Amsterdam, killing two of the eight occupants. S/L Cole and two others fell into

enemy hands, while three retained their freedom through the selfless courage of Dutch civilians. A secret German report would suggest a 20% loss of production for a limited period.

While this operation was in progress, matters were going seriously awry for the Wesseling force, and a catastrophic ordeal was befalling it, that would make the above casualty figure seem like a slight flesh wound. The Luftwaffe Nachtjagd got amongst the Lancasters during the approach to the target, and were responsible for the majority of the casualties resulting from this operation. Those reaching Wesseling had also expected to find clear skies, and conditions ideal for the 5 Group low-level marking method, but were met instead by ten-tenths low cloud and accurate predicted heavy flak. This meant, that low-level marking was not an option, and, faced with this situation, the Master Bomber, W/C James "Willie" Tait, had ordered a blind attack, forcing the Lancaster crews to bomb on H2S or the feint glow of red TIs. After the war, a secret German report would suggest a 40% loss of production at the site, but this was probably of very short duration, as the limited number of casualties on the ground pointed to a scattered and largely ineffective raid. Whatever the level of success, it was gained at the high cost of thirty-seven Lancasters, a massive 28%, and all but two of them belonged to 5 Group Squadrons. 44, 49, 57 and 619 Squadrons each lost six Lancasters, although one from 57 ditched off the English coast and the crew was rescued, while 207 and 630 Squadrons each had five empty dispersals to contemplate in the cold light of dawn.

F/L Keith stepped up temporarily to replace S/L Cole as B Flight commander, and W/C Frogley was posted in from 51 Base on the 22nd to succeed the recently departed W/C Heward as commanding officer. While more than four hundred aircraft of 3, 4, 6 and 8 Groups targeted four flying-bomb sites on the 23rd, 1 and 5 Groups were sent respectively against railway yards at Saintes and Limoges in western France. Ninety-seven Lancasters and four Mosquitos were detailed for the latter, with 53 Base squadrons among those in action, including sixteen representing 50 Squadron. They departed Skellingthorpe between 22.26 and 22.56 with F/Ls Botha and Mouat the senior pilots on duty, and all reached the target area to find clear skies and good visibility, in which ground features like the River Vienne and the railway sidings stood out prominently. Red spotfires and green TIs marked out the aiming-point, which the 50 Squadron crews bombed from 5,000 to 8,000 feet between 02.00 and 02.08, observing a number of large explosions and much smoke. F/L Mouat and crew reported a very large explosion when one hundred miles into the return flight at 02.46, and post-raid reconnaissance would confirm a highly accurate and concentrated attack.

617 Squadron had attempted to continue the Tallboy assault on the constructional works at Wizernes in daylight on the 22nd, but the attack had been abandoned in the face of ten-tenths low cloud. The squadron returned the bombs to store, and brought them back to France on the 24th to score a number of direct hits. Seventeen 50 Squadron crews were called to briefing on the 24th to learn of their part in a busy night of operations involving more than seven hundred aircraft targeting seven flying-bomb sites. 5 Group was assigned to Pommeréval and Prouville, situated respectively some fifteen miles south-east of Dieppe, and east of Abbeville, and detailed 103 Lancasters and four Mosquitos for each. The 53 Base squadrons were among those assigned to the latter, and 50 Squadron's seventeen participants departed Skellingthorpe between 22.30 and 23.06 with F/L Botha the senior pilot on duty. All reached the target area, where clear skies prevailed, and only slight ground haze lay between the Lancasters and the aiming-point. The preliminary Oboe Mosquito was punctual, but the subsequent marking was hampered by intense searchlight activity working in co-operation with flak and night-fighters,

and bombing was delayed while the aiming-point was positively identified and marked. It took until all of the illuminator flares had been expended before the low-level Mosquitos dropped red spotfires and the heavy brigade from 97 Squadron backed up with red and green TIs. The 50 Squadron crews delivered their attacks from 9,500 to 13,000 feet between 00.21 and 00.40 in accordance with the instructions of the Master Bomber, and the impression was of a somewhat haphazard attack that lacked concentration. Thirteen Lancasters failed to return, possibly as a result of the delay in opening the attack, and among them were two from 50 Squadron. ME798 was in the vicinity of the aiming-point when hit by fire from a night-fighter, which detonated the bomb load and distributed the Lancaster over a wide area, killing the experienced P/O Wood and his crew. JA899 also came down within three miles of the aiming-point to the south, but P/O Peters and one gunner survived, the former falling into enemy hands and the latter evading a similar fate.

S/L Stubbs was posted in from 9 Squadron on the 26th to succeed the missing S/L Cole as B Flight commander. More than seven hundred aircraft were detailed for operations against six flying-bomb sites on the 27th, while two railway yards would occupy the attention of other elements. There were two targets for 5 Group, a flying-bomb site at Marquise, situated some five miles inland from Cap Gris-Nez, and railway yards at Vitry-le-Francois south-east of Reims. 103 Lancasters and four Mosquitos were assigned to the latter, 53 Base squadrons providing the main force element, of which fifteen belonging to 50 Squadron departed Skellingthorpe between 21.35 and 22.02 with W/C Frogley the senior pilot on duty for the first time. All reached the target, where varying amounts of cloud were reported, between zero to seven-tenths at around 7,000 feet, but the visibility was good, and the aiming-point was clearly marked by red spot fires and green TIs. Bombing took place from 5,000 to 7,000 feet between 01.45 and 01.52, at which point the Master Bomber called a halt and ordered crews with bombs still aboard to take them home. Four 50 Squadron crews were among these, including that of W/C Frogley, and he was critical of the decision to abandon the attack, suggesting that, if the first spotfire had not been accurate, the bombing should never even have started. In fact, it had been smoke obscuring the aiming-point that prompted the Master Bomber to send the final wave home with their bombs.

F/L Botha and crew were posted to 97 Squadron on the 28th, while the squadron remained at home. Although the month's operational activity was over for some elements of 5 Group, 53 and 54 Bases were alerted on the 29th to provide eighty-five Lancasters and four Mosquitos as part of an overall force of 286 Lancasters and nineteen Mosquitos of 1, 5 and 8 Groups for a daylight attack on two flying-bomb launching sites and one storage site. Fifteen 50 Squadron Lancasters took off between 11.56 and 12.33 bound for the previously-attacked Beauvoir storage site, located twenty miles inland from the Pas-de-Calais coast. S/Ls Chadwick and Stubbs were the senior pilots on duty, the latter for the first time, but the former was forced to return early after the failure of his port-outer engine. The others reached the target to find clear conditions beneath the 15,000-foot cloud level, and bombed either visually or on red TIs from 15,000 to 19,000 feet between 13.45 and 13.56, observing large volumes of smoke, which partially obscured the site. The attack was believed to have been concentrated around the aiming-point, and losses amounted to a single Lancaster and Mosquito. F/L Shortt returned from 1660 Conversion Unit on the 30th to start another tour. During the course of the month, the squadron operated on thirteen occasions, and dispatched 209 sorties for the loss of five Lancasters and crews.

July 1944

Sadly, July would bring further traumas for 5 Group, the first occurring early on, while the disaster of Wesseling was still an open wound. The month began as June had ended, with flying-bomb sites providing employment for over three hundred aircraft on both the 1st and 2nd. It was the 4th before the Independent Air Force was invited to re-enter the fray, when it was called upon to attack a V-Weapon storage site in caves at St-Leu-d'Esserent, some thirty miles north of Paris. The caves had originally been used for growing mushrooms, and they were protected by some twenty-five feet of clay and soft limestone, to say nothing of the anti-aircraft defences brought in by the Germans. There is some confusion concerning the timing of the operation, which involved not only seventeen Lancasters, a Mustang and a Mosquito from 617 Squadron, but also 211 other Lancasters and eleven Mosquitos from the group, with three ABC Lancasters to provide RCM cover and three Pathfinder Oboe Mosquitos to carry out the marking of an initial reference-point. Some accounts suggest that 617 Squadron attacked early in the evening, and was followed by the group later on, when, in fact, both elements took off at the same time. There were actually two aiming-points, the road and railway communications to the area dump for the main force, and the tunnel complex at Creil, a settlement located three miles north-east of St Leu, for 617 Squadron.

50 Squadron supported the operation with eighteen Lancasters, which departed Skellingthorpe between 23.00 and 23.37 with W/C Frogley the senior pilot on duty. P/O Norbury and crew turned back as they reached the English coast, after their mid-upper turret became unserviceable, while F/O MacConnell and crew were within forty miles of the target, when they misinterpreted a signal from the Master Bomber at 01.13, and also abandoned their sortie. The others pressed on to reach the target area under clear skies and in good visibility, which would prove to be of equal benefit to the night-fighters. There were no searchlights, but the expected volume of flak was thrown up at the Skellingthorpe crews as they ran across the aiming-point to deliver their eleven 1,000 and four 500 pounders each from 14,000 to 18,000 feet onto green TIs between 01.35 and 01.40. Night-fighters pounced on the bombers over the target and on the route home, and thirteen Lancasters failed to return, although there were no empty 50 Squadron dispersals on this occasion. It was during this operation that the Squadron's veteran Lancaster, ED588 VN-G, logged her one-hundredth sortie in the hands, on this occasion, of F/L Enoch and crew, but sadly, she would not survive the war. Post-raid reconnaissance revealed that a large area of subsidence had blocked the side entrance to the caves and that the road and railway links had been cut over a distance of four hundred yards.

On the 6th, over five hundred aircraft were engaged on operations against V-Weapons targets, and 617 Squadron was assigned to a V-3 super-gun site at Mimoyecques. Originally planned as one of two sites near Cap Gris Nez containing twenty-five barrels each, angled at 50 degrees and aimed at London, test failures and delays meant that a single three-barrel shaft stretching a hundred metres into the limestone hill, five miles from the coast and 103 miles from its target, was all that existed at the time. Each fifteen-metre-long smooth-bore barrel, which was designed on the multiple-charge principle to progressively boost the acceleration of the one-ton projectile as it travelled towards the muzzle, was to be capable of pounding London at the rate of hundreds per day without let-up. It was protected by a concrete slab thirty metres wide and five-and-a-half metres thick, which was correctly believed by the designers to be impregnable to conventional bombs. It had been attacked on a number of occasions without success, but 617 Squadron scored direct hits with Tallboys, and provisional reconnaissance revealed four deep craters in the immediate target area, one causing a large corner of the concrete slab to collapse. The extent of the damage underground would not be apparent to the planners at Bomber Command, but the shafts and tunnels had been rendered unusable and would remain so. Although Cheshire did not know it, this was to be his final operation, not only with 617 Squadron, but also of the war in Europe.

The authorities were not convinced that the site at St-Leu-d'Esserent had received terminal damage, and scheduled another attack on it for the late evening of the 7th. Before they took off, more than 450 aircraft from 1, 4, 6 and 8 Groups had carried out the first major operation in support of the Canadian 1st and British 2nd Armies, which were trying to break out of Caen. The target had been changed from German-fortified villages to an area of open ground north of Caen, where almost 2,300 tons of bombs were dropped somewhat ineffectively, and, ultimately, that decision proved to be counter-productive by causing damage to the northern suburbs rather than to German forces. 5 Group detailed 208 Lancasters and fifteen Mosquitos for St-Leu, the 50 Squadron element of nineteen taking off between 22.05 and 22.47 with W/C Frogley again the senior pilot on duty and demonstrating excellent leadership qualities, which would not go unnoticed by his crews. There were no early returns, and they arrived in the target area to find medium-level cloud, which prevented the moonlight from providing illumination, although, below the cloud level, the visibility was good. The Master Bomber was the former 207 Squadron flight commander, W/C Ed Porter, and he oversaw the delivery of the Oboe yellow TI at 01.06, which was followed by the first stick of flares four minutes later. The first red spotfire went down at 01.08, a hundred yards south of the aiming-point, but in line with the direction of the bombing run, and backing-up by red and green TIs continued until 01.13. The marking was assessed as sufficiently accurate to call in the main force at 01.15, and the 50 Squadron crews dropped their loads of eleven 1,000 and four 500 pounders from 11,000 to 15,000 feet between 01.13 and 01.27. The Master Bomber's VHF was indistinct, so 83 Squadron's S/L Eggins assumed control, and sent the force home at 01.25. Twenty-nine Lancasters and two Mosquitos failed to return, after night-fighters got amongst them, and this represented 14% of the force.

It was a sobering night for Skellingthorpe, to which three 50 Squadron and two 61 Squadron Lancasters failed to return, all of them now smoldering wrecks on French soil. For 207 Squadron at Spilsby, it was the second time in under three weeks that five of its crews had failed to return from a single operation, and five had also been lost by 106 Squadron at Metheringham. Of the 50 Squadron casualties, DV363 had crashed some fifteen miles west-south-west of Beauvais, probably on the way home, killing F/Sgt Davies and his crew. There were also no survivors from the crew of Sgt Lloyd in DV277, which came down at around 02.00 some thirty miles short of the coast at Dieppe. At about the same time and, perhaps, fifteen miles to the west, PA996 exploded in the air, and, as so often happened on such occasions, the pilot, P/O Laidlaw RCAF, was thrown clear as the lone survivor of his crew, and he ultimately evaded capture. Photo-reconnaissance revealed that both ends of the tunnel complex had collapsed, as had a section in the middle, and the approach road and rail links had been heavily cratered and blocked.

There was no immediate opportunity for the squadrons to "get back on the horse", and there must have been a sombre air, while the station staffs at Skellingthorpe, Metheringham and Spilsby came to terms with the loss between them of more than a hundred familiar faces in one night. A special congratulatory message arrived on the participating stations from A-O-C,

AVM Sir Ralph Cochrane, who considered it the finest effort by the group to successfully press home the attack in the face of the fiercest opposition. F/L Lascelles was posted in from 1654 Conversion Unit on the 10th, as the new navigation leader, and he was followed by F/L Mills from 44 Squadron as the new gunnery leader on the 12th. Arriving at the same time from 5 LFS were F/Ls Flint and Ward and their crews.

Operations were posted at Skellingthorpe and then cancelled on each of the four days after St-Leu until the 12th, when twelve crews were called to briefing to be given the details about that night's operation against railway installations at Culmont-Chalindrey in eastern France. Two aiming-points were planned, at the western and eastern ends, for which a force of 157 Lancasters and four Mosquitos was made ready. While this operation was in progress, another by elements of 1 Group further south at Revigny would, hopefully, help to dilute the night-fighter response. The 50 Squadron crews departed Skellingthorpe between 21.53 and 22.05 with no senior pilots on duty, but no fewer than nine of flying officer rank. They flew out over eight-tenths low cloud until shortly before reaching the target area, where the conditions improved to provide clear skies, and, promisingly, no sign of defensive activity from the ground. The controller at the eastern aiming-point experienced VHF communications problems, which delayed that part of the attack, and eventually the entire force was directed to the western aiming-point. The 50 Squadron crews delivered their seven 1,000 and four 500 pounders each onto two red spotfires from just 5,250 to 8,500 feet between 01.56 and 02.19, and explosions were observed, followed by fires that remained visible for fifty miles into the return flight. The high proportion of delayed action fuses in use prevented an immediate assessment of results, but post-raid reconnaissance would confirm an effective operation.

Just eight 50 Squadron crews were detailed to operate on the 14th, and were informed at briefing that their target was to be the huge marshalling yards at Villeneuve-St-Georges situated on the southern rim of Paris. They would be part of a force of 111 Lancasters, six Mosquitos and an American twin-engine P38 Lightning containing the Master Bomber, W/C Jeudwine. The 50 Squadron crews departed Skellingthorpe between 21.57 and 22.15 led by W/C Frogley, each Lancaster loaded with a mix of 1,000 and 500 pounders, and all reached the target area to find a large amount of cloud with a base at 5,000 feet, but clear conditions below. W/C Jeudwine was having compass trouble, and would arrive on target twelve minutes late, so contacted his Deputy, 83 Squadron's W/C Joc Northrop, to take matters in hand. Joe could clearly see the target, and judged the Oboe marker to be within fifty yards of the planned aiming-point. He called in the 5 Group marker force, which lobbed the TIs within the confines of the yards, and the operation appeared to be proceeding smoothly and precisely according to plan. The 50 Squadron crews bombed on red and green TIs from 6,000 to 11,000 feet between 01.30 and 01.46, and most of the hardware hit the yards, while a proportion also fell outside to the east. Meanwhile, 1 Group had returned to Revigny, but had been thwarted by ground haze, which forced the Master Bomber to abandon the attack before any bombing could take place. Seven Lancasters were lost for no gain, and it would fall to 5 Group to finish the job a few nights hence at great expense.

Flying-bomb sites and railways dominated the target list on the 15th, and 5 Group was handed a railway junction at Nevers, a city on the North Bank of the Loire in central France. 50 Squadron contributed eight Lancasters to the force of 104 with four Mosquitos to carry out the low-level marking, and they departed Skellingthorpe between 22.13 and 22.25 with F/L Mouat the senior pilot on duty. All reached the target after an outward flight of more than three-and-a-half hours, and were greeted by clear skies and a little haze. The marker force exploited the favourable conditions to mark promptly and accurately, and the 50 Squadron crews delivered their ten 1,000 and three 500 pounders each onto a red spotfire and green TIs from 4,000 to 5,000 feet between 01.59 and 02.10. The entire force was carrying delayed-action ordnance, and no immediate assessment could be made, but a large explosion suggested, perhaps, that an ammunition train or dump had been hit. Two Lancasters failed to return, one each from 207 and 467 Squadrons, both crashing at Ligniéres-de-Touraine, a few miles west-south-west of tours, after an apparent collision witnessed by other returning crews. Photographic reconnaissance later in the day revealed that the site had been all but obliterated, and there was much damage to rolling stock.

Seventeen 50 Squadron crews were called to briefing at midnight on the 17/18th to learn of their part in a tactical support operation to be carried out at dawn by a force of 942 aircraft, of which 201 of the Lancasters were provided by 5 Group. It was the start of the ground forces' Operation Goodwood, which, Field Marshal Montgomery hoped, would be a decisive breakout into wider France as a prelude to the march towards the German frontier. The aiming-points were five enemy-held villages to the east of Caen, Colombelles, Mondeville, Sannerville, Cagny and Manneville, all of which stood in the path of the advancing British 2nd Army. The 50 Squadron element took off between 03.26 and 04.28 with W/C Frogley and S/L Chadwick leading from the front, and all reached the target area to find their aiming-point, the Mondeville steel works, already marked by red and yellow TIs, but about to be swallowed up and obscured by drifting smoke. The target, which the Germans had converted into a strongly defended fortress, was actually situated south of the River L'Orne in an industrial suburb of the city itself, to the east of the marshalling yards. Bombing by the 50 Squadron crews was carried out from 6,000 to 9,750 feet between 05.45 and 06.08 in accordance with instructions from the Master Bomber, and, as far as could be determined, it fell accurately onto the markers. The RAF dropped five thousand tons of bombs to good effect onto the two German divisions in just half an hour, and the Americans followed up with a further two thousand tons.

F/L Oram and crew were posted to 617 Squadron later on the 18th, after giving outstanding service to 50 Squadron, while their former colleagues attended briefing for the second operation of the day. Following two failed attempts by 1 Group to cut the railway junction at Revigny, in France's Marne region, at a cost of seventeen Lancasters, the job was handed to 5 Group, which assembled a force of 109 Lancasters, four Mosquitos and a P38 Lightning containing the Master Bomber, W/C Jeudwine. It was to be a busy night of operations, which included another railway and two oil targets, along with support and diversionary activities involving a total of 972 sorties. Eight 50 Squadron crews attended briefing at teatime, to learn of their part in what promised to be an unspectacular and routine operation, six of them, those of F/L Milne and F/Os Balance, Davis, Enoch, Millikin and Whyte, about to undertake their second sortie of the day. They departed Skellingthorpe between 22.52 and 23.11 with F/L Milne the senior pilot on duty, and crossed the French coast near Dieppe, before passing through an intense searchlight belt some twenty miles inland. They were harried all the way into eastern France by night-fighters, which had been fed into the stream shortly after it entered enemy airspace, and it was at this stage of the outward flight that matters began to go awry. In just forty-five minutes, sixteen Lancasters had fallen victim to night-fighters and one to flak, the seventeenth victim, the 50 Squadron Lancaster, DV312, having wandered off track. It contained the experienced crew of F/O Long RCAF, who was undertaking his sixteenth sortie, while his crew had completed three more, and only the bomb-aimer managed to save himself, fortunately, falling into the hands of the Resistance.

The surviving crews reached the target to find clear skies, but haze obscuring ground detail, and this elusive target continued to present problems, beginning with the first wave of flares, delivered at about 01.30, which were too far to the east. More flares were ordered, and the bombing was put back by five minutes, while Wanganui markers were dropped by Mosquito, and the situation was assessed. The whole attack seemed chaotic, and the use of many delayed-action bombs meant that it was difficult to see what was happening on the ground. The 50 Squadron crews were over the target at 7,000 to 9,000 feet between 01.41 and 01.52, and released their eleven 1,000 and three 500 pounders each onto a red spotfire, in accordance with instructions from the Master Bomber. Photo-reconnaissance revealed, that the operation had been successful in cutting the railway link to the battle front, but had cost twenty-four Lancasters, almost 22% of those dispatched. *(For a full and highly detailed account of the three Revigny raids, read the amazing book, Massacre over the Marne, by Oliver Clutton-Brock.)*

F/L Keith moved on to 11 O.T.U at the conclusion of his tour on the 19th, while his 5 Group colleagues stood-by for a possible daylight operation. It was evening before orders came through to prepare for an attack on a flying-bomb storage site at Thiverny, situated just to the north of St-Leu-d'Esserent, for which a force of 103 Lancasters and two Mosquitos was made ready, eight of the former provided by 50 Squadron. They departed Skellingthorpe between 19.08 and 19.30 with W/C Frogley the senior pilot on duty, and F/Ls Flint and Ward undertaking their first sorties with the squadron. The attack was to take place in daylight under the protection of a Spitfire escort, which was picked up at the south coast. All from the squadron reached the target in fine weather conditions, but with ground haze making it difficult to identify the aiming-point. Late preliminary marking by the Pathfinder element and communications problems between the Master Bomber and his Deputy added to the frustrations, and led to most crews having to bomb visually in the face of moderate to intense heavy flak bursting as high as 18,000 feet. They were over the target between 21.30 and 21.34 at altitudes ranging from 14,000 to 18,000 feet, and the operation was concluded without loss. Reconnaissance revealed some loose bombing, but sufficient aiming-point photographs were brought back to suggest a successful outcome.

On a busy night on the 20th, when three of the four campaigns were to be prosecuted, oil at Bottrop and Homberg, and V-Weapons sites at Ardouval and Wizernes, elements of 1, 5 and 8 Groups were detailed to attack railway yards and a triangle junction at Courtrai (Kortrijk) in Belgium. 50 Squadron contributed sixteen Lancasters to the 5 Group force of 190 Lancasters and five Mosquitos, and they departed Skellingthorpe between 22.57 and 23.27 with W/C Frogley the senior pilot on duty. They all reached the target area to find it free of cloud, if slightly obscured by ground haze, but the Oboe marking was well-placed in the marshalling yards, and backed up by green TIs, onto which the squadron's participants delivered their eleven 1,000 and four 500 pounders each from 10,000 to 13,500 feet between 00.57 and 01.02. They returned home safely to report a large, orange explosion at 00.57 and a successful outcome, which was confirmed by post-raid reconnaissance, that revealed both aiming-points to have been obliterated in return for the loss of nine Lancasters.

Following two nights at home for 5 Group and a two-month break from city busting, Harris sanctioned a major raid on the naval port of Kiel on the 23rd, for which a force of 629 aircraft was made ready. 5 Group contributed ninety-nine of the Lancasters, nine of them representing 50 Squadron at Skellingthorpe, which, unusually for an urban target, were loaded with eleven 1,000 and four 500 pounders. They took off between 22.47 and 23.58 with W/C Frogley and S/L Stubbs the senior pilots on duty, and headed for the rendezvous point, where they formed up behind an elaborate "Mandrel" jamming screen laid on by 100 Group, before setting course for Denmark's western coast. *(In November 1943, 100 Group had been formed to take over the Radio Countermeasures (RCM) role, which had been the preserve of 101 Squadron since its introduction a number of months earlier. 101 Squadron, however, would remain in 1 Group and continue to provide RCM for the remainder of the war.)* When they arrived unexpectedly and with complete surprise in Kiel airspace, they rendered the enemy night-fighter controller confused and unable to bring his resources to bear. Kiel was covered by a nine to ten-tenths veil of thin cloud with tops at 4,000 feet, and a skymarking plan was put into action, which enabled the main force to bomb on the glow, first of the flares, and then of fires. The 50 Squadron crews confirmed their positions by H2S, before bombing from 14,000 to 20,000 feet between 01.26 and 01.33, aiming at the glow of red and green Wanganui markers as they disappeared into cloud. Flak was mostly in barrage form and exploding at 15,000 to 22,000 feet, but was not overly troublesome. It was not possible to determine the outcome, but the glow of fires remained visible for a hundred miles into the return journey, which suggested an effective raid. This was confirmed by local reports, which conceded that this had been the town's most destructive raid of the war, and had inflicted heavy damage on the port and shipyards, and cut off water supplies for three days and gas for three weeks. Many delayed-action bombs had been dropped, and these continued to cause problems for some time.

5 Group divided its forces on the 24th to enable it to support the first of a three-raid series in five nights on the city of Stuttgart, and an oil refinery and fuel dump at Donges. Situated on the North Bank of the Loire to the east of St Nazaire, this target had been attacked successfully by elements of 6 and 8 Groups on the previous night, but clearly required further attention. The group detailed ninety-nine Lancasters for southern Germany in an overall force of 614, while 104 Lancasters and four Mosquitos were made ready for western France, with five 8 Group Mosquitos in attendance. 50 Squadron would support both operations with nine Lancasters each, and those bound for Stuttgart took off first, between 21.43 and 21.53 with S/L Stubbs the senior pilot on duty, and they were followed into the air between 22.12 and 22.30 by the others, led by F/Ls Flint, Milne and Mouat. They reached their respective destinations at the same time, at Stuttgart to find nine to ten-tenths cloud cover with tops at 4,000 to 7,000 feet, which required the employment of Wanganui flares to mark the aiming-point. The 50 Squadron crews bombed on the red glow on the cloud base from 18,000 to 20,500 feet between 01.52 and 02.00 in accordance with the instructions of the Master Bomber, and set course for home fairly satisfied with the outcome, although it was impossible to make an accurate assessment. At debriefings across the Command, crews reported a glow of fires covering an area of perhaps five square miles, which remained visible for eighty miles into the return journey. No local report came out of Stuttgart for this night, but it had been a successful and destructive raid, although gained at a cost of seventeen Lancasters and four Halifaxes. LL842 had been outbound for two hours when it crashed at Nogent-le-Rotrou at 23.51, roughly midway between Caen and Orleans, and claimed the lives of F/O Parker RCAF and four of his crew, while one of the survivors ultimately evaded capture.

Meanwhile, 290 miles to the west of Stuttgart, clear skies and good visibility greeted the 5 Group crews, who were able to pick out ground detail in the light of the illuminator flares. Bombing by the 50 Squadron element took place on concentrated red and green TIs from 8,250 to 11,200 feet between 01.41 and 01.56 in accordance with the Master Bomber's instructions, and the glow of fires through thick smoke, along with a large explosion at 01.49, indicated a successful outcome. Post-raid photo-reconnaissance confirmed the success of the operation, revealing the site to have been devastated at a cost of three Lancasters, among which was the squadron's PA968. It crashed at Pontchâteau, ten miles north of the target, with total loss of life among the predominantly Canadian crew of P/O Haaland RCAF.

5 Group split its forces again on the 25th to support the second of the raids on Stuttgart with eighty-three Lancasters, and a daylight attack on an aerodrome and signals depot at Saint-Cyr involving ninety-four Lancasters and six Mosquitos. *(There are at least four locations called Saint-Cyr, and it is believed that the one targeted on this night was in the Ile-de-France to the west of Paris.)* 50 Squadron briefed fourteen crews for the latter operation, while loading their Lancasters with a cookie, a single 1,000 pounder and fourteen 500 pounders each, before dispatching them from Skellingthorpe between 17.26 and 17.53 with W/C Frogley and S/L Chadwick the senior pilots on duty, the latter undertaking the final sortie of his second tour. They all enjoyed an incident-free outward flight, and arrived at the target to find good visibility below the 12,000-foot cloud base and Oboe preliminary marking in progress. Each of the three aiming-points was marked by a red spotfire, and, after the bombs had been delivered from 9,500 to 11,200 feet between 19.56 and 19.58, a huge pall of smoke rose through the cloud. Post-raid reconnaissance confirmed a successful attack, which had left all of the buildings severely damaged.

Meanwhile, the aircraft for the main event were crossing France and entering Germany, accompanied by layers of cloud, which, over the target, was at five to ten-tenths with tops in places as high as 20,000 feet. There was haze below the cloud level to create further challenges for the marker force, and the red and green TIs appeared to the main force crews to be somewhat scattered. Bombing took place from around 17,000 to 21,000 feet either side of 02.00 area, but it was impossible to assess the outcome, and there was little optimism at debriefings that a successful operation had taken place. In fact, this was probably the most destructive of the three raids in this current series, but it would be only after the third one that cumulative reports came out of the city to confirm much destruction and heavy casualties.

The hectic round of operations continued for 5 Group on the 26th with preparations for an attack on two aiming-points in the marshalling yards at Givors, situated on the West Bank of the River Rhône in south-eastern France. 178 Lancasters and nine Mosquitos were made ready, thirteen of the former by 50 Squadron, and they departed Skellingthorpe between 21.00 and 21.31 with F/Ls Flint, Milne Mouat and Ward the senior pilots on duty, and a round-trip of eleven hundred miles ahead of them. Bad weather had been anticipated, but the conditions during the outward leg over France were even worse than forecast, with icing and electrical storms, and fourteen aircraft turned back in all. There were no 50 Squadron crews among these as they covered the almost five-hour outward flight to reach the target and be greeted by severe weather conditions in the form of rain, thunderstorms and lightning. The cloud was down to around 7,000 feet with poor visibility below, and the flare force made a number of runs across the target, between 01.42 and 02.07, and orbited in between, awaiting instructions. There were occasional glimpses of the ground, but the Master Bomber was experiencing great difficulty in getting Mosquito TIs onto the two aiming points. Eventually, one of the Deputies managed to put a green TI onto the southern aiming-point, and the main force began to bomb at around 02.00. The 50 Squadron crews carried out their attacks from 5,500 to 8,000 feet between 02.12 and 02.23, using the light from flares and aiming at green TIs, all in accordance with instructions. They could offer little to the intelligence section at debriefing, but post-raid reconnaissance revealed that the tracks to the north of the junction were closed, and the locomotive depot in the yards had been damaged.

The night of the 28/29th would prove to be busy, eventful and expensive as the Command prepared for major operations against Stuttgart and Hamburg and a number of smaller undertakings involving a total of 1,126 aircraft. The final raid of the series on Stuttgart was to be an all-Lancaster affair of 494 aircraft drawn from 1, 3, 5 and 8 Groups, while 307 Lancasters and Halifaxes of 1, 6 and 8 Groups carried out the annual last-week-of-July attack on Hamburg, a year and a day after the devastating firestorm of Operation Gomorrah. 5 Group put up 176 Lancasters, thirteen of them made ready by 50 Squadron, and they were each loaded with a 2,000 pounder and thirteen or fourteen 500lb J cluster bombs. They departed Skellingthorpe between 21.53 and 22.14 with W/C Frogley the senior pilot on duty, and were not represented among the five early returns of 5 Group aircraft. They flew across France in bright moonlight above the cloud layer, and exposed themselves to the night-fighter hordes that had infiltrated the bomber stream as it closed on the target. It was the Luftwaffe's Nachtjagd that would gain the upper hand on this night, but the 50 Squadron crews must have been in a section of the bomber stream that remained unmolested, as they reported an uneventful outward flight, and not one reported seeing a night-fighter. There was a layer of up to ten-tenths thin cloud over the city, with tops in places at around 10,000 feet, and the Pathfinders initially employed skymarker flares (Wanganui), at which the 50 Squadron crews aimed their bombs from 14,500 to 21,000 feet between 01.56 and 02.04. LM210 was still some twenty miles short of the target when it crashed at 01.30 on the southern outskirts of Pforzheim, killing F/O Curphey RCAF and his crew, and this was one of thirty-nine Lancasters that would fail to return, fourteen of them from 5 Group. Night-fighters also caught the Hamburg force on its way home, and a further twenty-two aircraft were shot down, bringing the night's casualty figure to sixty-one aircraft. Although it was difficult to make an accurate assessment of this night's attack on Stuttgart, the series had severely damaged the city, leaving its central districts devastated, with most of its public and cultural buildings in ruins, while 1,171 of its inhabitants had lost their lives.

Fourteen 50 Squadron crews were briefed and put on stand-by at Skellingthorpe late on the 29th in anticipation of an early-morning tactical support operation in the Villers Bocage-Caumont region of the Normandy battle area south-west of Caen. They were to be part of an overall force of 692 aircraft to attack six enemy positions facing predominantly American forces, and they departed Skellingthorpe for their aiming-point at Cahagnes between 05.51 and 06.14 with S/L Stubbs the senior pilot on duty. They approached the target over ten-tenths cloud with tops at 5,000 feet and a base at 3,500 feet, and were five minutes from the bombing run at 07.59, when the Master Bomber sent them home.

5 Group prepared for two daylight operations on the 31st, one of them an evening attack on a flying bomb storage tunnel at Rilly-la-Montagne, some five miles south of Reims. A 5 Group force of ninety-seven Lancasters and three Mosquitos included sixteen Lancasters of 617 Squadron, led by its recently appointed successor to Cheshire, W/C James "Willie" Tait. Tait

was well-known to 5 Group crews as a member of the Master Bomber fraternity at Coningsby, but had spent most of his long operational career in 4 Group, and was among the most experienced pilots in the entire Command. A second operation was to be directed at locomotive facilities and marshalling yards at Joigny-la-Roche, situated north of Auxerre and some ninety miles south east of Paris, and would involve 127 Lancasters and four Mosquitos of 1 and 5 Groups. 50 Squadron would support both operations, assigning five Lancasters to the former and nine to the latter, which departed Skellingthorpe together between 17.15 and 17.47 with W/C Frogley leading the Joigny element and F/Ls Flint, Mouat and Ward the other. They made their way south to rendezvous with the rest of the two forces, 83 Squadron forming into two vics, one at 15,000 and the other at 18,000 feet, to lead the Rilly force to the target under a fighter escort. Weather conditions at the target were clear, and it could be identified visually, but once the tallboys went down, dust and smoke made it difficult to assess the outcome, and the use of delayed fuses added to that problem. The 50 Squadron element identified the target visually, and four of them bombed through four-tenths cloud from 15,000 to 17,000 feet within seconds of each other at 20.18, while F/O Mountain and crew withheld their bombs after failing to identify the aiming-point. Meanwhile, the Joigny-la-Roche force had arrived in the target area, also with a fighter escort, to find no more than three-tenths cloud with tops at 7,000 feet, and good enough visibility to enable a visual identification of the aiming-point. The marking was concentrated, as was the bombing onto the red TIs, and the 50 Squadron crews delivered their standard bomb loads from 12,000 to 14,750 feet almost as one at 20.27. Post-raid reconnaissance confirmed both operations to have been successful for the loss of a single Lancaster from Joigny and two from Rilly, one of the latter containing the 617 Squadron crew of F/L Bill Reid VC, who survived with one of his crew after their Lancaster was hit by bombs from above.

During the course of the month, the squadron carried out eighteen operations, and dispatched 209 sorties for the loss of seven Lancasters and crews.

August 1944

August would bring an end to the flying bomb offensive, and also see a return to major night operations against industrial Germany. Flying bomb sites were to dominate the first half of the month, and sites would be targeted in daylight on each of the first six days. It began with 777 aircraft being committed to operations against numerous flying bomb-related sites on the afternoon of the 1st, although there were serious doubts about the weather conditions, which were poor over England. 5 Group's targets were at La Breteque, situated in Normandy, some ten miles east-south-east of Rouen, Mont Candon, a mile or two south-west of Dieppe, and Siracourt, located some thirty miles east of the coastal town of Berck-sur-Mer. Forces of fifty-three Lancasters, fifty-nine Lancasters and a Lightning and Mosquito and sixty-seven Lancasters and four Mosquitos respectively were made ready, the two last-mentioned supported by 50 Squadron with eight and five Lancasters. Those bound for Siracourt departed Skellingthorpe between 15.05 and 15.16, each captained by a pilot of flying officer rank, and they were followed into the air between 16.45 and 17.08 by the Mont Candon element led by S/L Stubbs. They joined forces with the others of their respective formations as they made their way towards the south, and lost the cloud as they began the Channel crossing, only for it to build again to nine to ten-tenths strato-cumulus with tops at between 2,000 and 5,000 feet over the Pas-de-Calais region. F/O Balance and crew had already turned back long before, after the failure of their starboard-outer engine when over Surrey. One Lancaster bombed at

La Breteque, before the Master Bomber called a halt to proceedings, and the other two attacks were abandoned before any bombing took place. It was a similar story for the other groups, and, in total, only seventy-nine aircraft bombed.

On the following afternoon, 5 Group contributed 194 Lancasters, two Mosquitos and a P38 Lightning to operations by 394 aircraft against one flying bomb launching and three supply sites. Ninety-four Lancasters and two Mosquitos were assigned to a storage site at Trossy-St-Maximin, situated north of Paris and close to St-Leu d'Esserent, and a hundred Lancasters and the P38 to the Bois-de-Cassan facility. 50 Squadron loaded fifteen Lancasters with a mix of 1,000 and 500 pounders destined for the latter, some with a delay fuse of up to thirty-six hours, and dispatched them from Skellingthorpe between 14.25 and 15.00 with S/L Stubbs the senior pilot on duty. All reached the target to find three to five-tenths patchy cloud over the target, but few saw the Oboe proximity markers go down, and most bombed on visual reference, the 50 Squadron crews from 15,000 to 19,000 feet between 17.10 and 17.21. The lead aircraft turned suddenly at the last moment and caused a number of those following to overshoot the aiming-point, among them 50 Squadron's S/L Stubbs and F/O Oliver, and their bombs were seen to fall wide of the mark. A patch of cloud obscured the target from F/Os Haynes and Holseth, and they withheld their bombs. F/O Davis was hit by flak seconds before bombing, but he managed to release his load, and described the attack as generally scattered towards the north-east of the aiming-point. Post-raid reconnaissance revealed fresh damage to both sites, with many new craters, and, at Trossy, a large rectangular building stripped of its roof and sides, and the southern end of two road-over-rail bridges demolished.

Despite the effectiveness of the operation, the Trossy-St-Maximin site was included among targets for more than eleven hundred aircraft on the following day. The reason given to the 1 and 5 Group crews at briefing was, that the importance of the site to the Third Reich demanded that no building be left intact, and one or two may have escaped damage during the previous day's attack. 187 Lancasters, one Mosquito and the P38 Lightning were made ready as 5 Group's contribution to the operation, the fourteen 50 Squadron participants departing Skellingthorpe between 11.40 and 12.05 with every Lancaster captained by a pilot of flying officer rank. Each was loaded with a dozen 1,000 pounders and four of 500lbs, all of which reached the target area intact. The 5 Group element was to attack about fifteen minutes after 1 Group, and, as they reached the target, smoke could be seen rising to 8,000 feet, and this, combined with a fierce flak defence, presented the crews with challenging conditions. The 50 Squadron element bombed from 17,000 to 19,000 feet between 14.32 and 14.34, doing so by visual reference under instruction from the Master Bomber, having been prevented by the smoke from seeing the markers. Many aircraft returned to their respective stations bearing flak damage, although 50 Squadron crews made no mention of that, and they mostly commented on the slightly scattered nature of the bombing. Photo-reconnaissance was unable to confirm that the site had been obliterated, and it would need to be attacked again on the following day, a job that would be handed to 6 Group, while most of 5 Group stayed at home.

The 5th dawned bright and clear, and brilliant sunshine glinted off the Perspex of sixteen 50 Squadron Lancasters as they took off from Skellingthorpe between 10.30 and 11.10 bound for familiar airspace over St-Leu-d'Esserent with S/L Stubbs the senior pilot on duty. They were part of a 5 Group force of 189 Lancasters and one Mosquito, which, in turn, represented about 25% of the effort by 4, 5, 6 and 8 Groups against two flying-bomb sites, the other in the Forét-de-Nieppe, close to the Belgian frontier. It was an almost intact force that homed in on the target to find it partly protected by up to six-tenths patchy cloud with tops at about 12,000 feet. This prevented the Master Bomber from picking up the aiming-point until thirty seconds from it, which meant a very late course change to bring the bombers into position. This was achieved, however, although smoke and cloud hid the markers from view, and most crews picked up the aiming-point by means of ground features. The 50 Squadron crews ran through a spirited flak defence at 16,000 and 17,000 feet, and, with the exception of S/L Ward, whose bomb-aimer lost sight of the aiming-point under the drifting smoke, bombed between 13.33 and 13.39. Returning crews reported a fairly concentrated attack, which PRU photos seemed to confirm with views of fresh damage, and heavily cratered approaches.

S/L Chadwick was posted to 5 Group HQ on the 6th at the conclusion of his second tour, and his experience would be missed by the junior crews. He would be succeeded as A Flight commander by F/L Flint on his promotion to acting squadron leader rank on the 9th. 50 Squadron detailed nine crews for operations on the morning of the 6th, and they were in their Lancasters before 09.00 to carry out the checks before departing for another swipe at the flying-bomb launching site at Bois-de-Cassan in the L'Isle-Adam, a few miles to the south-west of St-Leu. They were part of a 5 Group force of ninety-nine Lancasters and the P38 Lightning, and took off between 09.30 and 09.50 to join up with the rest of the formation as they made their way south. The heavy element was led by 83 Squadron's G/C Deane with F/L Drinkall acting as his deputy, but Deane began to experience problems with his navigation homing equipment as he crossed the English coast outbound, and decided to hand over to F/L Drinkall. When about forty miles inland of the French coast, a large cumulus cloud barred the way up to 20,000 feet, and F/L Drinkall communicated his intention to take the force below it, descending to 16,000 feet. G/C Deane warned him not to go below 15,000, and advised him not to enter the cloud, but to turn to starboard. However, they were immediately enveloped in cloud, and G/C Deane did his best to hang on to F/L Drinkall's tail, as he continued to descend, and the two eventually became separated. Emerging on the other side of the cloud, Deane saw a large formation in the distance, and followed it. Passing through the cloud had caused the formation to become widely scattered, and it could not be reformed. Only thirty-eight aircraft bombed after picking up the aiming-point visually, three from 50 Squadron carrying out their attacks from 14,000 feet between 12.16 and 12.21. Fifty-eight crews were unable to bomb but still had to contend with a fierce flak and fighter defence. Three Lancasters failed to return, and among them was that of F/L Drinkall and crew, who failed to survive. Another was 50 Squadron's veteran W4824, which crashed near Pontoise, north-west of Paris, killing F/O Coombs and four others, while the flight engineer and navigator evaded capture. Photo-reconnaissance revealed some fresh damage to the eastern side of the target, but two large buildings on the main roadway immediately south of the aiming point remained intact, and further operations would be required.

Other than night flying tests (NFTs), there was little activity during the day on the 7th, the first time during the month that no daylight operations had been mounted. It was from teatime onwards that the feverish activity began, to prepare 1,019 aircraft for attacks on five enemy positions facing Allied ground forces in the Normandy battle area. The aiming-point for 179 Lancasters and one Mosquito from 5 Group was the fortified village of Secqueville, situated some fifteen miles east of Le Havre. Sixteen 50 Squadron Lancasters departed Skellingthorpe between 21.10 and 21.41 with F/L Ward the senior pilot on duty, and joined up with the others as they travelled south. The target could be seen by the approaching bombers to be under clear skies, although haze shrouded ground detail to an extent, and star shells were fired from the ground to illuminate the aiming-point. This enabled the Pathfinder aircraft to drop red TIs onto it for the main force crews to aim at, and the first phase of bombing proceeded according to plan in concentrated fashion, lasting fifteen minutes. It was then that smoke began to obscure the markers, and the Master Bomber called a halt to proceedings and sent everyone home, including the 50 Squadron contingent. 50 Squadron posted missing the crew of F/L Richard Palandri who were, by now, well into their first tour of operations. LL922 crashed some fifteen miles east of Le Havre near the town of Lillebonne, situated on the northern side of the Seine. The pilot and two others lost their lives, while three of the four survivors managed to retain their freedom. The squadron ORB makes no mention of the fact that ME813 overshot its landing at Skellingthorpe at 01.30 on return in the hands of F/O Mountain and crew, and was written off after hitting an air-raid shelter, without injury to the occupants.

A rare day off for 5 Group crews on the 8th led to another for them on the 9th until late afternoon, when briefings took place for that night's operation against an oil storage dump in the Forét-de-Châtellerault, situated south of Tours in western France. It was to be predominantly a 5 Group show involving 171 Lancasters and fourteen Mosquitos, but with five 101 Squadron Lancasters to provide RCM cover. 50 Squadron dispatched thirteen Lancasters between 20.39 and 21.06 with F/L Ward the senior pilot on duty and all other pilots of flying officer rank. F/O North and crew lost their port-outer engine within two hours and returned early, leaving the others to arrive in the target area under clear skies. However, the presence of considerable ground haze created poor visibility for the marker crews attempting to identify the two aiming-points. The flares dropped by the first two waves of the marker force were scattered, and this prompted the Mosquito marker leader to drop a Wanganui flare as a guide to the third flare-force crews. This meant that some crews had to orbit for up to twenty minutes before the Master Bomber was satisfied that the green TIs were in the right spot and called in the main force. They produced accurate bombing, resulting in three large explosions and volumes of black smoke, which, within five minutes, completely obscured the aiming-point. A pause in the bombing was called, before it recommenced, until the lack of a verifiable marker compelled the Master Bomber to call a halt. All but three of the 50 Squadron crews are known to have carried out an attack from 5,000 to 7,500 feet between 00.04 and 00.17, while two suffered bomb-sight failure and LM435 was one of two Lancasters failing to return. It crashed four miles west-north-west of the target without survivors from the crew of F/O Best, and it is not clear whether this was before or after bombing.

The mighty Gironde estuary, situated on France's Biscay coast, narrows as it leads inland towards the south-east, before dividing to become the Garonne River to the west and the Dordogne to the east. Its banks and islands were home to a number of important oil production and storage sites at Pauillac, Blaye, Bec-d'Ambe and Bordeaux, and the region was a frequent destination for gardening activities. Bordeaux itself was a vitally important port to the enemy, contained U-Boot pens and was heavily defended along the entire length of the waterway. Orders were received on 54 and 55 Base stations at teatime on the 10th to prepare sixty-two Lancasters and five Mosquitos to bomb oil storage facilities at Bordeaux. Returning crews were confident of a successful attack, but, as few explosions were observed, it was difficult to accurately assess the outcome.

On the 11th, while 617 Squadron took care of the U-Boot pens at la Pallice, 5 Group detailed thirty-nine Lancasters from 53 Base and two Mosquitos for an attack on a similar target at Bordeaux under the protection of six Mosquitos of 100 Group. 50 Squadron dispatched nine flying officer-captained Lancasters between 11.58 and 12.32, each loaded with 2,000lb armour-piercing bombs, but had two return early, one after taking off late and the other after setting course late. The others reached the target area to find good bombing conditions, which enabled them to make a visual identification of the T-shaped basin and U-Boot pens. The attack took place from 17,000 to 18,000 feet between 16.32 and 16.54 and appeared to be concentrated on the aiming-point.

That evening, 5 Group was switched to communications targets at Givors, located about twenty miles to the south of Lyon in south-east-central France. There were to be two aiming-points, the town's marshalling yards to the north, and a railway junction to the south, and 50 Squadron's four participants were assigned to the latter in an overall force of 175 Lancasters and ten Mosquitos. The quartet, consisting of the crews of F/Os Balance, Frew, Mountain and Oliver, departed Skellingthorpe between 20.25 and 20.50, each loaded with eight 1,000 and four 500 pounders, and all reached the target area to find clear skies and a little haze. While confusion reigned over the marshalling yards, matters proceeded smoothly at the junction, which was marked by green TIs and bombed from 6,500 to 8,000 feet between 01.02 and 01.06 by the 50 Squadron crews. They all returned to home airspace, many of those involved in the attack on the marshalling yards, critical of some aspects of the raid, but confident that it had been concluded successfully. Photo-reconnaissance revealed heavy damage to both aiming-points, with the ground badly-cratered and many tracks severed, and the middle span of the railway bridge over the River Rhône was seen to have received a direct hit.

The main operation on the 12th was an experiment to gauge the ability of main force crews to locate and attack an urban target on the strength of their own H2S equipment in the absence of a Pathfinder element. This resulted from the huge volume of operations generated by the four concurrent campaigns, each of which called upon the finite resources of 8 Group, compelling it, in the short term at least, to spread itself more and more thinly. The conclusion of the flying-bomb campaign at the end of the month, together with the end of tactical support for the ground forces, would remove the pressure, and the planned independence of 3 Group through the G-H bombing system from the autumn would solve the problem altogether. In the meantime, however, no one knew what demands might be made of the Command, and it would be useful to see what main force crews could do when left to their own devices. The target was to be Braunschweig, for which a force of 379 aircraft was assembled, seventy-two of the Lancasters provided by 5 Group. It was a night of heavy Bomber Command activity at numerous locations involving more than eleven hundred sorties. A second large operation over Germany was directed at the Opel motor factory at Rüsselsheim, some two hundred miles away to the south, and involved 297 aircraft, sixty of them provided by 5 Group. This would not weaken the enemy night-fighter defences, and powerful elements of the Nachtjagd were waiting for the Braunschweig force as it crossed the German coast at around 18,000 feet. Night-fighter flares were in evidence from then until the coast was crossed again on the way home, and it would prove to be an expensive night for the Command as a whole. Some of the bombing did hit Brunswick, but there was no concentration, and, typically at this target, many outlying communities also reported bombs falling.

53 Base was not involved at Braunschweig, but 50 Squadron contributed eleven Lancasters to the Rüsselsheim operation, dispatching them from Skellingthorpe between 21.32 and 21.41

with the now familiar line up of all-flying officer-ranked pilots. All reached the target with their single 2,000 pounder each and twelve 500lb J Cluster bombs, and found up to three-tenths cloud with tops as high as 20,000 feet. Despite the presence of ground haze, the conditions for an attack were favourable, and the red and green TIs marking out the aiming-point were clearly visible, if a little scattered. Bombing by the 50 Squadron element took place from 19,000 to 21,000 feet between 00.15 and 00.19, but they found it difficult to assess what was happening on the ground, and bombing photos would provide little detail. It was left to post-raid reconnaissance to ascertain that a number of buildings had been damage within the Opel factory complex, but nothing vital to production, and fires had spread through a wood three miles away and adjacent housing estates to the south-east. There were also many bomb craters in open country, confirming that this target would need further attention. Twenty aircraft failed to return from this disappointing effort, and among them was 50 Squadron's NE135, which crashed near Liege in Belgium, killing F/O Haynes RAAF and his crew, which contained three other members of the RAAF.

While the above was in progress, a "rush job" called upon the services of 144 crews to attack German troop concentrations and a road junction north of Falaise. 5 Group supported the attack with twenty-five Lancasters, the crews of which found a blanket of ten-tenths stratus cloud with tops at 2,000 feet, through which the green TIs were clearly visible and bombed. Post-raid reconnaissance confirmed that the area around the junction had been heavily cratered and the roads leading from it were mostly blocked.

Later, on the 13th, 5 Group notified 617 Squadron to prepare aircraft for an attack on the U-Boot pens and a cruiser at Brest, and fifteen Lancasters from 53 Base to target an oil storage depot at Bordeaux. 50 Squadron loaded four of its Lancasters with six 2,000 pounders each, and dispatched them from Skellingthorpe between 16.17 and 16.33 with W/C Frogley the senior pilot on duty. Three of them are known to have reached the target, where conditions were favourable, and the aiming-point was identified visually, before bombing took place from 15,000 to 17,800 feet at 20.04. The bombs were seen to straddle the aiming-point and U-Boot pens, but it was not possible to assess damage. PD237 failed to return to Skellingthorpe, the fifth 50 Squadron aircraft to go missing in the first two weeks of the month, but news soon came through that five of the crew had landed in Allied-held territory, and were safe. It took a little longer before it became known that F/Sgt Lorimer and the other crew member were also safe, after being picked up by the French Resistance.

The main activity during the afternoon of the 14th was an operation in support of Canadian divisions in the Falaise area, which involved 805 aircraft targeting seven enemy troop positions. 5 Group took part, by sending sixty-one Lancasters to the village of Quesnay, where accurate bombing left the village in ruins. Master Bombers were on hand to control the bombing at each aiming-point because of the close proximity of the opposing armies, but, despite the most stringent efforts to avoid friendly fire incidents, some bombs did fall into a quarry occupied by Canadian troops, killing thirteen men, injuring fifty-three others and destroying a large number of vehicles. The group had actually begun the day with an attack by elements of 617 and 9 Squadrons on the derelict French cruiser Gueydon at berth at Brest, which, it was believed, the enemy might sink strategically along with other ships in the harbour, to render it unusable if liberated. In the evening, 128 Lancasters and two Mosquitos were made ready to send back to Brest for another go at the Gueydon, a tanker and a hulk, and among those taking part were twelve crews from 50 Squadron, who departed Skellingthorpe between 17.21 and 17.54 with S/L Stubbs the senior pilot on duty. They arrived over the port to find clear skies and excellent visibility, but also a fierce flak defence, and a number of aircraft would return bearing the scars of battle. The 50 Squadron crews bombed from 15,500 to 16,500 feet between 20.19 and 20.25, and a number of direct hits were observed on both vessels, with smoke issuing out of the tanker. Photo-reconnaissance revealed that the tanker had settled on the bottom, and the cruiser had suffered a similar fate with its decks awash.

In preparation for his new night offensive against Germany, Harris called for operations against enemy night fighter airfields in Holland and Belgium. In response, a list of nine such targets was prepared for attention by daylight on the 15th, and they would involve a thousand aircraft. 5 Group was handed Deelen in central Holland and Gilze-Rijen in the south, and prepared forces of ninety-four Lancasters and five Mosquitos for the former and 103 Lancasters, four Mosquitos and the P38 Lightning for the latter. The P38 contained S/L "Count" Ciano and W/C Guy Gibson, who was desperate to get back onto operations. 53 Base was assigned to Gilze-Rijen, and 50 Squadron dispatched thirteen Lancasters between 09.52 and 10.16 with W/C Frogley the senior pilot on duty, each carrying eleven 1,000 pounders and up to five of 500lbs. They found the target under clear skies in excellent visibility, and were able to identify the aiming point visually to deliver their payloads from 15,500 to 17,000 feet between 12.09 and 12.11, in accordance with instructions from the Master Bomber. Bombs were observed to fall on runway intersections, and building could be seen burning as the force withdrew, Many bomb bursts were observed on the aerodrome, and post-raid reconnaissance confirmed almost eight hundred craters on the landing ground and a hundred on the runways.

The new offensive began with simultaneous attacks on Stettin and Kiel on the night of the 16/17th, 5 Group contributing 145 aircraft to the overall all-Lancaster force of 461 assigned to the former. 50 Squadron launched thirteen Lancasters from Skellingthorpe between 20.53 and 21.33 with S/L Flint the senior pilot on duty, and there were no early returns to reduce the squadron's impact. It took some three-and-a-half hours to reach the target, where the force was greeted by up to nine-tenths high cloud with a base at 18,000 to 20,000 feet and sufficient breaks to register clear visibility below. Concentrated red and green TIs could be seen marking out the aiming-point, and the 50 Squadron crews bombed these from 14,000 to 20,000 feet between 01.02 and 01.19, and reported fires taking hold. Not all returning crews were confident about the outcome, some suggesting the raid had been scattered, when, in fact, it had been highly successful, destroying fifteen hundred houses, numerous industrial premises, and sinking five ships in the harbour, while seriously damaging eight more.

Sixteen 50 Squadron crews were called to briefing early on the 18th to be told of that morning's operation against two flying-bomb dumps in the Forét-de-L'Isle Adam, north of Paris. 158 Lancasters, six Mosquitos and the P38 Lightning were to be involved, with 83 Squadron leading, and providing the back-up marking on the heels of the low-level Mosquitos at the two aiming-points in the east and west. The 50 Squadron element departed Skellingthorpe between 11.20 and 11.50 with W/C Frogley the senior pilot on duty, and each Lancaster carrying ten 1,000 and three or four 500 pounders. They headed south in squadron formation to rendezvous with the rest of the force and pick up the fighter escort, and, when over the mid-point of the Channel at 13.15, sixty or seventy American Liberators passed across the bows of the gaggle, heading east a thousand feet higher, prompting the lead Lancaster to change course. This may have been what prompted comments by some crews on return, that not all had observed station keeping as set out at briefing, a situation that would result in aircraft bombing out of the planned sequence and on wrong headings. On arrival in the target area they encountered five to seven-tenths cloud with tops at around 8,000 feet, which hampered identification of both aiming-points, and instructions were issued to not bomb unless a clear view of the target had been established. Some were able to pick out the aiming-points assisted by smoke markers, and fourteen of the 50 Squadron crews bombed from 12,000 to 13,000 feet between 14.08 and 14.11, observing a number of bursts. W/C Frogley retained his bombs when uncertain that the correct target was being bombed, and F/O Sweetman's bomb sight became unserviceable at the critical moment. Bombing photos suggested that the attack had overshot to the north, and this was confirmed later by PRU pictures.

53 Base was called into action on the 19th to provide fifty-two Lancasters for an attack on La Pallice, and, of these, 50 Squadron made ready thirteen, loading them with eleven 1,000 pounders each and four 500 pounders. They departed Skellingthorpe between 05.02 and 05.37 with S/Ls Flint and Stubbs the senior pilots on duty, and all reached the target area, where six to nine-tenths cloud hung over the western aiming-point, and seven to eight-tenths over the eastern one, with tops at 15,000 feet. This created challenging conditions in which to identify the targets, made more so by intense light flak, but crews claimed to have done so visually before bombing from 7,000 to 15,000 feet between 09.09 and 09.16. This was the first day of a spell of wet, cloudy and, sometimes, windy weather, which would last for the next week, and, although crews at Skellingthorpe were detailed for operations daily, nothing came of it. F/L Ward was posted to 57 Squadron on the 25th to assume the role of flight commander, while P/Os Slywchuk and Pethick moved on to 24 and 22 O.T.Us respectively at the end of their first tours.

This was the day on which major operations resumed, and more than nine hundred sorties would be launched against three targets, Rüsselsheim and nearby Darmstadt in southern Germany, and Brest, while a further four hundred would be engaged in a variety of smaller endeavours. The largest operation would be the all-Lancaster affair involving 461 aircraft from 1, 3, 6 and 8 Groups in a return to the Opel motor works, while 334 others attended to eight coastal batteries around Brest. 5 Group was assigned to Darmstadt, a university city and centre of scientific research and development, and one of a few almost virgin targets considered to be worthy of attention. 5 Group assembled a force of 191 Lancasters and six Mosquitos, eighteen of the former made ready by 50 Squadron, and they departed Skellingthorpe between 20.28 and 21.07 with W/C Frogley the senior pilot on duty. The Master Bomber was one of five crews to return early, leaving his two Deputies from 83 Squadron, F/L Meggeson DFC and S/L Williams DFC to step into the breach, and F/O Carter of 50 Squadron was another "boomerang", after losing his W/T.

The target area was found to be free of cloud, and some ground haze was present, but this was not responsible for matters going awry early on. VHF communication proved to be weak, which made it difficult for the Deputy Master Bombers to pass on instructions, but five aircraft dropped flares at 01.05, which turned out to be too far to the west, and the low-level Mosquitos reported at 01.07, that they were unable to find the aiming point. H-hour was pushed back to 01.22, although bombing actually began at 01.19, and, soon after, someone left their VHF on transmit, creating a noise that drowned out all voice communications, at the same time that W/T became jammed. One of the Deputies was heard indistinctly instructing the crews to "bomb on the box" (H2S), and then he and the other Deputy were shot down. The main force crews did their best to comply, among them ten of those from 50 Squadron, who were over the target at 8,000 to 10,000 feet between 01.16 and 01.41 and described a widely scattered attack. The lack of marking persuaded six 50 Squadron crews to seek alternative targets, and W/C Frogley, F/L North and F/O Horsepool joined in the attack on Rüsselsheim fifteen miles to the north-west, which they identified by red and green TIs, while F/O Korpala bombed Fischbach, and F/Os Davis and MacConnell bombed unidentified built-up areas. ED856 was abandoned over France, and was initially, one of seven missing Lancasters, until news came through within hours that it had been abandoned at 23.00 by F/O Frew and crew over Allied territory near Le Mans, and they had arrived safely on the ground, albeit with a number of injuries to report.

The German port of Königsberg, now Kaliningrad in Lithuania, is located on the eastern side of the Bay of Danzig, and was being used by the enemy to supply its eastern front. It lay some 860 miles in a straight line from the bomber stations surrounding Lincoln, which increased to a round trip of 1,900 miles when routing across Denmark was taken into account. This made it the most distant location ever targeted by the Command, and was exceeded only by SOE flights to Poland. Such a distance required sacrificing bombs for fuel, and it was a reduced load of a single 2,000 pounder and twelve 500lb J cluster bombs that was loaded into each of 50 Squadron's seventeen Lancasters, which were part of an overall force of 174 Lancasters. Having been briefed for this target twice before without going, there was some doubt as to whether or not this one would go ahead, but it did, and the first 50 Squadron Lancaster began to roll at Skellingthorpe at 20.05 to be followed by the others over the ensuing thirty-eight minutes with F/Ls MacConnell and North the senior pilots on duty. Accompanying the force to the target area would be ten Lancasters carrying mines for delivery into the sea-lanes off Pillau at the entrance to the estuary serving Königsberg. Ahead of them lay a ten-hour marathon, which all from 50 Squadron would complete. When they arrived in the target area almost five hours later, after flying through electrical storms and icing conditions over Denmark, the skies were clear and the visibility good, and they were greeted by around a hundred searchlights and an intense flak defence. The flare force went in at 14,000 to 15,000 feet between 01.05 and 01.12, to be followed minutes later by the heavy markers at a lower level. The 50 Squadron crews identified the aiming-point by red TIs, and bombed them from 7,500 and 9,500 feet between 01.13 and 01.27. Returning crews were fairly enthusiastic about the outcome, reporting punctual marking, concentrated bombing and fires that could be seen, according to some, from 250 miles into the return journey. Photo-reconnaissance revealed that the main weight of the attack had fallen into the town's north-eastern districts, where fire had ripped through many building blocks at a cost of just four Lancasters. However, the job was not yet done, and a second operation would have to be mounted.

The final operations in the long-running flying-bomb campaign were conducted by small Oboe-led forces against twelve sites on the 28th, and Allied ground forces took control of the Pas-de-Calais a few days later. It was clear, that a decisive blow had not been delivered on Königsberg, and, at 17.30 on the 29th, seventeen 50 Squadron crews attended briefing at Skellingthorpe to learn that they were to be part of a returning 5 Group force of 189 Lancasters. They took off between 20.20 and 20.45 with F/Ls MacConnell and North the senior pilots on duty, and, because of the extreme range, they again carried between them only 480 tons of bombs to deliver onto four aiming points. The bomber stream made its way across the North Sea and Denmark and reached the target to encounter eight to ten-tenths cloud with a base at around 10,000 feet. The Master Bomber, W/C Woodroffe, one of 5 Group's most experienced raid controllers, having decided on a visual attack, instructed the first flare force wave to drop below the cloud, and kept the spearhead of the main force circling for twenty minutes before the marking began. The later arrivals could see the markers going down as they approached for what was a complex plan of attack that proceeded with the first flares going down at around 01.05 and continuing at regular intervals thereafter. At 01.24 the third flare force wave was instructed to illuminate the red spot fire, and a minute later an instruction was given to overshoot by 400 yards to the east of the aiming-point. At 01.26 a marker aircraft was told to run over the red marker and overshoot by 300 yards, while, at 01.27, another was ordered to overshoot by 600 yards east of the aiming-point, before the visual backers-up were sent to track over the reds and greens and overshoot by 300 yards. The flare force was invited to go home at 01.30, and, at 01.34, the visual marker crews were instructed first to back up the greens by 600 yards on a westerly heading, and, two minutes later, the concentrations of reds and greens. The 50 Squadron crews identified the target by the red and green TIs and searchlight concentrations, and confirmed their positions by H2S before bombing from 8,000 to 9,000 feet between 01.38 and 01.53.

The Master Bomber called a halt to bombing at 01.52 and sent the crews home, at which time F/O Davis and crew still had their bombs on board, having circled for twenty-seven minutes, during which time they became increasingly agitated at the controller's refusal to let them bomb until further backing up had taken place. Enemy night-fighters were much in evidence over the target, and one latched onto ND991 at 01.42 at 20,000 feet some twenty-five miles south-south-east of the target. At the same time, they were coned and lost 18,000 feet before escaping, only to find another night-fighter on their tail, from which three cannon shells struck home and caused fires in the mid-upper turret and bomb-aimer's compartment. When they landed after more than ten hours aloft to find that four 50 Squadron Lancasters were among fifteen missing, the Davis crew was scathing about the performance of W/C Woodroffe, and blamed his stubbornness for the high casualty rate of 7.9%. They maintained that the backers-up had confirmed the marking to be on the mark, despite which, he kept some crews orbiting for up to forty minutes. The demise of ED588 to a crash in Sweden with the loss of F/O Carver and his crew was doubly sad, because she had been with the squadron since arriving from 97 Squadron in early 1943, and had participated in all of the campaigns since, notching up what was probably an unprecedented fifteen trips to Berlin during the twelve months to March 1944. Her total operations tally was, according to various records, 126, 128 or 130, and it seems that 116 of these were undertaken with 50 Squadron. The crews of F/O Clarke and F/O Holseth were both lost without trace in LM222 and NF921 respectively, presumably having been chased out to sea and shot down by night-fighters. The operation's other casualty from Skellingthorpe was PA994, in which F/O Horspool and all but one of his crew were killed, the survivor falling into enemy hands. Post-raid reconnaissance confirmed that the operation had been an outstanding success, which destroyed over 40% of the town's residential and 20% of its industrial buildings.

The flying-bomb campaign may now have ended, but a new one against V-2 rocket storage and launching sites began on the 31st with raids on nine suspected locations in northern France. 5 Group sent three forces, of forty-nine, forty-six and fifty-two Lancasters with two Mosquitos each to respectively target sites at Auchy-les-Hesdin, Rollancourt and Bergueneuse, all situated some twenty miles inland from the coast at Berck-sur-Mer. 53 Base was assigned to the last-mentioned, for which 50 Squadron made ready a dozen Lancasters, and dispatched them from Skellingthorpe between 15.48 and 16.20 led by S/L Flint. All reached the target area to find five-tenths cloud with a base at 6,000 feet and tops as high as 18,000 feet, out of which issued occasional heavy rain showers. The Mosquitos dropped smoke markers, which nine of the 50 Squadron crews bombed from 10,500 to 14,000 feet between 18.19 and 18.39, while F/O Warrington and F/L MacConnell and their crews failed to identify the aiming-point through the cloud and smoke, and F/O Bland suffered a hang-up. The operation appeared to be successful, and the collapse of a probable tunnel entrance was observed. This concluded a month of feverish and record activity for most heavy squadrons, during which 50 Squadron took part in twenty-one operations, and dispatched 255 sorties for the loss of eleven Lancasters and eight complete crews.

September 1944

The destructive power of the Command was now almost beyond belief. Each of its heavy bomber groups was capable of laying waste to a German town and city at one go, and, from now until the end of the war, this would be demonstrated in awesome and horrific fashion. Much of the Command's effort during the new month would be directed towards the liberation of the three French ports remaining in enemy hands, but operations began for 5 Group with an attack on shipping at Brest on the 2nd, for which sixty-seven Lancasters were detailed from 55 Base. They flew through thunderstorms on the way out, and, on arrival in the target area, initially found a layer of five to seven-tenths cumulus cloud between 2,000 and 9,000 feet affording a range of visibilities between good and poor. However, as the cloud appeared to be drifting away, they were ordered to orbit until the aiming-point could be identified visually. The bombing was carried out unopposed and was observed to straddle the quays, although some of it hit the town also. Post-raid reconnaissance revealed damage to a number of the vessels at berth.

Preparations were put in hand on the following morning to launch attacks on six Luftwaffe-occupied aerodromes in southern Holland. A total of 675 aircraft were to be involved, 5 Group detailing 103 Lancasters and two Mosquitos for its target at Deelen, while again, 53 Base remained at home. Cloud on the way out created challenging conditions for formation-keeping, and, at the target, varying amounts of cloud up to nine-tenths with tops at 7,000 feet forced the crews to orbit while they awaited gaps through which to identify the aiming-point visually. Despite a spirited flak defence from the airfield, there were no losses, and returning crews were relatively confident that they had fulfilled their brief, although it would be the 6th before photo-reconnaissance provided a partial cover of the target area and revealed at least sixty craters around runway intersections and taxiways.

Most of 5 Group remained at home over the ensuing five days, while enemy strong-points in and around Le Havre received daylight visitations from other elements of the Command on the 5th, 6th, 8th and 9th. These operations took place during a spell of unhelpful weather conditions, and the attacks of the 8th and 9th were not fully pressed home. As this campaign began, 53 Base was roused from its inactivity on the 5th to provide aircraft for an evening daylight attack on a coastal battery holding out at Brest. The force of sixty Lancasters and seven Mosquitos included a marking element from 54 Base, with thirteen of the former representing 50 Squadron. They departed Skellingthorpe between 16.12 and 16.26, with W/C Frogley the senior pilot on duty and first away. Cloud conditions at the target varied from zero to five-tenths in a layer between 2,500 and 6,800 feet, and the aiming-point was identified by smoke markers backed up by green TIs. The 50 Squadron crews carried out their part in the two-phase attack from 5,000 to 9,000 feet between 19.35 and 20.02, but F/O Carter and crew suffered a hang-up on their first pass, and the bombs fell out as soon as the bomb doors were opened at the start of the second run.

Mönchengladbach was posted as the target for 113 Lancasters and fourteen Mosquitos of 5 Group on the 9th, in the absence of a contribution from 53 Base. The aiming-point was the centre, which, with Operation Market Garden looming, was expected soon to be within striking distance of the advancing Allied forces. The crews would have to wait until the early hours of the 10th before departing their stations, eventually to set course for the target by way of Ostend. They found clear skies and good visibility as they followed on the heels of the flare forces, and bombed on red TIs, observing a number of large explosions and the glow of fires from the Dutch coast up to eighty miles away. There were no losses, and photo-reconnaissance confirmed the town centre to be in ruins.

A further attack on German positions around Le Havre was carried out on the 10th and involved almost a thousand aircraft. 5 Group supported the effort with 108 Lancasters and two Mosquitos from 53 and 54 Bases, 50 Squadron loading nineteen of its own with eleven 1,000 and four 500 pounders each, and dispatching them from Skellingthorpe between 14.57 and 15.40 with S/L Stubbs the senior pilot on duty. There were no early returns, and the crews were greeted at the French coast by clear skies and just a little ground haze, which enabled them to identify the target visually. They released their bombs onto red TIs from 11,000 to 12,000 feet between 17.22 and 17.29, and observed the area to become enveloped in smoke.

The 11th would bring the final attacks on the environs of the port, and would involve 218 aircraft drawn from 4, 5, 6 and 8 Groups. 5 Group contributed ninety-three Lancasters from 53, 54 and 55 Bases, 50 Squadron providing ten of them, which took off between 04.10 and 04.42 with W/C Frogley the senior pilot on duty. They arrived in the target area under clear skies with slight haze, and located their aiming points, to the north and south of the outer defences at Cadillac, just after dawn. Initially, there were no markers on the northern aiming-point, and nothing was heard from the Master Bomber, which left the crews to their own devices. The 50 Squadron crews mostly bombed on red and green TIs at the southern aiming-point from 9,000 to 13,000 feet between 07.33 and 07.42, and, once the northern aiming-point had been marked at 07.41, the attack continued until around 07.50. Photo-reconnaissance confirmed accurate and concentrated bombing, and, within hours of this operation, the German garrison surrendered to British forces.

With the exception of W/C Frogley, all of the crews who had participated in the morning operation, found themselves on the Order of Battle and back in the briefing room at Skellingthorpe later in the day, along with eleven others, to learn of their part in 5 Group's return to Darmstadt, which had escaped serious damage at its hands during the last week of August. A force of 221 Lancasters and fourteen Mosquitos was made ready, and the 50 Squadron element took off between 20.10 and 21.09 with F/Ls Enoch and North the senior pilots on duty. F/O Hewett and crew returned early with an unserviceable mid-upper turret, leaving the others to arrive in the skies over southern Germany to find them clear of cloud, and, despite some ground haze, good visibility prevailing as the flare force went in at 17,000 feet at 23.52, homing in on a green Mosquito-laid TI. The Master bomber seemed satisfied with the illumination, and required no further flares, leaving the backers-up to drop their TIs over the ensuing four minutes, before being sent home at 23.59. The main force followed up with extreme accuracy and concentration, the 50 Squadron crews bombing on red and green TIs from 13,500 to 15,000 feet between 23.58 and 00.08. The city centre became engulfed in flames, which spread outwards to consume large parts of the built-up area, and the glow, according to some, could be seen from the French coast, 250 miles away. The conditions had been ideal for the 5 Group marking method, and photo-reconnaissance confirmed the main weight of the attack to have fallen in the centre and surrounding districts to the south and east. It was learned after the war, that the attack had resulted in a genuine firestorm, only the third to be recorded after Hamburg and Kassel in 1943, although a number of local ones may have occurred in other cities like Berlin and Stuttgart. More than twelve thousand people died in the inferno, and a further seventy thousand, 60% of a total population of 120,000, were made homeless. The operation cost the group twelve Lancasters, among which were 50 Squadron's NF919 and PD294, both of which were heading out of the target area when the end came. The former crashed at 00.15 some ten miles south-west of the centre of Ludwigshafen, killing the crew of F/Sgt McLean RCAF, while the latter came down twenty-five minutes later near Lampertheim, on the eastern side of the Rhine between Worms and Mannheim. F/O Odgers RNZAF perished with three members of his crew, and the three survivors were taken into captivity.

Orders were received on 5 Group stations on the 12th to prepare for a return to southern Germany that night, this time to target Stuttgart. Nineteen 50 Squadron crews attended the briefing at Skellingthorpe, and learned that they were to be part of a force of 195 Lancasters and fourteen Mosquitos, which would be accompanied by nine ABC Lancasters from 1 Group's 101 Squadron. A simultaneous operation by 378 Lancasters and nine Mosquitos of 1, 3 and 8 Groups would take place at Frankfurt, a hundred miles to the north. The 50 Squadron element took off between 18.36 and 19.29 with F/L North the senior pilot on duty, but the lateness of the departures of F/Os Hewett and Nisbet and their crews, and the failure of the latter's rear turret, persuaded them to turn back early. The others mostly enjoyed an uneventful flight across France to Stuttgart, which was found to be under clear skies with moderate visibility and ground haze, and, therefore, ideal conditions for the low-level markers. The marking and backing up was very accurate, and the main force bombing concentrated upon the city centre, with a slight tendency to creep back towards the north-eastern district of Bad Canstatt and beyond into Feuerbach. The 50 Squadron crews bombed on red TIs from 14,000 to 16,000 feet between 23.10 and 23.28, and all but one returned safely to report a successful operation. Returning crews reported a huge explosion at 23.25, which lasted for about five seconds, and, when a PRU aircraft photographed the city on the following morning, the entire centre was obscured by the smoke from numerous and widespread fires. Only four Lancasters were missing from this operation, but 50 Squadron's LM162 crashed on the north-eastern outskirts of Lincoln at 02.33, after being involved in a mid-air collision at 1,200 feet. F/O Hickling and his crew survived, although two were reported to have sustained injury. Local reports from Stuttgart described the central districts as "erased", and it seems that a firestorm erupted in northern and west-central districts, wiping them from the map. Almost twelve hundred people lost their lives, the highest death toll ever in this much-bombed city.

Other than 617 Squadron's first of three attacks on Tirpitz on the 15th, 5 Group undertook no further operations until the morning of the 17th, when contributing to a total of 762 aircraft made ready to attack troop positions at seven locations around the port of Boulogne. The raids would be staggered over a four-hour period, and would benefit from a 5 Group effort of 195 Lancasters and four Mosquitos, twenty-one of the former representing 50 Squadron and departing Skellingthorpe between 07.33 and 08.15 with F/L North the senior pilot on duty. The Skellingthorpe squadrons were in the second wave of aircraft to attack one of two aiming-points assigned to the group, and were an hour behind the first wave. They found clear skies with good visibility, and a little flak from a coastal position to the north, which did not impede their progress. They saw red TIs marking out the aiming-point, and delivered their eleven 1,000 and four 500 pounders each from 6,000 to 8,000 feet between 09.42 and 09.48, failing to observe the results because of smoke drifting across the area. A total of three thousand tons of bombs was sufficient to pave the way for Allied ground forces to move in shortly afterwards to accept the surrender of the German garrison. This left only Calais of the major French ports still under enemy occupation.

5 Group stations received orders on the 18th to prepared for an operation that night against the port of Bremerhaven, located on the East Bank at the mouth of the River Weser, some thirty miles north of Bremen. It was to be a classic 5 Group-style attack, employing the low-level visual marking method and involved 206 Lancasters and seven Mosquitos. At Skellingthorpe, 50 Squadron loaded nineteen Lancasters with a mix of 2,000 pounders and 500lb J cluster bombs plus incendiaries, and sent them off between 17.50 and 18.31 with F/L Steele the senior pilot on duty. There were no early returns, allowing the squadron to arrive intact in the target area to find favourable weather conditions and good visibility. They ran in on the aiming-point at medium level to release their loads onto red TIs from 14,000 to 15,500 feet between 20.59 and 21.07, mostly in accordance with the Master Bomber's instructions. A number of huge explosions were witnessed at 21.02 and 21.07, and, as they headed out of the target area, they could see many large fires spreading throughout the built-up area, the glow from which remained visible for at least 150 miles. Post-raid reconnaissance revealed that this first major attack on the port, carried out by what, at the time, could be considered to be a modest force, had devasted the built-up areas north and south of the harbour entrance, wiping out installations and warehousing, and only the most northerly and southerly suburbs had escaped complete destruction. Local reports produced a figure of 2,670 buildings reduced to rubble and thirty-thousand people bombed out of their homes, all at the modest cost to 5 Group of a single Lancaster and a Mosquito.

Nineteen 50 Squadron crews assembled for briefing at Skellingthorpe on the 19th, and learned that they were to be part of a predominantly 5 Group attack on the twin towns of Mönchengladbach and Rheydt. This represented a shallow penetration into Germany, just ten minutes from the Dutch border, and, therefore, a short round trip of four-and-a-half to five hours, followed by a night in bed. 217 Lancasters and ten Mosquitos were made ready, along with ten ABC Lancasters from 101 Squadron, and the 50 Squadron participants took off between 18.33 and 19.08 with S/L Stubbs the senior pilot on duty, each Lancaster carrying a 2,000 pounder and eleven 500lb J cluster bombs. The Master Bomber for the operation was W/C Guy Gibson VC, DSO, DFC, who had been agitating to get back into the war before it was over, and didn't want his service to end in a backwater, while others gained the glory by being in at the death. Gibson was a warrior, and the war had brought out of him qualities, which, in peacetime, may have lain dormant. War had also given him a direction, and he revelled in the company of fellow operational types, particularly those of the officer class. Having been torn away from the operational scene following the success of the Dams operation, his direction had gone, and he had become listless, frustrated and discontented. His time in the operational wilderness had not, however, deprived him of his arrogance and self-belief, and when the opportunity to fly as Master Bomber on the coming raid presented itself, he grabbed it. He was driven the three miles from Coningsby to Woodhall Spa to collect his 627 Squadron Mosquito, which, for whatever reason, he rejected, and swapped with F/L Mallender, causing a degree of resentment. Gibson had already set the tone for the evening by rejecting the advice of W/C Charles Owen, who had been Master Bomber at this target ten nights earlier. Owen had advised him to leave the target by a south-westerly route, and cross north-eastern France to the coast, and also to observe orders to remain above 10,000 feet. Gibson insisted that he would fly home via a direct route across Holland at low level, and would not be dissuaded. He took off ahead of the 627 Squadron element at 19.51, to meet up with the main force over the target, where two aiming-points were to be marked.

Some crews reported icing clouds at around 9,000 feet as they made their way to the target over Belgium at around 9,000 feet, and chose to keep below, before climbing fast to 15,000 feet as the cloud dispersed. The marking was complex, with a green marker to be dropped on a factory in a western district of Mönchengladbach, and a yellow marker on railway yards in the north, while a red marker was to be placed on railway yards in Rheydt, two miles to the south. It would have been a demanding plan even for an experienced Master Bomber, which Gibson was not, but, even so, his instructions were heard clearly. All seemed to be going to plan, with accurate and punctual marking for the green and yellow forces, but late, though accurate marking for the red force, and some of the red force crews were diverted to the green aiming-point. The 50 Squadron crews were assigned to the green force, and identified it by flares and TIs, before bombing from 10,000 to 11,300 feet between 21.51 and 21.57, observing the target to be well ablaze with the glow visible for at least a hundred miles into the return flight. Post-raid reconnaissance confirmed a highly destructive attack on both towns for the loss of four Lancasters and a Mosquito. Gibson had returned low over Holland, just as he said he would, and crashed on the outskirts of Steenbergen in south-western Holland, with fatal consequences for him, and Coningsby's recently appointed station navigation officer, S/L James Warwick.

It was now time to turn attention upon Calais as the final port still under enemy occupation. Only one 5 Group Lancaster was involved in the first round of attacks on enemy positions on the 20th, after which, the group remained inactive until the 23rd. Orders came through on that morning to prepare 136 Lancasters and five Mosquitos for an attack that night on the aqueduct section of the Dortmund-Ems Canal south of Ladbergen, a target associated with the group since June 1940. It was also the scene of a disaster for 617 Squadron in September 1943, during which the former 50 Squadron pilot, F/L Les Knight RAAF, had lost his life while protecting the lives of his seven-man crew. An element from 617 Squadron would be on scene also on this night, to open the attack with Tallboys, to which the raised banks containing the waterway were particularly vulnerable. Germany's canal system was a vital component in the transport network, and facilitated the import of raw materials and the export of finished goods to support the war effort. Its wide thoroughfares allowed the passage of large barges, and, as the slack in Germany's war production was taken up during 1944, traffic was being pushed through at increasing levels. While this operation was in progress, a second 5 Group force of 108 Lancasters, four Mosquitos and the P38 Lightning would hit the Handorf night-fighter airfield some ten miles to the south to prevent it from interfering. The main operation on this night, however, would be conducted by 549 aircraft from 1, 3, 4 and 8 Groups seventy miles to the south-west at Neuss, situated across the Rhine opposite Düsseldorf, and this, hopefully, might help to split the enemy defences.

50 Squadron prepared nineteen Lancasters for the Dortmund-Ems Canal, and they departed Skellingthorpe between 18.39 and 19.30 with S/L Flint the senior pilot on duty. All reached the target area to encounter a layer of ten-tenths cloud between 8,000 and 9,500 feet, but with good visibility beneath. The Master Bomber found himself unable to direct the attack, and experienced great difficulty in communicating the fact to his Deputy because of intense interference on VHF. Identification and marking of the aiming-point proved to be difficult, and only two green TIs could be seen by a few crews. There would be complaints later that there was no control, and some crews orbited and remained in the target area for up to thirty-five minutes before bombing either on green TIs at Handorf or on yellows at Münster, which was selected as the last-resort target. F/Os Drinkell, Nisbet and Warrington joined in at Handorf, F/O McEachern bombed Münster and F/L Enoch backtracked to Neuss to deliver his load, while F/O Lillies failed to identify a suitable target and brought his load home. This left the remainder to try their hand at the primary target, and eleven of them are known to have bombed from 6,700 to 15,750 feet between 21.50 and 22.09, aiming at the glow of red TIs. Two others of the 50 Squadron element were among fourteen Lancasters failing to return after the Canal-Busters were badly mauled by night-fighters on the way home. LM212 crashed near Zelhem in east-central Holland, killing F/O Sweetman and all but his mid-upper gunner, who became a PoW. ME700 came down further north between Ommen and Zwolle at 23.40 after F/L Korpela RCAF and two of his crew had abandoned it to its fate, and they evaded capture, while four others died in the wreckage. Post-raid reconnaissance revealed no new damage at Handorf, where only twenty-two aircraft had bombed, but two Tallboys were probably responsible for breaches in both branches of the canal, which left a six-mile stretch drained and unnavigable.

The second of the series of raids on enemy positions around Calais was mounted by 188 aircraft on the 24th, for which 5 Group detailed thirty Lancasters from the 53 Base stations of Skellingthorpe and Waddington. 50 Squadron dispatched eight Lancasters between 17.20 and 17.35 with S/L Flint the senior pilot on duty, and, apparently, all reached the target, which was obscured beneath ten-tenths cloud with a base at 2,000 feet. However, we are left with a confusing picture of events, the squadron ORB recording a series of messages received by most crews between 18.20 and 18.26 to "cease bombing". According to the map references provided by the crews, they were over Kent at the time, which harmonizes with the likely distance covered since take-off, but some reported observing red TIs at 18.38, and F/O Bloor and crew received no signal before carrying out a bombing run, which ended with a total hang-up. F/O Carter and crew also picked up no message, but, despite observing the glow of TIs, failed to positively identify the aiming-point and did not bomb. In the event, only 126 aircraft bombed, eight of them from 5 Group, and they attacked either on a reference provided by Oboe skymarkers or came below the cloud base to bomb visually. At such a height, they were sitting ducks for the heavy and light flak batteries, which accounted for seven Lancasters and a Halifax. LM264 failed to return to Skellingthorpe, and disappeared into the sea, taking with it to their deaths the crew of F/O Warrington. This was an unusually mature crew, in which the gunners were thirty-seven and thirty-nine years old, and the flight engineer thirty-six.

It was a similar story on the following day, when only a third of more than eight hundred aircraft were able to deliver their bombs, before the Master Bomber called a halt to proceedings in the face of low cloud. The campaign continued on the 26th, with two separate raids against seven enemy positions around Cap Gris Nez and nearer Calais involving more than seven hundred aircraft. This time the conditions were favourable, and bombing was observed to be concentrated around the aiming points. On the afternoon of the 26th, fourteen 50 Squadron crews attended briefing, and learned that the night's operation was to be against Karlsruhe in southern Germany, for which 216 Lancasters of 5 Group were made ready, along with ten of the ABC variety from 101 Squadron and eleven Mosquitos. It was to be a two-phase attack with a two-hour gap between, and the 53 and 55 Base elements assigned to the second phase. This meant a late take-off, and it was between 00.27 and 01.02 that the 50 Squadron crews departed Skellingthorpe with F/L Wake the senior pilot on duty. They flew out over France with ten-tenths cloud beneath them, which persisted all the way to the target, but thinned to a narrow band with the base estimated to be between 6,000 and 7,000 feet. The plan was to bomb through the cloud on H2S, guided by Wanganui flares, and some approaching crews observed a red TI cascade above the cloud at 03.54. The 50 Squadron crews focused on the glow of red and green TIs, and bombed them between 04.02 and 04.09 in accordance with the instructions of the Master Bomber, from a variety of heights ranging from below the cloud base at 6,000 feet to 12,250 feet. All returned safely to report what appeared to be a city in flames and the glow of fires visible for up to 150 miles into the return journey. There were no plottable bombing photos, but reconnaissance confirmed that the attack had been spread throughout the city and had left a large part of it devastated.

As the crews returned to their stations after 07.00, elements of 1, 3, 4 and 8 Groups were preparing to leave theirs for a further attack on the Calais area. On arrival, the Master Bomber ordered the 340-strong force to come below the cloud base to bomb visually, and another successful operation ensued. Later that day, sixteen 50 Squadron crews attended briefing for an operation that night against Kaiserslautern, an historic city on the edge of the Palatinate Forest, some thirty miles west of Mannheim. It would be the first major attack of the war on this location, for which a force of 217 Lancasters, including ten from 101 Squadron, and ten Mosquitos, was made ready. The 50 Squadron Lancasters were loaded between them with seven 2,000 pounders, eighty-four 500lb J cluster bombs and twenty-four thousand 4lb incendiaries, which they lifted into the air between 21.44 and 22.17 with F/L Enoch the senior pilot on duty. Clear skies over England gave way to a build-up of cloud over the Channel, and, from the French coast to near the target, they encountered ten-tenths cumulus with a base at 2,800 feet. The target was partially covered by a thin layer of five to eight-tenths cloud with tops at 3,000 feet, with a further layer at 6,000 to 7,000 feet. The marking with red and green TIs was punctual and accurate, and a green TI visible in the centre of the town became the objective for the main force crews in accordance with the Master Bomber's instructions at 00.58. The 50 Squadron crews attacked from 4,000 to 5,750 feet between 01.03 and 01.13 and observed the bombing to be concentrated. Two yellow explosions were seen at 01.02, and fires were beginning to take hold as the force retreated towards the west. Reconnaissance revealed massive damage within the city, caused by more than nine hundred tons of bombs, and an estimated 36% of the built-up area was reduced to ruins.

The final raids on German positions around Calais were carried out by 490 aircraft of 1, 3, 6 and 8 Groups on the 28th, and the garrison surrendered to Canadian forces shortly thereafter. During the course of the month the squadron participated in twelve operations and dispatched 197 sorties for the loss of six Lancasters and five crews.

A theme running throughout October was a campaign against the island of Walcheren in the Scheldt estuary, where heavy gun emplacements were barring the approaches to the much-needed port of Antwerp some forty miles upstream. Attempts to bomb these positions in September had proved unsuccessful, and it was decided to flood the land, both to inundate the batteries, and to render the terrain difficult to defend when the ground forces moved in. 252 Lancasters were drawn from 1, 5 and 8 Groups and made ready on the 3rd to attack the seawalls at Westkapelle, the most westerly point of the island. 5 Group contributed 128 Lancasters, allotted to four of eight waves of thirty aircraft each, with the Tallboy-carrying 617 Squadron Lancasters standing off to be called in only if required. A breach was opened by the fifth wave, which was extended by those following behind, and the flood waters had reached the town by the time the last Lancasters turned for home. 50 Squadron had not been invited to take part, and had to wait until 5 Group's first major outing of the month, which was posted on the 5th, as a daylight attempt to bomb the port of Wilhelmshaven through ten-tenths cloud on H2S. A force of 227 Lancasters, one Mosquito and the P38 Lightning was assembled with 50 Squadron providing twenty-one aircraft, and they set out from Skellingthorpe between 07.29 and 08.22 with W/C Frogley the senior pilot on duty. Whether or not it was part of the plan, the controller led the force around the northern side of Heligoland, before heading for Jade Bay, and all but one made it to Germany's north-western coast. Here, they found the target, as forecast, concealed under a layer of ten-tenths cloud between 3,000 and 5,000 feet with good visibility above. The 50 Squadron crews established their positions by H2S-fix or by observing others, and eighteen of them delivered their ten 1,000 pounders and four 500lb J cluster bombs each from 18,000 to 19,000 feet between 11.04 and 11.11. F/L Wake dropped his load on Carolinensiel on the coast to the north-west of the primary target, F/L North attacked a railway line six miles to the west, and F/O Marris a built-up area four miles to the north-west. No results were observed, and there was no possibility of making an assessment, but the impression of a scattered attack was confirmed later when photo-reconnaissance became possible.

From this point until the end of the war, German towns and cities were to be subjected to a new and terrible bomber offensive, beginning with a new Ruhr campaign, which was to open at Dortmund, and for which a 3, 6 and 8 Group force of 523 aircraft was made ready on the 6th. 5 Group, meanwhile, had its own target, and prepared 237 Lancasters and seven Mosquitos for what would prove to be the thirty-second and final raid of the war on the city of Bremen. 50 Squadron loaded twenty-one Lancasters with a total of two cookies, twenty 1,000 pounders and 45,750 x 4lb incendiaries, and dispatched them from Skellingthorpe between 17.12 and 17.52 with S/L Flint the senior pilot on duty. Having climbed out and set course, they left the cloud behind and headed into crystal clear skies with a three-quarter moon. They found the target area to be free of cloud, which was ideal for the 5 Group low-level marking method, and the conditions handed the hapless city on a plate to the bombers. The 50 Squadron crews carried out their attacks in the face of many searchlights and the usual flak response, and aimed for the red and green TIs from 15,750 to 18,000 feet between 20.27 and 20.33. They turned away from a city in flames, the glow from which remained visible for a hundred miles and more. The success of the operation was confirmed by post-raid reconnaissance and local reports, which described a huge area of fire, and catalogued the destruction of more than 4,800 houses and apartment blocks, and severe damage to war industry factories, all achieved at the modest cost of five aircraft. The number of sorties to complete a tour had been reduced from thirty-five to thirty-three, and this meant that F/L Enoch could now be screened from operations.

The crews of F/L Wake, F/O Osborne, F/O London and F/O Bland were posted to Bardney on the 7th to add experience to the newly-reforming 227 Squadron, which was being created out of 9 Squadron's A Flight and 619 Squadron's B Flight. Following the failure of Operation Market Garden, the German frontier towns of Cleves (Kleve) and Emmerich were earmarked for attention by daylight on the 7th. Five miles apart and separated by the Rhine, both would suffer massive damage at the hands of large forces from 1, 3, 4 and 8 Groups. 5 Group, meanwhile, was to return to Walcheren, to target the seawalls near Flushing, and made ready 121 Lancasters and three Mosquitos, twelve of the former representing 50 Squadron. They took off between 12.24 and 12.36 with W/C Frogley the senior pilot on duty, and all reached the target area to identify the two aiming-points visually and by red TIs. The 50 Squadron crews delivered their fourteen 1,000 pounders each from 5,400 to 6,500 feet almost as one between 14.10 and 14.11. Many of the bomb carried by other squadrons contained a thirty-minute delay fuse, but others detonated on impact, and the dyke was already beginning to crumble as the bombers headed home, where confirmation of a successful outcome would catch up with them.

Focus remained on the Scheldt defences, and the gun battery at Fort Frederik Hendrik near Breskens on the East Scheldt was targeted by elements of 1 and 8 Groups on the 11th, while 115 Lancasters from 5 Group were assigned to others near Flushing on the North Bank of the West Scheldt. At the same time sixty-one Lancasters and two Mosquitos from the group were to attempt to breach the seawalls at Veere, situated on the eastern side of Walcheren opposite Westkapelle. 50 Squadron contributed twenty Lancasters to Flushing, and they departed Skellingthorpe between 13.00 and 13.19 with W/C Frogley the senior pilot on duty. On arrival in the target area the crews encountered varying amounts of cloud between two and seven-tenths with tops at 4,000 to 5,000 feet, and the 50 Squadron crews carried out their attacks from 5,200 to 7,500 feet between 14.59 and 15.04. Post-raid reconnaissance revealed an area of flooding of 800 x 250 yards at Veere, but no new damage to the gun positions.

The 14th brought the opening salvoes of Operation Hurricane, a terrifying demonstration to the enemy of the overwhelming superiority of the Allied air forces ranged against it. Bomber Command ordered a maximum effort from all but 5 Group to attack Duisburg, for which 1,013 Lancasters, Halifaxes and Mosquitos answered the call. The American 8th Air Force would also be in business on this day, targeting the Cologne area further south with 1,250 bombers escorted by 749 fighters. The RAF force took off at first light, picked up its own fighter escort, and delivered 4,500 tons of high-explosives and incendiaries into Duisburg shortly after breakfast time, causing unimaginable destruction. That night, similar numbers returned to press home the point about superiority, bringing the total weight of bombs over the two raids to 9,000 tons from 2,018 sorties. The only involvement by 5 Group were single sorties by a Lancaster and a Mosquito to conduct a photo-reconnaissance of the operation.

However, 5 Group was not otherwise inactive, and took advantage of the evening activity over the Ruhr to return to Brunswick, the scene of quite a number of unsatisfactory previous attempts to land a really telling blow. A force of 232 Lancasters and eight Mosquitos was made ready, of which twenty of the former were provided by 50 Squadron. They departed Skellingthorpe between 22.20 and 23.06 with F/Ls North and Steele the senior pilots on duty and all others of flying officer rank. All reached the target area to find conditions ideal for low-level marking method, but, approaching the aiming-point at 18,000 feet from the south-west over Hallendorf/Salzgitter, the crews had to run the gauntlet of searchlight cones and heavy flak for the three minutes it took to pass through. They were greeted by clear skies and good visibility, which facilitated accurate marking, and, although the early stages of bombing tended to undershoot, the Master Bomber quickly brought it back on track, calling for crews to overshoot by up to nineteen seconds, depending on their time of arrival. The 50 Squadron contingent passed over the aiming-point between 02.30 and 02.44, and delivered their payloads onto red TIs from 16,000 to 17,500 feet to contribute to a highly effective raid. 83 Squadron's F/O Price complained that main force crews were jettisoning incendiaries all the way back as far as the Rhine, and thereby illuminating the track for any stalking night fighters, and this was confirmed by a number of 50 Squadron crews. In the event, only a single Lancaster failed to return from what was, indeed, confirmed to be an outstanding result, which had wiped out the entire centre of this historic city, and visited damage on almost every district.

On the 17th, 5 Group posted the seawalls at Walcheren as the target for an afternoon attack by forty-seven Lancasters and three Mosquitos from 55 and 54 Bases. They found favourable conditions in which to deliver their delay-fused bombs, and most brought back an aiming-point photo, despite which, the photos from a reconnaissance aircraft, which had remained over the target from 14.55 to 15.10 to record the bomb blasts, revealed no extension to the breach in the dyke.

Following a break of four nights, twenty-one 50 Squadron crews reported to the Skellingthorpe briefing room on the 19th, to be given details of the operation that night against Nuremberg, which was to be a 5 Group affair involving a new record for the group of 263 Lancasters and seven Mosquitos. Meanwhile, 560 aircraft from the other groups would be plying their trade at Stuttgart, some ninety miles to the south-west. The 50 Squadron crews took off between 17.16 and 17.51, led by F/L North, and, unusually in recent times, suffered an early return in the shape of F/O Lillies and crew, who lost the use of their intercom and mid-upper turret and turned back some twenty miles short of the French coast at 19.00. For the others, the outward flight across France was uneventful, but the target was found to be covered by a wedge of eight to ten-tenths cloud between 3,000 and 10,000 feet, with poor visibility below. The marker force laid down flares and backed them up with others along with red and green TIs, which were observed to be somewhat scattered, and bombing had to take place on their glow observed through the cloud. The 50 Squadron crews carried out their attacks from 16,500 to 17,200 feet between 20.59 and 21.08 in accordance with the Master Bomber's instructions, before returning home uncertain as to the outcome. The impression given by the glow of fires was of an effective attack, but post-raid reconnaissance revealed the bombing to have fallen not on the intended city centre aiming-point, but predominantly into the more industrial southern districts, where almost four hundred houses were destroyed, along with forty-one industrial buildings.

It was back to Walcheren on the 23rd for 112 Lancasters of 5 Group, this time to target the coastal battery at Flushing. 50 Squadron loaded twenty-one Lancasters with a total of 217 x 1,000 pounders, and sent them skyward between 14.37 and 15.06 with S/L Stubbs the senior pilot on duty. They were greeted at the target by eight to ten-tenths cloud with a base at between 3,000 and 5,000 feet, and poor visibility below caused by haze and rain. The force was led in on what appeared to be a decent approach, but was ordered to "orbit port" as the lead crews experienced great difficulty in identifying their respective aiming-points. A second run was no more revealing, even for those crews who ventured down as low as 2,000 feet, and twenty would still have their bombs on board when ordered to go home. Nine 50 Squadron crews carried out a visual attack from 3,750 to 4,600 feet between 16.18 and 16.34, and observed their bombs to fall within the target area. Post-raid reconnaissance revealed evidence of seventy bomb bursts, including four near-misses, and the destruction of a number of buildings on the site.

That evening, a new record force of 1,055 aircraft was sent against Essen as part of the Hurricane "message", and dropped 4,538 tons of bombs, more than 90% of which was high explosive. This number was achieved without 5 Group, which took the night off, and committed only twenty-five Lancasters to gardening duties in northern waters on the following night. Essen was pounded again by more than seven hundred aircraft in daylight on the 25th, after which, it ceased to be an important source of war production. S/L Stubbs was posted to 54 Base on the 26th, having given magnificent service to 50 Squadron. Operation Hurricane moved on to Cologne on the 28th, when two districts east of the centre were totally devastated by more than seven hundred aircraft.

5 Group occupied the 28th with the preparation of a force of 237 Lancasters and seven Mosquitos for an operation that night against the U-Boot pens at Bergen in Norway. 50 Squadron made ready twenty-one Lancasters, and dispatched them between 22.12 and 22.52 with F/L Steele the senior pilot on duty. There were only two early returns from the entire force, which reached the target area after a three-and-a-half-hour outward flight, having battled their way through electrical storms. They had been told to expect clear conditions, although some doubts had been expressed about the forecast, and these were confirmed when the force was met by eight to ten-tenths cloud between 4,000 and 14,000 feet, which obscured the aiming-point. This would not have been a problem over Germany, however, the risk to Norwegian civilians was uppermost in the mind of the Master Bomber as he pondered his options before calling for the main force to descend. Even then, most were unable to pick out any markers, and the situation was exacerbated by intermittent VHF reception, which persuaded 83 Squadron's F/L Cornish to fly up and down the coast acting as a communications link between the Master Bomber and the main force. The flare force contingent did what they could between 12,500 and 15,000 feet, and the main force supporters flew as low as 4,500 feet, without being able to identify the target. The operation was abandoned after only forty-seven aircraft had bombed, among which were those containing the 50 Squadron crews of F/Os Groves, Marris, Fairbairn, Day and Rennie, who carried out their attacks from 6,000 to 7,500 feet between 02.02 and 02.06. Three Lancasters failed to return, including 50 Squadron's PD326, which was lost without trace with the crew of F/O Wonders.

The final operations against Walcheren were undertaken by 5 Group on the 30th, when two forces of fifty-one Lancasters and four Mosquitos each were sent against coastal batteries at Westkapelle and Flushing. They ran into four to seven-tenths cloud at 6,000 feet over the target, despite which, visibility was good, and the aiming-point was identified visually and marked by red TIs. Some of these became buried in the dunes and were partially concealed, leading to a little overshooting, but the operation proceeded more or less according to plan, and ground forces went in on the following day to begin a week of heavy fighting, culminating in the island's capture. Even then, the clearing of mines from the approaches to Antwerp would keep the port out of commission for a further three weeks. On the evening of the 30th, nine hundred aircraft returned to Cologne, and almost five hundred went back again twenty-four hours later to complete the destruction of the Rhineland Capital. During the course of the month the squadron carried out eight operations and dispatched 157 sorties for the loss of a single Lancaster and crew.

November 1944

The new month began with a daylight operation on the afternoon of the 1st, against the Meerbeck synthetic oil plant at Homberg, on the West Bank of the Rhine facing Duisburg. This target had inflicted heavy casualties on a number of 3 Group squadrons during the summer, but its reputation probably meant less to the likes of 50 Squadron, which briefed nineteen crews as part of an overall 5 Group force of 226 Lancasters and two Mosquitos, which were to be joined by fourteen 8 Group Mosquitos to provide the Oboe marking. Some good news before they made their way to their aircraft was that the number of sorties for a tour had been reduced again to thirty. They took off from Skellingthorpe between 13.41 and 14.04 with S/L Flint the senior pilot on duty, and all reached the target to find it completely obscured by cloud with tops at between 6,000 and 9,000 feet. Wanganui flares from earlier arrivals were well-scattered over a circle with a ten-mile radius, prompting a backer-up from 83 Squadron to drop a yellow TI over the built-up area, in the hope of attracting some bombing. Some 50 Squadron crews caught a glimpse of the target area through a chink in the cloud, while others carried out a time-and-distance run from the last visual pinpoint, before aiming at red skymarkers with green stars to deliver their thirteen 1,000 pounders each from 16,000 to 17,000 feet between 16.08 and 16.10. The problem seemed to be, that crews at the head of the stream had seen no markers, or were past them by the time they became evident, and had taken their bombs home. Among these was S/L Flint, who lost the Master Bomber's signal, and did not trust the widely spread markers sufficiently to aim at one. The attackers had faced an intense flak response, and, on return to their respective stations, there was plenty of work to occupy the airframe and engine fitters. At debriefing many crews reported difficulty in hearing the Master Bomber, after his VHF transmissions became jammed by someone in another aircraft leaving the transmit button on. Ultimately, the conditions rendered the whole attack ineffective, and, although 159 crews released their bombs, it is unlikely that any hit the intended target.

A large influx of new crews for 50 Squadron began on the 2nd, and included the arrival of S/L Blair from 49 Squadron, while others came in from 5LFS. Düsseldorf's turn to face a massive force came on that day, when 992 aircraft were made ready for what would prove to be the final major raid of the war on this much-bombed city. 5 Group put up 187 Lancasters, nineteen provided by 50 Squadron, for this rare experience for the "Lincolnshire Poachers" to operate with the rest of the Command. The 50 Squadron element took off between 16.19 and 16.53 with no senior pilots on duty, and all arrived at the target to find clear skies, moonlight and only ground haze to slightly mar the vertical visibility. The moonlight nullified the searchlights ringing the city, but, of greater concern was the heavy flak bursting at 17,000 to 20,000 feet. The main force crews found the aiming-point to be well illuminated and marked with red and green TIs, which the 50 Squadron participants bombed from 17,000 to 25,000 feet between 19.15 and 19.35. The 25,000-foot altitude was registered by F/O McEachern and crew, and, if accurate, was among the highest, if not the highest, recorded by a Lancaster crew. Returning crews reported fires beginning to take hold and smoke rising to 2,000 feet as they turned away, and were confident of a successful attack. This was confirmed by post-raid reconnaissance, which revealed that the northern half of the city had received the main weight of bombs, and that five thousand houses had been destroyed or seriously damaged.

The continuing campaign against Ruhr cities would be prosecuted by 749 aircraft at Bochum on the 4th, while 5 Group renewed its acquaintance with the Dortmund-Ems Canal, which had been repaired following the successful breaching of its banks near Münster in September. Now that Germany's railways were being pounded, the Dortmund-Ems and the nearby Mittelland Canal, took on a greater significance as vital components in the transportation system, particularly with regard to the movement of raw materials like coal and coke to the steel works of the Ruhr region. A force of 168 Lancasters and two Mosquitos contained twelve 50 Squadron aircraft, which took off between 17.37 and 17.55 with no senior pilots on duty. They were headed for the familiar aqueduct section of the canal south of Ladbergen, and hoped to sneak in under cover of the main operation sixty miles to the south, and, hopefully, avoid the attentions of night-fighters. The first marker aircraft of 83 Squadron arrived at the target at 19.19, after making a GPI run (ground position indicated) by means of H2S from Münster, and encountered clear skies with ground haze. A blind-dropped green TI burst on the canal bank four hundred yards short of the aiming-point, and the flare force went in between 19.20 and 19.28. Red TIs were observed to fall between the two aqueducts, after which, the Master Bomber cancelled the third wave of flares and sent them all home to leave the way clear for the main force. The first bombs tended to overshoot, but, thereafter, the main force produced an accurate and concentrated attack, the 50 Squadron crews bombing from 9,500 to 12,800 feet between 19.30 and 19.40. Photo-reconnaissance confirmed that both branches of the canal had been breached and drained, leaving barges stranded and the waterway unnavigable.

To capitalize on the success, an attack was planned for the 6th against the Mittelland Canal at Gravenhorst, a point about a mile north of Das Nasse Dreieck, the "Wet Triangle" at Bergeshövede. This was a triangular basin, where the two waterways converge about ten miles north of Ladbergen, the Dortmund-Ems continuing on to the west, and the Mittelland north and then to the east. It was a 5 Group show involving 239 Lancasters and seven Mosquitos, nineteen of the former representing 50 Squadron. They departed Skellingthorpe between 16.19 and 17.00 with the newly promoted F/L Arden the senior pilot on duty, and all reached the target area to find clear skies but haze up to around 4,000 feet affecting the visibility. The Master Bomber called in the flare force, despite which, the low-level Mosquito markers experienced great difficulty in identifying the aiming-point. A single Mosquito piloted by F/L De Vigne eventually did deliver its target indicator accurately onto the aiming-point, where it fell into the water and was extinguished. Only thirty-one aircraft bombed before the Master Bomber called a halt to proceedings, and all from 50 Squadron withheld theirs, jettisoning the delayed-action 1,000 pounders before setting course for home and encountering not only night-fighter activity, but also very challenging weather conditions of electrical storms and low cloud. F/O Nisbet and crew found it difficult in deteriorating weather conditions to find somewhere to land, and were running short of fuel when Snetterton Heath accepted them. LM368 was attacked by a night-fighter in the target area, and, during the corkscrew, Sgt Grange's rear gunner shot it down in flames. Ten Lancasters were less fortunate, and failed to return, among them 50 Squadron's LM628, which crashed near Heerde, some eight miles south of Zwolle in central Holland, killing F/O Rennie RCAF and his crew, who, with the exception of the flight engineer, were also members of the RCAF.

Earlier on the 6th, a series of raids on Ruhr oil refineries had begun with an area attack by more than seven hundred aircraft at Gelsenkirchen, where the Nordstern plant (Gelsenberg A.G.) was the aiming-point, and this was followed by smaller-scale operations at Homberg on the 8th, Wanne-Eickel on the 9th and Castrop-Rauxel on the morning of the 11th. Later, on the 11th, twenty 50 Squadron crews assembled in the briefing room to learn that they would shortly be attacking the Rhenania-Ossag synthetic oil plant at Harburg, a town situated on the South Bank of the Elbe opposite Hamburg. 237 Lancasters and eight Mosquitos were to take part in another all-5 Group show, while elements of 1 and 8 Groups targeted a similar plant at Dortmund. Each of the 50 Squadron Lancasters was loaded with a cookie, four 1,000 and four 500 pounders, and seven Nº14 cluster bombs in time for another early evening take-off between 16.13 and 16.45, with F/Ls Arden, Drinkell and North leading the way. F/O Hickling RAAF lost his starboard-outer engine, and, after jettisoning his bombs in the North Sea, was instructed to land at East Kirkby. We will return to pick up the story later. The others reached the target area to find largely clear conditions, with only a thin layer of stratus at 8,000 feet and another at 17,000 to 18,000 feet between them and the aiming-point. This they identified either by H2S or red and green TIs, before delivering their loads from 16,000 to 19,000 feet between 19.13 and 19.24. The defenders threw up a heavy flak barrage, which reached as high as 23,000 feet, but there were no Skellingthorpe Lancasters among the seven that failed to return. At debriefing, crews reported a large explosion at 19.28, followed by an oil fire, and local reports would confirm that heavy damage had been inflicted upon the town's residential and industrial districts.

While the above events were playing out over north-western Germany, LM360 was heading inland towards East Kirkby, with the starboard-inner engine now beginning to falter. It was decided to make for Fiskerton, and they were on final approach when the lack of power decided the issue, and the Lancaster came down three hundred yards short of the runway. F/O Hickling and crew emerged unscathed, but LM360, the Lancaster in which 61 Squadron's Bill Reid had earned the Victoria Cross twelve months earlier, was declared to be beyond economical repair. As 61 Squadron shared Skellingthorpe, both squadrons were able to mourn the passing of a legend, which had also had to undergo a major repair after Bill Reid's exploits. It will be recalled that this was the Hickling crew's second crash-landing, having narrowly escaped death following the mid-air collision two months earlier.

The 16th was devoted to the erasure from the map of the three small towns of Heinsberg, Jülich and Düren, located respectively in an arc from north to east of Aachen, and close to the German lines being advanced upon by American ground forces. A total of 1,188 aircraft were involved, and 1, 5 and 8 Groups provided the heavy bombing and marking force of 485 Lancasters for the first-mentioned. 50 Squadron contributed eighteen aircraft to the 5 Group effort of 214, and they took off from Skellingthorpe between 12.18 and 12.57 with F/Ls Arden, Drinkell and North the senior pilots on duty, and each Lancaster carrying a dozen 1,000 pounders. They flew to the target over ten-tenths cloud, which cleared to three-tenths stratus above 6,000 feet as they approached the aiming-point in the final wave of the attack. They bombed in accordance with the instructions of the Master Bomber from 10,000 to 13,000 feet between 15.26 and 15.41, and observed smoke rising through 9,000 feet as they turned for home, confident in the success of the attack. F/L Drinkell and crew were too occupied in a life and death struggle to notice what was happening around them, after LM296 was struck in the starboard mainplane by a bomb from above while flying at 10,000 feet. The payload was jettisoned immediately, both starboard engines shut down and the master fuel cocks cut, but the Lancaster became uncontrollable, and began to spiral downward with fuel igniting in the slipstream. Drinkell gave the bale-out order, but regained control and rescinded the order seconds before any crew members acted upon it. A course was set for home, but the Lancaster continued to sink, and at 2,000 feet, some forty minutes after the incident, Drinkell decided to restart the two starboard engines, which responded and enabled them to reach home. All of the other 50 Squadron crews claimed to have hit the target, but most of the bombing photos were unplottable because of the smoke covering the area. At debriefing, F/L Drinkell complained that the Master Bomber's instructions must either have been unheard or disobeyed by the crew responsible for the bomb from 13,000 feet that almost killed him and his crew, which suggested that the order had been to bomb from 10,000 feet. The operation was a complete success at a cost of just three aircraft, post-raid reconnaissance confirming that the town had been all-but erased from the map, and local reports gave a death toll in excess of three thousand inhabitants. In the event, unfavourable ground conditions prevented the American advance from succeeding.

F/L Enoch was posted to 1654 Conversion Unit on the 19th at the conclusion of his tour. Nineteen 50 Squadron crews were called to briefing on the 21st, to be told, that 53 Base would be going back to the Dortmund-Ems Canal on a night of multiple operations involving 1,345 sorties. 1, 4, 6 and 8 Groups were involved in three operations, each by 270 aircraft, against railway yards at Aschaffenburg, situated about twenty miles south-east of Frankfurt, and oil plants at Castrop-Rauxel and Sterkrade in the Ruhr. 5 Group prepared two forces of 137 and 123 Lancasters respectively, with Mosquito support, for the Mittelland and Dortmund-Ems Canals, while a whole host of minor operations would complete the Order of Battle. The 50 Squadron element departed Skellingthorpe for the latter between 17.15 and 17.48 with S/L Blair the senior pilot on duty for the first time. They encountered a layer of six to ten-tenths cloud in the target area between 4,000 and 8,000 feet, which did not inhibit the accuracy of the marking, and the canal could be identified visually during the run-up, but could not be seen from above. That mattered little as red TIs clearly marked out the aiming-point, and clear instructions from the Master Bomber kept the attack on track. The 50 Squadron crews bombed from 3,000 to 4,500 feet between 21.01 and 21.08, and all returned safely to report a successful operation, many also praising the performance of the Master Bomber.

In contrast, his opposite number at Gravenhorst was accused of causing confusion by issuing contradictory instructions, despite which, post-raid reconnaissance revealed that the canal had been breached over a distance of fifty feet on the western bank, south of the road bridge, and had been drained over a thirty-mile stretch to leave fifty-nine vessels stranded and damaged by direct hits. Reconnaissance at Ladbergen revealed success also, showing the left-hand channel, which was the only one repaired since the last attack, to have been breached again where it crossed the River Glane, which had been unable to cope with the volume of water released, leading to extensive flooding on both sides of the canal. The two operations were concluded for the loss of just two 49 Squadron Lancasters. The Germans recognized that repairing the canals was an open invitation to Bomber Command to return, and, so vital were they to the transportation system, that they could not be abandoned. The answer was to complete repairs, but to leave the sections drained and apparently still under repair, until sufficient traffic had built up to push through in one night. They would then be flooded and re-emptied to dupe RAF reconnaissance flights and maintain the deception.

On the following night the group dispatched 171 Lancasters and seven Mosquitos to attack the U-Boot pens at Trondheim in Norway, a straight-line distance from Skellingthorpe of some eight hundred miles. 50 Squadron launched twelve Lancasters into the air between 15.35 and 16.23 with F/L Arden the senior pilot on duty, and all arrived in the target area some five-and-a-half hours later to find clear skies and excellent visibility. However, an effective smoke screen prevented the marker force from finding the aiming-point, and the Master Bomber had no option but to send the force home, where they arrived after 02.00 after more than ten hours aloft. 5 Group mounted a rare daylight mining operation on the 23rd, for which fourteen Lancasters were detailed, while 53 Base remained at home.

The weather was mainly responsible for curtailing operations over the next few days until the 26th, when briefings took place on 5 Group stations at 20.00. The eighteen attending 50 Squadron crews learned that Munich was to be their target for an all-5 Group affair involving 270 Lancasters and eight Mosquitos, which represented a maximum effort. They departed Skellingthorpe between 23.10 and 23.50 with F/L Arden the senior pilot on duty, and each carrying a 4,000lb cookie and thirteen Nº14 J-cluster bombs. Forming up and climbing to operational altitude was a time-consuming business, and it would be five hours before the target was reached. F/O Danyluk and crew were skirting the Swiss/German frontier when deciding to turn back through a lack of power in both inner engines and an inability to maintain height, which would prevent them from reaching the target in time. To their credit, they retained their bombs and returned them to store. The others found the target area under clear skies with good visibility, and confirmed their positions by means of H2S. Aside from one errant red TI, the low-level Mosquito marking was accurate, and the Master Bomber ensured that the crews focused upon the reds and greens on and close to the planned aiming-point, calling on some to carry out a twenty-two second overshoot. The 50 Squadron crews bombed from 16,500 to 20,000 feet between 05.01 and 05.22, and returned safely to praise the quality of the route, the target marking and the performance of the Master Bomber. They reported smoke rising through 18,000 feet as they turned away, and fires visible for a hundred miles into the return flight. The confidence in a concentrated and effective attack was justified, when post-raid reconnaissance confirmed it as such, and a local report singled out railway installations as being particularly hard-hit.

This was the final operation of the month for 5 Group, but among operations taking place before the end was an attack by 1 and 8 Groups on Freiburg in southern Germany. It was a minor railway centre within thirty-five miles of advancing American and French ground forces, and was thought to be harbouring large numbers of enemy soldiers. The force of over 330 Lancasters delivered 1,900 tons of bombs, missing the railway yards, but destroying two thousand houses and killing over two thousand inhabitants. During the course of the month the squadron carried out nine operations and dispatched 156 sorties for the loss of two Lancasters and one crew.

December 1944

There were no operations for 5 Group for the first three nights of the new month, largely because of the weather, and, in the meantime, 1, 4, 6 and 8 Groups pounded the Ruhr town of Hagen on the 2/3rd. Worthwhile targets were becoming more and more scarce at a time when the Command was at its most powerful, and this final period of the war would bring the most devastating attacks to date on the German homeland. When 50 Squadron returned to action in the early evening of the 4th, it was to provide nineteen Lancasters as part of a record 5 Group force of 282 of the type and ten Mosquitos. Their target was the town of Heilbronn, situated thirty miles due north of Stuttgart, which had the River Neckar and a north-south rail link running through it, but, otherwise, had no genuine strategic importance, and would not have been expecting to be attacked. The main operation on this night was actually by 535 aircraft of 1, 6 and 8 Groups at Karlsruhe, some fifty-six miles west-south-west of Heilbronn, and the concentration of aircraft in this area would be certain to bring out the night-fighters. The 50 Squadron element took off between 16.10 and 16.47 with W/C Frogley the senior pilot on duty, but lost F/O Sagar immediately because of intercom failure, and F/O Beer shortly after beginning the Channel crossing when a starboard engine caught fire. The others made their way across France in good conditions to find three to five-tenths thin stratus over the target at around 12,000 feet. The aiming-points were the marshalling yards and the town, which were illuminated by the flare force ahead of the low-level Mosquitos' run to drop red TIs for the visual markers to back up. The marshalling yards were marked with yellows, which the main force element was unable to distinguish in the burgeoning fires, and this persuaded them to focus on the town instead. The 50 Squadron crews attacked from 11,600 to 13,800 feet between 19.29 and 19.37, adding to the general destruction, and, as the force retreated westwards into electrical storms, 82% of the city's built-up area was in the process of being destroyed by what probably amounted to a firestorm. The post-war British Bombing Survey estimated 351 acres of destruction, and a death toll of at least seven thousand people. It cost the group twelve aircraft, but all from Skellingthorpe returned safely.

The town of Giessen was 5 Group's objective on a night of heavy Bomber Command activity on the 6/7th. Other operations centred on the oil refinery at Leuna (Merseburg), which was the target for 475 Lancasters of 1, 3 and 8 Groups, while 450 aircraft from predominantly 4 and 6 Groups attacked railway installations at Osnabrück. 50 Squadron briefed nineteen crews as part of an overall 5 Group heavy force of 255 Lancasters, and they set off between 16.34 and 17.11 with F/L North the senior pilot on duty, and each Lancaster carrying a dozen 1,000 pounders. Their destination lay some eighty-five miles south-east of Cologne in west-central Germany, and thirty-five miles north of Frankfurt. The main force crews had been assigned to two aiming-points, two-thirds of them to the town, and the remainder to the marshalling yards, and, on arrival in the target area, they found predominantly clear skies and good visibility. The flare force began illuminating three minutes early and to the west of the target, but the Mosquito-laid red TIs fell close to the aiming-point and the Master Bomber ensured that they were backed up by greens. The 50 Squadron crews bombed from 10,000 to 11,100 feet between 20.14 and 20.24, and all returned safely to report another successful raid, which would be confirmed by reconnaissance photographs, and which cost eight Lancasters. This was the final sortie of their tour for F/O Nisbet and crew.

The Urft Dam was one of a number of similar structures in the beautiful Eifel region of western Germany, close to the Belgian frontier. There was a fear that the enemy might strategically release flood water to hamper the American advance into Germany, and it was decided to attempt to breach the dam, to allow any excess water to drain away. The first of a number of attacks on the region began on the 3rd at Heimbach, the small town nestling against the northern reaches of the reservoir, but the 1 and 8 Group force failed to identify it, and no bombs fell. On the following day, a small 8 Group effort against the dam was unsuccessful, as was a 3 Group attack on the nearby Schwammenauel Dam on the 5th. The job was handed to 5

Group on the 8th, for which a force of 205 Lancasters was made ready, fourteen of them by 50 Squadron and nineteen from 617 Squadron, which would be carrying Tallboys. The 50 Squadron element departed Skellingthorpe in a snow shower between 08.12 and 08.41 with W/C Frogley the senior pilot on duty and first away. All reached the target to be greeted by six to nine-tenths cloud at between 6,000 and 8,000 feet and moderate visibility, which partially obscured the aiming-point for some as they ran in to bomb. F/Os Boyle, Hatcher and Amey withheld their bombs after being denied a sight of the aiming-point by cloud, F/O Boyle after making four runs. At the end of his second run, while complying with the Master Bomber's instructions to orbit to starboard, and blinded by the sun, F/O Boyle's port wingtip made contact with the port tailplane of another aircraft, but neither was apparently seriously damaged. The others bombed from 6,800 to 10,600 feet between 10.55 and 11.03, and were among 129 crews to carry out an attack before the Master Bomber called a halt and sent the force home.

The conditions had prevented any assessment of results, which meant that another attempt on the dam would be necessary, and preparations were put in hand on the 10th to return with a force of 217 Lancasters. 50 Squadron launched fourteen aircraft at around 04.30 on a cold and frosty morning, but the entire force was recalled before it reached the English coast. F/L Arden was declared tour-expired on this day after completing twenty-five operations. 233 Lancasters and a Mosquito were scheduled to take off in the early morning of the 11th to join five 8 Group Mosquitos at the target, but take-off was postponed until late morning, when the fifteen 50 Squadron participants took off between 11.44 and 12.06 with F/L Drinkell and Steele the senior pilots on duty. They met icing conditions at the French coast, and found that conditions at the target area were hardly an improvement on the previous day, with up to nine-tenths cloud topping out at 8,000 feet and making life difficult for the Master Bomber. He tried to bring the crews down to below the cloud base, and some complied, while others were able to identify the aiming-point through a four-mile-long gap. Nine of the 50 Squadron crews bombed from 7,000 to 9,500 feet between 14.37 and 14.41, while five others were thwarted by the cloud and smoke and retained their payloads. Reconnaissance revealed a number of hits on the dam and its stepped apron, and cratering all around, but no actual breach occurred.

The final heavy night raid of the war on Essen was carried out by 540 aircraft from 1,4 and 8 Groups on the 12/13th, and was sufficiently accurate to be complimented by Albert Speer in his diaries. Centred upon the Krupp works, the attack inflicted severe industrial damage and also destroyed almost seven hundred houses, while damaging thirteen hundred more. The main operation on the night of the 15/16th was directed at Ludwigshafen in southern Germany, home to a number of I.G.Farben factories, which, as mentioned a number of times before, were using slave workers in the production of synthetic oil and other products. The attack by elements of 1, 6 and 8 Groups was highly destructive, and had a greater effect on synthetic oil production at this plant than any previous raid. It was on the 16th that German ground forces began a new offensive in the Ardennes, in an attempt to break through the American lines and reach the port of Antwerp in what would become known as the Battle of the Bulge.

Munich remained a 5 Group preserve, and a further operation against it was planned for the 17th, which would turn out to be another night of heavy Bomber Command activity. The main raid was to be by more than five hundred aircraft, predominantly of 4 and 6 Groups, on Duisburg, while 1 Group targeted Ulm with over three hundred Lancasters, leaving 5 Group to send 280 Lancasters some seventy miles beyond to the Bavarian Capital City. 50 Squadron briefed twenty crews, while their Lancasters were being prepared for the 1,300-mile round-trip, and they departed Skellingthorpe between 16.09 and 16.45 with F/L Drinkell the senior pilot on duty. The others reached the target area to find generally clear skies and good visibility, with F/O Fairbairn and crew flying at 11,500 feet at the sharp end of the 50 Squadron element and among the first to begin a bombing run. Suddenly, another Lancaster, which turned out to be PD215 of 467 Squadron RAAF, began to cut across from 150 feet to starboard at 21.50, and F/O Fairbairn, pushed the yoke forward in an attempt to get underneath. The two aircraft made contact, however, denting the roof of PD346's fuselage, knocking off the upper aerials and damaging the port-outer propeller, which would eventually fall off. They continued on to be the first from the squadron to bomb at 22.00, and were followed by the others to bomb in accordance with the instructions of the Master Bomber on red and green TIs from 9,700 to 12,750 feet between 22.00 and 22.13. At this point, F/O Firmin and crew were still some distance behind the rest of the squadron, and received the Master Bomber's instruction to not bomb at 22.15. This prompted them to seek out an alternative recipient for their payload, and dropped it on what they believed to be the town of Murnau, nestling on the south-east corner of the Staffelsee, twenty-five miles south-west of Munich. The operation proceeded according to plan, and the resultant fires were visible from a hundred miles into the return journey. Seven Lancasters failed to return, and among them were LM676 and NG302 from 50 Squadron, the former exploding over the target after being hit by flak. F/O Amey and his flight engineer were thrown clear and survived, while the rest of the crew died in the crash. The two survivors fell into enemy hands, and, sadly, F/O Amey DFC, succumbed to pneumonia on New Year's Eve. There is a suggestion that the latter may have been brought down by Allied flak over Belgium, as it crashed near Antwerp, but, whatever the cause, there were no survivors from the crew of F/O Beer. The 467 Squadron Lancaster was abandoned by its crew on the way home over Châlons-sur-Marne, and all arrived safely on the ground in Allied territory. No local report was available from Munich to confirm or deny the outcome of the attack, but the Command claimed severe and widespread damage to the city.

On the following night it was the turn of the distant Baltic port of Gdynia to play host to 5 Group, for which 50 Squadron put up seventeen Lancasters in an overall force of 236 of the type. The intention was to catch elements of the German fleet at anchor, in particular the Lützow, and also to destroy harbour installations, as well as cause damage within the town. *(The original Lützow was actually never completed, and was sold to the Russian navy in 1940 as a hull minus superstructure. The pocket battleship, Deutschland, was renamed Lützow, to avoid humiliation for the nation should she be lost in battle.)* While this operation was in progress, fourteen other Lancasters of the group were to sneak in under cover of the main activity to deliver mines to the Privet and Spinach gardens in Danzig (Gdansk) Bay. The 50 Squadron element departed Skellingthorpe between 16.51 and 17.21 with S/L Blair the senior pilot on duty, and all reached the target area, after an outward flight of almost five hours, to find clear skies and good visibility. As was usually the practice, the initial identification was by H2S, but the harbour and town could be picked out visually until a smoke screen was activated. The illumination and marking proceeded according to plan, and the 50 Squadron crews bombed aiming-point B, believed to be the town, on red and green TIs from 11,000 to 14,000 feet between 22.01 and 22.15 in accordance with the Master Bomber's instructions, and, in the face of intense light flak. The smoke screen eventually obscured the view of those attacking aiming-point A, the Lützow, and crews with bombs still to deliver turned their attention to the port area and town. It was not possible to make an accurate assessment of results, but bomb bursts were seen across the docks and quaysides. Reconnaissance photos confirmed that damage had been inflicted upon shipping, port installations and residential property in the waterfront districts, at a cost of four Lancasters.

Thick fog kept the crews on the ground on the 20th, and threatened to do so also on the 21st, but an operation was called on the basis that the weather over Scotland after midnight would be clear for returning aircraft, even if Lincolnshire remained fogbound. In briefing rooms across southern and south-eastern Lincolnshire, crews learned that their target would require them to retrace their recent steps to Germany's eastern Baltic region, although the Wintershall oil refinery at Politz, situated less than ten miles north of the port of Stettin, was some two hundred miles short of their trip to Gdynia. *(This location is often wrongly spelled Pölitz, which is a town in Germany's Schleswig-Holstein region at the western end of the Baltic.)* A force of 207 Lancasters and a single Mosquito was assembled, and, unusually, it included an element from 617 Squadron carrying Tallboys. 50 Squadron made ready seventeen Lancasters, which departed Skellingthorpe between 16.27 and 17.18 with F/Ls Drinkell and Whalley the senior pilots on duty, the latter having recently arrived from 5LFS. F/O McEachern and crew turned back from a position over the Baltic some fifty miles south of the Swedish coast after the starboard-inner engine caught fire. F/O Rolston and crew took off late and were unable to make up time. At 22.24, with Stettin ten miles to the north-east and the target a further ten miles beyond, the jettisoned their bombs and turned back. The others reached the target under clear skies with ground haze, which may have been a smoke screen, and found this highly important war-industry asset to be protected by around fifty searchlights. Heavy flak accompanied the Lancasters as they ran in on the red and green TIs, which had fallen some two thousand yards north-north-west of the plant. This was a situation recognized by the Master Bomber, but he was unable to persuade the backers-up to shift the point of aim accordingly, and most of the bombing would miss the mark. The 50 Squadron crews bombed on red and green TIs from 15,500 to 19,000 feet between 22.05 and 22.19, and observed most of the bomb bursts to be around the markers. Fires remained visible for almost a hundred miles into the return journey, but the plant had not been destroyed, and it would be necessary to mount further raids.

The final wartime Christmas period was celebrated on 5 Group stations undisturbed by operational activity between the 22nd and Boxing Day, which was not the case for the other groups. The peace came to an end on the 26th, when crews from all groups were roused from any resulting stupor to attend briefings for operations against enemy troop positions at St Vith in Belgium. The German advance towards Antwerp had run out of steam after its earlier successes, and, starved of fuel and ammunition, it was now attempting to withdraw back into Germany. 5 Group contributed twenty-six Lancasters to the force of 296 aircraft for the first joint operation since October. The crews found the target to be under clear skies with good visibility and could identify the aiming-point visually by a red TI. When this became obscured by smoke, the Master Bomber ordered them to descend to 10,000 feet and bomb the upwind edge of the smoke. All indications suggested the attack to be well concentrated and effective.

53 Base was called into action on the 27th, to provide aircraft for an attack on marshalling yards at Rheydt, for a which a force of two hundred Lancasters and eleven Mosquitos was drawn from 1, 3, 5 and 8 Groups. 50 Squadron provided eight of the forty-four 5 Group Lancasters, and they departed Skellingthorpe between 12.00 and 12.28 with F/L Steele the

senior pilot on duty. They all reached the target, where the skies were clear, and the aiming-point could be identified visually, although red and green TIs marked it out to provide a more solid reference. The 50 Squadron element bombed from 18,000 to 20,000 feet between 15.00 and 15.06 in accordance with the instructions of the Master Bomber, and dust and smoke was obscuring the area as they turned away. The attack was well concentrated, but no explosions or fires were reported, and, it seems, there was no post-raid reconnaissance.

On the 28th, five 50 Squadron crews were told, that they would be part of a 5 Group force of sixty-seven Lancasters targeting shipping, specifically the cruiser Köln, at Horten and Moss, located respectively on the western and eastern coasts of Oslo Fjord, thirty miles south of Norway's capital city. The 50 Squadron ORB specified Moss as the target for its crews, who departed Skellingthorpe between 19.18 and 19.35 with S/L Blair the senior pilot on duty. They all reached the target area after an outward flight of four-and-a-half hours, and found the skies to be relatively clear and the visibility good, but a thin layer of alto-cumulus cloud at between 15,000 and 20,000 feet reduced the brightness of the moonlight and cast deceptive shadows on the water to prevent a clear identification of the target. The aiming-points at Horten were marked by Wanganui flares, but most crews followed the Master Bomber's instructions after establishing their own reference point. A patch of light flak to the north-east of the harbour mole was thought to be concealing a large naval unit, and this area was marked and bombed. Some crews would claim to have attacked a large vessel moving from this area in a southerly direction, and other shipping in the harbour, all in the face of intense shipboard and shore-based light flak. The 50 Squadron crews identified a number of vessels at the northern end of the narrow strait between Moss and Jeløya island, about a mile south of Kambo, and marked them with flame floats, before bombing from 6,000 to 8,000 feet between 23.41 and 23.57. It was difficult to assess the outcome, and no direct hits were claimed, but S/L Blair and crew believed that they could see smoke issuing from one vessel.

A dozen 50 Squadron crews were called to briefing late on the 30th to learn that they were to be part of a 5 Group force of 154 Lancasters and thirteen Mosquitos to attack an enemy supply line at Houffalize in the Ardennes region of Belgium. They took off between 01.58 and 02.27 with S/L Blair the senior pilot on duty, and found the target area under five to seven-tenths stratus cloud at 5,000 to 6,000 feet, with another layer of eight-tenths with tops at 9,000 feet, all of which made identification very difficult. The marking was punctual and accurate, but the red TIs were observed only by a proportion of the crews, who chanced upon a gap in the clouds directly over the aiming-point. Eight of the 50 Squadron participants bombed from 6,000 to 11,750 feet between 05.02 and 05.10, but four others were unable to establish the location of the aiming-point and aborted their sorties. A number of crews in the force descended to below the cloud base and confirmed that the bombing was concentrated around the markers, but it would be deemed necessary to revisit this objective within a short time. During the course of the month the squadron took part in ten operations and dispatched 145 sorties for the loss of two Lancasters and crews.

RAF Skellingthorpe. 50 Squadron Navigators' Section. 1944

50 Squadron Lancaster W4119 VN-Q

*L to R: Fred Clark (FE) Dougie Cruickshanks RNZAF (BA), Bert (Bob) Martin (W/Op),
Hugh Skilling RNZAF (pilot), Len Retford (Nav), Johnnie Meadows (MUG), Alan Macdonald (RG).*

Station commander, G/C Jefferson, and S/L Stubbs With The "Lord Camrose" Bombing Trophy.

50 Squadron Lancaster LM480 VN-U Mailly-le-Camp, 3/4th of May 1944
Shot down soon after clearing the target area and crashed at St. Mesmin (Aube), a village on the railway between Romilly-sur-Seine and Troyes. With the aircraft on fire, Blackham fought to keep the aircraft flying until all his crew had baled out safely; after which a sudden explosion knocked him senseless, hurling him through a glass panel. He recovered consciousness to find himself surrounded by flames and jumped clear moments before the aircraft blew up. Parachuting into Maquis country, Blackham narrowly escaped being hanged as a German spy, but another airman in the vicinity was able to vouch for him. For months Blackham lived and fought with the Maquis, until he was sent to Paris for return to England along the Comete line. In Paris, he was betrayed by the French traitor Jacques Desoubrie on 27th of July 1944 and handed over to the Gestapo. After interrogation, Blackham was imprisoned in Fresnes prison where he was beaten, stripped of clothing and put under cold showers, surviving on weak soup and sleeping on filthy lice-infested straw. At one point during a two week stay at Fresnes, Blackham was among a group of inmates to face a firing squad manning machine guns, but for some unknown reason, the order to fire was never given. He was sent to the Buchenwald concentration camp. There, the airmen were fully shaved, starved, denied shoes, and for three weeks forced to sleep outside without shelter in one of the sub-camps known as "Little Camp".

The crew: F/L T.H.Blackham DFC (Pilot), P/O C.E.Stephenson RAAF, (2nd pilot), P/O C.R.E.Walton, F/O D.G.Jones, F/Sgt S.J.Godfrey, evading, he was assisted by Mme Deguilley of Romilly-sur-Seine before being passed to a Resistance group. Killed by the Germans, on 24th of June 44, whilst in the company of the French Resistance, when the Wehrmacht attacked their camp. He has no known grave. Sgt S.C.Wilkins killed, Sgt H.G.Ridd killed, Sgt W.D.Dixon killed. Both of the reported evasions failed.

W/C James (Jim) Flint DFC, GM, DFM, AE.
The last wartime Commanding Officer of 50 Squadron 1944-45.
Vice President of 50 and 61 Squadrons Association.

W/O Reg Payne

F/L M J Beetham 1944
(Marshal of the Royal Air Force Sir Michael Beetham
GCB CBE DFC AFC FRAeS)

F/L Mike Beetham and Crew
L-R Fred Ball Rear Gunner, Les Bartlett (BA), Mike Beetham (Pilot). Frank Swinyard (Nav),
Reg Payne (W/Op), Don Moore (FE), Jock Higgins (MUG).

VN-T the aircraft of S/L Bill Drinkell being de-iced on dispersal at Skellingthorpe.
S/L W.G. (Bill) Drinkell, DFC, AFC.

Crew and ground crew in front of VN-T showing Ron squatting centre in front of Bill Drinkell.
(Photo from the grandson of LAC Ronald Schofield),

Terry Barber BA, back right, and his crew, his skipper Bill Firmin front centre. Gordon Bulmer (FE) kneeling next to him. Other crew are: Reg Hughes (MUG), Don Smith (W/Op), Larry Watts (RG), Bert Bright (Nav). Terry affectionally became known as "Ali Barber" by the rest of the crew.

Terry Barber (RG)

Pilot Bill Firmin

Logbook of Terry Barber (Bill Firmin's Crew)

The Crew: F/L R.S. Palandri, (pilot), Sgt J.B. Firth, (FE), F/Sgt R.J. Owen, F/O H.A. Manos, (BA), Sgt A.D. Mellish, (W/Op), Sgt W. Johnson, (MUG), F/Sgt A.R. Meredith, RCAF, (RG). On 7th of August 1944, while bombing Secqueville, Palandri was shot down on his 20th operation. The aircraft, LL992, VN-T, crashed at La Frenaye, Palandri, Mellish, and Owen were killed. Firth, PoW, Hearn, Johnson and Meredith evaded. (F/O E.A. Hearn, the Bombing Leader of 50 Squadron, had taken F/O Manos's place in the crew).

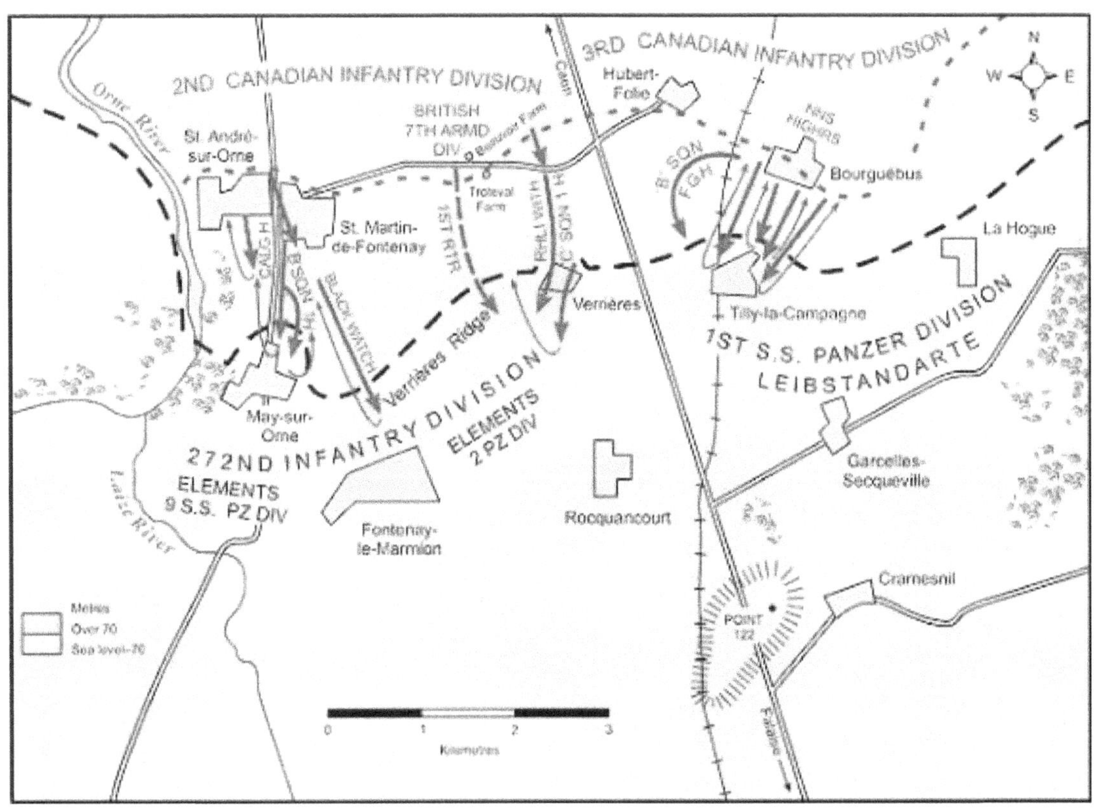

August 1944. Map of Secqueville area showing nearby troop concentrations.

W/O John B Firth (FE) of F/L Palandri's crew

On the 7th of August 1944 we were detailed to bomb a German troop concentration near Secqueville, France (Our troops being quite close). By the time we arrived at the target the T.I.s had extinguished so we were ordered to return to base without bombing the target. As we flew past Rouen on our return journey a German fighter attacked us spraying our wings from port to starboard. One cannon shell flew through the side near the Skipper and then smashed through the windscreen. With the aircraft now in a steep dive to port, and with the fire extinguishers unable to put out the raging fire, Skipper gave the order to bale out. My exit from the aircraft was somewhat delayed. However, I did manage to successfully get out. After parachuting down, I landed fairly close to the crashed aircraft and was caught quite soon by the enemy. I spent the rest of the war in Stalag Luft V11 in Silesia.

On the night of the 23/24th of September 1944, George Kelly's Lancaster was shot down near Slangenberg Castle, Guilderland, Holland, returning from the Ladbergen Raid. The German pilot was Nachtjager (Night fighter) ace Heinz-Wolfgang Schnaufer. George was the only survivor, his life saved by his parachute. F/Sgt Kelly's crew mates, F/O J Sweetman, F/Sgt E Gully, F/Sgt E Hobbs, F/Sgt A Johnstone, F/Sgt W Wilcox and F/Sgt G Keens were buried at Zelhem. He was taken into the jurisdiction of the Dutch Resistance, moving from house to house. He was particularly touched when helpers, mainly Protestant, made sure he and other fugitives were visited by a Catholic priest. For 2 months, in a dangerous, volatile and deeply scarring experience, he was on the run in occupied Holland. On November 18th, he joined in the failed attempt, known as Pegasus II, to cross the Rhine with other isolated troops from Operation Market Garden, but was captured. He was taken to the Dulag (central interrogation camp) in Frankfurt-am-Main, before transfer to Stalag Luft VII Bankau (Polish Bakow) in Silesia (now Poland) in December 1944. He made the 'Long March' in 1945.

F/Sgt George Kelly

F/Sgt Ronald Marlow (RG)

On the 5th of May 1944 Sgt Ronald Marlow was posted to 50 Squadron

He completed 11 operations on Lancaster VN-K before occupying a new Lancaster, LM591 VN-B, on the 3rd of June 1944. Throughout his entire tour with 50 squadron his pilot was P/O (later F/O) Pethick.

Crew were: P/O L W Pethick (Pilot), Sgt J Potter (FE), F/O J D Bald (Nav), Sgt W V Wallace (W.Op), Sgt L Taylor (BA), Sgt R Marlow (MUG), Sgt T R McKenley (RG).

F/Sgt Herbert (Bob) Reginald Martin flew as a wireless operator with 50 Squadron.

F/Sgt Donald Watson KIA on the 12th of April 1944.

Donald Watson & Friend, South Africa, Nov 1942   *P/O Ernest Skillen during training*

Observer training at RAF Dumfries. Don Wilson is standing far right.
He was posted to 50 Squadron at RAF Skellingthorpe on 24 March 1944, the crew being: P/O E Skillen RAAF (Pilot), F/Sgt D Watson (Nav), F/Sgt D T Mackintosh (FE), F/Sgt P M Davies (RG), F/O E Fletcher (BA), F/Sgt A M Stickells. (W/Op), F/Sgt C C McKenna, (MUG).

The crew of P/O Ernest Skillen RAAF (Top middle), F/Sgt Donald Watson (front right). They disappeared without trace in Lancaster I ME572 VN-Z. on the night of the 11/12th of April 1944, during an operation to Aachen. All are Commemorated on the Runnymede Memorial.

Sgt Dennis R. Allen from F/O Curphey's crew.

F/O T Curphey and his crew, were posted to 50 Squadron from 5 LFS, on the 11th of June 44, and were on their 14th operation when lost. The crew consisted of: F/O T.G. Curphey RCAF, (Pilot), Sgt L.W. Lewis, (FE). Sgt D.R. Allen (Nav), F/O D.G. Sholte, RCAF (AB), Sgt H. Lambert, (W/Op), F/O M.L.G. Lovering RCAF, (MUG), Sgt J.I. Fisher, (RG).

50 Squadron Lancaster VN-D in formation with other Lancasters during a daylight operation (c.1944/45)

Lancaster LL842 VN-F failed to return from a raid to Stuttgart on the 24/25th of July 1944. All on board were killed. F/Sgt D S Campbell, Sgt R Hampton, F/O J M Neal, F/O G H Parker (Pilot), Sgt L Salway, F/Sgt J H Spencer, Sgt T W Thompson.

50 Squadron Lancaster LL842 VN-F. P/O Parker & crew.

50 Squadron Lancaster LL842 VN-F

Lancaster SW249 VN-R. F/O Jeff Leach and crew, Sgt Larry V Sharpe (FE) is second from the right. Other crew members are F/O Wally Cheeseman (BA), F/Sgt Geoff Mosley (W/Op), Sgt Jerry Davies (Nav), F/Sgt D Price (RG).

50 Squadron Armourers at RAF Skellingthorpe.

50 Squadron Armourers at RAF Skellingthorpe, 1944.

444

This picture and the one below shows Lancaster NF922, VN-U of 50 Squadron with crew members. At the front are, from the left Bob Baber (Nav), Frank Turner (MUG), and Ginger Lee (RG). At the back are Ginger Franklin (BA), Geoff Carslake (W/Op), Bill Endean (Pilot) and Tom Hall (FE). The other two are the ground crew. Probably 1944/45 at Skellingthorpe.

50 Squadron Lancaster VN-N bombing up July 1944

Skellingthorpe

Posed for the camera, "Attention 50 Squadron, 'Scramble'"

F/O H William Enoch (Pilot)

Top: H. Southcott (AG), J.Hugh (BA). Middle: G Pritchard (FE), Patch, Andy George (Nav), E. Goymer (AG). Bottom row: William Enoch (Pilot). Eddie Garstang (W/OP).

Ivor's crew pose for a picture on top of their aircraft with two members of VN-G's ground crew. Top row: Member of ground crew, then Patch, Joe, Harry, Andy. Bottom: Member of ground crew.

Ezra Goymer paints the 116th bombing symbol onto the fuselage of VN-G as the rest of the crew look on.

Top: Tom (F/E), Bill (Pilot), Ezra (A/G), Patch, (F/E). Bottom row: Eddie (W/Op). Andy (Nav), Joe (BA), Harry (AG).

After Enoch and crew completed their 23rd and last operation in ED588 "George", a new crew took over the aircraft. On the 29/30th of August, F/O A.H.Carter and crew took her to Königsberg and crashed in Sweden without survivors.

On the night of the 30/31st of March 1944, R5546 VN-T was shot down by a night-fighter when bound for Nuremberg. F/Sgt D.G. Gray (pilot) F/Sgt Campbell RAAF and F/Sgt G Wallis RAAF became PoW's. Sgt. J Grant, Sgt. H A Wright, Sgt F B Patey and Sgt D Maughan were all killed.

F/L John Edward and crew were posted to 617 Squadron and failed to return from an attack on a flying bomb storage site at Wizernes on the 24th of June 1944. F/L Edward and four others were killed.

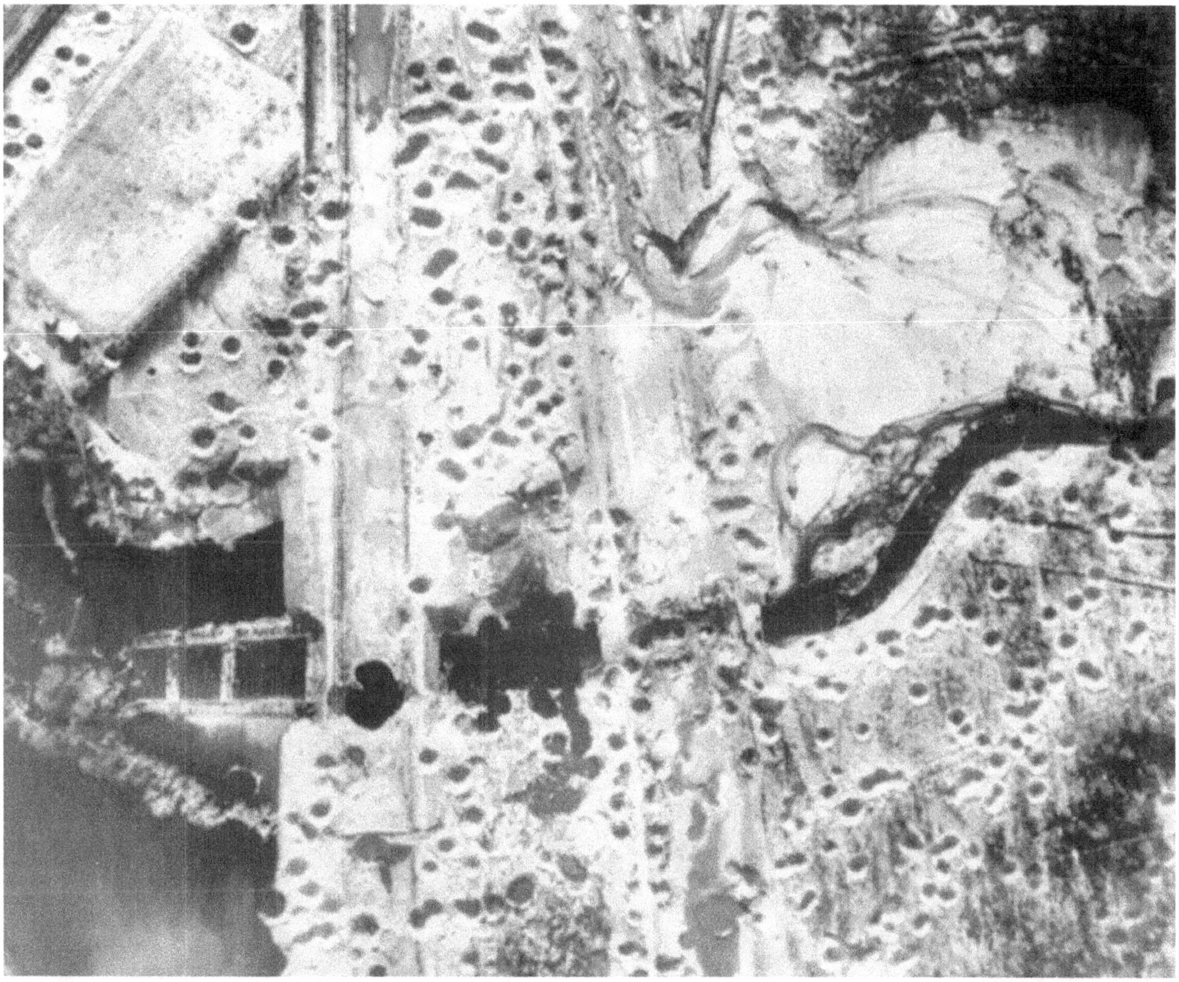

November 1944. The twin aqueduct section of the Dortmund Ems Canal at Ladbergen.

The picturesque Wet Triangle, the joining point of the Dortmund-Ems and Mittelland Canals at Bergeshövede, near Gravenhorst.

January 1945

The final year of the war began with a flourish, as the Luftwaffe launched its ill-conceived and, ultimately, ill-fated Operation Bodenplatte (Baseplate) at first light on New Year's Day. The intention to destroy the Allied air forces on the ground at the recently liberated airfields in France, Holland and Belgium was only modestly realized, and it cost the German day fighter force around 250 aircraft. Many of the pilots were killed, wounded or fell into Allied hands, and it was a setback from which the Tagjagd would never fully recover, while the Allies could make good their losses within hours from their enormous stockpiles.

5 Group was also active that morning, having roused the crews early from their beds to attend briefings for an attack on the recently-repaired Dortmund-Ems Canal near Ladbergen, for which 102 Lancasters and two Mosquitos were made ready. 50 Squadron loaded eight Lancasters with the appropriate canal-busting ironware, namely 1,000 pounders, some with delayed-action fuses, and dispatched them between 07.30 and 07.54 with F/Ls Drinkell, North and Whalley the senior pilots on duty. The 54 Base squadrons fell in line behind 83 Squadron, with the 55 Base squadrons about three miles further back, and a third section, made up of 53 Base units, some twenty miles to the rear, which were allowed to catch up, putting the force two minutes behind schedule at point C, over the North Sea. It was between points C and D that the fighter escort was expected to join them, and, although it was not immediately apparent, it did eventually put in an appearance. The gaggle held together fairly well, although the controller would complain later that the legs were too short to keep the gaggle tight, and some aircraft were seen to break formation. When about eight minutes from the target, smoke from a Mosquito-laid red TI could be seen, which was assessed as being on the southern tip of the island between the two branches of the canal. It was clearly visible to all crews, who were able to home in on it without difficulty. A six-gun flak battery greeted their arrival with accurate salvoes, but this did not inhibit the bombing runs, and the 50 Squadron crews carried out their attacks from 10,200 to 12,000 feet between 11.19 and 11.21. F/O Marris and crew were about to bomb, when another Lancaster passed within a hundred feet directly underneath, forcing them to withhold their bombs and jettison them two miles north-east of the target. On return, they would complain that the gaggle was too tight and put crews at risk from "friendly" bombs. The impression was of an effective operation, the use of delay fuses having prevented an immediate assessment of the results, but photo-reconnaissance revealed later, that the canal had been breached again, and the surrounding fields had become flooded.

Operations for the day were not yet done for 5 Group, which now had an appointment with the Mittelland Canal at Gravenhorst, for which 152 Lancasters and five Mosquitos were made ready. 50 Squadron dispatched ten aircraft between 16.43 and 16.52, each captained by a pilot of flying officer rank, but NG127 swung off the runway and was written off in the subsequent crash, which the squadron ORB failed to mention. F/O Sagar and his crew emerged unhurt from the wreckage, but had used up their ration of good fortune. The others reached the target area to find that the clear conditions enjoyed during the morning raid nearby, had persisted, and, so accurate were the initial TIs and illumination, delivered visually or by H2S, that the third flare force was not required and was sent home. The main force was called in ahead of H-Hour at around 19.10, and the 50 Squadron element bombed on red TIs from 9,250 to 12,000 feet between 19.12 and 19.17, before being diverted to Kinloss on return. NF984 was homebound when blown by a change of wind over the Belgian city of Liege, now in Allied hands, and was damaged by a single burst of predicted heavy flak, sending it into a dive. F/O

Skilling RNZAF issued the order to bale out, and the Kiwi bomb-aimer complied before some control was regained after the loss of 2,500 feet, and the order was rescinded. In fact, the intercom to the rest of the aircraft had been cut, and no other crew members heard the order. With temperatures rising in both port engines, they were shut down, and permission was granted to land at Juvincourt. A forced-landing was carried out, which ended the Lancaster's career, but the crew was flown home on the following day and was reunited with their bomb-aimer on the 6th. One of the perils of operating on New Year's Day was the risk of falling victim to trigger-happy American flak gunners, who had been spooked by the German raids at dawn, and now fired at anything that moved. A number of RAF aircraft and crews would be lost in such "friendly fire" incidents, and, unquestionably, the above was one of them. The employment of predominantly delayed-action bombs again prevented an immediate assessment of results, but a highly successful operation was confirmed later by photo-reconnaissance.

5 Group remained on the ground when Nuremberg and Ludwigshafen were raided by large forces on the night of the 2/3rd, and both operations were hugely destructive. A controversial attack was planned against the small French town of Royan in the early hours of the 5th, in response to requests from Free French forces, which were laying siege on their way to the port of Bordeaux. Situated on the eastern bank at the mouth of the Gironde estuary, it was occupied by a German garrison, the commander of which had offered the inhabitants the opportunity to evacuate the area. However, around two thousand had declined, and would suffer the consequences. 1, 5 and 8 Groups put together a force of 347 Lancasters and seven Mosquitos, of which fifteen of the former represented 50 Squadron. They departed Skellingthorpe between 00.42 and 01.28, again all captained by flying officers, and were in the first of two waves heading for the unsuspecting target, separated by one hour. It was approaching 04.00 as they lined up for the bombing run in cloudless skies and excellent visibility, but the start of the attack was delayed for two minutes to allow misplaced markers to be corrected. A red TI went down at 04.01 very close to the aiming point, and another fell in the middle of the town, near the beach, at which point, the Master Bomber called in the main force. The 50 Squadron crews delivered their cookie and sixteen 500 pounders each from 6,250 to 8,500 feet onto Pathfinder markers between 04.02 and 04.10, and witnessed a yellow oil fire at 04.08, which began to emit volumes of black smoke. This was just one of a number of large explosions created by the first phase of bombing, and the resultant fires would act as a beacon to the 1 Group force following behind. PD292 failed to return to Skellingthorpe, and no trace of F/O Sagar and his crew was ever found. The attack destroyed about 85% of the town, and between 500 and 800 people lost their lives. In the event, the town was not taken, and it would be mid-April before the garrison surrendered.

5 Group was not involved in a major attack on Hannover by more than 650 aircraft on the night of the 5/6th, the first on this northern city since the series in the autumn of 1943. However, a rushed battle order came through to 5 Group stations at 18.30, which would lead to another late briefing and take-off for 131 crews, and it was actually between 00.04 and 00.52 on the 6th that eleven 50 Squadron crews departed Skellingthorpe bound for a German supply column trapped at Houffalize in the Belgian Ardennes. The all-flying officer-captained crews they made their way south on a clear night above low cloud, which, over the target, formed thin layers of eight to ten-tenths cover between 4,000 and 10,000 feet. The marker force crews were able to identify it visually, and the first red Mosquito-laid TIs were seen to go down close together, followed by greens at H-3. They were backed up to leave a compact

group of reds and greens visible by their glow through the clouds, and the Master Bomber, who was circling at 10,000 feet, called in the main force to bomb. The 50 Squadron crews complied from 9,000 to 12,000 feet between 03.00 and 03.08, although F/Os Danyluk, Marris and Wells were among around a third of the force to retain their bombs in accordance with instructions at briefing, if they failed to identify the aiming-point. Afterwards, one of the marker crews descended to 3,500 feet between the cloud layers, where they saw two large columns of smoke, the source of which could not be identified. Post-raid reconnaissance confirmed that the target had been bombed with great accuracy, and the success had been gained for the loss of two Lancasters.

A major operation against Munich was planned for the 7th, for which a two-wave force of 645 aircraft was drawn from all five of the Lancaster-equipped groups. 5 Group, which was unused to sharing this target, would lead the way with 213 Lancasters and three Mosquitos, leaving the second wave to follow on two hours later, the tanks of the heavy brigade containing sufficient fuel for a nine-hour round-trip. The 50 Squadron element of fourteen Lancasters departed Skellingthorpe as dusk was descending between 16.30 to 16.52, with a single pilot officer captain breaking into the otherwise exclusively flying officer club. F/O Farrer and crew had reached the Kent coast at Gravesend, when starboard-inner engine failure ended their sortie, and F/O Tarrant and crew turned back from a position south of Reims, having been the last to take-off and being further delayed by icing conditions that left them with an impossible thirty minutes to make up. The others arrived to find broken medium level cloud above 14,000 feet, with haze or thin cloud below, by which time the Master Bomber had made a visual identification, and sent the first two primary blind markers in to deliver their TIs at the same time thirty seconds ahead of the planned opening of the attack. The flare force went in immediately afterwards, and illuminated the city very effectively, allowing ground detail to be identified. Red TIs went down west and east of the River Isar, bracketing the aiming point, and the Master Bomber ordered the backers up to drop their TIs between the reds, after which, the next batch of flares formed a circle around the aiming point. The main force was then called in, and the 50 Squadron participants delivered their loads accurately within the specified area from 17,500 to 20,000 feet between 20.30 and 20.36. The city was seen to be burning well as the force withdrew, and the glow of fires could be seen from up to 130 miles away. Two hours after the 5 Group attack, in what would become an established pattern, the 1, 3, 6 and 8 Group force arrived to complete the destruction of the central and some industrial districts, and this proved to be the final large-scale attack of the war on Munich.

With the exception of 617 Squadron, 5 Group remained on the ground for the ensuing six days, with snow-clearing providing exercise for all capable of wielding a shovel. The crews were, therefore, no doubt relieved to be called to briefing on the 13th, when they learned that the group would be operating alone in a return to the Wintershall oil refinery at Politz near Stettin. The plant had sustained damage in the previous attack in December, but production had not been halted. A force of 218 Lancasters and seven Mosquitos was assembled, of which seventeen of the Lancasters were provided by 50 Squadron. Another dusk departure saw them taking off between 16.23 and 16.58 with S/L Blair the senior pilot on duty, and F/O Harrop and crew were 120 miles out from the Yorkshire coast when the navigator became ill and forced them to turn back. The others arrived in the target area on time to find clear skies with slight haze, by which time the blind marker crews had identified the target by means of H2S, and delivered their green TIs in a line approaching the target shortly after 22.00. The illuminators then dropped their flares, which caused ground detail to stand out, highlighted by the snow on the ground. A blind-bombing attack had been planned, but, because of the excellence of the conditions, Mosquitos were able to go in at low level. The main force was called in, and the 50 Squadron crews bombed from 14,000 to 16,750 feet between 22.15 and 22.24 to help seal the fate of the plant. Photographic reconnaissance confirmed that the site had been severely damaged, and Bomber Command claimed it to be in ruins. This was the thirtieth and final sortie of their tour for F/O McEachern and crew, who, no doubt, had a party planned for the following night. Sadly, the majority of their invited guests would be busy elsewhere.

Oil targets would continue to dominate during the remainder of the month, and a two-phase attack was planned for the following night against the refinery at Leuna, near Merseburg in eastern Germany, as previously mentioned, one of many similar sites situated in an arc to the west and south of Leipzig. The first phase would be carried out by 5 Group, which detailed 210 Lancasters and nine Mosquitos, fifteen of the former contributed by 50 Squadron. They took off from Skellingthorpe between 15.55 and 16.35 with F/Ls Drinkell and Whalley the senior pilots on duty, but would lose two crews to technical issues. F/O Fairbairn and crew were twenty miles out from Brighton when their intercom failed at 17.10, and, thirty minutes later, F/O Day and crew turned back from thirty miles out after the rear turret guns jammed during testing. The others pressed on and reached the target area to find clear skies but poor vertical visibility due to a layer of haze, which was no hindrance to the primary blind markers, whose job was to establish their position over the aiming-point by means of H2S. They delivered their TIs from 18,000 feet, after which, the first element of the flare force went in. The Master Bomber called for ground marking only, which was carried out by the low-level Mosquito element, and, by 20.50, he was satisfied and sent the marker aircraft home. The main force produced what appeared to be concentrated bombing, the 50 Squadron crews dropping their loads of a cookie and nine 500 pounders each onto red and green TIs from 16,000 to 18,400 feet between 21.02 and 21.12, doing so with a fourteen-second overshoot in accordance with the Master Bomber's instructions. A proportion of main force crews were often detailed to support the flare force by accompanying them over the aiming-point, before going round again to deliver their bombs. F/O Jones and crew were hit by heavy flak as they went in with the flare force, but, remarkably, were unaware of the extent of the damage until after they had bombed, when the starboard-inner engine began to race and had to be shut down. The port-outer engine lasted until they reached the front line, and it was decided to put NF918 down at Juvincourt. Returning crews reported explosions and smoke rising upwards as they turned for home, and left behind a beacon for the second wave of 363 Lancasters and five Mosquitos of 1, 6 and 8 Groups following three hours behind. They would add to the massive destruction, which effectively put the plant out of action for the remainder of the war. Ten Lancasters failed to return, and among them was LM234, which was hit by flak and crashed at Reichmannsdorf, sixty miles south-west of Leipzig, killing F/O Nicol RAAF and four of his crew, while the two gunners survived to fall into enemy hands.

Three oil plants were selected for attention on the night of the 16/17th, at Zeitz, near Liepzig, Wanne-Eickel in the Ruhr, and Brux in north-western Czechoslovakia (now Most in the Czech Republic), some 140 miles due south of Berlin. It was for the last-mentioned that fifteen 50 Squadron crews were briefed as part of a 5 Group force of 224 Lancasters and six Mosquitos, which would be accompanied by seven 101 Squadron ABC Lancasters for RCM duties. They were each carrying a cookie and nine 500 pounders for what would be a nine-hour round-trip, and departed Skellingthorpe between 17.56 and 18.19 with F/Ls Drinkell, North and Whalley the senior pilots on duty. There were ten early returns from the force, and among them was the Drinkell crew, who were just south of Ipswich when it became clear that the generator was not charging. The others reached the target area to encounter nine to ten-tenths low cloud with tops at 3,000 feet, which interfered with the low-level marking system. The four primary blind markers identified the target by means of H2S, and dropped green TIs, and they were followed by the first illuminators, who also relied on H2S to deliver their flares. It seems that a number of Mosquitos managed to get below the cloud base to put red TIs onto the aiming-point, and reported that the greens were among the oil tanks. However, the reds were not generally visible through the clouds, and the Master Bomber called for skymarking, while informing flare force 3 that it would not be required. The 50 Squadron participants bombed either on the glow of the red TIs or on the cascading greens from 14,000 to 16,750 feet between 22.31 and 22.45, and observed many explosions and large columns of thick, black smoke emerging through the cloud-tops. Photo-reconnaissance would confirm, that massive damage had been inflicted upon the plant, and a severe setback delivered to the enemy's oil production.

There would be no further operations for 5 Group during the month, although a number would be posted before being cancelled. The squadron spent the period inducting new crews, attending lectures, training, and, during the last few days, clearing snow from the runways. During the course of the month the squadron operated on eight occasions and dispatched 105 sorties for the loss of four Lancasters and two crews.

February 1945

The weather at the start of February provided difficult conditions for marking and bombing, particularly for 5 Group, and a number of operations would struggle to achieve their aims in the face of thick, low cloud and strong winds. The group was back in harness immediately at the start of the new month following the long lay-off, and 271 Lancaster and eleven Mosquito crews were called to briefings on all 5 Group stations on the 1st to learn that their target was to be the marshalling yards in the town of Siegen, situated some fifty miles east of Cologne. This was a 5 Group show, and was one of three major operations planned for the night, the others, by larger forces, taking place at Ludwigshafen and Mainz further into southern Germany. A high wind during the night had helped to clear some of the snow, and the nineteen 50 Squadron Lancasters took off without incident between 15.36 and 16.38 with F/Ls Drinkell and Steele the senior pilots on duty. They all reached the target area shortly after 19.00, and encountered ten-tenths cloud between 3,000 and 7,000 feet, which was causing problems for the flare and marker forces, some of which were finding it difficult to obtain a clear H2S image on their screens. Eventually one of the primary blind markers ran in and dropped green TIs at 19.05 from 15,000 feet, and their glow was visible through the clouds. This prompted the first flares, followed by an attempt to mark at low-level with red TIs, which were not visible through the clouds, and, when the Master Bomber called for skymarking at 19.10, the remaining illuminators were superfluous to requirements and were sent home. The bombing phase was put back by four minutes until 19.20, forcing crews to either orbit or dogleg to waste time if they were still on approach, and then instructions were issued to aim at the skymarkers, which were being driven by the strong wind across the intended aiming-point and beyond the target. The glow of red target indicators was faintly visible through the clouds, but this was most likely a decoy fire site. It attracted many bomb loads, perhaps some from the 50

Squadron participants, who bombed from 8,500 to 12,000 feet between 19.20 and 19.30, contributing to what became a widely scattered raid. Much of the bombing fell into open and wooded country, and, although the railway station sustained damage, the marshalling yards escaped. PD346 was one of three Lancasters missing, and came down somewhere near the Ruhr with F/O Fairbairn DFC, RAAF and four of his crew. The two gunners managed to save themselves, and they were taken into captivity. Further bad news was that a tour was now to be increased again to thirty-six sorties.

Eighteen 50 Squadron crews were called to briefing at 15.00 on a drizzly afternoon on the 2nd, to be told of that night's operation to Karlsruhe in southern Germany. This was to be another 5 Group effort involving 250 Lancasters and eleven Mosquitos, and, was again, only one of three major operations taking place. Wiesbaden was to receive its one and only major raid of the war at the hands of almost five hundred aircraft, while a 320-strong predominantly Halifax force dealt with an oil plant at Wanne-Eickel in the Ruhr. The 50 Squadron element departed Skellingthorpe between 19.37 and 20.35 with S/L Blair the senior pilot on duty, and headed for the assembly point over Reading. The winds turned out to be lighter than forecast, and this caused a change in route, which now took the force directly from Reading to the target, straddling the Franco-Belgian frontier all the way to Germany, where they encountered heavy cloud between 3,000 and 15,000 feet. The flare force arrived over the target at 17,500 to 18,500 feet between 23.03 and 23.28, and its crews tried to perform their assigned tasks in difficult conditions, some with malfunctioning H2S boxes. The Mosquitos tried to establish an aiming-point, but the illumination was not getting through to the ground, and, even had they dropped red TIs, it is unlikely that they would have been visible. At 23.11 the Master Bomber called for skymarking, and sent the Mosquitos and remaining illuminators home. The 50 Squadron crews bombed on the glow of markers, as instructed by the Master Bomber, from 14,000 to 16,000 feet between 23.20 and 23.30, and all but two returned safely. This final raid of the war on Karlsruhe was a complete failure, and cost fourteen Lancasters, among which were NG381 and PA223. F/O Tarrant RNZAF and his crew were all killed when the former crashed in southern Germany, while one man was blown clear to survive when the latter exploded fifteen miles north-west of the centre of Strasbourg near the Franco-German border, killing F/O Harrop and the rest of his crew.

While the frontier towns of Goch and Cleves were being pounded by the other groups on the night of the 7/8th, ahead of the advancing British XXX Corps, 5 Group would return to the Dortmund-Ems Canal with 177 Lancasters and eleven Mosquitos, the former carrying delayed action bombs. 50 Squadron made ready twelve Lancasters, which departed Skellingthorpe between 20.43 and 21.18 led by W/C Frogley, and all reached the target area to find seven to ten-tenths cloud between 6,000 and 9,000 feet. They bombed onto what were believed to be accurate red and green TIs that were observed through gaps in the cloud, releasing their twelve 1,000 pounders each from 9,000 to 11,500 feet in the minutes either side of midnight on the instructions of the Master Bomber. F/L Steele and crew suffered the frustration of a hang-up caused by a short in the release circuitry, during what turned out to be a rare unsuccessful attack on this target, photographic reconnaissance revealing that the bombs had fallen into fields, and had failed to cause any breach. Among three missing Lancasters was PD316, which contained the experienced crew of F/L Boyle, who died with four others, while the two survivors fell into enemy hands.

Seventeen 50 Squadron crews found themselves being briefed on the following day for another long round-trip to the Wintershall oil refinery at Politz, as part of a 5 Group force of 227 Lancasters and seven Mosquitos. They were to act as the first wave in a two-phase attack, which would be completed two hours later by 248 Lancasters from 1 and 8 Groups. They departed Skellingthorpe between 16.35 and 17.17 with F/Ls Ling and Whalley the senior pilots on duty, and all reached the target area, where, ahead, the blind markers and the flare force crews were going in at 13,000 to 14,500 feet between 21.03 and 21.15 to carry out their assigned tasks in the face of an ineffective smoke screen, but, more seriously, fierce night fighter activity on approach to and over the target. The operation was favoured by clear skies and excellent visibility, and the 50 Squadron crews identified ground detail in the light of the illuminating flares before delivering their loads onto red TIs in accordance with the Master Bomber's instructions from 9,000 to 11,500 feet between 21.15 and 21.25. A large explosion was witnessed eight hundred yards north of the TIs at 21.17, and up to six others were also reported, along with smoke rising through 3,000 feet as they turned away to the west, confident in the quality of their work. Ten Lancasters would not arrive back in home airspace, and among them was NG385, the fifth 50 Squadron failure to return already this month. P/O Hewett and his flight engineer were taken into captivity, while the bodies of the remaining five crew members were recovered from the wreckage of the Lancaster in shallow waters off Wollin, some fifteen miles north of the target. 1 and 8 Groups completed the destruction of the plant, and no more synthetic oil would be produced before war's end.

Briefings took place on the 13th for the first round of Operation Thunderclap, the Churchill inspired offensive against Germany's eastern cities, which was devised partly to act in support of the advancing Russians, and also as a demonstration to them of Allied air power. The historic and culturally significant city of Dresden was selected to open the offensive in another two-phase affair, with a 5 Group force of 246 Lancasters and nine Mosquitos leading the way, to be followed three hours later by 529 Lancasters of 1, 3, 6 and 8 Groups. It had proved to be a successful policy thus far, with the 5 Group low-level marking system and main force attacks providing a beacon for the second force, and, should it be required on this night, 8 Group would provide any necessary marking for phase two from high level. The 50 Squadron contingent of sixteen Lancasters took off between 17.38 and 17.53 with S/L Blair the senior pilot on duty, and had absolutely no concept of the ramifications of the operation, both in terms of its outcome on the ground, and its hysterical aftermath. Dresden was Germany's seventh largest city, and its largest remaining partially un-bombed built-up area, which, according to American sources, contained more than a hundred factories and fifty thousand workers contributing to the war effort. It was also an important railway hub, to the extent that the marshalling yards had been attacked twice in late 1944 by the USAAF.

The spearhead of the heavy brigade was two hours out when W/C Maurice Smith of 54 Base, the Master Bomber for the 5 Group attack, lifted off the runway at a few minutes before 20.00 hours in Mosquito KB401 AZ-E, a 627 Squadron aircraft on loan, and he was followed away by eight others from 627 Squadron. The Mosquitos would arrive in the target area at the same time as their less fleet-footed cousins to encounter three layers of cloud, between 3,000 and 5,000 feet, 6,000 to 8,000 feet and 15,000 to 16,000 feet, but otherwise good visibility. The first primary blind marker delivered green TIs from 15,000 feet at 22.03, and was followed in by the flare force, which lit the way for the low-level Mosquitos. The main force Lancasters were carrying eight hundred tons of bombs, made up into loads containing various mixes drawn from cookies, 2,000 and 500 pounders and cluster bombs, and these were delivered by the 50 Squadron crews from 10,000 to 13,900 feet between 22.15 and 22.23 onto the glow of red TIs in accordance with the Master Bomber's instructions. As far as the crews were concerned, this was no different from any other attack, and the fires visible for a hundred miles into the return journey nothing out of the ordinary. S/L Blair and crew had other matters on their minds, having lost their port-outer engine to low oil pressure over the target, and had only half power on the starboard-inner as they were confronted by severe icing conditions on the way home. Unable to climb above the front, they came down to 4,000 feet, and made it to debriefing, where S/L Blair had comments to offer. The Master Bomber's "patter", over the target expressed great satisfaction with the results, but S/L Blair questioned how he could make that assessment when the ground was obscured by cloud.

By the time that the second force of 1, 3, 6 and 8 Group Lancasters arrived over Dresden three hours after 5 Group, the skies had cleared, and the fires created by the earlier attack provided the expected beacon. A further eighteen hundred tons of bombs rained down onto the historic and beautiful old city, setting off the same chain of events that had devastated parts of Hamburg in July 1943, and a number of other cities since. Dresden's population had been swelled by masses of refugees fleeing from the eastern front, and many were engulfed in the ensuing firestorm. On the following morning, three hundred American bombers carried out a separate attack under the umbrella of a fighter escort, and completed the destruction. Initial propaganda-inspired reports in Germany falsely claimed a death toll of 250,000 people, but an accurate figure of twenty-five thousand has been settled upon since.

The destruction of Dresden has been used by some as a weapon with which to beat Bomber Command and Harris, and label them as war criminals. To this day, in Germany, survivors claim that RAF aircraft strafed civilians in the streets and open spaces, an accusation absolutely without foundation. It should be remembered, that American bombers arrived over the city on the following morning under the umbrella of escort fighters, and it was they that strafed the ground to increase the level of confusion. Curiously, no accusations have been levelled at them. It should also be understood, that Harris had no interest in attacking Dresden, and had to be nagged by Chief-of-the-Air-Staff Portal to fulfil Churchill's wishes. The aircrew simply did the job asked of them, and the raid on Dresden was no different from any other attack on a city. The death toll at Hamburg was much higher, and yet, there has been no similar outcry. The legacy of this operation served to deny Harris and the men under his Command their due recognition for the massive part they played in the ultimate victory, and only in recent times has a monument been erected in Green Park in London and a campaign clasp awarded, sadly, far too late for the majority. Churchill, with his eyes set on a peacetime election, betrayed Harris and the Command in a typical politically motivated U-turn, leaving Harris as the only commander in the field to be omitted from the Honours List.

Round two of Thunderclap was planned for the following night, when Chemnitz was posted as the target for 717 aircraft drawn from 1, 3, 4, 6 and 8 Groups, while 224 Lancasters and eight Mosquitos of 5 Group targeted an oil refinery in the small town of Rositz, situated twenty-five miles due south of Leipzig and thirty miles north-west of Chemnitz. Fourteen 50 Squadron Lancasters were made ready, and they all became safely airborne between 16.40 and 17.05 with F/Ls Drinkell, Ling and North the senior pilots on duty, but with W/C Birch and crew also taking part, while on attachment to the squadron to gain operational experience before taking command of 619 Squadron. F/O Cain and crew had been experiencing a port-inner engine problem since take-off, and had reached the midpoint of the Channel crossing when they admitted defeat and turned back. The route out took the bomber stream across France, before traversing Germany to be greeted by two layers of six to ten-tenths thin cloud in the target area, one at 6,000 to 8,000 feet, and the other at 10,000 to 12,000 feet. The primary blind marker made a good run on H2S at 15,000 feet at 20.48 to drop green TIs, and the illuminators followed up between 20.51 and 20.58 from a similar height. Designated main force crews arrived at the same time to carry out support runs with the marker element, before the entire main force was called in to bomb at 21.07, the 50 Squadron crews releasing their cookie and nine 500 pounders each onto red and green TIs, or on their glow, from 8,000 to 11,000 feet between 21.02 and 21.12. Returning crew reported explosions and fires, and, generally, expressed confidence in the success of the operation, but, it was established afterwards that only the southern part of the oil plant had been damaged, and it would be necessary to return to finish the job. The Chemnitz raid had been compromised by adverse weather conditions, and it would be March before success was achieved against this target.

An oil refinery at Böhlen, another in the Leipzig area and some ten miles north of Rositz, was posted as the target on the 19th for a 5 Group force of 264 Lancasters and six Mosquitos. 50 Squadron dispatched twenty Lancasters in a late take-off between 23.06 and 23.47 with F/L Ling the senior pilot on duty, and W/C Birch and crew also taking part. They all completed the three-and-a-half-hour flight out, and would meet up with the later-departing Mosquito element at the target. Master Bomber for the occasion was 54 Base's W/C Benjamin, who was flying the same Mosquito used by W/C Smith at Dresden six nights earlier. They encountered ten-tenths cloud over the target in two layers at 5,000 to 8,000 feet and 10,000 to 14,000 feet, and this would introduce a challenging element to the operation. The illuminators went in at around 15,000 feet between 04.05 and 04.13, and the VHF chatter suggested that a Mosquito had been able to mark a factory building with a red TI, and that that had been backed up. The main force was called in, before W/C Benjamin's VHF was suddenly cut off, and his Deputy took over. It would be established later, that the Master Bomber's Mosquito had been shot down by flak, and that W/C Benjamin DFC & Bar had died alongside his navigator. The 50 Squadron crews carried out their attacks in accordance with confusing instructions, doing so from 7,000 to 13,000 feet between 04.18 and 04.29, and aiming mostly at the glow in the cloud of red and green TIs. Post-raid reconnaissance revealed only superficial damage to the site, which would have to be attacked again.

The following night, the 20th, proved to be a busy one, with more than five hundred Lancasters targeting Dortmund, while 268 Halifaxes from 4 and 6 Groups provided the heavy elements for raids on Rhenania-Ossag oil refineries in Düsseldorf and Monheim. 5 Group, meanwhile, prepared itself for a further attempt on the Mittelland Canal at Gravenhorst, for which ten 50 Squadron crews were briefed as part of an overall force of 154 Lancasters and eleven Mosquitos. They departed Skellingthorpe between 21.36 and 21.57 with S/L Blair the senior pilot on duty, and all reached the target area to find a layer of ten-tenths cloud between them and the aiming-point. The primary blind marker succeeded in delivering two green TIs by H2S from 12,000 feet at 00.53, and they fell on the starboard side of the canal. After the flare force went in, the Mosquito element descended to 4,500 feet, but could not identify the aiming-point, and, just before H-Hour, the Master Bomber sent the markers home, to be followed almost immediately by the main force as he abandoned the operation.

The operation was rescheduled for twenty-four hours later, when Duisburg and Worms were also to be attacked by heavy forces of 362 and 349 aircraft respectively. 5 Group detailed 165

Lancasters and twelve Mosquitos, and, among those attending the briefing at Coningsby was G/C Evans-Evans, the station commander, who would be taking the bulk of G/C Ingham's highly experienced crew with him. The ten 50 Squadron participants took off between 16.57 and 17.14 with no senior pilots on duty, and lost the services of F/O Hills and crew to starboard-inner engine failure ten minutes after take-off. The others reached the target area to find moonlight beaming down from clear skies with some ground haze. One of the primary blind markers was able to deliver his green TIs, doing so two minutes late because of a change in the wind, and they fell about a mile south of the aiming-point, quite close to the Wet Triangle meeting point of the Mittelland and Dortmund-Ems Canals. After the flare force had done its job, the Mosquitos delivered their red TIs, which were backed up successfully, before the main force was called in at 20.25. The 50 Squadron participants released their loads of thirteen 1,000 pounders each from 8,000 to 10,500 feet between 20.34 and 20.40, but could not assess the outcome because of the use of long-delay fuses. The familiar hostile reception took its toll, and nine Lancasters failed to return, among them a further two belonging to 50 Squadron. LL741 crashed at Helenaveen, in liberated territory between the German frontier and Eindhoven, killing F/O Anderson RCAF and all but the flight engineer. Three others among the dead were members of the RCAF. RF138 came down on the German side of the frontier, killing F/O Hatcher and all but his rear gunner, who was taken into captivity. Another sad loss was that of G/C Evans-Evans, the Coningsby station commander, and his massively experienced and decorated seven-man crew, who had no need to take part in the operation, but could not resist the opportunity. Only the rear gunner survived, and, among those killed was the twenty-two-year-old navigator, S/L Wishart DSO, DFC & Bar, who had completed sixty-one operations in Lancasters with 97 Squadron and eighteen in Mosquitos as navigator to Master Bombers.

53 Base was not involved in the 5 Group operation by seventy-four Lancasters to bomb what was believed to be a U-Boot base at Horten in Oslo Fjord on the night of the 23/24th. Whether or not a U-Boot base existed is uncertain, but no shipping was seen by the crews, and a local report described heavy damage in the port area and a shipyard, and the sinking of a tanker and floating crane. The main operation on this night was conducted by more than 350 Lancasters and thirteen Mosquitos of 1, 6 and 8 Groups against Pforzheim, situated some thirty miles north-west of Stuttgart in south-western Germany. In a twenty-two-minute orgy of destruction, 1,825 tons of bombs destroyed by fire an area of 3km x 1½ km and killed more than 17,000 of the inhabitants, the third largest death toll in a single night after Hamburg and Dresden.

A daylight attack on the Dortmund-Ems Canal was planned for the afternoon of the 24th, and would involve 166 Lancasters and five Mosquitos, eighteen of the former provided by 617 Squadron with Tallboys on board, while 50 Squadron put up sixteen. They departed Skellingthorpe between 13.38 and 14.08 with W/C Frogley and S/L Blair the senior pilots on duty, and all reached the target, where ten-tenths cloud was encountered, with tops at 7,000 to 9,000 feet, at which point the Master Bomber abandoned the operation and sent the force home with its bombs. During the course of the month the squadron carried out ten operations, including those aborted, and dispatched 152 sorties for the loss of seven Lancasters and crews.

<h1 align="center">March 1945</h1>

The new month would see the Command bludgeon its way across Germany, concentrating on oil, rail and road targets, along with the few towns still boasting a built-up area. Mannheim was raided for the last time in numbers by more than 450 Lancasters, Halifaxes and Mosquitos from 1, 6 and 8 Groups on the 1st, while 5 Group remained at home. On the 2nd, Cologne was pounded for the final time, first by a force of seven hundred aircraft, which inflicted huge destruction across the city, particularly west of the Rhine, and, later, by a 3 Group force, of which only fifteen bombed because of a faulty G-H station in England. The city ceased to function, thereafter, and was still paralyzed when American forces marched in four days later. Just when it seemed that German resistance to air attack might end, March would prove that the defenders were still capable of mounting a challenge, even though they were stretched beyond their capacity to protect every corner of the Reich.

5 Group opened its March account with a return to the Ladbergen aqueduct section of the Dortmund-Ems Canal on the evening of the 3rd, for which 212 Lancasters and ten Mosquitos were made ready. Fifteen 50 Squadron crews attended briefing, and they departed Skellingthorpe between 18.24 and 18.50 with F/Ls North and Steele the senior pilots on duty. All reached the target area to encounter eight to ten-tenths cloud between 3,500 and 6,000 feet, noting that the defences had been strengthened since the last attack and was throwing up a curtain of intense light flak as high as 15,000 feet. H2S allowed the two 83 Squadron primary blind markers to locate the canal and deliver their green TIs from 14,000 feet at 21.47 and 21.49 respectively, and the first illuminators went in a minute later to light the way for the Mosquitos, after which, a large red glow could be seen through the clouds. At 21.59 the Master Bomber called in the main force to bomb on the glow or on sight of the TIs through gaps in the thin cloud, and the 50 Squadron crews complied from 7,700 to 10,000 feet between 22.00 and 22.10, contributing to the breaching of both branches, which rendered the waterway unnavigable and out of action for the remainder of the war. Seven Lancasters failed to return, the last to do so during this long-running campaign that had started in those dark days of the summer of 1940. The recently-mentioned W/C Birch of 619 Squadron reported shooting down a V-1 near the target. A second operation on this night was directed by a main force of two hundred 4 Group Halifaxes at the synthetic oil refinery at Kamen in the Ruhr, and, together with all other activity, this put almost eight hundred RAF aircraft in the air and at the mercy of the Luftwaffe's Operation Gisella. Some two hundred intruders stalked the bombers as they prepared to land, and they succeeded in shooting down twenty for the loss of three of their own.

Nineteen 50 Squadron crews attended briefing on the 5th, to learn that the group would be sending 248 Lancasters and ten Mosquitos back to Böhlen, for another crack at the synthetic oil refinery. A simultaneous operation by a Thunderclap force of 760 aircraft would attempt to redress the recent failure at Chemnitz, some thirty-five miles to the south. Take-off from Skellingthorpe was completed by the 50 Squadron crews without incident between 16.50 and 17.37 with S/L Blair leading the way, but F/O Wood and crew dropped out when thirty miles short of the French coast because of an unserviceable rear turret. The others battled through severe icing conditions to reach the target area and encounter ten-tenths cloud in layers between 2,000 and 11,000 feet. Uncertainty concerning the prevailing conditions on arrival led to the preparation of two marking plans, low-level and skymarking, and the lead primary blind marker made his first run at 14,000 feet to drop green TIs at 21.40. He did not see them burst because of the cloud, but thought that the illuminator flares were well-placed. Some of the Coningsby crews had H2S difficulties, and not all were able to pinpoint on Leipzig for the run-in. This meant that they were unsure of their position, and, when the Master Bomber called for Wanganui flares at 21.45, they withheld them, rather than risk dropping them inaccurately and attracting some of the bombing. A large explosion was witnessed at 21.50, and, three minutes later, Wanganui flares were observed by the approaching main force crews. Those from 50 Squadron bombed from 8,000 to 13,500 feet between 21.53 and 22.01, observing another large explosion at 21.57, before the Master Bomber called a halt at 22.01 and sent everyone home, leaving evidence of fires and smoke behind them. F/O Skilling and crew were struggling with icing at the time, and were orbiting, trying to identify the aiming-point after dumping a proportion of their load "live" ten minutes earlier. The Master Bomber's call brought an end to their search and they retained the rest of their bombs to return to store. At debriefing, S/L Blair offered his customary uncomplimentary comments about the conduct of the operation and decisions of the Master Bomber, probably borne out of the frustration of having to battle the conditions while trying to establish position over the aiming-point. Four Lancasters failed to return, and among them was 50 Squadron's F/O King's NF918, which crashed in Germany with no survivors. Post-raid reconnaissance revealed extensive damage to the coal-drying plant, and some hits in other areas of the site, but it was still not a knockout blow. Meanwhile, the Thunderclap force had succeeded in inflicting severe fire damage in central and southern districts of Chemnitz.

The target posted on 5 Group stations on the 6th was the town and port area of Sassnitz, located on the Baltic island of Rügen, about thirty miles north of Peenemünde. This was a region with memories of heavy casualties sustained by the group during Operation Hydra in August 1943. The two-fold purpose of the operation was to destroy its installations and facilities, and sink shipping to render it unusable as a port. 150 Lancasters and seven Mosquitos were made ready, ten of the former by 50 Squadron, and they departed Skellingthorpe between 18.06 and 18.23 with F/Ls North, Walls and Whalley the senior pilots on duty, the last-mentioned having just completed a Flight Commanders course at Metheringham. All reached the target area to find five to nine-tenths drifting cloud with tops up to 8,000 feet, over which an 83 Squadron blind marker made a run at 22.50 to drop green TIs over the port from 12,000 feet, and the flare force maintained illumination of the town and outer harbour for the next twenty-five minutes. Apart from a short break, when cloud slid across the aiming-point, the markers remained visible to the main force crews, and those from 50 Squadron bombed with a seven-second overshoot on red and green TIs from 7,500 to 10,000 feet between 23.02 and 23.16, in accordance with instructions from the Master Bomber. Post-raid reconnaissance revealed extensive damage in the northern part of the town, and three large ships in the harbour had been sunk.

It was back to the oil campaign for 5 Group on the following night, for an attack on an oil refinery at Harburg, the town facing Hamburg from the southern side of the Elbe. A force of 234 Lancasters and seven Mosquitos was made ready, which would not be alone over Germany, as more than a thousand other aircraft would be engaged against similar targets at Dessau and Hemmingstedt and in minor and support operations. 50 Squadron provided seventeen Lancasters, which took off between 17.25 and 18.03 with S/L Blair the senior pilot on duty, and all arrived over the target to find eight-tenths thin cloud and red and yellow target indicators clearly visible. F/O Halliwell and crew supported the flare force, which made them too late to get back to a starting point for their bombing run, and they had to jettison the eight delay-fused 500 pounders in their bomb bay, but retained the rest. F/O Berriman and crew became caught up in the support run, and also failed to complete a second run before the Master Bomber called a halt. Acting in accordance with the Master Bomber's instructions to overshoot the TIs by seven-seconds, the others bombed from 12,000 to 15,000 feet between 22.02 and 22.09. Bomb bursts were clearly seen, along with explosions and black smoke rising to 9,000 feet, and all set course for home confident in the success of the operation. Night-fighters were waiting for returning bombers at the German coast, and S/L Blair and crew ran into one at 22.42, when at 2,000 feet and some twenty miles out from Jade Bay. The fixed aerial was shot away, but no other damage sustained, and this, it seems, was sufficient to work out any frustrations lurking within S/L Blair, who described the marking and controlling as excellent. It was a good night also for 5 Group gunners, who claimed seven night-fighters as destroyed. Post-raid reconnaissance confirmed further damage to this previously attacked target, with oil storage tanks taking the most hits, and revealed that a rubber factory had also been severely damaged.

The squadron welcomed a new commanding officer on the 11th, who would see it through to the end of hostilities. W/C Flint had risen through the 50 Squadron ranks from sergeant pilot, and, even now, held a substantive rank of flight lieutenant, elevated to acting wing commander rank so that he could now succeed the long-serving and highly-respected W/C Frogley, who was posted to 5 Group HQ after an outstanding tour as commanding officer. An all-time record was set on this day, when 1,079 aircraft, the largest Bomber Command force ever for a single target, was assembled to attack Essen for the last time. 5 Group contributed 199 Lancasters and a single Mosquito, 50 Squadron loading fourteen Lancasters with a cookie and sixteen 500 pounders each, and dispatching them between 11.48 and 12.05 with a handful of flight lieutenant pilots leading the way. The city was covered by ten-tenths cloud with tops at 6,000 feet, which required the Pathfinder element to employ skymarkers in the form of red and blue smoke puffs, and these were bombed by the 50 Squadron crews from 16,000 to 19,000 feet between 15.16 and 15.31. More than 4,600 tons of bombs were dropped into the already ravaged city and former industrial powerhouse, and left it in a state of paralysis, from which there was no recovery. American ground forces would capture it unopposed on the 10th of April.

A little over twenty-four hours later, the short-lived record was surpassed by the departure from their stations in the early afternoon of 1,108 aircraft, which had Dortmund as their destination. This time 5 Group provided 211 Lancasters, fifteen of them from 50 Squadron, which departed Skellingthorpe between 13.08 and 13.31 with F/Ls Chadwick, Day, Ling and North the senior pilots on duty. They found the Ruhr still under a blanket of ten-tenths cloud, this time with tops at 6,000 feet, and the Pathfinders marked the aiming-points with green and blue smoke puffs. Some of the 50 Squadron crews were directed by the Master Bomber to aim for the northerly blues, and the others the greens, which they did from 15,000 to 18,750 feet between 16.47 and 16.56. Returning crews spoke of brown smoke climbing through the clouds to 7,000 feet from the northern end of the city, and also a ring of smoke encircling the area. A new record of 4,800 tons of bombs was delivered, and photo-reconnaissance revealed that the central and southern districts of the city had received the greatest weight of bombs, and had been left in chaos, with all industry silenced permanently and railway tracks torn up. That night, there would be a party for F/O Firmin and crew, who had now finished their first tour of operations.

5 Group's next objective was the Wintershall oil refinery at Lützkendorf, another site to the west of Leipzig and south-west of Leuna. *(Lützkendorf no longer exists on a map of Germany, and is now known as Krumpa)*. The briefing of 244 Lancaster and eleven Mosquito crews took place on the 14th, eighteen of the former representing 50 Squadron, and they departed Skellingthorpe between 16.31 and 17.01 with F/Ls Chadwick, Ling, North, Walls and Whalley the senior pilots on duty. The bomber stream headed out over the Wash and the bulge of East Anglia en-route to the Scheldt estuary, before crossing Belgium to swing south of Cologne and then point their noses to the east for the long leg to the target. F/L Chadwick had just crossed the Franco/German frontier south of Strasbourg when the rear turret became unserviceable, and forced them to turn back at 20.37. The others were met on arrival by conditions described variously as ten-tenths cloud, no cloud, thin layer of cloud, thin banks of stratus with tops at 12,000 feet, a little medium cloud, poor visibility and good visibility, but there was unanimity with regard to the haze. Ahead, the primary blind marker aircraft could be seen delivering their green TIs at 21.49, followed by the illuminators immediately afterwards between 21.51 and 22.00 to drop flares and bombs. Finally, the low-level Mosquitos did their job to accurately mark the aiming-point before the main force was called in, the 50 Squadron participants bombing on red and green TIs in accordance with the Master Bomber's instructions from 8,000 to 9,950 feet between 22.02 and 22.11. Returning crews claimed an accurate attack, reporting explosions and fires, and thick black smoke drifting across the plant and ascending through 7,000 feet, which rendered impossible a detailed assessment. Night-fighters were very much in evidence over the target and during the return flight, and eighteen Lancasters failed to return, an alarming 7.4% of those dispatched. Among them was 50 Squadron's NG177, which was lost without trace with the experienced crew of F/L Ling. Reconnaissance revealed a partially successful raid, which meant that a further visit would be required.

Sixteen 50 Squadron crews assembled in the briefing room at 14.00 on the 16th, to learn that they were to attack the virgin target of Würzburg, a small city on the River Main, situated some sixty miles south-east of Frankfurt in southern Germany. A 5 Group force of 225 Lancasters and eleven Mosquitos was made ready for an early-evening take-off, and the 50 Squadron element got away between 17.24 and 17.53 with F/Ls Chadwick, Drinkell, Jung and Whalley the senior pilots on duty. While this operation was in progress, a similar-sized force, drawn from 1 and 8 Groups, would be delivering the final attack of the war on Nuremberg, fifty miles to the south-east. All from 50 Squadron reached the target area to find clear skies with ground haze, and the marking and flare forces having carried out their assigned tasks between 21.25 and 21.34. When the main force crews followed up to exploit the favourable bombing conditions, the 50 Squadron crews found red and green target indicators marking the aiming-point, and complied with the Master Bomber's call for a twenty-four-second overshoot, to deliver their bomb loads from 9,300 to 10,000 feet between 21.33 and 21.38. They returned to Skellingthorpe without incident to report a successful operation, but had to wait for the reconnaissance reports to discover the extent of the destruction. The bombing had lasted just seventeen minutes, during which period 1,127 tons of bombs had fallen into the historic old cathedral city, destroying an estimated 89% of the built-up area and killing four to five thousand people. The Nuremberg operation had also been highly destructive, but had cost 1 Group twenty-four Lancasters, thus proving, that the enemy defences were not yet spent, and could still give the Command a bloody nose.

S/L Oldacre was posted in from 9 Squadron on the 19th to assume the role of flight commander. He would find that there was still business to attend to at the Böhlen oil refinery, and 5 Group prepared a force of 236 Lancasters and eleven Mosquitos on the 20th, to deliver what was hoped to be the knockout blow. Briefings began at 20.00, and, at Skellingthorpe, was attended by seventeen 50 Squadron crews, with a handful of flight lieutenants the most senior pilots present. They learned also that a dozen Lancasters from the group would be conducting a diversionary raid on Halle some twenty miles to the north-west of Leipzig. They departed Skellingthorpe between 23.18 and 23.53, and set out on the now familiar path to eastern Germany, where conditions in the target area were fairly good, with three to six-tenths cloud with tops at 6,000 to 8,000 feet. The bomber stream arrived early because of stronger-than-forecast winds, and the main force had to orbit while the first primary blind marker crew delivered green TIs at 03.33. They fell 750 yards south of the plant, to be followed at H-16 by a yellow TI bursting two miles short of the target. A cluster of illuminator flares ignited ahead, revealing that a smoke screen had been activated and was generating much smoke, which might impede the efforts of the Mosquito low-level markers, but they deposited red TIs on the button, and the main force was called in. A few dummy TIs attracted a number of bomb loads, but the 50 Squadron crews complied with the instructions of the Master Bomber to bomb on specific reds, greens and yellows, doing so from 12,300 to 14,000 feet between 03.46 and 03.53. The main weight of the attack was concentrated around the target, and numerous explosions were witnessed, as was smoke rising through 5,000 feet as they turned away. The diversion at Halle may have helped to reduce losses from the main event, but, even so, nine Lancasters failed to return, including 50 Squadron's ME441. It is believed that this Lancaster may have crashed in Belgium, based on the fact that one crew member is buried in that country, and the sole survivor from the crew of Sgt Levy RAAF, the navigator, was not listed as a PoW or evader. The operation finally put the plant out of action, and it was still idle when American forces moved in a few weeks later.

It was after 22.00 on the 21st that 151 Lancaster and eight Mosquito crews of 5 Group were informed that the Deutsche Erdölwerke synthetic oil refinery at Hamburg was to be their target that night. 50 Squadron was not to be involved in this operation, which was attended by thin stratus cloud at around 2,000 feet, and resulted in the destruction of twenty storage tanks at a cost of four Lancasters. After its night off, 50 Squadron was alerted on the 22nd, and sixteen crews attended briefing to learn of their target for that afternoon, which turned out to be a railway bridge at Bremen, while 617 Squadron attended to a similar structure at Nienburg, situated some twenty-five miles to the south-east. A force of eighty-two Lancasters was assembled, and the 50 Squadron crews departed Skellingthorpe between 11.14 and 11.45 with S/L Oldacre the senior pilot on duty for the first time. F/Sgt Evans and crew peeled off from the bomber stream when over the North Sea ten miles north of Sheringham, and returned home with a dead starboard-outer engine. The others pressed on to find clear skies and good visibility in the target area, which enabled them to pick out the River Weser and the bridges spanning its length within the city. The 50 Squadron crews delivered their attacks visually, in accordance with the instructions of the Master Bomber, doing so from 15,500 to 17,500 feet between 14.08 and 14.11, some of them having to aim at the smoke that was enveloping the bridge, while dodging the moderate to intense heavy flak. It was impossible to assess the outcome, but photo-reconnaissance would reveal the bridge to be still intact.

On the 23rd, orders came through that five former members of W/C Frogley's crew were to be declared tour-expired with immediate effect, having completed between twenty-three and twenty-six sorties. F/O Groves and crew finished at the same time, but their plans for a joint party that night were scuppered by further orders referring to that night's operation. The town of Wesel had the misfortune to lie close to the Rhine and in the path of advancing British ground forces. Since the 16th of February it had been systematically reduced to rubble by repeated air attacks, and now had one final onslaught to face, having already endured one by 3 Group earlier in the day. 195 Lancasters and eleven Mosquitos were made ready, the 50 Squadron element of fourteen departing Skellingthorpe between 19.02 and 19.33 with F/L Jung the senior pilot on duty. The crews found the target under clear skies with slight ground haze, and were able to identify it visually. The aiming point was well-marked by red and green TIs, which were bombed from 8,250 to 12,000 feet between 22.35 and 22.41 in accordance with the Master Bomber's instructions. They noted that, despite the Master Bomber ending the attack at H+8, bombing had continued for some minutes afterwards. While outbound at 21.40, F/O Lillies RAAF and crew had been forced to shut down their starboard-outer engine, but pressed on hoping to reach the target in time to bomb by H+8, and were actually on the bombing run when, frustratingly, the Master Bomber had called a halt. They were disciplined enough to hang on to their bombs, some of which they hoped to unload in the jettison area on the way home, but a faltering starboard-inner engine put paid to that idea, and, as they began to lose height, they let the bombs go and set a course for Juvincourt. When the port-inner began to show signs of stress, it was clear that they needed to land soon, and called "Darkie", eventually receiving a signal to land at Florennes in Belgium, where they hit a pothole and wrote off NG171, happily, without crew casualties. Post-raid reconnaissance confirmed the effectiveness of the raid, which left only 3% of Wesel's buildings standing. After the war it would claim justifiably to be the most completely destroyed town in Germany.

The month's final operations for 5 Group took place on the 27th, when twenty Lancasters of 617 Squadron were sent with Tallboys and Grand Slams to the U-Boot pens at Farge, a small port on the eastern bank of the Weser, northwest of Bremen. In his classic book, The Dambusters, Paul Brickhill described the target as the largest concrete structure in the world, measuring some 1,450 by 300 yards, which boasted a reinforced-concrete roof twenty-three-feet thick. The massive structure contained a tank large enough for completed U-Boots to be tested under water. At the time of the attack it was still under construction and was not operational. In fact, the concrete for the roof had only recently been poured, and had not had time to set before the attack took place. A simultaneous operation by ninety-five Lancasters against a nearby underground oil storage facility involved fourteen from 50 Squadron, which departed Skellingthorpe between 10.04 and 10.40 with S/L Oldacre the senior pilot on duty. They all arrived at the target to find clear skies and good visibility, and identified the aiming-point visually, before bombing from 15,000 to 17,500 feet between 13.00 and 13.05. They were unable to assess the outcome, but three explosions and thick, brown smoke suggested a successful attack, and their attention was drawn inevitably to the 617 Squadron activity, where a sheet of flame was observed. F/L Lees and crew had forgotten to prime the bomb-release master switch, and failed to release their bombs on the primary target. They sought out an alternative on the way home, and found the town of Friesoythe, forty miles due west of Bremen, to bomb at 13.13 from 16,400 feet. The 617 Squadron attack was another masterly display of precision bombing, and photo-reconnaissance confirmed two direct hits by Grand Slams, which had penetrated the partially completed roof and caused a great deal of it to collapse. The structure was still incomplete at the end of hostilities, having never been used, and its enormous bulk remains to this day as a permanent monument to a failed regime.

During the course of the month the squadron took part in twelve operations and dispatched 184 sorties for the loss of four Lancasters and three crews. Fewer than four weeks of operations remained ahead of the crews before the bombing war finally came to an end.

April 1945

There would be a gentle introduction to April for 5 Group, and it was not until the 4th that the "Independent Air Force" was called into action. The operation was against what was believed to be a military barracks at Nordhausen, situated in the Harz Mountains between Hannover to the north-west and Leipzig to the south-east. It had been attacked on the previous day by 1 Group, and was, in fact, a camp for forced workers at the V-2 factory that had been constructed in tunnels under the mountains after the destruction of Peenemünde. There, the workers endured the most appalling conditions and brutal treatment as an increasingly desperate regime sought to change the course of the war. The 5 Group attack, by 243 Lancasters, was to be divided between the barracks and the town, ninety-three to the former and 150 to the latter, the twenty 50 Squadron crews allotted, it is believed, to the former. They departed Skellingthorpe between 05.44 and 06.36 with F/Ls Gifford, Lees and Walls the senior pilots on duty, and arrived at the target to encounter five-to-seven-tenths cloud with tops as high as 7,000 feet. They were able to visually identify the barracks and the marshalling yards serving the site until smoke began to obscure it, at which point, those still with bombs were redirected to the town. The 50 Squadron crews bombed mostly the barracks, but some the town, doing so from 13,000 to 16,250 feet between 09.15 to 09.24, and, although some of the early bombing of the town was seen to undershoot, the Master Bomber corrected this by calling for a five-second overshoot, and, thereafter, the markers were soon obscured by smoke. Returning crews were able to report a concentrated attack on both aiming-points, with severe damage, and, sadly and inevitably, there were heavy casualties among the unfortunate slave workers. On return from this operation, F/O Farrer and crew were declared tour-expired after thirty-five sorties.

53 Base was called into action on the 6th to attack blockade-runners at the Dutch port of Ijmuiden, and a force of fifty-four Lancasters and a Mosquito was made ready. Eleven 50 Squadron Lancasters departed Skellingthorpe between 08.27 and 09.02 with S/L Oldacre the senior pilot on duty, but NG271 lost its port-outer engine almost immediately, and, despite the jettisoning of twelve of the fourteen 1,000 pounders, height could not be maintained. F/O Turrell RCAF put the Lancaster down in Waddington village under some semblance of control, and only the rear gunner sustained minor injury. On arrival at the target, the others found a band of cloud between 3,000 and 5,500 feet lying across the area, which persuaded the Master Bomber to abandon the operation and send the crews home.

The only sizeable effort on the night of the 7/8th was by 175 Lancasters and eleven Mosquitos of 5 Group, which had a benzol plant at Molbis, near Leipzig, as their target. Situated south of the city, and less than two miles east of Böhlen, it was becoming a familiar destination for the group, with a well-trodden route across Belgium to pass south of Cologne. 50 Squadron made ready seven Lancasters, which departed Skellingthorpe between 17.52 and 18.03 with no senior pilots on duty, but, fifteen minutes after setting course, F/O Campbell and crew lost their port-inner engine and turned back. Some crews found themselves delayed by wrongly forecast head winds, and would arrive too late to deliver an attack. All of the 50 Squadron crews reached the target area to find clear skies with ground haze, or, perhaps, a smoke screen in operation, but not all from the force would get to the aiming-point before the call to cease bombing was issued. The two 83 Squadron primary blind markers formed the tip of the spear, and identified Zeitz on H2S, before making the ten-mile north-easterly run from there to the target. Green TIs were released from 15,000 feet at 22.48, and the flare force followed up between 22.50 and 22.57 to enable the low-level Mosquitos to drop red and green TIs among the chimneys of the plant. This was an invitation for the main force to plaster it with high explosives, which most of the 50 Squadron element did from around 16,500 feet between 23.01 and 23.07, leaving them in no doubt, that the operation was a complete success. This was confirmed by photo-reconnaissance, and no further production would be possible on the site.

Two major operations were scheduled for the 8th, the larger one involving 440 aircraft from 4, 6 and 8 Groups to be directed against Hamburg's shipyards, while 5 Group would take on the Lützkendorf refinery, following a failed attempt on the 4th by 1 and 8 Groups to conclusively end production at the site. A force of 231 Lancasters and eleven Mosquitos was put together, and the seven 50 Squadron participants departed Skellingthorpe between 18.09 and 18.49 with F/L Day the senior pilot on duty. F/O Skilling and crew were back in the circuit within three hours after a hydraulics pipe broke in the rear turret, leaving the others to reach the target and find the conditions as they had been twenty-four hours earlier, with clear skies and either ground haze or generated smoke. The primary blind markers ran in at 14,000 feet at 22.33 to deliver green TIs, and the illuminators followed between 22.35 and 22.42, after which, the main force was called in. The 50 Squadron crews attacked in accordance with the Master Bomber's instructions to bomb the southerly red and yellow TIs after an eleven second overshoot, doing so from 11,000 to 14,000 feet between 22.46 and 22.53. Many explosions were reported by returning crews, including a large one at 22.47, which was surpassed in size by another one two minutes later, which produced flames said to have reached up to 3,000 feet. The complete destruction of the site was confirmed by photo-reconnaissance, and the plant would remain out of action for what remained of the war. Earlier in the day, the official length of a tour had been reduced from thirty-six to thirty-three sorties, but there seemed to be a degree of discretionary early release in operation.

On the 8th, F/L North and most of his crew were posted to the Bomber Command Film Unit at Fulbeck. Orders were received on 53 Base stations on the 9th to prepare for an attack on oil storage tanks at Finkenwerder, on one of the islands in the Elbe to the west of Hamburg city centre. A force of forty Lancasters was made ready, ten of them provided by 50 Squadron, and they departed Skellingthorpe between 14.27 and 14.50 with S/L Oldacre the senior pilot on duty. F/L Jung and crew returned early with an engine issue, leaving the others to press on to be greeted by clear skies and good visibility, which enabled them easily to identify the docks area, before bombing visually from 15,800 to 18,000 feet between 17.37 and 17.39. On return, there were reports of concentrated bombing, which produced many fires and much black smoke, but not among them at debriefing was the crew of F/O Berriman RAAF. NG342 had crashed in the target area without survivors, and this crew, therefore, bore the sad honour of being the very last from 50 Squadron to lose their lives on offensive operations.

53 Base squadrons were not called into action on the 10th, when other elements of 5 Group returned to the Leipzig area to hit a railway line at Wahren, situated to the north-west of the city. A larger operation on this night, involving more than three hundred aircraft from 1 and 8 Groups, was to be directed at the Plauen marshalling yards to the south-west of Dresden, and

the two forces would adopt a similar route until shortly before reaching Leipzig. 5 Group contributed all seventy-six Lancasters and eleven Mosquitos, with 8 Group providing the other eight Oboe Mosquitos, which, now that mobile Oboe stations had been set up on the Continent, could operate over the whole of Germany. Clear skies over the target provided excellent conditions for bombing, and photo-reconnaissance would confirm serious damage to the eastern half of the targeted stretch of track. On the 11th, acting F/L Steele and three of his crew were declared tour-expired after completing between twenty-eight to thirty sorties, and F/O Groves and four of his Canadian crew were posted to Warrington for repatriation to Canada.

5 Group was used to being handed the most distant targets, and, as the final days of the bombing war approached, it found itself facing three long-range trips on consecutive nights, all to railway targets. The first of these was at Pilsen in Czechoslovakia, for which a force of 222 Lancasters and eleven Mosquitos was made ready. The fifteen 50 Squadron crews attended briefing in the early evening, and took off between 23.22 and 23.53 with F/Ls Gifford, Walls and Whalley the senior pilots on duty. They found clear skies in the target area, and only slight haze, and, ahead, watched the first primary blind marker aircraft deliver green TIs at 03.38, before the flare forces followed between 03.51 and 03.56. The main force was called in at 03.58, and the 50 Squadron participants bombed from 12,000 to 15,000 feet between 03.59 and 04.04, aiming at the north-westerly red and yellow TIs with an eight-second overshoot in accordance with the Master Bomber's instructions. Returning crews reported a large explosion at 04.00, followed by oily smoke, and it was concluded that the raid had been successful.

There was good news to celebrate on the 17th, when the length of a tour was reduced further to thirty successful sorties, although, as previously mentioned, it didn't seem to make a lot of difference. As a result, F/Ls Drinkell, Jones and Jung and their crews were now to be screened. That evening, the target posted for ninety 5 Group Lancasters and eleven Mosquitos was the marshalling yards at Cham, on Germany's border with Czechoslovakia. 53 Base was not involved in the operation, which delivered delayed-action bombs, and left the crews guessing as to the outcome. Photo-reconnaissance confirmed later that another concentrated and accurate attack by the "Independent Air Force" had left tracks torn up and rolling stock damaged.

5 Group was not involved when a force of over nine hundred aircraft reduced the island of Heligoland to the appearance of a cratered moonscape during the day on the 18th, but, 53 Base stations were alerted to another long-range operation that night, for which a force of 113 Lancasters and ten Mosquitos was put together. The target was the railway yards at Komotau (now Chomutov), also in Czechoslovakia, which proved to be the last raid in the communications offensive, begun more than a year earlier. 50 Squadron made ready eighteen Lancasters, which departed Skellingthorpe between 23.05 and 23.46 with S/L Blair the senior pilot on duty and first off the ground. W/O Nethery and crew returned early with a starboard-outer engine issue, leaving the others to find two layers of broken cloud over the target, one at 6,000 feet and the other between 10,000 and 12,000 feet. The Master Bomber directed crews to bomb on red and yellow TIs with an eight-second overshoot, and do so from the clear lane between the cloud layers. The 50 Squadron crews complied from 8,000 to 10,000 feet between 03.58 and 04.05, and post-raid reconnaissance revealed the yards to be heavily cratered with most of the tracks cut, and severe damage also to locomotive sheds and

workshops.

617 Squadron employed Grand Slams and Tallboys to complete the destruction of Heligoland by daylight on the 19th, while the rest of 5 Group remained at home with a sense that it was all coming to an end. It was the 23rd, before orders came through again to prepare for the next operation, which was to be directed at the railway yards and port area of Flensburg on the eastern side of the Schleswig-Holstein peninsular. The ten 50 Squadron crews departed Skellingthorpe between 15.02 and 15.29 with S/L Blair the senior pilot on duty, and, according to his post-raid comments, also acting as the Master Bomber. He reported contacting his two Deputies for a conference by VHF at H-29, while his bomb-aimer identified the target and led him to the start of the bombing run, at which point he ordered an overshoot in the case of cloud obscuring the ground. That was precisely what happened, when a layer of ten-tenths cloud with tops at 4,500 feet slid across the area as he began his final approach, and, judging it impossible to bomb by any method, issued further orders to maintain the gaggle in the hope of going round again. However, the gaggle had begun to break up, and, despite reducing speed to 130 knots for a considerable time, he was unable to rescue the situation, and ordered the crews to disperse and go home. His frustration at debriefing was clear, as he made the point that they could have bombed if the formation had remained together.

5 Group operated for the final time on the 25th, with an operation in the morning on the SS barracks at Hitler's Eaglesnest retreat at Berchtesgaden in the Bavarian mountains, and later that night on an oil refinery at Tonsberg in Norway. 5 Group supported the former with eighty-eight Lancasters and a single Mosquito in an overall 1, 5 and 8 Group force of 359 Lancasters and sixteen Mosquitos. 50 Squadron was not involved in the attack, during which it proved difficult to identify the barracks in the absence of visible markers, but a nearby lake and the town stood out clearly, and the bombing took place under clear skies in the minutes either side of 09.00. 50 Squadron had to wait until mid-evening before embarking on what would prove to be its final offensive operation of the war. Fifteen of its Lancasters departed Skellingthorpe between 20.05 and 20.35 with F/Ls Brunskill, Chadwick, Walls and Whalley the senior pilots on duty, but lost the services of F/O Skilling and crew, who were forced to turn back after bursting a tyre and damaging the starboard undercarriage on take-off. The others reached the target, situated close to the western shore of Oslo Fjord, a dozen or so miles south of the recently attacked Horten. They encountered a layer of eight to ten-tenths cloud between 7,500 and 10,500 feet, prompting the Master Bomber to call the crews down to clear air, with which some of the 50 Squadron crews complied to bomb on red and yellow TIs from 7,000 to 10,750 between 23.45 and 23.52. Not all could pick out the aiming-point, however, and five crews withheld their bombs. When F/O Halliwell and crew touched down at Skellingthorpe at 03.29 on the 26th, they had the honour to bring to a close 50 Squadron's offensive service, which had spanned the entire five years and eight months duration of the war. Returning crews reported many fires and explosions together with much black smoke, which suggested a successful conclusion to the squadron's and group's offensive activities. During the course of this final month of the bombing war, the squadron took part in nine operations and dispatched 113 sorties for the loss of a single Lancaster and crew.

The very first sorties in support of Operation Exodus, the repatriation of prisoners of war, were launched later on the 26th, when forty-two Lancasters from the group were dispatched to an unnamed continental airfield, which may have been Melsbroek in Belgium. W/C Flint,

F/Ls Gifford and Hills and F/Os McKinnon, Danyluk, Evans, Lillies and Filmer took off in the late morning, and returned their passengers to Wing in Buckinghamshire. Sadly, while returning to Skellingthorpe, PD339 hit a tree while low-flying, and crashed at 16.55 at Hardingstone, situated on the south-south-eastern outskirts of Northampton. F/O Evans RNZAF and four of his crew, including three other members of the RNZAF, were killed and the two gunners injured, one seriously, and these proved to be the squadron's final fatalities of the war. The squadron would continue to support Operation Exodus, but there is no mention of participation in Operation Manna, the supply of food to the starving Dutch people still under occupation, which began during the final few days of April and continued until the cessation of hostilities on the 8th of May.

It had been a long and testing war for all concerned, and one which 50 Squadron negotiated with distinction. It took part in more bombing operations than any other heavy squadron in the Command, flew the highest number of sorties, and dropped the greatest tonnage of bombs in 5 Group, and carried out the highest number of Hampden operations in the Command. 50 Squadron was, without doubt, one of the premier units in Bomber Command, with an unparalleled reputation. It counted many amongst its number who were, or would become characters and legends, Henry Maudslay, Mickey Martin and Les Knight all finding fame as Dambuster pilots, and others from the squadron also joined 617 in various crew capacities. The spirit and morale of 50 Squadron contributed to its experiencing one of the lowest percentage loss rates of any that went right through the Battle of Berlin, and this was an indication of the quality of leadership enjoyed by the squadron throughout, through the likes of W/Cs Walker, Russell and Frogley, to name but a few.

The Friends of Skellingthorpe website is dedicated to the memory of 50 and 61 Squadrons, and provides a focal point for those who wish to keep alive a record of the deeds of these gallant men and women, who served in the air or on the ground, and who have now mostly departed this world.

Damage to the Dortmund-Ems Canal the 24th of February 1945 following a Lancaster Daylight Operation

22 March 1945 Lancaster daylight operation to Bremen with the liner "Europa" in dock.

March 1945 RAF Skellingthorpe. John Lawrey's crew behind VN-L LOVE.
James Flowers (RG), Jack Morrison, (Nav), Arthur Smith, (FE), Henry Flowers, (MUG).
In front of Frank Wallis (BA), John Lawrey, (Pilot). H.W. Kent (W/Op).

June 1944 Air Gunner Training. RAF Stormey Down. Front Row: lst James. 2nd Henry.

AC2 Flowers

Harry and Eunice Flowers

F/O John S Lawrey RNZAF

F/S H. James Flowers and Sgt Birch

Photograph above was taken by Jack, the Nav. just before the Lawrey crew climbed aboard VN-K for the trip to Böhlen.

F/O John Strathern Lawrey RNZAF

Sgt Jack Morrison Scottish (Nav).

Sgt Frank Wallis, RNZAF (BA)

Sgt H.W. Kent RNZAF. (W/Op)

Sgt Arthur G. Smith, (FE)

Sgt Henry J Flowers (MUG)
Sgt H. James Flowers (RG)

F/Sgt A G Smith

Sgt H.J.Flowers
Served on 50 Squadron from January to June 1945

H James Flowers in his turret.

Henry in his mid-upper-turret.

F/O Eric Harrop

50 Squadron Lancaster PA223 VN-D

This picture, believed to have been taken at the end of the war, shows Lancaster RE135, with Ron Schofield lying down on the top of the aircraft the last one of the four.
RE135 was on the Squadron during April 1945 and flew around 5 operations according to the ORB's.

LAC Ronald Schofield - Trained as a Flight Mechanic Engines, he was posted to 50 Squadron.

A Lancaster over Hitler's Eaglesnest Bavarian mountain retreat at Obersaltzberg on the last day of bombing operations of the war, 25th of April 1945.

50 SQUADRON

MOTTO **FROM DEFENCE TO ATTACK**   Code **VN**

Stations

WADDINGTON	03.05.37. to 10.07.40.
HATFIELD WOODHOUSE/LINDHOLME (from 17.08.40)	10.07.40. to 9.07.41.
SWINDERBY	19.07.41. to 26.11.41.
SKELLINGTHORPE	26.11.41. to 20.06.42.
SWINDERBY	20.06.42. to 17.10.42.
SKELLINGTHORPE	17.10.42. to 15.06.45.

Commanding Officers

WING COMMANDER L YOUNG	12.07.38. to 10.04.40.
WING COMMANDER D W REID	13.02.40. to 10.04.40.
WING COMMANDER R T TAAFE OBE	10.04.40. to 12.06.40.
WING COMMANDER N D CROCKART	12.06.40. to 27.06.40.
WING COMMANDER G W GOLLEDGE	27.06.40. to 16.12.40.
WING COMMANDER G A WALKER DSO DFC	16.12.40. to 26.10.41.
WING COMMANDER R J OXLEY DSO DFC	26.10.41. to 20.10.42.
WING COMMANDER W M RUSSELL DFC	20.10.42. to 11.08.43.
WING COMMANDER R McFARLANE DSO DFC	11.08.43. to 06.12.43.
WING COMMANDER F PULLEN DFC	06.12.43. to 21.12.43.
WING COMMANDER A W HEWARD DFC AFC	21.01.44. to 14.06.44.
WING COMMANDER R T FROGLEY	22.06.44. to 11.03.45.
WING COMMANDER J FLINT DFC GM DFM	11.03.45. to 25.01.46.

Aircraft

HAMPDEN	12.38. to	05.42.
MANCHESTER	04.42. to	06.42.
LANCASTER I/III	05.42. to	11.46.

Operational Record

Overall

Operations	Sorties	Aircraft Losses	% Losses
767	7135	176	2.5

Category of Operations

Bombing	Mining	Leaflet
620	124	23

Hampden

Operations	Sorties	Aircraft Losses	% Losses
368	2299	57	2.5

Category of Operations

Bombing	Mining	Leaflet
266	88	14

Manchester

Operations	Sorties	Aircraft Losses	% Losses
44	126	7	5.6

Category of Operations

Bombing	Mining	Leaflet
15	10	9

Lancaster

Operations	Sorties	Aircraft Losses	% Losses
365	4710	112	2.4

Category of Operations

Bombing	Mining	Leaflet
339	26	0

Aircraft Histories

HAMPDEN. **To May 1942.**

L4062	Crashed while landing at Lindholme on return from Calais 26.9.40.
L4063	Crashed in Scotland on return from patrol 16/17.3.40.
L4064	FTR Kristiansand in Norway 12.4.40.
L4065	FTR from mining sortie 13/14.4.40.
L4073	FTR Kristiansand in Norway 12.4.40.
L4074	To 44Sqn.
L4075	To 16 O.T.U.
L4076	To 14 O.T.U.
L4077	To 49Sqn.
L4078	FTR Langenhagen airfield Hannover 26/27.6.40.
L4079	FTR Mönchengladbach 30/31.8.40.
L4080	Damaged beyond repair in taxying accident at Waddington 17.10.39.
L4081	FTR Kristiansand in Norway 12.4.40.
L4083	FTR Kristiansand in Norway 12.4.40.
L4084	To 25 OTU.
L4096	Crashed soon after take-off from Waddington while training 31.10.39.
L4097	FTR Ostend 10/11.9.40.
L4099	To 44Sqn.
L4149	From 106Sqn. FTR Mannheim 10/11.11.40.
L4150	From 106Sqn. To 16 O.T.U.
L4164	From 7Sqn. To 1 AAS.
L4168	From 44Sqn. Returned to 44Sqn.
P1152	From 44Sqn. Crashed in Yorkshire following early return from mining sortie 16.11.41.
P1156	To 455Sqn.
P1166	From 144Sqn. Returned to 144Sqn.
P1202	Force-landed near Skellingthorpe on return from Hamburg 1.12.41.
P1223	To 1404Flt.
P1228	To 106Sqn.
P1239	To 420Sqn.
P1317	Crashed on approach to Hemswell on return from Leipzig 26/27.8.40.
P1321	From 106Sqn. Landed on a Norfolk beach on return from Castrop-Rauxel 26.7.40.
P1327	SOC on return from a mining sortie 1.8.40.
P1329	FTR Hannover 26/27.6.40.
P1330	To Farnborough.
P1356	From 83Sqn. To 16 O.T.U.
P2070	FTR Berlin 25/26.8.40.
P2093	To 1 AAS.
P2094	From 144Sqn. To 420Sqn.
P2124	Ditched off Yorkshire coast on return from Berlin 26.8.40.
P4285	To 44Sqn.
P4286	To 44Sqn.
P4287 VN-J	FTR Hamburg 8/9.9.40.

P4288	Crashed near Waddington while training 9.7.40.
P4289 VN-X	Crashed on approach to Waddington while training 8.6.40.
P4382	FTR from a training flight 10/11.8.40.
P4383	FTR from a mining sortie 31.7/1.8.40.
P4389	Crashed soon after take-off from Lindholme for air-test 18.6.41.
P4395	Crashed on take-off for Berlin 30.9.40. To 14 O.T.U after repair.
P4408	Crashed in North Sea during air-sea rescue operation 15.8.41.
P4409	From 49Sqn. Crashed on take-off from Lindholme while training 1.4.41.
P4411	Crashed on landing at Docking on return from Berlin 1.10.40.
P4417	FTR Cologne 5/6.10.40.
P5335	From 7 AAU. To 144Sqn.
X2896	Crashed in Scotland on return from Hamburg 3.10.40.
X2897	To 83 Sqn..
X2902	FTR Stuttgart 29/30.9.40.
X2907	FTR Magdeburg 5/6.11.40.
X2908 VN-Y	Crashed at Goole on return from Hamburg 15.11.40.
X2919	Crashed near Wittering on return from Berlin 3.9.41.
X2968	To 16 O.T.U.
X2983	FTR from mining sortie 14/15.2.41.
X2984	Crashed in Yorkshire on return from Cologne 2.3.41.
X2991	Crashed on take-off from Swinderby when bound for Mannheim 27/28.8.41.
X2992	To 25 O.T.U.
X2993	FTR Berlin 14/15.10.40.
X2994	Abandoned over Norfolk on return from Essen 8.11.40.
X3000	Abandoned near Linton-on-Ouse on return from Berlin 30.10.40.
X3003	To 16 O.T.U.
X3004	FTR Düsseldorf 7/8.12.40.
X3022	Converted for use as torpedo bomber. To Russian Navy.
X3117	FTR Mannheim 10/11.12.40.
X3125	Force-landed in Lincolnshire on return from Kiel 26.11.40.
X3133	FTR Kiel 29/30.6.41.
X3141	FTR Lorient 28/29.12.40.
X3143	Crashed on landing at Lindholme on return from Bremen 2.1.41.
X3145	Converted for use as torpedo bomber. To 415Sqn.
X3146	FTR Hamburg 13/14.3.41.
AD721	FTR Berlin 12/13.3.41.
AD728	FTR from mining sortie 28/29.4.41.
AD730	Crashed in Eire on return from Berlin 17/18.4.41.
AD742	Crashed on approach to Lindholme on return from mining sortie 21.3.41.
AD753	Crashed in the sea when bound for Brest 5.4.41.
AD764	Converted for use as torpedo bomber. To 5 O.T.U.
AD766	To 144Sqn.
AD789	FTR Düsseldorf 10/11.4.41.
AD795	From 83Sqn. Converted for use as torpedo bomber. To 144Sqn.
AD797	FTR Düsseldorf 2/3.6.41.

AD824	To 49Sqn.
AD828	FTR Düsseldorf 10/11.4.41.
AD830	Crashed in Leicester while training 10.4.41.
AD834	FTR from mining sortie 28/29.4.41.
AD836	Converted for use as torpedo bomber. To 455Sqn.
AD839	FTR Frankfurt 29/30.8.41.
AD843	FTR Frankfurt 23/24.7.41.
AD844	FTR Hamburg 16/17.7.41.
AD852	Converted for use as torpedo bomber. To 489Sqn.
AD853	To 420Sqn.
AD854	Crashed in Bedfordshire on return from Kassel 9.9.41.
AD867	Crashed near Lindholme during air-test 30.5.41.
AD897	Crashed near Lindholme during practice 19.7.41.
AD902	Crashed while landing at Swinderby following early return from mining sortie 29.7.41.
AD908	To 144Sqn.
AD927	Converted for use as torpedo bomber. To 489Sqn.
AD928	To 144Sqn.
AD929	From 106Sqn. To 144Sqn.
AD977	Converted for use as torpedo bomber. To 455Sqn.
AE115	To 420Sqn.
AE116	Converted for use as torpedo bomber. To 489Sqn.
AE124	Crashed on take-off from Swinderby for mining sortie 8/9.8.41.
AE137	FTR Karlsruhe 5/6.8.41.
AE157	Hit X3025 (44Sqn) on the ground at Waddington on return from mining sortie 3.9.41.
AE158	To 144Sqn.
AE159	FTR from mining sortie 28/29.7.41.
AE184 VN-Z	Crashed on landing at Ratcliffe Yorkshire while training 25.10.41.
AE185	FTR Bremen 17/18.8.41.
AE218	From 44Sqn. Crashed on approach to Skellingthorpe on return from Kiel 28.2.42.
AE226	FTR Bremen 12/13.7.41.
AE228	To 455Sqn.
AE229	Crash-landed on Lincolnshire decoy site on return from Frankfurt 29/30.8.41.
AE230	FTR Bremen 12/13.7.41.
AE231	Converted for use as torpedo bomber. To 144Sqn.
AE234	Crashed soon after take-off from Swinderby when bound for Hannover 25/26.7.41.
AE248	To 144Sqn.
AE250	Crashed in Cumberland on return from mining sortie 10/11.1.42.
AE251	FTR Cologne 13/14.10.41.
AE256	From 455Sqn. FTR Kiel 23/24.10.41.
AE291	To 455Sqn.
AE305	Crash-landed in Norfolk on return from Berlin 3.9.41.
AE306	FTR from mining sortie 7.2.42.
AE316	To 144Sqn.

AE318	FTR Kiel 7/8.9.41.
AE320	FTR Mannheim 25/26.8.41.
AE367	FTR Hüls 12/13.10.41.
AE369	FTR Norway 27.12.41.
AE370	Converted for use as torpedo bomber. To 415Sqn.
AE373	To 408Sqn.
AE375	To 408Sqn.
AE380	FTR Ostend 15/16.12.41.
AE381	Crashed in Derbyshire while training 21.1.42.
AE383	FTR Bremen 20/21.10.41.
AE386	To 14 O.T.U.
AE387	Crashed on take-off from Skellingthorpe while training 7.3.42.
AE388	From 83Sqn. Converted for use as torpedo bomber. To 144Sqn.
AE394	Partially abandoned and crashed in York on return from Koblenz 22.2.42.
AE400	FTR from mining sortie 7/8.3.42.
AE401	To 420Sqn.
AE420	From 83Sqn. FTR Hamburg 14/15.1.42.
AE422	To 420Sqn.
AE423	Converted for use as torpedo bomber. To 5 O.T.U.
AE427	FTR from mining sortie 6/7.11.41.
AE428	From 44Sqn. FTR Norway 27.12.41.
AE429	FTR from mining sortie 24/25.3.42.
AE431	FTR Hamburg 14/15.1.42.
AE435	Converted for use as torpedo bomber. To 455Sqn.
AT109	Converted for use as torpedo bomber. To 455Sqn.
AT118	From 49Sqn. Force-landed in Cornwall while on air-sea-rescue patrol 26.3.42.
AT125	Converted for use as torpedo bomber. To 144Sqn.
AT139	To 408Sqn.
AT140	Converted for use as torpedo bomber. To 144Sqn.
AT142	Crashed on approach to Cottesmore on return from Münster 22.1.42.
AT146	To 106Sqn.
AT147	Converted for use as torpedo bomber. To 489Sqn.
AT151	FTR Essen 25/26.3.42.
AT152	Converted for use as torpedo bomber. To 415Sqn.
AT153	Converted for use as torpedo bomber. To 5 O.T.U.
AT158	FTR from mining sortie 25/26.3.42.
AT173	Abandoned over Norfolk on return from Essen 11.3.42.
AT177	FTR from shipping strike (Channel Dash) 12.2.42.
AT216	Crashed in Lincolnshire soon after take-off from Skellingthorpe when bound for Cologne 6.4.42.

MANCHESTER.   **From April 1942 to June 1942.**

| L7277 | Flew on the last Manchester operation, to Bremen 25/26.6.42. To 1654CU. |
| L7289 | From 83Sqn. FTR Bremen 25/26.6.42. |

L7291	From 106Sqn. No operations. To 1654CU.
L7294	From 97Sqn. To 1654CU.
L7301 ZN-D	From 106Sqn on loan. FTR Cologne (Operation Millennium) 30/31.5.42. P/O Manser awarded posthumous V.C.
L7401	From 61Sqn. To 1485 T.T.Flt.
L7415	From 61Sqn. To 1654CU.
L7416	To 1654CU.
L7419	From 61Sqn. To 1654CU.
L7432 VN-Z	From 207Sqn. FTR Bremen 3/4.6.42.
L7455	From 97Sqn. To 1661CU. Completed 23 operations.
L7456 ZN-T	From 106Sqn on loan. FTR Cologne (Operation Millennium) 30/31.5.42.
L7460	From 97Sqn. To 1656CU.
L7464	From 61Sqn. To 460Sqn.
L7468	From 207Sqn. Completed 19 ops. Became ground instruction machine.
L7469	From 49Sqn. Returned to 49Sqn.
L7471	From 61Sqn. FTR Emden 6/7.6.42.
L7475	From 97Sqn. Completed 21 operations. Crashed 16.8.42.
L7476 VN-Z	From 207Sqn. To 1654CU.
L7486	From 207Sqn. Crashed on landing at Skellingthorpe during training 25.3.42.
L7489	From 97Sqn. FTR Warnemünde 8/9.5.42.
L7491	From 207Sqn. To 1654CU.
L7492	From 97Sqn. To 1654CU.
L7496	From 207Sqn. To 1654CU.
L7516 VN-N	From 61Sqn. FTR from mining sortie 29/30.4.42.
L7519	From 61Sqn. Crashed in Lincolnshire while training 13.5.42.
L7521	Crashed while landing at Waddington 5.9.42.
L7525	From 83Sqn. To 1485Flt.
R5769	From 106Sqn. To 9Sqn.
R5778	From 207Sqn. Damaged beyond repair during operation to Warnemünde 8/9.5.42.
R5782	From 207Sqn. FTR Hamburg 17/18.4.42.
R5784	From 61Sqn. To 1660CU.
R5786	From 61Sqn. To 1654CU.
R5833	From 83Sqn. FTR from mining sortie 5/6.6.42.
R5835	From 49Sqn. To 408Sqn.

LANCASTER.　　　**From May 1942.**

L7532	From 61Sqn. No operations. To 207Sqn.
L7534	From 44CF. Undercarriage collapsed when landing at Swinderby while training 13.8.42.
R5503	From 1660CU. To 1664CU.
R5546 VN-T	From A&AEE. FTR Nuremberg 30/31.3.44.
R5625	From 83Sqn. No operations. Returned to 83Sqn.
R5626	From 83Sqn. No operations. Returned to 83Sqn.
R5639 VN-J	FTR Osnabrück 17/18.8.42.

R5680 VN-O	To 106 Sqn.
R5685 VN-P	To 44Sqn on loan. Returned to 50Sqn. To 460Sqn.
R5687 VN-N/D	FTR Hamburg 27/28.7.43. (Firestorm).
R5688 VN-G	To 12 Sqn.
R5689 VN-N	Crash-landed in Lincolnshire on return from mining sortie 18/19.9.42.
R5690 VN-H	To 1654CU via 50CF.
R5691 VN-K	FTR Milan 24.10.42.
R5702 VN-S	To 106Sqn.
R5725 VN-F	FTR Düsseldorf 10/11.9.42.
R5726 VN-B	To 44Sqn.
R5728 VN-L	FTR Saarbrücken 29/30.7.42. Squadron's first loss of a Lancaster on operations.
R5733 VN-O	Flew 31 operations. To 44Sqn.
R5735 VN-G	FTR Düsseldorf 15/16.8.42.
R5739 VN-X	To 1654CU.
R5746 VN-Q	FTR Le Havre 11/12.8.42.
R5747 VN-G	To 83Sqn and back. To 1654CU.
R5753 VN-C	Crashed on landing at Skellingthorpe while training 17.11.43.
R5851	From 207Sqn. To 1654CU.
R5902 VN-T	FTR Wismar 12/13.10.42.
R5909	FTR Wismar 23/24.9.42.
W4112 VN-L	Destroyed in explosion at Scampton 15.3.43.
W4115	To 1651CU via A.V.Roe and A&AEE.
W4117 VN-R	Crashed on landing at Skellingthorpe during training 11.12.42..
W4119 VN-Q	From 207Sqn via 1661CU. Abandoned over East Kirkby 12.2.44.
W4131	To 1660CU via 50CF.
W4135 VN-Q	Flew 21 operations. To 44Sqn.
W4154 VN-A	Flew 21 operations. To 100Sqn.
W4155 VN-M	To 9Sqn and back. Returned to 9Sqn.
W4161 VN-J	Became ground instruction machine.
W4163 VN-M/N	To 622Sqn via 1667CU.
W4194 VN-F	FTR Hamburg. 9/10.11.42.
W4196	From 156Sqn. Destroyed when W4834 (57Sqn) blew up at Scampton 15.3.43.
W4232	From 57Sqn via 1660CU. To 5LFS.
W4250	Crashed at Woodhall Spa on return from Turin 9/10.12.42.
W4266 VN-N/S	To 44Sqn and back. FTR Soltau 17/18.12.42.
W4267	To 44Sqn.
W4303	No operations. To 1654CU.
W4315	To NTU. Returned to 50Sqn. To 61Sqn.
W4367	To 106Sqn.
W4380 VN-E	From 467Sqn. To 12Sqn.
W4381 VN-G	To 207Sqn.
W4382	From 467Sqn. FTR Soltau 17/18.12.42.
W4383	From 467Sqn. To 207Sqn.
W4762	From 61Sqn. FTR Duisburg 12/13.5.43.
W4772	Conversion Flt only. To 1654CU.
W4800 VN-T	FTR Duisburg 8/9.1.43.

W4823	From 467Sqn. Destroyed on the ground at Scampton when W4834 (57Sqn) blew up 15.3.43.
W4824 VN-Z	From 467Sqn. FTR Bois-de-Cassan 6.8.44.
W4905 VN-H	From 83Sqn. FTR Frankfurt 4/5.10.43.
W4932	From 97Sqn. Crashed near Dunholme Lodge during night flying training 19.6.43.
W4933	From 44Sqn. Crashed at Skellingthorpe 30.3.44.
W5004	To 5LFS.
DV156 VN-C	From 617Sqn. FTR Turin 12/13.7.43.
DV161	From 9Sqn. To 1653CU.
DV167 VN-M	FTR Reggio Emilia 15/16.7.43.
DV178 VN-N	From 49Sqn. FTR Berlin 26/27.11.43.
DV197 VN-T	Crash-landed in Northamptonshire on return from Remscheid 31.7.43.
DV217 VN-C	FTR Frankfurt 20/21.12.43.
DV223	Destroyed in forced-landing in Algeria following operation to Milan 7/8.8.43.
DV227 VN-F/L	FTR St Leu d'Esserent 7/8.7.44.
DV234 VN-M	FTR Frankfurt 20/21.12.43.
DV312 VN-J	From 207Sqn. FTR Revigny 18/19.7.44.
DV324 VN-N	FTR Hanover 8/9.10.43.
DV325 VN-B	FTR Berlin 2/3.12.43.
DV363 VN-H/O/K	Flew 13 Berlin operations. FTR St Leu d'Esserent 7/8.7.44.
DV366 VN-R	FTR Berlin 22/23.11.43.
DV368	To 5LFS. Flew on 11 Berlin operations.
DV375 VN-E	FTR Berlin 29/30.12.43.
DV376 VN-F	FTR Berlin 15/16.2.44.
DV377 VN-X	Destroyed in ground accident at Melbourne on return from Berlin 27.11.43.
DV384 VN-V	From 44Sqn. FTR Frankfurt 22/23.3.44.
ED308 VN-J	From 57Sqn via 1661CU. FTR Frankfurt 18/19.3.44.
ED309	From 467Sqn. To 44Sqn.
ED358	To 106Sqn.
ED387	From 49Sqn. FTR Nuremberg 25/26.2.43.
ED388	FTR Berlin 17/18.1.43.
ED393 VN-K	Crashed in Yorkshire on return from Berlin 26/27.11.43.
ED394 VN-R	Crashed while landing at Crosby Cumberland during training 9.1.43.
ED409 VN-S	To 106Sqn.
ED415 VN-N	FTR Mannheim 23/24.9.43.
ED423 VN-N	FTR Berlin 1/2.3.43.
ED429	FTR Bochum 12/13.6.43.
ED430	From 97Sqn. To 622Sqn.
ED437	To 617Sqn.
ED442	To 207Sqn.
ED445 VN-L	From 49Sqn. FTR Berlin 23/24.12.43.
ED449 VN-T	FTR Essen 12/13.3.43.
ED468 VN-A	Crashed on take-off at Skellingthorpe when bound for Hamburg 29.7.43.
ED470 VN-O	To 61Sqn.

ED471	FTR Berlin 17/18.1.43
ED472	FTR Bochum 12/13.6.43.
ED473	To 15Sqn via 1667CU.
ED475 VN-E	Ditched off Hastings on return from Gelsenkirchen 10.7.43.
ED478 VN-G	Lost in the North Sea on return from Frankfurt 10/11.4.43.
ED482	FTR from mining sortie 2/3.4.43.
ED483 VN-R	FTR Kassel 22/23.10.43.
ED484 VN-Q	FTR Lorient 13/14.2.43.
ED486	Crashed after take-off for Düsseldorf 27.1.43.
ED488 VN-M	FTR Cologne 2/3.2.43.
ED491 VN-H	To 115Sqn.
ED527 VN-B	Crashed in Morocco after raid on Turin 4/5.2.43
ED585 VN-G	To 1656CU.
ED588 VN-G	From 97Sqn. Flew 116 operations, 15 to Berlin. FTR Königsburg 29/30.8.44.
ED592 VN-B	FTR Berlin 1/2.3.43.
ED617	From 57Sqn. FTR Gelsenkirchen 9/10.7.43.
ED690	To BDU 3.43.
ED691 VN-K	FTR Pilsen 16/17.4.43.
ED693 VN-H	FTR Pilsen 13/14.5.43.
ED712	FTR Wuppertal 24/25.6.43.
ED753 VN-M	FTR Essen 25/26.7.43.
ED755 VN-Q	FTR Berlin 3/4.9.43.
ED784 VN-N	FTR Pilsen 16/17.4.43.
ED800 VN-U	FTR Pilsen 16/17.4.43.
ED810 VN-Z	FTR Oberhausen 14/15.6.43.
ED828 VN-B/S	FTR Bochum 12/13.6.43.
ED856 VN-K/A	From 156Sqn. FTR Darmstadt 25/26.8.44.
ED870 VN-I/J	From 97Sqn. Completed 11 Berlin raids. FTR Mailly-le-Camp 3/4.5.44.
EE124 VN-B/Z	To 300Sqn.
EE174 VN-A	From 97Sqn. FTR Nuremburg 30/31.3.44.
EE189 VN-S	FTR Hanover 27/28.9.43.
JA899 VN-D	Flew 13 operations to Berlin. FTR Prouville 24/25.6.44.
JA961 VN-A	Damaged in ground accident at Melbourne on return from Berlin 27.11.43.
JB143 VN-L	FTR from mining sortie 29/30.9.43.
LL741 VN-X	FTR Mittelland Canal at Gravenhorst 21/22.2.45.
LL744 VN-B	FTR Brunswick 22/23.5.44.
LL786	To 5LFS.
LL791 VN-O	FTR Augsburg 25/26.2.44.
LL840 VN-M	FTR Gelsenkirchen 21/22.6.44.
LL841 VN-O	FTR Rennes 8/9.6.44.
LL842 VN-F	FTR Stuttgart 24/25.7.44.
LL922 VN-E/T	FTR Secqueville 7/8.8.44.
LM162	Crashed in Lincolnshire after collision on return from Stuttgart 12/13.9.44.
LM210 VN-D	FTR Stuttgart 28/29.7.44.

LM212 VN-L	FTR Dortmund-Ems Canal 23/24.9.44.
LM222 VN-Y	FTR Königsburg 29/30.8.44.
LM234 VN-K	FTR Leuna 14/15.1.45.
LM236	To 1651CU.
LM264 VN-J	FTR Calais 24.9.44.
LM296 VN-T	Completed 50 operations.
LM360	From 61Sqn. Written off at Fiskerton 11.11.44.
LM368 VN-S	From 467Sqn. To 1653CU.
LM394 VN-R	FTR Nuremberg 30/31.3.44.
LM428 VN-O	FTR Berlin 28/29.1.44.
LM429 VN-T/C	FTR Lille 10/11.5.44.
LM435 VN-E	FTR Chatellerault 9/10.8.44.
LM437 VN-P	FTR Mailly-le-Camp 3/4.5.44.
LM480 VN-U	FTR Mailly-le-Camp 3/4.5.44.
LM591	To ECDU.
LM628 VN-M	FTR Gravenhorst 6/7.11.44.
LM629 VN-O	To 5LFS.
LM656 VN-W	From 619Sqn. FTR Munich 17/18.12.44.
LM676 VN-W	FTR Munich 17/18.12.44.
LM680	To 630Sqn.
ME295 VN-P	To 463Sqn.
ME319 VN-M	
ME429	
ME441 VN-W	FTR Böhlen 20/21.3.45.
ME483 VN-A	
ME567 VN-G	To 1664CU.
ME572 VN-Z	FTR Aachen 11/12.4.44.
ME578 VN-K	FTR Frankfurt 22/23.3.44.
ME700 VN-N/V	FTR Dortmund-Ems Canal 23/24.9.44.
ME797 VN-J	FTR Duisburg 21/22.5.44.
ME798 VN-Z	FTR Prouville 24/25.6.44.
ME813	Crashed while landing at Skellingthorpe 8.8.44.
ND874 VN-R	FTR St Pierre de Mont 5/6.6.44.
ND876 VN-Z	FTR Munich 24/25.4.44.
ND953 VN-S	FTR Mailly-le-Camp 3/4.5.44.
ND989	Crashed on approach to Benson on return from Tours 19/20.5.44.
ND991	To Flight Refuelling Ltd.
NE135 VN-F	FTR Rüsselsheim 12/13.8.44.
NF918 VN-N	FTR Böhlen 5/6.3.45.
NF919 VN-D	FTR Darmstadt 11/12.9.44.
NF921 VN-Q	FTR Königsburg 29/30.8.44.
NF922 VN-G/U	
NF930	To 433Sqn.
NF984	FTR Mittelland Canal at Gravenhorst. Crash-landed at Juvincourt 1/2.1.45.
NG127 VN-D	Crashed on take-off from Skellingthorpe when bound for Mittelland Canal at Gravenhorst 1.1.45.
NG171	Crashed on landing at Florennes when bound for Wesel 23.3.45.

NG177 VN-L   FTR Lützkendorf 14/15.3.45.
NG271   From 1651CU. Crashed near Waddington when bound for Ijmuiden 6.4.45.
NG302 VN-R   Shot down by allied flak over Holland on return from Munich 17/18.12.44.
NG326 VN-Q
NG342 VN-S   FTR Hamburg/Finkenwerder 9.4.45.
NG381 VN-A   FTR Karlsruhe 2/3.2.45.
NG385 VN-P   From 1669CU. FTR Pölitz 8/9.2.45.
NN694 VN-L   FTR Lille 10/11.5.44.
PA222 VN-K
PA223 VN-D   FTR Karlsruhe 2/3.2.45.
PA968 VN-S   FTR Donges 24/25.7.44.
PA994 VN-H   FTR Königsburg 29/30.8.44.
PA996 VN-J   FTR St Leu d'Esserent 7/8.7.44.
PB755 VN-Y
PB821 VN-E
PD237 VN-D   FTR Bordeaux 13.8.44.
PD291   To 1656CU.
PD292 VN-H   FTR Royan 4.1.45.
PD294 VN-A   FTR Darmstadt 11/12.9.44.
PD316 VN-A   FTR Dortmund-Ems Canal at Ladbergen 7/8.2.45.
PD326   FTR Bergen 28/29.10.44.
PD339 VN-J   Crashed in Northamptonshire during transit following Exodus sortie 26.4.45.
PD340 VN-C
PD346 VN-V   FTR Siegen 1/2.2.45.
PD362   To 467Sqn.
PD368   To 9Sqn.
RA565
RA591 VN-P
RE133 VN-D
RE135
RF138 VN-D   FTR Mittelland Canal at Gravenhorst 21/22.2.45.
RF153   To 49Sqn.
RF175   To 463Sqn.
RF180   To 467Sqn.
RF249 VN-L
RF267 VN-M
SW249
SW253
SW261   To 83Sqn.
SW262   To 83Sqn.
SW264 VN-F

HEAVIEST SINGLE LOSS.

12.04.40. Kristiansand Norway.   4 Hampdens FTR.

03/04.05.44. Mailly-le-Camp.   4 Lancasters FTR.
29/30.08.44. Königsberg   4 Lancasters FTR.

KEY TO ABBREVIATIONS

A&AEE	Aeroplane and Armaments Experimental Establishment.
AA	Anti-Aircraft fire.
AACU	Anti-Aircraft Cooperation Unit.
AAS	Air Armament School.
AASF	Advance Air Striking Force.
AAU	Aircraft Assembly Unit.
A/C	Air Commodore
ACM	Air Chief Marshal.
ACSEA	Air Command South-East Asia.
AFDU	Air Fighting Development Unit.
AFEU	Airborne Forces Experimental Unit.
AFTDU	Airborne Forces Tactical Development Unit.
AGS	Air Gunners School.
AMDP	Air Members for Development and Production.
AOC	Air Officer Commanding.
AOS	Air Observers School.
ASRTU	Air-Sea Rescue Training Unit.
ATTDU	Air Transport Tactical Development Unit.
AVM	Air Vice-Marshal.
BAT	Beam Approach Training.
BCBS	Bomber Command Bombing School.
BCDU	Bomber Command Development Unit.
BCFU	Bomber Command Film Unit.
BCIS	Bomber Command Instructors School.
BDU	Bombing Development Unit.
BSTU	Bomber Support Training Unit.
CF	Conversion Flight.
CFS	Central Flying School.
CGS	Central Gunnery School.
C-in-C	Commander in Chief.
CNS	Central Navigation School.
CO	Commanding Officer.
CRD	Controller of Research and Development.
CU	Conversion Unit.
DGRD	Director General for Research and Development.
EAAS	Empire Air Armament School.
EANS	Empire Air Navigation School.
ECDU	Electronic Countermeasures Development Unit.
ECFS	Empire Central Flying School.
ETPS	Empire Test Pilots School.
F/L	Flight Lieutenant.
Flt	Flight.
F/O	Flying Officer.
FPP	Ferry Pilots School.
F/S	Flight Sergeant.

FTR	Failed to Return.
FTS	Flying Training School.
FTU	Ferry Training Unit.
G/C	Group Captain.
Gp	Group.
HCU	Heavy Conversion Unit.
HGCU	Heavy Glider Conversion Unit.
ITW	Initial Training Wing.
LFS	Lancaster Finishing School.
MAC	Mediterranean Air Command.
MTU	Mosquito Training Unit.
MU	Maintenance Unit.
NTU	Navigation Training Unit.
OADU	Overseas Aircraft Delivery Unit.
OAPU	Overseas Aircraft Preparation Unit.
OTU	Operational Training Unit.
P/O	Pilot Officer.
PTS	Parachute Training School.
RAE	Royal Aircraft Establishment.
SGR	School of General Reconnaissance.
Sgt	Sergeant.
SHAEF	Supreme Headquarters Allied Expeditionary Force.
SIU	Signals Intelligence Unit.
S/L	Squadron Leader.
SOC	Struck off Charge.
SOE	Special Operations Executive.
Sqn	Squadron.
TF	Training Flight.
TFU	Telecommunications Flying Unit.
W/C	Wing Commander.
Wg	Wing.
WIDU	Wireless Intelligence Development Unit.
W/O	Warrant Officer.

www.ingramcontent.com/pod-product-compliance
Lightning Source LLC
Chambersburg PA
CBHW080344030726
47598CB00009B/2620